A Companion
to Psychological
Anthropology

Blackwell Companions to Anthropology

The *Blackwell Companions to Anthropology* offer a series of comprehensive syntheses of the traditional subdisciplines, primary subjects, and geographic areas of inquiry for the field. Taken together, the series represents both a contemporary survey of anthropology and a cutting edge guide to the emerging research and intellectual trends in the field as a whole.

Forthcoming

A Companion
to Psychological
Anthropology

Modernity and Psychocultural Change

Edited by Conerly Casey and
Robert B. Edgerton

Blackwell
Publishing

OCT 0 5 2005

© 2005 by Blackwell Publishing Ltd

BLACKWELL PUBLISHING
350 Main Street, Malden, MA 02148-5020, USA
108 Cowley Road, Oxford OX4 1JF, UK
550 Swanston Street, Carlton, Victoria 3053, Australia

First published 2005 by Blackwell Publishing Ltd

Library of Congress Cataloging-in-Publication Data

A companion to psychological anthropology: modernity and psychocultural change / edited by Conerly Casey and Robert B. Edgerton.
   p. cm. — (Blackwell companions to anthropology)
   Includes bibliographical references and index.
   ISBN 0-631-22597-8 (hardback: alk. paper)
   1. Ethnopsychology.   I. Casey, Conerly Carole, 1961-   II. Edgerton, Robert B., 1931-
   III. Series.
   GN502.C64 2005
   155.8′2—dc22

                                                                    2004012927

A catalogue record for this title is available from the British Library.

Set in 10/12pt Galliard
by Graphicraft Limited, Hong Kong
Printed and bound in the United Kingdom
by TJ International Ltd, Padstow, Cornwall

The publisher's policy is to use permanent paper from mills that operate a sustainable forestry policy, and which has been manufactured from pulp processed using acid-free and elementary chlorine-free practices. Furthermore, the publisher ensures that the text paper and cover board used have met acceptable environmental accreditation standards.

For further information on
Blackwell Publishing, visit our website:
www.blackwellpublishing.com

For Andrew

Contents

Synopsis of Contents

3   "Effort After Meaning" in Everyday Life
Linda C. Garro

A process oriented perspective of cognition need not limit the cultural contribution to content, or the process merely to biochemical cognitive processes. Rather, it can highlight cultural–historical and social processes as well as the range of artifacts and culturally available resources for "effort after meaning" while advancing an understanding of variation and change in cultural settings. The constructive and situated nature of knowing is explored through the distributed nature of cognition, transformative learning processes, schemas, and narrative as a mode of thinking.

4   Culture and Learning
Patricia M. Greenfield

Over the last forty years, concepts of culture and learning have moved from strict and separate operational definitions to integrations of these concepts as they are used within the fields of psychological anthropology and developmental psychology. Culture and learning have become cultural learning, and cultural learning is fast becoming part and parcel of developmental psychology. At the same time, the domain of culture and learning is no longer contextualized in separate and timeless cultures; the perspective is now historical, evolutionary, and global.

5   Dreaming in a Global World
Douglas Hollan

In this chapter it is argued that the study of dreams is one of the ways we can examine the degree to which "global" processes, however defined, gain cognitive, emotional, and motivational saliency for a person. Because dreams exist at the interface of self and social experience, they can illuminate how and in what ways aspects of self, desire, and fantasy become intertwined with the experience of body, world, and people. They can give us a sense of how the self projects itself into the world, but also a sense of how "the world," no matter how large or small, affects the development and organization of self.

6   Memory and Modernity
Jennifer Cole

This chapter reviews the relationship of memory to modernity, arguing that the experience of modernity has both increased scholarly and popular interest in memory and shaped the study of memory in problematic ways by separating the analysis of individual memory from that of social memory. Arguing for the importance of viewing memory as a key site at which to examine the complex interplay of individual and social experience, the chapter reviews social psychological and anthropological approaches to memory and constructs a history of different regimes of memory in the West. It then proposes an alternative genealogy from which to recuperate a view of memory that takes account of the dual social and individual nature of memory, tracing out the relevance of the work of Halbwachs, Bartlett, Vygotsky, and Voloshinov to such an approach. The final section of the chapter explores some concrete instantiations of the proposed approach through a review of specific work on discourse and ritual as they relate to memory.

Part II   Language and Communication

7   Narrative Transformations
James M. Wilce, Jr.

Narrative is changing globally. Stories, genres, and languages themselves shift. The relevance of such change to psychological anthropology may be clearest vis-à-vis emotional genres like lament, but new communicative forms are shaping shared subjectivities – widely shared identities. These shifts putatively reflect a grand narrative, the meta-story we call modernity. A limited version of this claim is embraced, based on evidence that newer forms of narrative participation can fit the so-called age of the spectacle.

8   Practical Logic and Autism
Elinor Ochs and Olga Solomon

This chapter examines the practice-based paradigms of Bourdieu and Garfinkel, specifically the relation between structure and agency, through the prism of autism. It is argued that practical logic is not a homogeneous domain of competence, as it presents degrees of complexity when applied to the flow of local and extended actions and expressed/implicated propositions. The practical proclivities of children with autism illuminate the primacy of structure over improvisation.

9   Disability: Global Languages and Local Lives
Susan Reynolds Whyte

This chapter proposes a pragmatic approach to the study of global discourses on disability. Like many languages of misfortune, these languages offer hope, but do so in contexts where opportunity is socially patterned. Analyzing disability discourses suggests that problems are defined in terms of the solutions being offered. Analyzing the pragmatics of empirical situations shows that discourses of disability are unevenly relevant to people in different positions. We cannot assume that discourse shapes subjectivity in any simple or regular way. Instead, we must examine how it is used and what social implications it has in practice.

Part III   Alienation, Ambivalence, and Belonging

10   Identity
Daniel T. Linger

Contemporary studies of identity focus on emergent gender, ethnic, and transnational identities, simultaneously engaging sharp debates within anthropology over the nature and locus of meaning. This chapter explores controversies over the instability and proliferation of identities, arguing that significant future work requires continued elaboration of a model of the person. Such a model is a theoretical precondition of all approaches to meaning, all attempts to link public and private domains, and thus all accounts of identity.

11 Self and Other in an "Amodern" World
A. David Napier

This chapter reviews the major assumptions about culture and identity that have shaped the fields of social and psychological anthropology. Beginning with philosophical questions about ideological commensurability and incommensurability – that is, are different embodied practices exclusive? – the chapter goes on to examine the degree to which contemporary anthropologists may have silenced this discussion, not only by failing to admit to the potential importance of learning about new domains of experience, but also by denying that one can have any knowledge outside of the self. Consequently, the chapter sets out to demonstrate how postmodern views of the discipline are actually dependent on traditional ideas about personal development and transformation – how, in Latour's sense, *We Have Never Been Modern*. Here, the author maintains that the conservative views that characterize postmodern anthropology can only be transcended by acknowledging, in ways stated by those "others" we study, that creativity is dependent upon the risk of encountering that which is different enough to appear at first unknowable.

12 Immigrant Identities and Emotion
Katherine Pratt Ewing

The inbetweenness of those who migrate is not easily captured in the models that dominate the anthropology of emotions. This chapter examines situations in which this inbetweenness is foregrounded: the medical clinic, where many migrants seek help in managing the stresses of migration; the emotional structurings of the memory of home; and the relationships between first and second generations, in which emotional structures and identities are transmitted across a gulf of cultural difference.

13 Emotive Institutions
Geoffrey M. White

This chapter explores the social and cultural character of emotion, outlining a model for comparative ethnographic research on the meaning and force of emotions in everyday life. After briefly reviewing differences between psychological and anthropological approaches to the social dimensions of emotion, the chapter introduces the idea of "emotive institution" as a means of focusing attention on the role of cultural models, social context, and social relational factors in producing emotional experience.

14 Urban Fear
Setha M. Low

This chapter uncovers some of the underlying motivations of moving into a residential gated community by exploring how the discourse of fear of violence and crime and the search for a secure community legitimates and rationalizes class-based exclusion strategies and residential segregation embodied in the walls, gates, guards, and surveillance technology of these built environments. The chapter expresses the concern that these physical changes in suburban design and planning will become normative and ultimately encode fear in a relatively open, suburban landscape. Secondarily, it attempts to untangle the relationship of emotion and environment, through the examination of this built form.

15   Race: Local Biology and Culture in Mind
Atwood D. Gaines

This chapter considers concepts of "race" from several perspectives: psychological and medical anthropology, cultural history, psychoanalysis, and the Cultural Studies of Science. From these perspectives, it views "race" as cultural and psychological constructs, as professional medical and scientific constructs, and in the contexts of "racial" justifications and psychological defenses. The chapter focuses on medical and scientific discursive formations of "race" in the United States, since social racial categories are transmuted into a "Local Biology" that is exported in part or in whole to other countries. While for some time researchers have demonstrated the lack of empirical bases for any conception of "race," it remains a (clearly declining) paramount cognitive, cultural, medical, and scientific reality.

16   Unbound Subjectivities and New Biomedical Technologies
Margaret Lock

This chapter argues the concept of subjectivity has a genealogy best contemplated through the practices, technologies, and discourses that change through time and space. Using three illustrative case studies – organ transplantation, the recognition of brain dead bodies as corpse-like and no longer alive, and the production and globalization of the technology of immortalized cell lines – it is argued that not only subjectivity, but also the bounded material body, has a history. Both subjectivity and material embodiment are radically challenged by new biomedical technologies in which the body is fragmented and commodified, resulting in an exchange of cells, tissues, and organs among people and places.

17   Globalization, Childhood, and Psychological Anthropology
Thomas S. Weisner and Edward D. Lowe

The psychological anthropology of childhood and adolescence accounts for the marvelous variety of childhoods found around the world, and how children and adolescents acquire, transform, share, integrate, and transmit cultural knowledge. Psychological anthropologists focus on topics in human development impacted by global processes: identity, self, trust and attachment, cognition and memory, parenting, childhood stages, health, social behavior, personality, and character. The opportunities are stunning for new research and applied knowledge about children engaging global processes.

18   Drugs and Modernization
Michael Winkelman and Keith Bletzer

Attitudes toward substance use in the United States and Europe have shifted from prehistory through postmodernity. Premodern use of natural substances was sanctioned for cultural practices that sought improved integration of the individual within society. European colonization altered the religiosity of early substance use by commercializing it and eventually taking legal control of it, restricting and prohibiting the popular use of some substances. The modernization of substances has led to an emphasis on individual pursuit rather than communal well-being.

19 Ritual Practice and Its Discontents
Don Seeman

This chapter maps three broad approaches to the study of ritual practice. Psychological approaches pioneered by the students of Freud and cultural approaches pioneered by the students of Boas have competed with and contributed to one another in the foundation of their respective disciplines. However, neither has yet succeeded in escaping the charge of reductionism first sounded by Edward Sapir. This chapter argues for a rethinking of ritual practice along poetic and phenomenological lines that responds to this early critique.

20 Spirit Possession
Erika Bourguignon

Spirit possession beliefs are ancient, very widespread, and dynamic. Rapid changes in numerous aspects of existence in the context of globalization have affected the most intimate aspect of people's lives virtually everywhere. Frequent among the effects of change are alterations in people's relations to spirits and ancestors, as well as in their own sense of identity. Ritualized possession trance states project human concerns to a cosmic plane and may assist in restructuring relationships within a community.

21 Witchcraft and Sorcery
René Devisch

Seeking some endogenous understanding of lethal bewitchment, primarily among blood relatives in Bantu African contexts, this chapter is concerned with the captivating intercorporeal and intersubjective transactional dynamics mobilized between a victim and the suspected aggressor's congenital capacity for fatal attack. It focuses on the prereflective consciousness (at play in the skin, the "flesh," the senses, the belly), as a magma of "forces" of abjection, transgression, and annihilation gradually consumes it. Without a bewitched, there is no witch. A fatal bewitchment only comes about at the level of the affects of some weakened individuals who, while imagining an evildoer regarding their weakening or ill-fate, turn themselves into victims or counter-attack.

Part IV Aggression, Dominance, and Violence

22 Genocide and Modernity
Alexander Laban Hinton

This chapter maintains that, as opposed to being an "aberration" or a "regression" to a state of "barbarism," genocide is powerfully influenced by modernity. Reflecting on the work of Zygmunt Bauman, the chapter argues psychological anthropology provides an important and distinct vantage on the interconnection between genocide and modernity, illustrating how modern genocides, while unfolding within particular cultural contexts, involve issues of identity, motivation, upheaval and revitalization, meaninglessness, existential dread, and manufacturing difference.

23   Corporate Violence
Howard F. Stein

Taking a psychoanalytic approach to understanding culture, this chapter explores American corporate violence that takes the forms of downsizing, reductions in force, restructuring, reengineering, outsourcing, deskilling, and other euphemized forms of "managed social change." Language is shown to be a key to disguising human disposability in the idiom of rational economic necessity. Much national attention has been given in recent years to physical forms of "violence in the workplace." This chapter explores ongoing symbolic violence that is no less brutal.

24   Political Violence
Christopher J. Colvin

This chapter's examination of political violence begins by looking at post-conflict traumatic storytelling in South Africa. It is particularly focused on the globalization of psychological discourses of trauma and argues the narrative and emotional labors demanded of victims (and perpetrators) by these discourses are both intensely personal and political acts. The chapter suggests that increasingly global languages of trauma make it more difficult to understand the many internal and external causes and effects of political violence.

25   The Politics of Remorse
Nancy Scheper-Hughes

This chapter treats the politically and morally ambiguous task of recording the experience of violence and truth-telling from the point of view of a small cross-section of white South Africans. Their narratives of suffering, remorse, and reconciliation reflect the experiences of ordinary people existentially "thrown" into a political drama in which they participate as active collaborators, passive beneficiaries, or revolutionary "race traitors" vis-à-vis the apartheid state. Today, they are trying to make sense of their country's violent history and of their role in that history, to undo past wrongs, and to mend spoiled identities, so as to resume interrupted lives.

Notes on Contributors

Kevin Birth is Associate Professor in the Department of Anthropology at Queens College, City University of New York. He is the author of *Any Time is Trinidad Time: Social Meanings and Temporal Consciousness* (1999) as well as articles on Trinidadian music, kinship, and ethnicity.

Keith Bletzer completed formal training in medical anthropology and public health. His substantive interests include critical medical anthropology, social epidemiology of risk behavior (including substance use, HIV/AIDS, violence), and the long-term ethnography of agricultural labor.

Erika Bourguignon is Professor Emerita in the Department of Anthropology at Ohio State University. Her major interests are in psychological anthropology and the anthropology of women. Among her publications are *Religion, Altered States of Consciousness, and Social Change* (1973), *Possession* (1976, 1991), *Psychological Anthropology* (1979), *A World of Women* (1980) and (edited with Barbara Rigney) *Exile: A Memoir of 1939 by Bronka Schneider* (1998).

Conerly Casey is a Fulbright IIE sponsored Visiting Lecturer in the Departments of Psychiatry and Sociology at Bayero University in Kano, Nigeria. In 1998, her article "Suffering and the Identification of Enemies in Northern Nigeria" won the Association for Political and Legal Anthropology Student Essay Prize and was published in the *Political and Legal Anthropology Review*. Her book chapter "Identity and Difference in Today's Nigeria" will appear in *The Workbook on Ethnic Conflicts*, edited by Vamik Volkan and George Irani (in press).

Jennifer Cole is a cultural anthropologist and member of the Committee on Human Development at the University of Chicago. She has written extensively on the social and cultural construction of memory, including a book entitled *Forget Colonialism? Sacrifice and the Art of Memory in Madagascar* (2001). She is currently writing a book about youth, families, and the intimate bodily and moral politics of globalization in urban Madagascar.

Christopher J. Colvin has a Ph.D. in Anthropology from the University of Virginia and is currently a Post-Doctoral Fellow at the Center for Comparative Literature and Society at Columbia University. His research with a victim support group in Cape Town examines the politics of "traumatic storytelling" among victims of apartheid era violence. His book chapters include " 'Brothers and Sisters, Do Not Be Afraid of Me': Trauma, History and the Therapeutic Imagination in the New South Africa," in *Contested Pasts* (2003), edited by Kate Hodgkins. Related research interests include reparations and the globalization of psychological discourses of trauma.

René Devisch is Professor of Anthropology at the Catholic University of Louvain in Leuven, Belgium. A past coordinator there of the Africa Research Centre, and a member of the Belgian Royal Academy of Overseas Sciences, and the Belgian School of Psychoanalysis, he has published a number of books, including *Weaving the Threads of Life: The Khita Gynecological Healing Cult Among the Yaka* (1993) and *The Law of the Life-Givers: The Domestication of Desire* (1999). His major topics of interest concern the relations between culture, cosmology, bodily and psychic symbolism, and symptom formation, and the management of misfortune and healing in Bantu African cults and Christian healing churches.

Robert B. Edgerton is a University Scholar and Professor of Anthropology at the University of California, Los Angeles. A past president of the Society for Psychological Anthropology, he has published a number of books in the field, including *The Individual in Cultural Adaptation* (1971), *Alone Together* (1979), *Rules, Exceptions and Social Order* (1985), *Sick Societies* (1992), and *Warrior Women* (2000).

Katherine Pratt Ewing is Associate Professor of Cultural Anthropology and Religion at Duke University. Her publications include *Arguing Sainthood: Modernity, Psychoanalysis and Islam* (1997) and numerous articles based on research in Pakistan, in Turkey, and among Muslim migrants in Europe, including "The Illusion of Wholeness: Culture, Self, and the Experience of Inconsistency" (*Ethos* 1990), "Legislating Religious Freedom: Muslim Challenges to the Relationship between 'Church' and 'State' in Germany and France" (*Daedalus* 2000), and "Between Turkey and Germany: Living Islam in the Diaspora" (*South Atlantic Quarterly* 2003).

Atwood D. Gaines is Professor of Anthropology, Bioethics, Psychiatry, and Nursing in the College of Arts and Sciences and the Schools of Medicine and Nursing of Case Western Reserve University. A medical/psychiatric anthropologist with public health training, he has published a number of articles on ethnopsychiatry, theory in medical anthropology, ethnicity, aging, and the cultural studies of science. He has co-edited several volumes, with Robert Hahn, on *Physicians of Western Medicine* (1982, 1985) and edited *Ethnopsychiatry* (1992). He is currently finishing books on identity in Alsace, the cultural studies of science, and theory in medical anthropology.

Linda C. Garro is a Professor in the Department of Anthropology at the University of California, Los Angeles. Recipient of the Stirling Award for Contributions to Psychological Anthropology in 1999, she is co-author, with James C. Young, of *Medical Choice in a Mexican Village* (1994) and co-editor, with Cheryl Mattingly, of *Narrative and the Cultural Construction of Illness and Healing* (2000).

Patricia M. Greenfield is Professor of Psychology at the University of California, Los Angeles and founding Director of the Foundation for Psychocultural Research/ UCLA Center for Culture, Brain, and Development. She has authored or co-authored a number of books, including *Studies in Cognitive Growth* (1966, with Bruner, Oliver, et al.), *The Structure of Communication in Early Language Development* (1976, with J. H. Smith), *Mind and Media: The Effects of Television, Video Games and Computers* (1984), and *Weaving Generations Together: Evolving Creativity in the Maya of Chiapas* (forthcoming).

Alexander Laban Hinton is Assistant Professor of Anthropology at Rutgers University. He has published *Why Did They Kill? Cambodia in the Shadow of Genocide* (2005) and three edited volumes: *Biocultural Approaches to the Emotions* (1999), *Genocide: An Anthropological Reader* (2002), and *Annihilating Difference: The Anthropology of Genocide* (2002).

Douglas Hollan is Professor and Chair of Anthropology and Luckman Distinguished Teacher at the University of California, Los Angeles and an instructor at the Southern California Psychoanalytic Institute. He is the co-author of *Contentment and Suffering: Culture and Experience in Toraja* (1994) and *The Thread of Life: Toraja Reflections on the Life Cycle* (1996). Much of his published work examines the interface of cultural and psychological processes.

Charles Lindholm is University Professor of Anthropology at Boston University. His most recent books are *The Islamic Middle East: Tradition and Change* (2002), *Culture and Identity: The History, Theory and Practice of Psychological Anthropology* (2001), and (co-authored with John. A. Hall) *Is America Breaking Apart?* (1999). His book *Charisma* is available on-line at www.bu.edu/uni/faculty/publications/. He is presently working on a book on authenticity and modernity.

Daniel T. Linger is Professor of Anthropology at the University of California, Santa Cruz. He has done ethnographic research in Brazil and Japan. His published works include *Dangerous Encounters: Meanings of Violence in a Brazilian City* (1992), *No One Home: Brazilian Selves Remade in Japan* (2001), and *The Double Lens: Public and Personal Worlds in Anthropological Theory* (forthcoming).

Margaret Lock is Marjorie Bronfman Professor in Social Studies in Medicine affiliated with the Department of Social Studies of Medicine and the Department of Anthropology at McGill University. She is a fellow of the Royal Society of Canada, received a Canada Council Izaak Killam Fellowship, was awarded the Prix Du Québec, domaine Sciences Humaines in 1997, and in 2002 the Canada Council for the Arts Molson Prize. Her monographs include *Encounters with Aging: Mythologies of Menopause in Japan and North America* (1993) and *Twice Dead: Organ Transplants and the Reinvention of Death* (2002), both of which received prizes. She has edited or co-edited nine other books, including *New Horizons in Medical Anthropology* (2002), and written over 150 scholarly articles.

Setha M. Low is Professor of Environmental Psychology and Anthropology and Director of the Public Space Research Group at the Graduate Center of the City University of New York. She is the author and/or editor of numerous articles and books, including *Theorizing the City* (1999), *On the Plaza: The Politics of Public Space and Culture* (2000), *The Anthropology of Space and Place: Locating Culture* (2003, with D. Lawrence), and *Behind the Gates: Life, Security and the Pursuit of Happiness in Fortress America* (2003). Her most recent research with the Public Space Research Group is a post 9/11 ethnography of Battery Park City, New York. Currently, she is finishing a book on how to maintain cultural diversity in large urban parks and historic sites (*Common Ground: The Cultural Life of Parks*, forthcoming) as a fellow in residence at the Getty Center in Los Angeles.

Edward D. Lowe is a Research Anthropologist in the Department of Psychiatry and Biobehavioral Sciences at the University of California, Los Angeles. His recent publications include "A Widow, a Child, and Two Lineages: Exploring Kinship and Attachment in Chuuk" (2002) and "Identity, Activity, and the Well-Being of Adolescents and Youths: Lessons from Young People in a Micronesian Society" (forthcoming).

Catherine Lutz is Professor of Anthropology at Brown University. She is the author of *Homefront: A Military City and the American Twentieth Century* (2001). She has also co-authored *Reading National Geographic* with Jane Collins (1993), co-edited *Language and the Politics of Emotion* with Lila Abu-Lughod (1990), and written *Unnatural Emotions* (1988). She has conducted studies on militarization and on domestic violence for activist organizations, including *Micronesia as Strategic Colony for Cultural Survival* and *Making Soldiers in the Public Schools: An Analysis of the Army JROTC Curriculum* (with Lesley Bartlett) for the American Friends Service Committee.

A. David Napier is Senior Lecturer in medical anthropology at University College London. He is the author of three books on the cultural construction of the self: *Masks, Transformation and Paradox* (1986), *Foreign Bodies* (1992), and *The Age of Immunology* (2003). He has conducted fieldwork in Indonesia and India, and has spent several years working with the homeless and with primary care doctors in rural settings. He is the founder and current Executive Director of Students of Human Ecology, a non-profit organization that sponsors mentor–apprentice learning opportunities in the areas of medicine, the environment, and culture.

Elinor Ochs is Professor of Anthropology and Applied Linguistics, and Mac Arthur Fellow (1998) at the University of California, Los Angeles. Her books include *Culture and Language Development: Language Acquisition and Language Socialization in a Samoan Village* (1988), *Developmental Pragmatics* (1979, co-edited with B. B. Shieffelin), *Language Socialization across Cultures* (1986), *Interaction and Grammar* (1996, co-edited with E. Schegloff and S. A. Thompson), and with

L. Capps: *Constructing Panic: The Discourse of Agoraphobia* (1995) and *Living Narrative: Creating Lives in Everyday Storytelling* (2001).

Nancy Scheper-Hughes is Professor of Anthropology at the University of California, Berkeley, where she also directs the doctoral training program in Critical Studies in Medicine, Science, and the Body. Among her publications are two award winning ethnographies: *Saints, Scholars and Schizophrenics: Mental Illness in Rural Ireland* (new, updated and expanded edition, 2000) and *Death without Weeping: The Violence of Everyday Life in Brazil* (1993). She has published two edited volumes, *Commodifying Bodies* (2003) with Loic Wacquant, and *Violence in War and Peace* (2003) with Philippe Bourgois. Her next book is *Parts Unknown*, a multi-sited ethnographic study of the global traffic in human organs. Scheper-Hughes is the Director of Organs Watch, a medical human rights project.

Don Seeman is an Assistant Professor in the Department of Religion at Emory University. A former NIMH fellow in clinically relevant medical anthropology at Harvard Medical School, his recent publications focus on social suffering in ethnographic contexts and on religious ritual as a mediator of social experience, including the phenomenology of religious violence in Israel. He previously taught in the Department of Sociology and Anthropology at the Hebrew University in Jerusalem.

Olga Solomon is a Post-Doctoral Fellow in the Department of Anthropology at the University of California, Los Angeles. She brings together her graduate training in applied linguistics and clinical psychology to examine discourse competence of children with autistic spectrum disorder to participate in everyday narrative activity with family members. She is a guest co-editor with Elinor Ochs of a special issue, *Discourse and Autism*, of the journal *Discourse Studies* (forthcoming). She is currently the director of the UCLA Ethnography of Autism Project on the everyday lives of high functioning children with autistic spectrum disorders.

Howard F. Stein, a psychoanalytic anthropologist, is a Professor in the Department of Family and Preventive Medicine at the University of Oklahoma Health Sciences Center. A past president of the High Plains Society for Applied Anthropology, he is the author of 22 books, including *Listening Deeply* (1994), *Euphemism, Spin, and the Crisis in Organizational Life* (1998), *Nothing Personal, Just Business: A Guided Journey into Organizational Darkness* (2001), and *Beneath the Crust of Culture: Psychoanalytic Anthropology and the Cultural Unconscious in American Life* (2003).

Thomas S. Weisner is Professor of Anthropology, Departments of Psychiatry and Anthropology, University of California, Los Angeles, Center for Culture & Health (NPI). His publications include "The American dependency conflict: Continuities and discontinuities in behavior and values of countercultural parents and their children" (*Ethos* 2001), "Anthropological aspects of childhood" for the *International Encyclopedia of the Social and Behavioral Sciences* (2001), *African Families and the Crisis of Social Change* (1997, co-edited with C. Bradley and P. Kilbride), and *Discovering Successful Pathways in Children's Development: New Methods in the Study* *of Childhood and Family Life* (ed., forthcoming). He is President-elect of the Society for Psychological Anthropology.

Geoffrey M. White is Professor of Anthropology at the University of Hawai'i and Senior Fellow at the East–West Center. His publications include *Perilous Memories: The Asia-Pacific War(s)* (2001, co-editor), *New Directions in Psychological Anthropology* (1992, co-editor), *Identity Through History: Living Stories in a Solomon Islands Society* (1991), and *Person, Self and Experience: Exploring Pacific Ethnopsychologies* (1985, co-editor). He served as president of the Society for Psychological Anthropology 2001–3.

Susan Reynolds Whyte, a Professor at the Institute of Anthropology, University of Copenhagen, has done research in the areas of misfortune, health, disability, medicines, and international development. She has co-edited two books, *The Social Context of Medicines in Developing Countries* (1988) and *Disability and Culture* (1995), written a monograph, *Questioning Misfortune* (1997), and co-authored *Social Lives of Medicines* (2003).

James M. Wilce, Jr. is Associate Professor of Anthropology at Northern Arizona University and has also served as Visiting Lecturer at the École des Hautes Études en Sciences Sociales, Paris. His first book, describing his fieldwork on language, the self, and medicine in Bangladesh, was *Eloquence in Trouble: Poetics and Politics of Complaint in Rural Bangladesh* (1998). He has published articles related to language and emotion in *Comparative Studies in Society and History, Culture, Medicine, and Psychiatry*, and *Ethos*. He is the editor of *Social and Cultural Lives of Immune Systems* (2003) and is currently working on a new book, *Crying Shame: Metaculture, Modernity and Lament*.

Michael Winkelman is Director of the Ethnographic Field School and Head of the Sociocultural Subdiscipline, Department of Anthropology at Arizona State University. He is the author of several books, including *Shamans, Priests and Witches* (1992), *Shamanism: The Neural Ecology of Consciousness and Healing* (2000), and *Ethnic Relations in the US* (1998). He has recently examined the role of shamanism as part of an evolved human psychology in "Shamanic universals and evolutionary psychology" (*Journal of Ritual Studies*, 2002) and the applications of shamanism to contemporary health problems, particularly addiction, in "Alternative and traditional medicine approaches for substance abuse programs: A shamanic perspective" (*International Journal of Drug Policy*, 2001) and "Complementary therapy for addiction: 'Drumming out drugs'" (*American Journal of Public Health*, 2003). His website is at www.public.asu.edu/~atmxw.

Acknowledgments

We offer our heartfelt thanks to all of the volume's contributors, many of whom have provided valuable advice and suggestions along the way, and to our anonymous reviewers. The volume would not have been conceived or produced without Jane Huber's editorial guidance, laced with her unwavering perseverance, diplomacy, and charm. For the loving indulgence of our families and friends, Conerly thanks Carole and Michael Landon, Andrew Wilson, Margaret Ostermann, Lelia Casey, and Carolina Izquierdo. Bob thanks his wife Karen Ito. We both thank Kristen Hatch for her editorial assistance in pulling the manuscript together.

Introduction

Within the past two decades, planetary computerization, burgeoning media industries, and other global processes have significantly altered the ways in which individuals experience local and global, interdependent, cultural communities. Individuals, and the emerging or dissolving communities to which they belong, enter dialogical, often paradoxical relations. While scholars from many fields question these life changes, this anthology demonstrates the vitality and relevance of psychocultural approaches that emerge through the sub-field of psychological anthropology. Psychological anthropology, or the study of individuals and their sociocultural communities, helps us to understand what Jackson (1998: 21) refers to as "the many refractions of the core experience that we are at one and the same time part of a singular, particular, and finite world and caught up in a wider world whose horizons are effectively infinite." While critiques of ethnocentrism have brought attention to the politics of identity and equality, as well as to the mutual recognitions and attunements that are necessary for coexistence, the relationship and balance of the particular and the universal, the individual and the global, as examined through various life processes, vary dramatically among individuals and across communities. Psychological anthropologists bring unique approaches to these dynamic relations. Ethnopsychological research, in-depth case studies, studies of transference and counter-transference, person-centered ethnographies, and ethnographies of communication, enable psychological anthropologists to draw out the experiential lives of subjects and informants who shape, and are shaped by, their communities.

Psychological anthropology, which marked the birth of American anthropology, has been credited with early attention to racism and ethnocentrism, while simultaneously discredited for developing cultural and national stereotypes. Part of our revisionist approach to the historical, theoretical genealogy of psychological anthropology is to chart the ambivalence with which scholars have viewed the linking of people's "psychologies" with their sociocultural communities. This ambivalence emerged out of critiques of imperialism, colonialism, Social Darwinism, capitalism, and development industries, all of which have supported the production of "psychologically underdeveloped" cultural communities as objects for modern intervention. Not surprisingly, ambivalence about the relationship between the particular and the universal has been poignant during major world crises and events – World War II and its aftermath, during the 1960s and 1970s decolonizations, civil rights' and women's movements, and in the 1990s with increased attention to the inequities of global cultural economies. During these periods of rapid social change, rich concepts of the "individual," the "self," an "authoring self," a "person," and "intersubjective selves" – self-formations that are embedded in social realms of meaning and significance – have been attached to thin or poorly understood notions of power, agency, and changing sociocultural communities.

Critiques of psychocultural studies tend to oscillate between those of totalization and Euro-American centrism, to those of extreme dialogism, where heteroglossia and polynarrative supposedly make it difficult to hear or to interpret the experiences of individuals. Within this range of critique, scholars have widely accepted social speech and visible bodily practice as ways to understand others, while intrapsychic processes such as Freud's unconscious motivations or Bakhtin's (1981) "inner speech," speech directed toward oneself, have been considered impossible to study across cultures, or racialized and "othered" in such a way as to be unthinkable, even unknowable.

In his 1935 preface to Zora Neale Hurston's *Mules and Men*, Franz Boas wrote: "It is the great merit of Miss Hurston's work that she entered into the homely life of the southern Negro as one of them and was fully accepted as such by the companions of her childhood. Thus she has been able to penetrate through that affected demeanor by which the Negro excludes the White observer effectively from participating in his true inner life" (Hurston 1935: xiii). A conscious champion of cultural difference and anti-racism, Boas, like many other psychological anthropologists, nonetheless lived within racist, segregated academic and political, cultural communities.

It was not until the late 1950s and 1960s that scholars in psychological anthropology and psychology began to address the connections between racism, ethnocentrism, and psychology, and the sociohistorical ruptures that make listening to the "inner lives" of others so profoundly difficult. However, listening has never been enough. As many scholars show, intersubjectivity is not simply the dialectic of conceptual intentions, but it is lived through our bodies and our five senses (Fanon 1963, 1967; Jackson 1998; Merleau-Ponty 1962; Stoller 1995). It is marked by conscious perspectives, intentions, and attunements, and by those less conscious, unconscious, or habitual (Hollan and Wellenkamp 1994; Obeyesekere 1981); it is neither well-integrated neurophysiologically nor consonant, so that persons may perceive and relate the same occurrence, yet experience and remember it differently. We also witness human consciousness shift among diverse senses of self, from ontologically secure and whole, to selves that are "epidermalized," anxious, fragmented, or engulfed (Casey 1997; Fanon 1963, 1967; Laing 1969), to those that integrate many different selves (Ewing 1990; Holland et al. 1998). We now recognize as many selves as people who recognize us and who engage us in their thoughts, words, or actions (Goffman 1959; Jackson 1998). We note the temporal and spatial dimensions of self and other recognitions, sometimes drawing ourselves into synchronicity with global cultural communities or sharply diverging in our perceptions, cognition, or memory. While many theorists describe intersubjectivity and dialogism as mere styles of representation, we do not consider them the same as the intersubjectivity that makes empathy, transference, synchronicity, or analogy even possible. We suggest that, in hindsight, the historical genealogy of psychocultural studies exemplifies both substantial nuance *and* stereotyping in relational accounts of others and ourselves, infused with the complexities and contradictions of rapidly changing concepts of the "individual" and of "culture," of individuality and of cultural diversity.

Our intention is revisionist: we open with a brief overview of the theoretical developments associated with psychological anthropology, then present psychocultural ethnography and theory that has been ignored, neglected, or subsumed within sociocultural studies, particularly under the rubrics of postcolonial and cultural studies. Part of our explicit focus is the splitting of psychological anthropology, which defined the birth and early work of American anthropology, into diverse sub-fields that sustain strands of psychocultural work, but fail to identify them as psychocultural. At the same time, we would like to underscore the sustained efforts of scholars whose work has given depth and shape to this sub-field, most prominently, our contributors. Contributors to this volume demonstrate the vitality of integrative, psychocultural approaches – those that engage and synthesize multiple historical, theoretical genealogies of psychological anthropology, whether psychoanalytic/psychodynamic, phenomenological, linguistic, psychoadaptive ecological, medical, cognitive, embodied, or informed by the neurosciences, psychology, cultural studies, and social history. We address the anthology to readers within and outside of the field of anthropology who seek to understand relations of the particular and the universal, the individual and his or her communities.

HISTORICAL GENEALOGY OF PSYCHOCULTURAL STUDIES

As early as the mid-1800s, psychology and anthropology shared an interest in the relationship between culture and psychology, and by the 1870s German anthropologists such as Waitz and Bastian joined British anthropologist Edward Tylor in efforts to link culture to psychology. In 1888, Franz Boas was hired by Clark University, where he began his long study of the "mind of primitive man." Empirical research on this topic soon followed. British psychologist W. H. R. Rivers took part in Cambridge University's Torres Straits Expedition in 1898. He showed that the same optical illusions that puzzled Europeans had little effect on the native peoples. German psychologist Wilhelm Stern and anthropologist Richard Thurnwald soon after carried out similar research in the South Pacific.

The first theoretical orientation to have an impact on this field came from Freud's psychoanalytic work. In 1900, he published his first great book, *The Interpretation of Dreams*. By 1910, Freud had turned his interests to a demonstration of how psychoanalysis could help to explain how cultural institutions arise and how they function. His book *Totem and Taboo*, published in 1913, had a dramatic impact, attracting to psychoanalytic theory such influential "Freudians" as Erich Fromm, Ernest Jones, J. C. Frügel, Geza Róheim, George Devereux, and Erik Erikson. In arguing that social prohibitions – "taboos" – were comparable to the self-imposed inhibitions of "neurotic" individuals, Freud sought to explain why taboos such as those surrounding rulers and the dead came into being and how they were maintained.

The Freudian impact focused psychological anthropologists on child training, including such often criticized topics as toilet training, and on the general question of the relationship between personality and culture. In 1928 one of Freud's disciples, Hungarian Geza Róheim, went to the Aranda of Central Australia to describe what he called "delayed infancy," the length of time that humans are dependent on adults. He argued that each culture is founded on a specific childhood trauma which produces the type of personality of people in that society. Other Freudian scholars such as Weston LaBarre, Bruno Bettleheim, and George Devereux produced influential work as well, but their psychoanalytic writings were soon eclipsed by an emerging field known as culture and personality.

Edward Sapir was the first to describe the unconscious configuration of grammar and sound, and his work led to the study of how personality and culture were configured. In her book *Patterns of Culture,* published in 1934, Ruth Benedict compared the basic configurations of culture and personality among the Pueblo and Plains Indians, the Kwakiutl of the Northwest Coast, and the Dobu of Melanesia. Portraying the Pueblo Indians as "Apollonian," the Plains Indians as "Dionysian," the Dobuans as "Paranoid," and the Kwakiutl as "Megalomaniac," Benedict argued each culture had its own personality and that because some individuals could not cope with their culture's demands they became alienated and frustrated. Her book was enormously popular, making her one of the best known anthropologists of all time.

Benedict's friend and colleague, Margaret Mead, was also a major psychological anthropologist. She helped to found configurationism, but went on to make important contributions to many other areas of psychological anthropology, including childhood development, sex roles and temperament, personality and culture change, national character, and cross-cultural socialization. Her first three books were based on her fieldwork in the South Pacific: *Coming of Age in Samoa* (1928), *Growing Up in New Guinea* (1930), and *Sex and Temperament in Three Primitive Societies* (1935). Mead also wrote numerous articles in popular magazines, her name becoming a household word.

While Mead was having her early impact on psychological anthropology, anthropologists Cora DuBois, Ralph Linton, and Thomas Gladwin joined psychoanalyst Abram Kardiner in the study of "basic" and "modal" personality. They posited a causal chain from primary institutions such as household form, subsistence activities, and child training to basic personality and then to secondary institutions including religion, ritual, and folklore. Cora DuBois put this paradigm to the test with 18 months of fieldwork in the Dutch East Indies in 1938–9. The result was *The People of Alor* (1944), in which she argued that not everyone in such a society developed the same basic personality. Instead, she spoke of a "modal" or most frequent form of personality.

The attempt to measure modal personality led to the widespread use of projective tests, especially the Rorschach and Thematic Apperception Test (TAT). During the 1940s and 1950s the Rorschach was widely used. One of the most widely known uses of this test was by A. F. C. Wallace among the Iroquois Indians in New York. He found that only 26 of the 70 individuals tested fell into a modal class, although another 16 were close to this class (Wallace 1952).

A year after Wallace's study was published, anthropologist Thomas Gladwin and psychiatrist Seymour B. Sarason collaborated to produce a projective test study of people on the island of Truk. In a 650-page book, *Truk: Man in Paradise* (1953), Gladwin and Sarason described the many anxieties about food and sexuality, as well as the pressure of much gossip and fear of sorcery. They strongly recommended the use of the Rorschach and the TAT as means of identifying personality attributes that might otherwise be missed.

The next major development in psychological anthropology was the study of national character – the personality of most members of an entire nation. Characterizations of the national character of the British, Germans, French, Italians, and other Europeans go far back in history. In 1928, for example, Salvador de Madariaga wrote *Englishmen, Frenchmen and Spaniards*, contrasting English "action" with Spanish "emotion" and French "thought." But it was the eruption of World War II that initiated the empirical study of the national character of our enemies and even our allies. As early as 1939, Margaret Mead, Gregory Bateson, Eliott Chapple, and other anthropologists tried to devise ways that psychological anthropology could support the war effort. After the United States entered the war, others moved to Washington, where they attempted to analyze the national character of the Japanese and the Germans.

Ruth Benedict did much research on the Japanese, trying to reconcile their restrained aestheticism with their fanatical militarism. Although her book *The Chrysanthemum and the Sword* (1946) has been roundly criticized by Americans and Japanese alike, it was studied by our military leaders and used by the postwar MacArthur occupation forces. Benedict considered it her finest work. In *Escape From Freedom* (1941) Erich Fromm tried to explain the appeal of Nazism to the German people in terms of their national authoritarian personality. Such a person is obedient and subservient to superiors, but overbearing and scornful to social inferiors. Walter C. Langer wrote *The Mind of Adolf Hitler* for the American Office of Strategic Services soon after the war broke out, but it was not published for the public until 1973. Erik Erikson also studied Hitler for our military, characterizing him as a superhuman leader who created terror among his followers and involved them in crimes which they could not deny.

After the war, national character studies focused on the Russians. British anthropologist Geoffrey Gorer and his collaborator John Rickman wrote *The People of Great Russia* (1948), arguing that Russian infants were tightly swaddled and unable to move except for a brief period each day when they were released, cleaned, and actively played with. This phenomenon was to produce the Russian propensity for mood swings between long periods of introspective depression and brief spurts of frantic social activity. The need for strong authority was also learned and symbolized through swaddling. Clyde Kluckhohn followed Gorer and Rickman by comparing traditional Russian personality with the new ideal Soviet personality type. There were many differences. The traditional personality was warm, trusting, expansive, and responsive, while the Soviet ideal was formal, controlled, distrustful, and conspiratorial (Kluckhohn 1962).

Other scholars studied American modal personality. Margaret Mead wrote *And Keep Your Powder Dry* in 1942 as a wartime morale booster. Geoffrey Gorer wrote *The American People* in 1948, arguing that the American and British national characters contrasted dramatically. David Riesman, Nathan Glazer, and Reuel Denney followed with *The Lonely Crowd* in 1950, describing Americans as "other-directed," constantly scanning their environment for cues to the correct attitudes and behaviors. They also emphasized perceived American behaviors of rivalry, jealousy, and individualism. Philip Slater, in his book *The Pursuit of Loneliness* (1970), suggested that our core of individualism must be replaced in our value system if our society is to remain viable, while the Chinese-born anthropologist Francis L. K. Hsu argued American national character is one of self-reliance, the search for political, economic, and social equality.

There were other studies of national character as well, but this kind of approach increasingly came under fire from many quarters for its political prejudice and lack of objectivity, as well as its assumption that there was a causal relationship between culture and personality. The most powerful criticism came from someone within culture and personality itself, Melford E. Spiro. In 1951 he wrote a detailed article in the journal *Psychiatry* entitled "Culture and Personality: The National History of a False Dichotomy," arguing persuasively that the field of culture and personality had failed to show any causal relationship between culture and personality because the development of personality and the acquisition of culture were a single process.

In response to criticisms like that of Spiro, the study of culture and personality fell by the wayside to be replaced by a new cross-cultural comparative research strategy championed by G. P. Murdock, who possessed an encyclopedic knowledge of world ethnography. Murdock established the Human Relations Area Files (HRAF) at Yale, making available a host of cross-indexed data on hundreds of non-Western societies. One of Murdock's students was John W. M. Whiting, whose earliest field research in New Guinea provided rich empirical data about the process of socialization. Joined by psychologist Irvin L. Child, Whiting then employed what they called the correlational method of testing hypotheses utilizing HRAF data. This work resulted in their influential book *Child Training and Personality* (1953). Other correlational research appeared as well. At the same time, Robert A. LeVine and Melford E. Spiro, both of whom were trained in anthropology and psychoanalysis, carried out ethnographic field research on various ways in which people adapt psychologically to the world in which they live. Spiro focused on Burma and LeVine worked in East Africa. While they produced their stimulating findings, John Whiting and his wife Beatrice were developing their highly influential "Six Cultures Project." Six pairs of investigators, usually husband and wife teams, were sent to six different societies to observe the behavior of children aged three to eleven as they interacted with infants, other children, and adults, in effort to learn in what ways culture impacts children's lives. Their findings were presented in three major books: *Six Cultures* (1963), *Mothers of Six Cultures* (1964), and *Children of Six Cultures* (1974). The research was the most meticulous yet conducted and it continues to attract attention. However, it did not lead to any conceptual breakthroughs. At the same time that the Whitings were carrying out their intensive data collection, a team organized by Walter Goldschmidt was conducting controlled interviews and observations with samples from eight populations in East Africa, searching for psychological and behavioral differences between farmers and pastoralists. *The Individual in Cultural Adaptation: A Study of Four East African Societies* (1971) is Robert Edgerton's assessment of the changing lives of individuals living in four of these eight East African societies. He demonstrated the variability of psychological adaptations within and across social and cultural settings.

In the 1960s and 1970s, psychocultural variability within and across cultures, worldwide decolonization, the Cold War, and the civil rights' and women's movements, worked their way into a critical disruption within anthropology. Criticisms about collaborations of anthropologists with colonial and other regimes of power led to grave reflections about the relations of anthropologists to their subjects. The idea of culture itself became suspiciously connected to regimes of power that discipline and construct, rather than study, their subjects (Fanon 1963, 1967; Foucault 1965).

Claude Lévi-Strauss's "structuralism" posited human activity as constructed, rather than natural or essential, with culture as a system of organization and of structural differences homologous to Saussure's concept of "langue." Jacques Lacan's theory of the unconscious organized like a language also had affinities to structuralism, drawing together psychoanalytic and linguistic perspectives on psychology. A revival of psychoanalytic anthropology brought new approaches to dreams, sexuality, religious symbolism, and psychopathology, integrating psychoanalytic, linguistic, and social, historical perspectives.

In *Black Skin/White Masks* (1967), Franz Fanon, a psychiatrist born in Martinique and schooled in France, described his personal experience as a black intellectual in a white world and the ways in which the colonizer/colonized relationship became normalized as psychology. Fanon wrote that being colonized by a language is to support the weight of a civilization that identifies blackness with evil and sin. To escape this, colonized people don a white mask so as to consider themselves universal subjects equally participating in colonial and world societies. The cultural values of the colonizers, internalized or "epidermalized" into consciousness, created a fundamental disjuncture between a black man's consciousness and his body. Fanon integrated Jung's psychoanalytic notion of "collective unconsciousness" with embodied experiences of colonization and racism in Algeria, locating the historical point at which certain psychological formations become possible and begin to perpetuate themselves as psychology.

During the 1960s and 1970s, "madness" and "badness," as defined by medical establishments and criminal justice systems, became early sites of struggle for self-expression, identity, and agency. Robert Edgerton, in *The Cloak of Competence* (1967), highlighted individual motives and the social adaptations of people with mental retardation to expose the frailty – even cruelty – of institutionalized forms of psychological assessment that fail to consider one's individuality in cultural life contexts. In *The Death and Rebirth of the Seneca* (1969), A.F.C. Wallace traced the dramatic revitalization of a demoralized people living in a shattered culture. The struggle for life by terminally ill children received attention, as the work with leukemic children by Myra Bluebond-Langer poignantly illustrates: *The Private Worlds of Dying Children* (1978). There was also a growing concern with child abuse and neglect, as an edited volume by Jill Korbin in 1981 illustrates: *Child Abuse and Neglect: Cross-Cultural Perspectives*. Work on this same issue has continued to the present time with perhaps the most dramatic example coming from Nancy Scheper-Hughes in her powerful book *Death Without Weeping* (1992), in which she explored the mechanisms used by women in a Brazilian "shanty-town" to cope with the high death rate of their children.

Psychological anthropologists continued with familiar topics such as dreaming, altered states of consciousness, possession, trance, shamanism, fantasy, emotion, and mental illness. Puberty rites and adolescence came under study as well, and so did shame, guilt, and bereavement. Research on conceptions of personhood and self continued. An influential example was provided by Geoffrey M. White and James Kirkpatrick in their edited volume *Person, Self, and Experience: Exploring Pacific Ethnopsychologies* (1985). While research interests in the self, perception, cognition, emotion, language, learning, decision-making, and other psychological concerns continued, a new focus emerged as more and more psychological anthropologists turned their attention to cultural change and urbanization, including global issues relating to modernization.

Marc Manganaro describes a shift in the 1960s from fieldwork based on principles of "science" to postmodern, discursive processes of "text-making": *Modernist Anthropology: From Fieldwork to Text* (1990). Repudiating the claims of "objectivism," postmodern and poststructural theorists began to address such issues as authorship, ideology, power, and readership, contributing to a general trend toward meaning-centered, self-reflexive, narrative accounts of people and their cultures (Geertz 1973; Rosaldo 1989). "Experience-near" approaches to intersubjectivity, identity, and other relational forms emerged as scholars recognized the primacy of lived experience, meanings, and significance over analytic categories (Csordas 1994; Desjarlais 1992; Hollan and Wellenkamp 1994; Kleinman and Kleinman 1991; Levy 1973; Lutz 1990; Wikan 1991). Many psychological anthropologists shifted from Darwinian, Marxist, and Durkheimian groundings of individual experience in ecological adaptations and institutions toward ethnopsychological, sociolinguistic, phenomenological, and symbolic approaches. In contrast to standard ethnography, psychocultural scholars developed "person-centered ethnography" to "represent human behavior and subjective experience from the point of view of the acting, intending, and attentive subject, to actively explore the emotional saliency and motivational force of cultural beliefs and symbols (rather than to assume such saliency and force), and to avoid unnecessary reliance on overly abstract, experience-distant constructs" (Hollan 2001: 49). This approach was not meant to displace the power of ecological adaptions and institutions in shaping one's life, but to address the tensions between individual agency and culturally hegemonic forms.

MODERNITY AND PSYCHOCULTURAL CHANGE

> To speak . . . is to exist absolutely for the other . . . it means, above all, to assume a culture, to support the weight of a civilization. (Fanon 1967: 17)

Fanon's thoughts are particularly relevant today, wherein present pasts haunt the Ethernets, and people continue to don "white masks" so as to consider themselves universal subjects, equally participating in societies that advocate equality, abstracted from appearance. The real–virtual interface of global cultural relations places a heavy emphasis on the intercultural accountings of identity, memory, and consciousness. These transmissions affect real–virtual remappings of ourselves in relation to others, and newly forming intersubjective assemblages of self-reference that alter psychocultural processes such as consciousness and time, emotion, cognition, learning, memory, and identity. Such remappings reflect and constitute psychocultural experiences, yet vary in their impacts on individuals and communities.

As Wilce, Ochs and Solomon, and Whyte (this volume) illustrate, people blend internal and external, temporal and spatial dimensions of experience to rearrange, to transform, and to narrate themselves and others. Cultural representations in speech, thought, or imagination may be paths to unconscious processes or objects of inquiry in and of themselves. No longer do we separate individual and social experiences (Cole, this volume), or process and content (Garro, this volume). Capps and Ochs (1995: 15) explain:

> What "actually happened' in some past event in our life is inextricably tied to the phenomenological meaning we ascribe – that is, to our experience of the event. And this meaning changes as we continually respond to the blending of external and internal forces that make up our ongoing experience – as we revise and reshape the story of our lives.

Global and local forms of communication introduce narrative improvisations and structures that map into assemblages of self-reference and meaning-making. We make experiences our own and our own "truths" – lenses through which we see, evaluate, and remember differing accounts of life events.

South Africa's Truth and Reconciliation Commission (Scheper-Hughes and Colvin, this volume) and the bombing of the World Trade Center (White, this volume) are notable examples of what Huyssen (2001) refers to as the "traumatic side of memory culture, the evermore ubiquitous discourses of trauma, recovering memories, genocide, AIDS, slavery, drugs, alcohol, and sexual abuse, and the increasing numbers of memorials, commemorations and apologies." Shifts in remembering and forgetting appear to be under (re)forming individual and sociocultural pressures, but there is little ethnographic work documenting these changes, and their relations to historical events, consciousness, and time (Antze and Lambeck 1996; Birth 1999; Cole 2001). Furthermore, remembering, and the emotions it evokes, may be channeled through "emotive institutions" (White, this volume) such as the media, the Truth and Reconciliation Commission, and gated communities (Low, this volume), which as Low suggests emerge in response to discourses of fear of violence.

While scholars from many disciplines concern themselves with the social impact of global time-space compression, few offer insights about the resonance of this compression with psychical, spiritual, or corporeal processes, even those that so profoundly affect us, such as biological rhythms, dreaming, and remembering (Birth, Hollan, Cole, Scheper-Hughes, Colvin, and Lock, this volume). How do psychocultural processes such as consciousness or memory mediate or become mediated by racism, genocide, a politics of inequitable globalization, migration, worldwide desecularization, or corporate instability (Gaines, Hinton, Ewing, and Stein, this volume)? What differential aspects of globalization produce increased witchcraft afflictions in Africa and South America (Casey 1997; Comaroff and Comaroff 1998; Izquierdo and Casey 2003), yet decreased afflictions and resulting violence in Melanesia (Knauft 2002)? How are such experiences lived and remembered through our emotions, our bodies, and our five senses (Stoller 1995; Bourguignon, Devisch, Seeman, Winkelman and Bletzer, this volume)? How do they shape the way in which we feel, think, or learn about our world (Lindholm, Garro, Greenfield, this volume)?

Intersubjectivity and the impacts of biomedical sciences and new technologies are an important area of interest for psychocultural scholars. Gaines (this volume) locates the historical and cultural epistemologies of "race," tracing the ways in which "race sciences" have been exported around the world. Lock (this volume) argues new biomedical technologies may fragment and commodify the body, resulting in new forms of intersubjectivity and the global exchange of cells, tissues, and organs. Ewing (this volume) describes the inbetweenness of those who migrate and the emotional restructurings of memory and generation that occur within medical clinics. Addressing debates about the effects of global processes on the identifications that people make with others, Linger (this volume) asks us to consider what it means to be a "person" in today's world. Linger and Napier (this volume) both question the moral and ethnical dimensions of self and other, and the cultural and historical contexts, including the biomedical sciences, that reflect and constitute these identifications. How are moral and ethical dimensions of identity codified, evoked, deployed, or remembered by individuals and groups, local and global?

Increased world violence is a phenomenon linked to time-space compression and the development of new technologies. Nandy (1996) argues that a violent retooling of the self, particularly in the so-called "developing" countries, has gone hand in hand with the loss of large parts of remembered pasts. Irrelevant aspects of the past have been excised, while only those conducive to modern Euro-American forms of development remain. He feels that individuality has been denuded of much of its substantive content, with personal initiative and choice handed over to a bureaucratic false sense of freedom. Nandy (1996), in much of the world, finds contextual and relational roles of communities removed from situations of choice so that individuals are left to deal with global forces. Like Bauman (1989), Nandy posits the functional division of labor, distantiation, and the substitution of technical for moral responsibility as features of modern global bureaucracies that may not cause violence, but certainly make it possible – an idea that Hinton and Stein (this volume) develop further in their discussions of genocide and corporate "downsizing." What is different about their arguments is the importance of affective, personal and symbolic aspects of bureaucratic violence, dimensions which are also focal points in Scheper-Hughes' and Colvin's work with victims and perpetrators in South Africa. What options are available for the victims, collaborators, or passive observers of violence? How do people evaluate ubiquitous discourses of violence or maintain a sense of security (Low, and Colvin, this volume)? How do people recover in the aftermath of violence (Colvin, and Scheper-Hughes, this volume)? Are there alternatives to violence in the face of continuing social injustice and global inequities?

While modern global processes create anxieties for scholars and laypeople alike, the conflicts of modern life are not homogeneous in their impact on individuals and communities. Appadurai (2001: 3) suggests "grassroots globalization" or "globalization from below" may offer "democratic and autonomous standing in respect to the various forms by which global power further seeks to extend its dominion." "Alternative," "parallel," and "multiple" modernities require a self-fashioning of what is considered modern across relational experiences (Ewing 1997; Knauft 2002; Ewing, Linger, Napier, and Weisner and Lowe, this volume). Contributors to this volume focus on the variability between and among individuals and communities with respect to power, agency, and the possibilities of modern life. A central human preoccupation, as Jackson (1998) aptly points out, is control over the relationship and balance of the particular and the universal, the individual and the global, the self and non-self, themes prevalent throughout this volume.

Within the past two decades, new technologies in the cognitive and neurosciences, the importance of global communications, ethnographies of communication, and person-centered ethnography have reinvigorated psychocultural studies of modern life. With increased media and telecommunications, "imagined communities" and "global villages" create further propinquity in our world, but with little sense of place or origin, the value of which, in some communities, defines one's identity or access to resources. Psychocultural research strengthens our evaluations of the saliency, force, and impact of modern persons and communal forms, including "imagined" ones, and the intersubjectivities and assemblages of self-reference that emerge in diverse, often rapidly changing world conditions.

A WORD ABOUT THOSE WHO ARE MISSING

With this volume we hope to introduce new readers to the sub-field of psychological anthropology and to contribute to its growing vigor. In compiling the chapters for this volume we sought to provide a sampling of contemporary psychocultural perspectives, those that creatively synthesize concepts of "individuality," "society," and "culture." We also asked contributors to envision how psychological anthropologists might address important new theoretical and social issues in an interdisciplinary way. We specifically urged contributors to focus upon their key concept or topic, while engaging scholarly debate about the ways in which people incorporate, or are incorporated into, modern, global cultural relations. For us, a vibrant psychological anthropology retains close relations with psychology and the neurosciences and with other anthropological sub-disciplines. Consequently, contributors to the volume, while varied in their approaches and backgrounds, tend to have explicit interests in psychocultural aspects of modern life. Missing from this volume are works generated from computational or lab studies that are primarily oriented toward evolution or the cognitive and neurosciences.

REFERENCES

Antze, Paul, and Michael Lambeck, 1996 *Tense Past: Cultural Essays in Trauma and Memory.* New York: Routledge.

Appadurai, Arjun, 2001 *Globalization.* Durham, NC: Duke University Press.

Bakhtin, M. M., 1981 *Dialogic Imagination: Four Essays by M. M. Bakhtin.* Michael E. Holquist, ed. Caryl Emerson and Michael Holquist, trans. Austin: University of Texas Press.

Bauman, Zygmunt, 1989 *Modernity and the Holocaust.* Ithaca, NY: Cornell University Press.

Benedict, Ruth 1946 *The Chrysanthemum and the Sword: Patterns of Japanese Culture.* Boston, MA: Houghton-Mifflin.

— 1989 [1934] *Patterns of Culture.* Boston, MA: Houghton-Mifflin.

Benjamin, Walter, 1983–4 Theoretics of Knowledge; Theory of Progress, *Philosophical Forum,* xv, 1–2 (Fall–Winter): 7.

Birth, Kevin, 1999 *Any Time is Trinidad Time: Social Meanings and Temporal Consciousness.* Gainsville: University of Florida Press.

Bluebond-Langner, Myra, 1978 *The Private Worlds of Dying Children.* Princeton, NJ: Princeton University Press.

Capps, Lisa, and Elinor Ochs, 1995 *Constructing Panic: The Discourse of Agoraphobia.* Cambridge, MA: Harvard University Press.

Casey, Conerly, 1997 Medicines for Madness: Suffering, Disability and the Identification of Enemies in Northern Nigeria. Ph.D. dissertation, University of California, Los Angeles.

Child, Irvin L., and John W. M. Whiting, 1953 *Child Training and Personality: A Cross-Cultural Study.* New York: Yale University Press.

Cole, Jennifer, 2001 *Forget Colonialism? Sacrifice and the Art of Memory in Madagascar.* Berkeley: University of California Press.

Comaroff, John, and Jean Comaroff, 1998 Occult Economies and the Violence of Abstraction: Notes from the South African Postcolony. ABF Working Paper, No. 9724. Chicago: American Bar Foundation.

Csordas, Thomas, 1994 *Embodiment and Experience: The Existential Ground of Culture and Self.* Cambridge: Cambridge University Press.

Damasio, Antonio, 1999. *The Feeling of What Happens: Body and Emotion in the making of Consciousness.* London: Harcourt.

Desjarlais, Robert, 1992 *Body and Emotion: The Aesthetics of Illness and Healing in the Nepal Himalayas.* Philadelphia: University of Pennsylvania Press.

DuBois, Cora, 1961 [1944] *The People of Alor: A Social-Psychological Study of an East Indian.* New York: Harper.

Edgerton, Robert B., 1967 *The Cloak of Competence: Stigma in the Lives of the Mentally Retarded.* Berkeley: University of California Press.

— 1971 *The Individual in Cultural Adaptation: A Study of Four East African Societies.* Los Angeles: University of California Press.

Ewing, Katherine Pratt, 1990 The Illusion of Wholeness: Culture, Self, and the Experience of Inconsistency, *Ethos* 18 (3): 251–278.

— 1997 *Arguing Sainthood: Modernity, Psychoanalysis, and Islam.* Durham, NC: Duke University Press.

Fanon, Frantz, 1963 *The Wretched of the Earth.* New York: Grove Weidenfeld.

— 1967 *Black Skin, White Masks.* New York: Grove Weidenfeld.

Feldman, Allen, 1997 Violence and Vision: The Prosthetics and Aesthetics of Terror. *Public Culture* 10 (1): 24–60.

Foucault, Michel, 1965 *Madness and Civilization: A History of Insanity in the Age of Reason.* R. Howard, trans. New York: Random House.

Freud, Sigmund, 1950 [1913] *Totem and Taboo: Some Points of Agreement Between the Mental Lives of Savages and Neurotics.* James Strachey, trans. London: Routledge and Kegan Paul.

— 1956 [1900] *The Interpretation of Dreams.* James Strachey, ed. and trans. New York: Basic Books.

Fromm, Eric, 1941 *Escape From Freedom.* New York: Farrar and Rinehart.

Geertz, Clifford, 1973 *The Interpretation of Cultures.* New York: Basic Books.

Gladwin, Thomas, and Seymour B. Sarason, 1953 *Truk: Man in Paradise.* New York: Wenner-Gren Foundation for Anthropological Research.

Goffman, Erving, 1959 *The Presentation of Self in Everyday Life.* Garden City, NY: Doubleday Anchor Books.

Gorer, Geoffrey, and John Rickman, 1949 *The People of Great Russia: A Psychological Study.* London: Cresset Press.

— 1964 [1948] *The American People: A Study in National Character.* New York: Norton.

Hollan, Douglas, 2001 Developments in Person-Centered Ethnography. In *The Psychology of Cultural Experience.* Carmella Moore and Holly Mathews, eds. Pp. 48–67. Cambridge: Cambridge University Press.

Hollan, Douglas, and Jane Wellenkamp, 1994 *Contentment and Suffering: Culture and Experience in Toraja.* New York: Columbia University Press.

Holland, Dorothy, with William Lachicotte, Jr., Debra Skinner, and Carole Cain, 1998 *Identity and Agency in Cultural Worlds*. Cambridge, MA: Harvard University Press.

Hurston, Zora Neale, 1990 [1935] *Mules and Men*. New York: Perennial Library.

Huyssen, Andreas, 2001 Present Pasts: Media, Politics, Amnesia. In *Globalization*. Arjun Appadurai, ed. Pp. 57–77. Durham, NC: Duke University Press.

Izquierdo, Carolina, and Conerly Casey, 2003 Global Consumption of Resources: Examples from Amazonia and Africa. Paper presented at the Congresso des Americanistas, Santiago, Chile.

Jackson, Michael, 1998 *Minima Ethnographica: Intersubjectivity and the Anthropological Project*. Chicago: University of Chicago Press.

Kleinman Arthur, and Joan Kleinman, 1991 Toward an Ethnography of Interpersonal Experience. *Culture, Medicine, and Psychiatry* 15: 275–301.

Kluckhohn, Clyde, 1962 *Culture and Behavior: Collected Essays*. Richard Kluckhohn, ed. New York: Free Press of Glencoe.

Knauft, Bruce, 2002 *Exchanging the Past: A Rainforest World of Before and After*. Chicago: University of Chicago Press.

Korbin, Jill, ed., 1981 *Child Abuse and Neglect: Cross-Cultural Perspectives*. New York: New American Library.

Lacan, Jacques, 1977 [1966] *Écrits: A Selection*. New York: W.W. Norton.

Laing, R. D., 1969 *The Divided Self*. New York: Pantheon Books.

Langer, Walter C., 1973 [1972] *The Mind of Adolf Hitler: The Secret Wartime Report*. New York: Basic Books.

Levy, Robert I., 1973 *Tahitians: Mind and Experience in the Society Islands*. Chicago: University of Chicago Press.

Lutz, Catherine A., 1990 *Unnatural Emotions: Everyday Sentiments on a Micronesian Atoll and Their Challenge to Western Theory*. Chicago: University of Chicago Press.

Madariaga, Salvador de, 1928 *Englishmen, Frenchmen and Spaniards*. Oxford: Oxford University Press.

Manganaro, Marc, 1990 *Modernist Anthropology: From Fieldwork to Text*. Princeton, NJ: Princeton University Press.

Mead, Margaret, 1928 *Coming of Age in Samoa*. New York: William and Morrow.

— 1930 *Growing Up in New Guinea*. New York: William and Morrow.

— 1935 *Sex and Temperament in Three Primitive Societies*. New York: William and Morrow.

— 1942 *And Keep Your Powder Dry*. New York: William and Morrow.

Merleau-Ponty, Maurice, 1962 *Phenomenology of Perception*. Colin Smith, trans. London: Routledge and Kegan Paul.

Minturn, Leigh, and William Lambert, 1964 *Mothers of Six Cultures*. New York: John Wiley.

Nandy, Ashis, 1996 Development and Violence. In *Genocide, War, and Human Survival*. C. Strozier and M. Flynn, eds. Pp. 207–18. Lantham, MD: Rowman and Littlefield.

Obeyesekere, Gananath, 1981 *Medusa's Hair: An Essay on Personal Symbols and Religious Experience*. Chicago: University of Chicago Press.

Riesman, David, with Nathan Glazer and Reuel Denney, 2001 [1950] *The Lonely Crowd: A Study of the Changing American Character*. New Haven, CT: Yale University Press.

Rosaldo, Renato, 1989 *Culture and Truth*. Boston, MA: Beacon Press.

Scheper-Hughes, Nancy, 1992 *Death Without Weeping: The Violence of Everyday Life in Brazil*. Berkeley: University of California Press.

Shore, Bradd, 1996 *Culture in Mind: Cognition, Culture and the Problem of Meaning*. New York: Oxford University Press.

Slater, Philip Elliot, 1990 [1970] *The Pursuit of Loneliness: American Culture at the Breaking Point*. Boston, MA: Beacon Press.

Spiro, Melford E., 1951 Culture and Personality: The National History of a False Dichotomy. *Psychiatry* 14: 19–46.

Stoller, Paul, 1995 *Embodying Colonial Memories: Spirit Possession, Power and the Hauka in West Africa*. New York: Routledge.

Wallace, A. F. C., 1952 The Modal Personality Structure of the Tuscarora Indians as Revealed by the Rorschach Test. Bureau of American Ethnology, Bulletin No. 150. Washington, DC: Smithsonian Institution.

Wallace, A. F. C. 1970 [1969] *The Death and Rebirth of the Seneca*. New York: Knopf.

White, Geoffrey, 1991 *Identity through History: Living Stories in a Solomon Islands Society*. Cambridge: Cambridge University Press.

White, Geoffrey, and J. Kirkpatrick, eds., 1985 *Person, Self, and Experience: Exploring Pacific Ethnopsychologies*. Berkeley: University of California Press.

Whiting, Beatrice, ed., 1967 [1963] *Six Cultures: Studies of Child Rearing*. New York: John Wiley.

Whiting, Beatrice, and John Whiting, 1975 *Children of Six Cultures*. Cambridge, MA: Harvard University Press.

Wikan, Unni, 1991 *Managing Turbulent Hearts: A Balinese Formula for Living*. Chicago: University of Chicago Press.

PART I Sensing, Feeling, and Knowing

In a curious way, consciousness begins as the feeling of what happens when we see or hear or touch. Phrased in slightly more precise words, it is a feeling that accompanies the making of any kind of image – visual, auditory, tactile, visceral – within our living organisms.

(Damasio 1999: 26)

An image is that in which the past and the now flash into constellation. In other words: image is dialectic at a standstill.

(Benjamin 1983–4: 7)

Contributors to this section take up classic topics in psychocultural studies: consciousness and time, emotion, cognition, learning, dreaming, and memory. Using a variety of theoretical orientations – phenomenological, psychoanalytic/psychodynamic, ecological adaptive, cultural models of mind, symbolic, and historical – contributors make obvious the reverberations between individuals and their sociocultural communities. Individuals' psychologies, and in many cases biochemistries, shape and are shaped by social, cultural, and historical processes.

Contributors address a number of critical questions: How are concepts of time and consciousness changing around the world? What are the constraining effects of cultures, histories, and social structures on the felt qualities of emotions and emotional expressions? How do people in diverse cultural settings experience and interact with people who express multiple cultural and historical forms of learning, cognition, emotion, dreaming, or memory? What aspects of self, desire, and fantasy become intertwined with the experiences of bodies and people living locally or around the world? In what ways do academic categories, theories, and dualisms, such as mind/body, internal/external, process/content, affect our senses, perceptions, and knowledge of psychocultural processes? Whether entering this question from the perspective of an experiencing self, or through cultural concepts and activities, contributors evaluate the extent to which psychocultural processes elude categorizations popular in academia, as refractions of them are channeled through epistemologies, or captured by various disciplines, bounded by disciplinary practices and methods. In doing so, contributors offer new directions for the study of psychocultural processes.

CHAPTER 1

Time and Consciousness

Kevin Birth

"Fine" watches are wonderful distillations of the complicated, interwoven dimensions of the relationships of culture and time. What makes a watch "fine" are accuracy in time-keeping to a tiny fraction of a second and an analog, rather than digital, display in which accuracy is obscured because time is judged by the relative position of the hands. The combination of physics, technology, conspicuous consumption, and function manifested by such watches attests to time being more than human awareness of the relationship of duration, sequence, and cycles.

Time engages culture, nature, and experience, making the study of time a fruitful domain for exploring the relationship of natural and cultural cycles and sequences mediated through individual and collective experiences. Because cultural concepts of time link human ideas and activities to astronomical and biological cycles, time generates a problem for anthropologists; as Greenhouse observed: "Anthropologists know that people conceptualize time differently around the world, but they have tended to treat social time as a paradox, seeming to be both culturally relative and universal" (1996: 1).

This paradox is a manifestation of the deeper anthropological quandary of psychic unity versus cultural diversity, but it goes beyond debates about universals in human psychology and includes extra-human phenomena such as seasons, lunar cycles, and solar cycles. To complicate matters further, some of these cycles are not the same at every location on the globe: the difference between the equal amounts of daylight throughout the year at the equator versus the long nights and days at extreme northern and southern latitudes is one example, and the difference between those parts of the world where the seasons are "rainy" and "dry" versus those parts of the world where there are weather patterns identified with winter, spring, summer, and fall is another example. Consequently, building a claim that all humans share a common idea of time through their noticing "natural" phenomena elides local differences in such "natural" phenomena.

As Shore (1996) argues with regard to the paradox of psychic unity and cultural relativism, the resolution of this quandary requires relating culture to mind.

The implication for the study of time is that there is a need to relate time to culture, cognition, perception, and biology. In considering the latter two issues, perception and biology, one must keep in mind that culture influences our choices of what in our surroundings we notice, and cultural knowledge recognizes and even has some power to influence biological cycles.

While time draws together many issues associated with both nature and culture, part of the challenge of studying time is that time is connected to ideas of space. Most of the connections made between time and space are cosmological and onto-logical. The endeavor to understand what time *is* should not be confused with the attempt to understand cultural constructions of time or the human experience of time. The former can easily be related to theoretical physics, such as Einstein's time-space continuum or Steven Hawking's discussions of the origin of the universe. Furthermore, the connection between space and time in such theories should not lead to the assumption that the cultural constitution of the relationship between space and time is the same across cultures. Instead, one must leave open the possibility that, in human experience, the relationship of time to space is culturally constructed and culturally, even contextually, variable.

Looking at the concept of time in the context of globalization powerfully demonstrates both the multiple connections of time to culture, perception, and biology and the constructed connections of time to space. Those who study globalization often assume that time and space can be compressed through technology that allows interactions to transcend space almost instantaneously (Featherstone 1995; Harvey 1990; Ohmae 1996), or that such space-transcending technologies even create a sense of "timelessness" (Castells 1996). Such perspectives neglect the features of living on a rotating "globe" that revolves around the sun. In processes of globalization, space and time do not have a consistent or clear relationship – their relation is consistently mediated by the speed of communication or travel. Communications and travel must take into account connecting points on a globe – a fact that results in different times relative to the rotation of the earth and biological cycles in different places at the same instant. Contact via the Internet or by telephone is experientially different from physical, face-to-face interaction. Indeed, this is one of the weaknesses of claiming timelessness or time-space compression as a result of current telecommunications and information technology.

Castells rightly emphasizes the significance of "the annihilation and manipulation of time by electronically managed global capital markets" (1996: 467), but while capital and information may move instantaneously and be immune to the differences in daylight versus darkness, the experience of our bodies is quite different. Compared to information and capital, people do not move very fast; when they do move long distances along an east–west axis as quickly as they can, they experience jet lag – a well-documented experience of how the transfer of people is phenomenologically different from the transfer of information; and when they are awakened while deeply sleeping by a telephone call from another time zone, they are generally not appreciative of the instantaneous electronic movement of information across large distances (particularly if it is a wrong number).

Moreover, as Sassen (1998, 2000) argues, globalization is not a homogeneous process, but one that generates conflicts and in which a small number of global cities play particularly important roles. With global telecommunications, it is the times of these cities, and consequently the circadian cycles as defined by their time zones, that are beginning to play a significant role in how time is globally experienced and conceptualized. The opening of the stock market in New York is temporally signific- ant for many people far from the Eastern time zone of the United States in ways that are not true for many events in other time zones.

The human experience of the relationship of consciousness of time to globalization is largely unexamined. This relationship is historically contingent and culturally deter- mined. With regard to transnationalism, the immediate contact many communities maintain through telephones or computers is a different experience from the travel time and jet lag that often accompanies moving from one location to another. Media decisions about broadcasting "live" events when they occur or during "prime time," such as the major controversy about NBC's broadcast of the 2000 Summer Olympics in the United States, highlight the temporal dimensions of living on a rotating globe. The ability to broadcast an event in one location globally raises the problem that an event in, say, Sydney occurs at the same time as the viewing audience in, say, eastern North America is sleeping. For that matter, in the United States, the exit polling conducted by the media during presidential elections is increasingly viewed as skewing results in the western part of the nation (e.g., voters in California often know how the east coast has voted before they cast their own votes). Consequently, contrary to claims of how technology has created a sense of timelessness, globalization has highlighted the issue of timeliness and has created dilemmas about time and timing that did not exist in the past. It also highlights the negotiated relationship of media to time and events. Whereas there was debate over when to broadcast the Olympics, and whereas there is continuing debate over the broadcasting of election projections, when hijacked aircraft struck the World Trade Center there was no question but that the broadcast be immediate. In the wake of that tragedy many say that they will remember the exact time and place they heard the news.

The instantaneous quality of the media thereby creates memories embedded in particular times and places. Consequently, any discussion of cultural ideas of time in relationship to consciousness at the beginning of the twenty-first century must synthesize the traditional anthropological and historical discussions of conceptions of time with phenomenological discussions of the interaction of globalization and time. This is a daunting task and a necessarily incomplete one – the distribution of media and travel technology is uneven and reflects political economic differences of class, ethnicity, gender, legal status, and age in highly localized fashions. The inter- action of multiple physiological manifestations of biological cycles, multiple experiences of time, multiple conceptions of time, multiple technologies of representing time, and the effect of movement and telecommunications on all of these multiplicities is difficult to theorize. Here, I'm going to be more modest and primarily explore circadian cycles and daily experiences of time, rather than larger slices of time.

ANTHROPOLOGICAL APPROACHES TO TIME

In the last decade there have been several excellent reviews of the anthropology of time (Gell 1992; Greenhouse 1996; Munn 1992), so there is no need to cover that ground here. Instead, through my discussion of time, I shall continue to wrestle with the issue of psychic unity in terms of cognition and biological circadian cycles. Underlying both issues is the question of what, for humans, are "natural" and "unnatural" ways of experiencing and thinking about time.

The classic ethnographic treatments of time, such as Mauss's *Seasonal Variations of the Eskimo* (1979), Evans-Pritchard's *The Nuer* (1940), or Hallowell's "Temporal Orientation in Western Civilization and in a Pre-Literate Society" (1955), establish a set of tacit assumptions that include (1) among non-industrialized peoples, time-keeping is closely related to cultural knowledge about the environment, and (2) this cultural knowledge is then tied to the cycle of social activities. The most frequently cited example of this is Evans-Pritchard's description of "oecological time" and "structural time" among the Nuer. In his description, the daily cycle of activity, the annual cycle of movement, and the relationship of space to time allowed him to trace connections between interactions with the environment and his idea of Nuer social structure – a naturalizing of time. In contrast, Mumford's roughly contemporary book, *Technics and Civilization* (1934), emphasized the unnaturalness of clock time. The contrasts between primitive and industrialized, and natural and humanly created, became intertwined and suggested incommensurable ways of thinking about time and experiencing it. The incommensurability remained a theme in works such as Geertz's "Person, Time and Conduct in Bali" (1973) or E. T. Hall's *The Dance of Life* (1983). It was also implicit in E. P. Thompson's article "Time, Work-Discipline, and Industrial Capitalism" (1967), which argued that the shift from agrarian to industrial time was one of the fundamental cognitive changes of the industrial revolution.

The tendency of early anthropological approaches to time to emphasize alterity has been rightly criticized as unduly exoticizing and naturalizing "the Other" (Greenhouse 1996). Several important studies develop this point and focus on de-essentializing Western versus Eastern times (Gupta 1994), or establishing that there are certain ideas about time in daily living that are shared pan-culturally (Bloch 1977), or criticizing either the idea of the ethnographic present or any ethnographic representation that portrays ethnographic subjects as existing in times separate from history or from the "West" (Fabian 1983). These perspectives lay the groundwork for claiming pan-cultural and global elements of time consciousness.

Yet such studies do not develop a critique of studies of clock time that parallels the critique of studies of ritual or ecological times (i.e., there has been no close scrutiny of the assumption that time in "industrial" societies is at odds with nature). This position continues to be manifest in social scientific treatments of clock time, as is the case with Adam's research on reproduction (1995). Adam assumes the clock is antagonistic to the body, and therefore to nature. Is this claim tenable, however? There is abundant evidence that the clock entrains biological processes. For that matter, if one examines the literature on humans' supposed "natural" free-running circadian cycles studied in conditions where all social and temporal cues were controlled (see Wever 1979), one realizes that so-called "natural" human circadian cycles bear no resemblance to the cycles of any human society, and that they are highly sensitive to light duration, light intensity, intensity of physical activity, and especially social contact. Consequently, not only must the association of "traditional societies" with "natural time" be discarded, but the association between "modern societies" and "unnatural time" must also be undone. To view times of modernity as being culturally constructed and unnatural is just as misleading as viewing the times of premodernity as being constructed out of a pragmatic closeness to nature. Biological cycles are not immutable, but are, instead, very sensitive to the environment, whether it be a factory or a pastoral setting. This is true for humans and the animals that they domesticate. Because of the biological flexibility in organisms, the relationship between clock time and biology is complex.

Discarding this assumption about natural time blurs the conceptual barriers between industrial time and non-industrial time by returning to the initial anthropological formulation of viewing time as emerging out of cultural ways of thinking about all environments and cycles. Instead of using the clock as the conception of time against which all others are compared, thereby exoticizing non-horological cultural constructions of time, this shift views clock time as serving the same purposes as the cultural models of time described by Mauss, Evans-Pritchard, and Hallowell. Furthermore, precisely because of the multiplicity and flexibility of social and biological rhythms, it is difficult to separate the "natural" from the "culturally constructed." Time consciousness involves the recognition and definition of all sorts of sequences and cycles. Time serves to orient people cognitively and biologically to one another and their environment.

TEMPORAL ORIENTATION

Hallowell's (1955) concept of behavioral environment blurs the boundary between nature and culture in ways useful for thinking about time. The behavioral environment emphasizes the environment as experienced. Hallowell (1955: 93) claims that one of the major functions of the relationship between the self and its behavioral environment is the orienting of the self in time. This can also be said of institutions, collectives, and societies. In a sense, all seek to orient their participants through recognizing or creating cycles and sequences. As Foucault emphasizes in *Discipline and Punish* (1979), a significant technique for the imposition of power is implementing definitions and organizations of time. In his treatment of discipline what he neglects is the establishment of a dominant concept of time by which discipline is structured. While he traces the origin of temporal discipline to the Benedictine monks, he does not acknowledge other conceptions of time or the conflicts that emerged about how time is defined, as opposed to how time is applied. As E. P. Thompson (1967) points out, the victory of clock time over other conceptions of time was apparent at the point that the workers negotiated with their managers over work hours, as opposed to the original confrontations over the imposition of the clock.

Thus, Foucault emphasizes conformity without exploring the orientational function of time and the possibility of multiple times providing different, and even conflicting, temporal orientations. This is despite the orientational function of time being central to his argument about how power works. It is temporal orientation that allows the definition of conformity and non-conformity; for example, a clock-defined hour that defines when work begins is a necessary condition for the definition of tardiness, and a conception of how much work can be performed in an hour is a necessary orientational condition for the definition of laziness. In the slave system of the United States, the efforts of those enslaved to challenge authority were based on cycles, sequences, and durational measurements of activity shared by those enslaved and their supervisors (Smith 1997).

It seems that temporal orientations are necessary for economic systems to function. The market days crucial to commerce are an example of people culturally creating temporal systems to mark, measure, and coordinate their economic activity. What makes assertions of time-space compression or timelessness in the global, networked society fascinating is the claim that temporal orientations have come to be defined by immediateness detached from local times. This may be true in the sense that financial activities are no longer bound by local times, but the concepts of sequence and cycles are still profoundly important. The hourly cycle imposed to define and measure labor in the industrial revolution may be finding itself superseded in global financial networks, but quarterly and annual cycles continue to be marked by earnings reports that have immense influence over the flow of capital. The use of "timelessness" or "time-space compression" falsely indicates that time is irrelevant, when what seems to be happening is that the temporal, clock-bound, culturally constructed orientation that was essential to the industrial revolution is decreasing in importance relative to other temporal orientations.

The insight that time orients also must be viewed in light of the fact that humans are not reliable timekeepers. When placed in isolation from temporal cues, humans tend to develop rest–activity cycles of around 25 hours. Changes in activity cycles due to jet lag or shift work result in de-synchronization of the cycles of body temperature and of different hormones. While there are several biological cycles that are viewed as timekeepers in humans, the fact that these cycles are identifiable through isolating people from social and temporal cues suggests the extent to which human temporal orientation is a product of the interaction of internal, biological cycles and external social and environmental cycles.

Temporal orientation is, then, not produced independent of the environment. It is also not simply a matter of passively observing the environment. Nature provides a cacophony of cycles from which humans select, and human ingenuity has added a number of potential time cues, whether it be the vibration of a cesium 133 atom in one of the atomic clocks used by the United States Naval Observatory or the duration of sports' seasons, shopping seasons, academic semesters, or budget cycles. People thinking about cues in their socially structured, culturally determined environment produce time. These environmental cues are an excellent example of what Vygotsky meant when discussing cognitive tools and the extension of cognition outside of our bodies (Steel 2000). It is of great importance that the orientations in time occur through the relationship of the embodied mind/mindful body to the environment. Time is profoundly material and profoundly cognitive at the same time.

Consciousness of temporal orientation is consequently both inward- and outward-looking. It is a matter of individual cognition, as a multitude of psychological studies have shown, but it is also a matter of modes of production, class distinctions, social relationships, and power, as the large literature on political economy and time has demonstrated.

Time Is What You Make It

Whether it is with regard to the Nuer, the Eskimo, the Balinese, eighteenth-century English workers, or Trinidadians, when social scientists discuss time they are not discussing an essentialized definition of time but cultural models of time. Discussing time as a circle versus time as a line or an arrow is not discussing what time is, but how time is thought – the metaphorical underpinning of this discourse gives this away. Cultural models of time are tools with which people think about and structure their world.

The culturally constructed nature of time is most easily seen in the history of calendars. For instance, in 1752 the government of Great Britain decreed that the day after September 2 would be September 14. This seemingly odd change of dates was to bring the calendar being used in Britain in line with the other calendars of Western Europe (Steel 2000). Indeed, in 1752, September 1 in Great Britain was September 13 across the English Channel in France. This created a bit of a problem, particularly as the pace and extent of international commerce increased.

This is not, by any means, the first or last such time adjustment of a calendar. In 1993, Kwajalein, part of the Marshall Islands, skipped Saturday, August 23. This island is near the International Date Line, and for many years its people had set their clocks as if they were on the same side of the date line as the United States. After the Marshall Islands gained independence, Kwajalein was the only island in the nation that acted as if it were on the United States' side of the date line – so its residents decided to change their time and calendar in order to be consistent with the rest of the Marshall Islands. This meant losing a day.

Actually, we make such changes regularly, and call those occasions leap years. These adjustments call into question the naturalness of calendars, however. Something to contemplate is that, even for those places that had adopted the Julian calendar, the beginning of the millennium on January 1, 1001 AD took place on different days in different places, because different principalities dealt with the inaccuracies of the calendar differently. As January 1, 2000 media promotion of the new millennium showed, now the beginning of a new calendar year is a global event displayed and coordinated by a global network of technology and media.

Not only have we adjusted our calendar, but we have adjusted our watches, as well. These calculations – our seconds, minutes, and hours – themselves have only a tangential relationship to their origins in reckoning time by the sun. All the watches we wear and employ are set to standard mean time. This is based on the average length of a day during the year. In fact, the length of solar days varies during the year. The idea of standard *mean* time – the average length of the day – emerged during the early industrial revolution both as a means of standardizing labor hours throughout the year and as an important step in simplifying mechanisms for clocks, so that they could be made smaller and mass produced.

In effect, our calendars and watches are important cognitive tools, but they are not extensions of cognition designed to measure actual time. Historically, the way in which calendars and watches have evolved makes it clear that these timekeeping tools are devices for coordinating ourselves vis-à-vis others and activities. The ideology that they measure some ontologically existing time importantly obscures the social origins of our time reckoning, and gives it an air of naturalness that places time beyond challenge. This ironic combination of factors, namely, naturalized culturally constructed time that is beyond challenge, is what makes the study of time such a fascinating window into the relationship of cognition/emotion, activity, and social relationships.

All of this challenges the naturalness of clock time and calendars derived from the Gregorian calendar. The processes by which natural phenomena are selected to mark, measure, and reckon time takes on an existence more closely linked to human activity than to the originally selected natural phenomena. This is probably a pan-cultural practice. The socio-ecological cycles of the Nuer (Evans-Pritchard 1940) and the Eskimo (Mauss 1979) are very different, but the end result of ecological cycles only becoming important because of their relevance to human activity is the same. Indeed, Evans-Pritchard hints that although Nuer "time" is based on ecology, it tends to privilege social cycles above environmental change: "Ultimately most, perhaps all, concepts of time and space are determined by the physical ambient, but the values they embody are only one of many possible responses to it and depend also on structural principles" (Evans-Pritchard 1940: 94). Thus, for all the "naturalness" of Nuer time, it shares with clock time and the Gregorian calendar a derived, socially influenced relationship to the environment, rather than a direct one.

TRAINING IN TIME

The body is not immune to culturally created tools of keeping time. Not only do social relationships structure human circadian cycles, but humans also tend to challenge their bodies in unusual ways. Carnival, all-night rituals, shift work, and jet lag are examples of human attempts to overcome typical biological circadian patterns. Because shift work and jet lag are products of societies which also relentlessly pursue biological research to improve "productivity," the biological implications of these two have received the vast majority of scientific and governmental attention (see US Congress, Office of Technology Assessment 1991). Some of what has been learned can be conservatively applied to activities such as carnival or ritual. First, the body's multiple circadian rhythms do not all respond in the same fashion or at the same rate to a radical change in circadian activity. For instance, in shift work there is a phase shift in prolactin and growth hormone so that nighttime workers have levels similar to those in daytime workers, but there is not a similar shift in cortisol or thyrotropin cycles (Weibel and Brandenberger 1998). Second, from jet lag studies, people find shifts in activity that result in staying awake longer – traveling in an eastward direction – easier to accommodate than shifts that require getting up earlier – traveling in a westward direction. Third, physical exertion affects hormone levels and helps people to stay awake at night. Fourth, there is a great deal of variation from individual to individual.

The body's sensitivity to temporal structures is culturally recognized separate from the biological research. Due to the persistence and ubiquity of clocks and watches in some societies, people in those societies are born into a world of timekeeping. Anyone who has recently had children has been beset upon by lactation consultants providing moral directives about feeding schedules. Some pediatricians will hold forth on the importance of feeding schedules, whereas others will argue for feeding on demand. In the United States, the classic guides for raising children address this issue. Dr. Spock writes: "The baby can be greatly influenced by the parents' *management*. Suppose a mother wakes her baby boy whenever he's still asleep 4 hours after the last feeding; she is helping him to establish a 4-hour hunger habit"

(Spock and Rothenberg 1985: 95; emphasis added). The child's earliest experiences are consequently structured by a horological obsession. *What to Expect the First Year* extols: "For all babies, the absence of structure in their lives early on can interfere with their developing, and then exercising self-discipline later in life. Getting to school on time, completing homework, and getting papers in on schedule can be inordinately difficult for children who have never been exposed to any kind of structure previously" (Eisenberg et al. 1989: 175). I suggest these practices are part of a very early process of synchronizing biological rhythms to social and cultural rhythms. These practices associated with activity, sleep, and feeding patterns have all been demonstrated to influence and structure circadian rhythms at the level of biological processes (Moore-Ede et al. 1982). This means that the cultural environment of children begins to influence biological rhythms by bringing them in line with externally generated, culturally constructed conceptions of time. The embodiment of discipline through scheduling that Foucault stresses in *Discipline and Punish* is not limited to coordinating social groups or embodiment in a symbolic sense, but includes embodiment in the sense of affecting basic body functions at the level of the nervous system that is normally not associated with cognition, much less with discourse.

Time and Cognition

Time as a tool is not isolated from other issues. Methodologically, it does not generally work well to accost an informant and ask, "What is your cultural model of time?" or even, "What is time?" Cultural models of time are not models that act autonomously, but instead are models that are connected to other models. In fact, models of time are usually constituted by metaphors – itself a fact that emphasizes connections. From the perspective of understanding cognition, then, it is not useful to view cultural models of time as self-contained schemas or as elements of sequential logical thinking. Instead, cultural models of time are more consonant with connectionist models of cognition.

Examples of this are parapraxes that are commonly heard in university environments: saying "yesterday" when one means the previous class, even if the class met two or more days before, or saying "tomorrow" when one means the next class, even if it meets two or more days in the future. This is an example where two parallel models of time, one having to do with the sequence of classes and the other having to do with the sequence of days, interact to affect what is said and to cause a slip of the tongue.

It is also an example of the interaction of the behavioral environment and temporal consciousness and orientation. Classes are part of the university environment. Often they constitute a means of organizing the world. Models for organizing the world but not the self always utilize a chronological organization of time. The chronology may not always be a clock or a calendar; any marker in the world by which one can measure and mark change can serve as a temporal marker. Meetings and class periods temporally organize the university. Therefore, class periods are temporal markers during the academic year. Class periods are used to organize the week, but generally not for periods longer than a week. As a result, "last class" and "next class" are the main expressions utilizing class periods as temporal markers.

There are other interesting features of these parapraxes that demonstrate the extent to which metaphors penetrate and structure temporal consciousness. Implicit in the temporal structuring of university classes is, seemingly, the travel metaphor of time. This metaphor involves expressions such as the "preceding class" and the "up-coming class" as synonymous with the "last class" and the "next class." This travel metaphor of the past and future is closely associated with linear time and ideas of chronology, rather than with other metaphors.

"Yesterday" and "tomorrow" are words that are used to orient oneself in time vis-à-vis the world through a model of time based on chronology and sequence. "Next class" and "last class" also orient one in time vis-à-vis a specific educational context, and they also imply a sequential, chronological model of time. Such parallelism suggests both models of time are connected to the same underlying temporal model. Or, put in more connectionist terms, the network into which "yesterday" and "tomorrow" integrate is the same network into which "last class" and "next class" integrate. This does not mean the "last class" is synonymous with "yesterday" and "next class" is synonymous with "tomorrow," but that their orientational function utilizes the same logic. Obviously, if the last class was three days ago, then it was not "yesterday." Yet, since "yesterday/tomorrow" are based on the same sequential temporal logic as "last class/next class," it is quite easy, although incorrect, to segue from the one to the other, thereby creating a slip of the tongue. Thus, in cognition, cultural models of time relate different ideas. They are used to coordinate actions with one another, but they are also employed in the ideological work of linking unrelated ideas in order to naturalize cultural constructions of the world.

TIME IS MONEY IN TRINIDAD

The metaphorical system "time is money" has been explored by Lakoff and his colleagues in several books (Lakoff and Johnson 1980; Lakoff and Turner 1989; Lakoff and Johnson 1999), and would seem to qualify as a cognitive/cultural model of time that indicates the effect of industrial capitalism on cognition. If industrial capitalism has the sort of ideological and cognitive influences implied by the essentialist contrasts between industrial time and agrarian time, then one would expect a close correspondence between the metaphorical system described by Lakoff and Johnson and industrialism – basically, where one is found, one would find the other. But reality is far too messy for such essentialisms.

Rural Trinidad is the place in which this fact came to the fore for me. In studying cultural conceptions of time, I went through the classic metaphors associated with the "time is money" metaphorical system:

Time is money
Spend time
Waste time
Save time
Budget time
Invest time
Manage time/time management

The context in which I did this was a rural community in which most residents had attended school, and in which many of the men had worked in factories. Everyone I interviewed on this topic (16 people) reported that they had heard the phrases "spend time," "waste time," and "save time." They could all produce examples of how these phrases are used that correspond with Lakoff and Johnson's discussion and with the usage of the phrases that I was accustomed to in the United States. No individual I interviewed reported that they had heard the phrases "invest your time," "manage your time," or "time management." One individual reported hearing the phrase "budgeting time," and then said, "Budgeting time is the time of year when the government makes its budget." Two individuals reported hearing "time is money," and they were both tailors. While my sample is admittedly small, the results are extremely clear: the metaphorical system "time is money" has been adopted only partially in the region of Trinidad in which I worked. The distribution of the phrases that have been adopted is interesting, in that it was not the individuals who had worked in factories that reported awareness of the metaphor "time is money," but individuals who worked as tailors – individual artisans, so to speak – who used this metaphor.

This suggests that temporal ideologies do not adhere to well-defined modes of production or economic formations; instead, these temporal ideas are unevenly distributed in their cognitive manifestations. Such manifestations are distributed according to social relations. This distribution allows for strategic action based on self-presentations of knowledge or naïveté. With transport and communication spanning multiple time zones, the possibilities for sometimes disrupting others' lives purposefully and with impunity are great. An example of a tailor's visiting the United States, who had manifested much of the "time is money" system in Trinidad, is instructive in exploring how cultural models of time, ideologies, and the use of time are combined strategically.

Ted had arrived from Trinidad and was waiting for his friend, Mark, who lived in California, to make arrangements for Ted to visit. Mark had promised a good time and work for Ted while Ted was in the United States, and Ted, who had arrived with a green card but very little cash, was anxious to get a paying job. For several weeks, he had visited family and friends in New York City, and he was staying with my family and me for part of this time. After the first week, he became increasingly forward with Mark, who had not yet purchased plane tickets for Ted. One morning, around 8:00 EST, Ted picked up the telephone and announced, "I'm calling Mark." My wife, in a moment of sympathy for Mark, said, "Don't you know it is five in the morning there?" Ted beamed, replying, "Is it? Really?" and as he chuckled, he dialed the number.

Ted, who had been calculating time zone differences for a long time, was still able to play the naive, just-off-the-airplane Trinidadian. In a fascinating use of time through a performance of a lack of knowledge about time, Ted was able to disrupt Mark's day and get away with it – even though calling Mark at 8:00 a.m. would have been calling too early for him, much less at 5:00 a.m. Ted the tailor demonstrates that, in representing individual knowledge of models of time, and agency in negotiating time and subjectivities of time, neither the traditional anthropological approach of associating a cultural model of time with a society, nor more recent approaches to globalization that assert timelessness in constructing global homogeneity, suffice.

Conclusion

The anthropological study of time has been enmeshed in implicit assumptions that essentialize biology and exoticize cognition. It has also tended to view clock time as something completely different from other forms of conceptualizing and reckoning time, and has avoided exploring the influences of culture on biological cycles. To overcome these conceptual obstacles, it is necessary to discard discourse about natural versus unnatural ways of reckoning time. Instead, time must be viewed as a culturally created cognitive tool for thinking about our body's cycles, our world, our activities, and our relationships. Consequently, cultural models of time integrate these different dimensions of experience, and allow for manipulating each dimension, including our biological rhythms. Our bodies have multiple cycles, some of which are culturally sensitive and others that are slow to change, and many of which are consciously and culturally noted.

This integration of the biological, social, and cultural experience of the world found in cultural models of time has implications for understanding globalization. A consequence of globalization is that people can be bombarded by temporal rhythms emanating from all over the world in ways that directly conflict not only with local times, but also with the body's biological cycles. A further consequence of the form that globalization processes take is that, because of the dominance of certain global cities, there are relatively few time zones that have global significance. A feature of this situation is that there are growing numbers of people who orient themselves to what a clock reads in a distant time zone, such as that containing New York, London, or Tokyo time. Because of the multiple ways of defining time and, consequently, of temporally orienting oneself, there are significant conflicts of time and contradictions generated by such conflict, and because of the integrative possibilities of cultural models of time, these conflicts and contradictions can be manifested from the level of society down to the level of individual biological processes.

REFERENCES

Adam, Barbara, 1995 *Timewatch: The Social Analysis of Time.* Oxford: Blackwell.
Bloch, Maurice, 1977 The Past and the Present in the Present. *Man* 12: 278–292.
Castells, Manuel, 1996 *The Rise of the Network Society.* Oxford: Blackwell.
Eisenberg, Arlene, with Heidi E. Murkoff, and Sandee E. Hathaway, 1989 *What to Expect the First Year.* New York: Workman.
Evans-Pritchard, E. E., 1940 *The Nuer.* Oxford: Oxford University Press.
Fabian, Johannes, 1983 *Time and the Other.* New York: Columbia University Press.
Featherstone, Mike, 1995 *Undoing Culture.* London: Sage.
Foucault, Michel, 1979 *Discipline and Punish.* New York: Vintage.
Geertz, Clifford, 1973 Person, Time, and Conduct in Bali. In *The Interpretation of Cultures.* Clifford Geertz, ed. Pp. 360–411. New York: Basic Books.
Gell, Alfred, 1992 *The Anthropology of Time.* Oxford: Berg.
Greenhouse, Carol, 1996 *A Moment's Notice.* Ithaca, NY: Cornell University Press.
Gupta, Akhil, 1994 The Reincarnation of Souls and the Rebirth of Commodities: Representations of Time in "East" and "West." In *Remapping Memory.* Jonathan Boyarin, ed. Minneapolis: University of Minnesota Press.

Hall, Edward T., 1983 *The Dance of Life*. Garden City, NY: Anchor.

Hallowell, A. Irving, 1955 *Culture and Experience*. Philadelphia: University of Pennsylvania Press.

Harvey, David, 1990 *The Condition of Postmodernity*. Oxford: Blackwell.

Lakoff, George, and Mark Johnson, 1980 *Metaphors We Live By*. Chicago: University of Chicago Press.

— 1999 *Philosophy in the Flesh*. New York: Basic Books.

Lakoff, George and Mark Turner, 1989 *More Than Cool Reason*. Chicago: University of Chicago Press.

Mauss, Marcel, 1979 *Seasonal Variations of the Eskimo*. New York: Routledge.

Moore-Ede, Martin C., Frank M. Sulzman, and Charles A. Fuller, 1982 *The Clocks That Time Us*. Cambridge, MA: Harvard University Press.

Mumford, Lewis, 1934 *Technics and Civilization*. New York: Harcourt Brace.

Munn, Nancy, 1992 The Cultural Anthropology of Time. *Annual Review of Anthropology* 21: 93–123.

Ohmae, Kenichi, 1996 *The End of the Nation State*. London: Harper Collins.

Sassen, Saskia, 1998 *Globalization and its Discontents*. New York: New Press.

— 2000 Spatialities and Temporalities of the Global: Elements for a Theorization. *Public Culture* 12: 215–232.

Shore, Brad, 1996 *Culture in Mind*. Oxford: Oxford University Press.

Smith, Mark M., 1997 *Mastered by the Clock*. Chapel Hill: University of North Carolina Press.

Spock, Benjamin, and Michael B. Rothenberg, 1985 *Dr. Spock's Baby and Child Care*. New York: Pocket.

Steel, Duncan, 2000 *Marking Time*. New York: John Wiley.

Thompson, E. P., 1967 Time, Work-Discipline, and Industrial Capitalism. *Past and Present* 38: 56–97.

US Congress, Office of Technology Assessment, 1991 *Biological Rhythms: Implications for the Worker*. Washington, DC: US Government Printing Office.

Weibel, L., and G. Brandenberger, 1998 Disturbances in Hormonal Profiles of Night Workers during Their Usual Sleep and Work Times. *Journal of Biological Rhythms* 13: 202–208.

Wever, Rütger, 1979 *The Circadian System of Man*. Berlin: Springer Verlag.

SUGGESTED FURTHER READING

Aschoff, Jürgen, ed., 1981 *Handbook of Behavioral Neurobiology, Vol. 4: Biological Rhythms*. New York: Plenum.

Birth, Kevin, 1999 *Any Time Is Trinidad Time*. Gainesville: University Press of Florida.

LeVine, Robert, 1997 *A Geography of Time*. New York: Basic Books.

McEachron, Donald L., and Jonathan Schull, 1993 Hormones, Rhythms, and the Blues. In *Hormonally Induced Changes in Mind and Brain*. J. Shulkin, ed. Pp. 287–355. San Diego, CA: Academic Press.

O'Malley, Michael, 1990 *Keeping Watch: A History of American Time*. New York: Viking.

Rutz, Henry J., ed., 1992 *The Politics of Time*. Washington, DC: American Ethnological Monograph Series.

Smith, Michael French, 1982 Bloody Time and Bloody Scarcity. *American Ethnologist* 9: 503–518.

CHAPTER **2**

An Anthropology of Emotion

Charles Lindholm

In the modern world where computers are capable of calculating faster and more accurately than any person, we like to believe our emotions, not our analytic abilities, make us human. In other words, instead of "thinking animals" we see ourselves as "feeling machines." Accordingly, we say that people who are cerebral and unemotional are "inhuman" and "heartless." We want our friends and lovers to be compassionate and ardent, not rational and calculating. For the same reason, our leaders never portray themselves as logically minded technocrats, but as empathetic individuals who "feel our pain." For entertainment, we appreciate the books and movies that stimulate us to experience the maximum amounts of fear, grief, indignation, or joy. In our personal lives, we make our choices on the basis of whether something "feels right." In light of our pervasive concern with feelings, the philosopher Alasdair MacIntyre has persuasively argued that the dominant modern creed ought to be called emotivism (MacIntyre 1981).

ANTHROPOLOGISTS AVOIDED THE STUDY OF EMOTION

Yet even though emotions take center stage in our daily lives, until quite recently anthropology has had very little to say about how emotions are interpreted, how they differ cross-culturally, or whether emotions have any universal character (for reviews of the literature, see Lutz and White 1986; Jenkins 1994; Rorty 1980). The disciplinary neglect of such a crucial aspect of the human condition is especially remarkable since anthropologists have long relied on emotional relationships of rapport, empathy, and compassion to gain the trust of informants. Moreover, anthropologists often find the ties established during research to be among the most powerfully moving of their lives.

The strong affective bonds with people that occur in anthropological fieldwork are not to be found in academic psychology, where emotional relationships with one's subjects (when they are humans instead of white rats) are discouraged; nor are they found in sociology, where impersonal surveys of large samples are the favored methodology. Only in psychoanalysis is the emotional relationship between therapist and patient (termed, in the depersonalizing jargon of the discipline, transference and counter-transference) made part of the intellectual equation, and even there the bond is formed only to be severed at the end of treatment – just as the academic psychologist must kill her rat after the experiment is concluded.

It is worth considering why anthropologists have been so unconcerned with the analysis of the meaning and context of emotion when their whole disciplinary practice is based on feelings of empathy. To a degree this disinterest has reflected a deep and recurrent anthropological anxiety about the validity of participant observation as a methodology. Hoping to be accepted as legitimate scientists, most anthropologists in the past have cautiously heeded Durkheim's warning that emotions cannot be properly studied because they are fluid, mixed, not easily defined, and consequently impossible to analyze (see Durkheim and Mauss 1963). From this point of view, emotions are too "soft" and too subjective to be appropriate topics for research by anthropologists seeking above all to be impressively "hard" and empirical.

However, although Durkheim admitted the difficulty of attaining an adequate analysis of emotion, he nonetheless made emotion – specifically the ecstasy of immersion in the collective and the sense of depression and alienation that occurs when excluded from the group or deprived of a sense of significance – the core of his social theory. This crucial aspect of his work has often been forgotten by sociologists and anthropologists more impressed with his empiricism and functionalism.

Yet Durkheim was certainly right to point out that emotion is a notoriously obscure concept, as is indicated in the ambiguity of the word itself: "emotion" has its etymological origins in the Latin word *emovere* – to move away – indicating both elusiveness and agitation. Nor is the word emotion easily translatable cross-culturally (Wierzbicka 1993). The French, for example, unite feeling and emotion in one word: *sentiment*. And even in English the use of the word "emotion" is relatively recent, dating only from the eighteenth century. Formerly, English referred only to the passions – derived from the Latin *passus* – suffered, submitted – which suggests the overwhelming power of desire and the passivity of the individual, who is believed not to control feelings but to be enslaved by them.

This etymology suggests a further reason for the general exclusion of emotion from serious study by earlier anthropologists: the association of emotion with irrationality and sentimentality. In Western thought women have been regarded as the more emotional sex, making them best suited for homemaking and the helping professions, while men have been viewed as the reasonable ones, capable of success in the rational fields of business and science. For anthropologists seeking professional legitimacy in the sciences, a masculine meaning-centered and cerebral model of research naturally trumped any serious study of effeminate, irrational emotional states. (This point has been made most cogently by Lutz 1988.)

There is perhaps yet another disciplinary reason why emotion is not a traditional topic for anthropologists. Because emotion has been viewed in the West as a natural force that arises in the core of the individual, it falls within the disciplinary realm of psychology and physiology and not within the domain of anthropology, which has usually been concerned with the study of culture and symbolic relationships. As a result, when emotion has been the object of scientific scrutiny, it has been studied solely by psychologists and biologists who, naturally enough, measured, codified, and analyzed feelings within laboratory settings, leaving aside all cultural contexts.

THE PHILOSOPHERS OF EMOTION

In contrast to the remarkable lack of anthropological interest in the emotions, the nature of the passions and their relationship to the human condition has been very much a matter of fundamental concern in many non-Western societies, especially in religions devoted to achieving mystical communion. For example, in India the cultivation and intensification of prescribed passions (*rasa*) was thought to be a pathway to divine knowledge; as a result, specific emotional states were exhaustively described and invoked. Muslim Sufis, too, had a complex understanding of the vacillations of the heart that were said to occur upon the pathway to enlightenment. These indigenous theories of emotional capacities and transformation deserve much more attention from anthropologists than they have so far received.

Closer to home, throughout Western history many centrally important philoso phers have occupied themselves with understanding emotion: Plato, Aristotle, Aquinas, Descartes, Hobbes, Kant, Hume, and Adam Smith are among those who developed partially overlapping and partially competing theories. (For a synopsis of some of these, see Gardiner et al. 1937.) All of them recognized at the outset that the passions, however conceptualized and categorized, were powerful and often dangerous motiv- ators of human action. The question for these thinkers was not so much what the passions are (Aristotle argued for desire, fear, pleasure, and pain; Descartes proposed love, hate, desire, joy, astonishment, and grief), but how to control or channel them so they will not have destructive consequences.

One of the most sophisticated and influential theories was put forward by David Hume, who made the radical argument that human beings are in truth motivated primarily by their fears, desires, and passions. As he wrote in 1737: "Reason alone can never be a motive to any action of the will . . . it can never oppose passion in the direction of the will . . . Reason is, and ought to be the slave of the passions, and can never pretend to any other office than to serve and obey them" (Hume 1978: 413, 415). Hume believed that primary passions, derived from sensation, give rise to secondary passions derived from reflection. He further distinguished direct emotions arising immediately from the experience of pleasure or pain (desire, aversion, joy, hope, fear, despair, security) from indirect feelings that have the self as their object, and arise from various associations and impressions. Pride, humility, love, and hate are the primary indirect emotions; ambition, vanity, envy, pity, malice, and generosity are the secondary indirect emotions. There are as well other passions – revenge, sympathy, hunger, and lust – issuing from original instincts. Opposing emotions, Hume thought, could be aroused by proper stimuli and then marshaled against one another, leading to their mutual negation, and hence to peace. Many of his later writings consisted of meditations on how to achieve this beneficent goal.

Hume's theory was contested and complicated in 1759 by Adam Smith, who based his system on the human capacity for entering into sympathetic emotional communion with the feelings of others. For him, the tendency to sympathize depends on the type of passion felt, and Smith subdivides feelings into those derived directly from the body, such as pain, which excite little real sympathy, and those derived from the imagination, which arouse much more. As he says, "a disappointment in love, or ambition, will call forth more sympathy than the greatest bodily evil" (Smith 1982: 29). The passions of the imagination are subdivided into unsocial passions of resentment and hatred, which onlookers do not enter into easily, and the social passions of generosity, kindness, and compassion, which are particularly compelling. Between these extremes are the selfish passions of grief and joy. Smith's case histories, though certainly culturally bound, nonetheless give credit to the complex interaction of personality, context, and custom on human emotions, and raise the important question of the degree to which those emotions arouse a sympathetic response in others, and therefore are a source of social cohesion. His vision of the relation between emotion and community is one that anthropologists might well reconsider.

CAPITALISM AND THE TRANSFORMATION OF FEELING

With the brilliant exception of Smith, most later Utilitarian theorists greatly simplified Hume's system, though they too believed men and women were the slaves of passion, eternally seeking to avoid pain and attain pleasure. Like Hume, they also wanted to alleviate human violence, but instead of manipulating mutually negating desires, they argued that the "calm passion" of greed would make men and women single-minded, long-term calculators, impervious to the risky ambitions for glory that had caused so much havoc in the past. Avarice, a deadly sin for earlier moralists, became regarded by Utilitarian thinkers and their economist acolytes as both morally good and socially useful (Hirschman 1977). This is, in a nutshell, the argument made by Max Weber in *The Protestant Ethic and the Spirit of Capitalism* (1930), where he discovered the roots of capitalism in the moral fervor and this-worldly asceticism of Calvinism.

The transformation of greed from sin to virtue illustrates the way that changes in the cultural climate can effect the experience and expression of emotions over time. Certainly, nascent capitalists in the seventeenth and eighteenth centuries struggled hard to subdue their more aggressive and expansive impulses in order to pursue profit with a new, single-minded devotion. But there was also a romantic backlash against the Utilitarian model of feeling, demonstrating that human passions cannot be so easily confined to such a narrow band. When Johann Wolfgang Goethe published *The Sorrows of Werther* in 1774 he tapped into this wellspring of repressed sentiment. His tale of the suicide of an idealistic young artist spurned in love inspired hundreds of poetic young men throughout Europe to commit suicide themselves as the ultimate expression of their sensitive hearts and total contempt for the predominant ethos of cool calculation and hard cash.

The combination of the emotional constraints demanded by capitalism and the romantic resistance to those limits serves to demonstrate how shifts in social organization, cultural context, and life style may have profound effects on the ways in which individuals experience emotion. A modern example of this correlation has been documented by the sociologist Arlie Hochschild, who shows how the increasing importance of a service economy has led to increasing self-consciousness among Americans about the authenticity of their own feelings and the feelings of others.

This is because more people in the United States are presently working in positions that involve constant public interaction with customers and a high degree of emotional control. This pervasive "emotion work" can have pernicious effects.

For example, in her study of airline stewardesses, Hochschild found workers were required to smile and be friendly, regardless of their own moods, and were even expected to manipulate their inner feelings so they would correspond with the demanded outer expressivity. The obligatory professional maintenance of cheerfulness led many to experience deep feelings of self-estrangement and sometimes to a sense of emotional deadness. As Hochschild puts it:

> When the product – the thing to be engineered, mass produced, and subjected to speed-up and slow down – is a smile, a mood, a feeling, or a relationship, it comes to belong more to the organization and less to the self. And so in the country that most publicly celebrates the individual, more people privately wonder, without tracing the question to its deepest social root: What do I really feel? (Hochschild 1983: 198)

According to Hochschild, the value of "authentic" emotion, free of restraint or obligation, has risen greatly in the United States as a reaction against the pervasive management of feeling.

SCIENTIFIC THEORIES OF EMOTION

The type of study undertaken by Hochschild of the complex interrelationship between social structure, political organization, historical change, cultural ideals, and emotional expressivity remains unusual, but it does offer a paradigm for the future. However, to be completely adequate, any such study must also be grounded in a theory of the fundamental nature of emotions themselves. Clearly, in order to act as primary motivating factors in an individual's social and personal life, emotions must be understood to have a degree of force and autonomy.

To develop such a theory requires turning to the physical sciences, where study of the physiology of the emotions has a very long history, beginning in the West with Aristotle's linkage of emotions with "pneuma" or vital spirits. Later medieval thought elaborated this doctrine, dividing people into four distinctive physical/emotional types: "choleric" (angry), "splenetic" (spiteful), "phlegmatic" (dull), "melancholiac" (depressed), each shaped by the relative predominance of the elemental fluids in the body (blood, yellow bile, phlegm, black bile). Remnants of this theoretical framework may be seen in Jung's concept of archetypical character types (which, incidentally, had great influence on Gregory Bateson and other Culture and Personality theorists).

However, eventually most scientific investigators set aside notions of innate emotional types and instead followed Darwin's claim that emotions are adaptive mechanisms humans share with their animal cousins: fear and anger prepare the body for flight or fight, and so on (Darwin 1965). In the United States, William James followed in Darwin's path, proposing that emotion is best seen as a byproduct of the bodily responses caused by the stimulation of the senses. The various emotions, from this perspective, are unconscious, innate, adaptive physiological reactions that impel humans (and animals) to action (Lange and James 1922). James's argument was later championed by a number of neurobiologists (for example, Funkenstein 1955), who claimed that different emotions are associated with different autonomic processes and chemicals.

Yet this perspective did not immediately carry the day. Opponents contended that physical changes do not necessarily arouse specific emotions; rather, the same stimulus could be interpreted completely differently, according to context (Cannon 1927). The paradigmatic test of this theory was conducted by the psychologists Stanley Schachter and Jerome Singer. They injected their subjects with epinephrine, a drug that causes an accelerated heartbeat and a sense of excitement. Some were then put into situations where the stooges around them pretended to be irritated, while others were placed in situations where the stooges were euphoric. Not surprisingly, the experimental subjects surrounded by cranks felt cross themselves, while those surrounded by cheery people felt happy. Schachter and Singer concluded that appraisal "determines whether the state of physiological arousal will be labeled as 'anger,' 'joy,' 'fear,' or whatever" (1962: 380). For many researchers, Schachter and Singer's findings appeared to prove that emotions were best understood as a product of the evaluations of individuals – a conclusion that could easily be extended to favor a strongly cultural approach to the definition of emotion, since if the same sensation was interpreted differently by individuals according to context, then it followed that context made the emotion.

However, physiological explanations were soon resuscitated by sophisticated neurobiological research on the brain that showed that endorphins and other neuro-chemicals had significant and quite specific effects on mood. Schachter and Singer's experimental procedures were also brought into question (see Kemper 1987 for a review). Because of these problems, the purely cognitive-evaluative theory of emotions failed to convince many neurologists and psychologists who, like Hume, argued that "cognitions have largely evolved in the service of emotions" (Plutchik 1982: 544), or, somewhat less radically, that emotions exist in consciousness inde-pendent of cognition, aroused by unconscious drives or by other emotions (Izard 1971, 1972, 1977). For these researchers, choices we claim to have made for good logical reasons may well be generated by unconscious emotional preferences en-coded at a visceral level (Zajonc 1980). This latter perspective obviously validates Freud's view of the importance of unconscious drives in human action, and it also tends to confirm Durkheim's picture of the manner in which emotional involve-ment in the collective propels human beings to act in ways that are against their own self-interest.

In an attempt to mediate between a cognitive-interpretive and an essentialist-biological argument, Silvan Tomkins asserts emotion might best be seen as a biological motivating system: "Without its amplification nothing else matters, and with its amplification anything else can matter" (Tomkins 1982: 356). Similarly, anthropo-logist David Parkin has written: "emotions are non-judgmental shapers of decisions. That is to say, emotions act autonomously, or at least appear to do so, in giving sense to an interpretation, not through comparison with other possible decisions, but by making that particular interpretation seem fitting" (Parkin 1985: 142). (For a recent neuroscientific linkage of emotion with cognition and perception, see Damasio 1999.) These authors have accepted the position (taken by Freudians as well) that emotion is the mechanism for directing the trajectory of unconscious drives. Some aspects of these emotions hold across human beings everywhere: sudden intense input, for instance, causes a startle reaction; increased stimulus leads to distress; lowered stimulus is pleasurable; some emotional reactions, such as disgust, are innate.

Tomkins and others of his persuasion have also accepted the proposition that the vast majority of emotional responses are a result of a process of cultural learning; they can be blended, channeled, increased, reduced, and transformed almost infinitely. It follows that cultural differences in the revelation and experience of feelings may be a result of divergent attitudes toward those particular feelings, and not a consequence of differences in the innate character of the basic emotions (Izard 1980).

THE SEARCH FOR BASIC EMOTIONS

This leaves open the task of defining the emotions. As Durkheim warned, emotions do not form a natural class; they are perplexing even to describe, much less to categorize into any clear taxonomy or hierarchy such as that proposed by Hume. In consequence, despite considerable advances, the catalogue of emotions posited by psychologists remains confused. For example, Carol Izard (1980) has proposed nine primary emotions: interest, excitement, joy, surprise/startle, distress/anguish, disgust/contempt, anger/rage, shame/humiliation, fear/terror; Paul Ekman and his colleagues (1982a) claim to have discovered five essential emotional states: happiness, fear/surprise, sadness (or distress), anger, disgust; Theodore Kemper (1978) has restated Aristotle's case for the existence of only four primary emotions: fear, anger, depression, and satisfaction. These are only a few of the best known of the many categorizations of emotion suggested by modern science. Yet, despite disagreements among empirical researchers and commentators, it is clear that all the categorizations of primary emotions include at least the four posited by Kemper (and Aristotle). These appear among infants only 2 months old, who cry to elicit care, show fear when surprised, become angry when frustrated, and are happy when suckled (Trevarthen 1984: 152).

In this vein, psychological anthropologist Robert Levy has concluded "the central tendencies named by various emotional terms are probably universal but that the borders of the categories may differ" (1984: 229). He has been seconded by the experientialist linguist George Lakoff and his colleagues, who have argued that whenever emotions are described, the same set of metaphors is always utilized. For example, anger is invariably characterized in terms of an increase in body heat, internal pressure, and agitation that builds within the container of the body until there is an explosion. People are "red hot" and "ready to burst" when they are "inflamed" with rage. According to the experientialists, this linguistic prototype "corresponds remarkably well with the actual physiology" of anger; thus "the physiology corresponding to each emotion has a great deal to do with how the emotion is conceptualized" (Lakoff and Kovecses 1987: 221; see also Lakoff 1987; Ekman et al. 1983). Cognitive anthropologists have made similar assertions for the continuity of emotional experience. For example, there is a remarkable cross-cultural correlation in the colors people pick to represent various primary emotions, such as happiness, sadness, anger, and fear (D'Andrade and Egan 1974).

EMOTIONS AS CULTURAL CONSTRUCTIONS

With empirical scientists having established at least the rudiments of a basic set of emotions, a reasonable contribution for anthropologists would seem to be to study how these emotions can be blended, transformed, expanded, or contracted by culture. However, this is not the direction research has taken. Instead, when they have written about emotion at all, anthropologists have tended, mostly for reasons of disciplinary ideology, to argue against any universal emotions and in favor of the total authority of culture over feeling. This trend existed but was muted among earlier writers, such as Margaret Mead and Ruth Benedict, who conceded in an off-handed manner that there was probably some kind of natural "arc" of human emotional potential that was wider in range than any particular social configuration allowed – though it was never stated what the range actually was, or what the basic emotions might be.

However, during the 1960s a more radical cultural constructivist position of emotion was asserted. This position was correlated with the rise of interpretive anthropology and was spearheaded by Clifford Geertz, who argued quite seriously that the Balinese have no emotions at all, except for stagefright. According to Geertz, the Balinese lacked "individuality, spontaneity, perishability, emotionality, vulnerability" (1965: 399); they did not grieve at funerals, smiled regardless of stress, and devoted their entire energies to a public aesthetic performance of rituals. They were, in effect, all surface. Somewhat less immoderately, in her widely cited ethnography of the Alaskan Inuit, Jean Briggs (1970) declared that anger did not exist among her informants, who, she said, were motivated solely by feelings of nurturance and rational judgment.

For some time, these strong claims for the authority of public culture over private feelings were allowed to stand without refutation, and their notoriety led other anthropologists to follow suit with their own demonstrations of the manner in which emotion is culturally constructed. But there was a break in the consensus when Briggs, in a reconsideration of her earlier findings, wrote that Inuit child-raising techniques relied heavily on frightening questions such as, "What a lovely new shirt. Why don't you die so I can have it?" (Briggs 1987: 12; see also Briggs 1978). According to Briggs, this type of frightening question, along with other social-ization practices, served to make Inuit children hyperaware of their own antisocial tendencies and increased pressure on them to control their violent impulses, which were presumed to be very near the surface. Briggs concluded that Inuit anger did not vanish, as she had earlier claimed, but rather was a dangerous potential held in check only by strict training and constant control. Nonetheless, rage and cruelty did sometimes surface, particularly in the treatment of animals, which were sometimes nurtured, but also were often sadistically mutilated and killed. A parallel argument was made by Robert Paul (1978) in his analysis of outbursts of extreme aggression among the famously non-violent Semai.

Geertz's portrait of the Balinese as masks without content was challenged on similar grounds by the Norwegian anthropologist Unni Wikan. Undertaking fieldwork in Bali to reaffirm Geertz's research, she found something quite different lurking beneath the smooth surface of the ubiquitous Balinese smile. As she writes, for the Balinese:

> The heart, seen as a seething cauldron of passions, is a power to be reckoned with, though it works undercover and surreptitiously. Indeed, Balinese see the "acted" or "expressed" order in the form of predictable politeness and cheerfulness as necessitated by the tumults that would threaten were hearts allowed to reign. (Wikan 1990: 229)

In other words, the Balinese maintain their smiling composure not because they have no feelings, but precisely because their feelings are too strong and would expose them to danger if revealed. Nonetheless, those who are culturally knowledgeable can detect the quiver in the eyelid, the slight flush, that betray the carefully concealed passions trembling just beneath the relentlessly happy exterior.

CULTURE AND EMOTIONAL CONTROL

The sort of strict emotional control found in Bali is in fact quite common in face-to-face societies where people cannot escape the long-term consequences of yielding to their immediate impulses in public. Examples include the "face" demanded in China or the stiff upper lip of the English upper class. Sometimes in such cultures there is a class division of emotional labor; for example, among the Wolof speakers of Africa the inferior Griot are permitted and even required to enact the strong feelings which more respectable persons are forbidden to show (Irvine 1990). Even more commonly, emotion is divided by gender; stolidity is most often masculine, expressivity feminine. For instance, among the Swati Pukhtun khans whom I studied, men sat expressionless and silent at funerals while women wailed and keened hysterically in the background. These stereotypical public differences carried over into private life as well, as women were expected to be emotional and impulsive while men were phlegmatic and rational. However, the stoic male front hid considerable anxiety, which surfaced in pervasive (but hidden) fears of suffocating night demons (Lindholm 1980).

Of course, the control and manipulation of emotional expression is not only found in less complex societies, as we have seen in the example cited above of American airline stewardesses and other "emotion workers." Probably the most thorough account of emotional control in a complex society was made by Norbert Elias, who showed how members of the Court society of France's Louis XIV had to be willing and able to enact emotional states that were pleasing to their superiors and to keep their own immediate reactions strictly in check in order to gain favor. Behind their well-controlled surface performance the courtier had feelings much like our own, though their attitudes toward their feelings differed: like the airline stewardesses obliged to smile continually and who suffer alienation as a result, we tend to believe that to maintain mental health and personal authenticity, our true feelings ought to be revealed; the courtiers, in contrast, believed that for safety and self-aggrandizement strong feelings had to be well disguised and false emotions displayed. Thus, the courtier, like the Pukhtun khan and the Balinese, hid his feelings because of a well-founded fear that revealing them would give his enemies an advantage. In none of these societies was there any of the modern Western notion that emotional suppression is alienating or inauthentic, though it could be very hard work indeed.

But there was also a fundamental difference in the concept of the nature of emotions in these societies. In Swat and France the public performance of emotion was always primarily for the other, not for the self. The Pukhtun wished simply to hide his feelings beneath a shell of invulnerability; the courtier had the more complex task of both hiding his real feelings and displaying false ones. However, neither had any desire to make the inner and the outer correspond; the courtiers and the khans certainly did not think that smiling would make them happy. Rather, for them, feelings were hidden or dissimulated for advantage, but the inner reality existed autonomously and was not easily obliterated or altered.

In contrast, in some societies, such as Bali, appearance was meant not only to convince others but also to convince the self. The Balinese presumed that by changing the exterior expression of emotion one can, over time, change the internal feeling. As the Balinese say, "laughter makes happiness, it takes sadness out" and "if you only think good thoughts, it is impossible to feel sad" (Wikan 1990: 123, 152). Furthermore, Wikan claims the Balinese do not clearly distinguish thought and feeling – they think with their feelings and feel with their thoughts, which implies that feelings can be controlled just as thoughts can be controlled. There is also no unconscious in Balinese folk psychology: emotions are not internal, but are believed to be socially generated by specific situations and to be quite controllable and effortlessly changed and channeled.

As much as I admire her work, I must point out that Wikan's ethnographic material does not validate the Balinese ethnopsychology: instead, she provides accounts of how strong feelings of sadness and anger sometimes overwhelm the Balinese, despite their best efforts at control; nor do the Balinese have a lucid idea of why they have some feelings and not others, and they themselves often debate over whether feelings or thoughts have precedence in ordinary life.

FEELING AS EMBODIED THOUGHT

In stressing the unity of thought and feeling, conscious control over emotions, and the absence of an unconscious, Wikan has followed the lead of a number of recent researchers who have worked in the Pacific. Most notable among them is Catherine Lutz, who takes her examples from her research on the small, peaceful, non-competitive island of Ifaluk. The central "feeling-thought" there is *fago*, which translates as a combination of compassion-love-sadness. Fago is said to be an automatic consequence of relationships of mutual exchange. As one woman says, "I fago you because you give me things . . . If I take care of you, give you things, and talk to you, I'll know you fago me." Yet fago turns out not to be quite as nurturing as it seems on the surface, since Lutz explains it as a functional technique for "sanctioning the display of resources and abilities in the act of helping others" (1988: 139, 152; for a critique, see Russell 1991); in essence, beneath nurturance is a hidden agenda – a quest for power in a small-scale social universe where overt power-seeking is repudiated. Much like an archetypical Jewish mother, the Ifaluk can dominate one another by the purportedly selfless giving of succor.

A number of other ethnopsychological studies have followed Lutz's lead and have claimed that small-scale sociocentric cultures experience emotion not as private and inner motivation, but as a consequence of the enactment of specific public roles: a person will always feel *x* when another person does *y*. *Contra* Lakoff, emotions in these cultures are described not in terms of inner sensations as they are in the West ("He acted so coldly that I just boiled over with rage") but in terms of formal obligations and public relationships ("I fago you because you are my relative"). These authors also follow Lutz in focusing on the way in which emotion is correlated with power and social hierarchy (for some examples, see the essays in Lutz and Abu-Lughod 1990). From this perspective, the claim is made that emotion can best be understood as a form of cognitive assessment that arouses the body as well as the mind.

One of the most influential spokespersons for this position was Michelle Rosaldo, who worked among the Ilongot of the Philippines. As she wrote:

> What distinguishes thought and affect, differentiating a "cold" cognition from a "hot," is fundamentally a sense of the engagement of the actor's self. Emotions are thoughts somehow "felt" in flushes, pulses, "movements" of our livers, minds, hearts, stomachs, skin. They are embodied thoughts, thoughts steeped with the apprehension that "I am involved." (Rosaldo 1984: 143; for a fuller account, see Rosaldo 1980)

As in the model put forward by Schachter and Singer, emotions are here depicted as socially constituted and reflective of the mental constructs that are believed to make up culture; they are the "felt thoughts" in which the cultural habitus of power is embedded (or resisted) within the physical being of the relational self. In a real sense, this is a return to the position of the Greek Stoics who imagined the passions to be types of judgment, reliant on opinion. For them, as for the Balinese, the compulsions of desire could be eliminated by the exercise of proper logic.

There is much to be said for this point of view, which extended Geertzian interpretivism in a more complex manner and allowed anthropologists to analyze emotions as cultural artifacts for the first time. But a fundamental problem remained: viewed from an overwhelmingly cognitive position, emotions lose their autonomy and structure; there are no drives, no repression, no conflicts between internal desire and external constraint, no variations in emotional intensity and force. Feelings simply serve as the physical expression of authority (or protest against authority). And so, in principle, it would seem that anything can be felt, so long as it is expressed and defined in a discourse of power and opposition (for an example, see Kapferer 1995).

This constructivist and discourse oriented view flies in the face of a convincing array of physiological and evolutionary evidence already cited that indicates emotions are not infinitely malleable, nor totally cognitive, nor completely relational; nor is the quest for power the only motivation of human beings. Primary affects are more varied than this, and the drives that impel them do have some autonomy, force, and structure and do press toward expression no matter how thoroughly they are denied. To ignore this is to make analysis one-sided, without an oppositional dialectic.

A DIALECTICAL VIEW OF EMOTION AND CULTURE

A different and more adequate understanding of emotion was achieved by Michelle Rosaldo's husband Renato in a well-known paper he wrote shortly after her tragic death in a fall while doing fieldwork. He reports that previous to her accident he did not believe the Ilongot when they told him a man killed an enemy to vent the rage caused by heart-rending grief over the death of a loved one. Headhunting, he thought, was a form of exchange, and death was an occasion for a ritual performance of reciprocity. But after the death of his wife he realized viscerally how overwhelming rage can indeed arise from profound grief. With his ordeal fresh in his mind, Rosaldo argued that compelling emotions can exist without ritual expression, while rituals can exist without emotional content, as mere platitudes. Ignoring the autonomous force and intensity of basic emotions such as anger, fear, and love, Rosaldo asserted, is to dehumanize others, making it impossible to understand their deepest motivations (Rosaldo 1983; see also Chodorow 1999 on Rosaldo's later repudiation of this position).

The view of the emotions as active elements motivating an individual's relationship with culture makes better sense of ethnographic data than does the notion that emotions are really a form of cognition, wholly socially and linguistically constituted. For example, the anger that the Ilongot "throw away" when at home is expressed against others in headhunting, which not only relieves painful feelings of grief, but also displaces rage at their own neighbors and kin, which cannot be expressed without tearing apart the social fabric of their egalitarian communal society (Spiro 1984; for an example of the same phenomenon among the Mundurucu in South America, see Murphy 1960).

Similarly, the Balinese ethnopsychology of emotions as easily regulated feeling-thoughts cannot explain the fear of sorcery that is so pervasive there. It is more reasonable to see this fear as the consequence of the severe repression demanded in ordinary interaction; witchcraft accusations and ecstatic possession trance are a response to this pervasive repression and serve, as Linda Connor writes, to "release violent pent-up emotions in uncontrolled behavior without having to take any direct personal responsibility" (1982: 225). In a like manner, among the Ifaluk the apparent surface harmony of society is also undermined by an overwhelming sense of fear; in this case fear of ghosts and an unrealistic anxiety about the sharing of food. Charles Nuckolls (1996) has argued that these frightening aspects of Ifaluk emotional life are transformations of the anger aroused by the severe suppression of childhood sibling competition over the affection of the mother. The strong cultural value placed on charity and empathy by the Ifaluk coincides with equally powerful, though repressed, feelings of anger, expressed in ubiquitous irrational fears.

Other recent ethnographies of the Pacific tell a similar story. Samoans, like the people of Ifaluk and Bali, do not speak of physical states when they talk of emotions but of stereotyped situations and appropriate responses – of "feeling-thoughts" in Wikan's phrase. Ethnopsychologists have sometimes taken this to indicate that their actual feelings are detached and relational. But when Samoans are engaged in an emotionally loaded situation it is easy to see the physiological signs of strong affect (flushing, tears, clenched teeth), despite the fact that these signs are unmentioned. Like the Ilongot and Ifaluk, Samoans also vehemently deny the existence of certain feelings, especially any resentment toward one's parents, since such animosity is considered to be absolutely immoral. But nonetheless Samoans sometimes do lose control of their pool of unexpressed anger, which floods into violence. This occurs especially during periodic drinking bouts, when drunken men rage against their peers, not against their elders; such violence is not "owned" by the perpetrator – he was "under the influence" of alcohol – and therefore his anger has no subversive meaning (alcohol has a similar function in the United States, allowing violent actions forbidden in daily life). By such unconscious balancing mechanisms, the equilibrium between social constraint and proscribed emotional impulse is maintained (Gerber 1985).

While the Ifaluk, Ilongot, and the Samoans deny anger, the Tahitians do the opposite; among them anger is "hypercognized"; that is, there is a large vocabulary available for discussing it. Sadness, in contrast, is minimally elaborated; it is "hypocognized." This means that in situations where we would talk about grief, the Tahitians talk about sensations of fatigue, aches and pains, and other forms of physical distress: "I have been feeling tired since my mother died." Sadness is "somatized" as an objective perception of a bodily state, but not felt to be subjectively involving. (Robert Levy calls the first state a feeling, the second an emotion. His useful distinction makes emotion an internalized and subjective subsystem of the larger objective physical category of feeling.) Yet the lack of a vocabulary to describe sadness does not mean that grief disappears. On the contrary, Levy (1984) asserts the emotions denied in discourse are manifested in powerful and uncanny ways; for example, as "ego-alien" sensations of being overcome by malevolent spirits or illness. His model gives much-needed credit to the force and autonomy of primal emotional impulse and explores how they are dialectically involved in culture and experience.

Anger and sadness are not the only emotions repressed on the surface only to resurface in disguised forms. Among the rivalrous Pukhtun the advice of their national poet Khushal Khan Khattack made good sense: "The eye of the dove is lovely, my son, / but the sky is made for the hawk. / So cover your dovelike eyes / and grow claws" (quoted in Khan 1958: 12). Yet in this agonistic universe emotions of love, mutuality, and nurturance were indirectly revealed in performances of unstinting hospitality and idealized bonds of friendship. Deprived of attachment in reality, the Pukhtun sought it in symbols and fantasies. I should think the same would occur in any society where fundamental emotions are forbidden or denied (Lindholm 1980).

CULTURALLY SPECIFIC EMOTIONS

This is not to say that emotions are exactly the same everywhere, but it is to say that the psychological substrate out of which mixtures come is universal, though the specific colorations and intensities will differ across cultures and individuals. Each culture will produce its own blend of basic feeling states, since these states do not have hard and fast boundaries and can be mingled in specific ways. Fago (compassion, love, sadness) is one such culturally specific emotion; the Inuit have a parallel category of *nallik*, implying nurturance, love, pity, and the suppression of all anger. Ekman found in his survey of facial expressions that many preliterate societies merge fear and surprise. But even though some cultures may separate categories of emotion that others mix and elaborate experiences that other societies do not, this does not mean there is no commonality among them. We have already cited the consensus among neurobiologists and psychologists that such a substrate exists and must include at least the four basic emotions of fear, anger, sadness, and happiness and their permutations.

There also are culturally specific "emotions" that are barely emotions at all, since they do not move anyone; they are vague feeling states like "nostalgia for the lilies of the field"; narrowly defined, shallow, and culturally specific, with little if any motivating affect behind them. The Samoan concept of "respect" may be one such shallow feeling; while some Samoans say it is indeed a feeling inside, most say it is merely a form of ritual behavior. Nonetheless, such "affectless affects" probably are modeled after more highly charged feelings; in this case, a combination of love and fear (Gerber 1985: 130).

Alternatively, the unique emotional category may be a culturally specific transformation of a more fundamental impulse. One such is the Japanese emotion of *amae*, defined as an asymmetric adult bond of helpless dependency modeled after early infantile attachment. In showing amae, Japanese subordinates commonly act in a childlike and dependent way toward superiors, expecting to elicit nurturance in return. This highly valued emotion – often called "passive love" – favors "a considerable blurring of the distinction between subject and object" (Doi 1981: 8; see also Kumagai and Kumagai 1986.) Amae makes sense in the intensely group-oriented and hierarchical atmosphere of Japan, where it obliges a kindly superior to offer protection and provides a safe way for subordinates to act in a weak and needy manner. But it is an emotional constellation that is neither recognized nor valued in the United States, where personal independence is prized and where public expressions of helplessness and dependency among adults are strongly disapproved. Yet this does not mean that a need for nurturance and attachment is biologically unimportant for Westerners, only that we have ways of expressing it that are culturally specific, such as romantic love (Averill 1980, Lindholm 1999).

As a result of these and other arguments, overbalanced anthropological claims for the power of culture over emotion have of late been very much muted. Richard Shweder, who has often been a major spokesman for a relativist, interpretive view of culture, now concedes "it is ludicrous to imagine that the emotional functioning of people in different cultures is basically the same. It is just as ludicrous to imagine that each culture's emotional life is unique" (1991: 252).

THE FUTURE OF THE ANTHROPOLOGY OF EMOTION

We can determine then that an adequate psychological anthropology ought not to try to prove that every culture is emotionally unique (this is both obvious and fruitless), but that differences are culturally, structurally, and historically motivated variations resting upon a common psychic ground. The real task is the double one of seeking to discover what that ground may be and of finding what factors determine the alternative paths taken in the repression, expression, and interpretation of emotion.

In terms of comparative research agendas for the future, it might be worth considering whether some emotional blends (such as the love–sadness–pity constellation) are more common while others are rare or impossible. For example, can there be an emotional category which combines sadness and joy? Do certain combinations of emotion and types of emotional control correlate with certain types of social organization? Does Hume's categorization of emotions as primary and secondary, direct and indirect, have any validity cross-culturally? Or, to take a modern example, how applicable is Robert Plutchik's (1982) "emotion wheel," which distinguishes primary transient emotions of joy, acceptance, fear, surprise, sadness, disgust, anger, and satisfaction from secondary enduring ones of love, submission, awe, disappointment, remorse, contempt, aggression, and optimism? What sorts of cultures favor the Balinese notion that appropriate emotions can be manufactured through controlling one's behavior and thoughts, and what sort follow the Pukhtun/courtier belief that emotions exist autonomously, though they can and should be hidden or manipulated (Lindholm 1988, 1999)? What types of cultures display the modern American faith that spontaneous emotional expressivity equals authenticity?

We also ought to follow up the lead of ethnopsychology, but on a more sophistic-ated level, and spend time understanding and comparing the emotional theories put forward in various mystical traditions such as Sufism and Hinduism. This investigation should coincide with an in-depth study of the actual content and implications of the theories of emotion proposed by Western philosophers. In particular, Adam Smith's notion that mutual sympathy is at the core of civilization may be worth reevaluating.

Finally, it is worth stressing that the investigation of emotion is not simply an academic exercise. The infectious spread of terror and violence in today's world ought to lead us to think more about Hume's fundamental question: How can dangerous desires be re-channeled and toleration inculcated? To answer this inquiry, we first need to understand the passionate impulses that motivate popular uprisings, ethnic revivalism, and cultic zealotry; we need to think about what occurs when identity is challenged and about the kinds of emotional transformations that are aroused when individuals lose themselves in a mass movement. As I have argued elsewhere (Lindholm 1990), this requires thinking again about crowd psychology, a topic that was central to both Durkheim (1965) and Freud (1959) but one that has been forgotten by anthropologists, who have focused instead on "meaning-making" among free agents who appear to be suspiciously rationalistic and individualistic, regardless of their cultural heritage.

To restate: the evidence from many different fields strongly supports the existence of a constellation of fundamental emotional impulses within each individual; these impulses, which vary in strength and duration according to each person's psychic makeup, are expressed within and against the constraining and ordering framework of culture, history, and structure. This way of thinking about emotion does not under-mine anthropological analysis. Instead, it provides a better foundation for comparative work and, perhaps more importantly, gives a basis for the humane claim that others are not so different from ourselves. They too are driven by contradictory desires for attachment and for autonomy; they too are overcome by rage and grief; they too are transported by love and joy. And all of us, however rational we are and whatever our meaning systems, can sometimes be swept away by the passions of the collectives that surround us.

REFERENCES

Averill, James, 1980 Emotion and Anxiety: Sociocultural, Biological and Psychological Deter-minants. In *Explaining Emotions*. A. Rorty, ed. Pp. 37–72. Berkeley: University of California Press.

Briggs, Jean, 1970 *Never in Anger: Portrait of an Eskimo Family*. Cambridge, MA: Harvard University Press.

— 1978 The Origins of Nonviolence: Inuit Management of Aggression. In *Learning Non-Aggression: The Experience of Non-Literate Societies*. Ashley Montague, ed. Pp. 54–93. New York: Oxford University Press.

— 1987 In Search of Emotional Meaning. *Ethos* 15: 8–15.

Cannon, W., 1927 The James–Lange Theory of Emotion: A Critical Examination and an Alternative Theory. *American Journal of Psychology* 39: 106–124.

Chodorow, Nancy, 1999 *The Power of Feelings: Personal Meaning in Psychoanalysis*. New Haven, CT: Yale University Press.

Connor, Linda, 1982 The Unbounded Self: Balinese Therapy in Theory and Practice. In *Cultural Conceptions of Mental Health and Therapy*. Anthony Marsella and Geoffrey White, eds. Pp. 251–267. Dordrecht: Reidel.

D'Andrade, Roy, and Michael Egan, 1974 The Colors of Emotion. *American Ethnologist* 1: 49–63.

Damasio, Antonio, 1999 *The Feeling of What Happens: Body and Emotion in the Making of Consciousness*. New York: Harcourt Brace.

Darwin, Charles, 1965 *The Expression of Emotions in Man and Animals*. Chicago: University of Chicago Press.

Doi, Takeo, 1981 *The Anatomy of Dependence*. Tokyo: Kodansha International.

Durkheim, Emile, 1965 *The Elementary Forms of Religious Life*. New York: Free Press.

Durkheim, Emile, and Marcel Mauss, 1963 *Primitive Classification*. Chicago: University of Chicago Press.

Ekman, Paul, with Wallace Friesen, Phoebe Ellsworth, 1982a What Emotion Categories or Dimensions Can Observers Judge From Facial Behavior? In *Emotion in the Human Face*. Paul Ekman, ed. Pp. 39–55. Cambridge: Cambridge University Press.

— 1982b What are the Similarities and Differences in Facial Behavior Across Cultures? In *Emotion in the Human Face*. Paul Ekman, ed. Pp. 128–143. Cambridge: Cambridge University Press.

Ekman, Paul, with R. Levinson, Wallace Friesen, 1983 Autonomic Nervous System Activity Distinguishes between Emotions. *Science* 221: 1208–1210.

Freud, Sigmund, 1959 *Group Psychology and the Analysis of the Ego*. New York: Norton.

Funkenstein, D., 1955 The Physiology of Fear and Anger. *Scientific American* 192: 74–80.

Gerber, Eleanor Ruth, 1985 Rage and Obligation: Samoan Emotion in Conflict. In *Person, Self and Experience*. G. White and J. Kirkpatrick, eds. Pp. 121–167. Berkeley: University of California Press.

Gardiner, Howard M., with Ruth Metcalf and John Beebe-Center, 1937 *Feeling and Emotion: A History of Theories*. New York: American Book Company.

Geertz, Clifford, 1965 *Person, Time and Conduct in Bali: An Essay in Cultural Analysis*. Southeast Asia Studies. New Haven, CT: Yale University Press.

Hirschman, Albert O., 1977 *The Passions and the Interests: Political Arguments for Capitalism before its Triumph*. Princeton, NJ: Princeton University Press.

Hochschild, Arlie Russell, 1983 *The Managed Heart: Commercialization of Human Feeling*. Berkeley: University of California Press.

Hume, David, 1978 *A Treatise of Human Nature*. Oxford: Oxford University Press.

Irvine, Judith, 1990 Registering Affect: Heteroglossia in the Linguistic Expression of Emotion. In *Language and the Politics of Emotion*. Catherine Lutz and Lila Abu-Lughod, eds. Cambridge: Cambridge University Press.

Izard, Carrol, 1971 *The Face of Emotion*. New York: Appleton-Century-Crofts.

— 1972 *Patterns of Emotions*. New York: Academic Press.

— 1977 *Human Emotions*. New York: Plenum.

— 1980 Cross-Cultural Perspectives on Emotion and Emotion Communication. In *Handbook of Cross-Cultural Psychology*. H. Triandis, ed. Pp. 185–221. Boston, MA: Allyn and Bacon.

Jenkins, Janis, 1994 The Psychocultural Study of Emotion and Mental Disorder. In *Psychological Anthropology*. Philip Bock, ed. Pp. 97–120. Westport, CT: Praeger.

Kapferer, Bruce, 1995 From the Edge of Death: Sorcery and the Motion of Consciousness. In *Questions of Consciousness*. Anthony P. Cohen and Nigel Rapport, eds. London: Routledge.

Kemper, Theodore, 1978 *A Social Interactional Theory of Emotion*. New York: John Wiley.

— 1987 How Many Emotions Are There? Wedding the Social and the Autonomic Components. *American Journal of Sociology* 93: 263–289.

Khan, Ghani, 1958 *The Pathans: A Sketch*. Peshawar: University Books.

Kumagai, Hisa, and Arno Kumagai, 1986 The Hidden "I" in Amae: "Passive Love" and Japanese Social Perception. *Ethos* 14: 305–320.

Lakoff, George, 1987 *Women, Fire and Dangerous Things*. Chicago: University of Chicago Press.

Lakoff, George, and Zoltan Kovecses, 1987 The Cognitive Model of Anger Inherent in American English. In *Cultural Models in Language and Thought*. Dorothy Holland and Naomi Quinn, eds. Pp. 195–221. Cambridge: Cambridge University Press.

Lange, C. and William James, 1922 *The Emotions*. New York: Macmillan, Hafner Press.

Levy, Robert, 1984 Emotion, Knowing, and Culture. In *Culture Theory: Essays on Mind, Self and Emotion*. Richard Shweder and Robert LeVine, eds. Pp. 214–237. Cambridge: Cambridge University Press.

Lindholm, Charles, 1980 *Generosity and Jealousy: The Swat Pukhtun of Northern Pakistan*. New York: Columbia University Press.

— 1988 The Social Structure of Emotional Constraint: The Court of Louis XIV and the Pukhtun of Northern Pakistan. *Ethos* 16: 227–246.

— 1990 *Charisma*. Oxford: Blackwell.

— 1999 Love and Structure. In *Love and Eroticism*. Michael Featherstone, ed. Pp. 243–263. London: Sage.

Lutz, Catherine, 1988 *Unnatural Emotions: Everyday Sentiments on a Micronesian Atoll and their Challenge to Western Theory*. Chicago: University of Chicago Press.

Lutz, Catherine, and Lila Abu-Lughod, eds., 1990 *Language and the Politics of Emotion*. Cambridge: Cambridge University Press.

Lutz, Catherine, and Geoffrey White, 1986 The Anthropology of Emotions. *Annual Review of Anthropology* 15: 405–436.

MacIntyre, Alasdair, 1981 *After Virtue: A Study in Moral Theory*. London: Duckworth.

Murphy, Robert, 1960 *Headhunter's Heritage*. Berkeley: University of California Press.

Nuckolls, Charles, 1996 *The Cultural Dialectics of Knowledge and Desire*. Madison: University of Wisconsin Press.

Parkin, David, 1985 Reason, Emotion and the Embodiment of Power. In *Reason and Morality*. Joanna Overing, ed. Pp. 135–151. London: Tavistock.

Paul, Robert, 1978 Instinctive Aggression in Man: The Semai Case. *Journal of Psychological Anthropology* 1: 65–79.

Plutchik, Robert, 1982 A Psychoevolutionary Theory of the Emotions. *Social Science Information* 21: 529–553.

Rorty, Amélie, 1980 Explaining Emotions. In *Explaining Emotions*. Amélie Rorty, ed. Pp. 1–8. Berkeley: University of California Press.

Rosaldo, Michelle, 1980 *Knowledge and Passion: Ilongot Notions of Self and Social Life*. Cambridge: Cambridge University Press.

— 1984 Toward an Anthropology of Self and Feeling. In *Culture Theory: Essays on Mind, Self and Emotion*. Richard Shweder and Robert Levine, eds. Pp. 137–157. Cambridge: Cambridge University Press.

Rosaldo, Renato, 1983 Grief and a Headhunter's Rage: On the Cultural Force of Emotions. In *Text, Play, and Story: The Construction and Reconstruction of Self and Society*. Edward Bruner, ed. Pp. 178–195. Washington, DC: Proceedings of the American Ethnological Society.

Russell, James, 1991 Culture and the Categorization of Emotions. *Psychological Bulletin* 110: 426–450.

Schachter, Stanley, and Jerome Singer, 1962 Cognitive, Social and Psychological Determinants of Emotional States. *Psychological Review* 69: 379–399.

Shweder, Richard, 1991 *Thinking Through Cultures: Expeditions in Cultural Psychology*. Cambridge, MA: Harvard University Press.

Smith, Adam, 1982 *The Theory of Moral Sentiments*. Indianapolis, IN: Liberty Classics.

Spiro, Melford, 1984 Some Reflections on Cultural Determinism and Relativism with Special Reference to Emotion and Reason. In *Culture Theory: Essays on Mind, Self and Emotion*. Richard Shweder and Robert Levine, eds. Pp. 323–346. Cambridge: Cambridge University Press.

Tomkins, Silvan, 1982 Affect Theory. In *Emotion in the Human Face*. Paul Ekman, ed. Pp. 352–395. Cambridge: Cambridge University Press.

Trevarthen, Colwyn, 1984 Emotions in Infancy: Regulators of Contact and Relationships with Persons. In *Approaches to Emotion*. Klaus Scherer and Paul Ekman, eds. Hillsdale, NJ: Erlbaum.

Weber, Max, 1930 *The Protestant Ethic and the Spirit of Capitalism*. New York: Scribner.

Wierzbicka, Anna, 1993 A Conceptual Basis for Cultural Psychology. *Ethos* 21: 205–231.

Wikan, Unni, 1990 *Managing Turbulent Hearts: A Balinese Formula for Living*. Chicago: University of Chicago Press.

Zajonc, R., 1980 Feeling and Thinking: Preferences Need No Inferences. *American Psychologist* 35: 151–175.

CHAPTER 3

"Effort After Meaning" in Everyday Life

Linda C. Garro

Cognition, defined concisely by psychologist Ulric Neisser, is "the activity of knowing: the acquisition, organization, and use of knowledge" (1976: 1). Casting a wide net, D'Andrade portrays the study of cognition within anthropology as concerned with "the relation between human society and human thought" (1995: 1). The implications of "the need and ability to live in the human medium of culture" (Cole 1996: 1) for an understanding of cognition is a historically enduring topic (D'Andrade 1995; Hutchins 1995; Jahoda 1982; Shweder 1984; Shore 1996; Cole 1996). The broad range of orientations points in many directions and is underpinned by a diversity of perspectives concerning culture.

Some time ago, the psychologist Frederick Bartlett pointed out that remembering, a form of cognitive activity, "is a function of daily life, and must have developed to meet the demands of daily life" (1932: 16). He maintained "it is fitting to speak of every human cognitive reaction – perceiving, imagining, remembering, thinking and reasoning – as an *effort after meaning*" (1932: 44), which does not necessarily involve conscious effort or even awareness. Judging it impossible to divest meaning from cognitive activities, Bartlett rejected the prevailing approach to memory which attempted to control for meaning and prior experience by investigating the learning and forgetting of artificial nonsense syllables. Although his vision exceeded the experimental findings and observations he reported, it is noteworthy that he stressed the social, cultural, and affective grounding of cognitive activities. This message went essentially unheeded.

The cognitive revolution of the 1950s "was intended to bring 'mind' back into the human sciences" after a "long hard winter of objectivism" dominated by behaviorism and verbal learning theory (Bruner 1990: 1). According to Jerome Bruner (1990: 1–3), a key player from the very beginning, the ascendance of the computational metaphor technicalized the cognitive revolution, diverting attention away from and even undermining the "impulse that brought it into being," which "as originally conceived virtually required that psychology join forces with anthropology and linguistics, philosophy and history" in order to "establish meaning as the central concept of psychology." Cognitive science "took as its domain of study the internal mental environment largely separated from the external world" with an "apparently unintended side effect: the hands, the eyes, the ears, the nose, the mouth, and the emotions all fell away when the brain was replaced by a computer" (Hutchins 1995: 371, 363). In a retrospective look at cognitive science published in 1985, Gardner observed that, despite an appreciation for the potential power of interdisciplinary studies, "in practice" cognitive scientists de-emphasize and attempt to factor out culture, emotion, context, and history "to the maximum extent possible" as a matter of "practicality," so that "an adequate account can be given without resorting to these murky concepts" (1985: 41–2).

This chapter, as in some earlier writings (Garro 2000a, 2001, 2003), works toward a process oriented account relating to cognitive activities in everyday life. While I draw on a diverse range of studies and insights, by no means does this chapter encompass all that could be considered. This would be beyond the scope of a single chapter. I do not, for instance, address psychodynamic processes as highlighted in work by scholars with a psychoanalytic orientation. And I can only allude to ways that broader political–economic forces and socially structured arrangements impact on "effort after meaning."

The arguments advanced here are consistent with the constitutive claim that the "effort after meaning" in everyday life is a jointly cultural–cognitive–social process, linked to and dependent upon our social involvements within specific settings; for example, as an interacting participant, through exposure to the actions, ideas, and/ or recounted experiences of others, relationships with others mediated through artifacts. This process oriented perspective revolves around the interplay between the range of historically contingent cultural resources available for "effort after meaning" and the socially and structurally grounded processes through which individuals learn about, orient towards, and may become participants in ways of knowing. The ways of construing reality that we learn from experience, our own or vicariously, may equip us with resources useful for acting in the world and for trafficking in alternative interpretive plausibilities – for our own experiences, future social interactions, and aspects of the world around us. A strength of a process oriented perspective is that it provides an entrée for exploring variability and change.

To ground this discussion, the initial sections of this chapter provide a selective historical backdrop. I start with Hallowell, as aspects of his general approach are compatible with a process oriented perspective. A discussion of the beginnings of cognitive anthropology follows.

PERCEIVING AND ACTING IN A CULTURALLY CONSTITUTED BEHAVIORAL ENVIRONMENT

Hallowell situated perceiving and acting persons in specific cultural worlds. He stated: "the organism and its milieu must be considered together" and any "inner–outer dichotomy with the human skin as a boundary is psychologically irrelevant" (1955: 88). He maintained:

> The psychological field in which human behavior takes place *is* always culturally consti-
> tuted, in part, and human responses are never reducible in their *entirety* to stimuli derived
> from an "objective" or surrounding world of objects in the physical or geographical sense.
> For the world of human awareness is mediated by various symbolic devices which, through
> the learning and experience of individuals, establishes the concepts, discriminations,
> classificatory patterns, and attitudes by means of which perceptual experience is person-
> ally integrated. In this way assumptions about the nature of the universe become, as it
> were, a priori constituents in the perceptual process itself. (Hallowell 1955: 84)

The world in which the experiencing self develops is a "culturally constituted
behavioral environment" (Hallowell 1955: 87). The effort to assume, as much as
possible, "the outlook of the self in its behavioral environment" allows for the possibility of apprehending "the most significant and meaningful aspects of the world of
the individual as experienced by him and in terms of which he thinks, is motivated
to act, and satisfies his needs" (Hallowell 1955: 88). Learned culturally shaped dispositions may enter into and organize perceptual discriminations, motivating cognitive, affective and behavioral responses. In his writings on the Ojibwa of Manitoba,
Hallowell provides numerous examples of specific environmental situations, which
from the "naive orientation" unconsciously assumed by a cultural outsider, appear
to be "objectively" innocuous but which to the Ojibwa afford information about
potentially significant harm. Importantly, the behavioral environment is also a moral
order with prevailing frameworks of moral accountability for one's own behavior
and that of other persons.

Hallowell's work is ethnographically relevant, as some of what is presented later
draws on my fieldwork in an Anishinaabe community (also known as Ojibwa). My
work owes an immense debt to Hallowell. Still, while his writings posit a pre-contact
unified cognitive outlook, mine reflects an appreciation that the "behavioral environment" is not the same for all individuals and may even vary for the same individual
across time.

COGNITIVE ANTHROPOLOGY

Emerging in the 1950s, the field of cognitive anthropology coalesced around Goodenough's definition of culture:

> A society's culture consists of whatever it is one must know or believe in order to
> operate in a manner acceptable to its members, and do so in any role that they accept
> for any one of themselves. Culture . . . must consist of the end product of learning:
> knowledge, in a most general, if relative, sense of the term . . . [C]ulture is not a
> material phenomenon; it does not consist of things. It is the forms of things that people
> have in mind, their models for perceiving, relating, and otherwise interpreting them.
> (Goodenough 1957: 167)

The view that "culture" be reserved "for what is learned, for the things one needs
to know in order to meet the standards of others" (Goodenough 1981: 50) has been
quite influential and much critiqued. Goodenough saw the linking of knowledge
and behavior as encompassing the study of naturally situated real-world activities

(as noted in Goodwin's (1990) exploration of how urban children constitute their social world through verbal interactions, and in Young and Garro's (1994) research on medical decision-making). Nevertheless, in a 1981 article by D'Andrade, culture is depicted as a "socially transmitted information pool," "the shared information – the cognitive content" – "with which we do our thinking" and upon which "the cognitive processes operate" (1981: 181, 182, 193). This agenda directs attention to describing and representing aspects of the way the world is understood within cultural settings. Writing at a relatively early point, Frake describes his objective as developing an "operationally-explicit methodology for discerning how people construe their world of experience from the way they talk about it" (1969: 29). Considerable work addresses the conceptual organization of cultural domains (e.g., kinship, illness, plants, color), which may include associated propositional knowledge ("beliefs").

As "one of the characteristics of human society is that there is a major division of labor in who knows that" (D'Andrade, 1981: 180), cognitive anthropologists have explored what is known as intracultural variation. Differential opportunities to learn, perhaps structured by gender and other social roles, may contribute to variability, with some individuals knowing more about specific domains and specialized practices than others (Boster 1985; Garro 1986). Cultural consensus theory offers a method for assessing how much an individual knows about the "smaller, coherent segments of the total information pool constituting culture" (Romney et al. 1986: 314).

Beginning around the 1980s, and for the most part proceeding independently from work described in the preceding paragraph (though see Garro 1988, 2000a), considerable attention was directed toward "cultural models" (or cultural schemas/schemata). A recurring theme across the cognitive anthropological literature is a commitment to theories compatible with what is known about human cognition. The development of cultural schema theory can be seen in this light. A number of cognitive theories converge on the schema construct (D'Andrade 1995) and the idea that "in large measure information processing is mediated by learned or innate mental structures that organize related pieces of our knowledge" (Strauss and Quinn 1997: 49).

Acknowledging Goodenough's influence, Quinn and Holland portray cultural models as "presupposed, taken-for-granted models of the world that are widely shared . . . by members of a society and that play an enormous role in their understanding of that world and their behavior in it" (1987: 4). Cultural model theorists tend to rely on analyses of talk – often interviews – inferring the existence of cultural models from what informants say (though see Shore 1996). Quinn, for example, says her strategy "has been to exploit clues in ordinary discourse for what they tell about shared cognition – to glean what people must have in mind in order to say the things they do" (Strauss and Quinn 1997: 140).

Much work on cultural models is consonant with the longstanding cognitive anthropological concern with discovering and representing "cultural knowledge . . . embedded in words, stories, and artifacts, and which is learned from and shared with other humans" (D'Andrade 1995: xiv). This thematic continuity can be seen in research strategies advocated by two prominent scholars quoted above: Quinn and Frake. Both – despite notable differences in methodology and objectives, not to mention a separation in time of more than thirty years – are engaged in portraying cognitive cultural content based on what people say in interviews and in other settings. In his synthesizing book *The Development of Cognitive Anthropology*, D'Andrade reaffirmed the basic problem of cognitive anthropology as understanding "how cultural knowledge is organized in the mind" (1995: 248).

> The cognitive anthropologist studies how people in social groups conceive of and think about the objects and events which make up their world – including everything from physical objects like wild plants to abstract events like social justice. Such a project is closely linked to psychology because the study of how particular social groups categorize and reason inevitably leads to questions about the basic nature of such cognitive processes. (D'Andrade 1995: 1)

The last sentence recalls an earlier article by D'Andrade (1981) that proposed an intellectual division of labor, with psychologists responsible for the cognitive processes and anthropologists for the cognitive content. This is a rather restricted view of culture's contribution to cognition.

BROADENING FRAMEWORKS FOR RELATING COGNITION AND CULTURE

In response to critiques within anthropology against culture as an expressly ideational phenomenon, Strauss and Quinn contend that culture depends on "two sorts of relatively stable structures": "extrapersonal, world structures" and "intrapersonal, mental structures" ("schemas," "understandings") (1997: 6). Their focus is on "people's (more-or-less) shared experiences" of "regular occurrences in the humanly created world" (objects, events, and practices) and the "schemas they acquire on the basis of those experiences" (1997: 7). Schemas are not like "sentences in the head"; they "are not distinct things" but, drawing on "connectionist" models of cognition, they are cognitive networks "of elements that work together to process information at a given time" (1997: 49). According to Strauss and Quinn: "cultural schemas differ not at all from other schemas learned from humanly mediated experiences, except in being shared. Schemas unique to individuals are built up from idiosyncratic experience, while those shared by individuals are built up from various kinds of common experience" (1997: 122). Schemas can be seen as orchestrating what Sapir described as "deep-seated cultural patterns" which are "not so much known as felt, not so much capable of conscious description as naive practice" (1985a: 548; cf. Bourdieu 1990). But schemas are also implicated in what Strauss and Quinn call cultural meaning: "the typical (frequently recurring and widely shared aspects for the) interpretation of some type of object or event evoked in people as a result of their similar life experiences . . . To call it a *cultural* meaning is to imply that a different interpretation would be evoked in people with different life experiences" (1997: 6).

Setting up a contrast with what could be called a "fax model" in which "publicly accessible symbols" as "extrapersonal messages are simply reproduced in people's psyches," thus straightforwardly determining "people's understandings," Strauss and Quinn's account of internalization explicitly rejects "misleading connotations of taking in whole" for an "appropriative process" that can be "selective and transformative" (1997: 23, 9). Bringing "the knowing subject back into social process" (1997: 256), they recognize that conflicting schemas may be inferred from what people say or do – perhaps through being voiced in different ways or in different contexts and/or different points in time, or through efforts to reconcile or integrate divergent ways of understanding. A focus on meanings as "mental while being learned from and sensitive to the public world" (1997: 84) means variability among individuals can be seen as knowing differently and not just knowing more or less (see also Garro 2000a).

Hutchins, although also confronting "the fact that human cognition is always situated in a complex sociocultural world and cannot be unaffected by it" (1995: xiii), takes a different tack. Hutchins sees the marginalization of anthropology in cognitive science as stemming from the focus on content. If culture is conceptualized as "simply a pool of ideas that are operated on by cognitive processes" (1995: 353), then detailing how contents vary across cultures has relatively little to contribute. Hutchins's alternative vision looks outward to diverse sources of material and conceptual structure in the world, to situated practices that are socially organized, distributed, culturally structured, and historically contingent. His research on team navigation activities on large ships is not primarily concerned with internalization but with connecting "what is in the person to what is around the person" through "an architecture of cognition that transcends the boundary of the individual" (Hutchins 1995: 64–5, 289). Detailed observational records document how the navigation task is distributed across and coordinated among multiple actors and humanly created artifacts. For Hutchins, team navigation provides a setting for studying how human cognition "adapts to its natural surroundings" – to "naturally occurring culturally constituted human activity" (1995: xiv, xiii). Clearly, "natural surroundings" are not "natural environments": "They are artificial through and through. Humans create their cognitive powers by creating the environments in which they exercise those powers" (1995: 169). Through "what our culture knows for us in the form of the structure of artifacts and social organization," environments are "organizers of cognitive activity" and play a role "in the construction of thought" (Hutchins 1995: 361, 169).

A backdrop for Hutchins's arguments can be found in the growing interdisciplinary literature critiquing explanations localizing "everything cognitive as being *possessed* and residing *in the heads* of individuals" in light of the varied ways individuals "appear *to think in conjunction or partnership* with others and with the help of culturally provided tools and implements" (Salomon 1993: xiii; italics in original). An instructive example of what can be learned through a fine-grained observational analysis comes from Charles Goodwin's research examining how proficient practitioners instruct the less expert. Goodwin examines how "participants build and contest *professional vision*, which consists of socially organized ways of seeing and understanding events that are answerable to the distinctive interests of a particular social group" (1994: 606). Professional vision legitimates the power of practitioners as having authoritative knowledge in relevant settings.

According to Goodwin: "All vision is perspectival and lodged within endogenous communities of practice. An archaeologist and a farmer see quite different things in the same patch of dirt" (1994: 606). One example comes from a moment in practice at an archeological field school where a student is being guided by a professor to see relevant information at a site and inscribe it on a map. Through embodied participation involving talk, gesture, and artifacts in interaction with each other and with the world, the apprentice progressively learns to see relevant information in the environment and to inscribe it according to professional standards. The refining of individual perceptual discrimination to become attuned to affordances available in the perceptual world can be seen as embedded within a socially grounded ongoing transformation of participation through which the novice becomes a competent practitioner. The emerging competence in taking the perspective of a skilled practitioner is accompanied by increasing intersubjectivity:

> The relevant unit for the analysis of the intersubjectivity at issue here is . . . not these individuals as isolated entities but archaeology as a profession, a community of competent practitioners, most of whom have never met each other but nonetheless expect each other to be able to see and categorize the world in ways that are relevant to the work, tools, and artifacts that constitute their profession. (Goodwin 1994: 615)

Similarly, in team navigation, the learning of individual practitioners unfolds over time in adapting their behavior to meet standards of competent performance: "Human beings are adaptive systems continually producing and exploiting a rich world of cultural structure" (Hutchins 1995: 288). In the work of the navigation team, individual cognition is but a part of the overall social coordination of cognition distributed across participants and artifacts. With the "proper unit of analysis for talking about cognitive change" encompassing the "socio-material environment of thinking," learning is defined as "adaptive reorganization in a complex system" (Hutchins 1995: 289; see also 361–363; D'Andrade 1995; and Csikzentmihalyi 1996 for comments explaining how even what seems to be a prototypical act of cognitive activity/creativity localized in an individual mind, such as a mathematician working out a calculation – or writing a book chapter – is best viewed in a broader systems perspective). Hutchins considers cognition to be a "fundamentally cultural process" and changes in the skills and knowledge as individual practitioners develop are "mental residua of the process" (Hutchins 1995: 374).

The cultural structure of navigation practice "evolves over time as partial solutions to frequently encountered problems are crystallized and saved in the material and conceptual tools of the trade and in the social organization of the work" (1995: 374). External cognitive artifacts take shape through cultural–historical–cognitive processes. The "accumulation of structure in the tools of the trade" – "a physical residuum of generations of . . . practice" – "is itself a cognitive process" (1995: xv, 97).

As Hutchins reminds us, "the ways we have of doing things, the ways that seem to us to be natural and inevitable or simply the consequences of the interaction of human nature with the demands of a given task, are in fact historically contingent":

> It is really astounding how much is taken for granted in our current practice. The difficulties that were overcome in the creation of all these techniques, and the power they provide relative to their predecessors, are not at all apparent to the modern practitioner. Only when we look at the history can we see just how many problems had to be solved and how many could have been solved differently. A way of thinking comes with these techniques and tools. (Hutchins 1995: 114–115)

Along with viewing cognition as a "fundamentally cultural process," Hutchins considers culture to be "a human cognitive process that takes place inside and outside the minds of people. It is the process in which our everyday cultural practices are enacted" (1995: 354). Unlike cognitive-content definitions of culture, culture is not divorced from its material aspects. Emphatically, however, culture is "not a collection of things," whether tangible (e.g., a book, a navigational device) or abstract (e.g., "some collection of ideational contents" or "knowledge"). "The 'things' that appear on list-like definitions of culture are residua of the process. Culture is an adaptive process that accumulates partial solutions to frequently encountered problems" (1995: 354).

Navigation is an example of a domain through which humans "have managed to open up new perspectives on reality based on information mediated by symbols" (Csikzentmihalyi 1996: 36). Controversially defining creativity as bringing "into existence something genuinely new that is valued enough to be added to the culture," and thus becoming a vehicle for future perspective-taking by others, Csikzentmihalyi considers the existence of such domains as "perhaps the best evidence of human creativity" (1996: 25, 37). Creativity is situated "in the interaction between a person's thoughts and a sociocultural context" (1996: 23). Innovators are well schooled as competent practitioners, but innovations are linked to political/social/economic conditions in a particular time and place and may draw on other aspects of "material/ cognitive residua" available in the cultural surround, cultural resources which may be imports from other locales "separated by time and/or space" (Csikzentmihalyi 1996, ch. 2).

In more ways than can be detailed here, the work by Hutchins and others enriches an understanding of cognition in relation to cultural-historical and social processes. Still, the situated activities examined here – navigating, and recording relevant information at an archeological site – have heavy cultural scaffolding. For the most part, the effort after meaning in these activities occurs in contexts where both the problems and their solutions are culturally structured and the emphasis is on reproduction/replacement through transforming apprentices into competent practitioners. A key component involves the individual's "fitting in" and gaining the competency to carry out the requisite tasks, through a process of transforming participation in coordination with others and with culturally provided materials. The attention is on coordinating actions, the artifacts, and the development of the practice: mental constructs like schemas have been noticeably absent. It is time to bring them back into the discussion.

SCHEMAS AS DYNAMIC PROCESSES

Consistent with the division mentioned earlier between basic psychological processes and culturally variable cognitive content, anthropologists have tended to present content oriented views of cultural models. But many of these efforts recognized that schemas are not static. Notably, Strauss and Quinn (1997) offer a process oriented account of how cultural schemas are internalized.

Schemas are dynamic and constructive cognitive processes mediating our understanding of the world that develop through embodied interaction with the world (physical, social, cultural). Schemas are seen as integral to perceiving, attending to, exploring, organizing, interpreting, remembering, representing, making inferences about, and coordinating action in the world (e.g., D'Andrade 1995; Strauss and Quinn 1997). Meaning-making as a constructive and creative process depends upon the dynamic involvement of schemas (see, for example, Shore 1996). Current work in cognitive science examines processes like conceptual blending and analogical blending as central to both everyday meaning and exceptional human creativity – "imaginative operations of meaning construction that work at lightning speed, below the horizon of consciousness, and leave few formal traces of their complex dynamics" (Fauconnier and Turner 2002: 15). Further, the complex sociocultural world offers multiple affordances for meaning-making and through social involvements individuals come to learn that alternative perspectives may be taken on what is "objectively" the same experiential situation (cf. Tomasello 1999).

Contemporary theories about schemas owe much to the pioneering work of Bartlett (mentioned earlier), who introduced the phrase "effort after meaning" and sought to understand cognitive processes in relation to everyday life. Akin to Bourdieu's (1990: 73) view that what is " 'learned by body' is not something that one has, like knowledge that can be brandished, but something that one is," Bartlett extended the notion of bodily schemas, as developing within situated contexts of embodied participation (1932: 203–204; note parallel to Bourdieu 1990: 63; Sapir 1985a, Shore 1996), to schemas as involved in other cognitive activities. Bartlett concentrated on remembering, but asserted that remembering cannot be understood in isolation but only in relation to other mental processes: "in order to understand how and what we remember, we must set into relation to this how and what we perceive" (Bartlett 1932: 15).

Operating outside of awareness, schemas are "living and developing" (Bartlett 1932: 214) generic mental representations ("organized settings," in Bartlett's wording), actively anticipating and selectively appraising incoming information and which may be modified by new experiences. Our understanding of new information is influenced by what we already know; interpretations are actively constructed as meaningful in relation to prior knowledge and experience. Perception, as Hallowell understood, is where "cognition and reality meet" (Neisser 1976: 9). Neisser, relating the notion of schemas as anticipatory perceptual processes with Gibson's ecological perspective, sees diverse involvements in the physical–social–cultural world as providing opportunities for educating attention and learning to perceive in ways that are meaningful for navigating the world. It is through ongoing engagements in specific cultural worlds and in purposeful activities, as in the example involving the archeology student, that perceptual processes become attuned to pick up culturally/socially relevant information. As Neisser puts it: "Perception and cognition are usually not just operations in the head, but transactions with the world. These transactions do not merely *in*form the perceiver, they also *trans*form him. Each of us is created by the cognitive acts in which he engages" (1976: 11). Given the sheer magnitude of what is potentially available in the world, the aforementioned ability for "perceiving" multiple possibilities is complemented by a necessary selectivity (discrimination, differentiation), informed by past experiences, in what is detected, attended to, retained, and recollected.

Another key component of Bartlett's theory is the notion of "attitude," rather amorphously characterized as "a complex psychological state or process" which is "very largely a matter of feeling, or affect" (1932: 206–207). At once personal and social, attitude is an orienting and permeating characteristic of cognitive activity. Motivation, interests, and values all interact with attitude to "direct the course and determine the content" of cognitive activities (1932: 33). As what is meaningful, emotionally engaging, and/or familiar varies across different contexts, Bartlett acknowledged the importance of "social influences" on cognition. By participating in social and cultural groups, individuals develop a "bias in . . . dealings with external circumstances," an "active tendency to notice, retain, and construct specifically along certain dimensions" (1932: 255). Bartlett's notion of schemas conjoins thinking, feeling, and motivation in relation to a culturally meaningful world. Bartlett's perspective provides a useful starting point for exploring cognitive processes within everyday life contexts (see Garro 2000a, 2001). As in the writings of Hallowell, the position that culture is integral to cognitive process and not just content can be seen as challenging the notion of psychic unity.

Psychic Unity

Within anthropology, the "'psychic unity' of our species – the degree to which we could characterize human psyche as essentially the same despite the effects of cultural differences" (Shore 1996: 5) – is less often an empirical question than a starting assumption. In a clear statement, Price-Williams asserts: "As a rule anthropologists have accepted the doctrine of psychic unity to settle for the view that cognitive processes are the same all over the world; it is only the product or content that is different" (1980: 156). But terms like "psychic unity" and "basic universal" are often left underspecified and "devoid of any substantive content" (Jahoda 1982: 52), resulting in what Shore views as the psychic unity "muddle": "Anthropologists have typically defended cultural difference as a defining human characteristic while repeatedly affirming their faith in humankind's psychic unity, usually without noting the apparent tensions between these two views" (1996: 15). Lucy, lamenting the paucity of research on linguistic relativity (the hypothesis, associated with Sapir and Whorf, that culture, through the language we speak, influences the way we think), suggests that many researchers may be "reluctant to challenge the universality of cognitive processes given historical experience with evolutionary and racial interpretations of purported differences in mentality. By contrast, ideological universalism is ethically well received" (1996: 42; see also Shore 1996).

This separation of process and content does not mesh well with current understandings of human development and learning across the life span. With three-quarters of the human brain developing after birth and neural plasticity throughout life driven by experience (Bransford et al. 2000: 235), part of our evolutionary heritage is an "eco-logical brain," organized by and "dependent throughout its life on environmental input" – "finely designed for cognitive adaptation to diverse and changeable environments" (Shore 1996: 3, 312). Our relationship with the world is an active one; our brains are "*essentially* the brains of embodied agents capable of creating and exploiting structure in the world" (Clark 1997: 220). Each person's mind is constituted through experiences in particular and complex sociocultural environments. In light of the diverse range of cultural environments, accepting that uniformities (cognitive universals) exist, acknowledging the equipotentiality of infants in terms of "being like other infants," and recognizing that cognitive activities may come to be patterned along cultural lines, does not necessarily lead to the conclusion that "it is only the product or content that is different." "Properly understood, the common architecture of the human nervous system accounts for important local differences in cognition, just as it accounts for universals of human cognition" (Shore 1996: 312). If it can be said that process and content are mutually implicated in our active cognitive engagements in culturally meaningful social worlds, there is little justification for separating process and content in our theoretical constructs. This includes the constructs highlighted in this chapter, namely schemas and, as discussed in a later section, narrative as a mode of thinking. Still, our position on these matters must (as will become clear in the remaining sections of this chapter) allow for variability in cognitive processes within cultural settings as well as between cultural settings.

WHAT ONE NEEDS TO KNOW IN ORDER TO MEET THE STANDARDS OF OTHERS

I turn now to a specific example, one that provides a glimpse at cultural learning seemingly compatible with a content oriented perspective and that includes an ethnographer as culture learner. This section intentionally appears at a rather late point, after arguing for the need to attend to process and content. I have not selected a piece representative of cognitive anthropology. Instead, I have chosen Evans-Pritchard's book, *Witchcraft, Oracles and Magic Among the Azande*, published in 1937. The book serves, in my view at least, as an initial exploration of some of the terrain later staked by Goodenough and others.

Evans-Pritchard's objective was "not to describe in full every social situation in which magic, oracles, and witchcraft are found, but to study the relations of these practices and beliefs to one another, to show how they form an ideational system, and to inquire how this system is expressed in social behavior" (1937: 2). He detailed how gender and socially relevant positions – through constraint, empowerment, and divination – impacted the way the "ideational system" mediated action in everyday life. He reported that witchcraft is so "commonplace" that to use the idiom to account for misfortune does not allow one to suppose that "emotions are deeply stirred." His own learning process comes in for several comments, including the following:

> I found it strange at first to live among Azande and listen to naive explanations of misfortunes which, to our minds, have apparent causes, but after a while I learned the idiom of their thought and applied notions of witchcraft as spontaneously as themselves in situations where the concept was relevant. (Evans-Pritchard 1937: 65)

> I, too, used to react to misfortunes in the idiom of witchcraft, and it was often an effort to check this lapse into unreason. (Evans-Pritchard 1937: 99)

Stressing the logical grounding, the interdependence, and the "intellectual consistency of Zande notions," Evans-Pritchard reported "no difficulty using Zande notions as Azande themselves use them" (1937: 540, 541). Indeed, he pragmatically regulated everyday household affairs in accordance with answers given by oracles communicated through the consequences of poison administered to chickens, reporting this practice to be "as satisfactory a way of running my home and affairs as any other I know of" (1937: 270). In some ways at least, Evans-Pritchard appears to have met the objective of describing the things one needs to know to meet the standards of others.

Some recent studies serve as points of contrast. Luhrmann, in her book on "magicians" and ritual magic in contemporary England, described the process of "interpretive drift" – the "slow, often unacknowledged shift in someone's manner of interpreting events as they become involved with a particular activity," and the "ease with which we all come to see a given view as valid, and the skills we gain in explaining it so that its limitations, biases, and contradictions with other views never seem apparent" (1989: 312, 344). The process of becoming a magician involves learning skills to perceive differently, to pick up information in a way that others do not have access to, affording a significant shift in the interpretation of events. Luhrmann writes: "Magical ideas begin to seem normal in the process of becoming a magician: in this way, the involvement is more similar to becoming a certain sort of specialist than to producing a new theory" (1989: 312). Good (1994: ch. 3), based on ethnographic research at Harvard Medical School, identifies a set of "distinctive interpretive practices" as fundamental to American medicine and as important to learn as the language and knowledge base of medicine. Becoming a physician is a "process of coming to inhabit a new world" built up as a "distinctive world of experience" through praxis, constituted by "specialized ways" of "seeing," "writing," and "speaking" – of formulating "reality in a specifically 'medical' way."

Through embodied engagement, the novices studied by both Luhrmann and Good underwent powerful phenomenological experiences. As earlier, the situation can be seen as one in which existing schemas undergo transformation through participation and interactions with others in practice relevant settings. In time, the transformative processes of learning to see with new eyes, to perceive in new ways (the evidential basis of reality), become naturalized and orient experience within the culturally constituted behavioral environment. With much of this transformation occurring outside of awareness, what comes to be noticed, retained, and constructed is observable in situated actions as well as in reflections on and talk about experience past, present, and future (see, for example, Good and Good (2000) on changing narrative practices as part of becoming a physician).

The transformations in the learners as described by Luhrmann and Good seem dramatically different from what Evans-Pritchard reported as a participant observer. While witchcraft, oracles, and magic were integral to the "texture of . . . thought" for the Azande, the situation was quite different for Evans-Pritchard. In contrasting his way of knowing with his portrayal of Azande ways of knowing, Evans-Pritchard was explicit that witchcraft has "no real existence" and is not "an objective reality." His account of his own learning focuses on cultural content; his knowledge about witchcraft was a resource he could draw upon to understand how others viewed happenings in the world. While Evans-Pritchard's way of knowing cannot stand as a model for others in this setting, the process through which he acquired this cultural knowledge is not unusual. Hearing about the experiences of others, recounted through narrative in situated contexts and interactions, is an important means through which cultural understandings about misfortune or illness are acquired, confirmed, and refined. Evans-Pritchard does not need to personally suffer from witchcraft to understand that this is a perspective on reality that may be adopted by others.

ON VARIATION

Except for Evans-Pritchard, attention has primarily been on processes that contribute to shared outlooks on reality within an "identified" cultural group (the Azande) or a community of practice. Much of my own work has concerned both sharing and variability within a cultural setting, especially with regard to meanings conferred upon conditions with the potential to be seen as illness. My writings on the Anishinaabe community, for example, convey how some explanatory frameworks for illness pervasively known among adults in the community (though not necessarily shared) are essentially unknown (not culturally available) among individuals in nearby communities who are descendants of European settlers. Other cultural frameworks for illness appear to be widely known throughout North America (Garro 2002).

It is now commonplace to point out that the notion of bounded and separable "cultures" is problematic. In an effort to recognize cultural similarities that are not limited "only to spatially and temporally contiguous communities," Strauss and Quinn focus on shared cultural meanings and their experiential groundings:

> To the extent that people have recurring, common experiences – experiences mediated by humanly created products and learned practices – that lead them to develop a set of similar schemas – it makes sense to say they share a culture . . .
>
> You share some experiences with people who listen to the same music or watch the same television shows you do, and still others with people who have had formal schooling like yours, even if you live on opposite sides of the world. This makes each person a junction point for an infinite number of partially overlapping cultures. (Strauss and Quinn 1997: 7)

I am somewhat uncomfortable with any reference to "a culture" and "an infinite number of partially overlapping cultures." I agree with Sapir's assertion: "it is difficult to see how cultural anthropology can escape the ultimate necessity of testing out its analysis of patterns called 'social' or 'cultural' in terms of individual realities" (1985b: 572). Yet, for Sapir, "a culture" was a theoretical construct (a model of reality useful for some purposes) often reified by anthropologists. Although I cannot develop this argument fully here, my reading of Sapir and my own work have led me to be wary of construing the cultural around what is shared. Following Sapir, my position is that "culture" – including its framing in the two quotes above – is problematic as a basic unit of analysis.

It is important to note that this should not be interpreted as denying that there are ways of knowing and ways of being in the world that may be widely shared among those identified as members of a social group or an "enduring collectivity" (Hannerz 1996: 33) – regularities that persist across time, and that may be found across successive generations. Rather, given the presence of variation and the potential for change, this is an empirical matter and not an *a priori* assumption. In my view, one of the advantages of a process oriented perspective is that it does not require the concomitant adoption of designations like "Anishinaabe" culture and, if I am interpreting Strauss and Quinn correctly, thinking about a (any) person living in the Anishinaabe community as a "junction point" for "Anishinaabe" culture and "Canadian" culture.

During fieldwork in another spatially removed Anishinaabe community, where, as in the first, many are bilingual speakers of English and Anishinaabemowin, I learned that some explanatory frameworks commonly known in the first community were basically unknown, while others were found in both. A plausible explanation revolves around historical differences in the conversion efforts of missionaries, along with the virtual disappearance of practicing Anishinaabe medicine persons in the second community, but not the first. Is it the common subset of explanatory frameworks that provides a basis for asserting a shared "Anishinaabe" culture?

Although many of my writings have dealt with "intracultural variation," I have come to feel less and less comfortable with that phrase because it suggests variability can be localized within "a culture." I currently simply prefer to refer to variability in a cultural setting, or to variability present in other socially constructed groupings, attempting to illuminate, when possible, the processes leading to the observed variability.

While the focus in this chapter is on cognition in specific settings, whatever bounding this involves is permeable, as the example of the missionaries illustrates. In the Anishinaabe community, members routinely travel in and out of the community, for varying periods of time, and their interactions outside the community can impact on their interactions with others when they return. Others who are not originally from the community are present for varying periods. Community members interact with a variety of biomedically trained health professionals but, as we shall see later, how individuals interpret and respond to these messages is highly variable. And these interpretations often enter the social arena with the potential to influence others or be influenced by others. Media – through print, radio, and television – are widespread and I have written about cases where individuals corroborate their own illness accounts with reference to something they learned through television or a film (e.g., Garro 2000b: 82; 2003: 18). A process oriented perspective allows for any form of relational experience to become part of activities of knowing. This includes experiences when others are not co-present and mediated through humanly created artifacts, as well as with regional and transnational media (Strauss and Quinn 1997, 7; Anderson-Fye 2003; Robbins 1997). Such relational experiences can occur across historical time and space, as when one reads a book from another time and place and applies what one has read to everyday experiences and events. As Hannerz states: "as soon as people make themselves accessible to the senses of others, through physical co-presence or artifactual extensions, they render themselves interpretable. Whether it is what you intended or not, some meaning can always be attributed to you" (1992: 4).

It is through relationships that the "outside," the "new," or the "imported" (e.g., people, ideas, artifacts, media) become part of the local cultural flow (Hannerz 1992). The channeling of the cultural flow may reflect the ways societies and states are organized by lines of social difference, like gender, race, social class, and ethnicity (Hannerz 1996). Thus, the existing sociocultural and political–economic organization may constrain or facilitate certain kinds of interactions with others and/or with artifacts and lead to differential and socially patterned opportunities for gaining new perspectives for meaning-making. As well, some of what is in the cultural flow may be more psychologically salient, meaningful, or interesting, and may lead to an active seeking of or attending to certain information in the flow (Anderson-Fye

2003; Robbins 1997) and/or attempts to test its relevance in light of preexisting understandings (Hollan 1988: 282, Garro 2000b: 82).

Further, overall social contexts change. In the Canadian Anishinaabe community, schooling at different historical periods, for example, took different forms and is associated with different patterns of involvement with Anishinaabe medicine persons (see Garro 2003: 19–20). And although this aspect can only be mentioned here, the increased presence or waning of cultural resources for meaning construction may be linked to historical processes and changes in power relationships. Within Canada, the trend toward self-government in First Nations communities has been accompanied by widespread and positive interest in Aboriginal healing traditions. This has taken different and complex shape in the two Anishinaabe communities mentioned earlier. An example of one trend can be seen in periodic visits of medicine persons to the second Anishinaabe community, with the consequence that explanatory frameworks previously available only in the first have entered into social life in the second community and impacted on how instances of illness are understood by some community members.

The penultimate section of this chapter concerns narrative thinking: an active and constructive mode of cognitive engagement which allies the culturally plausible with singular circumstances.

The Narrative Framing of Experience

Narrative thinking can be seen as a type of culturally informed perspective taking on situated experiences and events. A fundamental human way to understand life in time, through narrative we try to make sense of how things have come to pass and how our actions and the actions of others have shaped our history (see Garro and Mattingly 2000). The effort after meaning can be seen in the predilection to render experience, especially troubling experiences, in narrative form. Here, the focus is on troubling experiences that come to be seen as indicating the presence of an illness.

Through narrative, present troubles are situated, however provisionally, within a larger temporal surround. Narrative activity, as a distinctive way of "ordering experience, of construing reality" (Bruner 1986: 11), concerns not just the past and the present but also possible future, "as yet unrealized" experience (Ochs and Capps 2001: 2). Narrative thinking draws attention to how jointly cognitive, cultural, and social processes offer potentialities for organizing and endowing experience with meaning. To borrow some of Bartlett's phrasing, schemas are active organizations of past experience that mediate our ongoing transactions with the world. As Hallowell first pointed out, our worlds become culturally meaningful worlds in concert with the development and attunement of orientational frameworks (namely schemas) for selectively attending to and organizing experience in those worlds. Narrative is an active and constructive mode of cognitive engagement, with implicit interpretive frameworks, or schemas, orchestrating both the production and interpretation of narrative.

As noted above, narrative is a mode of thinking that depends upon past involvements in situated contexts and interactions – one's personal experiences and learning about illness and misfortune from and through others. The notion of cultural resources draws attention to historically situated and socially embedded interpretive frameworks – the range of interpretive possibilities afforded within a cultural setting. These culturally available interpretive frameworks (some widely shared and others not) serve as resources variably relied upon by individuals to help make sense of one's own, another's, or collective experience. When there is widespread awareness of a cultur- ally available framework, it can be seen as a form of collective memory. Culturally available understandings afford plausible narrative frames for understanding a par- ticular troubling experience in one way or another (e.g., a certain kind of illness), oriented to the present in a way that anticipates future possibilities (e.g., treatment actions) while organizing the past (e.g., probable cause). Alternative interpretive frameworks may be entertained simultaneously and what is seen as relevant may change through time and in relation to unfolding events (see Garro 1998a, 1998b). As perhaps first discussed in Frake's (1961) study on the diagnosis of "skin diseases" among the Subanun, the evaluation of illness may at times become a "social activity" that involves negotiating the relevance of culturally shared understandings about illness and treatment to particular cases.

Narratives may be co-constructed. This can happen in a variety of ways. Those in the position of authoritative knowledge, a physician or a healer for example, may guide the co-construction along certain paths, which may only give the appearance of shared interpretive agreement. Thus, social context may encourage the voicing of statements consistent with some narrative framings and discourage others (Garro 2000a, 2001; Ochs and Capps 2001). In other instances, alternative, even new, cul- tural resources may come to be seen as applicable through interactions with others, for example through a consultation with a physician or other healer, or through the application of ideas gleaned from cultural artifacts, such as a television program, website, or book.

Culturally available understandings both enable and constrain interpretive pos- sibilities; they are resources for navigating the ambiguity surrounding illness and other troubling experiences. Cultural resources are historically situated. Some narrative framings persist across long periods of time, others are more ephemeral. Historical circumstances, such as increased interaction with biomedically trained practitioners or collectively experienced changes, may impact on preexisting ways of understand- ing or give rise to new understandings. In the Anishinaabe community, some of the available narrative frames reflect social processes of colonization. In the case of illness, boarding schools, missionaries, and a variety of other outsiders sought to introduce changes in thinking and promote some narrative framings and disparage others. These introduced explanatory frameworks may come to be collectively understood in light of preexisting knowledge (see Garro 2002: 84) and become transformed as they are used in their new locale. Still, other available narrative frames link illness to detrimental changes occurring consequent to the arrival of Europeans.

Maturity-onset diabetes is a relatively new illness in the Anishinaabe community, but one that has gone from being unknown prior to World War II to being so common that some express fears that everyone might have it at some future point. At a very general level, it is possible to say that talk about diabetes reflects both con- cern about the ever-increasing numbers of community members who have been diagnosed with the condition as well as the view that diabetes is a result of the types of foods that one eats. It is also talked about as a white man's illness, seen as occurring after Europeans came to North America, thus embedding the emergence of diabetes within the continuing disruption and destruction of the Anishinaabe way of life. Talk about diabetes often brought up strongly articulated contrasts between the healthy and fortifying foods obtained through Anishinaabe subsistence activities in the past and the comparatively unhealthy reliance on the store-bought foods of the Anishinaabe present. I heard many other things about diabetes as well. In an attempt to discover whether there were culturally shared understandings about diabetes (a cultural content approach), I interviewed individuals diagnosed with diabetes. While there was considerable evidence of shared understandings about diabetes, what I found more interesting was patterning in the way individuals appropriated particular narrative frames and situated themselves and their own experiences with diabetes in relation to these narrative frames.

I noticed a tendency for younger and older individuals (see Garro 2000a) to talk about diabetes in different ways. Younger individuals tended to talk about their own case of diabetes in terms of over-consumption, especially being overweight and over-consuming sugary foods and drinks, often pointing to physicians as sources of authoritative knowledge. To the extent that diabetes was seen to run in families, it was the younger individuals who made such a link. When younger individuals made comments about diabetes as a white man's sickness, such comments tended to be apart from their own personal experiences and little elaborated beyond viewing diabetes as something relatively new and tied to changes in diet. In contrast, older individuals often concentrated on diabetes as a white man's sickness; and rather than the quantity of foodstuffs, their comments stressed the change in quality. While the amount of sugar was mentioned by a few, by far the most common source of bodily imbalance linked to foods of today was through poisons ingested with foods, including chemicals and other substances sprayed on crops and injected into animals, as well as those added during food processing and canning.

These patterns suggested to me that variability in understandings about diabetes in this setting often appears to be a matter of thinking differently, of knowing differently. And while this is not a deterministic form of explanation (these are patterns or tendencies), the differences in how individuals explain diabetes are linked with historically divergent life experiences (for which age is a convenient marker). The older individuals grew up during a time when diabetes was not a presence in the community and many said they could remember a time when they first learned someone had been diagnosed as having diabetes. Diabetes first appeared in the community around the same time as community members were becoming more dependent on store-bought foods and canned foods. Many noted the incongruity of diabetes running in the family with their knowledge that it is of quite recent origin.

Knowing differently has implications that go beyond content – it is intertwined with how individuals remember their past and envision their futures. Knowing and remembering mutually implicate each other, such that remembering is not separate from what is known. And this is a dynamic process involving reflexive assessments which may be altered by new experiences (see Garro 2000a: 309–311). Ideas about poisons in foods and over-consumption are culturally available resources which offer narrative frames for ordering experience: two versions of past, present, and possible future. When a younger person, relying on an over-consumption framing, explains her own diabetes as a consequence of drinking too many sodas and eating too many candy bars, a culturally available narrative framework becomes situated knowledge, connected to a particular person, context, and illness history. The same occurs when an older person, who sees diabetes as a "white man's sickness," speaks of time spent working in a demanding agricultural job off the reservation and situates the emergence of diabetes to "poisons" in the canned foods she had no choice but to eat during that time. In this case, the narrated account is an example of the collective history of the Anishinaabe married to individual circumstances.

The situation is not one where individuals are unaware of alternative framings; some of those who focused exclusively on the white man's sickness or over-consumption explanatory frameworks often made comments revealing their awareness of the re-jected viewpoint and reasons for their divergence from it. One can have "awareness" knowledge about a culturally available framework (at the level of content) without "living by" the construal of reality it entails. Further, what is known and remem-bered has significance for meeting the present and future. The younger woman, who connected diabetes with the over-consumption of foods high in sugar, sees limiting sugar intake as most critical. The older woman, who linked diabetes with eating canned foods, adopted the food ingredients and cooking styles of her mother, crediting this change with the remission of her diabetes.

A more dynamic view of the narrative framing of experience can be seen in cases of what is known in the community as Anishinaabe sickness. For simplicity, the discussion of Anishinaabe sickness will be restricted to "bad medicine" which may be seen as the cause of illness and other misfortune. Bad medicine involves the intentional, covert, and morally censured wielding of power by human beings which leads others to "perform acts or enter a state that they wouldn't have if left to their own autonomy" (Black 1977: 150). While certain clues are considered highly suggestive that bad medicine is involved, there is often considerable ambiguity and a lack of definitive signs. At the time of my fieldwork, there was significant diversity in the extent to which individuals deemed bad medicine as a credible account of illness and misfortune (see Garro 1990, 1998b, 2003). For some, going to see an Anishinaabe medicine person is an action that they state they would not contem-plate. For others, under some situations, including when bad medicine is suspected, an Anishinaabe medicine person is the only possible recourse.

One of my close friends was among those who steadfastly disavowed any belief in Anishinaabe sickness and especially bad medicine, a stance apparently shared by her parents and siblings (as well as a number of others in the community). When young, her parents had spent considerable time in a religiously oriented boarding school and through that experience came to discredit accounts of Anishinaabe sickness and bad medicine (patterning linked to social processes). Yet this friend helped me to understand the local cultural logic of bad medicine by pointing out situations where fears of bad medicine were likely to arise, as well as on whom suspicions might fall. Her way of knowing was like that of Evans-Pritchard. While she understood it was a reality for others, as far as she was concerned it simply didn't exist; it was not something that could touch her life in any way. Her knowledge about bad medicine was a resource she could draw on to understand the narrative constructions of others. The situation was quite different for another friend who was considered by some as inclined to act too readily upon evidence potentially indicative of bad medicine. She, as well as others with whom she was close, told of past misfortunes where they had personally experienced the effects of bad medicine and had been restored to health through the intercession of an Anishinaabe healer. Adopting Hallowell's phrasing, her behavioral environment was one in which bad medicine was objective reality, and for her, its seeming ubiquity structured the psychological field within which she was prepared to act. Primed and attentive to indications that individuals outside her home were upset with her or could possibly be envious of her, the interpretive possibility (anticipatory schema) of bad medicine fueled the ongoing (unconscious and conscious) monitoring of the social environment. Even after pinning protection medicine on herself and other family members, she altered plans on more than one occasion to avoid contact with those whom she feared might cause harm through bad medicine. And, during my period of fieldwork in the community, there were several occasions when she perceived that something was amiss and her suspicions were subsequently confirmed by an Anishinaabe medicine person. There were also times when bad medicine was suspected but not confirmed and the medicine person led her to adopt an alternative construction of what had happened (with an impact on remembering) and what should be done in response.

In a few other cases, individuals who initially told me they gave little credence to bad medicine later sought the help of a medicine person for a troublesome problem, motivated by apprehensions that Anishinaabe sickness might be involved. The problem was unfolding in ways that suggested this possible narrative framing. Or in some instances, others suggested bad medicine as a possible explanation. Sometimes, subsequent events were seen to confirm their preexisting skepticism, but not always. For example, one young woman, originally from the reserve but who grew up in an urban environment and only returned to the community when she married, initially relayed to me, in an incredulous and dismissive manner, what she had been told about bad medicine. She fully expected that I would share her view. Some time later, after I had been absent from the community for a period of several months, I learned of several misfortunes that had befallen her and members of her family. She came to see me, rather distressed, with the warning that the unbelievable was true; bad medicine really existed. She described, in great detail, the distressing experiences that ultimately led her to seek the help of a medicine person, after considering, actively assessing, and then rejecting a variety of other narrative possibilities. Rather than experiencing interpretive drift, in a short space of time she had undergone interpretive "shift," entering a quite distinctive behavioral environment without leaving the community. While previously she had been very active socially, for the next few months before she moved off the reservation she was almost housebound. She was not sure who might have evil intentions toward her and it was far safer to remain at home. In a number of the cases I recorded, the effort after meaning did not run along a single path. There were often multiple, sometimes conflicting, interpretive frameworks that were potentially applicable to a given situation. Sometimes the ambiguity of whether an illness was an Anishinaabe sickness or not persisted, even after symptoms receded, and could be revived under changed circumstances (see Garro 1998b).

The diversity in these examples poses challenges for an approach that centers only on cultural content. In this community, with regard to bad medicine, one can act in a way that acknowledges its reality, act in a way that denies its existence, switch from one pole to another, act in a manner akin to Evans-Pritchard through learning the idiom and comprehending the circumstances where it may be considered relevant by others, and perhaps other ways as well. It would indeed be surprising if someone who had lived for any length of time in the community had no awareness about bad medicine. Comments and stories about bad medicine enter into everyday conversation and may make evident social tensions and carry political ramifications. Thus, whether one credits such talk or not, a certain level of understanding is essential for full participation in social life.

Within the community, as mentioned above, it is possible to consider this cultural resource as a form of collective memory, a source that, historically, others have variably relied upon in reconstructing the past, making sense of the present, and anticipating the future in relation to unfolding events in the social world. Still, depicting what could be called the core understandings, the basic cognitive content, is but an ethnographic starting point, especially with regard to illuminating the effort after meaning in this cultural setting. Variability appears to be more a matter of knowing differently, of being in the world differently. Ways of understanding and interpretive proclivities to frame experience along particular lines may be linked to ways of being in the world, with attentional, perceptual, emotional, and moral ramifications. Knowing about bad medicine seems to be fundamentally different when it is a real possibility in one's behavioral environment than when it is not. The world is a different place when populated with persons who may have the power to covertly cause harm to you and to those you hold dear. However, even for those attuned to the possibility of bad medicine, the emotional salience and the likelihood of this interpretive process entering into everyday life varies across individuals, and for individuals, across time. Even when one is disposed toward a particular narrative construction, one may still remain open to alternative construals of reality that may emerge in socially situated interactions. The intertwining of cultural, social, and cognitive processes offers interpretive and experiential possibilities without being deterministic.

CONCLUDING REMARKS

Everyday cognitive activities conjoin content and process. One of the objectives of this chapter is to highlight the role of culture in cognition as process as well as content. Understanding cognition in everyday life requires attention to the constructive and situated nature of cognition. This includes the "murky concepts" that cognitive science put to one side at the beginning of the cognitive revolution in the late 1950s: culture, emotion, context, and history (cf. Hutchins 1995). These "concepts" underpin the framework of intertwining cognitive, social, and cultural processes explored here.

We enter the world as active, embodied, meaning-seeking, and meaning-generating agents whose further development is contingent on ongoing engagements in physically, culturally, and socially rich worlds. While the attention has been on localized cultural settings (or worlds), these are worlds where it is always possible for the new to enter the cultural flow – perhaps emerging in direct interpersonal relations or mediated by artifacts, perhaps generated from within the setting or co-constructed with what is introduced from without.

Schemas, as content bearing processes, are constituted through our relational experiences and transactions with the world. We seek patterning (structure) in the world and our schemas enter into and are modified by this effort after meaning. While some knowledge is explicit (declarative) and accessible to conscious awareness, much implicit (tacit) knowledge is gained through our embodied participation. We are also predisposed to learn not just from but through the experiences and interpretations of others; implicitly, we come to understand that multiple perspectives on the world are possible. Our everyday efforts after meaning are informed by what we already know and by anticipating what may come to pass while remaining open to new possibilities. As we become attuned to what is known for us in the cultural surround, it becomes part of our way of being in the world, part of the recurring effort after meaning. We enter as novices and progressively undergo transformations of participation in socially situated activities; activities that may be cognitively distributed across, and require coordinated involvement with, others and/or with artifacts. We continue to learn and are transformed through our interactions with the world throughout our lives (cf. Strauss and Quinn 1997). As we come to understand that multiple perspectives, often with divergent implications, may be taken on an experiential situation, the potential exists for alternative construals of reality. The effort after meaning, as seen in the discussion of the narrative framing of troubling experiences, need not run along a single path but may admit alternative interpretive possibilities.

In addition to undergoing transformative processes ourselves, we may be agents facilitating the transformation of others. We are cultural resources for others as others are resources for us. In one or more settings we may, for example, become involved in organizing the participation of the less expert. Along with artifacts and other forms of cultural structure in the world, our talk and other actions may become resources in the effort after meaning of others. Narrative is a mode of cognitive engagement that may serve as a cultural resource in the sensemaking processes of others. Our everyday acts of insight, imagination, and creativity, as well as those more extraordinary, are enabled by our varied participations and engagements in the world. Our insights and innovations may not take concrete form, even though they may enter the cultural flow with the potential to impact others. Or they may result in artifacts (or modifications to existing artifacts) with the potential to enter into the effort after meaning of others without requiring our presence. But not all resources may be equally available to all. We are in worlds that are historically situated and socially structured in ways that channel relational experiences and participatory engagements for each person – some particular forms of involvement are more likely than others, some are encouraged or compelled and others are discouraged or impeded.

What is proposed is a view of human cognition as inextricably linked to the social and cultural contexts within which lives take shape as culturally meaningful lives and, equally importantly, as uniquely individual lives. While this orientation draws attention to specificity, the argument is a general one, independent of time and place. The view of culture relied on here moves away from thinking about individuals as belonging to different cultures, even when it is recognized that individuals may participate in variable numbers of multiple cultures. Taking Sapir's recommendation that we test the patterns we call social or cultural in terms of individual realities requires a more dynamic and processual view of culture that reflects the actions of people in a social world as well as understanding the complexities of the socio-cultural world and the availability of cultural resources for cognitive activities and meaning-making. Variation is not a problem for culture theory, it is at its heart. Culture as cognitive process and cognition as sociocultural process infuse the recurring effort after meaning in everyday life.

REFERENCES

Anderson-Fye, Eileen P., 2003 Never Leave Yourself: Ethnopsychology as Mediator of Psychological Globalization among Belizean Schoolgirls. *Ethos* 31: 77–112.

Bartlett, Fredrick C., 1932 *Remembering: A Study in Experimental and Social Psychology.* Cambridge: Cambridge University Press.

Black, Mary B., 1977 Ojibwa Power Belief System. In *The Anthropology of Power: Ethnographic Studies from Asia, Oceania, and the New World.* Raymond D. Fogelson and Richard N. Adams, eds. Pp. 141–151. New York: Academic Press.

Boster, James S., 1985 "Requiem for the Omniscient Informant": There's Life in the Old Girl Yet. In *Directions in Cognitive Anthropology.* Janet W. D. Dougherty, ed. Pp. 177–197. Urbana: University of Illinois Press.

Bourdieu, Pierre, 1990 *The Logic of Practice.* Palo Alto, CA: Stanford University Press.

Bransford, John D., with Ann L. Brown and Rodney R. Cocking, eds., 2000 *How People Learn: Brain, Mind, Experience, and School,* Expanded Edition. Washington, DC: National Academy Press.

Bruner, Jerome, 1986 *Actual Minds, Possible Worlds.* Cambridge, MA: Harvard University Press.

— 1990 *Acts of Meaning.* Cambridge, MA: Harvard University Press.

Clark, Andy, 1997 *Being There: Putting Brain, Body, and World Together Again.* Cambridge, MA: MIT Press.

Cole, Michael, 1996 *Cultural Psychology: A Once and Future Discipline.* Cambridge, MA: Harvard University Press.

Csikzentmihalyi, Mihaly, 1996 *Creativity: Flow and the Discovery of Invention.* New York: Harper Collins.

D'Andrade, Roy, 1981 The Cultural Part of Cognition. *Cognitive Science* 5: 179–195.

— 1995 *The Development of Cognitive Anthropology.* Cambridge: Cambridge University Press.

Evans-Pritchard, E. E., 1937 *Witchcraft, Oracles and Magic Among the Azande.* Oxford: Clarendon Press.

Fauconnier, Gilles, and Mark Turner, 2002 *The Way We Think: Conceptual Blending and the Mind's Hidden Complexities.* New York: Basic Books.

Frake, Charles O., 1961 The Diagnosis of Disease among the Subanun of Mindanao. *American Anthropologist* 63: 113–132.

— 1969 [1962] The Ethnographic Study of Cognitive Systems. In *Cognitive Anthropology.* S. A. Tyler, ed. Pp. 28–41. New York: Holt, Rinehart, and Winston.

Gardner, Howard, 1985 *The Mind's New Science: A History of the Cognitive Revolution.* New York: Basic Books.

Garro, Linda C., 1986 Intracultural Variation in Folk Medical Knowledge: A Comparison between Curers and Non-Curers. *American Anthropologist* 88: 351–370.

— 1988 Explaining High Blood Pressure: Variation in Knowledge about Illness. *American Ethnologist* 15: 98–119.

— 1990 Continuity and Change: The Interpretation of Illness in an Anishinaabe (Ojibway) Community. *Culture, Medicine and Psychiatry* 14: 417–454.

— 1998a On the Rationality of Decision Making Studies: Part 1: Decision Models of Treatment Choice. *Medical Anthropology Quarterly* 12: 319–340.

— 1998b On the Rationality of Decision Making Studies: Part 2: Divergent Rationalities. *Medical Anthropology Quarterly* 12: 341–355.

— 2000a Remembering What One Knows and the Construction of the Past: A Comparison of Cultural Consensus Theory and Cultural Schema Theory. *Ethos* 28: 275–319.

— 2000b Cultural Knowledge as Resource in Illness Narratives: Remembering through Accounts of Illness. In *Narrative and the Cultural Construction of Illness and Healing.* Cheryl Mattingly and Linda C. Garro, eds. Pp. 70–87. Berkeley: University of California Press.

— 2001 The Remembered Past in a Culturally Meaningful Life: Remembering as Cultural, Social, and Cognitive Process. In *The Psychology of Cultural Experience.* Carmella C. Moore and Holly M. Mathews, eds. Pp. 105–147. Cambridge: Cambridge University Press.

— 2002 Hallowell's Challenge: Explanations of Illness and Cross-Cultural Research. *Anthropological Theory* 2: 77–97.

— 2003 Narrating Troubling Experiences. *Transcultural Psychiatry* 40: 5–44.

Garro, Linda C., and Cheryl Mattingly, 2000 Narrative as Construct and Construction. In *Narrative and the Cultural Construction of Illness and Healing.* Cheryl Mattingly and Linda Garro, eds. Pp. 1–49. Berkeley: University of California Press.

Good, Byron, 1994 *Medicine, Rationality, and Experience: An Anthropological Perspective.* Cambridge: Cambridge University Press.

Good, Byron, and Mary-Jo D. Good, 2000 "Fiction" and "Historicity" in Doctors' Stories: Social and Narrative Dimensions of Learning Medicine. In *Narrative and the Cultural Construction of Illness and Healing.* Cheryl Mattingly and Linda Garro, eds. Pp. 50–69. Berkeley: University of California Press.

Goodenough, Ward H., 1957 Cultural Anthropology and Linguistics. In *Report of the Seventh Annual Round Table Meeting in Linguistics and Language Study.* P. Garvin, ed. Monograph Series on Language and Linguistics, 9. Washington, DC: Georgetown University.

— 1981 *Culture, Language, and Society,* 2nd edn. Menlo Park: Benjamin/Cummings Publishing.

Goodwin, Charles, 1994 Professional Vision. *American Anthropologist* 96: 606–633.

Goodwin, Marjorie H., 1990 *He-Said-She-Said: Talk as Social Organization Among Black Children.* Bloomington: Indiana University Press.

Hallowell, A. Irving, 1955 *Culture and Experience.* Philadelphia: University of Pennsylvania Press.

Hannerz, Ulf, 1992 *Cultural Complexity: Studies in the Social Organization of Meaning.* New York: Columbia University Press.

— 1996 *Transnational Connections: Culture, People, Places.* London: Routledge.

Hollan, Douglas, 1988 Pockets Full of Mistakes: The Personal Consequences of Religious Change in a Toraja Village. *Oceania* 58: 275–289.

Hutchins, Edwin, 1995 *Cognition in the Wild.* Cambridge, MA: MIT Press.

Jahoda, Gustav, 1982 *Psychology and Anthropology: A Psychological Perspective.* London: Academic Press.

Lucy, John A., 1996 The Scope of Linguistic Relativity: An Analysis and Review of Empirical Research. In *Rethinking Linguistic Relativity.* John J. Gumperz and S. C. Levinson, eds. Pp. 37–69. Cambridge: Cambridge University Press.

Luhrmann, Tanya, 1989 *Persuasions of the Witch's Craft: Ritual Magic in Contemporary England.* Cambridge, MA: Harvard University Press.

Neisser, Ulric, 1976 *Cognition and Reality.* San Francisco: W. H. Freeman.

Ochs, Elinor, and Lisa Capps, 2001 *Living Narrative: Creating Lives in Everyday Storytelling.* Cambridge, MA: Harvard University Press.

Price-Williams, Douglas R., 1980 Anthropological Approaches to Cognition and their Relevance to Psychology. In *Handbook of Cross-Cultural Psychology Vol. 4: Basic Processes*. H. C. Triandis and W. Lonner, eds. Pp. 155–184. Boston, MA: Allyn and Bacon.

Quinn, Naomi, and Dorothy Holland, 1987 Culture and Cognition. In *Cultural Models in Language and Thought*. Dorothy Holland and Naomi Quinn, eds. Pp. 3–40. Cambridge: Cambridge University Press.

Robbins, Joel, 1997 "When Do You Think the World Will End?": Globalization, Apocalypticism, and the Moral Perils of Fieldwork in "Last New Guinea." *Anthropology and Humanism* 22: 6–30.

Romney, A. Kimball, with Susan C. Weller and William H. Batchelder, 1986 Culture as Consensus: A Theory of Culture and Informant Accuracy. *American Anthropologist* 88: 313–338.

Salomon, Gavriel, ed., 1993 *Distributed Cognitions: Psychological and Educational Considerations*. Cambridge: Cambridge University Press.

Sapir, Edward, 1985a [1927] The Unconscious Patterning of Behavior in Society. In *Edward Sapir: Selected Writings*. D. G. Mandelbaum, ed. Pp. 544–559. Berkeley: University of California Press.

Sapir, Edward, 1985b [1938] Why Cultural Anthropology Needs the Psychiatrist. In *Edward Sapir: Selected Writings*. D. G. Mandelbaum, ed. Pp. 569–577. Berkeley: University of California Press.

Shore, Brad 1996 *Culture in Mind: Cognition, Culture, and the Problem of Meaning*. New York: Oxford University Press.

Shweder, Richard, 1984 Anthropology's Romantic Rebellion against the Enlightenment, or There's More to Thinking than Reason and Evidence. In *Culture Theory: Essays on Mind, Self and Emotion*. Richard Shweder and Robert LeVine, eds. Pp. 27–66. Cambridge: Cambridge University Press.

Strauss, Claudia, and Naomi Quinn, 1997 *A Cognitive Theory of Cultural Meaning*. Cambridge: Cambridge University Press.

Tomasello, Michael, 1999 *The Cultural Origins of Human Cognition*. Cambridge, MA: Harvard University Press.

Young, James C., and Linda C. Garro, 1994 [1981] *Medical Choice in a Mexican Village*. Prospect Heights, IL: Waveland.

CHAPTER **4** # Culture and Learning

Patricia M. Greenfield

In this chapter, I will outline how the meanings of "culture" and "learning" have changed over the last forty years since I went to Senegal to do a psychology dissertation on culture and cognitive development among the Wolof. Equally important, I will show how the way we define "culture" and "learning" in our research relates to the kinds of theoretical issues, findings, and conclusions that emerge from it. While drawing primarily on my own research, I will also attempt to situate it with other trends going on in psychocultural studies, both within psychology and within anthropology.

Operationalizing Culture and Learning in the 1960s

Operational definition is a positivistic concept that refers to how a psychological construct is actually "measured" in a research situation: What constitutes empirical evidence for its presence or absence? When I went to Senegal in 1963, the operational definition of "culture" in the not-yet-born field of cross-cultural psychology was primarily that of an independent variable "packaging" many ecocultural influences together (Whiting: 1976). (In psychology, an independent variable is an environmental factor or dimension causally related to some behavior, called a "dependent variable.") The two ecocultural dimensions whose effects I studied were the rural–urban contrast and, within the rural setting, the schooled–unschooled contrast.

More implicitly and secondarily, culture was also defined in terms of the normative reasoning processes used by a particular ecocultural group. My research centered on the development of Piaget's concept of conservation (the notion, from physical science, that, in any physical transformation, some qualities stay the same, are "conserved", while others change) and on the development of conceptual categories. Culture was therefore also defined as reasoning processes shared by a particular ethnic group under particular ecocultural circumstances.

Conservation Tests

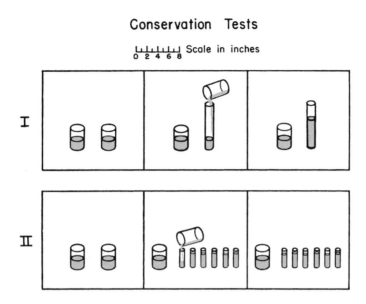

Figure 4.1 Standard test for conservation of liquid quantity. In this procedure, the child is first asked to equalize the water level in both the identical beakers. In I, the literal translation of the Wolof question was "Does this glass of yours and this glass of mine have equal water; or does this glass of mine have more water; or does this glass of yours have more water?" The follow up question depending on the answer to the first question was, literally, "What reason they are equal?" or "What reason this one has more than this one?" The questions for II followed the same pattern.

In sum, my basic research design compared children's development of conservation and categorization in rural and urban environments and, within the rural environment, compared children who went to school with those who did not (Greenfield 1966; Greenfield et al. 1966). For purposes of exposition, the basic conservation and concept formation tasks are shown in Figures 4.1 and 4.2; the figure captions contain the questions that were asked about each visual display.

What constituted learning in this research? Learning was two things, one explicit and one implicit. I will begin with the implicit because it was most basic to the research design. Contrary to Piaget's notion of universal cognitive development that was independent of learning processes, the goal of my research design was to show that learning opportunities, which should vary in different ecocultural environments, would affect developmental processes. In other words, cognitive development was not just a joint function of universal maturational processes and universal opportunities to interact with the physical environment, as Piaget had posited; it was also a function of culture-specific learning opportunities.

My major finding, and one that was extremely surprising at the time, was that cognitive development in both domains, conservation and categorization, depended on Western schooling. In Senegal, formal education was the direct result of French colonization, which had ended only three years earlier. These results implied learning: schooling apparently encapsulated learning opportunities that led to the familiar pattern of response to these two tasks. Figures 4.3 and 4.4 present the basic

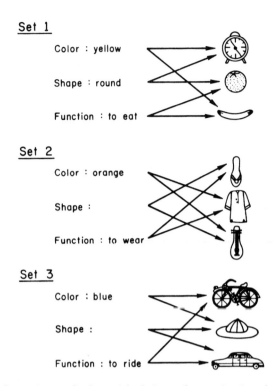

Set 1

Color : yellow

Shape : round

Function : to eat

Set 2

Color : orange

Shape :

Function : to wear

Set 3

Color : blue

Shape :

Function : to ride

Figure 4.2 The three picture displays with their attributes. Set 1 – clock, orange, banana; Set 2 – sandal, bubu (Wolof robe), guitar; Set 3 – bicycle, helmet, car. Children were asked to show the experimenter the two pictures out of each set of three that were most alike. They were then asked the reason for their choice. The same procedure was then repeated with instructions to show the experimenter "two others" that were alike in each trio, followed by a request for a reason.

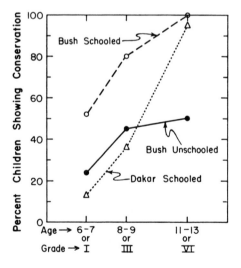

Figure 4.3 Percentage of children of different backgrounds and ages exhibiting conservation of continuous quantity on both parts of the procedure shown in Figure 4.1.

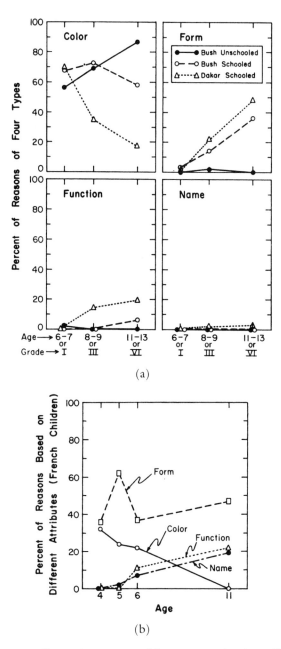

(a)

(b)

Figure 4.4 Percentage of grouping reasons of four types: color (e.g., "They are both yellow"); shape (e.g., "They are both round."); function (e.g., "They are both to wear") or name (e.g., "They are both vehicles"). Figure 4.4a shows the results for Wolof children tested in Wolof in three different ecocultural niches. Figure 4.4b shows the results for French children tested in French and living in Dakar, the same city as the urban Wolof children.

developmental results for conservation and categorization. Note that rural or urban residence made little difference, particularly in conservation; the main differentiating factor was schooling. This was particularly dramatic because schooled and unschooled rural participants not only lived in the same bush village, they were also sometimes brothers and sisters. In essence, the graph lines for the school children replicate the patterns that had been found in Geneva, in the United States, and among French children living in Dakar (Figure 4.4b) (Piaget and Inhelder 1962; Bruner et al. 1966). Here a cultural institution, the school, created a difference in opportunities to learn; this difference, in turn, influenced the construction of cultural modes of thought.

Learning also had an explicit role in the research program. What specific environmental opportunities and learning processes were favoring or disfavoring cognitive development under these task conditions and under varying ecocultural conditions? In the case of conservation, I noted that unschooled bush children had a culturally unique mode of reasoning against conservation (i.e., for explaining why the amount of liquid in Figure 4.1 changed when I transferred it to the long, thin beaker or six little beakers: the long thin beaker, for example, had less water "because you poured it"). I called this the "magical action reason" because children seemed to be attributing magical powers to me, the experimenter. So I tried to develop a learning procedure that would counteract this reasoning: I asked the children to transfer the water themselves (the basic transfers are depicted in Figure 4.1), rather than doing it for them. My reasoning was as follows:

> The child, while perfectly willing to attribute "magical" powers to an authority figure like the experimenter, would not attribute any special powers to himself . . . Any child, moreover, is bound to have more accurate cause–effect notions with regard to his own action than with regard to the actions of others. The child with little experience in manipulating environmental objects – as would be truer of children in the passive Wolof culture than of children in America – might also be more prone to attribute puzzling changes to extrinsic powers. Experience in producing effects on the physical world might combat this tendency. (Source?)

Price-Williams' (1961) results among Tiv children of Nigeria substantiated this interpretation. His participants were much more active than Wolof children in spontaneously performing and even reversing the pouring action themselves. Correlatively, he found 100 percent conservation judgments among unschooled children by age 8.

The results of pouring themselves are shown in Figure 4.5, which compares unschooled bush children who received the "do-it-yourself" training with another group who received training that was not relevant to action reasons against conservation. As is evident from the graphs, pouring yourself made a big difference, both immediately and on two post-tests where the experimenter once again did the pouring. Even where the impact was smallest (Post-test 1 for the younger group), the rate of success was still much greater than when the experimenter poured in the standard conservation test.

But what exactly did children learn as a result of pouring the liquid themselves? They did not seem to learn something about the effect of their own motoric action, because action reasons for conservation judgments (e.g., "It is the same because I only poured it") were quite rare. Instead, they seemed to learn to pay less attention to an authority figure and more attention to the initial equalizing operation they

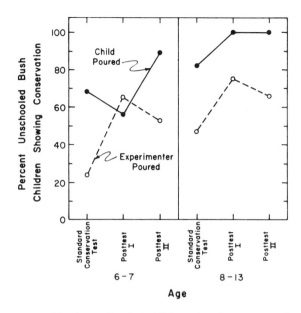

Figure 4.5 Percentage of bush unschooled children showing conservation after pouring themselves or watching the experimenter pour.

themselves had carried out in both the standard and "do-it-yourself" versions of the task (see caption to Figure 4.1). In the "do-it-yourself" condition, children most frequently supported their conservation judgment ("They are both the same") with reference to the initial equalizing operation: "I made them the same." The removal of the experimenter from the action situation made the children pay more attention to their own actions in the situation, actions that were actually the same under both the original and the "do-it-yourself" conditions. The take-home message about culture and learning is that there are different learning paths to the same cognitive end and these paths relate to cultural modes of reasoning about a problem situation.

Also relevant to an analysis of learning, the "packaged" variable of schooling could also be unpackaged into multiple learning components, including a linguistic one. Going to school in Senegal meant, for a Wolof child, learning French, the language of the school, as a second language. Language is a key component of human culture; correlatively, language differences should be a key component of cultural differences. In the case of categorization, I explored the effect of learning French on categorization of the stimuli in Figure 4.2.

This exploration began with the Sapir-Whorf hypothesis, that specific languages determine or influence specific modes of thought. However, Sapir and Whorf also realized that lexicon (vocabulary) reflected culture as well as affecting individual thought. Their famous example was the fact that Eskimos have many words for snow, whereas English has only one. However, as Roger Brown pointed out some years later, skiers also have a lot of descriptors for snow. In both cases, the Eskimos and the skiers, snow has particular relevance to shared cultural activities and the environment in which they take place. However, the notion that the language lexicon also reflected the culture did not become part of my thinking on this subject until decades

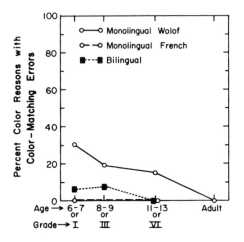

Figure 4.6   Percentage of Wolof monolinguals, French monolinguals, and Wolof-French bilinguals showing color matching errors.

later (see the 1990s, below). In essence, my question was whether acquiring and using a particular language would provide a learning experience that would change the way categorical concepts were constructed.

I first explored the role of language on the level of perceptual discrimination. A relevant fact was that Wolof did not have separate color terms for coding either red or orange; yet this distinction had to be the basis for correct color grouping in Set 2 (Figure 4.2), where the robe and the guitar were orange and the sandal was red. In Set 3, there was no Wolof term to characterize the two blue items. In Set 1, Wolof speakers sometimes use the same term to code yellow and orange, the two colors that must be discriminated in order to make a correct color match.

The first learning question was the following: Does the acquisition of color words that discriminate particular colors in the world constitute a learning experience that helps children make those color discriminations? The answer was "yes." To arrive at this answer, I compared Wolof monolinguals (unschooled children and adults) with Wolof–French bilinguals (schooled children) and French monolinguals (French children living in Dakar). More specifically, I compared these three groups at different ages for color-matching errors. I defined a color-matching error as occurring when a participant who claimed to group by color matched the wrong pictures, for example the clock and the orange in Set 1.

Figure 4.6 presents the results. Clearly, there is a developmental pattern as well as an effect of language. Among the youngest children, color matching errors are the greatest among the Wolof monolinguals, but nonexistent among French monolinguals; Wolof–French bilinguals fall in the middle. Yet, by adulthood, such errors have disappeared even in the Wolof monolinguals. The pattern of the graph lines in Figure 4.6 indicates that presence of color distinctions in a language's lexicon hastens the learning of color discriminations. The take-home message concerning culture and learning is that language acquisition in a particular cultural milieu is a learning input into perceptual discrimination.

A second level of exploration of the role of language in categorization related to flexibility in re-categorizing the same stimuli according to different criteria. For this level of analysis, I focused not on terminology within a domain such as color, but on the presence or absence of a hierarchically structured set of lexical terms, with both basic-level and superordinate terms (cf. Rosch 1973). Basic-level terms would, in the color domain, be "red," "green," "blue," "orange," etc. The superordinate term in this domain would be the word "color." In the case of our stimuli and task (Figure 4.2), the relevant difference between Wolof and French was the absence in French of equivalent superordinate terms to "color" and "shape." French, like English, possessed such lexical items. In Wolof, these domains are semantically structured with basic-level terms only. Consider the following diagram:

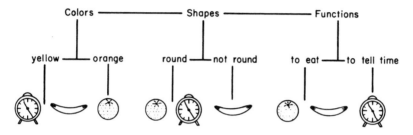

Figure 4.7   Hierarchical organization of categorization stimuli.

Does this hierarchical organization correspond to the type of conceptual structure generated by the participant in order to respond to the task? If so, then the presence of superordinate terms should indicate that the participant is at the highest level of the hierarchy where the domains of color, shape, and function are connected. If this is the case, then one would predict that a participant who used a superordinate term to rationalize a categorical grouping (e.g., "The orange and clock are similar because they are the same shape") would be more able to move from one domain to another when asked to make a second grouping than a participant who was limited to specific attribute words (e.g., "The orange and clock are similar because they are both round"). Indeed, the results indicated an association between superordinate terms and success in shifting the attribute basis for grouping in response to a request for a second grouping. Looking at Wolof school children, there is a definite difference at each age between superordinate word users and those who do not use such a lexicon (Figure 4.7). (Note that the use of such vocabulary involved inserting French superordinates into a Wolof frame.) At every grade level, we see that super-ordinate word users have greater conceptual flexibility in changing their grouping strategy to utilize a second attribute with the same stimuli. The take-home message is that superordinate terms provide a cultural learning tool that favors the development of conceptual flexibility in categorizing the real world.

Whereas this research began with Western concepts and then looked at how they were learned in an African cultural and linguistic context, Gay and Cole (1967) pioneered the study of indigenous cultural concepts and an analysis of their role in school learning. In *The New Mathematics and an Old Culture* Gay and Cole integrated the study of indigenous mathematical concepts into a traditional ethnography of the Kpelle of Liberia. However, the Western school was also a cultural focus of their attention. Indeed, their goal was to improve the teaching and learning of math in school by helping teachers to build on indigenous concepts in the domains of arithmetic, geometry, and measurement. In the course of reaching this goal they, too, investigated the effect of school learning on cognitive development among the Kpelle. In line with my results in Senegal, they found large positive effects of school learning with procedures that were culturally foreign, such as time estimation or resorting cards along multiple dimensions, similar to my categorization task. On the other hand, school learning did not improve performance in culturally familiar math tasks such as estimating volumes of rice. Gay and Cole also exported learning experiments from the US directly to Liberia, such as concept identification in which an arbitrary stimulus in an array is selected as the concept (e.g., different arrays of one circle and one triangle, where circle is always the correct choice), and the participant must infer which stimulus is the chosen "concept."

Procedures such as this one used indigenous concepts (here, shape), but they embedded them in learning procedures that were culturally foreign. In this research on culture and learning, culture is defined as indigenous concepts. Learning is, on the one hand, school learning; on the other hand, it is procedures taken from American learning theory. In my view, one enduring value of Gay and Cole's research lies in its suggestions for bridging cultures in instruction when school culture is markedly discontinuous with home and community culture. The other enduring value of this research lies in the study of indigenous concepts. Extended in 1971 with the appearance of *The Cultural Context of Learning and Thinking*, this work formed a transition to research on culture and learning of the 1970s.

OPERATIONALIZING CULTURE AND LEARNING IN THE 1970s

The 1970s saw a critique of measuring learning and cognition by means of assessments that come from the culture of the researcher, rather than the culture of the participant. If school was so important an influence in Africa and school was an instrument or residue of European colonialism, then clearly many learning experiments were missing indigenous forms of learning. *The New Mathematics and an Old Culture* stimulated a new learning question: What learning takes place as a result of everyday experience in cultures in which schooling is an imposition from the outside?

Inspired by Gay and Cole's study of indigenous concepts from everyday life, as well as by Price-Williams and colleagues' study of the cognitive effects of pottery making (albeit on Piagetian tasks), Carla Childs and I studied the effects of learning to weave on pattern representation in the Mayan community of Zinacantán (Greenfield and Childs 1977; Price-Williams et al. 1967). I developed the representational task out of the cultural skill of weaving itself; the task was not imported from our culture and country. For a Zinacantec girl, learning to weave was the functional equivalent of going to school.

We found that weavers (teenage girls) were analytical in their approach to representing familiar woven patterns – they frequently represented them as they were actually constructed with thread. In contrast, non-weavers (teenage boys) often represented the patterns in a global way, as they might look from a distance. Schooling (which had until recently been restricted to boys only) was an alternative learning experience that also made teenagers more analytical in their representations. Apparently both the cultural experiences, weaving and schooling (albeit originating in different cultures), encouraged an analytic approach to pattern representation.

Jean Lave, working with the Vai and Gola in Monrovia, Liberia, studied how the occupation of tailoring led to particular kinds of mathematical learning that were used in the tailor's craft. This type of research became "everyday cognition" in the 1980s and 1990s (Rogoff and Lave 1984; Schliemann et al. 1997). In both Zinacantán and Liberia, the researchers had an interest in seeing how situated learning generalized beyond itself to new problems. Our conclusion was that it did not necessarily transfer, that learning in concrete situations often remained there (Guberman and Greenfield 1991). Indeed, it was not until the 1990s that I realized that generalization is a form of novelty and that traditional cultures like the Vai or Zinacantec value conforming to tradition rather than creating novelty (Greenfield 1999).

In the 1970s, I (like a number of other investigators) began to integrate culture and learning in a new way. We began to study the sociocultural processes by which culture is learned and transmitted. We also began, almost unconsciously, to explore the ontogeny of these sociocultural processes. In the area of cultural transmission, I carried out a study of weaving apprenticeship in the same Zinacantec Maya community in Chiapas, Mexico. Relevant to the ontogeny of cultural development and co-construction was a study of language acquisition in the United States. In these research projects, my operational definition of both culture and learning differed from what it had been in the 1960s. For the study of weaving apprenticeship, we operationalized culture as indigenous techniques, such as weaving, that were transmitted from generation to generation. In this same study, we operationalized learning as the apprenticeship processes through which transmission took place. For the study of language development, culture became the co-construction of linguistic propositions by child and mother; the process of language acquisition constituted learning. This refocusing on the actual transmission and creation of shared culture in everyday life entailed a corresponding change on the level of methodology: I therefore moved from experiment to naturalistic ethnography, sometimes involving video records. At this point, my methodology became more anthropological, less psychological in nature.

Through the earliest use of video in the field, we were able to show that weaving apprenticeship involved an exquisitely sensitive process of learning and teaching in the service of cultural transmission. Teachers were sensitive both to the skill level of the learner and to the difficulty level of each component process. For example, our video microanalysis showed that observation of models was most frequent for the least experienced learners and least frequent for the expert weavers. It was also most frequent on the more difficult components of the weaving process and least frequent on the easier parts of the process. Perhaps most important was the help that teachers, most often mothers, gave to their daughters. Weaving apprenticeship was highly scaffolded, so that teachers provided whatever help the learners needed to complete the weaving without any gross errors or missteps. Four hands on the loom was the paradigmatic image of weaving apprenticeship in 1970 (Figure 4.8).

Figure 4.8 Four hands on the loom: Zinacantec weaving apprenticeship in 1970. Video image by Patricia Greenfield.

The close analysis afforded by video also allowed us to correct some accepted generalizations from anthropology about informal education in non-literate societies, notably that it is non-verbal. Instead, we found that verbalization was intrinsic to the teacher's role and that, like non-verbal guidance, it too was sensitive to the skill level of the learner. So, for example, teachers used mostly commands with inexperienced learners, who needed more direction. The proportion of commands decreased, while statements increased, as we analyzed the apprenticeship processes of more experienced learners. In this research, culture and learning had now been integrated into cultural learning; this was a new operationalization of both "culture" and "learning." Cultural learning was tied much more to everyday practices in a given culture, much less to standardized learning assessments that could simply be imported from one culture to another (cf. Greenfield 2000). Cultural learning and apprenticeship were expanded and generalized in the 1990s with the publication of Barbara Rogoff's important book, *Apprenticeship in Thinking* (1990).

In language, the notion of co-construction as the ontogeny of culture emerged, and a model for the construction of human culture, was born. From today's vantage point, I can see that I operationalized culture as co-constructed discourse, while learning became the acquisition of normative language structures. In my study of the one-word stage of language development, I identified a basic form of co-construction: a two-person sentence in which the child provided a one-word component, and mother provided the rest. For example, here is an instance of paradigmatic substitution whereby a child, Nicky, age 22 months, implicitly inserts his word into his mother's sentence to make a new two-person structure. Mother says, "Can Matthew have your Teddy?" and Nicky replies, "Nicky," implicitly substituting his name for Matthew's and thus indicating that he wants his Teddy (Greenfield and Smith, 1976). This type of shared meaning, we now realize, is the essence of and early manifestation of the co-construction of culture on a micro-level. It demonstrates the early capacity for intersubjective sharing that makes human culture possible. This co-construction is a cultural process that ensures one particular kind of cultural learning, language learning.

In the 1970s other language researchers, notably Ochs, Schieffelin, and Platt (1979), came up with similar ideas and data about the co-construction of linguistic communication in early ontogeny. Most important to the notion of culture as social sharing was the establishment of a shared focus of attention. In this same period, Jerome Bruner (1975, 1983) investigated preverbal co-construction of normative routines by even younger infants, in concert with their mothers. In essence, these are ontogenetic processes of cultural learning that mirror and provide the foundation for what we observed in early weaving apprenticeship: a two-person (learner and teacher) co-construction incorporating language within its boundaries.

Operationalizing Culture and Learning in the 1980s

One important new development in the 1980s was an appreciation of the role of cultural tools as mediators of learning. Vygotsky (1978) provided the theoretical foundation for this work. On the empirical side, Scribner and Cole published their classic book, *The Psychology of Literacy*, in 1981. This book explored print literacy as a cultural tool of learning and cognitive development among the Vai of Liberia. Its theme was that almost all effects of literacy on learning are not general, but are specific and arise from the particular uses to which a given type of literacy is put. The Vai were a wonderful "natural experiment" for Scribner and Cole because they have three different literacies, each with its own pattern of apprenticeship and uses: English learned at school, Vai script learned in community settings, and Arabic learned in Koranic schools. In this research, literacies constitute both learning experiences and cultural tools. They also have an impact on learning. For example, Scribner and Cole also included one explicit laboratory learning task – learning by rote memory – and found that it was enhanced by Koranic literacy.

In the same spirit, I explored the nature of and impact on learning of the newer cultural tools of television, video games, and computers (Greenfield 1984). Subsequent experimental research indicated that the virtual tool of video games enhances visual skills, develops parallel processing, and fosters a transition from written to iconic communication (Greenfield and Cocking 1996). These experimental studies utilize a before–after and control group learning paradigm to assess these impacts. In other words, this research program demonstrates short-term learning as a function of experience with these tools of electronic culture.

I have also made the argument that these symbolic cultural tools are responsible for much of the recent increase in non-verbal IQ performance in the United States (Greenfield 1998). Again, these cultural tools constitute both an aspect of culture and a medium of learning. As a medium, they impact various sorts of learning. For example, the skills they develop have potential applicability to learning computer and other technical skills, as well as learning visual spatial skills, skills in iconic representation, and strategic skills for processing simultaneous visual information in more than one location (Greenfield and Cocking 1996).

A second new development in the 1980s was the extension of cultural learning to include social learning. Most notable were the studies of the acquisition of morality, a universal attribute of shared symbolic culture. The cultural apprenticeship of morality was one important area of study, paralleling studies of the cultural apprenticeship of technical skills. As an example, Edwards found in Kenya that children learned moral and conventional rules through accusations, sanctions, commands, and responsible suggestions (Edwards 1987; Eckensberger and Zimba 1997). At the same time, different pathways of cultural learning in the domain of morality began to take shape, notably with Joan Miller's comparative studies of moral development and behavior in India and the United States (Miller and Luthar 1989). This line of research foreshadowed one of the notable new developments of the 1990s and the new millennium: the integration of research on cultural learning into mainstream areas of social and developmental psychology (Markus and Kitayama 1991; Greenfield 1994).

OPERATIONALIZING CULTURE AND LEARNING IN THE 1990s

Extensions of time scale, both historical and phylogenetic, characterized new developments in the way I, and others, characterized culture and learning in the 1990s. I begin with the evolutionary time scale. An influential article, "Cultural learning," by Tomasello et al. (1993) extended the concept of cultural learning into phylogenetic time. These authors started discussion of the evolutionary history of cultural learning by placing it in a species comparative framework. Their analysis centered on important human mechanisms of cultural learning, such as imitation and collaborative learning, and the extent to which these mechanisms were or were not shared by living non-human primates (chimpanzees) sharing a common phylogenetic ancestor in most recent evolutionary time (between five and seven million years ago).

With Tomasello et al.'s article in mind, Emily Yut, Christopher Boehm, Ashley Maynard, and I took a cross-species comparative approach to tool apprenticeship. We did a video-based analysis of the learning techniques used by chimpanzees in Jane Goodall's Gombe Reserve colony to transmit tool-based termite fishing from one generation to the next. Towards the end of the decade it became accepted that termite fishing was, in fact, a cultural skill, one possessed by only certain chimpanzee colonies (Whiten et al. 1999).

In our analysis we compared the learning techniques, both social and non-social, used by chimpanzees in the wild to acquire termite fishing with those used by the Zinacantecs to acquire weaving skill (Greenfield et al. 2000). Our logic was that techniques shared between the two species were good candidates for an ancestral foundation of cultural learning in the human species, that is, basic techniques that may have been present in some form or another in our common ancestor five to seven million years ago. We found evidence, for example, of heavy reliance on observational learning as young Gombe chimpanzees acquired skill in utilizing tools to extract termites from the ground. Hence, observational learning became a good candidate for an evolutionary precursor of the human capacity to learn and transmit cultural skills from generation to generation.

Let me now move to an expansion of the historical time scale for research on cultural learning. Here the question was the following: Would processes of cultural learning be historically contingent or historically constant within a given society? There had always been an implicit assumption of the latter, but I was not so sure that this assumption would hold up in the light of empirical investigation.

In order to find out, I returned to Zinacantán with my collaborator, Carla Childs, 21 years after our initial research. Our main purpose was to investigate historical changes in modes of weaving apprenticeship. In the intervening decades, Zinacantec society had transitioned from a mainly subsistence economy/ecology to a mainly commercial one. A major goal was to investigate the relationship of this ecological shift to modes of apprenticeship. I had hypothesized that heavy reliance of cultural apprenticeship on observation and close guidance was adapted to the maintenance of tradition, characteristic of cultures based on subsistence economies. In contrast, I expected a more independent, trial-and-error type of learning to be better adapted to entrepreneurial commerce in which innovation has a more positive value (Greenfield and Lave 1982). Returning to study the daughters, nieces, and goddaughters of our original 1970 sample of weaving learners, we found that the predicted change in cultural learning had indeed taken place. Learners were now more independent and separate from their teachers (Figure 4.9). However, as of the early 1990s, economic change had been uneven, and it was precisely the girls who, with their mothers, participated more in textile commerce (e.g., selling their weavings) who showed the more independent trial-and-error style of cultural learning (Greenfield 1999). These results indicated that styles of cultural learning are both historically contingent and adapted to particular ecocultural niches.

Closely related to historical change in cultural apprenticeship are the conflicting cross-currents of cultural learning that occur in situations of immigration from one society to another. Weaving apprenticeship (and other aspects of socialization) had moved, in Zinacantán, from a more interdependent model to a more independent model of learning as the ecocultural niche changed. This shift over two decades was parallel to the more rapid shift experienced by many immigrants, as they moved from societies that value the cultural learning of interdependence into societies (such as the United States) that value the cultural learning of independence. An international and multidisciplinary group of researchers explored the relationship between cultural learning in ancestral societies in Asia, Africa, and Latin America and cultural learning by the same ethnic groups after their transition to the United States, Canada, or France (Greenfield and Cocking 1994). This project implicitly recognized not only historical change, but also the globalization of cultural learning as it occurs in transnational immigration.

Figure 4.9 Learner is more separate from and independent of teacher in the changed weaving apprenticeship of the early 1990s. The learner in this video image is the daughter of the girl learning to weave two decades earlier, shown in Figure 4.8. Video image by Patricia Greenfield.

THE NEW MILLENNIUM

In my own work of the new millennium, I began to make the interaction of contrasting goals of cultural learning experienced by immigrants an explicit focus of study. For example, our research demonstrated how Latino immigrant parents want their children to learn one set of cultural priorities (e.g., helping, sharing, family values) while their children's teachers want them to learn a different set (e.g., independence, respect for personal property, and individual achievement) (Greenfield, Quiroz, and Raeff 2000; Raeff, Greenfield, and Quiroz 2000; Raeff et al. in press).

A second focus of my work in the new millennium has been to mainstream notions of cultural learning into developmental psychology. A large body of research has congealed around the notion that cultural learning has a longitudinal trajectory with two major pathways through universal developmental issues, a pathway towards independence and a pathway towards interdependence (Greenfield et al. 2003). These cultural pathways refocus and link all of the classic topics in developmental psychology (e.g., attachment, cognitive development, adolescence) with each other and with cultural learning. This last development places culture and learning at center stage in developmental psychology. At the same time, there is resistance to this formulation from anthropology (e.g., Harkness et al. 2000), with its preference for particularities and local theory. Whether my own formulations of cultural learning and development spread and become typical of the millennium, only time can tell.

Over the last forty years, culture and learning have moved, in my own work and that of others, from strict and separate operational definitions to integration of the concepts of culture and learning with each other and with the field of developmental psychology as a whole; culture and learning have become cultural learning, and cultural learning is fast becoming part and parcel of developmental psychology. At the same time, the domain of culture and learning is no longer contextualized in separate and timeless cultures; the perspective is now historical, evolutionary, and global.

REFERENCES

Bruner, Jerome S., 1975 From Communication to Language. *Cognition* 3: 255–287.

— 1983 *Child Talk*. New York: W. W. Norton.

Bruner, Jerome S., with Rose R. Olver and Patricia M. Greenfield, eds., 1966 *Studies in Cognitive Growth*. New York: John Wiley.

Eckensberger, L. H., and R. F. Zimba, 1997 The Development of Moral Judgment. In *Handbook of Cross-Cultural Psychology, Vol. 2: Basic Processes and Human Development*. John W. Berry, Pierre R. Dasen, and T. S. Saraswathi, eds. Pp. 299–338. Boston, MA: Allyn and Bacon.

Edwards, C. P., 1987 Culture and the Construction of Moral Values: A Comparative Ethnography of Moral Encounters in Two Cultural Settings. In *The Emergence of Morality in Young Children*. Jerome Kagan and Sharon Lamb, eds. Pp. 123–154. Chicago: University of Chicago Press.

Gay, John, and Michael Cole, 1967 *The New Mathematics and an Old Culture: A Study of Learning among the Kpelle of Liberia*. New York: Holt, Rinehart, and Winston.

Greenfield, Patricia M., 1966 On Culture and Conservation. In *Studies in Cognitive Growth*. Jerome S. Bruner, Rose R. Olver, and Patricia M. Greenfield, eds. Pp. 225–256. New York: John Wiley.

— 1984 *Mind and Media: The Effects of Television, Video Games, and Computers*. Cambridge, MA: Harvard University Press.

— 1994 Independence and Interdependence as Developmental Scripts: Implications for Theory, Research, and Practice. In *Cross-Cultural Roots of Minority Child Development*. Patricia M. Greenfield and Rodney R. Cocking, eds. Hillsdale, NJ: Erlbaum.

— 1997 You Can't Take It with You: Why Ability Assessments Don't Cross Cultures. *American Psychologist* 52: 1115–1124.

— 1998 The Cultural Evolution of IQ. In *The Rising Curve: Long-Term Gains in IQ and Related Measures*. U. Neisser, ed. Pp. 81–123. Washington, DC: American Psychological Association.

— 1999 Cultural Change and Human Development. In *New Directions in Child and Adolescent Development*, Vol. 83. Elliot Turial, ed. Pp. 37–60. San Francisco: Jossey-Bass.

— 2000 History, Culture, Learning, and Development. *Cross-Cultural Research* 34 (4): 351–74.

Greenfield, Patricia M., and Carla P. Childs, 1977 Weaving, Color Terms and Pattern Representation: Cultural Influences and Cognitive Development Among the Zinacantecos of Southern Mexico. *Inter-American Journal of Psychology* 11: 23–48.

Greenfield, Patricia M., and Rodney R. Cocking, eds., 1994 *Cross-Cultural Roots of Minority Child Development*. Hillsdale, NJ: Erlbaum.

— eds., 1996 *Interacting with Video*. Norwood, NJ: Ablex.

Greenfield, Patricia M., with H. Keller, A. Fuligni, and Ashley Maynard, 2003 Cultural Pathways through Universal Development. *Annual Review of Psychology* 54: 461–490.

Greenfield, Patricia M., and Jean Lave, 1982 Cognitive Aspects of Informal Education. In *Cultural Perspectives on Child Development*. D. Wagner and H. Stevenson, eds. Pp. 181–207. San Francisco: Freeman.

Greenfield, Patricia M., with Ashley Maynard, Christopher Boehm, and E. Yut, 2000 Cultural Apprenticeship and Cultural Change: Tool Learning and Imitation in Chimpanzees and Humans. In *Biology, Brains, and Behavior*. Sue T. Parker, Jonas Langer, and Michael L. McKinney, eds. Pp. 237–277. Santa Fe, NM: SAR Press.

Greenfield, Patricia M., with Blanca Quiroz, and Catherine Raeff, 2000 Cross-Cultural Conflict and Harmony in the Social Construction of the Child. In *New Directions in Child Development*. Sara Harkness, Catherine Raeff, and Charles R. Super, eds. Pp. 93–108. San Francisco: Jossey-Bass.

Greenfield, Patricia M., L. C. Reich, and Rose R. Olver, 1966 On Culture and Equivalence: II. In *Studies in Cognitive Growth*. Jerome S. Bruner, Rose R. Olver, and Patricia M. Greenfield et al., eds. Pp. 270–318. New York: John Wiley.

Greenfield, Patricia M., and Joshua H. Smith, 1976 *The Structure of Communication in Early Language Development*. New York: Academic Press.

Guberman, S. R. and Patricia M. Greenfield, 1991 Learning and Transfer in Everyday Cognition. *Cognitive Development* 6: 244–260.

Harkness, Sara, with Charles M. Super, and N. Van Tijen, 2000 Individualism and the "Western Mind" Reconsidered: American and Dutch Parents' Ethnotheories of the Child. In *New Directions in Child Development*. Sara Harkness, Catherine Raeff, and Charles R. Super, eds. Pp. 23–39. San Francisco: Jossey-Bass.

Lave, Jean, 1977 Tailor-Made Experiments and Evaluating the Intellectual Consequences of Apprenticeship Training. *Anthropology and Education Quarterly* 8: 177–180.

Markus, H. and S. Kitayama, 1991 Culture and the Self: Implications for Cognition, Emotion, and Motivation. *Psychological Review* 98: 224–253.

Miller, J. G. and S. Luthar, 1989 Issues of Interpersonal Accountability and Responsibility: A Comparison of Indians' and Americans' Moral Judgments. *Social Cognition* 3: 237–261.

Ochs, Elinor, with Bambi B. Schieffelin, and M. L. Platt, 1979 Propositions Across Utterances and Speakers. In *Developmental Pragmatics*. Elinor Ochs and Bambi B. Schieffelin, eds. Pp. 251–268. New York: Academic Press.

Piaget, Jean, and B. Inhelder, 1962 *Le Développement des quantités physiques chez l'enfant*, 2nd revd. edn. Neuchâtel: Delachaux & Niestlé.

Price-Williams, Douglas, 1961 A study concerning concepts of conservation of quantities among primitive children. *Acta Psychologica* 18, 297–305.

Price-Williams, Douglas, W. Gordon, and M. Ramirez, 1967 Manipulation and Conservation: A Study of Children from Pottery-making Families in Mexico. Paper presented at Memorias del XI Congreso Interamericano de Psicologia, Mexico City.

Raeff, Catherine, with Patricia M. Greenfield and Blanca Quiroz, 2000 Developing Interpersonal Relationships in the Cultural Contexts of Individualism and Collectivism. In *New Directions in Child Development*. Sara Harkness, Catherine Raeff, and Charles R. Super, eds. Pp. 59–74. San Francisco: Jossey-Bass.

Raeff, Catherine, Patricia M. Greenfield, and Blanca Quiroz, In press Developing Personal Achievement in the Cultural Contexts of Individualism and Collectivism. In *Bridging Cultures in Latino Immigrant Education: From Research to Practice*. New York: Russell Sage Foundation.

Rogoff, Barbara, 1990 *Apprenticeship in Thinking: Cognitive Development in Social Context.* New York: Oxford University Press.

Rogoff, Barbara and Jean Lave, 1984 *Everyday Cognition.* Cambridge, MA: Harvard University Press.

Rosch, E. H. 1973 Natural categories. *Cognitive Psychology* 4, 328–350.

Schliemann, A., D. Carraher, and S. J. Ceci, 1997 Everyday Cognition. In *Handbook of Cross-Cultural Psychology, Vol. 2: Basic Processes and Human Development.* John W. Berry, Pierre R. Dasen, and T. S. Saraswathi, eds. Pp. 177–216. Boston, MA: Allyn and Bacon.

Scribner, Sylvia, and Michael Cole, 1981 *The Psychology of Literacy.* Cambridge, MA: Harvard University Press.

Tomasello, Michael, with A. C. Kruger and H. H. Ratner, 1993 Cultural Learning. *Behavioral and Brain Sciences* 16: 495–552.

Vygotsky, L. S., 1978 *Mind in Society: The Development of Higher Psychological Processes.* Cambridge, MA: Harvard University Press.

Whiten, A., with Jane Goodall, W. McGrew, T. Nishida, V. Reynolds, Y. Sugiyama, C. E. G. Tutin, R. W. Wrangham, and C. Boesch, 1999 Cultures in Chimpanzees. *Nature* 399: 682–685.

Whiting, B. B., 1976 Unpackaging Variables. In *The Changing Individual in a Changing World.* K. F. Riegel and J. A. Meacham, eds. Pp. 303–309. Chicago: Aldine.

CHAPTER **5** # Dreaming in a Global World

Douglas Hollan

Psychocultural anthropologists have been criticized in recent years for failing to appreciate the extent to which the subjects and objects of their study have been shaped by forces that extend far beyond the boundaries of local fieldwork sites. By valorizing the local, the particular, and the isolated, psychocultural anthropologists have both deliberately and unintentionally blinded themselves to the transnational and transcultural flows of images, people, technologies, capital, and ideologies within which human psychologies grow and develop.

Many of these criticisms hit the mark, I believe. While it is well to remember that humans, as far as we know, have *always* been involved in the exchange of people, ideas, and artifacts, the scale, pervasiveness, and rapidity of these exchanges in the contemporary world, and their impact on human psychologies, *do* warrant special attention. But as *psycho*cultural anthropologists, we cannot just assume that transglobal processes have a dramatic or significant impact on personal experience and individual psychology. Rather, it is our difficult task to assess actively what individual actors *make* of these processes; to delineate carefully how and under what circumstances "the global," however defined, gains cognitive and emotional saliency (Spiro 1984: 326–330) or directive force (D'Andrade 1984: 96–101) for any given person. Otherwise, we risk making the same mistake of earlier researchers such as Benedict (1989) and Kardiner (1945, 1974) who assumed, incorrectly, they could infer individual psychology from cultural and institutional data alone (see Hollan and Wellenkamp 1994: 7–10).

Many strategies might prove helpful here, but in the present chapter I focus on the usefulness of dreams in understanding the personal and psychological consequences of global and transnational processes. Dreams are thought to be one of the most private experiences a person can have, and yet we know from Freud (1965) and many others that dreamers draw upon the outside world for their construction of dream images and dream processes. Existing at the interface of self and social experience, dreams offer an interesting perspective on the impact of changing social conditions on constructions of self and identity and on other aspects of individual psychology.

In the first part of the chapter, I discuss contemporary ideas about the ways in which dreaming processes link organizations of self to body and world. I then present dreams from New Guinea, Samoa, and West Los Angeles to illustrate both the permeability and impermeability of unconscious and non-conscious organizations of self to changes in the social and global environment.

DREAMS AND THE SELF

It has been argued that dreams serve a variety of biological, psychological, and communicative functions, including, among others, the preservation of sleep through the imaginary fulfillment of unconscious wishes (Freud 1965), the solving of problems (Cartwright 1986), the elimination of non-essential neural connections in the brain (Crick and Mitchison 1983, 1986), the working through and mastery of emotional conflict and trauma (Barrett 1996), and the integration of new experiences into emerging schemas of self, memory, and emotion (see, for example, Breger 1977; Fishbein 1981; Moffitt et al. 1993). Only recently, however, have theories emerged that attempt to specify the ways in which dreaming processes mediate the relationship between the dreamer's organizations of self and his or her social, emotional, and physical environment.

In my own work, for example, I have used the term "selfscape dreams" to refer to emotionally and imaginally vivid dreams that appear to reflect back to the dreamer how his or her current organization of self relates various parts of itself to itself, its body, and to other people and objects in the world (Hollan 2003, 2004). Such dreams provide the mind with an updated map of the self's contours and affective resonances: its relative vitality or decrepitude, its relative wholeness or division, its relative closeness or estrangement from others, its perturbation by conscious and unconscious streams of emotions, and so on. (For other anthropological perspectives on dreams, see D'Andrade 1961; Kennedy and Langness 1981; Tedlock 1987, 1992; Mageo 2003a; and Lohmann 2003.)

My thinking about selfscape dreams originally was stimulated by some of the work of the psychoanalysts Heinz Kohut and W. Ronald D. Fairbairn. In *The Restoration of the Self* (1977), Kohut distinguishes "self-state" dreams from those whose latent contents are rooted in repressed wishes, desires, fantasies, and drives. The latter dreams, those that Freud (1965) described and analyzed, can be deciphered and talked about through the process of free association. In contrast, self-state dreams are characterized by visual imagery that is not easily associated to or talked about. Rather, it can be manifestly and directly related to the dreamer's current life situation and to alterations in his or her conscious and unconscious sense of self-esteem and well-being. Such dreams and imagery, according to Kohut, usually involve unconscious efforts to cover over dramatic shifts in self-organization:

> Dreams of this . . . type portray the dreamer's dread vis-à-vis some uncontrollable tension-increase or his dread of the dissolution of the self. The very act of portraying these vicissitudes in the dream constitutes an attempt to deal with the psychological danger by covering frightening nameless processes with nameable visual imagery . . . free associations do not lead to unconscious hidden layers of mind; at best they provide us with

further imagery which remains at the same level as the manifest content of the dream. (Kohut 1977: 109)

The meanings of self-state dreams are on the surface, so to speak. Thus, people who unconsciously sense a disruption or dissolution of self-organization may dream of themselves in a rocket ship shooting off into empty space or sitting precariously on a swing that is swinging ever higher and higher, faster and faster (cf. Kohut 1971: 4–5).

Kohut thought self-state dreams are linked to dramatic and ominous shifts in the dreamer's self-esteem and overall psychological balance. However, later self psychologists, including Paul Topin (1983), have argued they are related to less ominous shifts in the condition of the self as well. Many contemporary self psychologists now believe that self-state dreams are more common that Kohut imagined and may be used to express shifts in self-organization of all kinds – not just potentially traumatic or perilous ones. Topin and others also argue, in contrast to Kohut, that free associations may indeed be helpful in interpreting self-state dreams, though primary emphasis is still placed on how the manifest imagery can be related to the dreamer's current life situation.

Long before Kohut, Fairbairn (1952) also was struck by the manifest contents of dreams and their relation to the dreamer's self. After analyzing a woman who spontaneously described her dreams as "state of affairs" dreams, he came to view dreams as "dramatizations or 'shorts' (in the cinematographic sense) of situations existing in inner reality" (1952: 99). The manifest contents of dreams did not disguise the fulfillment of repressed wishes and drives, he argued. Rather, they accurately depicted the unconscious relationships among part-selves and between part-selves and the internalized representations of other people.

Both Kohut and Fairbairn came to believe that the manifest content of dreams could be related in a fairly direct way to the state of the dreamer's self (for other discussions of the manifest content of dreams, see Hall and Van de Castle 1966 and Greenberg and Pearlman 1993). However, Kohut emphasized how dreams could illuminate the self's response to its relations with real people and objects in the world, while Fairbairn emphasized how they could shed light on a dreamer's internal organization of self. In my view, both may be right: the manifest content of dreams often can be related either to the self's perturbation from the outside, or to its internalized "state of affairs," or to both at the same time.

My thinking about the self and dreaming was also influenced by some recent work in the neurosciences. In *Descartes' Error* (1994) and in *The Feeling of What Happens* (1999), Antonio Damasio reminds us just how deeply the mind is rooted in the body and its biological processes. Perceptions and cognitions of the world are always influenced by emotional states that mediate between neural representations of the body as it acts on the physical and sociocultural environment, and as that environment in turn impinges upon the body. In effect, emotions are the glues that hold together representations of the body and representations of the world (see also Kramer 1993).

Damasio emphasizes how dependent the mind is upon continuously updated representations of the body and how these representations "qualify" our perceptions of the world. In the later stages of the first book and throughout the second, he begins to speculate about the origins and maintenance of the self and consciousness. He suggests that neural representations of the self must be continuously updated and modified in a manner similar to that of bodily processes. Further, he speculates that the earliest representations of the self very likely emerge from, or coincide with, representations of the body as it interacts with the world. Thus, according to Damasio, neural representations of the body, self, and world are inextricably tied together through complex emotional states and processes, all of which must be continuously updated and modified as they stimulate and impinge upon one another.

Interestingly, Damasio barely mentions dreams in either of his books, even though dreaming clearly involves many of the emotional processes and representations of body, self, and world that are his central concern. My contention here is that dreams may provide a vantage point from which we can observe how the mind continuously updates and maps out the self's current state of affairs.

That this mapping out does indeed include the self's relation to its own body is supported by Oliver Sacks who, in a paper entitled "Neurological Dreams" (1996), reports how people may dream of damage or repair to their brains or bodies long before such injury or repair becomes manifest in physical or behavioral symptoms (cf. Fosshage 1988; Fiss 1993). He discusses cases of migraine, sensory and motor seizures, lesions of the visual cortex, blindness, encephapitis lethargica, acute sensory neuronopathy, motor-neural reorganization, disturbances of body-image from limb and spinal injury, parkinsonism, Tourette's syndrome, and psychosis, all of which were foreshadowed in dreams before becoming manifest in symptoms. He comments:

> One must assume in such cases that the disease was already affecting neural function, and that the unconscious mind, the dreaming mind, was more sensitive to this than the waking mind. Such "premonitory" or, rather, precursory dreams may be happy in content, and in outcome, as well. Patients with multiple sclerosis may dream of remissions a few hours before they occur, and patients recovering from strokes or neurological injuries may have striking dreams of improvement before such improvement is "objectively" manifest. Here again, the dreaming mind may be a more sensitive indicator of neural function than examination with a reflex hammer and a pin. (Sacks 1996: 214)

I use the concept of "selfscape dreams" to integrate some of these ideas about dreams and psychological processes, as well as to highlight both similarities and differences I have with particular researchers. The term obviously is a play on those used by Kohut and Fairbairn, which emphasize the manifest contents of dreams and their relationship to self-organization. But along the lines of Damasio's work, I also wish to emphasize how dreams may provide a current map or update of the self's contours and affective resonances relative to its own body, as well as to other objects and people in the world. The self emerges and maintains itself in the biological and imaginal space between body and world. Selfscape dreams map this terrain, thus the "-scape" part of the term.

Although my own thinking about the relationship between dreaming and the self has come from the direction of psychoanalysis and the neurosciences, similar ideas are being inspired from other sources. Michele Stephen (2003) has argued, drawing on contemporary work in the cognitive sciences, that dreams that reach consciousness are those that link together two separate, distinct registers of memory in the human mind and brain: one that organizes sensory input in terms of verbal categories and semantic understandings, and one that organizes all information according to its emotional significance to the self. Consciously remembered dreams arise when experiences are not easily assimilated into the emotional, imaginal memory (read the self) and must be further evaluated and processed by the verbal, semantic register.

Derek Brereton makes some similar claims about the relationship of dreaming to the self, though he is inspired by evolutionary theory; and he is at pains, in contrast to Stephen and me, to note that he is interested primarily in the neurophysiological processes underlying dreaming, *not* in the content or subjective experience of the dream itself. According to Brereton:

> Dreaming was a pre-existing mammalian function that contributed to the development of human consciousness by providing the brain with virtual scenarios pertinent to the individual's success in an intensely social milieu. Individuals more capable of such risk-free scenario building, especially scenarios not wholly bound by the constraints of external reality, enjoyed a selective advantage. They were able to keep more neuronal options open, and thus locate themselves more effectively in a fluid, and manipulable, social milieu. (Brereton 2000: 380)

Thus, he suggests, "dreaming is an emotionally salient memory of individually recognizable bodies moving in space" (2000: 386).

While there remain significant differences in the models of dreaming I have reviewed here, there seems to be a remarkable convergence of opinion, based on a variety of disciplinary approaches, that dreams and the dreaming process help relate world, self, and body in a more direct way than Freud imagined one hundred years ago. And it is this relatively direct connection between self and world that is helpful to us in attempting to *specify*, rather than merely speculate about, which aspects of a rapidly changing social environment have cognitive and emotional salience for a given actor. Let me now illustrate this point with some ethnographic examples. My first example is meant to demonstrate how directly an organization of self can be affected by differentials in social, economic, and political resources. In contrast, my second example will show that a self can be organized in such a way as to make it virtually impenetrable from outside influence, no matter how ubiquitous and "global" that outside influence might be.

Example one: Race in a postcolonial world

How is race *experienced* in a postcolonial world? How does an awareness or perception of differences in the status, power, and prestige of people affect the organization of self and identity? Dreams, I argue, may offer an interesting perspective on this question. Dreams and dreaming can illuminate for us not only the similarities and differences that people consciously perceive between themselves and others, but also the similarities and differences they reckon at a less-than-conscious level. Let us consider, for example, the dreams of some Ngaing youth in the hinterland of Papua New Guinea's Madang Province as they undergo initiation rituals. Kempf and Hermann (2003) tell us that the Ngaing once lived in scattered, disconnected hamlets in which they practiced swidden agriculture and small-scale pig husbandry. In the aftermath of an Australian colonial administration and a seventy-year exposure to Lutheran and Catholic missionaries, however, their hamlets have become integrated into 16 villages, they earn money through the production of cash crops like coffee and cocoa and through wage labor, and most Ngaing now are practicing Catholics.

For many years, then, outsiders have had a profound impact on the development of Ngaing initiation rituals. Lutheran and Catholic missionaries have denigrated these rituals as part of the dark, dirty, and sinful "heathendom" that existed in New Guinea before the arrival of the lightness and redemption of Christianity. And administrators have alternately encouraged or prohibited them, depending on whether they could be seen as promoting or disrupting the establishment of law and order, hygiene, and economic development. The Ngaing, in turn, have reacted to these political, economic, and cultural incursions by developing an indigenous discourse about "tradition" that enables them to maintain some control over how they define and evaluate their own behavior and ritual actions.

At the end of the 1980s, when Kempf and Hermann were conducting their field-work, the Ngaing still held initiation rites for young men and women that involved periods of isolation and seclusion from village, family, and people of the opposite sex – though the period of isolation was shorter than in precolonial times, and though the rituals no longer involved much of the secret paraphernalia and dress they once did. Through penile superincision for males and through ritual purification of first menstruation for females, youths were transformed into adults who could become married and undertake other adult tasks and responsibilities.

What is interesting about some of the dreams that initiates report during seclusion is that they illustrate how youths associate the process of becoming powerful adults with the literal or symbolic process of becoming white. To a degree, this association is promoted by local belief and ethnopsychology: even traditionally, it was thought that light colored sources of power and vitality are covered over and concealed by darker, exterior substances – just as the dark bark of the sariwat palm tree conceals its inner white sap, and as black soil conceals the earth's interior layers of white limestone. But such an association also is promoted by the economic and geopolitical realities of modern-day New Guinea. Initiates' dreams illustrate, I think, how Ngaing youth experience themselves relative to whiteness and how they map their selves' desire for power and transformation onto the contemporary postcolonial world: to be powerful and prosperous is to be white or to possess the accoutrements of whiteness. Thus a young woman dreams during her seclusion:

> I thought I was in a city. It was a big city! Now it was like I was a child of the whites . . . Of course I was a black, but a white man adopted me and gave me medicine that turned me into a white. So I always called this man "father," and his wife I always called "mother." Both had adopted me, okay, and this country, well I thought we were in Australia. And then we went into a department store. There you could read "Australia . . ." Now although I couldn't read what this said, I asked the salesman, "read it out for me!," so he did just that. After he had read it out and I had heard it, he said: "You must not go in there and touch the various things on the display counter. Or you'll be put on trial!" Now I clearly heard what was said, but all the same I went and touched the things on the display counter. Then the "security" man came behind my back and seized me. As he seized me, he said to me: "Now you're going off to prison!" (Kempf and Hermann 2003: 75)

We see here not only how the initiate maps her desire for power and transformation onto her experience of whiteness, but also her anxiety that such desire might be punished. At the same time, we see how aspects of the global environment gain cognitive and emotional salience for a person, by becoming intertwined with desire, fantasy, and the organization of self.

Kempf and Hermann (n.d.: 198–204) report that a group of male initiates, on the other hand, dream that their seclusion site is really an urban area populated by white people (among others). When they begin to dream of themselves acquiring the things that urban whites wear and possess (like socks, shoes, and wristwatches), they become assured that the initiation process will be successful and that they will be reintegrated into village life in a new and empowered state.

Such implicit comparisons between self and other in dreams are not limited to the New Guinea hinterlands, however. In a number of publications, Jeannette Mageo has examined the impact of colonization on Samoan hearts and minds. Samoa, too, has undergone extensive and rapid social and cultural change in the aftermath of European contact. Mageo notes that even in pre-contact Samoa, "white was equated with high status and beauty and black with low status and ugliness" (2003b: 93). However, these distinctions became hardened and extended when Christian missionaries, as in New Guinea, began to associate whiteness with all that was newly "good" (missionization itself, literacy, the discourse of sincerity, lightness, cleanness) and blackness with all that was traditional and therefore "bad" (hypocrisy, darkness, sexuality, dirtiness, heathenism). Mageo argues the confusion and moral "hurricane" that was brought to Samoan lives through the processes of colonization is clearly evident in their dreams, where whiteness and blackness and the various things they are associated with and symbolize become jumbled, fused, and superimposed. For example, a school age young man dreams:

> I was at a party . . . dancing and laughing and having fun. Suddenly, the music stopped . . . I started walking home. Then a car stopped on the side of the road. It was a black car . . . I looked inside. There was nobody but it was white inside. Everything was all white. I got in the car, I started it and I drove home. When I got home, I got outside, and it was black inside and white outside. And then it changed again to black outside and white inside. It kept on changing back and forth. It drove me crazy. I started throwing rocks to the car, and then it stayed black for a long time . . . (Mageo 2003b: 76)

Mageo writes of this dream:

> The car's color revolutions can be read as a metaphor, not only for a slippage of meaning, but also for identity slippage. Taking possession is an act of identification. Indirectly, through the car's chromatic instability, the dreamer asks, "Am I black or am I white?" Black/white sandwiched in one identity is reminiscent of Fanon's title *Black Skin/White Masks* (1967), which contrasts a genuine skin to a false face. The dream car conflates a confusion about black and white with one about inside (interiority) and outside (exteriority) . . . Yet, unlike in Fanon's title or African American slang . . . here which part is black and which white is unreliable.
>
> However tempted or encouraged postcolonial Samoans may be to align themselves with one side, one color, of a black/white opposition . . . they experience themselves as relations between these opposites, which spin around them at dizzying speed . . . This accelerated play leaves people in a perpetual identity crisis that, like the ceaseless transformation of the dream car, is possibly (borrowing a term from Gregory Bateson,

1972) "schizophrengenic." In the dreamer's words, "It drove me crazy." (Mageo 2003b: 77)

These dreams illustrate how directly and deeply an organization of self and identity can be affected by differentials in social, economic, and political resources. Due in part to these differences in power and prestige, they are selfscapes of vulnerability. They depict selves attempting to organize themselves in response to a world in which other people, in these cases white Europeans, control many of the objects and imaginings of desire, including the freedom of self-definition. Of course, it does not have to be this way. We can imagine people dreaming and selves responding to the same social and economic conditions in a very different way; for example, defensively or defiantly. I will return to this point in the conclusion.

Example two: The "world" of the self is relative

Now let me present a counter-example. For several years now, I have worked in psychotherapy with a man who I will call Steve. Steve is a white, middle class, a-religious, high-tech specialist living and working in the Los Angeles area with extensive knowledge of computers, software engineering, and the Internet. In many ways, he is the new, quintessential transglobal citizen: he works for an international corporation, he spends countless hours exploring and helping to build the Internet highway and its myriad functions, and he lives in an exploding metropolis with one of the most diverse populations in the world. Steve swims in a sea of globally shaped relationships, images, goods, and ideas. Yet one would never know this from examining his dreams.

Unlike the real and virtual worlds Steve inhabits in his waking life, the imaginal horizons of his dreams are narrow and claustrophobic. With few exceptions, he dreams of himself in interaction with his parents or parent-like figures. The world depicted in his dreams is the world of his childhood and youth, when he and his already middle-aged parents lived in nearly complete social and emotional isolation, allowing their selves to intermingle and fuse in a symbiotic union that was both blissful and terrifying at the same time. Here, for example, is a recent dream:

> He is in bed at his father's house with his father lying beside him. His father is asking him, "Are you still confused?" Steve instantly understands the "hidden" meaning of this question: his father is really asking, "Are you still seeing a therapist?" He confesses that he is, but he knows that the admission "is like giving a knife to your enemy. You know he will use it against you."
> Then his father is saying, "It's OK. I'm here with you. You don't have to worry." But somehow Steve knows that this is not true. He struggles to remember that his father has been dead for almost two years. He wants to yell at his father, "No! You are not here! You are dead!" but is terrified that if he does, his father will disappear or "shrivel up like a corpse." Finally, though, he yells and awakens abruptly as his father's form begins to fade into an indistinct, shadowy outline.

Steve concluded the narration of this dream by telling me, "This is my mind. This is who I am." By this he means that the emotional ambivalences and struggle to establish his own identity (more literally, his attempts to get "out of bed" with his parents) that are depicted in this dream are characteristic of his whole life.

In another series of dreams that I refer to as his "car dreams" (see Hollan 2003), Steve imagines himself trapped in a car with his parents. Often, he is in the back seat of the car with his parents driving; in others, he is the driver with his parents riding beside or behind him. In almost all of these dreams, something happens to the car to prevent Steve from getting where he wants to go: the car breaks down or is crashed into by another car; he or his parents drive it off the road; his parents refuse to have it repaired properly, or they are unwilling or unable to understand how badly it is damaged; etc.

Dreams such as these illustrate in a remarkably revealing and accurate way the manner in which Steve struggles in his current relationships and situation in life – wanting desperately to get the things he values and desires in life, and failing miserably. However, from a Fairbairnian perspective (Fairbairn 1952), they also reveal how Steve's internal representations of part-self and other have come to be organized and experienced. Having internalized as part of himself parent-like images that prevent his growth and development, are oblivious to his incapacitation, and from which he cannot escape, Steve engages the world from a position of entrenched paralysis and passivity. He is a man who experiences himself as profoundly unfree, shackled, and dependent, despite his culture's valorization of self-sufficiency and autonomy.

In Spiro's (1984) terminology, Steve knows a lot "about" the global culture that is weaving its web about us, but that does not mean it shapes his *current* organization of self and desire in any significant way. To the contrary, Steve's organization of thought, emotion, desire, and identity became frozen and relatively impermeable in his early youth. Indeed, his primary therapeutic goal is to escape the misery of his early attachments so that he can open himself to the emotional impact of new experience.

Of course, the world *does* have an impact on Steve, but it is the world as sensed and perceived through a self-system that is organized defensively to protect him from further harm. An organization of self that once was relatively open to, and shaped by, the world, as mediated through the unhelpful personalities and behaviors of his parents, is now not so open. More accurately, Steve's organization of self imposes its *own* emotional map onto the people, events, and situations that Steve encounters, covering over and masking the unique particularities and contours of these encounters, rather than shaping the map and its topography in response to them.

Steve's dreams, too, illuminate a selfscape of vulnerability, but one different than those discussed above. Steve's problem is not that his lack of social, economic, and political resources leaves him unable to defend his definition of self from present-day outside influence and control. It is that he defends himself from this present-day outside influence all too well, thus leaving himself isolated, fearful, and unable to "read" accurately the social and emotional terrain that surrounds him. Of course, ironically, there *are* present-day realities that enable this organization of self, and its vulnerabilities, to struggle along. Were Steve not male, white, relatively wealthy, in a job that enables him to minimize his contact with others, and living in a culture that values privacy, if not secrecy, most likely he would not be able to continue on in the way he does. Nonetheless, this is a far cry from saying that his adulthood immersion in the sea of real and virtual globalization has radically, or even significantly, transformed the way he experiences himself or encounters with the world.

CONCLUSION

I agree with some of the critics who argue that psychocultural anthropologists have tended to underestimate the impact of globalization processes on the development and expression of human psychologies. However, I have argued that we cannot just *assume* their cognitive, emotional, and motivational impact. Rather, we must demonstrate and assess what individual actors *make* of their worlds, no matter how wide and complex those worlds may be. One way to do this, I have argued, is through an examination of dreams and the dreaming process. Selfscape dreams illuminate how and in what ways aspects of self, desire, and fantasy become intertwined with the experience of body, world, and people. They give us a sense of how the self projects itself into the world, but also a sense of how "the world" – no matter how large or small – affects the development and organization of self.

The examples I have discussed are contrastive deliberately. Selfscape dreams map the terrain of the self as it emerges from and negotiates the biological and imaginal space between body and world. Although self-processes always must initially bear the imprint of the world in which they develop (Mead 1934; Kohut 1977; Mitchell 1988) – whether egocentric or sociocentric, capitalistic or socialistic, extended family or nuclear family, etc. – the extent to which they remain open to outside influence beyond early developmental stages must remain an empirical question. The relative openness or closedness of a self-system is affected by a number of factors, including macro-social structural and systemic features (see Bateson 1972; Levy 1973, 1990), socialization practices, gender, social class, particularities of individual development, birth order, and so on. Selfscape dreams map the inner terrain of fantasy, memory, and desire as well as the outer terrain of people, objects, and world. A self-system's inner terrain may be just as "real" and determinative of its boundaries and characteristics as its outer. It depends.

The dreams of the New Guinea and Samoan youth I present here illustrate self-systems that remain relatively open and responsive to their encounters with the world – in these cases, a world in which white Europeans control many of the objects and imaginings of desire. The outer terrain of these self-systems become their inner terrain – probably more so than the youth themselves are consciously aware. In their dreams, at least, they imagine themselves becoming white, or they become confused over whether they are white or not. Steve's dreams illustrate the opposite possibility. Here we see a self-system that does not allow its inner terrain to be influenced much by its outer. Indeed, the inner terrain imposes itself on the outer to such an extent that Steve has a difficult time appreciating fully the unique particularities and contours of the people, events, and situations that he encounters – whether real or virtual.

This rigid organization of the self-system has come about for many complex reasons. In part, it is a response by the self-system to the intrusiveness, manipulation, and control experienced earlier in life, the consequences of which are a defensive sealing off of further noxious influence, whether real or imagined (see, for example, Kohut 1971, 1977; Winnicott 1965). In part, it is an inability or refusal of the self-system to give up inner, symbolic representations of itself in interaction with Steve's parents (see Fairbairn 1952). This representation of intimacy, though suffused with pain, anxiety, and ambivalence, is still the only intimacy that Steve has experienced, and so, though problematic, cannot be given up easily or without anticipatory fears of abandonment and disintegration.

But my examples illustrate the *extremes* of the extent to which self-systems become open or closed, shaped more by their outer terrain or their inner. Of course, there are New Guinea and Samoan youth who actively and successfully resist European and postcolonial influence on their lives and definitions of self, or who organize them-selves in a defensive posture against that influence, much as Steve protects himself from the world he lives in. And of course there are people similar to Steve living in the Los Angeles area who are much more responsive – viscerally, emotionally, and cognitively – to the complex environment in which they live than is he. But their dreams, I argue, will be *different* from those presented here. They would illuminate the whole continuum of possible selfscapes, from those that are heavily influenced by environmental factors to those that are not, and all the myriad types in between – depending on the variables mentioned above.

And that is my point: that what actors make of their worlds, no matter how "local" or "global," no matter how "real" or "virtual," is not transparent, but must be investigated. Certainly, we will discover patterns in these varieties of selfscapes, but they will not be obvious from the observation of macro-level social and globalization processes alone. Rather, we will discover them only after we have assessed how "the global" becomes internalized; that is, how and under what circumstances features of the social, cultural, economic, and political environment gain emotional saliency and directive force for people.

Observation and analysis of people's selfscape dreams is one of the ways this can be done. Dreams illuminate for us how the self-system is responding to environ-mental influences; more literally, they tell us what is being "taken in" and what not, both consciously and not so consciously. The fact that selfscape dreams can tell us something about the unconscious or non-conscious organization of self-processes is important because selves can be organized in conflict with themselves (see Hollan 2000). Consciously, people may tell us that they are deeply affected or not by the world around them. Yet their dreams may suggest a more complex, ambivalent relationship. And it is this more complex relationship that is likely to influence their behavior in the world – thus, the usefulness of dreams in the psychocultural analysis of globalization processes and their impact on people's lives.

REFERENCES

Barrett, Deirdre, ed., 1996 *Trauma and Dreams*. Cambridge, MA: Harvard University Press.
Bateson, Gregory, 1972 *Steps to an Ecology of Mind*. San Francisco: Chandler.
Benedict, Ruth, 1989 [1934] *Patterns of Culture*. Boston, MA: Houghton Mifflin.
Breger, L., 1977 Function of Dreams. *Journal of Abnormal Psychology* 72: 1–28.
Brereton, Derek P., 2000 Dreaming, Adaptation, and Consciousness: The Social Mapping Hypothesis. *Ethos* 28: 379–409.
Cartwright, R., 1986 Affect and Dream Work from an Information Processing Point of View. *Journal of Mind and Behavior* 7: 411–428.
Crick, F. and G. Mitchison, 1983 The Function of Sleep. *Nature* 304: 111–114.
— 1986 REM Sleep and Neural Nets. *Journal of Mind and Behavior* (Special Issue) 7: 229–250.

Damasio, Antonio R., 1994 *Descartes' Error: Emotion, Reason, and the Human Brain*. New York: Avon Books.

— 1999 *The Feeling of What Happens: Body and Emotion in the Making of Consciousness*. New York: Harcourt Brace.

D'Andrade, Roy G., 1961 Anthropological Studies of Dreams. In *Psychological Anthropology: Approaches to Culture and Personality*. Francis Hsu, ed. Pp. 296–332. Homewood, IL: Dorsey.

— 1984 Cultural Meaning Systems. In *Culture Theory: Essays on Mind, Self, and Emotion*. Richard A. Shweder and Robert A. LeVine, eds. Pp. 88–119. Cambridge: Cambridge University Press.

Fairbairn, W. Ronald D., 1952 *Psychoanalytic Studies of Personality*. London: Tavistock.

Fanon, Franz, 1967 *Black Skin, White Masks*. New York: Grove Press.

Fishbein, William, ed., 1981 *Sleep, Dreams and Memory*. New York: SP Medical and Scientific Books.

Fiss, Harry, 1993 The "Royal Road" to the Unconscious Revisited: A Signal Detection Model of Dream Function. In *The Function of Dreams*. Alan Moffitt, Milton Kramer, and Robert Hoffmann, eds. Pp 381–418. Albany: State University of New York Press.

Fossage, James L., 1988 Dream Interpretation Revisited. In *Progress in Self Psychology*. A. Goldberg, ed. Pp. 161–175. Hillsdale, NJ: Analytic Press.

Freud, Sigmund, 1965 [1900] *The Interpretation of Dreams*. New York: Avalon Books.

Greenberg, Ramon, and Chester Pearlman, 1993 An Integrated Approach to Dream Theory: Contributions from Sleep Research and Clinical Practice. In *The Function of Dreaming*. Alan Moffitt, Milton Kramer, and Robert Hoffman, eds. Pp. 363–380. Albany: State University of New York Press.

Hall, Calvin S., and Robert. L. Van de Castle, 1966 *The Content Analysis of Dreams*. New York: Appleton-Century-Crofts.

Hollan, Douglas W., 1989 The Personal Use of Dream Beliefs in the Toraja Highlands. *Ethos* 17: 166–186.

— 1995 To the Afterworld and Back: Mourning and Dreams of the Dead Among the Toraja. *Ethos* 23: 424–436.

— 2000 Constructivist Models of Mind, Contemporary Psychoanalysis, and the Development of Culture Theory. *American Anthropologist* 102: 538–550.

— In press Selfscape Dreams. In *Dreaming and the Self: New Perspectives on Subjectivity, Identity and Emotion*. Jeannette Marie Mageo, ed. 2004 The Anthropology of Dreaming: Selfscape Dreams. *Dreaming* 14: 170–82. Albany: State University of New York Press.

Hollan, Douglas W., and Jane C. Wellenkamp, 1994 *Contentment and Suffering: Culture and Experience in Toraja*. New York: Columbia University Press.

— 1996 *The Thread of Life: Toraja Reflections on the Life Cycle*. Honolulu: University of Hawaii Press.

Kardiner, Abram, 1945 *The Psychological Frontiers of Society*. New York: Columbia University Press.

— 1974 [1939] *The Individual and His Society: The Psychodynamics of Social Organization*. Westport, CT: Greenwood Press.

Kempf, Wolfgang, and Elfriede Hermann, 2003 Dreamscapes: Transcending the Local in Initiation Rites among the Ngaing of Papua New Guinea. In *Dream Travelers: Sleep Experiences and Culture in the Western Pacific*. Roger Ivar Lohmann, ed. New York: Palgrave.

Kennedy, John G., and L. L. Langness, eds., 1981 Issue Devoted to Dreams. *Ethos* 9: 249–390.

Kohut, Heinz, 1971 *The Analysis of the Self*. New York: International Universities Press.

— 1977 *The Restoration of the Self*. Madison, CT: International Universities Press.

Kramer, Milton, 1993 The Selective Mood Regulatory Function of Dreaming: An Update and Revision. In *The Functions of Dreaming*. Alan Moffitt, Milton Kramer, and Robert Hoffmann, eds. Pp. 139–196. Albany: State University of New York Press.

Levy, Robert I., 1973 *Tahitians: Mind and Experience in the Society Islands*. Chicago: University of Chicago Press.

— 1990 *Mesocosm: Hindusim and the Organization of a Traditional Newar City in Nepal*. Berkeley: University of California Press.

Lohmann, Roger Ivar, ed., 2003 Dream Travelers: Sleep Experiences and Culture in the Western Pacific. New York: Palgrave.

Mageo, Jeannette Marie, 1998 *Theorizing Self in Samoa: Emotions, Genders, and Sexualities*. Ann Arbor: University of Michigan Press.

— 2001 Dream Play and Discovering Cultural Psychology. *Ethos* 29: 187–217.

— ed., 2003a *Dreaming and the Self: New Perspectives on Subjectivity, Identity and Emotion*. Albany: State University of New York Press.

— 2003b Race, Post-Coloniality, and Identity in Samoan Dreams. In *Dreaming and the Self: New Perspectives on Subjectivity, Identity, and Emotion*. Jeanette Marie Mageo, ed. Albany: State University of New York Press.

Mead, G. H., 1934 *Mind, Self, and Society*. Chicago: University of Chicago Press.

Mitchell, Stephen A., 1988 *Relational Concepts in Psychoanalysis*. Cambridge, MA: Harvard University Press.

Moffitt, Alan, with Milton Kramer and Robert Hoffmann, eds., 1993 *The Functions of Dreams*. Albany: State University of New York Press.

Sacks, Oliver, 1996 Neurological Dreams. In *Trauma and Dreams*. Deirdre Barrett, ed. Pp. 212–216. Cambridge, MA: Harvard University Press.

Spiro, Melford E., 1984 Some Reflections on Cultural Determinism and Relativism with Special Reference to Emotion and Reason. In *Culture Theory: Essays on Mind, Self and Emotion*. Richard A. Shweder and Robert A. LeVine, eds. Pp. 323–346. Cambridge: Cambridge University Press.

Stephen, Michele, In press Memory, Emotion, and the Imaginal Mind. In *Dreams and the Phenomenology of the Self*. Jeannette Marie Mageo, ed. Albany: State University of New York Press.

Tedlock, Barbara, 1987 Dreaming and Dream Research. In *Dreaming: Anthropological and Psychological Perspectives*. Barbara Tedlock, ed. Pp. 1–30. Cambridge: Cambridge University Press.

— 1992 The Evidence From Dreams. In *Psychological Anthropology*. Philip K. Bock, ed. Pp. 279–295. Westport, CT: Praeger.

Topin, Paul, 1983 Self Psychology and the Interpretation of Dreams. In *The Future of Psychoanalysis: Essays in Honor of Heinz Kohut*. Arnold Goldberg, ed. Pp. 255–271. New York: International Universities Press.

Winnicott, Donald W., 1965 Ego Distortion in Terms of the True and False Self. In *The Maturational Processes and the Facilitating Environment: Studies in the Theory of Emotional Development*. Pp. 140–152. New York: International Universities Press.

CHAPTER 6 Memory and Modernity

Jennifer Cole

You have to begin to lose your memory, if only in pieces, to realize that memory is what makes our lives. Life without memory is no life at all . . . Our memory is our coherence, our reason, our feeling, even our action. Without it, we are nothing . . .

Luis Buñuel

The *American Heritage Dictionary* defines memory primarily as (1) the mental faculty of retaining and recalling past experience, and (2) an act or instance of remembrance, a definition that binds content to process in a single term. Why memory matters to us, however, is better captured in Buñuel's words that serve as an epigram for this chapter: memory is the foundation of the self, mind, and agency, enabling human beings to conceive of themselves as integrated wholes who have the capacity for both reflection and action. But memory – which one can also define more broadly than the dictionary does as the multiple practices through which we keep the past in mind – is also fundamentally social in nature. Since we rely on our memories of the past to know who we are and to make decisions about our present and future, memory is closely connected to political power. As Orwell reminds us, "He who controls the past controls the future; He who controls the present controls the past."

Memory has a peculiar, even vexed, relationship to modernity in two senses. First, the very definition of modernity is often premised on a rupture with the past and a sense of the perpetual creation of the new. As Habermas writes, modernity has been used since the early Christian era to designate "the consciousness of an era that refers back to the past of classical antiquity, precisely in order to comprehend itself as the result of a transition from the old to the new" (cited in Steedly 2000: 815). When paired with the rapid social and technological changes that occurred in the nineteenth century in Western Europe and have occurred subsequently, in different guises, in many parts of the world today, modernity entailed a particular structure of feeling – which as Raymond Williams reminds us is the affective dimension of experience rooted in particular material structures – predicated on a continued sense of newness. This continuous production of novelty also entails the continuous production of memories.

At the same time, a series of changes that emerged with modernity is largely responsible for Western approaches to understanding memory today. First, with the growth of individualism, a process that was part of changing social and economic structures, people tended to theorize the social and the individual as opposed to one another. In turn, a division of labor based on these kinds of premises split off psychology from anthropology and history into separate academic departments, each with their proper domain of inquiry. Taken together, this combination of factors meant that memory came to be perceived as the domain of the individual, and hence the domain of psychological inquiry. Such an understanding of memory is unfortunate for, like dreams (Hollan, this volume), memory connects the individual and private with the social and public in complex ways. As such, memory remains a key site at which one can witness the multiple ways in which individual subjectivity is tied to larger projects of political struggle and historical transformation. Such an understanding of memory is at odds with much current writing on the topic in both anthropology and psychology, requiring us to recuperate an earlier tradition of twentieth-century thought on the relationship of individuals to their social and historical context that is in the process of being (re)developed today.

PSYCHOLOGICAL APPROACHES TO MEMORY

Two common assumptions characterize Western cultural models of memory. First, memory is an individual phenomenon, triggered by outside stimuli, that happens largely inside our heads. Second, memory works like a camera, registering photos at the time of the experience that remain unchanged, crystallized images that we can later recall at will. When we cannot easily access a memory, it is not because it is not there, but because we are looking in the wrong place. This folk conception of memory is both refuted and substantiated in scholarly writing on the topic. Based on laboratory studies that have focused primarily on studying input and output, thereby deducing the kinds of encoding and retrieval processes presumably taking place within the subject, psychologists have amassed considerable knowledge of how individual memory works. These studies have shown that our memories are constructed from bits of information drawn from multiple sources, including perceptions, internal thoughts, and our interactions with others. One of the key ways that culture enters into these discussions of memory, albeit implicitly, is through efforts to demonstrate the nature of reconstructive processes or what is sometimes referred to as "memory distortion."

Today, most psychologists agree with Frederick Bartlett (1995), who first established that individual remembering takes place through an active process of reconstruction. In the experiment now referred to as the War of the Ghosts, Bartlett had people read a folk tale documented by Franz Boas twice and then, after an interval of 15 minutes, of months, or even years, asked them to repeat the story. Bartlett intentionally chose the story for two reasons. First, because it came from a cultural context very different from that of Cambridge, England circa 1917 in which he did his research. Second, because the story appeared to provide no rational sequence to the events. The goal of the experiment was to try and figure out what kinds of processes were at work as people remembered the story. What Bartlett found was that people recalled the story through a process of rationalization: they introduced a logical sequence of events where none had existed and transformed the stranger elements of the story into things that appeared familiar. He characterizes this process as "effort after meaning" and suggested that it takes place through the creation of "schemas," a term that he borrows, in modified form, from the neurologist Sir Henry Head.

Bartlett defines schemas as a densely layered network of past associations and experiences that constantly rearrange and modify themselves into "momentary settings" as new experiences confront old ones. In turn, Bartlett emphasizes that memories are a product of this imaginative process of reconstruction. More recently, psychologists have shown how cultural stereotypes, expectations, or moods, which may focus attention on particular details, goals, and the context of recall, all work to shape the ways in which individuals remember. These studies acknowledge the importance of context in shaping individual memory; however, they also reinforce the assumption that memory is an individual faculty rooted in the brain because of the ways in which cultural factors are reduced to "distortion." This conception of individual memory is further supported by recent advances in our understanding of memory that have taken place over the last forty years and which suggest that human memory is made up of multiple systems, and that these systems have a neurological basis in different parts of the brain. Studies using PET scans (positron emission tomography) which can show pictures of the brain as people remember, and clinical studies of amnesiac patients in which a specific part of the brain has been damaged, support distinguishing among five major memory systems. These include episodic memory, which refers to the explicit recollection of incidents that occurred at a particular time or place in one's personal past; semantic memory, which refers to general knowledge or information, like knowing that there are seven days in a week; and procedural memory, which refers to skills that are acquired gradually over time through repetition. In addition, the perceptual representation system allows us to identify words and objects on the basis of their form and structure, while the working memory system holds information in short-term memory for use in basic cognitive processing. Psychologists also distinguish between implicit and explicit forms of memory, and have demonstrated that even when the systems that support explicit, declarative forms of memory are damaged, those enabling implicit, procedural forms of memory may continue to function.

ANTHROPOLOGICAL APPROACHES TO SOCIAL MEMORY

In contrast to psychologists who have concerned themselves with how individuals encode and retrieve information, anthropologists, sociologists, and historians have followed Durkheim's dictum that representations are social facts *sui generis*. They have largely heeded his warning that the social scientist should avoid claims based on the operation of individual minds, focusing instead on collective representations of the past. In following this approach, most contemporary studies of social memory trace their roots to Maurice Halbwachs. Arguing against the accepted doctrine of the day, which emphasized the subjective perception of inner time, Halbwachs proposed that our memories are in fact fragmentary and diffuse, made coherent only through dialogue with our social surroundings. Memories only exist, Halbwachs argued, as long as the groups that sustain them exist and they are susceptible to constant reinvention. Since our memories constantly change as groups evolve, memories require stable anchorage either in space or through acts of commemoration. Thus, in one study, Halbwachs showed how successive occupiers of Jerusalem – Jews, Romans, Christians, and Muslims – each rewrote the city as they occupied it, shifting the center of the city to conform to their own collective sense of the past. For example, early Christians made the Holy Sepulcher the city's center because they believed that the second coming seemed imminent. By contrast, when the Crusaders reconquered the city, they reaffirmed the importance of the Via Dolorosa where the Stations of the Cross occur, since that street appeared to best embody their own pilgrimage filled with suffering.

In the 1980s, Halbwachs' work was rediscovered at a time of profound concern within the human sciences about the end of grand metanarratives, which was paired with the rise of identity politics. Many people both inside and outside the academy became keenly aware of the ways in which history can work as an instrument of domination. It became commonplace to challenge state or official narratives using what was often called "popular" memory – informal ways of representing the past. A basic assumption underlying much of this work was that popular memory possessed "hidden circuits of movement" (Stoler and Strassler 2000: 8), which, if properly decoded, could reveal critiques of the nation-state. The moral stance implicit in much of this work is captured in Milan Kundera's (1980: 1) observation that "the battle of man against power is the battle of memory against forgetting" or the Orwell quote above.

The focus on locating counter-memories was paired with an interest in demonstrating the socially and historically constituted nature of national memory in such a way that certain memories became silenced or excluded. Several scholars used this approach to explore the different ways in which East and West Germans remember the Holocaust, the transformations in Israel's representations of Masada, or the erasure of African-American experience from the commemoration of the US Civil War. In each of these cases, the authors interpret social memory as the myriad practices through which a society represents its relationship to the past. As one historian described his understanding of social memory, in terms that might be widely applied to many scholars writing on the topic, social memory is "the way in which a community understands its history or, more precisely, conceptualizes its experience through a variety of means including narrative, ritual, dance, customs, bodily practices, and other forms of socially meaningful action" (Larson 2000: 39). Many of these studies have demonstrated that debates over the past are also debates over access to resources, property, or even tools to resist ethnocide. In this context, social representations of the past appear to become a social fact that is made and remade to serve needs in the present. If memory is invoked, then the analysts' task is to ask by whom, in what context, and for or against whom.

Though studies of the politics of commemoration are correct to emphasize the ways in which particular groups may reshape representations of the past according to their own concerns, a number of studies have also reacted against a presentist tendency in studies of social memory, criticizing the neo-functionalism implicit in many accounts. After all, it is simply not the case that every time the past appears in the present it must be serving present needs. As both Michael Schudson (1997) and Arjun Appadurai (1981) have observed, there are limits to the power of actors in the present to remake and evoke the past according to their own interests. Studies of memory should try to understand not only how people use the past but also how the past shapes the present.

In a discussion of the Iran-Contra scandal, Schudson shows how the metaphor of Watergate imposed itself on the Iran-Contra proceedings because many of the people involved had also had experience of Watergate and used that experience to interpret events. People did not seek out the Watergate metaphor because it served their interests in the present; to the contrary, Schudson stresses that the metaphor of Watergate, and a host of legal actions and political interpretations that came with it, imposed itself on the Iran-Contra scandal. Rosalind Shaw (2002) makes a similar point through a historical study in Sierra Leone. During the era of the slave trade, rumors of leopard and crocodile killings circulated throughout the Sierra Leonian hinterland. These rumors of weir-animal killings erupted again during the colonial period, as people started to accuse their chiefs – whose power had been reconfigured under British colonial rule – of devouring, sacrificing, and making their dependents into medicines which they used to increase their power. Shaw argues that memories of the Atlantic slave trade embodied in weir-animals thus formed the prism through which the predatory relationships of the legitimate trade were understood. Attempting to theorize the ways in which the past may influence the present, Schwartz (1996: 921) suggests that we think of memory as a network of symbols whose function is semiotic, working to "make tangible the values for which resources and armies are mobilized in the first place." Though Schwartz's semiotic approach and the focus on meaning provides a welcome antidote to the neo-functionalism implicit in many studies of social memory, as with all meaning-centered approaches it runs the risk of occluding the sociological and political elements at play in any instance of remembering.

MEMORY'S HISTORY

This focus on social practices of commemoration has also enabled scholars to start to sketch a history of memory, for if memory is social, then it is necessarily historical. This history starts with Frances Yates's pathbreaking book *The Art of Memory* (1966), which documented how early Greek and Roman orators trained their memories by creating vivid images that they then located within a spatial framework. The image was supposed to cue the content of the memory while the spatial loci were supposed to provide the narrative sequence structuring the argument. Yates traces the development of this art from early Greek times through early Christianity and the Renaissance, emphasizing the complex ways in which key classical and early Christian thinkers saw memory as fundamentally tied to conceptions of knowledge, notions of personhood, and one's relation to God. With the rise of printing, the art of memory started to die out. However, several other studies have suggested that the replacement of oral arts of memory was not complete, coexisting over long periods of time with the existence of writing (Carruthers 1990). Though we tend to associate memory with the self and certain kinds of interior experience, Ian Hacking (1996) emphasizes that the *ars memoria* were a knowing *how*, not knowing *that*, an outer directed technique that was only incidentally connected with inner experience. They were fundamentally different from the cultural conceptions and uses of memory that emerged in the nineteenth century.

By the nineteenth century a combination of increased industrialization, urbanization, and secularization led to new forms of "modern memory," as well as to new conceptions of how memory was to be understood, some of the consequences of which I mentioned in the introduction. In particular, the increased pace of social change meant that people came to have an increasingly refined sense of a break from the past. In an oft-quoted introductory article to his massive history of French sites of commemoration, Pierre Nora (1989: 7) characterizes late-modern memory by writing: "we speak so often of memory because we have so little of it left." Nora goes on to oppose what he calls a *milieu de mémoire*, a kind of idealized premodern world where people live surrounded by memory, to modern contexts which have "sites of memory." This dichotomy between an unselfconscious *milieu de mémoire* and a later period characterized by a historically self-conscious sense of the past is certainly overdrawn, a product of modernity. Nevertheless, there is abundant evidence that in the modern and late modern era we have become increasingly conscious of memory, finding new ways of objectifying and externalizing it, though what is cause and what is effect is impossible to say.

Matt Matsuda (1996), for example, suggests that in late nineteenth and early twentieth century France new technologies like systematic record keeping, the expansion of archival resources of the state, or new arts of photography and cinema objectified memory in more tangible form. This concern with memory was also manifest in literature – one thinks of the writings of Proust and Joyce – but also in the medical profession, where a host of memory ailments, including nostalgia, amnesia, and hyperamnesia, became the topics of medical investigation. It was at the end of the nineteenth century that Freud and Janet began their investigations into hysteria, which would eventually result in the belief that trauma is a disease of memory, thereby creating a normative set of ideas positing what the individual's relationship to the past and present should be.

In the twentieth century this normative idea of the relationship between past and present has been applied to collectivities as well, perhaps because new understandings of memory have often emerged in relation to violence and war. Several scholars, for example, point to the role of World War I in the development of national forms of commemoration as well as the democratization of a now-as-opposed-to-then temporal sensibility that many scholars identify as characteristically modern (Fussell 2000). By contrast, studies of World War II have tended to emphasize the problematic nature of remembering the Holocaust. In a study of recent efforts in Germany to build monuments to the Holocaust, James Young (1992) documents the difficulties implicit in a state's attempt to commemorate its atrocities. He shows how artists tried to create new forms of monuments – anti-monuments – that would draw people into the process of remembering and thus not let them forget the events. Though most people associate the history of World War II and the Holocaust with the question of the limits of representation, in the United States the commemoration of Vietnam has also been deeply problematic. In his book *The Harmony of Illusions* (1995) anthropologist Allan Young examines the historical creation of post-traumatic stress disorder, a disease of memory in which people who have witnessed extreme violence experience flashbacks. He shows that while the idea that people could be haunted by painful memories is nothing new, the constitution of PTSD as a supposedly timeless natural entity was closely tied to the history of World War I and the concept of "shell shock," becoming further elaborated during the Vietnam War. Memory of Vietnam remained both painful and problematic at the national level, but was individualized, medicalized, and inserted into a state-run system of compensation and rewards. The medicalization of memory worked to deflect the larger question of moral responsibility for the war.

Bridging the Individual–Social Divide: Halbwachs, Bartlett, Vygotsky, and Voloshinov

The new discourse around social memory, as well as scholars' efforts to write the history of memory, have the advantage of socializing, historicizing, and politicizing a set of processes that we are otherwise prone to interpret as natural fact. It has led to an increasingly sophisticated awareness of the multiple ways in which the past exists in the present, and the different forces that authorize and stabilize collective representations of the past, thereby supporting particular, contingent cultural formations. And it has allowed us to write a history of different mnemonic techniques and their relationship to wider processes of social and cultural transformation. But in the desire to demonstrate that memory is social, there has been a broad tendency to forget that people, in addition to archives and monuments, are essential to the process of remembering as well as the content of what gets remembered. As Kerwin Klein (2000: 136) points out, "Freed of the constraints of individual psychic states, memory becomes a subject in its own right, free to range back and forth across time, and even the most rigorous scholar can speak of the memory of events that happened hundreds of years distant, or to speak of the memory of an ethnic, religious, or racial group." One possible response is to put individuals back into studies of social memory, but this must be done in a particular way.

   To argue that we need to put the individual back into our studies of memory is not to say that we should somehow forget the insights into the culture/power/ history nexus that have been such an important part of studies of social memory. Nor is it to advocate a return to either a simple cognitive or a psychodynamic approach, both of which would separate individual memory from the historical context in which it inevitably occurs. Nor is it to do away with the distinction between individual and social memory altogether. Individual and social memory each encompass a variety of different kinds of subsystems, and it would be wrong to reduce the one to the other. But we do need to shift our focus squarely onto the interplay between social and individual memory, and develop the conceptual tools for theorizing the relation between them.

   As it happens, we do not, in fact, have to look far to find useful tools for this task. While much of our thinking about memory has been shaped by the modern tendency to see the individual and the social as opposed, there have always been other, competing currents of thought, even in the writings of those whom we most associate with the individual–social divide. To start with, Halbwachs did not reject the idea of individual memory nearly so completely as his interpreters imply. In *The Collective Memory* (1980: 48) he explicitly states it is individuals who remember. Read in this light, Halbwachs's examples take on a different valence. In one example, Halbwachs describes how a group might be brought together by a shared task, but may disperse afterwards into various sub-groups. Since each group is too restricted to remember everything about the interaction, they each fasten on a particular aspect of the past. Once they are separated, of course, no one group can reproduce the total content of the original task. In an interpretation that appears to presage more recent writing on distributed cognition (see Salomon 1993) – a view that sees human thinking stretched across the social and material environment in which it occurs – Halbwachs suggests each individual comes to possess a particular facet of the past. In still other examples, Halbwachs emphasizes a virtual space of individual remembering, suggesting that we always carry others' voices within us and remember in the context of internal – yet never entirely individual – dialogues, a perspective that resonates with the work of Voloshinov, whom I turn to below. To be sure, Halbwachs did not elaborate a theory of how "indefinite" and "incomplete" fragments are rendered coherent in social interaction and even his discussion of what constitutes a group remains frustratingly vague. Nevertheless, it is useful to interpret Halbwachs as focusing on the ways in which memory is *both* individual and social; rereading him, one can argue that individual memory is "finished" and made coherent in social practices like ritual, even as rituals may work to sustain the social memory of particular groups.

Similarly, Bartlett – whose idea of schema was appropriated as part of the cognitive revolution in the 1960s – also contains a more social dimension. First, some recent scholars have argued that focusing on how memory is evoked in conversation – which I turn to below – is an overlooked dimension of Bartlett's work, one which places processes of remembering squarely within a social context (Middleton and Crook 1996). Second, Bartlett's concept of "conventionalization" provides a useful tool for thinking about social remembering and related processes of meaning-transformation in the case of what he called "intergroup contact," but which more contemporary scholars might describe as the kinds of cultural mixing that come with trade, colonial conquest, and contemporary processes of economic and cultural globalization. He suggested that whenever cultural material was introduced to a group, it underwent a process of transformation, so that the meanings associated with it were gradually assimilated to a local set of perceptions and understandings. This could take place through the exaggeration of some elements or the selective omission of others, but he proposed that it was always likely to occur in the particular direction in which the group was developing. To rephrase the point in more contemporary anthropological terms, conventionalization provides a way to conceptualize the re-cognizing that takes place as deterritorialized objects and practices are relocalized in new forms.

The Russian psychologist Lev Vygotsky provides another perspective on the social constitution of individual memory. Vygotsky argued that for all higher forms of mental activity, culture mediates the relationship between the subject and the world. The process of human development is always a process of internalization and subsequent externalization of culturally constructed tools that shape and direct thought. What this means is that to think is always to think through the medium of the specific tools and practices that are a part of a specific historically constituted cultural community. As Bakhurst (1990: 209) summarizes Vygotsky's general approach:

> The human child enters the world endowed by nature with only elementary mental capacities. The higher mental functions constitutive of human consciousness are, however, embodied in the social practices of the child's community. Just as the child's physical functions are at first maintained only through connection with an autonomous system beyond the child, so his or her psychological life is created through the inauguration into a set of external practices. Only as the child internalizes or masters those practices is he or she transformed into a conscious subject of thought and experience.

With regards to memory, Vygotsky distinguished between two kinds. On the one hand, there is involuntary memory, a lower mental function which refers to spontaneous forms of memory. On the other hand, there is voluntary or logical memory, where one deliberately recalls the past for a specific purpose. In a series of experiments, Vygotsky gave children a list of words, which they were asked to recall either through rote memorization or by using pictographs as an external, symbolic device. He found that when young children used the pictographs as a memory aid, their performance on the tests improved. When he conducted the same experiment with adults, using the external symbolic aids actually detracted from people's performance. Vygotsky concluded that adults were already using symbolic devices to aid their memory, which had been previously internalized. However, Vygotsky and his colleagues noted that in experimental conditions where children were allowed to choose pictorial representations as memory aids, instead of having pictorial representations chosen for them, they often incorporated the memory aids into a mini-narrative, or some event, in order to remember the needed word. As a result, Bakhurst argues that Vygotsky began to rethink his views about the nature of mediation, suggesting that "the structure of mediated memory must be seen as narrative, delivering its results in virtue of the meaning of the employed mediational means, and not as straightforwardly causal" (1990: 211).

Vygotsky's approach is appealing because of his focus on the mediational means that enable memory, a perspective that draws our attention to the historical constitution of the remembering subject. However, his insights into the semiotic nature of remembering are strengthened when paired with the insights of V. N. Voloshinov. Voloshinov argued we have no experience of the world prior to the language through which we imagine it. Rather, through a process of interpretation, we access a world that has already been organized by our modes of representation. All conscious states are thus essentially semiotic phenomena; as Voloshinov (1986: 14) puts it, the "word is the semiotic material of inner life – of consciousness." In turn, when we remember, we are giving a reading or interpretation of our past. There is no immediate relationship between an image and the rememberer – rather, this relationship is mediated by words, which owe their meanings to a historically constituted communicative community. Since "wherever the sign is present then ideology is present too" (1986: 16), remembering also partakes of the kinds of ideological struggles that characterize all semiotic states.

These insights gesture towards the importance of language, and the ways in which language partakes of ideological systems, including the distribution of power. Looking at how Voloshinov (1976) reinterprets Freud, however, further demonstrates the importance of his ideas for bridging individual and social processes of remembering. Recall that Freud argues that memories of every experience are stored in the unconscious and, although they may not be easily accessible, remain within. He suggests that in order to save itself from particularly painful or conflictual memories, the ego might ward them off over long periods of time by means of repression. Yet he also suggests that, despite – or perhaps because of – the functionalist demands of the ego, certain habits or practices might indicate a displaced reaction to previously experienced painful events. For Freud, remembering and forgetting are tied to individual, psychodyamic needs.

It scarcely needs to be said that Freud's analysis is anathema to the sociohistorical approach proposed by Voloshinov. However, Voloshinov (1976) recuperates Freud's ideas through the following move. He suggests that both the conscious and the unconscious are the same type of phenomenon; both are aspects of consciousness, so both partake of the semiotic nature of consciousness described above. The difference, however, is the degree of ideological elaboration. Whereas the unconscious remains in inner speech, a relatively idiosyncratic, unelaborated domain, the conscious partakes in the public world where ideologies are shared openly with others. Voloshinov thus renames Freud's "unconscious" the "unofficial conscious" in contrast to the "official conscious."

Though Voloshinov's use of the "official consciousness" and "unofficial consciousness" draws parallels between individual thought processes and official, state culture, he also makes some important distinctions. In particular, Voloshinov emphasizes that public ideologies are stable and fixed, whereas the ideology as it exists at the level of the individual is more labile. What this gap ensures is that while individual consciousness may be shaped by concrete social historical conditions, it never "fully replicates the structure of the society's public values" (Holquist 1981: 179). As a result, the traffic between the individual and the social goes two ways. However, insofar as the content of individual consciousness diverges from official ideology, it will be harder to communicate. As Voloshinov writes, "the wider and deeper the breach between the official and the unofficial conscious, the more difficult it becomes for motives of inner speech to turn into outward speech . . . wherein they might acquire formulation, clarity, and vigor" (1976; cited in Holquist 1981: 180). Several points may be drawn from these insights that are relevant to understanding memory. First, social forces may suppress certain kinds of individual memories, since memories that do not conform to publicly shared concerns may become *more* difficult to remember. Second, it is at the level of the individual that dynamism and the potential for new memories remain.

With these insights in hand, we can begin to cobble together an approach for thinking about memory as a historically situated, individual, cultural, and social phenomenon. I use the "cobble" metaphor, which implies a kind of bricolage, self-consciously. Like individual memory – which psychologists have demonstrated rests on multiple, interlocking memory systems – so too there are many forms and sites for producing social memory. Since memory is a hybrid set of intertwined processes, no single theory can encompass the diverse ways in which remembering takes place.

As a result, what we should seek is less an overarching theory of how memory works than a tool kit that will enable us to analyze remembering in specific cultural and historical situations.

Though Bartlett, Vygotsky, and Voloshinov focus primarily on the ways in which the social "gets under the skin," the vectors of influence move both ways. Of relevance here is the fact that from a phylogenetic perspective, humans are limited in their capacity to process information. In a classic article, George Miller (1956) argued the magic number 7 plus or minus 2 is the maximum amount of information humans can hold in mind at one time. He concluded: "the span of absolute judgment and the span of immediate memory are quite different kinds of limitations that are imposed on our ability to process information" (1956: 92). As Miller and sub-sequent scholars have shown, insofar as we can recode information and put it in more accessible form, we can retain or use more information. Aspects of individual memory thus *require* us to produce the kinds of supra-individual shared practices and artifacts that are a part of social memory. One example of this process that has been widely documented is our tendency to make cognitive artifacts – physical artifacts or even social behaviors – used by humans for the "purpose of aiding, enhancing, or improving cognition" (Hutchins 1999: 126). Most writing on cognitive artifacts treats them as value neutral instruments that simply "improve" cognitive capacity. However, technologies never exist free of the social, historical, and moral context in which they are embedded. As we will see in the next section, some kinds of memorializing rituals build or use cognitive artifacts in ways that highlight their inescapably political and moral dimensions.

At the same time, there is evidence that in some cases the memories of individuals – or at least of particular groups – may become generalized, stabilized, and homo-genized into the kinds of collective representations with which anthropologists and historians have been concerned. Borrowing from linguistic theory, Geoffrey White (2000a) calls this process "entextualization," a term that refers to how discourse may become routinized or widely shared through repetition and institutionalization. On a more cognitive level, this process may also help to produce new schemas, which in turn may work to shape individual memory.

Yet the fit between individual memory and collective representations of the past is never a total one. Rather, the social heterogeneity that drives processes of historical transformation is guaranteed by two factors. First, social practices shape individual memory, but never entirely determine it, since culturally produced schemas and memory artifacts will never be used or internalized in precisely the same way (Strauss 1992). Second, variation in social positioning ensures that if some individual's memories do become "universalized" as a part of shared collective representations, they rarely do so for long. As Voloshinov writes: "In the depths of behavioral ideology accumulate those contradictions which, once having reached a certain threshold, ultimately burst asunder the system of the official ideology" (1976: 88). We can put aside the Marxist idiom and still appreciate the dynamism to which Voloshinov refers.

These observations bring me to an added step that studies of social remembering, at least according to the set of precepts I have laid out here, must take. Earlier, I suggested that in the context of studies of social memory, if memory is invoked then the analyst's task is to ask by whom, where, in which context, and against what. To this we might add that we should also inquire into the processes that authorize and stabilize individual memories, examining the kinds of power dynamics or historical projects such memory techniques serve.

MNEMONIC PRACTICES IN SOCIAL AND HISTORICAL CONTEXT

The theories that I have been discussing gesture towards a set of shared ideas about the ways in which diverse social practices, including ritual, forms of spatial encoding, schemas, and language itself, sustain and enable individuals' memories, though none of them discuss the social dynamics through which this happens in concrete terms. It scarcely needs emphasizing that though they have separated out the various factors (schemas, ritual, speech, etc.) for the purposes of argument, these different aspects inevitably converge and intertwine in particular contexts. There is a dialectical movement that occurs among the different kinds of memory so that what is at one moment embodied in ritual may later be expressed in speech, just as what starts as episodic memory may over time become part of semantic structures of knowledge. Here, I turn to the variable ways in which these theoretical insights have been instantiated through explorations of specific kinds of mnemonic practices.

Discourse and narrative

A growing body of literature has addressed the role of discourse in the constitution of both individual and collective forms of memory. For example, in the tradition of both Bartlett and Voloshinov, several scholars have argued that because thoughts must be expressed in language, discourse provides a natural bridge between mental processes and social practice. One particular direction in which this idea has been developed is that of "conversational remembering," an approach that focuses on how remembering is achieved in talk, and how invocations of remembering become a rhetorical tool which people use to argue for particular goals. According to this approach, it is through the rhetorical organization of remembering and forgetting in arguments about contested pasts and plausible accounts of who is to blame, or to be excused, acknowledged, or praised, that our memories are negotiated. As the social psychologists Middleton and Edwards (1990) show through a series of transcripts of discussions of the movie *ET*, which aspects of the past are selectively emphasized depend upon the rhetorical goals of the moment. Such an approach has the advantage of tying particular memories firmly to the context in which they emerge. Middleton and Edwards found that if you shift the discursive frame, then you are likely to access different kinds of memories. But whereas more traditional psychological approaches might see this as cuing a memory that was always already there, Middleton and Edwards emphasize to the contrary that this signals the contextual production of memory. As they point out, "People's accounts of past events are treated not as a window on to the cognitive workings of memory, but as descriptions that vary according to whatever pragmatic and rhetorical work they are designed for, such that no single, decontextualized version can be taken as a reflection of the 'contents' of a person's 'memory'" (1990: 37).

Middleton and Edwards's approach is appealing because of its focus on the pragmatics of rhetorical remembering, highlighting precisely the kinds of social dynamics that are missing from either Bartlett's or Voloshinov's accounts of memory that I described earlier. However, as with any social interactionist approach, the danger is that the importance of structural forces in the shaping of both individual and social memory will be overlooked, along with the narrative or rhetorical conventions that make some memories – and not others – plausible. Individuals' remembering may emerge out of a particular rhetorical context, but some people have more power to universalize their perspective than others and the analyst needs to know not only the pragmatics of the present but also the history of people's interactions with each other. This is true even among the kinds of small groups discussed by Edwards and Middleton, but it is especially necessary to attend to in the many modern contexts in which state power is involved.

Narrative forms and conventions provide another important site at which to study the role of language in structuring memory. Narratives – which Wilce (this volume) defines as storytelling – of course, circulate – providing the structure through which we narrate (e.g., remember) autobiographical histories, as well as ones that can be used to recount the stories of wider collectives. As a result, they provide a concrete practice that ethnographers can analyze in order to better observe the ways in which certain narratives may move from personal to public arenas and back again (see White 2000b). At the same time this perspective provides an antidote to any lingering notions that we can simply oppose public and private, or subaltern and dominant memories, for it enables one to explore the circulation and appropriation of particular narratives and the way they shape individual and social memory in specific contexts.

Michael Kenny (1999), for example, examines the ways in which narratives move between public and private domains in the context of an Australian Aboriginal group's experience of modernization. Over the course of the twentieth century, Aboriginal history has been one of increasing erosion of Aboriginal land rights and their forcible incorporation as unequal participants in the Australian state. During this time, Aboriginals have held diverse views regarding their attachment to their country and their relationship with their white bosses. Older informants who had lived through the 1930s and 1940s remembered a "golden age" when whites and Aboriginals had lived harmoniously, but this narrative was in the process of disappearing. Recently, however, an alternative narrative – and with it an alternative scaffold for individuals' memories – has emerged. As Kenny (1999: 426) describes,

> economic change had since set in accompanied by a rise in Aboriginal ethno-national consciousness driven by the dynamic of the official land claims process and the emergence of an Australia-wide Aboriginal political voice. The myth of mutual comity is eroding in such a way as to force even memory of it underground and to ultimately drive it into extinction because of its untellability and irrelevance.

Collective identity disputes in turn yield new understandings of history, which in turn may be read back into the ways in which individuals remember and reconstruct their past. Kenny implies that the rise of certain kinds of narratives may render other narratives diffuse and irrelevant; without a narrative scaffold, individual memories may be lost. However, to imply as Kenny does that these narratives are totally lost, is wrong. Rather, we might think of these memories as forced into Voloshinov's "unofficial conscious," diffused, to be sure, but not necessarily permanently lost. As Maurice Bloch (1998) has argued, we need to distinguish between memory and narratives. To suggest that they are the same is to overlook the multiple affordances for memory that operate at any given time. Aspects of the past that we sometimes think are lost can make startling resurgences and we need to focus on the dialectic between inner and outer forms of memory, or the movement between discursive and embodied forms of memory, in particular cases (see Cole 2001).

Ritual

Bloch's point suggests the importance of examining other kinds of mnemonic practices such as ritual, which often involve the creation or use of mnemonic artifacts that anchor individual memories and collective memory simultaneously. Let me take two examples from Madagascar, an island famed for its memorializing practices that has endured a turbulent history of colonial conquest in the modern era. In a detailed ethnographic study of the Sakalava of northwestern Madagascar, Gillian Feeley-Harnik (1990) analyzes the ritual of the *menaty*, in which followers of the Sakalava monarchy, a precolonial monarchy that continues to play an important role in contemporary northwest Madagascar, rebuild the innermost fence around the royal tomb. This ritual, which is central to the regeneration of ancestors whose power, Sakalava believe, lies at the heart of the monarchy, was banned during the colonial era.

The ritual begins when people gather at the royal capital, where they open the ceremony with libations of rum and invocations of the royal ancestors and work on gathering the requisite materials together. The ceremonial group then moves to a camp in the forest, where they work on cutting and debarking trees, a process that in the past was said to have taken six to eight years. Once the trees are stripped, they are carried to the royal cemetery. The tomb is cleaned, the old fence is taken down, and the new fence is put up. The door to the tomb is "sealed" with the blood of a sacrificed ox. At this point the ceremony is complete. Throughout the process special songs are used to invoke the ancestors, people use a special kind of mead to wash the tomb, and people behave in accordance with special taboos that apply to all things that are related to royalty.

For Sakalava, ideas about remembering are deeply entwined with the *menaty* ritual in which commoners work to literally regrow their royal ancestor through the rebuilding of the tomb. As the Sakalava workers reconstruct the royal tomb, cleaning it and erecting the new fence around it, they also build a giant tree-person "composed of stones and trees, trunks and living branches, bones and flesh, dead and living persons, including royalty, commoners, and slaves" (1990: 136). As Feeley-Harnik (1990: 135) explains:

> The royal order that governs the work camp is conveyed non-verbally through the structure of the place and the organization of the work around the royal body. In working – moving about the camp, carrying out their allotted tasks according to the pervasive requirements of heads and pairs, leaders and followers – the Sakalava are incorporated into the body of royalty, specifically ancestral royalty. Conversely, the royal ancestors are regenerated through their incorporation into the bodies of the living.

This process is mediated through the cores of trees that people use to build the fence around the tomb, which are handled exactly in the same way as the royal body. In this process, the posts cause the royal corpse to symbolically multiply, becoming associated with the commoners who are brought in to perform the ritual.

This example clearly supports Halbwachs's insights into the importance of both space and ritual in the construction of memory. However, because Halbwachs's discussions of the way space scaffolds memory were based primarily on literary examples, they are better at conveying the role of space in supporting collective representations than in illustrating the interplay between social and individual kinds of memory with which we are concerned. By contrast, the Sakalava example shows how the process of socially commemorating the deceased monarch through the refurbishing of the tomb, a process that takes place through drawing people into particular places, is inseparable from the process of creating proprioceptive memories that are lodged throughout the body, into which other kinds of sensory memories may be incorporated. The process of constituting a social memory of royalty entails the creation of individual memories in the process. At the same time, the entire ritual is fundamentally about the recreation of social and political hierarchies. Not only does the ritual strip people of their ties to kin and make them work for royalty, but it also forces them to recommit to a Sakalava polity in the face of the alternative political orders created by the colonial state. In turn, Sakalava believe "tomb building recalls people to the struggle with outsiders to protect their ancestors from theft by regenerating them in the very bodies of those who remember them" (1990: 138).

Finally, let me explore another example of the role of ritual and memory in the context of the modernizing processes associated with colonization. The Betsimisaraka are a lineage-based people who live on the east coast of Madagascar. Like the Sakalava, they too have often come into contact with intrusive outsiders, in this case Creole settlers from the islands of Réunion and Mauritius, conquering Merina from the high plateau of central Madagascar, and later the colonizing French. Like the Sakalava's *menaty* service, their key ritual of sacrifice also aims at inciting people to remember their ancestors. However, in contrast to the Sakalava *menaty* service that makes remembering part of re-rooting the monarchy in the ground, the Betsimisaraka ritual of cattle sacrifice highlights the ways in which rituals may enable new practices to be re-cognized, providing a clear illustration of Bartlett's conception of conventionalization.

These points are especially visible in the ways in which Betsimisaraka used rituals of cattle sacrifice to incorporate two products associated with the colonial period, coffee and tin-roofed houses (see Cole 2001). When the French colonized this part of Madagascar, they tried to develop it as a cash crop region and introduced coffee. They also created a local system of government administration. Betsimisaraka perceived these administrators, who lived in houses with tin roofs in contrast to Betsimisaraka who lived in houses made of palm thatch, as prestigious. While Betsimisaraka do not organize themselves into a monarchy, they are extremely hierarchical, and constantly compete among themselves. Since Betsimisaraka believe that to have powerful ancestors is the mark of a powerful person, this competition is always mediated through their ancestors. However, the living also play a crucial role. Betsimisaraka believe it is frequently because of the "loose talk" of other people that an ancestor hears that his descendent is doing well and decides to demand a sacrifice.

During the colonial period, Betsimisaraka sought to gain access both to productive coffee plantations and houses with tin roofs. Oral narratives that I collected suggest that as some people gained access to these symbols of prestige, the belief emerged that whomever farms prolific, money-making coffee, or whomever lives in a tin-roofed house, would die unless a cattle sacrifice was performed. In response, people started the practice of a "house washing" and "coffee cleansing," rituals of cattle sacrifice that work to transform the meaning of either the tin-roofed house or the money-making coffee. Like all Betsimisaraka rituals of sacrifice, the ritual involves the gathering of the wider community. Then, the sacrificial bull is brought in and just prior to the actual sacrifice of the animal a long and elaborate speech is made announcing the reason for the event. The ritual appears to work as a memory technique through the strategic narration of emotion, as the speech, performed in front of the cheering crowd, recounts the real ancestral power that lies behind all actions, including the power to own a tin-roofed house or a productive coffee tree. As Bartlett observed long ago, intense emotion is likely to promote a particularly "constructive" type of remembering. Betsimisaraka use this type of constructive remembering to literally re-cognize their relationship to the signs of colonial rule. The articulation of individual memory with a wider collective memory of ancestral power takes place in the speech that narrates the reason for the sacrifice and it is also symbolized when people take the horns of the sacrificed bull and nail it to either the northeast gable of the house or the trunk of the most productive coffee tree. Through the process of conventionalization enacted in the ritual, what starts out as a symbol of colonial rule is transformed into a sign of ancestral power.

Many recent anthropological studies have emphasized the point that tradition as we have come to know it is in fact an effect of modernity, as I discussed earlier. What the Betsimisaraka example shows is that memory is integral to the process of constituting tradition, as Betsimisaraka use rituals of cattle sacrifice to reshape the ways they perceive colonial importations. In the context of sacrifice, cattle become a kind of cognitive artifact, but not one that works to extend a universally measurable standard of memory. Rather, Betsimisaraka use cattle sacrifice to create a continuous memory of who they are, over and against the historical disruptions that they have repeatedly experienced.

CONCLUSION

The modern era is characterized by a proliferation of memories. As we face the twenty-first century it is tempting to guess that this process will continue. The increased movement of people across the globe, whether as political refugees or people seeking new economic opportunities, means that more and more people continue to move away from homelands, remembering imagined ones in their place. For those people who are too poor to travel, the arrival of television, other media, and tourists has often led to a series of changes that may inspire people to remember an idealized nationalist past. Scholars of globalization have suggested that a dialectical interplay of deterritorialization and subsequent reterritorialization is central to how globalization plays out, as images, goods, and ideas are pulled away from their original contexts and reterritorialized in new contexts in different forms. If this is the case, then memory practices, which are so central to the process of imagining and constituting both individual and collective selves, and to the selective transmission of information from the past, will surely continue to play a prominent role in both public and private life. The tools I have offered here are drawn from the high modernist period and scholars' attempts to grapple with the relationship of individuals to their historical and cultural contexts. Combined with insights we have gained into the relationship between culture and power and contingency in the late modernist period, we have tools with which to think about the many facets of memory in years to come.

REFERENCES

Appadurai, Arjun, 1981 The Past is a Scarce Resource. *MAN* 16 (2): 210–19.

Bakhurst, David, 1990 Social Memory in Soviet Thought. In *Collective Remembering*. David Middleton and Derek Edwards, eds. Pp. 203–226. London: Sage.

Bartlett, Fredrick, 1995 [1932] *Remembering: A Study in Experimental Social Psychology*. Cambridge: Cambridge University Press.

Bloch, Maurice, 1998 *How We Think They Think*. Boulder, CO: Westview Press.

Carruthers, Mary, 1990 *The Book of Memory: A Study of Memory in Medieval Culture*. Cambridge: Cambridge University Press.

Cole, Jennifer, 2001 *Forget Colonialism? Sacrifice and the Art of Memory in Madagascar*. Berkeley: University of California Press.

Feeley-Harnik, Gillian, 1990 Finding Memories in Madagascar. In *Images of Memory: On Remembering and Representation*. Susanne Kuchler and Walter Melion, eds. Pp. 121–140. Washington, DC: Smithsonian Institution Press.

Fussell, Paul, 2000 [1975] *The Great War and Modern Memory*. Oxford: Oxford University Press.

Hacking, Ian, 1996 Memory Sciences, Memory Politics. In *Tense Past: Cultural Essays in Trauma and Memory*. Paul Antze and Michael Lambek, eds. Pp. 67–87. London: Routledge.

Halbwachs, Maurice, 1980 [1950] *The Collective Memory*. New York: Harper and Row.

Holquist, Michael, 1981 The Politics of Representation. In *Allegory and Representation*. Stephen Greenblatt, ed. Pp. 163–183. Baltimore, MD: Johns Hopkins University Press.

Hutchins, Edward, 1999 Cognitive Artifacts. In *The MIT Encyclopedia of Cognitive Science*. Robert A. Wilson and Frank C. Keil, eds. Pp. 126–127. Cambridge, MA: MIT Press.

Kenny, Michael, 1999 A Place for Memory: The Interface between Individual and Collective History. *Comparative Studies in Society and History* 41 (3): 420–437.

Klein, Kerwin, 2000 On the Emergency of Memory in Historical Discourse. *Representations* 69 (winter): 127–150.

Kundera, Milan, 1981 *The Book of Laughter and Forgetting*. New York: Alfred A. Knopf.

Larson, Pier, 2000 *History and Memory in the Age of Enslavement: Becoming Merina in Highland Madagascar, 1770–1822*. Portsmouth, NH: Heinemann.

Matsuda, Matt, 1996 *The Memory of the Modern*. New York: Oxford University Press.

Middleton, David, and Charles Crook, 1996 Bartlett and Socially Ordered Consciousness: A Discursive Perspective, Comments on Rosa. *Culture and Psychology* 2: 379–396.

Middleton, David, and Derek Edwards, 1990 Conversational Remembering: A Social, Psychological Approach. In *Collective Remembering*. David Middleton and Derek Edwards, eds. Pp. 23–45. London: Sage.

Miller, George, 1956 The Magical Number Seven, Plus or Minus Two: Some Limits on Our Capacity for Processing Information. *Psychological Review* 63 (2): 81–97.

Nora, Pierre, 1989 Between Memory and History: Les Lieux de Mémoire. *Representations*, 26: 7–25.

Saloman, Gavriel, ed., 1993 *Distributed Cognitions: Psychological and Educational Considerations.* Cambridge: Cambridge University Press.

Schudson, Michael, 1997 Lives, Laws and Language: Commemorative versus Non-Commemorative Forms of Effective Public Memory. *Communication Review* 2 (1): 3–17.

Schwartz, Barry, 1996 Memory as a Cultural System: Abraham Lincoln in World War II. *American Sociological Review* 61 (October): 908–927.

Shaw, Rosalind, 2002 *Memories of the Slave Trade: Divination and Atlantic Modernity in Sierra Leone.* Chicago: University of Chicago Press.

Steedly, Mary Margaret, 2000 Modernity and the Memory Artist: The Work of Imagination in Highland Sumatra, 1947–1995. *Comparative Studies in Social History* 42 (4): 811–846.

Stoler, Ann, and Karen Strassler, 2000 Castings for the Colonial?: Memory Work in "New Order" Java. *Comparative Studies in Society and History* 42 (1): 4–48.

Strauss, Claudia, 1992 Models and Motives. In *Human Motives and Cultural Models.* Roy D'Andrade and Claudia Strauss, eds. Pp. 1–20. Cambridge: Cambridge University Press.

Voloshinov, V. N., 1976 *Freudianism: A Marxist Critique.* R. Titunik, trans. New York: Academic Press.

— 1986 [1929] Marxism and the Philosophy of Language. Laddislav Matejka and I. R. Titunik, trans. Cambridge, MA: Harvard University Press.

Vygotsky, Lev, 1978 Mind in Society. In *The Development of Higher Psychological Processes.* Michael Cole, Vera John-Steiner, Sylvia Scribner, and Ellen Souberman, eds. Cambridge, MA: Harvard University Press.

White, Geoffrey, 2000a Emotional Remembering: The Pragmatics of National Memory. *Ethos* 27 (4): 505–529.

— ed., 2000b Histories and Subjectivities. Theme Issue. *Ethos* 28 (4): 493–510.

Yates, Frances, 1966 *The Art of Memory.* Chicago: University of Chicago Press.

Young, Allan, 1995 *The Harmony of Illusions: Inventing Post-Traumatic Stress Disorder.* Princeton, NJ: Princeton University Press.

Young, James, 1992 The Counter-Monument: Memory against Itself in Germany Today. *Critical Inquiry* 18 (winter): 267–296.

PART II Language and Communication

We experience events in association with an ongoing story about who we are, in which we struggle to achieve coherence and continuity rather than objective truth.

(Capps and Ochs 1995: 15).

Language, in its broadest sense, including speech, gesture, and other non-verbal forms, is critical to our coexistence. How we interpret, translate, and attune to others facilitates meaningful communications, even with people who have mental illnesses, autism or other conditions that may seem to challenge communication.

A revival of psychoanalytic anthropology in the 1960s integrated psychoanalytic, linguistic, and social-historical perspectives on individuals and their communities. This integration, in many ways, lessened the sharp distinction between psychoanalytically trained anthropologists who considered cultural symbols and expressions as paths to the unconscious, and others who considered representations in speech or gesture as objects of inquiry in and of themselves. Contributors to part two integrate ideas from both perspectives. For them, internal and external experiences, and language process and content, shape, and are shaped by, the tensions between narrative improvisation and structure. Whether individual or communal, these tensions depend on individual agency and the historical, cultural situations of everyday life.

Through ethnographies of communication, the contributors to part two draw upon linguistic, psychological, sociocultural, and historical perspectives, analyzing new, often global, language forms, language pragmatics, and the tensions between language improvisations and structures. They question the extent to which people internalize and use newly available language forms. How do new language forms facilitate self-expression, communication, and agency among marginalized peoples? In what ways might new language forms challenge our ideas about healing and social justice? How do new language forms shape shared subjectivities and identities?

CHAPTER 7 Narrative Transformations

James M. Wilce, Jr.

INTRODUCTION

This chapter concerns language use and particularly narrative as affected by globalizing modernity. Narrative is language put to the service of emplotment, weaving events into a coherent storyline. Stories are good to think with. Storytelling is as old as language itself and perhaps its root function, playing a significant role in brain evolution (Bruner 1990; Jerison 1976). Telling one's story constructs a continuous sense of self over time (Ochs and Capps 1996; Ochs 2004). Narratives concern anthropologists because they are social: they involve interaction and reflect culturally particular genres, performance values, etc. To be human is to communicate in a group according to its norms and genres; narrative genres are central to cultural participation. Narrating does not just reveal but *constitutes* the structure, processes, and contents of subjectivity.

Culture shapes the narratives in which the self emerges. Yet culture is process. Cultures have always been in motion, and narrative facilitates their movement. Movement potentiates change. Narratives and ways of narrating are changing in ways both obvious and subtle. Global change in human narrative activity includes the languages in which the stories are told. As hundreds of languages disappear, old stories are now being told in new languages (like English), or not at all. As psychological anthropologists have shown for decades, culture loss has traumatic effects. But our focus here is on subtler transformations. Languages can disappear, but so can ways of producing and receiving story-like chunks of language. Shifts in narrative may include genres, modes of transmission (oral, mass mediated) and thus of participation, key symbols and allegiances, and plot types. Proliferation of mass media entails shifts in dominant modes of popular participation in text production: narration requiring a high degree of audience participation can give way to practices and ideologies of narrative that are much more passive (Debord 1994), as some cases cited below will illustrate. And, as modes of participation shift, so do social processes of self-formation.

The sections below sketch global trends in narration. I start with trends in lamentation, weeping with words and melody. I then reflect on whether these trends reflect "modernity," before discussing two examples of self-conscious modernization of narrative transmission by Egyptian and Chinese nationalisms. I then describe a modern trend toward "speaking from nowhere" and explore how electronic communication participates in blurring national identities.

I focus throughout on *meta*culture (Urban 2001), *meta*narrative, and reflexive processes. I hope thereby to avoid essentializing processes we call "culture" and "narrative" and to treat culture as movement and reflection as a pervasive part of everyday life, not just scholarly analysis.

TRANSFORMATIONS IN FACE-TO-FACE ORAL GENRES: LAMENT

Something is happening to one narrative form – lament. A song punctuated with sobs and words, lament is a genre of face-to-face performance that once had even wider audibility around the world. Lament tunes and lyrics are improvised to fit the occasion. The ancient practice of improvised lamenting is changing, along with those forms of social life and cultural ideals in which it thrived.

Like storytelling and blues singing, lament is verbal art, oral literature. Lament's place has varied, as have the particular emotions through which societies encourage their members to construct the stories of their lives. To evoke audience sympathy by narrating one's life as one of suffering and grief is to constitute oneself as a good Paxtun woman (Grima 1991). But Balinese honor a person who laughs off sorrow with words of strength, or who alludes impassively to the heartbreaks she is transcending, showing her friends a glowing face (Wikan 1990). Grief is universal. And, though the metasentiments (feelings about feelings) surrounding it – fear or shame for Balinese, a kind of pride for Paxtun women – vary markedly, Balinese discomfort with grief displays are the exception (Rosenblatt et al. 1976). To tell one's life story as tragedy receives widespread support.

BENGAL AND THE IMPACT OF COLONIAL AND ISLAMIST RATIONALISMS

My survey of lament traditions starts with Bengal. This brief account offers no details of the ethnographic fieldwork provided in *Eloquence in Trouble* (Wilce 1998), and the time scale such a survey requires to make its point requires historical sources.

I have recorded isolated examples of lament in rural Bangladesh, along with interviews with a variety of people who say it is, *or should be*, disappearing. I asked several dozen interviewees why contemporary Bangladeshis often regard lamenting as shameful (Wilce 2001). Even a child – a middle-class child in rural Chandpur, Bangladesh – expressed his revulsion at the uneducated rural practice of weeping aloud with words and melody – *bilāp*. My interviews indicated that only the highly educated easily recognize that centuries old label. What has happened to this and other types of lament?

Bangladesh was designated "East Bengal" when the British ruled India, as they did from the late eighteenth to the mid-twentieth centuries. Bangladesh and West Bengal

(India) share a poetic and musical heritage, of which *bilāp* (lament) is a part. No colonial records I have found describe spontaneous funerary *bilāp*, but written exemplars of other sorts of lament predate colonization by centuries. They must represent a mass of less well preserved oral genres widespread across South Asia. Written *bāromāsyo* (seasonal laments) express longing – *biraho* – for an absent love; oral composition continued in twentieth-century Indian villages (Vaudeville 1986). Yet, even before the British Raj, some tried to "reform" the genre: Sufi poets transformed the sexual longing in earlier ("Hindu") *bāramāsyo* into longing for divine communion (Vaudeville 1986: 38). In this premodern chapter in cultural globalization, Persian and Indic metasentiments produced a hybrid poetics of longing and transcendence.

The nineteenth century intensified globalization and new forms of cultural hybridity emerged. Two immense shifts occurred in Bengal. Islam, whose spread in rural Bengal had been slow, finally flourished beyond the Mughal court in Dhaka; simultaneously, the British were asserting hegemony over South Asia. Thus two new rhetorics – appealing, respectively, to Islamic and European rationalities – impacted Bengali emotion performances. Bengali Muslims returned from the pilgrimage to Mecca with new sensibilities, spawning religious–political movements promoting scripturalist Islam over local traditions. Bengali Muslim-reformist tracts addressed the public performance of emotion, singling out for unique criticism "readings" or performances of a poetic genre suddenly deemed excessively emotional. They condemned the "riotous reading of *marsiyā* poems on the death of the martyrs" (Mannan 1966: 171) – poems reflecting Shia rites described below. Despite their apparently Islamic content – honoring Muslim martyrs – the emotionalism of these folk laments offended modernist sensibilities forged in contact with other Muslims in Mecca.

While reformist Muslim tracts condemned emotionalism, so did their contemporaries among the *bhadralok* – the "gentlemen," a largely Hindu and more obviously British-influenced elite. By the nineteenth century, *biraho* had come to signify a protest lament rather than a seasonal poem of longing. Some of these *biraho* used stories of Vaisnavite Hindu deities "as a vehicle for voicing women's grievances in contemporary society." The scandalized *bhadralok* condemned such subversive performances as the domain of "the . . . 'lower orders' whose base instincts, they said, needed to be tickled by such 'obscene' songs" (Banerjee 1988: 136, 139). Colonial dramas also poked fun at local performance genres. Such metanarratives spread a kind of shame over local narrative performances of emotion.

SHIA METANARRATIVE SENSIBILITIES: PERFORMING GRIEF FROM IRAN TO LADAKH

Shia Islam draws its meaning and unity from ritual commemoration of tragic events at Karbala in 680 AD: the martyrdom of Imam Husayn, the grandson of the Prophet Muhammad. During the Islamic month of Muharram, Shia communities from Iran to Pakistan and Ladakh reenact this sacred narrative in "passion dramas" (Beeman 1988) called *Tā'ziyeh* (hereafter *Taziyeh*), "mourning." *Taziyeh* forms, and theological directives concerning their enactment, circulate widely among Shia communities. *Mārāthī* or *marsiyā* are poems, elegies, or songs telling Karbala's story. They epitomize *Taziyeh* as the central inspiration of Shia arts.

Since such public displays of passion simultaneously reproduce and threaten social structure, tension pervades performances of the Karbala drama. Iranian Shias whose *Taziyeh* narratives allusively protested against the Iranian state now find *Taziyeh* and the culture of lament co-opted by the Shia state – a state of tension (Good and Good 1988). It was the "riotous reading of *marsiyā* [=*mārāthī*] poems" that nineteenth-century Bengali reformist Muslims condemned. Yet Pakistani Shia women, whose performances of these songs have long been accepted as pious displays, somehow maintain approval even as they push the envelope of modesty in new modes of participation with electronic amplification. One woman said, "I do it for fame!" Groups of women singers compete for control of the mikes (Hegland 1998: 254). And – like Shias around the world – Pakistani Shia women participate in the retelling of Karbala's story in bodily as well as verbal ways. Hegland calls internationally shared Shia rites like self-flagellation a sort of "religious transnationalism" (1998: 240). But we cannot miss the degree to which these women's performances entail substantial self-assertion.

Given the tensions surrounding commemorations of Husayn's martyrdom, it is not surprising that Shia clerics have long tried to regulate them. Shia clerics tell metastories of the impropriety of self-flagellation in *Taziyeh*. Related theological narratives pass judgment on the propriety of other dimensions of *Taziyeh* (e.g., on just when the riderless horse signifying Husayn's death should appear in a commemorative procession where Shias are a minority). Iranian clerical rulings on details of narrative reenactment now circulate widely and quickly. Distant Shia communities are now more open to Iranian clerical attempts to "curb controversial Muharram [*Taziyeh*] practices" (Pinault 1999: 293). Ibrahim Moussawi, a Shiite academic, says: "'I believe this has nothing to do with religious teachings, it's just a tradition that has been followed around the world. Many clerics have issued *fatwas* saying this is *haram*, that it's not allowed by religion. If you want to show how dedicated you are to Imam Husayn and you want to sacrifice your blood, then donate it to blood banks,' he added" (Ghattas 2001). A Lebanese Shia medical doctor, Ahmed Kahil, offers, among others, a biomedical warrant for opposing self-flagellation: "'We worry about the spread of infectious diseases, like . . . AIDS, as [*Taziyeh*] participants are very close to each other and often use the same blade to cut their heads. Also, we believe that it gives a very backward image of Islam . . .' he added" (Ghattas 2001).

HOW TO NARRATE THE CHANGE IN NARRATIVE?

The telling of some stories – at least stories of grief and grievance (laments) – seems to be changing profoundly. But what is the bigger metastory? Should we say that laments once performed in so many societies might give way to relatively bland mini-stories like "I feel sad"? Greg Urban contrasts rainforest *performances* of emotion to urban *reference* to emotion:

> In cultures with a developed ritual wailing or lamentation tradition, as in many central Brazilian Amerindian societies, grief is expressed by means of formalized crying. Your stylized weeping tells others of your grief. Contrast this expressive style with one in which an individual says referentially – as is so often the case in American culture – "I'm feeling sad." (Urban 1996: 175ff.)

Urban makes no explicit reference here to modernity, but nonetheless contrasts a "rainforest" mode with a "modern" mode of feeling-narrating. The shift from performed emotion to cool reference thereto might be just what Weber described in a passage that seems to describe lament's disappearance from Protestant funerals in Europe:

> That great historic process in the development of religions, the elimination of magic from the world [rationalization] . . . which . . . repudiated all magical means to salvation as superstition and sin, came here to its logical conclusion. The genuine Puritan even rejected all signs of religious ceremony at the grave and buried his nearest and dearest *without song or ritual* . . . (Weber 1958: 105; emphasis added)

Can we demonstrate that lament's disappearance exemplifies modernity's rationalism? To *narrate feelingly* and to *refer to one's feelings* are two different language games. But does a grand narrative like *All that is solid melts into air* (Berman's 1982 version of modernity's story) really find support in relation to my examples of local shifts in lament? Yes, nineteenth-century colonial metadiscourses probably stifled Bengali genres of narrative emotionality. But close inspection turns a metanarrative of European modernity's unilateral advance into one of cooperation between Islamist and British-inspired rationalisms. If modernity means globalization – a spatiotemporal collapse bringing people together in circumstances not of their own choosing – we see its hand not only in colonial encounters but also in Islamist reform movements in Bengal and in Lebanese Shia concern to speak about self-flagellation in *taziyeh* to its international audience of spectators. Metadiscourses co-produced by British colonialists and their counterparts among the *bhadralok* might have spread in large part because they resonated with Islamist critiques.

No grand story can accommodate all local histories of narrative change. Narrative forms like lament have changed profoundly, but they may not be disappearing, let alone perishing at the hand of (post)colonialist regimes. Joel Kuipers (1998) describes Dutch colonial influence on Weyewa genres of expressive performance on the Indonesian island of Sumba. Before Dutch hegemony, Weyewa leaders were proud to cast themselves as "angry men." The verbal form in which they established their authority was angry oratory delivered in couplets. Under the sway of Dutch governors and missionaries, more and more Weyewa speakers aligned themselves with a different affect – *milla ate* (humility) – whose ideal discursive form was *lawiti* – lament! Metastories like "colonialism unilaterally transforms all narratives" mislead.

What about claims central to psychological anthropology's interests, claims in relation to histories of feeling-narrative – that modernity creates new selves, individualized, oriented to psychological interiority? Traditional laments tell stories and must demonstrate affect, but audiences expect that affect to be quite conventional and predictable. Lament appears "traditional" in providing a public space for conventionally shared feelings. And recent objections to lament might reflect modernity's opposite obsession – with newness. In Bangladesh relatives dismissed one young woman's long improvisational performances as that "same old crying" (Wilce 1998).

Further evidence indicates that, in some societies, women's increased focus on private feelings alienates them from conventional forms, including Tongan lament (Cathy Small, pers. comm.). Benedicte Grima describes such a change among Paxtun women in Northern Pakistan. At least through the early 1980s, these women ex-changed lament-like stories of hardship in informal meetings. Such "meetings" were called *gham-khadi* – grief-hardship – for the emotional tone of those stories. If we define modernity as a psychologized and self-reflexively subjective ethos, the local sense of these gatherings and narratives is non-modern: "*Gham* and *Khadi* are two words that do not evoke for Paxtuns an image of internal emotional states" (Grima 1991: 87). Paxtuns take *gham-khadi* stories to constitute a moral, not a psychological, universe. Until recently, these narratives of the "endurance of hardship exemplif[ied] Paxtun womanhood" (1991: 79). But this equation began to shift in the 1980s, as urban women expressed discomfort about narrating their lives in terms of suffering – or, evidently, in any conventional terms at all. This left them telling folklorist Grima that, in contrast with rural tellers of *gham-khadi*, they "have no stories" (1991: 84). We could see here another tradition crushed by the monolithic juggernaut of modernity, or urban Paxtun women telling new (meta)stories of change to new audiences (folklorists).

The conventional Paxtun embrace of suffering resonates with Shia narrative con-ventions surrounding *Taziyeh*. If the "Shia ethos" has lost its grip on mostly Sunni urban Paxtun, is modernity to blame? Paxtun women require a new relation to narrativity when they move to the city; they desire, but have trouble self-consciously "owning," a more individuated narrative. Their longing and alienation might both indicate their participation in modernity. Is this related to the self-consciousness of Lebanese Shia leaders cited earlier, and is that, too, "modern"? When Professor Ibrahim Moussawi calls self-flagellation a mere "tradition" he adds a link in a long chain of modernist invocations of tradition as its Other. We can safely assume that, by the "religious teachings" in which self-flagellation ostensibly finds no grounds, he meant authenticated texts. Like Martin Luther, reformist Muslims oppose authoritative texts to mere tradition. And when Dr. Ahmed Kahil decries a traditional Shia practice – self-flagellation – because it might spread AIDS, we hear a modern, cosmopolitan, biomedical voice competing with theological rhetorics (both "traditional" and "textualist"). Moreover, we only have access to their words courtesy of reporter Ghattas (2001) and a website that collects "developing world news stories" for global distribution. We sense that this representation of Shia words makes sense only in a context of global media spectatorship. Dr. Kahil is media savvy, image conscious: self-flagellation "gives a very backward image of Islam and we [cosmopolitan con-sumers of media? Muslims?] have to move away from that."

Do individuation, globalization, media saturation, and legitimating practices through authoritative texts all reflect one metanarrative of modern transformation? Separately or collectively, these pieces have all been treated as indicators of a modern essence spreading triumphantly across the globe. In relation to lament-like narratives, the problem with forcing the pieces to tell one objectivist metastory becomes clear when we add one more piece: modernity's theories (narratives) are themselves stories of loss (Santner 1990). It is irresponsible to offer more metastories of loss – or to dwell on how cultural Others once coped with loss (death), but now might lose even those genres (lament's loss) – without admitting that we who invent these neo-laments are thoroughly invested in modernity. And the particularity of each local case casts doubt on any claim that modernity advances in a single straight line from Europe. Still, modernity *is* a narrative force to be reckoned with, even when resisted or played with. Tradition and modernity may *in fact* always coexist in a dialectic, yet globally circulating discourses – including Ghattas (2001) circulating Moussawi's denouncement of mere "tradition" – continually reproduce their duality, accomplishing in many imaginations the division that defines modernity.

TRANSFORMATIONS IN THE SUBJECT OF NARRATIVES: THE NATION-STATE AND BEYOND

For many in developing countries, self-identification with modernity emerges with allegiance to a new god, perhaps a Christian god with particular expectations regarding speaking. Religious identities leading converts in Oceania to new disciplines of truth-telling have transnational dimensions. Christian or Shia Muslim identities, for example, require learning and reenacting narratives whose spatiotemporal locus predates and transcends modern nationalism. Contemporary media have a transnational reach, beaming news/stories across large regions or the whole globe and creating new imagined identities. Reading stories on the Internet causes a particularly disorienting loosening of local ties that is a prerequisite to globalization of identity.

Nation-states are far from dead. Postcolonial nations in particular struggle to build an imagination of the nation and modern citizenship. Mass circulation narrative forms have played a key role in the emergence of modern nation-states. Benedict Anderson (1991) argues vernacular novels helped to create the sense of a context of fellow readers whose limits were imaginable as those of an ethnolinguistic nation. He describes Filipino novels whose readers imagine a modern city in which people share a unified timeline and a place – one day in Luzon, for example. Readers imagine a nation of people who might inhabit the novel, or be reading it simultaneously. Likewise, newspapers constitute in readers a sense of a broader, literate, middle-class audience of which they are a part. Thus, perhaps because of consumption as much as distribution patterns, print media have emerged hand in hand with nation-states. Nationalist subjectivities thrive on certain narratives. Key forms of narrative have continued to emerge, evolve, and play a role in constituting national self-imaginations.

Among the features of modern nationalist subjectivity is the desire to be seen as one nation like many others (Anderson 1991: 184). (Compare Ahmed Kahil's desire that Muslims be seen as "just as modern as any other group" – or so we might interpret him.) This desire represents a transformation in identity narratives. Brian Honyouti, a Hopi man speaking in the 1990 PBS video *The Mind: Language*, says "our language is the language of the animals, the earth itself." The sense of being a people with a *unique* claim on humanness – claims to an ahistoric or divine ascent from lower earth – contrasts sharply with the modernist desire to be seen as one nation among many others that have emerged in history.

The case studies below return to lament-like forms, exploring narrative genres as ideological objects, instruments in struggles to produce a *national* self-consciousness.

MEDIA, LANGUAGE(S), AND NARRATIVE IN EGYPT

Egyptian narrative forms and the subjectivities linked to them are undergoing a major shift. Egyptian middle-class intellectuals writing television melodramas intend to create a modern national consciousness. Old epic poetry now circulates widely in print. Both of these new forms depart in interesting ways from traditional oral genres. Abu-Lughod (2000) has long documented emotional genres in Egypt. In *ghinnāwa*, "little songs" of sorrow, women "cry" aloud with words; men only "weep" (i.e., silently). Bedouin *ghinnāwa*, like *adida*, laments by non-Bedouins, are emotional in a performative way, not by way of reference. That is, they make "few references to emotional states . . . either ascribed to the lamenter or to . . . the deceased after death" (Wickett 1993: 166). They refer to tears, not inner states.

Ghinnāwa helped shape the public sphere in which signs of sentiment circulate. So did centuries of oral performances of narrative poems like the Arabic Hilali epic, the story of Abu Zayd, traditionally "recited professionally by socially marginal poets with astonishing verbal talents, not to mention prodigious memories" and wit. Newer print versions of the epic are more "complete and sequential . . . but . . . they also lack the elaborate punning" of oral performances. (Abu-Lughod 2000: 97 citing Slyomovics 1987). We can describe a similar change in *ghinnāwa*. Bedouin women once performed them in ritualized settings – weddings and other occasions for oral recitation. Now the genre "has moved out of its context . . . into the *commercial cassette*, in the process excluding women reciters and being turned into a *nostalgic* form that marks regional or ethnic identity" (Abu-Lughod 2000: 113; emphasis added; note that nostalgia characterizes modernism). The once dynamic, local, improvisational genre of live narrative performance becomes a signifier not of women's lives but of regional identity.

We know too little about consumers of *ghinnāwa* cassettes to describe the genre's meaning to them. However, Abu-Lughod's field studies of television viewing shed light on the sorts of transformation entailed in another shift. Popular oral performances give way not only to print and cassettes, but also to TV – particularly melodramas. To collect evidence of the impact of changes in the mediated form of narrative on the subjectivity of Egyptians, Abu-Lughod watched along with, and interviewed, viewers. Abu-Lughod finds in one viewer, Amira, a particular kind of emotionality and individualism akin to that of the melodramas. Amira makes herself the subject of her own life in quite non-traditional ways, at least in interacting with Abu-Lughod (2000: 102). Her personal stories take on some of the form of the TV melodramas with which she identifies as explicitly as do some viewers of American soaps.

Egyptian melodrama writers have self-consciously nationalist–modernist agendas. Apart from conscious aims, however, their productions enact a broader agenda of subject formation related to the project of modernity. "Instead of formulaic phrases about tears and their plenitude . . . television drama tries to produce the inner beings who feel these emotions through close-ups of facial expressions and melodramatic acting" (Abu-Lughod 2000: 99). And in place of the Hilali epic performances' celebration of language itself through elaborate punning, emotion performances mediated by print or television conjure up individuated subjectivities transparent to the medium (especially television cameras) and to language. Narrators' language becomes less important than the newly constituted subjectivity of the highly individuated persons required by the modern state and constituted in the new media. As in science, news, and conversion narratives (described below), the will-to-truth joins a notion that language is for transparent reference (not play).

Egyptian melodramas, and even print versions of the Hilali epic, foster several sorts of change. The shift in medium – from oral performance to print or broadcast distribution – alters the relationship between narrators and audiences. Capitalist metaculture – forces that propel bits of culture along (Urban 2001), here print and prerecorded cassette circulation of once-live genres – have refunctionalized epic and *ghinnāwa* narratives. Oral performances of *ghinnāwa* once constituted venues where women reproduced rhetorical skills and identified their sufferings with those of others in a generic (genre potentiated) way. Oral performances of the Hilali epic similarly drew attention to local performers. By contrast, mediatized narratives (cassettes and booklets) now function like artifacts in a museum insofar as cassette-distributed *ghinna\wa* are widely consumed as icons of regional identities.

From Lament to "Speaking Bitterness": Narrative Evolution Under Chinese Socialist Modernism

China's twentieth-century history is one of profound transformations involving the evolution of social imaginaries. Old ways of narrating appeared backward as new ways took their place. Mueggler (2001) describes the "mortuary laments" and "orphans' poetry" of the Lòlop'ò, a Tibeto-Burman people who live in Southwest China. The laments they composed were personal and local. Agents of the Cultural Revolution came to see lament as an ineffectual "grievance rhetoric." They sought to replace it with a rhetoric that was goal oriented and national in its scope (McLaren 2000b). The Cultural Revolution spread the new genre, *suku* ("speaking bitterness" – i.e., denouncing the bitter suffering of old days and celebrating socialist liberation) through all of China. Though Confucian scholars and satirical representations of rural China had tried to rid respectable China of lament (McLaren 2000a, 2000b), the Cultural Revolution had more success. It left a permanent mark on rural per-formances of grief and grievance, shifting their focus from the personal-as-local to the personal-as-national. "In public 'speaking bitterness' sessions, peasants were trained to render their experiences of poverty, powerlessness, and exploitation in the old society into narrative form, working them into the national story of liberation from past injustice" (Mueggler 2001: 59). Neither the motifs (local, personal) nor the genres themselves ("orphans' poetry" and "lamentation songs") completely disappeared. Instead, speaking bitterness faded in the 1980s. But it had already transformed Lòlop'ò laments. Since being (forcibly?) hybridized with *suku*, Lòlop'ò laments have followed the required narrative frame of *suku*, juxtaposing personal and national suffering (bitterness) with mentions of Liberation (sweetness).

Radical Disruptions of Narrative: Truth-ing from Nowhere/Everywhere

Late modernity refracts and transforms narrative in two paradoxically related ways. Mediated voices *come from everywhere*: news stories from far away circulated by new technologies. News narratives claim a truth that is transparent and universal. Two cases illustrate how (post)modernity might scatter narratives and shift ways of narrat-ing. Global news media spread stories from/to everywhere, loosening the viewer's sense of being exclusively rooted in one locality. And Protestantism in Oceania has incited newly missionized speakers to put narrative language to the service of the truth of the personal self in a way that might reflect Christianity *anywhere*. Contrasting with this proliferation of narrative is the stance of science. Science discourages narratives, except of its own accomplishments (Lyotard 1984), while encouraging talk that seems to *come from nowhere*, or nowhere stable and particular – the voice of objectivity. The truth visions of biomedicine and literary modernism are so inward that they render narratives peripheral or burden narrative with such introspective intensity as to parallel schizophrenic discourse.

GLOBALIZATION AND SHIFTS IN WHAT IT MEANS TO SPEAK FROM SOME PLACE: MEDIATED STORIES

Late modern globalization effects a deterritorialization of discourse. Jacquemet (2003) defines deterritorialization as "the displacement and dispersion of a subjectivity unrestrained by territorial control." Early modern nationalist subjectivity was "contained within the territorial confines set up by centralized powers," but now even nationalist subjectivity appears to have been set free from those constraints, while transnational subjectivities even more naturally emerge in deterritorialized communication. Those who communicate online while sitting in Bangladesh, France, or the US sometimes experience themselves and their virtual interlocutors occupying non-territorial space.

This entails a shift in indexicality. Making meaning includes not only denoting and referring, but also *pointing* to context: indexicality. All words have indexical dimensions, but words like "this" or "here" (as in "this side of the Atlantic") depend radically on shared context for their interpretability. Face-to-face speech often indexes contextual features presupposable as available to participants' senses. Written discourse creates context through tense (which presupposes the narrator's time as its temporal center) and deixis (demonstratives, etc.). Whether oral or written, stories require listeners to shift from our time to the narrated time.

Most stories emerge in the give-and-take of conversation. Conversation often features short or long stories that have a key place in self-formation. Now, mass-mediated stories play an ever-increasing role (Thompson 1996). Print media laid the groundwork for our mediated age, for centuries creating audiences with looser senses of participation in the author or message-sender's context. Now broadcast and e-media float freely across local and even national territories. Cable news networks propagate stories. Such media may transport the viewer to the site of news reports, creating a sense of you-are-there verisimilitude, a pretense of letting the viewer see events unfolding for herself. Yet, relative to oral performances of Egyptian epic poems, cable news obscures the locus and act of spinning the story – creating, in this perspective, truth from nowhere rather than everywhere.

Reading news stories online can loosen indexicality to a head-spinning degree. Jacquemet (2003) describes sitting in his New York office, reading in the online version of an Italian newspaper a story by its New York correspondent about the Socialist Scholars Conference. Jacquemet developed a case of globalization vertigo when he read the author locating the conference *al di qua dell-Atlantico*, "on this side of the Atlantic." To interpret that indexical expression produced in Jacquemet "a deep sense of estrangement." The article assumes readers are in Italy, consuming the paper's print version, imagining their co-readers located in the Italian nation-state. Readers' subjectivities and publishing conventions lag behind deterritorialized realities.

Missionization, conversion, and narratives of truth: Indonesia and Papua New Guinea

The movement of missionaries and their religion around the world has often facilitated discursive modernization. Nowhere is their impact on narrative construction of selves clearer than in contemporary Oceania. Conversion narratives in Sumba (Indonesia) and Papua New Guinea invoke familiar binaries like now–before, modern–traditional, ignorant–cosmopolitan – rifts characterizing modernity's master narrative.

Stories told by Sumbanese Christians and their missionaries describe an increase in features some say constitute a universal modernity – individualization, interiorization, and eventual secularization (Keane 1997: 685). We recognize the modern will-to-truth in recent Sumbanese Christian expectations of each other's words. The universalist claims of the "project of modernity" might persuade us if we were not regularly reminded that modernity's partner is always local non-modern phenomena (Mitchell 2000). And indeed Sumbanese stories of "the progress of salvation" invoke a variety of divine and evil spirits foreign to other modern narratives (Keane 1997).

Kaluli Christians in Papua New Guinea associate traditional knowledge and discourse genres with the "time of ignorance." New genres like Christian literacy lessons are transforming Kaluli notions of truth and talk, constituting the rift between traditional and modern ways. The change is not only in the content of the narratives but also in their participant structure. Storytelling and all discourse forms were once profoundly dialogical, involving an obvious amount of give-and-take with audiences. The new genres – sermons, stories told by literacy instructors, etc. – are relatively monological. Literacy teachers tell stories their students repeat in unison (displacing older polyphonic forms of reception), explicitly calling for local acceptance (Schieffelin 2000) of truths claiming universality.

Everyday narratives of other missionized Kaluli reflect a sea change in narrative temporality. Cassette "letters" that young men send, by missionary airplane, to families from an isolated Bible school indicate regimentation of narratable life around clock time. The very language in which stories are told is shifting. The language of cassette "letters" is mostly Kaluli; however, most of the temporal expressions are borrowed from the postcolonial vernacular, Tok Pisin. Old verbal means are inadequate to convey the new sense of time.

Truth-telling takes on new significance as talk is transformed in Oceania. Until recently, the Urapmin of Papua New Guinea considered language inadequate to represent human subjectivity. People might tell stories about the self, but listeners did not take references to inner states as transparently true. Since conversion, Urapmin feel the burden to speak truthfully and sincerely "at all times." Urapmin – like so many peoples of the island Pacific – traditionally attribute to listeners the responsibility for assigning the meaning of talk. "From the point of view of modern linguistic and social ideology, including its Protestant form, this decentered model of speech and action encourages an irresponsible disregard for the power one's own intentions have to create meaning and shape social life" (Robbins 2002: 906). Given Urapmin tendencies to distrust the ability of words to accurately narrate subjectivity, Christianity's call to speak truth presents problems. For while they recognize that, as modern Christian subjects, they should always accurately and openly represent themselves in speech, their traditional linguistic ideology does not constitute them or their language as capable (Robbins 2002). Hybridity resolves this tension. Because Urapmin understand themselves in Christian prayer, including stories told therein, to be addressing a totally new kind of divine hearer, the hearer elicits/enables truth-telling.

No Time or Space for Stories: Biomedicine Exported

The "view-from-nowhere" objectivity of biomedicine as a Foucauldian discipline and science's discouragement of narrativity compete with patients' needs to tell highly personal stories. "Traditional healing" can take more time insofar as it embraces narrative and ritual speech. After 1950 or so, at least in America, doctors' orientation shifted from *listening* to patients' stories to *looking* at the results of expensive tests (Reiser 1987). In biomedicine, high-tech tests are read (visually). While not altogether displacing discursive therapeutic practices (from psychotherapy to alternative or complementary treatments), vision dominates institutions from medical schools and teaching hospitals (Good 1994) to the structures of HMO coverages and payments. In the US, psychiatrists rely increasingly on medications. They seldom meet patients for years of talk therapy as they once did. Thus, even that psychiatric realm of medicine where narrative played the most central role now allocates less time to talk. Sufferers now talk with family and friends, in local space or cyberspace. Indeed, sufferers and their families can trade stories of their struggles in electronic or face-to-face support groups where those touched by illnesses and behavioral disorders generate shared narratives and meanings. At least in the US, what Foucault (1990) calls an "incitement to discourse" produces a culture of therapy that encourages narrating events and emotions (Wilce 1999, 2004). We see it in large domains of culture – perhaps spreading beyond the West – even as prolonged narrative engagement less often typifies the psychiatrist's office. The hegemony of technology is partial, displacing but not effacing narrative.

In Bangladesh, the shift in medical care of the mentally ill involves similar forces but different contextual factors. Nothing like a culture of therapy exists for the vast majority of Bangladeshis. They have stories to tell but are painfully aware that information escaping the privacy of homes can damage their positions in social networks, which are much more economically and socially determinative than for most Americans. Some deride seeking help from psychologists – even having psychological pain – as a luxury (Wilce 2000).

Bangladesh has few psychiatrists, though madness is neither rare nor traditionally regarded as radically beyond the pale of various healing practices. Eliciting long stories is integral to "traditional" Bangladeshi healing – though the storytellers can be family members as well as patients (Wilce 1998) – but only marginal to the efficiencies psychiatrists cultivate. Psychiatrists with private clinics may see many dozens of families in an evening – virtually no patients come without relatives – for about three minutes each, providing a diagnosis and prescribing medications for each. The longer stories families have to tell are profoundly disturbing. Whether or not they have direct clinical relevance, their stories are extremely complex, and the gap between brief clinic talk and long stories I heard in patients' homes is striking. Families spin narrative worlds foreign to scientific sensibilities: stories of sorcery causing madness and of lawsuits against alleged sorcerers; stories of succubi causing nightly semen loss upsetting the balance of the victim's whole being; or claims that one woman's acts of grieving (and love charms planted in her courtyard by her ex-husband) caused her "madness" – family claims countered by her own insistence that such claims justified the family's "torturing" her (Wilce 1998). When families do choose to take deviant members to psychiatrists, stories stay at home. After seeing a psychiatrist, in at least a few cases, the patients' stories even come to reflect something of the psychiatrist's rationalized, disenchanted world.

LITERARY MODERNISM, MADNESS, AND CULTURAL CHANGE

Another modern nook – literature – offers narrative a friendlier if perhaps a transforming home. Literary modernism pushed the envelope of subjectivity. Faulkner and Joyce presented very new sorts of narrative. At least this form of modernism cultivates a very particular subjectivity:

> Modernism is associated with attempts to render human subjectivity in ways more real than [nineteenth-century literary] realism: to represent consciousness, perception, emotion, meaning and the individual's relation to society through interior monologue, stream of consciousness, . . . defamiliarization, rhythm, irresolution." (Childs 2000: 3)

Premodern narratives sometimes represented inner states, but modernist novelists made this their chief end. Indeed, modernism peripheralized the event chronologies that dominated realist narrative. Its organizing principle was not time but inward-facing tropes of space (Sass 1992: 33). This inward move reflects modern thought more broadly. Freud and Jung interpreted characters and events of classical mythology as operating intrapsychically, interpreting narratives of events in the world as tropes for subjective occurrences.

This hermeneutical strategy reappears in Lévi-Strauss's (1963) argument that the myth of Muu's journey, which Kuna shamans recite over a woman in difficult childbirth, is "being enacted in [her] internal body." That is the myth's point. "The modern version of shamanistic technique called psychoanalysis thus derives its specific characteristics from the fact that in industrial civilization there is no longer any room for mythical time, except within man himself" (1963: 204). Lévi-Strauss might have had it all wrong. Notions of modernity are themselves mythic in projecting a past that never was – a distant past in which races or ethnic groups existed as unchanging essences, or one in which nation-states existed at all, though they are a recent invention. "Narratives of the modern age – the mythologies, tonalities, and rhythms of nation, race, and ethnicity – are . . . tales of forgetfulness, memories of a time that never was" (Erlmann 1999: 6). Yet such modern grand narratives serve as charters of a new order – myth's chief function.

The inward turn of modernist novelists and thinkers reflects the twentieth century's sense of the inadequacy of linguistic surfaces and conventions, of older shared meanings. If only a new idiom could be invented (and reinvented in each new work of fiction), perhaps the individual author could find a voice, and find herself. Yet, for many folk and academic analysts (such as Childs), "modernity has not fostered individual autonomy or profitable self-knowledge . . . meaning . . . [or] spiritual life" (2000: 17). Why should the narrator's quest to uncover true selves meet with such frustration? The quest to transcend all narrative conventions and even the need to make/share sense cuts such seekers off from others (Sass 1992). Modernist narrative struggles so much to immerse readers in streams of consciousness that characters become lost as centered subjects. Sass calls this the "paradox of the reflexive" and notes that modernism finds remarkable parallels here with schizophrenia. In both, "acute self-consciousness actually contributes to an effacing of the self, while simul- taneously obscuring its own role in this effacement" (1992: 220). The person with schizophrenia loses what Blankenburg calls a capacity for "'temporation,' which is defined as a basic sense of retro-continuity that sustains the possibility of projecting oneself into the future" (Corin and Lauzon 1994: 7; citing Blankenburg 1991). The narrative capacity depends on temporation. Yet, in modernism as well, tropes of space fragment narrative temporality.

The modernist sense of loss of self appears in postcolonial literatures around the world. Anthropologist Stefania Pandolfo describes two modernist discourses in Morocco – the local psychoanalytic voice and the Arab-modernist-literary voice – that resonate with Freud's model of melancholia. For Pandolfo, Arab modernism entails perpetual loss without the ability to mourn; thus the subject of such discourse, like Freud's melancholic, "become[s] that loss" (Pandolfo 2000: 125). Postcolonial narratives brim with loss, offering no possibility of return to the past and no obvious path toward a less conflicted future.

TRANSNATIONALISM

The borders of nation-states are increasingly porous. Globalization threatens to erase them. CNN and al-Jazeerah, the Arabic network sometimes called the "CNN of the Middle East," help shape identities globally. In telling stories ("news") from a per- spective attractive to different sorts of audiences distributed over large regions of the planet, they foster transnational identity in ways unimaginable before the electronic age. Regional and especially global media transform identities by distributing myths and postmodern stories that reflect transnational connections.

Postmodern stories include episodes of television shows like *South Park*. Rupert Murdoch's Hong Kong-based Star TV now broadcasts a Mandarin version of *South Park* into Taiwan, where it has an enthusiastic and growing following of teens. Hollywood licenses these broadcasts, but each Taiwanese episode has a new, locally relevant script. The humor often entails off-color allusions to events current in Taiwan. Sometimes more than half the dialogue is rewritten. The title becomes "'Nanfang Sijianke' or '[South Park's] Four Slackers,' which in Mandarin also sounds like 'The Four Musketeers.'" "The Jewish mother in the original who gets upset over a Christmas parade at her son's school becomes an outraged Buddhist in the Taiwanese version, who suggests that her son, Kyle, recite Buddhist scriptures in the campus pageant" (Chu 2000). Jacquemet (2003) brought this example of global narrative circulation to my attention.

In each broadcast, some "thing" is circulating while much is made *new*. Indeed, this typifies what Urban (2001) calls the metaculture of modernity. Though new cultural productions follow past models, newness is modernity's obsession. Globalizing modernity means the rapid spread, not of unchanged Western narratives but the metacultural fusing of hybrid stories. Still, the metastory of *South Park*'s circulation represents some hierarchy, the exporting of subtle "sensibilities":

> In true Hollywood fashion, [*Nanfang Sijianke* producer Michael D. K.] Mak and [Michelle] Chen [*Nanfang Sijianke*'s head-writer] are . . . working on another animated show for Taiwan called "Mother Nature" – which, they promise, will have a "South Park" *sensibility*. (Chu 2000; emphasis added)

It is just such subtleties – the typically asymmetrical flows of metanarrative sensibilities, transforming old modes of cultural (narrative) reproduction – that this chapter emphasizes.

CONCLUSION

Narrative presents thought. But since narrative is public, it helps constitute shared thought and thus culture itself. Twenty-first century narrative circulation transforms participants and the very nature of participation and identity. Even local conversational narratives, including stories told by New Guinean Protestants about themselves and their self-transforming project, partake of globalizing modernity. As older narrative forms like the novel helped create national identities, newer forms help constitute transnational identities – in Islamist or Christian religious transnationalism or in youth-oriented media-fostered global savvy (*Nanfang Sijianke*). As the distribution of narrative rights and responsibilities shifts, some contexts (Western hospital encounters, at least in a busy doctor's dreams) might become narrative-free zones at least in terms of the salience of narrative's role in doctor–patient interactions now vis-à-vis earlier generations. Other zones for narrative, such as support groups, arise to take their place. But, at least in the case of rural Bangladeshi lament, there appears to be a rift between a future in which a woman-friendly civil society appears and the past when spontaneous lament once formed a commonly available venue for women to participate in local public discourse. Such narratives of loss are at modernity's core and are far from objective. Still, if narrative increasingly becomes spectacle, especially through mass media, this represents a profound transformation in the ways that social thought circulates and social and cognitive worlds are transformed.

REFERENCES

Abu-Lughod, Lila, 2000 Modern Subjects: Egyptian Melodrama and Postcolonial Difference. In *Questions of Modernity*. T. Mitchell, ed. Pp. 87–114. Minneapolis: University of Minnesota Press.

Anderson, Benedict, 1991 *Imagined Communities: Reflections on the Origin and Spread of Nationalism*. London: Verso.

Banerjee, Sumanta, 1989 Marginalization of Women's Popular Culture in Nineteenth-Century Bengal. In *Recasting Women: Essays in Colonial History*. K. Sangari and S. Vaid, eds. Pp. 127–179. New Delhi: Kali for Women.

Beeman, William O., 1988 The Many Forms of Ta'ziyeh. In *Ta'ziyeh: Ritual and Popular Beliefs in Iran*. M. C. Riggio, ed. Hartford, CT: Trinity College Press.

Berman, Marshall, 1982 *All that Is Solid Melts into Air: The Experience of Modernity*. New York: Simon and Schuster.

Blankenburg, W., 1991 [1971] Le Perte de l'évidence naturelle. J.-M. Azorin and Y. Totoyan, trans. Paris: Presses Universitaires de France.

Bruner, Jerome, 1990 *Acts of Meaning*. Cambridge, MA: Harvard University Press.

Childs, Peter, 2000 *Modernism*. London: Routledge.

Chu, Henry, 2000 Tian-ah! Kenny Bei Guadiao! *Los Angeles Times*. December 20.

Corin, Ellen, and Gilles Lauzon, 1994 From Symptoms to Phenomena: The Articulation of the Experience in Schizophrenia. *Journal of Phenomenological Psychology* 25 (1): 3–50.

Debord, Guy, 1994 *The Society of the Spectacle*. D. Nicholson-Smith, trans. New York: Zone Books.

Erlmann, Veit, 1999 *Music, Modernity, and the Global Imagination: South Africa and the West*. New York: Oxford University Press.

Foucault, Michel, 1990 [1978] *The History of Sexuality: An Introduction*. R. Hurley, trans. New York: Vintage.

Ghattas, Kim, 2001 Lebanon Religion: Blood Flows in Commemoration of Imam Husayn. Globalinfo (an online news source at globalinfo.org), Article 6008. April 2.

Good, Byron J., 1994 *Medicine, Rationality, and Experience: An Anthropological Perspective*. Cambridge: Cambridge University Press.

Good, Mary-Jo Delvecchio, and Byron Good, 1988 Ritual, the State, and the Transformation of Emotional Discourse in Iranian Society. *Culture, Medicine, and Psychiatry* 12: 48–63.

Grima, Benedict, 1991 The Role of Suffering in Women's Performances of Paxto. In *Gender, Genre, and Power in South Asian Expressive Traditions*. Arjun Appadurai, Frank Korom, and Margaret Mills, eds. Pp. 79–101. Philadelphia: University of Pennsylvania Press.

Hegland, Mary Elaine, 1998 Flagellation and Fundamentalism: (Trans)forming Meaning, Identity, and Gender Through Pakistani Women's Rituals of Mourning. *American Ethnologist* 25 (2): 240–266.

Jacquemet, Marco, 2003 Transidiomatic Practices: Language in the Age of Globalization. Paper presented at the meetings of the International Pragmatics Association, Toronto, Canada.

Jerison, Harry J., 1976 Paleoneurology and the Evolution of Mind. *Scientific American* 234: 90–101.

Keane, Webb, 1997 From Fetishism to Sincerity: On Agency, the Speaking Subject, and their Historicity in the Context of Religious Conversion. *Comparative Studies in Society and History* 39 (4): 674–93.

Kuipers, Joel C., 1998 *Language, Identity, and Marginality in Indonesia: The Changing Nature of Ritual Speech on the Island of Sumba*. Cambridge: Cambridge University Press.

Lévi-Strauss, Claude, 1963 *Structural Anthropology*. New York: Basic Books.

Lyotard, Jean-François, 1984 *The Postmodern Condition: A Report on Knowledge*. G. Bennington and B. Massumi, trans. Minneapolis: University of Minnesota Press.

McLaren, Ann, 2000a The Oral and Ritual Culture of Chinese Women: Bridal Lamentations of Nanhui. *Asian Folklore Studies* 59 (2): 205–238.

— 2000b The Grievance Rhetoric of Chinese Women: From Lamentation to Revolution. Intersections 4: Displacements, Transitions and Diasporas. Electronic Document. http://wwwsshe.murdoch.edu.au/intersections/issue4/mclaren.html.

Mannan, Qazi Abdul, 1966 The Emergence and Development of *Dobhāṣi* Literature in Bengal (up to 1855 AD). Dhaka: Department of Bengali and Sanskrit, University of Dacca.

Mitchell, Timothy, 2000 Introduction. In *Questions of Modernity*. T. Mitchell, ed. Pp. xi–xxvii. Minneapolis: University of Minnesota Press.

Mueggler, Erik, 2001 *The Age of Wild Ghosts: Memory, Violence, and Place in Southwest China*. Berkeley: University of California Press.

Ochs, Elinor, 2004 Narrative Lessons. In *A Companion to Linguistic Anthropology*. Alessandro Duranti, ed. Pp. 269–289. Oxford: Blackwell.

Ochs, Elinor, and Lisa Capps, 1996 Narrating the Self. *Annual Review of Anthropology* 25: 19–43.

Pandolfo, Stefania, 2000 The Thin Line of Modernity: Some Moroccan Debates on Subjectivity. In *Questions of Modernity, Vol. 11: Contradictions of Modernity*. T. Mitchell, ed. Pp. 115–147. Minneapolis: University of Minnesota Press.

Pinault, David, 1999 Shia Lamentation Rituals and Reinterpretations of the Doctrine of Intercession: Two Cases from Modern India. *History of Religions* 38 (3): 285–305.

Reiser, Stanley, 1987 *Medicine and the Reign of Technology*. Cambridge: Cambridge University Press.

Robbins, Joel, 2002 God is Nothing But Talk: Modernity, Language and Prayer in a Papua New Guinea Society. *American Anthropologist* 103 (4): 901–912.

Rosenblatt, Paul C., with Patricia Walsh and Douglas A. Jackson, 1976 *Grief and Mourning*. New Haven, CT: HRAF Press.

Santner, Eric L., 1990 *Stranded Objects: Mourning, Memory, and Film in Postwar Germany*. Ithaca, NY: Cornell University Press.

Sass, Louis Arnorsson, 1992 *Madness and Modernism: Insanity in the Light of Modern Art, Literature, and Thought*. New York: Basic Books.

Schieffelin, Bambi B., Slyomovics, Susan 1987 The Death-Song of 'Amir Khafaji': Puns in an Oral and Printed Episode of Sirat Bani Hilal. *Journal of Arabic Literature* 18: 62–78.

— 2000 Introducing Kaluli Literacy: A Chronology of Influences. In *Regimes of Language*. Paul Kroskrity, ed. Pp. 293–327. Santa Fe, NM: School of American Research Press.

Thompson, John B., 1996 Tradition and Self in a Mediated World. In *Detraditionalization: Critical Reflections on Authority and Identity*. P. Heelas, S. Lash, and P. Morris, eds. Pp. 89–108. Oxford: Blackwell.

Urban, Greg, 1996 *Metaphysical Community: The Interplay of the Senses and the Intellect*. Austin: University of Texas Press.

— 2001 *Metaculture*. Philadelphia: University of Pennsylvania Press.

Vaudeville, Charlotte, 1986 *Bārahmāsā in Indian Literatures: Songs of the Twelve Months in Indo-Aryan Literatures*. Delhi: Motilal Banarsidass.

Weber, Max, 1958 [1920–1] *The Protestant Ethic and the Spirit of Capitalism*. T. Parsons, trans. New York: Charles Scribners' Sons.

Wickett, Elizabeth, 1993 "For Our Destinies": The Funerary Lament of Upper Egypt. Ph.D. dissertation, University of Pennsylvania.

Wikan, Unni, 1990 *Managing Turbulent Hearts: A Balinese Formula for Living*. Chicago: University of Chicago Press.

Wilce, James M., 1998 *Eloquence in Trouble: The Poetics and Politics of Complaint in Rural Bangladesh*. New York: Oxford University Press.

— 1999 Healing. In Language Matters in Anthropology: A Lexicon for the Millennium. Theme issue. *Journal of Linguistic Anthropology* 9 (1): 93–95.

— 2000 The Poetics of "Madness": Shifting Codes and Styles in the Linguistic Construction of Identity in Matlab, Bangladesh. *Cultural Anthropology* 15 (1): 3–34.

— 2001 Genres of Memory and the Memory of Genres: "Forgetting" Lament in Bangladesh. *Comparative Studies in Society and History* 44 (1): 159–185.

— 2004 Madness, Fear, and Control in Bangladesh: Clashing Bodies of Knowledge-Power. *Medical Anthropology Quarterly*. Special Issue: Illness and Illusions of Control 18 (3): 357–375.

CHAPTER 8

Practical Logic and Autism

Elinor Ochs and Olga Solomon

INTRODUCTION

At the beginning of the twenty-first century, contemporary social theory remains at a loss to articulate the relation between structure and agency in constituting social life. The paradigm shift towards constructivist perspectives brought a new vocabulary to social and cultural analysis, one which cast members as players in the game of life, actively manipulating symbols and behavioral principles to strategically manage the contingencies of fluid social situations. Decades after Garfinkel and Bourdieu presented their brilliant treatises on practice, however, we are still hovering around the notions of practical reasoning and practical logic and their relation to social order and "common culture," including categories, rules, common sense, and other "objective regularities" of local knowledge. In Bourdieu's writings, for example, we learn far more about what practical logic is *not* than what it *is*: "Practice has a logic which is *not* that of the logician" (1990a: 86). Indeed, we are cautioned against rigorous probing of practical logic, with emphasis on the supposition that the relation of members' habitus to fluid circumstances is inherently vague:

> The *habitus* goes hand in glove with vagueness and indeterminacy. (Bourdieu 1990b: 77)

> And there is every reason to think that as soon as he reflects on his practice, adopting a quasi-theoretical posture, the agent loses any chance of expressing the truth of his practice. (Bourdieu 1990a: 91)

Bourdieu argues that the vagueness of practical logic is a non-issue, for the beauty of practice-based paradigms is that practical sensemaking is a psychological activity that teeters between structure and agency. In this perspective, practical logic is in part an acquired, sociohistorically rooted sense of the immanent practice and in part a set of intuitions and improvisations generated on the spot in response to novel situations. Similarly, in Garfinkel's framework, practical reasoning involves members' use of both "background expectancies as a scheme of interpretation" and ad hoc, contingent, artful methods for responding to "every exigency of organizationally situated conduct" (Garfinkel 1967: 36, 34).

For all the emphasis on practice as a fusion of orchestration and spontaneity, however, we know little about the interweaving of these tendencies in social life. Garfinkel and Bourdieu emphasize that sociocultural dispositions provide a tool kit of resources for social actors, but that these resources alone cannot account for temporally unfolding practical reasoning and practical action. We are left in the dark as to the specific role such a tool kit plays as social actors move through the complexities of practical worlds and as to what transpires when the experiential tool kit proves inadequate and social players are required to innovate strategies and courses of action or otherwise no longer evince a feel for the game.

This essay offers an outside-in perspective on the accomplishment of practical logic and the dynamics of structure and agency through an unusual path, namely an examination of social practices in which certain players have been diagnosed with autism. Face-to-face interaction is often anathema to persons with this disorder, and social practices can be challenging for them to apprehend, initiate, and sustain. Because these and other difficulties with sociality are its defining symptoms and because anthropologists have neglected to analyze this disorder in relation to the constitution of society, autism presents an ultimate, formidable frontier for the field of anthropology. Geertz has written that the anthropological attempt to capture the general features of social life of another people "is clearly a task at least as delicate, if a bit less magical, as putting oneself into someone else's skin . . . The trick is to figure out what the devil they think they are up to" (1983: 58). In line with phenomenologically oriented anthropologists like Geertz, the authors of the present study make no claim to reproduce the "native's point of view" of autism. We do, however, attempt to present "experience-near" autistic understandings of social practice that we captured in the course of following autistic children at home, school, and elsewhere with video cameras and wireless microphones. Our analysis draws upon manner and content of talk, gaze, demeanor, and actions of 16 children of normal intelligence diagnosed as either high-functioning autistic (HFA) or with Asperger Syndrome (AS), including *sotto voce* commentaries on unfolding situations at hand, especially perceived moments of confusion and failure in the face of practical expectations.

The present study applies the tools of anthropology to understand how these children with autism participate in social encounters that require fluid, contingent, practical strategies and behavior. In so doing, the study begins to unpack the relation between structure and agency/dispositions and practice. Autism refracts this relation in fascinating ways. For example, our ethnographic observations indicate that children with HFA or Asperger Syndrome have a heightened awareness of how mastery of certain social practices is critical to being perceived as a normal kid. This awareness is especially manifest at school when they strive but fail to meet some practical exigency or when their oddities are noticed by their unaffected classmates. For example, during a math test, Karl, a 9-year-old HFA boy, asks his aide for help, bemoaning that he "does not know anything." As she approaches, he sneaks a peak at the multiplication table on the wall and is reprimanded (Ochs 2002: 111, 112):

(1)

Karl: [°Would you help me? I don't know aa-nny-thing°
         [*((turns to his aide, whispers))*
Aide: [*((comes over to Karl's seat, squats))* What?
Karl: [*((looks at multiplication table on the wall and sees a possible answer))*
         It's thirty-six?
Aide: >You're not supposed to be <u>lookin'</u> at that (.)
         [Look<

At this point, Karl articulates a complex social relation between the practice in which he is now engaged, the kind of person he is not and the kind of person he is, and the implications of these social categories for "being a kid":

Karl: [I don't <u>like</u> math
         [*((turning to/away from aide))*
         I am not a <u>math</u> person.
         .hh I am a <u>robot</u> person
         not a [<u>math</u> person.
Aide: [You a: : ↑re
Karl: **Yes: : !**
Aide: Okay (.) right <u>no: w</u> (.) you are a <u>person</u> doing a <u>test</u> (.) okay?
Karl: **He is <u>not</u> a test °person <u>anymore</u>°**
         (.)
         Eight
Aide: And you are [not supposed to be looking up on that <u>cha: rt.</u>
Karl: [**Two**
         I am not <u>good</u> at being a <u>ki- d.</u>
Aide: You are good at <u>everything</u> you <u>wanna</u> be.

A similar awareness of practical competence was displayed by 9-year-old Erin when her classmates ridiculed her for flapping her hands in the air, rocking back and forth, bobbing her head, and making loud rhythmic vocalizations on a playground bench (Ochs et al. 2001). The classmates marked her practice as odd with comments such as "What's your problem?" and "What the heck is she doing?" and half-smiles at one another. After these reactions, Erin ceased her jiggling, solicited their attention again, and when it was finally secured, reenacted the same behavior as a clown act. In redefining her practice as a humorous performance, Erin attempted to convince her classmates that she, like them, has normal control over her actions. Karl and Erin make evident in startling clarity philosopher Margaret Archer's dictum: "We do not make our personal identities under the circumstances of our own choosing. Our placement in society rebounds upon us, affecting the persons we become, but also and more forcefully influencing the social identities which we can achieve" (2000: 10).

What Karl and Erin and others like them make remarkable is that social practice is fundamental to identity formation in human consciousness. Although sociality presents numerous hurdles for them, autistic persons of normal intelligence are nonetheless able to reflect upon practices and identities, sometimes able to strategically accommodate to normative expectations (like Erin) and other times voicing frustration at their limitations (like Karl).

Autism indicates that certain facets of social practice are comfortably handled, while others stretch capabilities, suggesting that practical logic is not a homogeneous domain of competence (Ochs et al. 2004). These distinctions in turn illuminate what is foundational to performing social life and what poses greater cognitive and social challenges. Autistic interfaces with the world also clarify the power of structure over agency. For example, when children with autism are practical actors in the games of social life, the exercise of practical agency in novel situations may be thwarted by a strong autistic predilection for ritualization and structural regularity (Hughes 2001; Turner 1997; Wing and Gould 1979). If we consider structure to be Mohammed and agency to be the mountain, the mountain bends to Mohammed and structure rules supreme.

Moreover, the distinction between structure and agency requires some rethinking in light of how autistic children strategically transform social practices into exercises of listing, configuring, and permuting objective structures. That is, in addition to the unidirectional conversion of objective structure into contingent social practice, we find semi-inversions as well (i.e., partial retreats into structural algorithms). In contrast to the vague conversion of objective structures into practical logic as described by Bourdieu, the children at times baldly insert such structures into immanent social interactions. For example, recounting his first day of school to his mother, Adam, an 11-year-old boy with AS, sums up his music teacher's instructions: "Ink, ink for the practice report. Pencil for the music. Pencil not for the practice report, and ink not for the music," thus relating members of two paradigmatic sets (assignment set: practice report, music/writing media set: ink, pencil) according to a one-to-one correspondence algorithm and then relating them again in a one-to-one contrast (Solomon 2000).

Neither wholly irrelevant nor wholly relevant, such inserted structures are what we call *proximally relevant* to the social practice underway. The phenomenon of proximal relevance challenges strict structure–agency and structure–practice dichotomies: in the case of autistic actors, asserting information about objective structures and regularities *is* a practical strategy and a comfortable one at that; logical logic *is* practical logic. Such cases, in which rules, principles, taxonomies, and other structural domains of habitus are baldly deployed in autistic social practice, lend insight into the more subtle practical logic required of ordinary actors in translating, transposing, and otherwise generating systems of dispositions into situated practical behavior.

THE ETHNOGRAPHY OF AUTISM PROJECT

Much of what we know about autism is drawn from elicited behaviors in structured experimental settings. Alternatively, the present corpus, collected under the direction of linguistic anthropologist Elinor Ochs and clinical psychologist Lisa Capps, includes not only experimental data but also extensive ethnographic observations of the everyday lives of 16 8–12-year-old children diagnosed with either HFA or AS. All the children were fully included in regular public school classrooms. To confirm diagnosis, researchers administered Autism Diagnostic Interview-Revised (ADI; Le Couteur et al. 1989) and the Autism Behavior Checklist (ABC; Krug et al. 1978). The children's abilities were assessed using the Wechsler Intelligence Scale

(WISC-III; Wechsler, 1992), and a series of theory of mind tasks (Baron-Cohen 1989; Baron-Cohen et al. 1985; Happé 1994b; Leslie and Frith 1988).

In addition, the children were observed and video recorded for up to a month at home and school, yielding a total corpus of over 320 hours of recorded data, and audio recorded in transit to and from school for a total of approximately 60 hours. Using remote wireless microphones, the researchers tracked the children at a distance in a range of social practices related to mealtimes, car rides, schoolwork, sports, and other recreational activities. Researchers also photographed quotidian environments in which the children routinely conducted their social life and interviewed parents about family history and the children's daily schedules and social networks.

While sociability is a central topic in psychological research on autism, it has been examined largely in terms of the achievement of intersubjectivity and interpersonal relationships between individuals. Although drawing upon this scholarship, our ethnographic study of autism and social life instead foregrounds how children with autism spectrum disorder function as *members of social institutions* such as families, schools, and peer groups. It analyzes their ability to both apprehend and construct social order and social practice in everyday environments.

AUTISTIC IMPAIRMENTS AND SOCIAL PRACTICE

Autism is a neurodevelopmental disorder that affects, by the most conservative estimates, 1 out of every 1,000 children (Castelli et al. 2002; Croen et al. 2002; Gillberg and Wing 1999). Approximately 75 percent of children with autism suffer from mental retardation, and about half never develop spoken language (Wing 1996; Wing and Attwood 1987). Autism is a spectrum disorder, with a range of severity encompassing the most profoundly affected non-verbal individuals at one end of the continuum and those with only subtle impairments at the other. The latter includes both high functioning individuals with autism (HFA) and those with AS.

Independently of the level of current functioning, children are given a diagnosis of autistic disorder if they have had a delay or anomaly in early language and in cognitive development (APA, 2000). If no such delay has been documented, the children receive the diagnosis of AS. This diagnostic differentiation can be problematic, however, because children with AS are usually diagnosed at an older age than children with autism, making it impossible to establish whether, in fact, their language development was proceeding normally (Landa 2000).

The hallmark of AS is an image of a "little professor" (Volkmar and Klin 2001: 84) incessantly talking in a loud, pedantic tone of voice about such unusual or esoteric topics of interest as rain drains or number encryption. Compared to children with HFA, those affected with AS have a social disability that, paradoxically, manifests in exaggerated reliance on language combined with limited awareness of conventions of its use. Thus, unlike children with HFA, who may appear socially withdrawn, children with AS are often garrulous, inexhaustible conversational partners, making bids for interaction in a persistent, repetitive, and forceful manner with little ability to interpret others' non-verbal communicative cues (Volkmar and Klin 2001).

Persons with an autism spectrum disorder are generally thought to have relatively intact grammatical ability but display pragmatic impairments in language use (Tager-Flusberg 2000). The children may appear, however, linguistically intact on the surface due to the "gestalt" pattern of language acquisition, which results in the use of memorized linguistic chunks (Prizant 1983; Landa 2000). Nevertheless, pragmatic impairments of children with autism spectrum disorders are indisputable. In the early stages of development, the children almost completely lack proto-declarative gestures (i.e., pointing to share an interest in an object) (Foster 1990; Happé 1994a). In later development, they have impaired use of deictic markers that shift meaning depending on the context of use, such as demonstratives and personal pronouns, which they often reverse (Bartok and Rutter 1974; Tager-Flusberg and Calkins 1990; Tager-Flusberg 1993, 2000).

Moreover, certain children with autism spectrum disorders have idiosyncratic use of repetition in conversation. They may echo utterances of little relevance that have been heard in another situation. Additionally, some children with autism spectrum disorders repeat questions or statements to maintain their conversational involvement in the absence of an ability to otherwise participate in conversation (Prizant and Wetherby 1987; Wetherby et al. 2000). HFA children may ask questions in a socially inappropriate, potentially offensive way (Landa 2000).

Furthermore, the children tend not to invite other interlocutors to engage in joint attention to objects (Kasari et al. 1990; Loveland and Landry 1986; Mundy et al. 1993), communicate only a relatively restricted range of interests (Mercier et al. 2000), and have an impaired ability to organize events and states in a coherent narrative (Bruner and Feldman 1993; Capps et al. 1992; Capps et al. 2000; Loveland and Tunali 1993; Tager-Flusberg 1996; Tager-Flusberg and Sullivan 1995). Children with autism also have been reported to make few contributions to ongoing conversation and have difficulty sustaining conversational topics (Tager-Flusberg and Anderson 1991; Tager-Flusberg 1996, 2000). Even HFA and AS adults have been noted to produce relatively incoherent written and spoken discourse that rambles and fails to consider the addressee's knowledge and perspective (Happé 1991). Alternatively, our research on children with autism spectrum disorders in everyday social interactions finds that children exhibit various *degrees* of pragmatic impairments and, moreover, that pragmatics itself is not a uniform domain of competence (Ochs et al. 2004).

For decades, researchers attempted to locate a core deficit of autism (Sigman and Capps 1997). The main candidates have included an impairment in (1) the drive for central coherence (i.e., the integration of parts into whole configurations); (2) the executive function (i.e., coordinating actions and mental states to solve a problem and reach a desired goal); and (3) theory of mind (i.e., interpreting others' psychological dispositions). All these impairments potentially interfere with the exercise of competent practical logic.

Central coherence
The Weakness of Central Coherence hypothesis argues that those with autism have a specific imbalance in information processing that inhibits their ability to integrate information into a coherent hierarchical organization (Frith 1989; Happé 1996; Plaisted

2000; Shah and Frith 1993). The drive for central coherence is over-powered by strong lower-level cohesive forces, which results in "an incoherent world of fragmented experience" (Frith 1989: 98). For example, autistic individuals excel at tasks involving attention to local information – such as copying block designs of little cubes or arranging shapes in rows and columns – but perform poorly in tasks requiring information processing at the global level – such as assembling a cardboard picture of a horse from its parts.

An understanding of how parts fit into conceptual wholes is central to both understanding cultural systems of classification and social order and their implementation in everyday social practice. Curiously, a number of the HFA and AS children in our study took delight in conceptual paradigms, listing and contrasting members of sets (Solomon 2000). In the excerpt below, for example, Mary, a 9-year-old HFA girl, first computes "please" and "thank you" as "magic words" then, inspired by her mother's explanation of "nicknames," she notes a candidate member ("golden state") of this category, which in turn elicits "California" as a category, which then evokes Mary's mentioning of the "golden poppy" as "the state flower for CaliFORnia":

(2)
Mary: Pass the crab!
           ((*walks back to seat, Mom hands her the bowl*)).
Mother: Please.
Mary: Please.
Father: Mmm hmm.
Mary: [THANK you!
           [(((*perky tone*)).
           [. . .]
Mary: "Please" and "thank you" are called magic words
           [. . .]
Mary: [Right, Mommy?
           [(((*looking down*))
Mother: Yup! That's kind of a nickname.
           [. . .]
Mary: WHAT's a NICKNAME?
Mother: You know, like a little fun name.
Mary: The golden state is a nickname state.
Mother: The [golden [state is a nickname for?
Mary: [State! [CaliFORnia!
                [(((*enthusiastically*))
Mother: Mmm hmm!
Mary: And (0.5 sec. pause), the golden poppy is (0.1 sec. pause) the state flower for (0.1 sec. pause) CaliFORnia.
Father: [That's right!
Mother: [That's right.
Mary: And I never saw a golden POPPY

In this dinner interaction, the family turns Mary's interest in categories into a game. At times, however, the children's structural flights were more off the point. Grasping the conveyed meaning of an interactional move entails part–whole understandings of the relation that move has to the larger body of actions, attitudes, and propositions unfolding in time and place.

Topic continuity, for example, involves attention not only to the immediately prior proposition but also to the relation of that proposition to the accumulation of thematically continuous propositions (Keenan [Ochs] and Schieffelin 1976; Sperber and Wilson 1986, 2002). In the excerpt that follows, for example, Erin, a 9-year-old HFA girl, links a narrative about her father's broken leg to an immediately prior reference to her father, but not to the global discourse topic of her father's family genealogy underway. Erin initiates this personal narrative in the middle of a family history interview that the researchers were conducting with Erin's mother (Solomon 2001):

(3)

Mother:	His- his grandmother was- was from Italy
Researcher:	Aha
Mother:	- and so
Researcher:	His father's mother?
Mother:	Yeah
Researcher:	Aha
Mother:	Well actually probably both
Researcher:	Both his parents, right, because the name is –
Mother:	And then (.) his father I believe is born .hmm here (.) in New York I mean
Erin:	**Oh, and -**
Mother:	- and then they migrated out here
Erin:	**Oh, and – well – .hhh**
	Dad was born in San Bernardino
	and about two months ago he broke-
	fractured his leg on a skateboard . . .
	((narrative continues))

Erin's first utterance "Dad was born in San Bernadino" can be seen as thematically coherent with her mother's immediately prior utterance about her husband's parents migrating from New York to "out here," meaning California. Erin's continuing discourse, however, leaps from the location and time frame of her father's birth to a skateboard accident he incurred just two months ago. Of course, interlocutors switch topics as a matter of course, but they generally mark such discourse as topically divergent. Instead, Erin emphasizes topical continuity by using the conjunction "and" to link her father's birthplace to his skateboard injury.

Discourse Topic 1
Father's Family History

- -

"Dad was born in San Bernadino"
"and"

- -

Discourse Topic 2
Father's Recent Skateboard Injury
"about two months ago he broke-
fractured his leg on a skateboard"

As evidenced by this excerpt from Erin's narrative, the ability to integrate parts into coherent structures is central not only to introducing a narrative but also to recounting the narrative itself. Those with autism spectrum disorders find it challenging to recount a narrative of personal experience, in part because it entails organizing component events to form larger narrative episodes along a narrative trajectory that configures the plot of a story (Loveland et al. 1990; Solomon 2001).

Executive function

The Executive Function hypothesis argues that autistic impairments are related to an executive function disorder, which compromises problem solving abilities, particularly those required to plan a goal directed course of action amid changeable, relatively unstructured environmental circumstances (Hughes 2001; Russell 1997). This deficit is particularly consequential to practical competence, as much depends upon sizing up a situation and deploying strategies that are pertinent to projected social moves. As Bourdieu notes, "a player who is involved and caught up in the game adjusts not to what he sees but to what he fore-sees." (1990b: 81). The Executive Function hypothesis may offer a fruitful explanation for autistic difficulties in spontaneous narration, in that narrative plots have the structure of plans and entail the ability to causally link a complicating event to subsequent goal setting attempts, psychological responses, and consequences.

As part of their executive function impairment, persons with autism spectrum disorders have difficulty generating new and flexible responses to shifting situational demands. This ability to recognize socially significant variability in situations and adjust one's strategies for engagement accordingly is fundamental to exuding a feel for the game at hand. As noted earlier, persons with autism have a fondness, which can turn to obsessiveness, for constancy and regularity. They sometimes perseverate on a certain stimulus or prior problem solving strategy, even though the parameters of a situation have changed (Turner 1997). Their orientation to sameness also may lead autistic persons to over-regularize social situations, treating similar but distinct social moments as abiding by the same social rules. A HFA child in our study, for example, introduced himself to each member of his soccer team at not only the first practice but also every practice thereafter. And in the excerpt below, Jason, a 12-year-old HFA boy, reports to his parents at dinnertime his frustration that a strategy he used previously to handle a bully at school failed to work in an incident earlier that day:

(4)
Jason: **Actually**
          (6.0 sec. pause)
          Actually
          (2.0 sec. pause)
          he pick on me- he picked on me today.
Mother: Really? °Why°?
Jason: **I don't know**
          [. . .]
Father: So how you handled it?
Mother: Like what Jason?
Father: How do you handle it?
          (1.0 sec pause)

Jason: I say "hello"-
            ((animated)) **When I say "hello" to him**
            He says "AAAAH"
            He gets scared.
Father: Pretend
Mother: [uh hmm
Father: [uh hmm
            (2.0 sec pause)
Mother: [It's OK, it's alright Jason
Jason: **[But I**
            Then he walked away,
            So I wanted **to** do **that**
            But it wo–
            (.)
            It worked in the first place but now it didn't.

Theory of mind

The Theory of Mind hypothesis argues that autism impairs the ability to attribute mental states to others and even to themselves. Practical logic and practical action rely upon theory of mind to successfully infer from others' conduct and ideas what they are likely to be thinking and feeling and what is likely to be their next social move. In experimental settings, autistic children are often unable to infer others' beliefs and intentions, a phenomenon known as First Order Theory of Mind (Baron-Cohen 1989; Baron-Cohen et al. 1985). Even the most able HFA and AS children need to reach the verbal mental age of 9 years in order to pass the first order Theory of Mind tests passed by typically developing 3 to 4 year olds (Happé 1995). Typically, developing children make Second Order Theory of Mind inferences – about what one person (other than self) thinks another person thinks – at the age of 6, while only a few HFA individuals reach this ability sometime in their adult years (Baron-Cohen 2000). For example, while riding in the car, Sylvester, an 8-year-old HFA boy, and his mother see "two guys near the . . . railroad tracks with (.) what looks like a shotgun," and his mother later reports this to police over her cell phone. During the call Sylvester becomes increasingly nervous that the men will track them down, which is not a farfetched assumption for an 8 year old and one demanding second-order perspective-taking. But then, as his mother waits on the line with the police, Sylvester loses perspective on the gunmen when he fears that they may hear his mother talking, even though he and his mother have passed them by and are inside the car:

(5)
Sylvester: **Are they- are they parts of gangsters?**
            Do they hear you?
            (3.0 sec. pause)
            Are you- do they hear you?
            What is it?
            What?
            >What what what what?<

Powerfully hermeneutic, the Theory of Mind hypothesis makes sense of much of young autistic children's communicative profile (e.g., language delay, lack of response when called by name, diminished range of facial expression and gesture, diminished ability to initiate and maintain shared gaze and shared object of interest with a primary caregiver, echolalia). Theory of mind impairments also may account for older autistic children's and adults' difficulty recognizing the informational needs of their interactional partners, distinguishing between their own and others' point of view, and interpreting non-literal meanings such as sarcasm, metaphors, and indirect speech acts (Baron-Cohen 1988; Frith 1989; Happé 1991, 1994b, 1995; O'Neill and Happé 2000).

SOURCES OF PRACTICAL COMPETENCE

What happens when intelligent, regularity-loving, detail-oriented, literal-minded, and intersubjectively myopic persons with autism spectrum disorder venture forth in the buzzing world of social practices? Despite the long list of social impairments associated with autism and the examples of gaps and failures presented above, we were surprised at how well the children in our study managed practical arrangements (Ochs et al. 2004). Consider, for example, the age-appropriate responses made by Don, a 10-year-old HFA boy, in an interaction that focuses on his mother's announcement that he will not be allowed to bring arrows to school as part of his Native American Halloween costume:

```
(6)
Mother:   What's the matter.
Don:      [((staring in front of him))
          [Just thinking.
Mother:   >What are you thinking about<
          (2 sec. pause)
Don:      [((dreamy, smiling))
          [<Hallowe: en>
Mother:   What? >What about Halloween.<
Don:      I w- I can't wait to be- to eh- to hold the-
          bow and arrows a: ↓nd (.)
          [((in a lower voice))
          [be a Native American.
Mother:   You know what?
Don:      Hmm?
Mother:   We're not gonna be able to take the arrows to schoo↑l.
Don:      [((puts left hand to side, upset))
          [Great
          (.)
          Mo: m! It's [no: t fai: r
Mother:               [Don
          [((straightens Don's hair))
          [You know what? (.)
          You're not allowed to take (.)
          any kind of v- violent weapon-thing to school!
Don:      But Mommy I just saw pretend swo: rd
          and a – pretend light saber!
Mother:   Then their mommy and daddy weren't following the rules!
```

In the context of this informal social interaction, Don responds relevantly to his mother's queries and reasoning, ably stating and maintaining his moral position and providing a relevant counter-argument.

Why did most of the HFA and AS children in the study generally seem to navigate the flow of social exchanges? Two interrelated explanations are posited: the autistic achievement of practical logic is enhanced by (1) properties of the *practical actors* in the social practices observed and (2) properties of the *social practices* in which the actors are engaged.

Actor-based explanation

One possible source of the frequent social success of most of the HFA and AS children in the study lies in the *relatively high intelligence of the children* and the cooperation of *generous interactional partners*. Previous researchers have surmised that older children at the high-functioning end of the autism spectrum use their intelligence to strategize how to participate in social situations. Rather than acquiring social heuristics as a matter of course, these children are thought to "hack" out meanings conveyed in social situations (Frith et al. 1994). "Hacking" implies that the children work through stored algorithms to decipher the encrypted logic of messages conveyed in the course of social interaction. This view appears apt for some exchanges involving HFA and AS children. There is ample evidence, for example, that many of the HFA and AS children we observed did indeed frequently seek didactic explanations for what they did not understand about a social situation (Ochs et al. in press), as in excerpt (7) in which Erin cannot fathom the non-literal meaning of an idiom, a problem predicted by Happé (1991, 1995):

(7)
Mother: So(.) it's gonna be a fun day on Saturday.
         Right?
         Don't forget when you get home, wash your hands.
         I don't want any illnesses breaking out between now and Saturday.
Sister: What if we get sick↑during (xxx)
         and we don't even know it.
Mother: We'll cross that bridge when we get to it.
         We're not gonna worry about that right now
Erin: **Wha: : t bridge?**
Mother: It's- it's an expression Erin.
         Something that people say,
         "we'll cross that bridge when we get to it."
         That↑ <u>means</u> that we will wait and see what happens first
         And then we will deal with it.
         (.)
         There's no point worrying about something
         that might not happen.

While queries of this sort abound, the fluidity of the children's responses in many everyday encounters with family members, classmates, and teachers suggests that they are not usually effortfully calculating or "hacking" out practical strategies. Rather, most of the time they appear to have internalized certain fundamentals of how to sustain the practical focus of attention. We propose that these practical fundamentals are building blocks of online social practical competence.

Another actor-based explanation may lie in the tendency of other participants, especially family members, to design their talk and conduct to be comprehensible and interesting to these children and to richly interpret the talk and conduct of the children. As illustrated in (1) and (3) above, these generous participants usually make certain they secure the child's attention, clarify possible misunderstandings, fill in missing information, and otherwise promote the child's social involvement.

Practice-based explanations

Properties of the practical actors alone cannot account for the practical logic exercised by the children in this study. Practical functioning of children with autism spectrum disorders – and we suspect for all practical actors as well – depends centrally on certain *fundamental properties of the social practices* underway. Social practices that exhibit certain properties appear well within the grasp of autistic children of normal intelligence, while others, we suggest, are more challenging.

We began to analyze the conditions that afford more or less successful participation in social practices. Our observations led us to propose that first, success as practical agents varied in relation to *two primary coordinates* of social practice, and second, persons with autism benefit from the *fuzzy constraints of coherence* in everyday social practice, allowing their *proximally relevant* contributions to pass as roughly acceptable behavior. The coordinates of social practice impact how well members with autism spectrum disorders are able to strategically deploy sociocultural dispositions and schemata to "appreciate the meaning of a situation instantly, at a glance, in the heat of the action, and to produce at once the opportune response" (Bourdieu 1990a: 104).

Among the coordinates of import to practical competence we focus on those of (1) *mode* and (2) *scope*. The *coordinate of mode* considers two mutually constitutive but analytically distinct properties of social practice, namely practice as a *flow of social actions* and as a *flow of propositions*. Bourdieu's conceptualization of practical logic dwells upon the relation of habitus to the flow of social actions, while Garfinkel focuses on practical reasoning as the ethnomethodology through which members accomplish both common understanding and concerted social action. Bourdieu's discourse highlights expressions such as "conduct," "acts," "enactments," "exchange," "game," "strategy," and "style." Alternatively, Garfinkel's ethnomethodology provides a more proposition-rich account of social action; indeed, interpretation itself is a social action, a set of procedures that unpack the indexical meanings underlying "members' talk and conduct" (1967: 10–11).

The second coordinate of practice is the *coordinate of scope*. A participant in a social practice may proceed competently in relation to the immediately preceding and following *local* social moves, as when someone shakes an extended hand or produces a relevant response to a compliment. Yet successful practical logic may also entail surmising how these immediate moves are relevant to more *extensive* practical considerations.

The grid below displays a cline of practical competence. In relation to the coordinates of mode and scope, with "1" representing the greatest degree of competence and "4" representing the least, the HFA and AS children in the study exhibited greater practical competence in responding to the flow of actions than to the flow of propositions and greater success in more locally circumscribed than more extensive social practices.

Coordinates of social practice			
		Mode	
		Actions	Propositions
Scope	Local	1	2
	Extended	3	4

This grid specifies that the social fluency of the verbally able children with autism spectrum disorders resided primarily in their ability to act relevantly and generatively in response to locally prior and upcoming actions (1). Linking their predications to the propositional content of locally prior and anticipated utterances was somewhat more challenging (2). This was especially the case when interlocutors conveyed non-literal meanings (Happé 1994b, 1995) and when the propositions concerned persons other than the autistic child or lay outside the current interests of the child. We noticed as well that when children became upset, they also might drift away from the local topical focus. It was considerably more challenging for the HFA and AS children to link their actions to their own and others' actions over a more extensive span of social interaction (3). As we shall see below, for example, one child had difficulty sustaining a dinner grace. As would be predicted by deficits related to central coherence, executive function, and theory of mind, the greatest difficulty for the children lay in grasping more global themes constructed across an extended series of utterances or relating an expressed proposition to an idea mentioned in the non-immediate past or projected to apply to a relatively distant unrealized time and place (4).

This hierarchy of coordinates and properties pertains not only to autism but also to practical logic as social competence more broadly. It suggests that not all facets of practical logic are equally accessible. It may be easiest for participants to master a feel for locally relevant social action, to draw from the cultural tool box of actions those optimal for the situational moment. Bourdieu's (1990a) metaphor of the tennis player who knows to approach the net to respond to an approaching ball and to direct it expertly in relation to the opponent fits this coordinate of practical logic. At the other extreme of practical logic, it may be most difficult to master a feel for the overall, extended body of propositions that participants are entertaining in an extensive social practice, to link current referents, ideas, and symbols to the past and future beyond the here-and-now.

A FEEL FOR ACTIONS

The flow of actions in social practices comprises recognizable, conventional gestures, physical demeanors, physical motion, speech acts, conversational turns and sequences, and a range of social activities, among other forms of conduct (Duranti 1997; Goodwin 1981; Goodwin and Duranti 1992; Levinson 2000; Ochs and Schieffelin 1989; Sacks 1992; Schegloff 1972; Searle 1969). Practical actors' presumptions about relevant meanings conveyed in the course of social practice involve their understanding of felicity conditions of particular speech acts, and possible trajectories and expectations of moment-to-moment conversational moves in the construction of organized sequences of talk. This point is eloquently argued by Schegloff:

> The structure of sequences will supply us as analysts with a crucial tool in understanding the coherence of stretches of talk that vary in sizes, from two utterances in consecutive turns to extremely long spates of talk. It will do so because sequences, both in minimal adjacency pair format and in multiply expanded forms, are a generic form of organization for parties to talk-in-interaction. (Schegloff 1990: 72)

In this perspective, an utterance that may appear to be incoherent in relation to the propositional flow of discourse may be coherent in relation to unfolding sequences of conversational actions (Goodwin 1981, 1990; Heritage and Sorjonen 1994; Jefferson 1978, 1984; Sacks 1987; Schegloff 1990).

It is this property of social practice that seems most within the grasp of the verbally able HFA and AS children in our study, particularly those actions that are locally circumscribed (Ochs et al. 2004). They generally displayed sophistication in the felicity conditions of speech acts and principles of sequentially relevant discourse. The children, for example, recognized and provided sequentially normative responses to speech acts such as:

Prompts
Mary: Pass the crab!
           ((*walks back to seat, Mom hands her the bowl*))
Mother: Please.
Mary: **Please.**

Announcements
Mother: You know what?
Don: Hamm?
Mother: We're not gonna be able to take the arrows to schoo↑l.
Don: [(((puts left hand to side, upset))
           [Great

Proscriptions
Karl: ((*looks at multiplication table on the wall and sees a possible answer*))
Karl: It's thirty-six?
Aide: >You're not supposed to be lookin' at that (.)
Karl: [Look<
           [**I don't like math**

Questions
Father: How do you handle it?
           (1.0 sec pause)
Jason: **I say "hello"**

The children were particularly apt responding to questions. They provided sequentially relevant next moves to 85 percent of the questions directed to them by their parents, but provided propositionally relevant answers to only 75 percent of the questions (Kremer-Sadlik 2001, 2004). Responding sequentially to questions is not simply a matter of identifying grammatical and phonological characteristics of these speech acts. The respondent also needs to discern the kind of question posed; for example, a basic request for information, a request to repair a problem in understanding or hearing, a request for confirmation, a rhetorical question, a test question, a prefacing question that projects another question to follow (Levinson 1983; Quirk et al. 1985; Schegloff 1980, 1990). Most of the HFA and AS children discerned the type of question being posed, indicating a capacity for fine-grained understanding of conversational sequences. For example, in excerpt (8), Jason relevantly responds both to his father's initial request for information and to a subsequent request for clarification:

(8)
Father: What's the name of the book?
Jason: *Across Five Aprils*
Father: What?
Jason: *Across Five APRILS*
Father: Okay

Jason displays awareness that he has been asked to repair his earlier response by the fact that he reformulates his response in a louder voice (indicated by capital letters).

The most able children in the study could handle more extensive social practices involving questions. In the interaction below, Jed, an 8-year-old boy with AS, is able to discern that his father poses a question that prefaces and projects a possible upcoming next question (i.e., a "pre-question") (Schegloff 1980):

(9)
Father: Jeddy, I have a question.
          ToMORRow, you guys are serving LUNCH to the parents?
Jed: >**Yeah, so?**<
Father: Well, what- what do yuh guys serve?
          How do you (XXX)?
          How's your (XXX) now?
          What do yuh –
          Am I gonna like it?
          What are you serving?
Jed: (**Dessert**),
Father: [What is it?
Jed: [**Stuff like that**.
          Salad, (0.2 sec. pause) **and STUFF!**

This exchange demands considerable practical logic. First, the father's preliminary assertion, "I have a question," does not mean that the question that the father has in mind is the very next question he is going to ask, and Jed does not take it to be so. Instead, Jed correctly understands that the next question is a preliminary query to a projected question that eventually follows (Schegloff 1980, 1990). His "Yeah, so?" both provides a relevant response to this query ("Yeah") and anticipates ("so?") the projected focal question. Unlike the researchers writing this essay, Jed does not have the foreknowledge of the question his father has in mind. Nonetheless, he has a feel for the social action sequence in play and the perspective-taking ability to finely tune a relevant response. These and other examples in our corpus indicate that certain HFA and AS children have the perspective-taking capability to tailor relevant, coherent responses to nuanced practical actions.

A FEEL FOR PROPOSITIONS

The flow of propositions includes the unfolding informational focus of attention, topics of concern, references, predications, and other facets of emerging, literal, and non-literal conveyed meanings that participants in a social practice continuously construct, interpret, and take into consideration in formulating moment-by-moment practical strategies (Brown and Yule 1983; Garfinkel 1967; Grice 1975; Halliday and Hasan 1976; Keenan [Ochs] and Schieffelin 1976; Kintsch and van Dijk 1978; Levinson 1983, 2000; Li and Thompson 1976; Sperber and Wilson 1986, 2002). Even verbally gifted autistic individuals sometimes experience difficulties constructing thematically coherent discourse and interpreting meanings underlying interlocutors' utterances. Using Sperber and Wilson's framework, Happé argues that autistic difficulties in discerning relevant meanings reside in an impaired ability to disambiguate an individual speaker's intentions (Happé 1991; Happé and Loth 2002; Sperber and Wilson 2002). We found as well that relative to their adeptness at providing relevant actions, maintaining the coherent flow of propositions could be problematic for the children we recorded. In excerpt (7), for example, Erin failed to grasp the non-literal meaning of "We'll cross that bridge when we come to it."

Excerpt (10) below illustrates a case of propositionally incoherent discourse that forms part of a relatively *extended* dinnertime prayer produced by Karl. Karl has some difficulty with the ritualized actional components of the genre, but even more difficulty with the improvised propositional content. When first asked to say the prayer, Karl abruptly introduces the mother of his imaginary friend Justin without explaining her relevance:

(10)
Mother: Karl let's try to say a prayer
Father: >How 'bout some lights?<
           ((*turns on the lights above the table*))
Karl: **Just- a: : – Justin's mom**

Nonetheless, Karl's mother is able to provide an approving expansion:

Mother: [Okay .hh you can pray for Justin's mom
           [((*looking in front her, nodding*))

She waits for Karl to begin the prayer then provides a series of prompts:

           (0.2 sec pause)
           Okay?
           Go ahead (.)
           "Dear-"↑

Karl: **Dear Go: d**
           (.)
           I mean (.) alien God
Father: [.hhhh
           [(((chuckling))

Karl's shift to addressing "alien God" aligns with his decision to pray for alien acquaintances, which is greeted with humor by Karl's father. After this promising start, however, Karl's grace loses direction, referring to a series of disconnected events:

Karl: **Alien God**
           (.)
           I thanked you for believing that
           Justhhhin's mom has heard a story
           a lo: ng↓ time a[go
Father: [> Put your – <
           [*((gestures to Karl to put his hands together for prayer))*
Karl: [*((lowers eyes, in a lower voice, pensively))*
           [and we have everything for- for- three years ago
           (.)
           and we have seen (.)
           [everything like this
           [*((opens hands to the table))*
           (.)
           and we have promised him to believe them
           (.)
           Your friend-
           Your – (.) J- Just God

While Karl maintains the semblance of prayer through genre features such as (1) calling out to the almighty ("Dear God"), (2) expression of thanksgiving ("I thanked you for believing . . ."), (3) commitment ("and we have promised him to believe them"), and (4) his prayerful voice quality and bodily demeanor, the prayer contains incomplete, enigmatic predications and abrupt transitions from one clause or phrase to the next. Moreover, Karl ends the prayer inappropriately, first with reference to himself as supplicant ("Your friend"), then to the supernatural addressee of the prayer ("Your (.) J- Just God").

PROXIMAL RELEVANCE

Radical incoherence such as exhibited in Karl's prayer, however, was *rare* in the spontaneous interactions involving HFA and AS children. The children's ability to maintain some semblance of coherence was aided by the fact that coherence is a *relative* rather than absolute concept. It is often, for example, difficult to discern whether an utterance is on-topic or off-topic, because topics tend to shade or transition step-wise from one to another (Schegloff and Sacks 1973). Social practices eschew tidy coherence and are loosely constructed by agents mobilizing fuzzy principles and semi-integrated schemata (Bourdieu 1990a: 102). Profiting by the fuzziness of situational coherence, the HFA and AS children routinely maintained social practices by expressing ideas that were *proximally relevant* (i.e., not quite in synch with the focal concern). Their proximally relevant remarks often followed statements, opinions, or emotional or ironic comments concerning persons other than themselves.

We have discerned two prevailing strategies that lead to proximal relevance. The first strategy is to make the interactional contribution locally relevant to what was just said or what just transpired, but not to the more extensive concern or enterprise under consideration. The second strategy is to shift the focus away from personal states and situations to topically relevant impersonal, objective cultural knowledge. Some children mixed the two strategies, proximally relating objective knowledge to a locally prior move. The strategies for achieving proximal relevance are rooted in autistic impairments. Specifically, the first strategy (i.e., make the interactional contribution locally relevant) may stem from the deficits in central coherence and executive function, while the second strategy (i.e., to shift the focus away from personal states) may originate in limited perspective-taking ability.

Local scope and proximal relevance

A case of strategy one, a proximally relevant comment that somewhat misses the point of an extended sequence of propositions, is illustrated in example (3) when Erin introduced a narrative about her father's recent broken leg in the midst of a discussion about the family's distant family history. Her narrative was neither completely irrelevant nor completely relevant, but rather proximally relevant to the more global practical concerns. Similarly, in (11) below, Adam, an 11-year-old AS boy, was unable to grasp how his parents' comments related to a very long narrative he recounted to them about his grandmother's ("Yaya") horrified reaction to his first bike ride on a major street with his grandfather ("Papu"). Adam had detailed how his grandmother mercilessly and repeatedly grilled Papu and him. Adam's exaggerated pitch contours, vowel lengthening, and emphatic finger-shaking in reporting his grandmother's speech and gestures as well as his laughter and sarcastic repartee give the impression that his grandmother's response to his bike adventure was excessive. Below is a short excerpt from this narrative interaction:

(11)
Adam: She said-
         she says –
         "This WAS the first time you were riding a bike.
         [WASN'T it, Philip?
         [((*gesticulates with both hands*))
         This <u>WA: S</u> isn't it?"
         [And – and -and then,
         [((*change in voice, calmly*))
         [and Papu goes –
         [((*looks to the side, away from parents*))
         says uh –
         says uh –
         ["WELL- Bu↑t-"
         [((*change of voice to imitate grandfather, calmly*))

> [You know how Yaya doesn't like that-
> [((*calm tone, back to own voice*))
> ["JUST ANSWER THE QUESTION!"
> [((*waves hands, agitated*))
> ["It's the FIRST time"
> [((*imitating grandmother's voice*))

Father: [((*laughs*))
Mother: [((*laughs*))

Following Adam's reenactment of Yaya's reactions, Adam's mother comments that Yaya should have been a lawyer, specifically a district attorney; Adam's father suggests that she could have been a detective:

Mother: **See she should have been a lawyer.**
       [((*laughs*))
       ((*shakes finger knowingly*))
Adam: **((*starts to rock*))**
Father: [That's right
       [((*laughing*))
Adam: = "It's the first time he rides a bike."
       ["Are you SU: : RE?"
       [((*rocking back and forth, continuously*))
Father: It's true!
       [She should have been
       [((*laughing*))
Mother: [She really <u>should</u> have been.
       She could have easily been a district attorney.
Father: **Or a detective of [some type.** And her skills – she had skills for that.
Mother: [That's where she missed her call –
       she had ALL the skills to be it.
       ((*Adam, who has been rocking up to this point, stops*))
       Yeah. Yeah. Easily.
       [That's too bad.
       [((*pensively*))

At first, Adam seems oblivious to this discussion, then appears to concentrate: he stops quoting his grandmother's remarks, ceases rocking back and forth in his chair, then joins into his parents' characterization of his grandmother with his own proximally relevant comment:

Adam: **[She FINDS things easily?**
       [((*intently looking into mother's face*))
Mother: Yeah.
       She is – that's too [bad=
Adam: **[De<u>TECTIVE</u>, see? =**
       ((*begins rocking again*))
Mother: = That's what she should have been=
       ((*pensively, points finger in Adam's direction*))
Adam: ((*stretches arm across the table, points finger close to mother's face,
       with excitement*))
       [=A DE-TECT-IVE!=
       [((*waves hands, very excited, speaking abruptly*))

Mother:	=A district attorney or a detective.=
Adam:	**She can find things <u>EA: Sily</u> you know!**
Mother:	Uhu
Adam:	**An-an-anyway – so – uh.** ((*leans forward, in a low voice conspiratorially,* *looking at mother*)) **She looks for bargains (in the supermarket).**

In this social exchange, Adam was unable to relate the social roles of lawyer, district attorney, and detective to his own extended recounting of his grandmother's ceaseless and unyielding interrogation of those suspected of wrongdoing. Instead, he proximally relates being a detective to "she FINDS things easily" and "she looks for bargains (in the supermarket)," which, while not unrelated to finding informational clues and an agreed-upon predilection of Yaya, misses the main point of his parents' commentary. It may well be that Adam is not aware that detectives routinely interrogate their suspects, but it is also the case that Adam does not draw upon his own narrative discourse to construe the conveyed meaning of his parents' comments.

Objective knowledge and proximal relevance

A hallmark strategy of the HFA and AS children was to draw the interlocutor's attention to *objective* domains of knowledge more or less relevant to the topical talk underway. This strategy differs from given notions of how structure and agency relate to one another, for in these cases the autistic child as practical agent not only draws upon the cultural tool box of knowledge domains to meet the exigencies of the situation, but also converts the situation to focus on *these* objective domains of knowledge. While those unaffected by autism also at times assert cultural knowledge, this possibility coexists with a broader range of practical strategies for responding to social discourse than are available to verbally able persons with this disorder. For example, Mary, a child with a verbal IQ in the low normal range (80) and an inability to pass the First Order Theory of Mind experimental task, was highly reliant upon her use of objective knowledge as a means of participating in a proximally relevant way in the ongoing conversation. Recall that in excerpt (2) she identified "please" and "thank you" as "magic words," then "golden state" as a "nickname," then "golden poppy" as California's state flower. In excerpt (12) below, Sylvester, who has a higher verbal IQ (97) and passed First Order but not Second Order Theory of Mind tasks, incorporates proximally relevant knowledge domains at first subtly, then explicitly. Sylvester draws attention to depersonalized, objective knowledge in responding to his mother's personal, affective comment about it being a long morning as they are riding in the car one day in June:

(12)

Mother:	Sylvester? °Thank God°. ((*sighs*)) It's a long morning, isn't it?
Sylvester:	**mmhm** ((**2.0 sec pause**)) **Long morning and short night.**

Mother: What's that mean?
            ((10.5 sec pause))
Sylvester: **Mommy, in the summer, there's long days and short nights.**
Mother: [Oh yeah?
            [((*yawning*))
Sylvester: **Yeah.**
Mother: What about the winter?
Sylvester: **There are short days and long nights.**
Mother: I like that.

Preceded by the softly spoken "Thank God" and accompanied by a sigh, Mother's utterance, "It's a long morning, isn't it?" conveys a negative evaluation of the morning, a metaphor that notes how "long" it seems, a morning that feels like it will never end. Given autistic difficulties in interpreting non-literal meanings and others' emotional states (Frith 1989; Happé 1994b), this type of reflection presents a challenge to Sylvester. After concurring with his mother ("mmhm"), he repeats the topic of "long morning" but takes it in a slightly different direction, seeming to interpret it chronometrically and contrasting it with "short night." Indeed, his proposition characterizes the length of days and nights at the time of year (June) in which Sylvester is speaking. This proposition then invokes an objective discussion of seasonal changes in length of days and nights. Is Sylvester's utterance "Long morning and short night" irrelevant vis-à-vis his mother's prior comment? This attribution is too strong. Rather, Sylvester's utterance is proximally relevant.

Sylvester and Mary create proximal relevance by focusing on cultural categories. Some children enjoyed contrasting alternative members of paradigms (Solomon 2000). Adam, for example, repeatedly noted which writing tools a teacher did and did not want the students to use. In addition, the children would provide dictionary meanings of relevant concepts, elaborate the structural components of topically related situational schemata, and state social rules regulating the social practice at hand. The detail and preponderance of these proximally relevant structural noticings contribute to the "odd" and "rambling" character of some autistic discourse and the profiling of some of the children as little professors spouting off lectures concerning some domain of expertise (Happé, 1991; Volkmar and Klin, 2001). The social exchanges in which this practical strategy takes hold seem to drift into pockets of structural minutiae.

CONCLUSION

This essay proposes that autism and social practice are mutually illuminative. Refracting social practice with the prism of autism, we have discerned that practical logic applies to the flow of local and extended actions and propositions. While the two are complexly intertwined, the generation of situationally apt practical actions – especially locally integrated actions – may be more accessible, more easily mastered, and in this sense more basic to practical logic than the generation of relevant propositions that build social practices.

We have also proposed that autism reconfigures the relation of objective structure and practical agency. When HFA and AS children bring objective cultural knowledge as a proximally relevant strategy to bear on current concerns, they illustrate with great clarity the enormous pull that structure exerts on practical improvisation. One way of analyzing this communicative phenomenon is to view HFA and AS children as strategically *inverting* right then and there the practical logic of immanent social exigencies into the logical logic of patterned objective knowledge, *reversing* the default directionality of the logic of objective structures transformed into practical logic required for on-the-spot situational exigencies. Yet another interpretation, however, is the following: the autistic proclivity for proximally relevant taxonomies, schemata, and rules in everyday social exchanges may actually *confound* the dichotomy between the atemporal logic of objective structures and temporally situated practical logic. The dissolution of boundaries is rooted in the paradoxical status of the autistic focus on objective structures in social practice as at once a manifestation of *logical logic and practical logic* and as both *a step away from and a step within the flow of social practice.* When Sylvester, for example, comments "Long morning and short night" after his mother's plaintive "It's a long morning, isn't it," he simultaneously constructs a logic of objective regularities and a practical logic suited to the extant situated practice in which he is engaged as a player.

Using social practice as a lens to illuminate autism, we have learned that children with autism spectrum disorders have the capacity to be social agents who exercise practical reasoning. The HFA and AS children in this study meet the criteria of practical agents, in that they are able to display a "practical sense that 'selects' certain objects or actions . . . in relation to the matter in hand'" (Bourdieu 1990a: 89–90). Our study of the children's ability to effectively engage in local sequences of conversational practice indicate that they have considerable social perspective-taking when lodged in reasonable understandings of members' conversational moves (Ochs et al. in press).

Yet the children in this study were humbled by many of the practical demands imposed on them. They sometimes voiced confusion or frustration or tried to cover up their practical ineptitudes. In many situations they maintained their status as practical players by sticking to immediate considerations and shifting the personal drift of the social exchange towards discussion of objective structures. We invite future researchers to apply the practical coordinates proposed in this essay to discern forms of expertise called for in being not just a player but a *good* player in the games and dramas that inform our human ways of practicing life.

TRANSCRIPTION CONVENTIONS (ADAPTED FROM ATKINSON AND HERITAGE 1984)

.	Indicates a falling, or final, intonation contour.
?	Indicates rising intonation as a syllable or word ends.
↑	Indicates a rising intonation, usually in the middle of a word.
,	Indicates "continuing" intonation, not necessarily a clause boundary.
: : :	Indicate stretching of the preceding sound, proportional to the number of colons.
-	A hyphen after a word or a part of a word indicates a cut-off or self-interruption.

word	Indicates some form of stress or emphasis on the underlined item.
(( ))	Double parentheses enclose transcriber's comments.
( )	Single parentheses indicate that something is being said, but it is unintelligible.
(1.2 sec. pause)	Numbers in parentheses indicate pauses in tenths of a second.
(.)	A dot in parentheses indicates a "micropause," hearable but not readily measurable.
[	Separate left square brackets, one above the other on two successive lines with utterances by different speakers, indicates a point of overlap onset; also, simultaneous verbal and non-verbal behavior of one speaker.
[. . .]	Several lines omitted in the transcript.
WORD	Indicates increased voice volume (loudness).
Word	Indicates relevance to the discussion.

REFERENCES

American Psychiatric Association, 2000 *Diagnostic and Statistical Manual of Mental Disorders*, 4th edn. Washington, DC: American Psychiatric Association.

Archer, Margaret S., 2000 *Being Human: The Problem of Agency*. New York: Cambridge University Press.

Atkinson, J. Maxwell, and John Heritage, 1984 *Structures of Social Action: Studies in Conversational Analysis*. Cambridge: Cambridge University Press.

Baron-Cohen, Simon, 1988 Social and Pragmatic Deficits in Autism: Cognitive or Affective? *Journal of Autism and Developmental Disorders* 18: 379–402.

—— 1989 The Autistic Child's Theory of Mind: A Case of Specific Developmental Delay. *Journal of Child Psychology and Psychiatry* 30: 285–297.

—— 2000 Theory of Mind and Autism: A Fifteen Year Review. In *Understanding Other Minds: Perspectives from Developmental Cognitive Neuroscience*, 2nd edn. Simon Baron-Cohen, Helen Tager-Flusberg, and Donald J. Cohen, eds. Oxford: Oxford University Press.

Baron-Cohen, Simon, with A. M. Leslie and Uta Frith, 1985 Does the Autistic Child Have a "Theory of Mind"? *Cognition* 21: 37–46.

Bartak, L., and Michael Rutter, 1974 The Use of Personal Pronouns by Autistic Children. *Journal of Autism and Childhood Schizophrenia* 4: 217–221.

Bourdieu, Pierre, 1990a *In Other Words: Essays Towards a Reflexive Sociology*. Palo Alto, CA: Stanford University Press.

—— 1990b *The Logic of Practice*. Palo Alto, CA: Stanford University Press.

Brown, Gillian, and George Yule, 1983 *Discourse Analysis*. Cambridge: Cambridge University Press.

Bruner, Jerome S., and Carol Feldman, 1993 Theories of Mind and the Problem of Autism. In *Understanding Other Minds: Perspectives from Autism*. Simon Baron-Cohen, Helen Tager-Flusberg, and Donald Cohen, eds. Pp. 267–291. Oxford: Oxford University Press.

Capps, Lisa, Molly Losh, and Marian Sigman, 2000 "The Frog Ate the Bug and Made His Mouth Sad": Narrative Competence and Emotional Understanding in Children with Autism. *Journal of Abnormal Child Psychology* 28: 193–204.

Capps, Lisa, Nurit Yirmiya, and Marian Sigman, 1992 Understanding of Simple and Complex Emotions in Non-Retarded Children with Autism. *Journal of Child Psychology and Psychiatry* 33: 1169–1182.

Castelli, Fulvia, with Christopher D. Frith, Francesca Happé, and Uta Frith, 2002 Autism, Asperger Syndrome and Brain Mechanisms for the Attribution of Mental States to Animated Shapes. *Brain* 125: 1839–1849.

Croen, Lisa A., Grether, Judith K., Jenny Hoogstrate, and Steve Selvin, 2002 The Changing Prevalence of Autism in California. *Journal of Autism and Developmental Disorders* 32: 207–215.

Duranti, Alessandro, 1997 *Linguistic Anthropology*. Cambridge: Cambridge University Press.

Foster, Susan H., 1990 *The Communicative Competence of Young Children*. London: Longman.

Frith, Uta, 1989 *Autism: Explaining the Enigma*. Oxford: Blackwell.

Frith, Uta, with Francesca G. E. Happé and Frances Siddons, 1994 Autism and Theory of Mind in Everyday Life. *Social Development* 3: 108–124.

Garfinkel, Harold, 1967 *Studies in Ethnomethodology*. Englewood Cliffs, NJ: Prentice-Hall.

Geertz, Clifford, 1983 *Local Knowledge: Further Essays in Interpretive Anthropology*. New York: Basic Books.

Gillberg, Christopher, and Lorna Wing, 1999 Autism: Not an Extremely Rare Disorder. *Acta Psychiatrica Scandinavica* 99: 399–406.

Goodwin, Charles, 1981 *Conversational Organization: Interaction Between Speakers and Hearers*. New York: Academic Press.

Goodwin, Charles, and Alessandro Duranti, 1992 Rethinking Context: An Introduction. In *Rethinking Context: Language as an Interactive Phenomenon*. Alessandro Duranti and Charles Goodwin, eds. Pp. 1–42. Cambridge: Cambridge University Press.

Goodwin, Marjorie H., 1990 Byplay: Participant Structure and the Framing of Collaborative Collusion. In *Les Formes de la conversation*, Vol. 2. B. Conein, M. de Fornel, and L. Quéré, eds. Pp. 155–180. Paris: CNET.

Grice, Herbert Paul, 1975 Logic and Conversation. In *Syntax and Semantics, Vol. 3: Speech Acts*. P. Cole and N. L. Morgan, eds. Pp. 41–58. New York: Academic Press.

Halliday, Michael A. K., and Ruqaiya Hasan, 1976 *Cohesion in English*. London: Longman.

Happé, Francesca G. E., 1991 The Autobiographical Writings of Three Asperger Syndrome Adults: Problems of Interpretation and Implication Theory. In *Autism and Asperger Syndrome*. Uta Frith, ed. Pp. 207–242. Cambridge: Cambridge University Press.

— 1994a *Autism: An Introduction to Psychological Theory*. Cambridge, MA: Harvard University Press.

— 1994b An Advanced Test of Theory of Mind: Understanding of Story Characters' Thoughts and Feelings by Able Autistic, Mentally Handicapped, and Normal Children and Adults. *Journal of Autism and Developmental Disorders* 24: 129–154.

— 1995 Understanding Minds and Metaphors: Insights from the Study of Figurative Language in Autism. *Metaphor and Symbolic Activity* 10 (4): 275–295.

— 1996 Studying Weak Central Coherence at Low Levels: Children with Autism Do Not Succumb to Visual Illusions: A Research Note. *Journal of Child Psychology and Psychiatry and Allied Disciplines* 37 (7): 873–877.

Happé, Francesca G. E., and Eva Loth, 2002 "Theory of Mind" and Tracking Speakers' Intentions. In Pragmatics and Cognitive Science. Theme issue. *Mind and Language* 17 (1–2): 24–36.

Heritage, John, and Marja-Leena Sorjonen, 1994 Constituting and Maintaining Activities Across Sequences: And-Prefacing as a Feature of Question Design. *Language in Society* 23 (1): 1–29.

Hughes, Claire, 2001 Executive Dysfunction in Autism: Its Nature and Implications for the Everyday Problems Experienced by Individuals with Autism. In *The Development of Autism: Perspectives from Theory and Research*. Jacob A. Burack, T. Chapman, N. Yirmiya, and P. R. Zelazo, eds. Pp. 255–275. Mahwah, NJ: Erlbaum.

Jefferson, Gail, 1978 Sequential Aspects of Storytelling in Conversation. In *Studies in the Organization of Conversational Interaction*. Jim Schenkein, ed. Pp. 219–248. New York: Academic Press.

Kasari, Connie, with Peter Mundy, and Nurit Yirmiya, 1990 Affective Sharing in the Context of Joint Attention Interactions of Normal, Autistic, and Mentally Retarded Children. *Journal of Autism and Developmental Disorders* 20: 87–100.

Keenan, Elinor Ochs, 1977 Making it Last: Uses of Repetition in Children's Discourse. In *Child Discourse*. Susan Ervin-Tripp and Claudia Mitchell-Kernan, eds. Pp. 125–138. New York: Academic Press.

— 1983 Conversational Competence in Children. In *Acquiring Conversational Competence*. Elinor Ochs Keenan and Bambi B. Schieffelin, eds. Pp. 3–25. Boston, MA: Routledge and Kegan.

Keenan, Elinor Ochs, and Bambi B. Schieffelin, 1976 Topic as a Discourse Notion: A Study of Topic in the Conversations of Children and Adults. In *Subject and Topic*. C. N. Li, ed. Pp. 335–384. New York: Academic Press.

Kintsch, Walter, and Teun A. van Dijk, 1978 Towards a Model of Text Comprehension: A Constructive Integration Model. *Psychological Review* 95: 363–394.

Kremer-Sadlik, Tamar, 2001 How Children with Autism and Asperger Syndrome Respond to Questions: An Ethnographic Study. Ph.D. dissertation. University of California, Los Angeles.

— 2004 *How Children with Autism and Asperger Syndrome Respond to Questions: A "Naturalistic" Theory of Mind Task*. Discourse Studies 6 (2): 185–206.

Krug, David A., with Joel R. Arick and Patricia J. Almond, 1978 *Autism Screening Instrument for Education and Planning*. Portland: ASIEP Educational.

Landa, Rebecca 2000 Social Language Use in Asperger Syndrome and High-Functioning Autism. In *Asperger Syndrome*. Ami Klin, Fred V. Volkmar, and Sara S. Sparrow, eds. Pp. 125–155. New York: Guilford Press.

Le Couteur, Ann, with Michael Rutter, Catherine Lord, Patricia Rios, S. Robertson, Mary Holgrafer, and John McLennan, 1989 Autism Diagnostic Interview: A Standardized Investigator-Based Instrument. *Journal of Autism and Developmental Disorders* 19: 363–387.

Leslie, Alan M., and Uta Frith, 1988 Autistic Children's Understanding of Seeing, Knowing and Believing. *British Journal of Developmental Psychology* 6: 315–324.

Levinson, Steven C., 1983 *Pragmatics*. Cambridge: Cambridge University Press.

— 2000 Presumptive Meanings: The Theory of Generalized Conversational Implicature. Cambridge MA: MIT Press.

Li, Charles, and Sandra Thompson, 1976 Subject and Topic: A New Typology of Language. In *Subject and Topic*. C. Li, ed. Pp. 457–489. New York: Academic Press.

Loveland, Katherine A., and Susan Landry, 1986 Joint Attention and Language in Autism and Developmental Language Delay. *Journal of Autism and Developmental Disorders* 16: 335–349.

Loveland, Katherine A., and Belgin Tunali, 1993 Narrative Language in Autism and the Theory of Mind Hypothesis: A Wider Perspective. In *Understanding Other Minds: Perspectives from Autism*. Simon Baron-Cohen, Helen Tager-Flusberg, and Donald J. Cohen, eds. Pp. 247–266. Oxford: Oxford University Press.

Loveland, Katherine A., Robin McEnvoy, Belgin Tunali, 1990 Narrative Story Telling in Autism and Down Syndrome. *British Journal of Developmental Psychology* 8: 9–23.

Mercier, Celine, L., Laurent Mottron, and Sylvie Belleville, 2000 A Psychosocial Study on Restricted Interests in High-Functioning Persons with Pervasive Developmental Disorders. *Autism* 4 (4): 406–425.

Mundy, Peter, Marian Sigman, and Connie Kasari, 1993 The Theory of Mind and Joint Attention Deficits in Autism. In *Understanding Other Minds: Perspectives from Autism.* Simon Baron-Cohen, Helen Tager-Flusberg, and Donald J. Cohen, eds. Pp. 181–203. Oxford: Oxford University Press.

Ochs, Elinor, 2002 Becoming a Speaker of Culture. In *Language Acquisition and Language Socialization: Ecological Perspectives.* C. Kramsch, ed. Pp. 99–120. London: Continuum.

Ochs, Elinor, and Bambi B. Schieffelin, 1989 Language Has a Heart. *Text* 9 (1): 7–25.

Ochs, Elinor, with Tamar Kremer-Sadlik, Karen G. Sirota, and Olga Solomon, 2004 *Autism and the Social World: An Anthropological Perspective.* Discourse Studies 6 (2): 147–183

Ochs, Elinor, with Tamar Kremer-Sadlik, Olga Solomon, and Karen G. Sirota, 2001 Inclusion as a Social Practice: Views from Children with Autism. *Social Development* 10 (3): 399–419.

O'Neill, Daniela K., and Francesca G. E. Happé, 2000 Noticing and Commenting on What's New: Differences and Similarities Among 22-Month-Old Typically Developing Children, Children with Down Syndrome and Children with Autism. *Developmental Science* 3 (4): 457–478.

Plaisted, Kate C. 2000 Aspects of Autism that Theory of Mind Cannot Explain. In *Understanding Other Minds: Perspectives from Developmental Cognitive Neuroscience,* 2nd edn. Simon Baron-Cohen, Helen Tager-Flusberg, and Donald J. Cohen, eds. Pp. 222–250. Oxford: Oxford University Press.

Prizant, Barry M., 1983 Language Acquisition and Communicative Behavior in Autism: Toward an Understanding of the "Whole" of It. *Journal of Speech and Hearing Disorders* 48: 296–307.

Prizant, Barry M., and Amy M. Wetherby, 1987 Communicative Intent: A Framework for Understanding Social-Communicative Behavior in Autism. *Journal of American Academy of Child Psychiatry* 26: 472–479.

Quirk, Randolph S., with Sidney Greenbaum, Geoffry Leech, and Jan Svartik, 1985 *A Comprehensive Grammar of the English Language.* London: Longman.

Russell, James, 1997 How Executive Disorders Can Bring About an Inadequate "Theory of Mind". In *Autism as an Executive Disorder.* James Russell, ed. Pp. 256–304. Oxford: Oxford University Press.

Sacks, Harvey, 1987 On the Preferences for Agreement and Contiguity in Sequences in Conversation. In *Talk and Social Organization.* G. Button and J. R. E. Lee, eds. Pp. 54–69. Clevedon, UK: Multilingual Matters.

— 1992 *Lectures on Conversation,* 2 vols. Oxford: Blackwell.

Schegloff, Emanuel A., 1972 Sequencing in Conversational Openings. In *Directions in Sociolinguistics: The Ethnography of Communication.* John J. Gumperz and Dell Hymes, eds. Pp. 346–380. New York: Holt, Rinehart, and Winston.

— 1980 Preliminaries to Preliminaries: "Can I Ask You a Question." *Sociological Inquiry* 50: 104–152.

— 1990 On the Organization of Sequences as a Source of "Coherence" in Talk-in-Interaction. In *Conversational Organization and Its Development.* Bruce Dorval, ed. Pp. 51–77. Norwood, NJ: Ablex.

Schegloff, Emanuel A., and Harvey Sacks, 1973 Opening up Closings. *Semiotica* 8: 289–327.

Schieffelin, Bambi B., 1983 Talking Like Birds: Sound Play in a Cultural Perspective. In *Acquiring Conversational Competence.* Elinor Ochs and Bambi B. Schieffelin, eds. Pp. 177–184. Boston, MA: Routledge and Kegan Paul.

Searle, John R. 1969 *Speech Acts: An Essay in the Philosophy of Language.* Cambridge: Cambridge University Press.

Shah, Amitta, and Uta Frith, 1993 Why Do Autistic Individuals Show Superior Performance on the Block Design Task? *Journal of Child Psychology and Psychiatry* 34: 1351–1364.

Sigman, Marian, and Lisa Capps, 1997 *Autism: A Developmental Perspective.* Cambridge, MA: Harvard University Press.

Solomon, Olga, 2000 Narratives of a Different Order: Autistic Children's Use of Connectives. Paper presented at the Sixth Annual Conference on Language, Interaction, and Culture, Westwood, CA.

— 2001 Narrative Introduction Practices of Children with Autism and Asperger Syndrome. Ph.D. dissertation. University of California, Los Angeles.

Sperber, Dan, and Deidre Wilson, 1986 *Relevance: Communication and Cognition.* Cambridge, MA: Harvard University Press.

— 2002 Pragmatics, Modularity, and Mind-Reading. *Mind and Language* 17 (1–2): 3–23.

Tager-Flusberg, Helen, 1993 What Language Reveals about the Understanding of Other Minds in Children with Autism. In *Understanding Other Minds: Perspectives from Autism.* Simon Baron-Cohen, Helen Tager-Flusberg, and Donald J. Cohen, eds. Pp. 138–157. Oxford: Oxford University Press.

— 1996 Brief Report: Current Theory and Research on Language and Communication in Autism. *Journal of Autism and Developmental Disorders* 26: 169–172.

— 2000 Language and Understanding Minds: Connections in Autism. In *Understanding Other Minds: Perspectives from Developmental Cognitive Neuroscience*, 2nd edn. Simon Baron-Cohen, Helen Tager-Flusberg, and Donald J. Cohen, eds. Pp. 124–149. Oxford: Oxford University Press.

Tager-Flusberg, Helen, and Marcia Anderson, 1991 The Development of Contingent Discourse Ability in Autistic Children. *Journal of Child Psychology and Psychiatry* 32: 1123–1134.

Tager-Flusberg, Helen, and Susan Calkins, 1990 Does Imitation Facilitate the Acquisition of Grammar? Evidence From Autistic, Down Syndrome, and Normal Children. *Journal of Child Language* 17: 591–606.

Tager-Flusberg, Helen, and Kate Sullivan, 1995 Attributing Mental States to Story Characters: A Comparison of Narratives Produced by Autistic and Mentally Retarded Individuals. *Applied Psycholinguistics* 16: 241–256.

Turner, Michelle, 1997 Towards an Executive Dysfunction Account of Repetitive Behavior in Autism. In *Autism as an Executive Disorder.* James Russell, ed. Pp. 57–100. Oxford: Oxford University Press.

Volkmar, Fred R., and Ami Klin, 2001 Asperger's Disorder and Higher Functioning Autism: Same or Different? In *International Review of Research in Mental Retardation: Autism*, Vol. 23. L. M. Glidden, ed. Pp. 83–110. San Diego, CA: Academic Press.

Wechsler, David, 1992 *Manual for the Wechsler Intelligence Scale for Children*, 3rd edn. New York: Psychological Corporation.

Wetherby, Amy M., with Barry M. Prizant and A. L. Schuler, 2000 Understanding the Nature of Communication and Language Impairments. In *Autism Spectrum Disorders: A Transactional Developmental Perspective.* Amy M. Wetherby and Barry M. Prizant, eds. Pp. 109–141. Baltimore, MD: Paul H. Brookes.

Wing, Lorna, 1996 *The Autistic Spectrum: A Guide for Parents and Professionals.* London: Constable.

Wing, Lorna, and Anthony J. Attwood, 1987 Syndromes of Autism and Atypical Development. In *Handbook of Autism and Pervasive Developmental Disorders.* Donald J. Cohen, Anne Donellan, and Rhea Paul, eds. New York: John Wiley.

Wing, Lorna, and Judith Gould, 1979 Severe Impairments of Social Interaction and Associated Abnormalities in Children: Epidemiology and Classification. *Journal of Autism and Developmental Disorders* 9: 11–30.

CHAPTER 9 Disability: Global Languages and Local Lives

Susan Reynolds Whyte

The universal human experience of misfortune is a central concern for social science, as it is for theology, literature, and medicine – and for us all at some time in our lives. In the 1960s, Clifford Geertz (1966) wrote that suffering raised a Problem of Meaning: a challenge to our capacity to explain and understand. He showed how religions, as systems of symbols, provided meaning in the face of pain and affliction. Since then, the linguistic and narrative turn has encouraged researchers to explore the ways in which people tell stories about their troubles – how they perform them, express them, or refer to them. Wilce (this volume) suggests that the very forms of narrative available for doing this are changing as a result of globalization.

In this chapter, we shall consider the problem from a pragmatic point of view. That is, we shall ask how people deal with misfortune, how different "languages" of affliction dispose them to action, and how they use them. Our example is the problem of disability: an infirmity of the mindful body that inhibits a person's social competence. The significance and management of such infirmities is everywhere embedded in culturally shared ideas about personhood and in social orders of family, gender, and political economy (Ingstad and Whyte 1995). A pragmatic approach requires that we attend to expectations, intentions, and consequences in particular situations: being a landmine amputee in a refugee camp on the Thai-Cambodia border (French 1994) or being a paralyzed anthropology professor in New York (Murphy 1987). At the same time, such an approach provides a way of analyzing the global disability movement, a powerful spread of ideas and ideals that mobilizes people through a language of hope and justice. Pragmatism leads us to ask who uses this discourse and with what consequences. When we talk about "global" languages, we must ask how emplaced actors with "projects" invoke globalism (Tsing 2000) and which kinds of actors are able and willing to engage in such practices.

Pragmatism looks towards consequences: what could happen? And in matters of misfortune, hope is an important part of dealing with possible outcomes (Whyte

2001). For individual selves, hope is an orientation towards a meaningful future in which one's sense of possibility, being, and worth is enhanced. But hope is a social as well as an individual psychological affair. As Ghassan Hage has argued, society is the distributor of hope in that it generates life meanings (what is worth hoping for) and allots possibilities "by offering people the opportunities to 'make a life for themselves,' to invest and occupy and thus create and give social significance to their selves" (Hage 2002: 16). In situations of misfortune, the availability of hope and opportunity for making a life is a pressing matter. What we want to consider here is how new languages of disability and hope have arisen, how they are socially distributed, and how they are differentially taken up and used.

LANGUAGE AND PROGRAMS

"Full participation and equality" was the slogan adopted by the UN General Assembly when it launched the Year of Disabled Persons in 1981. The UN campaign to raise awareness about the rights of people living with disability was extended from a year to a decade. When the UN decade ended, the African Decade for the Disabled was declared. During the last twenty years, we have seen the global spread of a language about disability used to express a set of interrelated ideas. Keeping to the metaphor of language, we could say that the current language of disability has several idioms.

There is the idiom of justice that refers to the human rights of people with disabilities. They are set out in documents such as the *Standard Rules on the Equalization of Opportunities for Persons with Disabilities* adopted by the UN in 1993. The Standard Rules, though not legally binding, are guidelines for UN member states about law and policy to "guarantee rights to education, work, social security, and protection from inhuman or degrading treatment" (Bickenbach 2001: 574). New legislation passed in many countries in the 1990s protects the rights of disabled people. The idiom of rights is fundamental to the language, and also to the programs and practices, through which this "ideoscape" (Appadurai 1990) flows across national boundaries.

Professional idioms of disability have evolved in the same period for the use of health practitioners and policy makers, social workers and welfare managers, and international development experts. Sociologists have pointed out the tension between medical and social models of disability within professional idioms (Barnes et al. 1999; Williams 2001). While an older professional approach to disability focused on impairments and functioning of the individual body, the social model points at the way societies impede or facilitate people classified as disabled. The combination of these approaches was the foundation for a standard manual for diagnosis of the kind favored by biomedical professionals. The International Classification of Impairments, Disabilities, and Handicaps appeared in a first version in 1980 and a second in 1999. The idea was to describe not just a medical pathology, but the social context that makes an organic impairment into a handicap. Thus, terms like accessibility, barriers, assistive devices, and mainstreaming are part of this vocabulary, as well as visual impairments and functional deficits.

Rehabilitation as a specialized field was established in Europe and North America during the struggle for professional authority over the damaged bodies of World War I. However, the current language has evolved a new idiom for those working in developing countries: that of Community Based Rehabilitation. CBR principles are that people should be helped in their own communities, using inexpensive and locally appropriate means, and mobilizing family and neighbors. Enablement, empowerment, local resources, community participation, and community ownership are key words. CBR, like community participation in general, is an idiom used in low income countries or concerning marginalized target groups.

A third important idiom is that of identity politics. The emphasis on rights and on the social as well as medical aspects of disability has been accompanied, indeed made possible by, self-awareness and assertion on the part of people with disabilities. Self-respect, pride, solidarity, and demands for recognition and autonomy are recurring terms in statements like: "These natives can speak for themselves"; "Nothing about us without us"; "Deaf culture/deaf pride"; and "Don't disablize us." This idiom is important in mobilization for change because it offers a new self-understanding to the individuals who are most motivated to advocate for change. A positive identity as disabled is a hopeful and worthy position from which to act. This is the idiom that most clearly links the subjectivity of individuals with social and political movements at community, national, and international levels.

The metaphors of language and idiom underline the interrelatedness of the three versions of disability talk distinguished above. Because there is a pragmatics as well as a semantics of language, the metaphor should also serve as a reminder that kinds of discourse are associated with groups of actors, types of institution, and varieties of practice. Lawmakers, politicians, organizations for and of disabled people, community development officers, consumer groups, and donor agencies use particular idioms to create an image of problems and strategies for dealing with them. The issue of how language is used, by whom and with what effect, is a central theoretical concern.

DISCOURSES AND THEIR USES

One of the most ambitious attempts to trace a cultural history of disability discourse in Western civilization is that by Henri-Jacques Stiker. In his *Corps infirmes et sociétés* (1982; English translation 1999) he traces discourses on the infirm body and practices of exclusion through a series of eras: the notions of evil and impurity in ancient Jewish culture, the ideal of suffering and charity of the Middle Ages, the ensuing medical classification of disability and the Enlightenment program of special education, followed by the discourse of rehabilitation that characterized most of the twentieth century. Perhaps one might add to that the discourse on human rights that is common today. Stiker paints with a broad brush; his sociology is Durkheimian, focusing on social bonds and forms of inclusion and exclusion (Ravaud and Stiker 2001). For him, the language of difference reflects and shapes social forms. But he does not examine how different interest groups or individuals might use language differently, nor does he consider the flows and disjunctures between different social formations.

In contrast, recent work on colonial history (Vaughan 1991; Comaroff and Comaroff 1992) has shown how Europeans imposed a language of misfortune upon their colonial subjects. That is, they identified problems, such as the disabling disease leprosy, and gave them a moral value in relation to their own discourses on subject peoples. Christian missionaries saw leprosy as a biblical disease: the taint of sin to be healed, if not cured, by faith. It has been argued that horror of leprosy was introduced into many African societies by missionaries convinced that lepers must be segregated in camps and asylums where they were subject to a regime of discipline and Christian faith. In these situations, leprosy came to be colored by the status of the caretakers; it was a religious rather than a medical condition, an occasion for charity and spiritual care. Examining historical materials, Watts suggests "the missionaries needed their lepers more than the lepers needed them" (Watts 1997: 72–73).

A historical study of leprosy and identity in Mali provides a rich picture of how definitions of problems and solutions played out. Eric Silla quotes from diaries and other materials that show the combination of pity and religious zeal with which missionary nuns cared for lepers. He notes: "Melodramatic encounters with needy Africans, especially lepers, provided perfect copy for published reports and mission magazines directed at potential donors in Europe" (Silla 1998: 94). The missionaries needed the lepers, perhaps. But Silla goes further to trace the perspective of the lepers, who also had needs and recognized opportunities. He suggests the Sisters exaggerated the significance that conversion had for patients who understood little of the rituals. What they did understand was the food, lodging, attention, and prospect of a proper burial offered by the missionaries. Through interviews with former patients and careful examination of sources, Silla shows how people given an identity as lepers and confined in a leprosarium, developed a sense of community. At the same time they pursued their own projects, often in opposition to the program of those who defined the problem and managed the solution.

We are faced with two questions about discourses and their uses. First, what is the logic of representation for those who speak a discourse with confidence? Here we need to explore how the definition of a problem and its proposed solution are connected, even interdependent. The solution needs the problem; the missionaries needed the lepers. Perhaps the solution even creates the problem (in the sense that a leprosy program creates lepers). In holding out a vision of what to hope for, a discourse implies a definition of what is real and meaningful. Secondly, what is the practical logic for people who are the object of the discourse? The actual effect of a discourse, the extent to which it shapes a situation, depends on a combination of local political and social structures, values, and personal agendas. The hope and possibility perceived by those on the receiving end may not be congruent with the intentions of the givers. Both of these issues can be considered pragmatically – in terms of the consequences (convenient, irrelevant, life changing) they have for actors in different positions and situations.

To ask about consequences is not necessarily to be cynical about ideals and good intentions. It should allow a more nuanced understanding of the social distribution of hope. This in turn provides a better basis for a critical constructive discussion of social values, and a better foundation for remaking institutions that might achieve those values.

REPRESENTING PROBLEMS AND SOLUTIONS

Arthur and Joan Kleinman (1997) explore the ways in which the representation of problems and solutions distorts the experience of those whose lives are pictured.

They suggest that suffering is represented in images that can be commodified through the media, professionalized and distanced through analytical tools such as Disability Adjusted Life Years, or denied by authoritarian regimes. While the first two representational strategies may be used to mobilize humanitarian intervention and rational public health programs, they also have other effects. By identifying and decontextualizing a problem, they dispose would-be helpers to imagine solutions in the form of pre-defined assistance to passive victims. They ignore whatever resources or concerns exist in the local world that is being so unidimensionally represented.

The solution and the representation of the problem evoke one another. Perhaps it is inevitable that any idiom of disability simplifies and exaggerates. An "exposure document" published to commemorate the 50th Anniversary of the Universal Declaration of Human Rights gives examples of violations of specific articles of the Declaration, and of the UN Standard Rules on Equalization of Opportunities for Persons with Disabilities. The violations are located by naming a country, a region, or simply by identifying the violation as "Worldwide." As an example of the infringement of civil rights, the following is entered:

> The disadvantages of disabled women begin in childhood, because parents look on their disabled daughters as a curse from God. There is no hope of you bringing cows and other material wealth to the family, since it is widely believed that you will not marry because you are disabled. As if that was not enough, parents say they won't waste their money sending disabled children to school when they don't have enough resources to send their able-bodied children. (DAA 1998: 17)

Under this, which is a quotation from an unidentified source, is written simply, "Uganda." The implication is that this is generally the case in Uganda and that there is a need for a rigorous enforcement of disability rights in the country. A disability rights organization identifies the problem as one with which it is uniquely able to deal. By underlining the prejudice of families, they make the problem one of attitude rather than resources, and thus create it as an issue that can be treated through legal and educational means.

Benedicte Ingstad (1995, 1997, 2001) characterizes the emphasis on negative cases and generalizations about families and local communities abusing people with disabilities as the "myth of the hidden disabled." She traces this myth, which we could call a professional idiom, from documents of the WHO to local rehabilitation workers in Botswana where she did field research. I have heard the same language in Uganda, from professionals who decry the ignorance of local people, and their shame over, neglect of, or outright cruelty towards a disabled family member. The representation of the problem calls for, and gives value to, the solution. For community-based rehabilitation programs funded by international donors, the existence of prejudice and abuse underlines the need for a community program of information and mobilization of support. For the frontline rehabilitation worker, the idiom works differently. The ignorance of the "target group" throws into relief the enlightenment of the professionals and supports their authority. As Ingstad points out, it also serves to focus attention on the failings of families, rather than on their efforts to overcome problems they experience.

The assumption of this approach to representation is that representations make a difference. They shape subjectivity in the sense of how people understand and act upon situations. But to what extent do they do that, and for which categories of actors? Kleinman and Kleinman point to the way that images of misfortune influence an international public. Ingstad focuses on local situations in which professional helpers picture an unenlightened target group. If we want to pursue the second question mentioned above, about how the people who are the objects of a discourse on misfortune might use it, then we must take up empirical examples. For the particularities of context and perspective are central to this question. My cases come from Uganda. Before turning to the hopes and actions of specific people in that country, it is necessary to describe the scene upon which they are acting.

From Global Language to National Vernacular

The new discourse on disability was appropriated somewhat differently in different developing countries. For some, the historical link between rehabilitation and the ravages of war was relevant. The powerful symbolic value of bodies maimed by machetes, guns, grenades, and landmines has been important for governments making a fresh start after conflicts (Nicaragua, Zimbabwe, Sierra Leone). For Uganda, the path took a different turn even though it too suffered war and has a landmine problem.

Uganda is considered one of the most progressive countries in Africa in terms of policy on disability. It has adopted a discourse on rights and political inclusion that is almost unparalleled. The appropriation of the international discourse can be understood in the light of a conjuncture of national political developments and international donor activity.

After 15 years of civil war, the National Resistance Movement (NRM) came to power in 1986 with a strong program of social development and equal opportunity. The constitution that was ratified in 1995 ensures the rights of women, children, minorities, and persons with disabilities and requires the state to take affirmative action in favor of marginalized groups (Article 32). Article 35 states:

> (1) Persons with disabilities have a right to respect and human dignity and the State and society shall take appropriate measures to ensure that they reach their full mental and physical potential.
> (2) Parliament shall enact laws appropriate for the protection of persons with disabilities.

Uganda is governed by a series of councils at levels from villages through sub-counties and districts. The Local Government Act 1997 requires that disabled persons be represented at every level and politicians proudly point out that there are 47,000 disabled councilors in local government councils. The Parliamentary Act of 1996 provides special seats for disabled people: in the national parliament there are currently four regional seats and one earmarked for women with disabilities. The Universal Primary Education Act 1996, which provided free primary education for four children per family, specified that disabled children must be given priority.

But the NRM inherited an economically weak state and has been highly dependent on donor funding. Overall, donors cover about half of the annual budget; the proportion is much higher in the areas of health and social welfare. This means that multilateral, bilateral, and NGO projects and programs have been extremely influential since 1986. They have employed and trained thousands of Ugandans and in this way international development discourses have been nationalized. Donor funded conferences, workshops, courses, and seminars are a national industry. The idiom of disability rights adopted by the government has been constantly reinforced by the donor funded dissemination of ideas, resources, people, and language. Mostly the flow is from North to South, but funds have also facilitated South–South exchanges at international conferences. These "global" movements have been institutionalized in various forms. DANIDA funded the Uganda National Institute of Special Education, which trains teachers and rehabilitation workers at a beautiful complex near the national teachers' college. The Norwegian Association of the Disabled supports a community-based rehabilitation program implemented through government community development officers. Schools for the deaf or blind and rehabilitation training institutes anchor and reproduce a language and a set of practices about disability. So do the NGOs, though not quite as firmly or permanently.

Perhaps the most striking phenomenon on the current disability scene in Uganda is the plethora of non-governmental organizations that have appeared in recent years. Many of these came into being with help from sister organizations in Europe and most have some kind of outside funding. They include Disabled People's Organizations (DPOs) whose membership is disabled people, as well as organizations for the disabled. Some are for all kinds of disabilities, others are specific. They are international, nationwide, and local: the Ugandan Society for the Disabled Children, Action on Disability and Development, the Community Based Rehabilitation Alliance, Sight Savers International (the Royal Commonwealth Society for the Blind), the Uganda National Association of the Deaf, the German Leprosy Relief Association, the Uganda Parents Association for the Deaf Blind, the Uganda Special Olympics Association, and the Gulu Landmine Survivors Association. All of these and many more come under the umbrella of the National Union of Disabled Persons of Uganda, which has branches in every district.

The people who work in disability projects and those who are leaders of disability organizations speak the language fluently, as was evident at a conference on Community Based Rehabilitation held in Uganda in 2000. The Minister of Gender, Labor, and Community Development spoke of efforts to "empower people with information so they can demand for services." For her, this was a matter of rights, not needs, welfare, and pity. The rehabilitation professionals emphasized identifying community beliefs, involving the beneficiaries to ensure ownership, and social integration of their clientele. People with disabilities complained that they, and especially their organizations, were not invited to plan, implement, and evaluate projects: "Our needs are defined by others, professionals disadvantage us by taking decisions for us." The metaphor of speaking a language is not just an academic figure. One of the speakers called upon the government to implement its declarations on disability rights. "Government should walk our talk," she said.

The people who talk this talk are engaged in identifying problems that match solutions, and by enacting solutions creating an awareness of certain kinds of problems. In principle there is a kind of teleology at work by which problems are shaped toward solutions. Building a freeway brings traffic. Offering accessible and effective treatment of epilepsy in Africa creates "epileptics" in the sense that people identify and act as epilepsy patients. If medicines for AIDS treatment were available for free in Uganda, many people would be willing to undergo testing and accept an identity as HIV positive. But it is not quite that simple.

In countries that are poor and donor dependent like Uganda, institutions and solutions often function badly. The talk may not walk at all. Some people are in a stronger position than others to access solutions and formulate appropriate problems. Those who talk the talk and make it meaningful for their lives are mostly urbanites (Charlton 1998: 107–111) and often people with certain kinds of disabilities (physical rather than mental). Men more than women, educated more than illiterate, middle class more than poor are able to take up the global languages in their vernacular forms. The crooked path that a "global" discourse takes as it moves from the UN in New York, or DANIDA in Copenhagen, to poor and uneducated people living lives in villages and small towns can be illustrated with the stories of two Ugandan women.

OLIVE AND VERONICA

Olive K. heads an organization founded in 1994: the Association of Parents of Children with Hydrocephalous and Spina Bifida. This is a relatively rare condition, and in a country with thousands of polio survivors and people who have lost sensory and mental abilities because of disease, hydrocephalous is hardly recognized as a problem. The association functions in many ways like patient organizations in Europe and North America: it gives counseling and moral support and acts as a consumer group evaluating treatment options and devices (the shunts). But it also serves as a conduit for funds and knowledge. On the one hand, it lobbies national and international organizations for support, which is allowing it to send representatives to the 13th International Conference on Spina Bifida and Hydrocephalous, and to organize a study tour of eight social workers to the UK and USA. On the other hand, it works to identify cases and encourage treatment in Uganda. The chairman acknowledges that this part is difficult. People have erroneous views; parents hide their children and deny the diagnosis. Many cannot afford the cost of the operation at an NGO hospital in the Eastern Ugandan town of Mbale, and the subsequent follow up. To top it off, impersonators have taken pictures of hydrocephalic children and used them to solicit funds for their own purposes.

Olive is a nodal point for globalization in that she and the organization she started are creating awareness and introducing new terms to Uganda. She herself is strong on social and cultural capital: she is a teacher at a prestigious senior secondary school, articulate and self-confident; her husband is the medical superintendent of one of Kampala's major hospitals. When they gave birth to a child with a disability, they dealt with their own misfortune in a way that could be shared with others. They have found a mode of treatment in Uganda; they try to locate children who would benefit and convince their parents to accept the treatment and their definition of the problem. They are creating hydrocephalous as a possible identification and plan of action. Ideally, the parents should also join the organization and pay the annual membership fee. But people who are poor, uneducated, and living in remoter rural areas are not likely to hear, or to accept the rationality, of their language and practice.

Veronica N. has a life like so many women in rural eastern Uganda. She has borne eight children and two have died. She and her family are subsistence farmers, who have difficulty in getting by. Her husband distills moonshine for people in the neighborhood, but he is paid in kind – an arrangement that supports his alcoholism more effectively than his family. They fit the Ugandan picture of a genuinely poor household: one that must use the wife's only gown as a blanket. Veronica lost her sight in 1983. She blames it on her co-wife, who put sorcery medicine in the hearth, so that the smoke from her cooking would carry it to her eyes. "She was envying my fertility," says Veronica. "She didn't produce any children and finally she left." A white film covered her eyes and her father helped her by applying "African" medicine. She got no biomedical treatment at that time. In 1989 she begged me to find someone who could cure the sickness of her eyes. I brought a nurse with training in eye disease from the local hospital, but he said that there was nothing to be done. Another time, a man with connections, what Ugandans call "technical know who," was courting her sister. He brought her to the local hospital to be examined by the visiting consultant who comes for an eye clinic every few months. Unfortunately, they missed the clinic – either they came on the wrong day or perhaps the surgeon did not show up. Veronica wanted to be cured and she tried to mobilize people with contacts to help her.

One day in 1997 someone from her Local Council brought two strangers to her house: one spoke the local language and the other was a *musungu*, a "European." They gave her a white stick and showed her how to use it to tap her way around the home and along the road. "But they did not examine my eyes," she complained. They promised to come back, but never did. Veronica likes her white stick, though when she is in a hurry she extends the stick by having a child go in front holding the other end. (Guide children with sticks rather than guide dogs with harnesses are the standard mobility aid for most rural visually impaired people.)

Is blindness an important part of Veronica's identity? Probably not – at least not until recently. When I spent time with her in 2001, she was still hoping to be cured some day. She did not know any other blind person, nor did she blame her problems on her blindness or feel that people discriminated her for that reason. I asked what her husband said about her eyes, and she answered indirectly. "I produce children, my co-wife was barren. Sometimes we quarrel and I go home to my parents. But my husband insists that I come back since he paid the bridewealth." When pushed on whether he abuses her because she cannot see, she repeated that they quarrel sometimes and he can insult her. Once when she asked him for money to buy paraffin so the family could have a little light at night, he retorted that she was useless, she certainly did not need a lamp. But she seemed to regard this as an insult thrown in the heat of an argument, more than an indication of a devalued blind identity. Asked whether her neighbors sympathized with her, she replied: "Yes, because we are so poor and my husband is bad and doesn't help the family." Veronica's understanding of her problems and her sense of what she could hope for were not formulated in terms of the language of disability rights. A central meaning of her life was having children, and her inability to provide well for them (linked to her husband's failures) was her misfortune.

Toward the end of 2001 and in 2002, a new identity was offered to Veronica. She was called for meetings of *baleme* (lame people, a term now conventionally used for disabled) in her country. When I spoke to her in 2002, she could not remember the name of the organization that had arranged the meetings. But she recounted that they were asked to report their problems, and she had requested help in sending her children to school, and in getting means of support, a proper house, food, clothes for the children, and bedding for the family. With great satisfaction she showed me the goat she had been given. Later, she was invited to a meeting at the district headquarters, about 35 km away. She managed to borrow money for transport (no advance was given, the cost was refunded later), but the prospect of having to try to raise money for fare every time there was a meeting meant that she "feared" to be chosen as an officer for disabled people at the district level. Also, there was the problem of having to pay a membership fee (about 75 US cents) and obtain a photo for the membership card. She was unsure about what she was to be a member of, but when I mentioned NUDIPO (National Uganda Disabled People's Organization) she smiled in recognition. When I asked what she learned at the meetings, she said: "They taught us to continue forming groups and what to eat."

Olive and Veronica are in vastly different situations. Olive is at home in a cosmopolitan world of English and Luganda. She not only knows the term disability and the language in which it belongs. She also knows hydrocephalous and spina bifida and is teaching them to others. Veronica speaks her local language, which has no word that translates well as disability – only words like blind, deaf, lame. Olive is attending meetings in the UK and the US, while Veronica finds it almost impossible to get to the district headquarters. Olive founded an organization devoted to giving information and treatment about a particular disability. Veronica was "found" by an organization; she does not remember its name, nor does she talk about it in terms of her disability. What is important for her is the prospect of material help for her family. Her worst problem may not be her blindness, but that was what entitled her to receive help. Perhaps in time she will identify herself as a blind person and learn to speak the language of disability rights.

THE PRAGMATICS OF DISABILITY

Even though global discourses on disability have reached Uganda, and even though there are many organizations and programs, these discourses and programs are unequally relevant to people. Many have heard, or just hopefully imagine, that there is something to be had. Some, like Veronica, imagine a cure; others hope for opportunities or assistive devices. They try to find someone who can serve as a contact, who can tell them where to go, put them in touch, or best of all, mobilize resources and take action. It is extremely difficult to find out what possibilities there are for a small deaf child, or to get calipers and a wheelchair for a polio survivor, when the family lives far from town and the services function poorly and cost money.

Solutions to problems shape the identification of problems to the extent that people see a practical opportunity. Doing a study in eastern Uganda on the response of families with mentally disabled children to the new opportunity of sending them to local schools, a researcher describes how people sought her out, when rumor spread about "the white woman concerned with such children."

They expected to find a "NGO" with a plan for help, but again and again I had to
disappoint them . . . I had no means of curing the children, no means of sending them
to a boarding school, no financial help to offer in the meantime, and I seldom even had
much advice to give. (Jacobsen 2000: 22)

The parents in Jacobsen's study connected her to schooling and the world of
donors, and therefore, as she writes, "it was unavoidable that the kind of hope they
saw and expressed in interaction with me was connected to schooling and external
help." "While I tried to find out how people in Molo engaged in efforts of making
their mentally disabled children improve, my very presence offered a hope and a
potential means for that engagement." Jacobsen considers that people not only told
her the stories of their children, but lived those stories in interaction with her in that
they tempered them hopefully for her ears. They told her of their satisfaction that
their children were going to school now, in case she might be able to provide help
in connection with schooling (Jacobsen 2000: 34). Parents were talking of their
mentally disabled children as the sort of children who required schooling. But more
than that, in making their lives and those of their children, they were pragmatically
looking for the kinds of relationships and opportunities that might fit into the story
and turn it in a happy direction.

MOBILIZATION ON THREE WHEELS

Busia is a town on the Uganda–Kenya border, a rowdy, lively kind of place – on the
Uganda side at least. It is famous for business, the cross-border trade, in which commodities like sugar and maize go to Kenya while manufactured items like mattresses,
cement, diesel, soap, and cigarettes come into Uganda. In the 1980s and early 1990s,
black market business was big on this stretch of the border. The first polio survivors
on big hand crank tricycles got started transporting for traders in the early 1990s.
Traders, who sent them with money to buy goods across the border, trusted them and
the customs officials tended not to bother them. Soon polio survivors came to work
in Busia from all over the country. They came from rural areas where there were no
opportunities for earning money. Almost all of them bought their own tricycles (no
donor organization helped them) and through their earnings they managed to marry
and start families. What they accomplished they did as others did: with help from
family members, by nurturing contacts, and by hard work. Very few had had any
involvement with disability projects; one or two had been a short time at vocational
training centers but had not been able to use that training for anything. They made
their lives as entrepreneurs. Their accomplishment was a spontaneous initiative to
exploit a niche where withered legs and tricycles gave a comparative advantage.

In a sense they became "disabled" in 1994 when they joined together to establish
the Busia Disabled Association (BDA). The immediate reason for doing so was that
the Uganda Revenue Authority started to get tough in 1993, as part of the NRM
campaign to increase the government's revenue basis. The tricycle transporters joined
together to deal with the URA and protect their business interests. About that time
the Ugandan version of the disability movement offered some useful opportunities.
A disabled man named Wandera, who had been working with a community-based

rehabilitation project, involved himself in the BDA. He was dynamic and had learned language and strategy during his years with the donor funded CBR project. At the first opportunity, he was elected to the District Council as representative for the disabled. He encouraged them to do "cultural activities" like putting on shows where they made music and danced on their hands and held wheelchair races. He got the Municipal Council to give them office space. Most importantly, he was their articulate advocate with the customs authorities. As he said:

> I sensitize the URA and other district officials. Every month I go to the border to talk to the officials. They look at it in terms of smuggling, but when they are sensitized, they can understand that it's better for people with disabilities to be self-sufficient. When the Revenue Protection Police come and arrest them, we ask them to let them go with their goods. We say, "Don't disablize our disabled people."

Wandera even spoke up to President Museveni, when on a visit to Busia the president mentioned the tricyclists as smugglers. "The government gives us no alternative," he told Museveni. With satisfaction, Wandera pointed out to us: "There are no disabled beggars in Busia. There used to be many, especially on Fridays. We told them not to shame us." Perhaps this is a Ugandan version of identity politics, choosing to be neither beggars, nor smugglers, but independent disabled people.

Wandera talks the talk and when he called all the members of the Busia Disabled Association to meet us, we heard others using familiar phrases such as "disability is not inability." Some addressed the group as "my fellow disabled" and told how they welcomed newcomers and supported each other in times of trouble. But they talked to us hopefully and pragmatically too. Tricycle transport is hard work, the URA officers are unreasonable in demanding payment of tax on the goods, and earnings are small and unreliable. "If only we had a project, a vocational training school and workshop, credit facilities to branch out into other business, a big project to employ us, money to educate our children, donors. We need donors." It was the Ugandan dialect of the global language of disability.

For the Busia tricyclists, the language of disability has use in particular contexts. They are speaking it with government officials to negotiate an entitlement, an extra advantage, in the cross-border trade. One might say they are using a rationality, a way of reasoning, expressed in a language – not only to work for justice in some abstract sense – but for something they hope for: to make a life with a family and an income. In their own homes, such talk was noticeably absent. They were family men and businessmen, introducing their wives and children, talking of business opportunities – a small restaurant, the milk trade.

CONCLUSION

This chapter began with a description of a global language about disability – global not just in the sense that it is widespread, but also in that it asserts universality. In the names of human rights, professional public health, democracy, common humanity, and self-respect, it appeals beyond particular interests and denies its own origin in particular contexts. It should be relevant to everyone everywhere. At the same time, such a language, like other discourses about the management of social issues, construes problems in ways appropriate to the solution it offers.

Anthropologists concerned with international health have drawn attention to the disjunctures between global formulations of health policy and the uneven local playing fields in which they must be implemented (Whiteford and Manderson 2000). Transnational agencies, donors, practitioners, and scholars generate languages of universal affliction experience. While they are often developed in countries of the global North, they are taken up in countries of the South, with very different histories and social conditions. There is an uneven playing field between countries. More than that, within countries, social actors play on different fields. Education, urban or rural residence, and economic resources affect the circumstances in which people have to deal with problems, and their cares may not be congruent with the ways that problems are formulated in global languages.

A pragmatic approach focuses on the concerns that situated actors seem to have in particular situations. It asks how the available version of a global language might be relevant or not to people encountering difficulties and hoping for a fuller sense of social being. It examines the question of relevance and hope empirically by following people over time and trying to see what they see of significance and potential in a white stick, a CBR program, or an organization of disabled people. It listens to their talk and notices who speaks and in which contexts and with which effects.

A general contrast can be made between representational (including discursive) and experiential approaches in cultural anthropology (Linger, this volume; Whyte 1995). Studying discourse, we examine the changing ways in which it is possible to communicate and thus to shape subjectivity and shared assumptions. Focusing on experience, we appreciate individual consciousness and personal situation/history. A pragmatic approach adds another dimension to that contrast in that it draws attention to the way that people dealing with problems orient themselves and act in terms of a possible future. They do so in the context of a social patterning of opportunity and hope that is as important for cultural psychology as the study of discourse and experience.

REFERENCES

Appadurai, Arjun, 1990 Disjunction and Difference in the Global Cultural Economy. *Public Culture* 2: 1–24.

Barnes, Colin, with Geoff Mercer and Tom Shakespeare, 1999 *Exploring Disability: A Sociological Introduction*. Cambridge: Polity Press.

Bickenbach, J. E., 2001 Disability Human Rights, Law, and Policy. In *Handbook of Disability Studies*. Gary Albrecht, Katherine Seelman, and Michael Bury, eds. Pp. 565–584. Thousand Oaks, CA: Sage.

Charlton, James, 1998 *Nothing About Us Without Us: Disability Oppression and Empowerment*. Berkeley: University of California Press.

Comaroff, Jean, and John Comaroff, 1992 *Ethnography and the Historical Imagination*. Boulder, CO: Westview Press.

DAA, 1998 *Are Disabled People Included?* London: Disability Awareness in Action.

French, Leslie, 1994 The Political Economy of Injury and Compassion: Amputees on the Thai–Cambodia Border. In *Embodiment and Experience: The Existential Ground of Culture and Health*. Thomas J. Csordas, ed. Pp. 69–99. Cambridge: Cambridge University Press.

Geertz, Clifford, 1966 Religion as a Cultural System. In *Anthropological Approaches to the Study of Religion*. M. Banton, ed. Pp. 1–46. London: Tavistock.

Hage, Ghassan, 2002 *Against Paranoid Nationalism: Searching for Hope in a Shrinking Society*. Sydney: Pluto Press.

Ingstad, Benedicte, 1995 Mpho ya Modimo – a gift from God: Perspectives on "Attitudes" toward Disabled Persons. In *Disability and Culture*. Benedicte Ingstad and Susan Reynolds Whyte, eds. Pp. 246–263. Berkeley: University of California Press.

— 1997 *Community-Based Rehabilitation in Botswana: The Myth of the Hidden Disabled*. Lewiston, NY: Edwin Mellen Press.

— 2001 Disability in the Developing World. In *Handbook of Disability Studies*. Gary Albrecht, Katherine Seelman, and Michael Bury, eds. Pp. 772–792. London: Sage.

Ingstad, Benedicte, and Susan Reynolds Whyte, eds., 1995 *Disability and Culture*. Berkeley: University of California Press.

Jacobsen, C., 2000 *Giving All Children a Chance: A Study of Personhood, Childhood, and Educational Integration for Children with Mental Disabilities in Uganda*. Master's thesis, University of Copenhagen.

Kleinman, Arthur, and Joan Kleinman, 1997 The Appeal of Experience, The Dismay of Images: Cultural Appropriations of Suffering in Our Times. In *Social Suffering*. Arthur Kleinman, Veena Das, and Margaret Lock, eds. Berkeley: University of California Press.

Murphy, Roger, 1987 *The Body Silent*. New York: Henry Holt.

Ravaud, J. F., and Henri Jacques Stiker, 2001 Inclusion/exclusion: An Analysis of Historical and Cultural Meanings. In *Handbook of Disability Studies*. Gary Albrecht, Katherine Seelman, and Michael Bury, eds. Pp. 490–512. London: Sage.

Republic of Uganda, 1995 *Constitution of the Republic of Uganda*. Kampala: Government of Uganda.

Silla, E., 1998 *People Are Not the Same: Leprosy and Identity in Twentieth-Century Mali*. Portsmouth, NH: Heinemann.

Stiker, Henri-Jacques, 1982 *Corps infirmes et sociétés*. Paris: Aubier Montaigne.

— 1999 *A History of Disability*. W. Sayers, trans. Ann Arbor: University of Michigan Press.

Tsing, Anna, 2000 The Global Situation. *Cultural Anthropology* 15 (2000): 327–360.

Vaughan, Megan, 1991 *Curing their Ills: Colonial Power and African Illness*. Cambridge: Polity Press.

Watts, Sheldon J., 1997 *Epidemics and History: Disease, Power, and Imperialism*. New Haven, CT: Yale University Press.

Whiteford, L. M., and L. Manderson, eds., 2000 *Global Health Policy, Local Realities: The Fallacy of the Level Playing Field*. Boulder, CO: Lynne Rienner.

Whyte, Susan Reynolds, 1995 Disability Between Discourse and Experience. In *Disability and Culture*. Benedicte Ingstad and Susan Reynolds Whyte, eds. Pp. 267–291. Berkeley: University of California Press.

— 2001 Subjectivity and Subjunctivity: Hoping for Health in Eastern Uganda. In *Postcolonial African Subjectivities*. Richard Werbner, ed. Pp. 171–190. London: Zed Press.

Williams, G., 2001 Theorizing Disability. In *Handbook of Disability Studies*. Gary Albrecht, Katherine Seelman, and Michael Bury, eds. Pp. 123–144. London: Sage.

PART III Ambivalence, Alienation, and Belonging

> Who, then, is this other to whom I am more attached than to myself, since, at the heart of my assent to my own identity it is still he who agitates me?
>
> (Lacan 1977: 172)

Throughout history, a politics of identity and difference, notions of self and other, and a language of "us" and "them" have shaped descriptions of people from other cultures and subcultures. Whether immigrants, nations, or network societies, one of the most pressing problems in today's world is the exclusion of people from communities that may already be more or less disenfranchised. Identities, subjectivities, socialization, and ritual practices, including spirit possession, witchcraft, and the use of substances, all become sites of contest, evocation, and deployment in larger debates about who belongs to our communities.

Tied to these debates are questions about the subjective experiencing of ambivalence, alienation, or belonging. Do global processes such as the exportation of biomedicine and new technologies, or "development agencies" with their canned approaches to health and education, fragment or colonize identities? Are people bricoleurs, able to accommodate, assimilate, or reject such processes? How are identities, subjectivities, and the emotions they evoke channeled in today's world?

Contributors to part three offer new concepts and methods for studying modern identifications, subjectivities, and ritual practices. They question the extent to which identities and subject positions may carry transgressive or oppositional weight, but beyond a focus on epistemological or ontological primacy, contributors explain the extent to which identities and subjects play constitutive rather than merely reflective roles in their relations with others. What does it mean to be a person in today's world? Whether sedimented or new, what are the histories and reverberations of global and local processes, identifications, subjectivities, and practices?

CHAPTER 10 Identity

Daniel T. Linger

IDENTITY AND CULTURAL ANTHROPOLOGY

In a hybrid world, identity has, paradoxically, become a pressing popular and scholarly concern. The accelerated circulation of people, goods, and messages has kindled widespread anxieties. Unease over identity feeds ambivalent attitudes toward cosmopolitanism, ethnic mixing, immigration, standardization, international investment, and supranational organization. It motivates, at least in part, innovations in tradition, anti-globalization protests, ethnic renovation projects, revisions of history, and, more menacingly, the xenophobic hatreds that have embroiled much of the planet in intractable wars.

At the same time, quickened communication has multiplied identity possibilities. A bigger menu of identity options would seem to offer greater opportunities for self-discovery, self-affirmation, and self-fashioning. Proliferating identities also afford foundations for new social movements defending groups – women, gay men, lesbians, ethnics, disabled people, and countless others – whose concerns were formerly ignored or obscured. But the explosion of identity alternatives also has its dangers, for it can be disorienting, alienating, and divisive.

The more the world shrinks, the more complicated it becomes to find one's place. However one evaluates these phenomena, their importance is evident. No wonder identity has drawn growing attention from social researchers.

The study of identity occupies a key position in contemporary work in cultural anthropology. In response to the historical trends outlined above, ethnographers have begun to scrutinize newly recognized, increasingly salient, and emergent concepts of relatedness, including gender, ethnic, national, and "postmodern" or "transnational" identities. Of course, intellectual disciplines have distinctive concerns as well. The recent ethnographies of identity, intrinsically valuable as they are, engage compelling debates within anthropology. In particular, identity has become a site of intense theoretical disputes over the nature and locus of meaning. Such disputes show no sign of impending resolution, and the close examination of identity, especially in a fluid moment such as the present one, sharpens them further. Are meanings, above all identities, fixed or dynamic, symbolic or psychological, public or personal? Does the contemporary study of identity invite a reformulation of such questions? The ethnographic inquiries are, in short, inevitably ensnared in and productive of theoretical issues.

This essay explores theoretical disagreements, paradigmatic studies, and new directions in the anthropological analysis of identity. I attend particularly to controversies over the instability and proliferation of identities. I argue that significant future work will require anthropologists to think through the *model of the person* that underpins all approaches to meaning, all attempts to link public and personal domains, and thus, *a fortiori*, all accounts of identity.

Discourse vs. Culture, Representation vs. Experience

Let me first, in very broad strokes, sketch the theoretical controversies, turning later to ethnographic matters. For decades, cultural anthropology has taken meaning as its primary analytical object, for the most part abandoning earlier projects to inventory traits, things, and behaviors. Cultural anthropologists have, however, differed among themselves as to what meaning is and where to look for it. Two general viewpoints have emerged, which I will call *representational* (or *public*) and *experiential* (or *personal*). Within the representational perspective, I also distinguish between *symbolic* and the newer *discursive* approaches. Identity has proved to be a point of contention within the representational camp (that is, between symbolic and discursive anthropologists), and, more generally, between representational and experiential camps.

Representational and experiential positions should be thought of as ideal types: many accounts, even when they clearly lean in one direction or the other, cannot resist equivocations. Such equivocations are symptomatic of the elusiveness of "meaning," a phenomenon that seems, depending on one's point of view, either extrinsic or intrinsic to human beings. I will initially treat the two perspectives as distinct, but they are not necessarily incompatible, and, I will later argue, the most interesting new studies are likely to grapple with their inherent tension.

Representational approaches dominate the field of cultural anthropology. Practitioners of symbolic anthropology, the classic representational practice, try to decipher public language, images, rituals, and performances. Their usual analytic procedure, termed "interpretation" or "thick description" by Clifford Geertz (1973) and his followers, has strong affinities to literary criticism. As Geertz once put it, "The culture of people is an ensemble of texts . . . which the anthropologist strains to read over the shoulders of those to whom they properly belong" (1973: 452). In recent years, however, many anthropologists, sympathetic to interpretivism but politically and intellectually drawn to issues of social oppression and change, have become wary of Geertz's analogy on the grounds that it suggests cultural stasis or, at the very least, overstates cultural inertia. They have adopted a more dynamic practice, tracing the emergence and circulation of "discourses," which they view for the most part as politically charged, generative linguistic formations. In its discursive variant, representational theory has thus acquired a temporal dimension, and with it a strongly political and linguistic slant. Nevertheless, the foundational assumption of representational anthropology persists in the work of the discursivists: that meaning is at root a public phenomenon, produced through the circulation of symbolic carriers amenable to interpretive analysis.

Though always influential and currently ascendant, representational approaches have not gone unchallenged. The dissent dates at least to Edward Sapir's (1917) critique of Theodore Kroeber's notion of culture as a "superorganic" entity, an evolutionary phenomenon detached from individual human beings. In later essays Sapir continued to warn against mistaking "fantasied universes of self-contained meaning" – that is, social scientific abstractions such as "culture" – for the complexities and immediacies of human lives (1949b: 580–581; see also 1949a). Following Sapir, later critics have questioned representational anthropology in all its guises for its focus on public tokens of meaning taken to be primordially social phenomena. In short, they have mistrusted reifications of collective abstractions disconnected from personal experience and biography (for recent statements of this position, see Strauss and Quinn 1997; D'Andrade 1995; Linger 1994; Parish 1996; Sperber 1996; Shore 1996; Rapport 1997; Bloch 1998).

The dissenters – psychological anthropologists and a variety of writers who favor phenomenological, humanist, and existential approaches – often disagree among themselves but generally place greater emphases on mental processes, individual particularities, experiential immediacies, and personal agency. They typically view culture as a distributed subjective phenomenon (Wallace 1961; Schwartz 1978) rather than social inscription or "a cloud over Cincinnati," in Julie Tetel's memorable phrase (quoted in Strauss and Quinn 1997: 19.) Instead of trying to read public texts or text analogues in the mode of literary criticism, such anthropologists mobilize psychological theories to infer personal subjectivities from evidence such as in-depth interviews and other forms of interpersonal engagement. In its most self-conscious form, this practice has been called "person-centered ethnography" (Levy 1994; Hollan 1997; Linger 2001).

In sum, the core issues dividing representational and experiential theorists are: Is meaning best regarded as symbolic-discursive or mental stuff? Is meaning located in public representations or in minds? And for those seeking to bring representational and experiential perspectives into conversation, a further question arises: If meaning can be seen as both public and personal, how might we conceive possible links between the two realms?

Identity emerged as a site of heated anthropological debate during the late twentieth century largely because it was a good topic through which to argue these theoretical issues. Inside the representational camp, discursive theorists, whose approach underscored the fluidity of meaning and the ubiquity of political and moral contestation, were eager to emphasize the multiplicity, instability, and even strategic invention of identities. For them, the proliferating identities and identity hybrids of the late twentieth century pointed to the inadequacy of conventional treatments, which froze tribes, ethnic groups, genders, and nations, along with their associated habits and cultures, pristinely in time. And identity, an object with a seeming double valence (as social category and as personal experience), was also excellent grist for the theoretical mills of experience oriented anthropologists anxious to underline their reservations about or differences from representational positions which, they claimed, reduced people to categorical specimens, and therefore disregarded the active personal forging of diverse and unique selves. I now take a closer look at this changing treatment of identity, beginning with the shift in the representational camp.

IDENTITY AS A DISCURSIVE PRODUCT

For most of the history of their discipline, anthropologists have treated identity as relatively unproblematic. That is, they have viewed group and culture as coterminous, mutually constituting, relatively enduring, and located in a bounded space. So "the Balinese," who live "in Bali," have "Balinese culture," cockfights and teknonyms, and an aversion to cumulative interactions; "the Japanese," living "in Japan," have "Japanese culture," status rituals and honor and moral debt. Although by mid-century some anthropologists had already begun to offer unorthodox analyses, suggesting that identities could be surprisingly labile (Leach 1977; Mitchell 1956) and that shared culture was not their defining aspect (Barth 1969), the commonsense model "a group with a culture" really began to fray only toward the century's end. Not coincidentally, this was also a period of intensive theorizing about "postmodernity" and "globalization."

According to any number of philosophers and social critics, globalization throws huge numbers of transnational migrants into radically disorienting social and cultural circumstances. Even those who stay at home inevitably bump into foreigners, foreign ways, foreign products, foreign enterprises, and foreign media. Postmodern theory claims that the rapid, relentless circulation of people and representations produces a novel array of extraordinary effects, including scrambled identities, deterritorialized meanings, and hybrid cultures.

The argument suggested to many interpretive anthropologists that their culture theory was outmoded, that traditional symbolic anthropology had lost its way in this inexorably relativizing world characterized by movement, fluidity, and crossings. Couched in exhilarating, high-flown language, the theoretical fascination with move-ment suggested that the holistic view of culture – a system of symbols passed from one generation to the next within a spatially circumscribed group – was a musty relic of an obsolete episteme. Was it clear anymore, for example, who was and wasn't "Japanese," when "Japanese people" lived everywhere? Could "Japanese culture," saturated with garish McDonald's and Hollywood films, still be regarded as a coherent, self-contained, enduring entity? And, as sushi bars and karaoke parlors proliferated in San Francisco and São Paulo, how could one any longer claim that "Japanese culture" was confined to "Japan"? Cultural anthropologists found them-selves hesitating before such questions, unsure how to think about cultures and identities in a rapidly shrinking planet.

Amplifying the theoretical uncertainty associated with globalization was the turn, increasingly evident in the 1980s, to literary and historical modes of social analysis, a shift impelled by some feminist writers, poststructuralist historians, and anthro-pological critics such as Clifford and Marcus (1986), all of whom, like the philoso-phers of postmodernity, emphasized the contingency of identities and meaning. The postmodernists' perceptions of epochal change dovetailed with the feminists' and poststructuralists' move to new analytical techniques, encouraging a theoretical innovation in the representational position. Emerging "discourses," rather than static "culture," became for many the prime object of anthropological accounts.

The substitution of "discourse" for "culture" is not just a change in terminological fashion. It signals skepticism over the Platonic connotations of the term "culture," dissatisfaction with fixed interpretations of symbol systems, and a corresponding commitment to regard meanings as multiply formulated, power-infused, and exceptionally volatile. The chief concern of anthropology therefore becomes the ongoing *production* of meanings through ever-changing categories and narratives. An important corollary of this new position is that identity categories themselves, traditionally the unquestioned starting points for ethnographic studies of culture and society, are likewise unstable and should therefore be treated as objects of discursive analysis rather than simple group markers.

If identities have become unsettled, cultures itinerant, and borders permeable, the formerly commonsense foundations of representational anthropology – its "who," "what," and "where" – are up for grabs. In short, the conceptual entities of previous theorizing – bounded groups and their associated cultural units – are now treated by discursive anthropologists as historical products; and those products, above all identities, become the new foci of their ethnographic studies.

EXPERIENCE ORIENTED RESPONSES

For those convinced that the world is in a state of extraordinary flux, for those attuned to the long sweep of history, and for those holding strong views of human plasticity, discursive theorizing has considerable appeal. But one of its effects has been to further privilege the public realm at the expense of the personal. That is, discursive theorists, like the interpretivists they criticize, treat identity as an overwhelmingly extrapersonal phenomenon. They either downplay its subjective aspects or regard them as derivative of public representations. Their approach yields "subject positions," or what one might call "virtual identities" – identity niches carved out by public discourses. Implicitly, the personal appropriation of identities is a secondary, or residual, phenomenon: persons occupy, or are prodded or coerced into, one of the shifting identity niches afforded them. But the suggestion that discursive analysis exhausts the process of identity-making seems untenable to many psychological anthropologists and other experience oriented theorists.

Such theorists have questioned the premise that lived identities correspond to or are simply cobbled from virtual identities. Few psychological anthropologists, whatever their theoretical leanings, can accept a model that reduces persons to effects of discourse or, at most, rational actors. And indeed, some other anthropologists, not necessarily self-identified as psychological anthropologists but nevertheless favoring a more complex model of the person (based, for example, in existential or phenomenological philosophy), find the representational approach uncongenial. Increasingly restless, many have sought to devise viewpoints that move persons into the orbit, or even to the center, of studies of identity.

Especially vocal have been those who emphasize the importance of "individuality," the "human *a priori*" (Rapport and Overing 2000: 187). Note that Rapport and

Overing distinguish "individuality," a theoretically enabling claim about human beings, from "individualism," a historically contingent ideology. Individuality "is tied inextricably to individual consciousness, to that unique awareness, and awareness of awareness, which is the mark of human embodiment" (2000: 185). This claim underwrites Anthony Cohen's (1994) call for an "alternative anthropology of identity," a project endorsed by several other European anthropologists, including Nigel Rapport (1997) and Martin Sökefeld (1999). Cohen (1994) insists it is incoherent and discriminatory to deny to others the self consciousness anthropologists inevitably assume for themselves. For Cohen, the stereotypical distinction between egocentric Western and sociocentric non-Western selves is both simplistic and invidious, an ideological move that borders on bad faith (see also Spiro 1993). Instead, he argues, the study of identity is in need of "decolonization of the human subject" (Cohen 1994: 162), a revolutionary reorientation that takes as its point of departure the self conscious individual rather than collective representations.

Nigel Rapport, decrying the "impersonalization" (1997: 23) of social science, has issued a philosophical manifesto consonant with Cohen's position. Rapport's *Transcendent Individual*, based in a human-rights perspective, looks askance at the notion of collective identity, promoting instead person-centered studies emphasizing "the individual's conscious and creative engagement with . . . sociocultural environments" (1997: 1). Martin Sökefeld (1999), likewise refusing to reduce an individual to a mélange of virtual identities, proposes a distinction between identity and self. Sökefeld discusses Ali Hassan, a man from Gilgit, Pakistan. A revelatory incident for the ethnographer is his friend's visit to a relative on the occasion of a wedding, an uneasy encounter that Ali navigates by invoking, qualifying, and retreating from various of his identities associated with religion and descent. In a word, Ali Hassan orchestrates his identities, adapting them to the changing contours of his interactions with others. Sökefeld draws a general conclusion: "It is impossible to conceive of the actions of individuals embracing a plurality of identities without referring to a self" (1999: 418) that underpins and integrates those identities. That self, Sökefeld contends, is a panhuman entity capable of reflection, reflexivity, and agency.

Sökefeld, like Cohen and Rapport, thus rejects the "cultural and social determinism [that] lurks behind [the usual] conceptualization of non-Western selves" (1999: 419). These authors all see identity as a product of self-conscious agency operating with (but not determined by) public representations circulated within a social milieu. Overtly or by implication they criticize Durkheimian sociology, functionalist social anthropology, Geertzian symbolic anthropology, and top-down discursive approaches, favoring instead existential and humanist philosophers (Nietzsche, Sartre, Rorty) and recuperating long-neglected theorists of the self (Hallowell, Bateson, G. H. Mead).

The current fault line between representational and experiential approaches separates discursivists, who privilege emergent public identity formations, from person-centered anthropologists, whose analyses focus on personal appropriations of identities. The following section, though not intended to be a comprehensive survey, seeks to highlight clear and contrasting claims offered in three conspicuous genres of the contemporary ethnography of identity: studies of gender, studies of nationality and ethnicity, and studies of postmodernism and globalization.

Exemplary Studies and Contrasting Claims

Gender identities

Over the last several decades, feminist scholars have increasingly questioned the naturalness of gender categories, arguing for the most part that gender is a socially and temporally variable discursive construct. In cultural anthropology, such scholarship has precedents in the discipline's longstanding skepticism toward received categories. A standard move in anthropological analysis – perhaps *the* standard move – has been relativization: the unmasking of ethnocentric assumptions about what is natural or universal. Earlier, anthropologists' critical attention focused on, for example, supposedly universal psychological features such as the Oedipus complex (Malinowski 1955), adolescent turmoil (Mead 1961), and the emotions (Lutz 1988). In a landmark critique, David Schneider (1980) forcefully argued that even kinship, apparently nature incarnate, is entirely a symbolic construct. Influential historians, too, notably Michel Foucault, insisted that the most intimate realms of human experience, including sexuality (Foucault 1990), are discursively determined and historically contingent.

Feminist writers, building on Simone de Beauvoir's famous aphorism "One is not born, but rather becomes, a woman" (1957: 267), brought similar critiques to gender. A now sizable and strongly entrenched corpus of feminist theory and ethnography asserts that gender categories, roles, meanings, and hence identities are neither biologically given nor natural, but are instead the products of historically changing, power-infused discursive practices (important representative works by anthropologists include Rosaldo and Lamphere 1974; di Leonardo 1991; Ortner 1996).

Nancy Chodorow's *The Power of Feelings* (1999) is respectful of this body of relativizing feminist work but takes a different tack, moving in the direction of individual subjectivities. Chodorow mobilizes psychodynamic theory and her own clinical observations to show how gender meanings are personalized. Note that she does not wholly oppose her work to the discursively oriented feminist scholarship described above. She criticizes psychoanalysis for its tendencies to generalize unjustifiably about gender differences, and she gives academic feminism its due. Hence, she emphasizes gender inequalities and contestation over gender meanings, and recognizes that the subjectivities of the women she discusses "build on historically situated, cultural, discursive constructions of gender" (1999: 91). At the same time, however, Chodorow rejects an approach that infers subjectivities directly from public sources.

Consider Chodorow's comparison, drawn from her clinical interactions, of the women she calls "J" and "B." In J's case, "male–female difference is central to the meaning of gender, and an emotion, anger, is one key to gender construction" (1999: 79). For J, male anger reflects invulnerability, insouciance, and freedom, whereas female anger is bad, destructive, and symptomatic of vulnerability. The fantasy of being male is J's defense against feelings of powerlessness and dependency. B, on the other hand, harbors "images of her mother and maternal femininity [that] are almost sordid" (1999: 82). Her mother, she feels, was a weak woman who could not satisfy her children's needs. Her psychological defense is splitting – good, pure father vs. bad, impure mother – but this leaves B with a second-order problem of shame over her own femininity. Chodorow (1999: 83) concludes:

> B's construction of gender has an emotional configuration that differs in emphasis from J's. B does not want to be, and does not fantasize herself as, a man. Rather, she emphatically wants to have a man. Emotionally, cognitively, and in conscious fantasy she emphasizes heterosexual femininity. B's idealization of men revolves around how they can rescue her; for J, men's and boys' seeming self-sufficiency and ability not to care are central. For B, shame and excitement are emotionally central to her gender feelings; for J, anger becomes a defining criterion of gender.

Note that both women's appropriations of gender identities respond to gender concepts, practices, and inequalities common in American society. Yet, as Chodorow (1999: 90) emphasizes, it would be a mistake to reduce their gendered subjectivities to purely linguistic or cultural constructions:

> None of the women I discuss simply entered the realm of the symbolic or placed herself within a cultural discourse or unequal society or polity. From birth to the present, all have actively constructed their gender with intense individual feelings and fantasies . . . and with characteristic defensive patterns . . . This personal cast and individual emotional tonality pervade any person's sense of gender.

In short, for Chodorow, gender identities are both cultural and personal: they cannot be reduced to either public representations or to intrapersonal inevitabilities. Rather, people build those identities as they engage representations and work their way along individual life trajectories.

National and ethnic identities

With the recent historical turn, national and ethnic identities have likewise come to seem increasingly transient and fictitious. The publication in the early 1980s of two important works on nationalism (Anderson 1983; Hobsbawm and Ranger 1983) occasioned a flood of research on "imagined communities" and "invented traditions." The phrase "imagined community" points to the fact that most members of a nation have never met: that, in other words, the creation of national solidarity requires extraordinary ideological work. A strong corollary is that nations do not naturally arise on preexisting foundations of shared blood, language, or culture; rather, historically situated *narratives* of sharing and consequent illusions of collective identity build the bases for solidarity. The imagined communities literature therefore suggests that nations, like all collectivities, are entities conjured through symbols, rituals, and narratives.

An outstanding ethnography in this discursive vein is Richard Handler's *Nationalism and the Politics of Culture in Quebec* (1988). Handler explicitly goes beyond his mentor David Schneider in insisting on the artificiality of relatedness. Schneider sought to identify the enduring core symbols of American kinship, but Handler discovered in Quebec an active *production* of symbols in what was essentially a cultural vacuum:

I no longer claim to be able either to present an account of "the" culture or to demonstrate its integration, but will focus instead on cultural objectification in relation to the interpenetration of discourses – that is, on attempts to construct bounded cultural objects, *a process that paradoxically demonstrates the absence of such objects.* (Handler 1988: 14–15; emphasis in original)

Unlike American kinship, the stuff of Québécois nationalism is crafted, invented, and propagated by elite specialists. "Quebec" is an empty category, widely assumed to have content but bereft of it until the culture-makers get to work:

To be Québécois one must live in Quebec and live as a Québécois. To live as a Québécois means participating in Québécois culture. In discussing this culture people speak vaguely of traditions, typical ways of behaving, and characteristic modes of conceiving the world; yet specific descriptions of these particularities are the business of the historian, ethnologist, or folklorist. Such academic researches would seem to come after the fact: that is, given the ideological centrality of Québécois culture, it becomes worthwhile to learn about it. But the almost *a priori* belief in the existence of this culture follows inevitably from the belief that a particular human group, the Québécois nation, exists. The existence of this group is in turn predicated upon the existence of a particular culture. (Handler 1988: 39)

For Handler, then, national identity is an ongoing, historically situated discursive production, not a static web of symbols and meanings. That is why he eschews a history of Quebec, for to provide one would be to collaborate in the very project he is attempting to analyze (and, it would seem, criticize). The account he presents is a *history of the discursive production of Quebec*, quite a different matter.

But like gender identities, national identities may also be approached from a personal angle. Such an approach emerges at the edges of Anastasia Karakasidou's (1997) sensitive, powerful study of the imposition of Greek identity in ("Greek") Macedonia. Karakasidou's controversial book, which earned her death threats, is an indictment of the Greek nation-state. The state's crime is a brutal lie: an invention of memory that rides roughshod over the past lived by Macedonia's inhabitants. In essence, a region that was highly diverse in ethnicity, language, and religion was reconstituted by the Greek state as "always Greek." Historical events were rewritten: the burning of a village by Greek soldiers became, in the official account, an atrocity perpetrated by Bulgarians. Like Handler, Karakasidou details the invocation of a community in public discourse delivered through the politically powerful voices of historians, educators, propagandists, and ministries. But if providing cultural substance to a nascent "Quebec" is the business of Handler's discursive specialists, in this case the operation is more sinister: the Greek state's determination to erase and redraft the past. Unlike Handler, Karakasidou forwards – indeed, highlights – a historical account of her own. She contrasts the imposed past with a lived historical past that has left haunting emotional residues in those who traversed it.

One such person is Paskhalina, "the Bulgarian," an old woman of Slavic ancestry. Karakasidou interviews Paskhalina on several occasions. Paskhalina begins by shaping her life story to the normative past; but in later interviews she presents a different (and by implication more authentic) tale, in which she recalls Greek brutalities at odds with official narratives. In Paskhalina we see an intersection, or collision, between state-sanctioned representations of the past and personal memories. Paskhalina's stories are inconsistent, suggesting that although the official narratives have intruded into her recall, they have not fully displaced memories grounded in life experience.

Paskhalina's experienced identity, which shifts between and splices "Greek" and "Bulgarian," suggests that personal appropriations of public narratives are complex and dynamic products of biography, memory, and consciousness. My own ethnography of Japanese-Brazilians who have gone to Japan to live and work amplifies and refocuses Karakasidou's account by, in effect, attending closely to many Paskhalinas. Nine people – workers, middle-school students, and cultural brokers such as bilingual teachers and factory translators – appear in *No One Home* (Linger 2001). Through the medium of ethnographic interviews each explores issues of personal ethnic identity that arise in face-to-face interactions in the factory, at school, and in leisure sites. I conclude that feelings of Brazilianness usually intensify among these transnational migrants who formerly, in Brazil, often considered themselves Japanese.

But to stop with this general observation would be to miss the most important point. The specific, emotionally charged meanings of the interviewees' ethnic identities are the biographically contingent, somewhat unpredictable products of their reflections on their particular experiences in Japan. Thus Bernardo Kinjoh, a former executive turned factory worker and carpenter, incorporates Brazilian "freedom" and Japanese "responsibility" into his cosmopolitan identity. Miriam Moreira, a middle-school student, astounded and injured by her Japanese colleagues' disdainful ignorance of Brazil, harbors Brazilianness, which she identifies with "human warmth," as secret knowledge. For Naomi Mizutake, a bilingual teacher in Japanese public schools, Brazil is a multicultural, multiracial homeland, her *terra natal*, a place in which she feels at ease. At the same time, Naomi values her Japanese descent, and, when all is said and done, can even occupy a self that transcends both her ethnicities.

Of course, there exist well-known public narratives of Japanese and Brazilian nationality, the former emphasizing blood relatedness and the latter intimate interethnic contact. But my interviewees' identity sentiments cannot be inferred from those identity narratives. Brought to the surface through day-to-day interactions, and further hammered out through the activity of reflective consciousness, such sentiments are highly idiosyncratic transformations and elaborations of public national and ethnic discourses, not simple copies.

Postmodern identities

Finally, writers on postmodernity have suggested that contemporary identities are fragmented, blurred, and unstable, owing to unprecedented speedups in transnational communication, flows of capital, and migration. Earlier theorists – Marx, Weber, Simmel, and others – proposed that modernity, arising after the Protestant Reformation and the Enlightenment and gaining force with the industrial revolution, supplanted the feudal world, first in northwestern Europe and later elsewhere. A swarm of institutional changes accompanied the advance of the capitalist economic system. These included the market, the assembly line, wage labor, class divisions, money exchange, economic and bureaucratic rationalization, and the rise of the nation-state and colonial enterprises. Hand-in-hand with such institutional transformations went supposed changes in subjectivity: increased rationality, the standardization of time and space, the decline of magic and religion, the corresponding rise of pragmatism and utilitarianism, and a growing sense of permanent flux (Marx's "all that is solid melts into air").

Some authors, notably Fredric Jameson (1991), have argued that another shift in Zeitgeist occurred in the late twentieth century, as modernity went into hyperdrive. The new era has been labeled, unimaginatively, postmodernity. Another economic revolution has spawned worldwide electronic media, genetic engineering, and computers; vast empires have been decolonized; workers, refugees, tourists, and adventurers cross national boundaries in massive numbers; and capital too has become aggressively multinational. Above all, postmodernity features "space-time compression": a shrinking of the globe and a quickening passage of time (Harvey 1989).

Like the prophets of modernity, postmodern theorists claim that the institutional upheaval has cultural and subjective correlates. The story they tell goes like this. The accelerated circulation of products, people, and media representations detaches culture from space (a process called "deterritorialization") and generates new hybrid expressive forms (multilingual literatures, mixtures of musical styles, and so on.). Such cultural creolizations are symptomatic, and productive, of postmodern subjectivities, a profusion of attenuated, jumbled identities.

If modernity killed God, postmodernity killed the self. Solid selves, like everything else, have melted into air, replaced by "heaps of fragments" (Jameson 1991: 25). As everything moves and as everyone collides with alien objects, persons, languages, messages, styles, and customs, postmodern people have lost their bearings. Presented with a host of bewildering options, they become experts in identity pastiche. They wander through the identity supermarket, experimenting with possibilities. Their mental state has been called "postmodern schizo-fragmentation" (Jameson 1991: 372), characterized by floating emotions, a persistent sense of anachronism, difficulty in producing coherent self-narratives, and cognitive compartmentalization.

Claudia Strauss (1997) examines the claim that contemporary identities exhibit "schizo-fragmentation." She observes, "at present we have too many discussions of postmodern subjectivities that do not come within hand-shaking distance of any putatively postmodern people" (1997: 370). Strauss closes the distance, seeking out quintessential postmodern people, First-Worlders living in consumerist North America who are employed by multinational corporations. She interviews 15 neighbors of and workers at the Ciba-Geigy chemical plant near Providence, Rhode Island.

Strauss's discussion focuses on the comments of Jim Lovett, a disabled former welder in his sixties who lives near the factory. She identifies three "discrepant cognitive schemas," or "voices," in Lovett's talk: (1) *Can't fight the system*, expressing resentment and pessimism, (2) *Achieving anything you want*, expressing optimism and enthusiasm, and (3) *Feeling responsible for others*, expressing contentment. These "voices" are associated, respectively, with the roles of blue-collar worker, potential capitalist and patriotic American, and father.

Superficially, Lovett looks like Jameson's fragmented subject. Upon closer examination, however, Strauss finds that Lovett's ideas are no "random pastiche": rather, "Lovett's responsible, ethical, caring family man seems to be playing a central narrative role" (1997: 383), a stance rooted in "the emotionally salient early childhood experience of yearning for his father to be involved in the family" (1997: 385). Moreover, his schemas are reworked versions of dominant discourses, not replicas.

Strauss concludes that Jameson is both right and wrong: his description, she claims, "misses the extent to which fragmentation coexists with some integration" (1997: 395). The general moral for anthropologists, she insists, "is to be wary of analyses of consciousness that rest largely on the evidence of high culture, such as the music of John Cage or the architecture of John Portman . . . Anthropologists can make an enormous contribution by studying these effects [of contemporary political economy] comparatively, which will help us go beyond rhetoric about postmodern selves and answer questions about precisely who is being affected, how, and why" (1997: 396).

In sum, I have outlined three arenas – gender, ethnicity, and postmodernity – of contemporary debate over identity. Discursive theorists emphasize the contingency of identities and their social construction through public communication and discourse. They usually treat personal aspects of identity as either correlates of public identities or as more or less irrelevant to the analysis. In contrast, experience oriented anthropologists such as Chodorow, Linger, and Strauss insist that a thorough treatment of the subjective aspect of identity requires serious attention to complex, singular personal worlds.

In the last portion of this essay I argue that *all* treatments of identity, whether representational, experiential, or in between, rely on some assumed model of the person. Making such models explicit, and evaluating their credibility and implications, should therefore be a high priority for identity theorists and ethnographers.

MODELS OF THE PERSON

A model of the person is a proposition about the entity that mediates between public representations and personal subjectivities. The different approaches to identity described above rest upon different assumptions about what human beings are and how they negotiate meaning.

If we include the *null model* (see below) among the possibilities, all accounts of meanings, above all identity meanings, can be said to employ a model of the person. Unfortunately, many authors – especially those who are wary of making psychological claims – leave their models tacit. Tacit models are elusive, and unspecified assumptions are, obviously, especially undesirable when they are central to, and consequential for, an analysis. I want to urge anthropologists to think through what model they are using and why. Below, I lay out some models and briefly explore their implications.

At one extreme, as suggested above, is the null model. The null model proposes that public representations fully constitute subjectivities, inscribing them on a tabula rasa.

This model warrants a strong version of discursive or cultural determinism, an analysis of public communicative forms as, in the words of Clifford Geertz, "vehicles for conceptions" or "embodiments of meaning" (Geertz 1973: 91). The domain of subjectivity is thus, more or less by default, "symbol systems" or "discourses." By implication, personal subjectivities are either derivative of those public representations or else of minor interest. As in Handler's and Foucault's accounts, public discourses would seem to exercise immense power on perceptions and meanings.

A slight elaboration on the null model yields *choice models*. An example of a chooser is the *bricoleur*. The bricoleur, like those who roam the aisles of the postmodern identity supermarket, mixes and matches bits of public representations. The *rational actor* who, on the basis of reckonings of advantage, selects from among subjective niches afforded by the representational environment, is a more calculating version of the bricoleur. Alternatively, persons might be thought of as *tool users*, a trope visible in some practice theories that (following Vygotsky and Bakhtin) stress the mediating functions of language. In sum, choice models emphasize more or less purposeful combination, or means–ends calculation, or practice, an often ill-defined term that suggests directed engagement with public forms. Note that in all these cases representations still have immense force, since they comprise components or chunks of personal subjectivities.

Most psychological anthropologists, and many others as well, find null and choice models unsatisfactory. They certainly do not regard persons as either blank slates or utility maximizers: such reductions seem to ignore or theoretically mutilate complex systems of human consciousness and experience. More sophisticated practice theories (e.g., Holland and Lave 2001), which suggest systemic dynamics such that agents use representations as levers to change themselves, are more attractive, but raise thorny questions of motivation. More robust options range widely, and it is not my intent here to provide an exhaustive inventory or to evaluate the variants. Nevertheless, it will be useful to consider briefly several of the possibilities discernible in the studies I have cited in this chapter.

As indicated, some anthropologists, such as Cohen, Rapport, Sökefeld, and Overing, argue for a *consciousness* (or *individuality*) *model* that strongly emphasizes awareness, reflection, imagination, creativity, and personal agency. For such theorists, consciousness should be the point of departure for both sociocultural anthropology and psychology, fields that in any case can only be separated on arbitrary grounds. In other words, mediating between public representations and subjectivity is an active, creative, self-conscious, biographical human agent; no interpretation of symbols can yield an account of subjectivity, which is irreducibly personal.

The consciousness model has profound implications for the analysis of identity. It is implicit in Karakasidou's treatment of Paskhalina and, more strongly, in Norma Field's (1993) provocative discussion of Japanese dissenters. It is explicit in the appeal to "reflective consciousness" that underwrites my discussion of Japanese-Brazilian identities (Linger 2001). Reflective consciousness, which encompasses the capacity for "self consciousness" so strongly emphasized by Cohen (1994), can generate "hierarchic discontinuities" (Bateson 1972: 252) in perception that permit selves to operate on multiple levels. Hence, as I argue in *No One Home*, one can be "Japanese" at one moment, "Brazilian" at another; "someone who is sometimes Brazilian and sometimes Japanese" at yet another; and, finally perhaps, "someone who experiments with identities" (Linger 2001: ch. 17). I am dealing with a population of transitory global migrants, exemplary "postmodern subjects." But to characterize their various identity constellations as merely fragmented, as in discursive accounts of postmodernity, would be to flatten and mystify the panoply of coherent, dynamic, distinctive, multi-leveled identity patterns generated by each person's reflective consciousness.

The possibilities for modeling persons are, of course, endless. Psychological anthropologists have long developed elaborate models within psychodynamic and cognitive paradigms. Nancy Chodorow's study of gender identities, for instance, presents a variant of a *psychodynamic model*, emphasizing the importance of what she regards as universal psychological processes of transference, projection, introjection, and fantasy. Claudia Strauss offers a *cognitive model*, portraying her Rhode Island informants as idea-makers and users, motivated by interrelated conceptual schemes. Although some, especially those associated with various post- forms of theorizing, might condemn consciousness, psychodynamic, and cognitive models as "essentialist," I do not think the accusation carries much sting. As I have stressed throughout, the use of *some* model – null, rational-actor, existentialist, cognitive, psychodynamic, whatever – is unavoidable. A null model is undeniably a strong model: it seems as "essentialist" as any other, and more far-fetched than most. Moreover, none of the experience oriented writers takes the naive position that persons are hermetic units, sealed off from their social environments. The point they reiterate and underline is that the public and the personal are open systems, connected to each other. No experience oriented anthropologist, in other words, is so naive as to employ a null model of society. The question is not whether one endorses a model of the person, but whether the model endorsed is credible and productive of insights. By making such models explicit, at the very least they become readily available for critique and refinement.

SUMMARY AND FUTURE DIRECTIONS

A model of the person is the heart and soul of any analysis of identity, and the pivot of anthropological theories of meaning more generally. Specifying such models will be a useful first step in the elaboration and refinement of the theoretical link between sociopolitical formations and subjectivities, an area of enormous current interest. Contemporary ethnographies of identity attentive to this crucial issue, several of which I have discussed above, offer important, suggestive guidelines for future studies.

Some assumption about human beings is inevitable in any anthropological account. The question is what constitutes a plausible assumption. Most experience oriented anthropologists, myself included, are skeptical of null and minimalist models, which seem to accord too much power to culture and discourse and to underestimate the complexities of both communication and consciousness. To be sure, one should be cautious about making ethnocentric assumptions. But prudence should not paralyze anthropologists or cause them to retreat unthinkingly to fuzzy or skeletal models. For *any* model, including a skeletal model, runs the risk of making unjustified, and even demeaning, assumptions. Skeletal models have their own implausibilities: the negation of personal agency, the reduction of motivation to means–ends calculations, the denial of the systemic and peculiar nature of consciousness, and the discriminatory reservation of critical and creative faculties to people such as those who write ethnographic accounts.

If anthropologists are to explore questions of identity, they must address the link between public representations and subjectivities. More persuasive and coherent accounts of identity (and of meaning) will demand the explicit formulation of credible models of the person, a task for which psychological and other person-centered anthropologists are especially well equipped.

REFERENCES

Anderson, Benedict, 1983 *Imagined Communities: Reflections on the Origin and Spread of Nationalism*. London: Verso.

Barth, Fredrik, 1969 Introduction. In *Ethnic Groups and Boundaries*. Fredrik Barth, ed. Pp. 9–38. Boston, MA: Little, Brown.

Bateson, Gregory, 1972 [1960] *Minimal Requirements for a Theory of Schizophrenia: Steps to an Ecology of Mind*. New York: Ballantine.

Bloch, Maurice E. F., 1998 *How We Think They Think: Anthropological Approaches to Cognition, Memory, and Literacy*. Boulder, CO: Westview Press.

Chodorow, Nancy J., 1999 *The Power of Feelings: Personal Meaning in Psychoanalysis, Gender, and Culture*. New Haven, CT: Yale University Press.

Clifford, James, and George E. Marcus, eds., 1986 *Writing Culture: The Poetics and Politics of Ethnography*. Berkeley: University of California Press.

Cohen, Anthony P., 1994 *Self Consciousness: An Alternative Anthropology of Identity*. London: Routledge.

Cohen, Anthony P., and Nigel Rapport, eds., 1995 *Questions of Consciousness*. London: Routledge.

D'Andrade, Roy, 1995 *The Development of Cognitive Anthropology*. Cambridge: Cambridge University Press.

de Beauvoir, Simone, 1957 [1949] *Le Deuxieme Sexe/The Second Sex*. Trans. H. M. Parshley. New York: Bantam Books.

di Leonardo, Micaela, 1991 *Gender at the Crossroads of Knowledge: Feminist Anthropology in the Postmodern Era*. Berkeley, CA: University of California Press.

Field, Norma, 1993 *In the Realm of a Dying Emperor: Japan at Century's End*. New York: Vintage Books.

Foucault, Michel, 1990 [1976] *The History of Sexuality*, Vol. 1. Robert Hurley, trans. New York: Vintage Books.

Geertz, Clifford, 1973 *The Interpretation of Cultures*. New York: Basic Books.

Hallowell, A. Irving, 1988 [1954] The Self and its Behavioral Environment. In *Culture and Experience*. Pp. 75–110. Prospect Heights, IL: Waveland Press.

Handler, Richard, 1988 *Nationalism and the Politics of Culture in Quebec*. Madison: University of Wisconsin Press.

Harvey, David, 1989 *The Condition of Postmodernity*. Oxford: Blackwell.

Hobsbawm, Eric, and Terence Ranger, eds., 1983 *The Invention of Tradition*. Cambridge: Cambridge University Press.

Hollan, Douglas, 1997 The Relevance of Person-Centered Ethnography to Cross-Cultural Psychiatry. *Transcultural Psychiatry* 34 (2): 219–234.

Holland, Dorothy, and Jean Lave, eds., 2001 *History in Person*. Santa Fe, NM: School of American Research Press.

Jameson, Fredric, 1991 *Postmodernism, or, the Cultural Logic of Late Capitalism*. Durham, NC: Duke University Press.

Karakasidou, Anastasia N., 1997 *Fields of Wheat, Hills of Blood: Passages to Nationhood in Greek Macedonia, 1870–1990*. Chicago: University of Chicago Press.

Leach Edmund R., 1977 [1954] *Political Systems of Highland Burma*. London: Athlone Press.

Levy Robert I., 1994 Person-Centered Anthropology. In *Assessing Cultural Anthropology*. Robert Borofsky, ed. Pp. 180–189. New York: McGraw-Hill.

Linger, Daniel T., 1994 Has Culture Theory Lost Its Minds? *Ethos* 22 (3): 284–315.

— 2001 *No One Home: Brazilian Selves Remade in Japan*. Stanford, CA: Stanford University Press.

Lutz, Catherine A., 1988 *Unnatural Emotions: Everyday Sentiments on a Micronesian Atoll and Their Challenge to Western Theory*. Chicago: University of Chicago Press.

Malinowski, Bronislaw, 1955 [1927] *Sex and Repression in Savage Society*. New York: Meridian Books.

Mead, Margaret, 1961 [1928] *Coming of Age in Samoa: A Psychological Study of Primitive Youth for Western Civilization*. New York: Dell.

Mitchell, J. Clyde, 1956 *The Kalela Dance: Aspects of Social Relationships among Urban Africans in Northern Rhodesia*. Rhodes-Livingstone Papers No. 27. Manchester: Manchester University Press.

Ortner, Sherry B. 1996 *Making Gender: The Politics and Erotics of Culture*. Boston, MA: Beacon Press.

Parish, Steven M., 1996 *Hierarchy and Its Discontents: Culture and the Politics of Consciousness in Caste Society*. Philadelphia: University of Pennsylvania Press.

Rapport, Nigel, 1997 *Transcendent Individual: Towards a Literary and Liberal Anthropology*. London: Routledge.

Rapport, Nigel, and Joanna Overing, 2000 Individuality. In *Social and Cultural Anthropology: The Key Concepts*. Pp. 185–195. London: Routledge.

Rosaldo, Michelle, and Louis Lamphere, eds. 1974 *Woman, Culture, and Society*. Stanford, CA: Stanford University Press.

Sapir, Edward, 1917 Do We Need a "Superorganic"? *American Anthropologist* 19: 441–447.

— 1949a [1938] Why Cultural Anthropology Needs the Psychiatrist. In *Selected Writings in Language, Culture, and Personality*. Pp. 569–577. Berkeley: University of California Press.

— 1949b [1939] Psychiatric and Cultural Pitfalls in the Business of Getting a Living. In *Selected Writings in Language, Culture, and Personality*. Pp. 578–589. Berkeley: University of California Press.

Schneider, David M., 1980 [1968] *American Kinship: A Cultural Account*. Englewood Cliffs, NJ: Prentice-Hall.

Schwartz, Theodore, 1978 Where is the Culture? Personality as the Distributive Locus of Culture. In *The Making of Psychological Anthropology*. George D. Spindler, ed. Pp. 419–441. Berkeley: University of California Press.

Shore, Bradd, 1996 *Culture in Mind: Cognition, Culture, and the Problem of Meaning*. New York: Oxford University Press.

Sökefeld, Martin, 1999 Debating Self, Identity, and Culture in Anthropology. *Current Anthropology* 40 (4): 417–447.

Sperber, Dan, 1996 *Explaining Culture: A Naturalistic Approach*. Oxford: Blackwell.

Spiro, Melford E., 1993 Is the Western Conception of the Self "Peculiar" within the Context of World Cultures? *Ethos* 21 (2): 107–154.

Strauss, Claudia, 1997 Partly Fragmented, Partly Integrated: An Anthropological Examination of Postmodern Fragmented Subjects. *Cultural Anthropology* 12 (3): 362–404.

Strauss, Claudia, and Naomi Quinn, 1997 *A Cognitive Theory of Cultural Meaning*. Cambridge: Cambridge University Press.

Wallace, Anthony F. C., 1961 *Culture and Personality*. New York: Random House.

CHAPTER 11

Self and Other in an "Amodern" World

A. David Napier

Hegel tells us that the self is born only in battle with another consciousness, through a struggle with the Other.

Massey, *Birth of the Self*

The individual who has not risked his life may well be recognized as a *person*, but he has not attained the truth of this recognition.

Hegel, *Phenomenology of Spirit*

THE CATEGORY OF THE PERSON

It is often said that social anthropology is the study of no more nor less than the modes of thinking by which a cosmology gives way among individuals to forms of embodied practice. In such a view, the act of examining another way of life must be based upon some willingness to consider the possible experiential differences that a galaxy of shared perceptions makes feasible. Out of such a structural sensibility, the notion of "culture" arose during the Enlightenment as the study of life forms and, in our era, of the lives of those individuals whose minds were inhabited by idiosyncratic manifestations of what were understood as shared cultural perceptions.

But already in the early twentieth century, it had been forcefully argued that the possible variations of any particular life form might be infinite (or, at least, that they could appear to be so) and, given this variability, that the proper domain of sociology ought rightly to *exclude* those psychological factors that accounted for perceptual variations among individuals. Durkheim (1898) was clear on this point, as were so many others who believed that the focus of our field of inquiry could be located in recognizing and elucidating the categorical mechanisms that framed the various images of the world that we each individually drew.

Much of the growth of British social anthropology (and of its younger cousin, American cultural anthropology) could be outlined as an outcome of this fundamental discrimination. However, the very French social theory that defined these parameters soon produced its own debunking, for the clear counter-argument was made that the distinction between individual and shared perceptions was, itself, a cultural construct. This construct, it turned out, could be easily challenged by the indisputable awareness that any one of us could only know the manner in which we individually embodied anything (because the only thing of which we have both subjective and objective knowledge was the very body we each inhabit), and because the growing corpus of ethnographic literature provided numerous examples of cultures in which the notion of the person was, itself, ameliorated by various claims on that notion's autonomy.

In fact, it was the latter of these two that was first recognized in the repeated instances in which Cartesian ideals were struck down by the daily living of life elsewhere – first this recognition, of course, because it is always easier to recognize difference in another than in oneself (see Bourdieu 1977). Perhaps the most gifted of all expositors of these, now "cultural," differences was the French cleric and ethnographer Maurice Leenhardt, who, by virtue of his experience in Melanesia over some four decades, was able to offer stunning examples of other modes of thinking that could challenge Descartes at every turn – examples unusual enough that they may never be equaled in the anthropological literature. Indeed, Leenhardt's expository skills were born out of a fascination and love that could only result from being himself so thoroughly transformed by the anthropological enterprise.

Here is one famous example (see Napier 1986: 17):

> Un jour que, sous ces impressions, je voulais mesurer cependant le progrès accompli chez ceux que j'avais instruits de longues années, je dis à l'un d'eux:
>
> – En somme, c'est la notion d'esprit que nous avons porté dans votre pensée.
> – Pas du tout, objecta-t-il brusquement, nous avons toujours connu l'esprit. Ce que vous nous avez apporté, c'est le corps. (Leenhardt 1937: 195)

Leenhardt time and again offered compelling cases in which a body image, and its boundaries, were enough negotiable so as nearly to *require* outright condemnation on the part of any psychoanalyst who might find himself trapped into fitting an alien worldview into his experiences at the couch. In "La Personne mélanésienne," Leenhardt makes his view unequivocally: "Un personnage est une figure et un rôle . . . Il ne discrimine pas entre le corps et le rôle" (1970: 104).

So compelling were such cases from the lived experiences of ethnographers that few, if any, psychological theorists dared allow themselves to be ensnared into "explaining away" what to all others seemed mysterious and, at times, ineffable. Indeed, in Hindu Bali, body image boundary seemed fluid enough that a state of possession could be linked not only to the active overtaking of the self by another with whom that self had interacted, but also that the distance between positive and negative magic could dissolve in a phenomenal encounter the moral value of which could not be known as it was experienced. Here, time and again, a vanquished spirit would even thank its vanquisher for being released from a life cycle that caused even its best intended actions to have destructive outcomes.

No less than Gregory Bateson, perhaps the most innovative of all ethnographers of this century, realized that abandoning his psychological inquiries on Bali was necessitated by both the way in which the complexities of Balinese thinking defied the potential range of his own intellectual gymnastics and by the problem of how one might translate what his experiences suggested into a language that fellow Westerners could appreciate. But his then-wife, Margaret Mead, did attempt this translation; and, though she no doubt started the contemporary women's movement by so doing for middle America, eventually she suffered the disapprobation both of her professional peers (who considered her work unverifiable) and, eventually, of a women's movement (that found her interest in gender differences troubling).

By the 1960s there was enough momentum in the profession to deny what these ethnographers claimed, renouncing their sincere efforts as the apparent exoticizing of life elsewhere. It is a pity, then, that those dissenting intellectuals were not required in making this case to display their hands before being allowed to speak at professional meetings, for were they so required we would almost certainly find excessive amounts of soft fatty tissue of the kind that Lord Byron felt made one a real gentleman – tissue that, while proving their gentility, in no way could stand for the embodied practices of those whose lives these ethnographers claimed to know intimately. Such a test would, no doubt, tell us more about how they spent their days than would their writing. Such a test could also expose their remoteness from those very peoples who moved Marcel Mauss (1938, 1973) to write our first deep essays on the topic of how self and non-self get sorted out in other places.

There is no reason to produce any inventory of attitudes about the manner in which a self can display a body image boundary that is quite flexible, especially when such an inventory can be so readily dispelled by skeptics. However, as Boas illustrated for the Kwakiutl long ago, there is little sense in talking about persons as we might know them if the ground rules admit from the start what for outsiders seems unacceptable. Citing Boas's pioneering work, Goldman noted many such examples among the Kwakiutl, including the idea that personae can be willfully discarded when removed masks fly back to the sky world:

- The Grizzly Bear masks and skin return home by themselves.
- Seals are surprised and seen as men before they have time to put on their masks . . .
- On owl masks: "Owls are men, for we all have owl masks." The dead go toward their owl masks and fly about as owls. "The owl names the name of the owner of the owl mask."
- Masks become excited behind their curtain at the sound of beating and yelling at a ceremony. (Goldman 1975: 228)

Yes, these are all "unusual" cases – unusual in that they will *always* appear improbable or sensational to a skeptical rationalist, to the involuted postmodernist, and to the old-fashioned psychoanalyst. They are also unusual in that – like illness itself – they are enough adaptive so as never to present themselves in a "usual" form. They demonstrate, in other words, instances of dissociative projection that only achieve "normality" once the transformations for which they are catalysts are assimilated recursively into a narrative of interconnected events.

I will not, therefore, make any extended argument for the need to take seriously anthropology's literature on animism from Tylor onwards, for this would be to repeat arguments that have already been made (Napier 1986, 1992). Nor will I address the defensive posture of anthropology's academic industry, especially the version of that industry that claims some moral high ground through the kind of rhetorical sentimentality that is our current fashion. What I will say, moreover, has nothing to do with recent theories of the person that get drummed up in academic high society. Instead, I will describe the damaging consequences of normalizing the exotic, since I would not, in this forum at least, be permitted to display my own hands as evidence of what I do on any given day.

GETTING POISONED

Getting poisoned in the field can be a good thing. It happened to me in 1981, while studying the uses and abuses of magic in Bali. I cite the year here because at that time our field was busy telling everyone that anthropology's earlier interest in structure and ritual had skewed the lived worlds of those we study. Magic and ritual – the things that had fascinated our professional ancestors – were thought to be part of the luxurious fantasizing of both intellectual and actual colonists.

Though years later it would seem no more nor less demanding than my stays in other Asian countries, I had initially been discouraged by professionals who had worked in Bali from going there in the first place. It was "over-studied" and "ruined by tourism" – perhaps too soft a fieldsite in a discipline whose members had traditionally fascinated one another by extraordinary tales of survival. But, for a recent philosophy graduate, it was an ideal setting in which to explore the cultural construct of the person, especially as that construct got tossed and torn in ecstatic dissociative trances. Of course, I had no idea at the time of what I was getting into. An experienced British ethnographer warned me that my topic (by then defined as the interpretation of masks) could be dangerous. However, more commonly I was confronted by the derision of fellow anthropologists who felt that studying masked ritual was a romantic thing of the past – even, potentially, an elitist endeavor, since it clearly involved things that, if they existed at all, were not part of the "everyday" world of Balinese commoners. Never mind that some of them have since come to write about the impact of magical beliefs upon those "everyday" Balinese; suffice it to say that the moment when I arrived was important because modernity seemed to have struck the island as well as those who studied it with something like a vengeance.

As it turned out, I began my work in the usual sort of way – finding out who made masks, where they were used, how many kinds there were, how they were consecrated. All seemed important to me, but it was the last of these that provided my introduction to a world that my professional peers appeared to know nothing about, for, despite the volumes of literature on my topic, I could find no examination of the correlation between woods used for masks and what was clearly an indigenous pharmacopoeia. My "over-studied" topic, in other words, turned out – despite the many books about it – to contain crucial dimensions that were "never-studied." Indeed, before long I realized that my inquiries were leading me deeper and deeper into a world of experience that was, indeed, *very* "exotic" and, moreover, almost wholly alien to me.

Now, you may ask at this juncture why I am telling this story, rather than, say, writing about Balinese ethnobotany. You may also ask why, as a professional anthropologist, I have never written any ethnography – for the experiences that I had could for some probably be elucidating or instructive. You may ask why my Balinese experiences inform everything I write, even though I rarely write about them directly – why I have never presented my experiences as "data" to be scrutinized by others. Well, the reason I am framing these experiences so narrowly is because, in fact, I am not going to describe them, to prove in some narrative form that they are "mine." Rather, what I am going to describe is how I came to see that there were certain doors of perception that were opened for me, thresholds that I had looked through but did not cross; for had I crossed them, I could not be writing what I write at this moment. I am not being coy here; I am merely pointing out that getting poisoned was a good thing for me.

It would, of course, be improper (if not, perhaps, dangerous) to describe in too much detail how my "initiation" occurred. But I can say that it all happened in a most unexpected way. In fact, it was probably the fault of my camera, for I had taken a photo of a magical covering over a powerful mask – a photo that a god would not have allowed were I not meant to have it. In other words, there was no prohibition on approaching a magical object other than the wrath or the patronage of the inhabiting spirit. Tourists, for instance, may happily walk across a graveyard at night; but if being in that powerful place were part of some calling, one had better be ritually prepared. On other occasions my thoroughly reliable camera had jammed under similar circumstances, so the outcome of taking such photos was, I was told, in the gods' hands, not mine.

Had I known more of Bali at the time, I would surely have recognized the request for a copy of the photo by a member of a competing clan as an urgent plea to control a potentially overpowering force. But there was no way for me to know that capturing an image on film could be construed as a power move of its own kind. Moreover, there were several other signals that I will not describe, but suffice it to say that my professional loneliness had led me to spending long days deciphering in my appalling German a copy of Wolfgang Weck's 1937 *Heilkunde und Volkstum auf Bali* (*Curing and Folk Wisdom on Bali*). The book intrigued me not only because of the fact that Weck was himself a medical doctor (a profession I had once considered), but also because, unlike most of the ethnographies I had read, what Weck said rang true to me. As I read what he wrote about magical attacks, I began to realize that I was myself in the midst of one.

So, when the day came that I was offered datura (brugmansia) in a traditional Balinese dish, I accepted the food politely, but disposed of it when I removed myself to dine. When a servant later appeared that day to inquire how I was doing in hospital, he was more than surprised to learn that I was in excellent health and only curious about why he should ask such a question. What he had anticipated was that sufficient poisoning would, were it not fatal, at least leave me in a restless panic the outcome of which would be a state of memory-less anxiety – a psychotic fear of each waking moment that eventually would leave me spending long, listless days in a zombie-like state.

Why, then, do I call my experience a poisoning, rather than an "attempted" poisoning? Because my survival made it clear to everyone familiar with the incident that my identity had been permanently changed by the experience. I had been, as it were, inoculated by a god's protective efforts. There was no other explanation for my survival. Now, for whatever reasons, I have been spared to tell a story, and that story is about transcendence.

THE ESSENTIAL FEAR

I remember the moment well. It was June of 1977. I was wearing my Oxford gown and sitting in the University Schools with a neatly printed examination book containing questions that would determine whether or not my year had been usefully spent. Some hours later, I reached the final page of the exam and found a question that made me laugh almost openly. Perhaps it was the near six hours already spent clutching a pen; perhaps it was the formality of the experience, but for whatever reason I was brought up short by a question that asked me to comment on British cultural traits.

Since we students were required to choose from a list of possible essay topics, I put this question aside and only recalled it that afternoon when we cracked the traditional bottles of champagne as we spewed into High Street following the completion of our exams. To my surprise, a number of my classmates had elected to answer this question, and it soon became clear to me that what I thought to be a humorous example of the "essentializing" of other cultures was for many a serious and legitimate inquiry. If there were, indeed, autonomous and potentially incommensurate ways of embodying experience, then did it not follow that some cultures would excel at certain domains of experience and knowledge? And if a collectivity can develop certain excellences, did it not then also follow that not all such social collectivities would excel in the same sorts of ways?

This basic idea – which, by the way, is also evident in a much more politically correct discourse on multiculturalism – comes dangerously close to openly racist discourse because its logic necessitates certain conclusions that are as unpalatable as they are morally suspect. Indeed, it was a small step from saying that specific modes of thinking develop unique techniques for experiencing the world to saying that some would be better than others for specific tasks. To call one thing "better" is to have established a hierarchy, and to have done that is to have set off down the bumpy road of Social Darwinism and, equally troubling, of eugenic programming. What, after all, do we mean at the social level when we believe biologically that the "fittest" survive, or when embryos or sperm are selected for the version of humanness they are meant to reproduce? "If you can't stand the heat," Richard Nixon used to love saying, "get out of the kitchen": it's the same idea. If you haven't got what it takes, you will never be one of the few good men that the Marines are always in search of.

Without revisiting the history of "planned parenthood" from Herbert Spencer to Julian Huxley, it is clear that there is no diversity to "honor" if there is no difference; and if there is *relative* difference, then there is choice. If there is preference, then there is hierarchy. As soon as we have hierarchy, alas, we have inequality – unless, as Phillips (1994: 79) points out, we are prepared to argue that a boxer's view of a psychoanalytic session is as insightful as a psychiatrist's view of boxing.

Though, indeed, the boxer may sometimes have the advantage of his own insights, our lists of psychiatrists holding down important institutional posts is enough evidence in itself to show that our love of novelty hardly matches our cultural obsession with achieved status (i.e., of social hierarchy). Otherwise, we would see no problem in having the psychiatrist devote her days to boxing as might the boxer to the analytical couch. In fact, though the novelty of either may endear us to a boxing psychiatrist or an analyzing boxer, our love of that novelty is hardly adequate to sustain the belief that those two worlds are anything like "equal." If, in other words, one manages to swallow the notion that relative difference can be maintained without preference (i.e., without one thing being "better" than another), then one need only ask why so many academic professionals who preach diversity from the pulpit are wholly reticent of living at all outside of the institutional networks that sustain them. I think here, especially, of my socialist colleagues who, in spite of their politics, still send their children to Oxford and Harvard – which, of course, brings us right back to having a better look at those hands before such gentlemen start their engines and we, in turn, express our hope, may the best man win.

Though historical examples are less discomforting because they are, by their distance, so easily dismissed, the process of stereotyping continues unchecked in a society in which achieved status reigns above all else. In this respect, America will never solve the ongoing oppression of its so-called minorities, because the presence of some minority is required to create a relative hierarchy of achievement in which heroes distinguish themselves from those less fortunate Others. The problem, in other words, with focusing on the everyday, or workaday, experiences of commoners, is that our doing so itself creates a hierarchy in which WE become the voice for THEM. In America, to salt the wound, we then hide our hierarchies within a rhetoric of equality. Show me the university professor who has no interest in working under the "bright lights" and I will show you either a professional second-class citizen or what his colleagues would consider a damned fool.

Yet I know for a fact that I will never learn to speak a new language as well as a 5-year-old native speaker. I know that I will never learn to ski as effortlessly as my son who grew up skiing. Likewise, I know that I can never fully appreciate the famine of an Ethiopian by watching television, or, indeed, know his or her hunger by visiting a refugee encampment. I can no better survive Saharan heat than a Bedouin can sense the presence of a whale beneath an ocean swell. The problem is that acknowledging these things so easily leads to views of the "Other" that are totally problematic, because for most of us it is but a short leap from "kids make good skiers," to "mountain dwellers make good skiers," to "Austrians make good skiers." And it is yet another small leap that can then lead us to even more problematic perceptions of Others, like the often-voiced racist stereotype that blacks make better athletes. Do Eskimos sense more about variations in weather? Do Japanese excel at collective endeavors? Here in Vermont, for instance, one can on most days hear political lobbyists arguing for special visas for low-cost Jamaican apple pickers on the grounds that they possess the inherent ability to handle fruit delicately – as if they somehow have a genetic disposition to this form of manual labor. Where do experiential considerations, in other words, give way to national, racial, and ethnic biases? And how are statistical generalities used to destroy real difference? Well, Hitler did very well at this (e.g., noting the numbers of Jews who are academic achievers, or numbers of unwed Catholic mothers); but so, unfortunately, did recent uses of the bell curve (see Fraser 1995; Napier 2002).

The problem, in other words, with essentializing shared experiences is that there is no lack of quantitative evidence to support almost any sort of conclusion, but the logical conclusions to which such essentializing draws us are nearly always both morally and democratically wrong. In extreme cases of such stereotyping (what we now call "profiling"), the tendency to adopt racially driven views of others leads to highly offensive assumptions. If Muslim terrorists only train other Muslims for acts of terror, people will always assume that such terrorists are Muslim, because generalizations are based on generalities that, in turn, are based on the repeated verification of those same assumptions. We employ, in other words, many kinds of shorthand just to get through a day, even if that very generalizing process so often leads to quite sloppy and morally inappropriate thinking. Only when our stereotypes are overturned before us through personal encounters, or when we can distance ourselves from them over time, do they actually stand out as wholly unacceptable.

So, this idea – that various culturally embedded forms of knowledge will be better suited to particular life forms – perforce places the notion of modes of thought in enough of a potentially bad light to make most of us uncomfortable about saying much of anything about the ways in which culture conditions values. At the same time, as long ago as Plato the idea was widely recognized that the character of our social institutions would be reflected in collectively valued notions of what makes us human. Aristotle's similar belief that "what makes the world one will also be what makes a person" is conditioned by like notions about how the human body and, say, a governmental body are more than metaphorically related. Why else, for instance, did Americans continue to "give blood for America" long after the September 11 hijackings? Why else do we describe terrorist organizations as "cells" and their behavior as "viral"? Why else were American news broadcasters so obsessed with reciting the word "anthrax" when so many more dangerous threats were being faced by Americans both at home and abroad? Clearly, a horrendous crisis was causing us to reify the connection between the self and that social body called "our culture."

Because we both take offense to, and recognize the social currency of, such assumptions, we also feel a natural urge to police them in ways that are sometimes appropriate and sometimes not. Either way, the fact of the matter is that if you think of the self as a negotiated terrain of host–pathogen balancing, you will by definition be less concerned about the presence of a little Otherness in your life. All French people, for instance, may not share the view that Americans are too antiseptic about the body, but it is a view that we, nonetheless (and with some accuracy), call "French."

So why continue to talk about cultural variation if it always leads either to stereotypical "profiling" or to the covert deployment of hierarchy within a rhetoric of equality? And does it really matter that the French possess a culturally driven notion of the self that sees individuals as made up in part of difference? Well, the answer to the first of these questions is that Hegel was right about the need for the Other in defining the self, even if he was wrong about this relationship as always being militant. And the answer to the second of these questions is, well . . . yes.

Transformation "c'est la moi"

In her popular account of the variations in healthcare practices in France, Germany, the United Kingdom, and the United States, the late Lynn Payer describes the importance in French society of thinking of the body as *la terrain* – a concept that has no easy English equivalent, but essentially one that encapsulates a cultural predilection for recognizing a disease as not only an invasion from outside, but as the combination of outside influences and the body's reaction to those influences. In this view, morbidity is not just a function of what pathogens do to us, but of how successfully or unsuccessfully that "Outsider" is assimilated – "a combination of some type of outside insult and the body's reaction to that insult" (Payer 1988: 61).

As a consequence of this view, French doctors by and large "are more likely to try to find ways to modify the reaction as well as fight off the insult" (Payer 1988: 61), whereas the healthcare practices of certain other Western nations tend to focus more on destroying completely the insult itself. French medicine, then, is more accommodating, more homeopathic, more attuned to health-related therapies that strengthen and condition the body. The French – as is evidenced in their national health policies – feel that paying for baths and spas is an important part of healthcare, the concrete outcome of which is not only evidenced in the French tendency to see clinical health as a function of "well-being" in some broad sense, but also apparent in such an equal distribution of health benefits that the WHO recently rated France number 1 in healthcare worldwide. Yes, there are French researchers just as adamant about eliminating HIV or malaria as their colleagues elsewhere, but there is actually as deeply embedded in France a cultural discourse about recognizing and assimilating the outside as there is about eliminating it. Vaccinology (the assimilation of pathogens) is an acknowledged theoretical domain in France, whereas in America (where pathogens are eliminated immunologically) the discipline only has meaning in a strictly scientific sense. We don't, in other words, talk about exposing ourselves to pathogens in the same way that we describe the need to fortify our immune systems. Try raising the subject of vaccinology at your next cocktail party and you will be dutifully impressed by the silence and vacant stares you have visited upon yourself.

What, then, might we make, Payer asks, of the cultural idea of the French as a people tolerant of "a little bit of dirt"? Well, if we look at the numbers of French doctors who are licensed homeopaths, or at the research on plasmodistatic drugs – that is, drugs that alter a body's response to plasmodia (the agents of malaria), rather than killing pathogens outright – the answer must be "a good bit." Are the French, then, likely to be better at addressing the problems of how the world might deal with the multi-resistant bacteria that have grown out of our overuse of antibiotics designed to eliminate the "Outside"? "Yes, of course." And if we, then, say that the French are more likely to succeed intellectually in balancing antibodies and antigens than are their American colleagues who are dead set on killing off those antigens, are we not also, then, saying that stereotypes about French bathing habits are enough "real" to be evidenced in their scientific research programs?

So what, one might ask, makes attending to this stereotype any more productive than the stereotypes that may as readily be constructed for other cultural groups? The answer here is easy – because the French assimilative treatment of biological (and cultural) differences creates a kind of transformational environment that is ideologically more creative than is, say, the cathartic relational model with which Americans by and large are more comfortable. The assimilative value of *la terrain*, in other words, itself stands as an indicator of some shared confidence about how a productive encounter with the "Other" (be it real or imagined) may be orchestrated. To put it differently, in acknowledging that the "self" is in part "other," we force ourselves also to acknowledge that social encounters only produce positive outcomes when their dynamic nature is attended to. As Ricoeur says of his own book title:

> Oneself as Another (*Soi-même comme un autre*) suggests from the outset that the self-hood of oneself implies otherness to such an intimate degree that one cannot be thought of without the other, that instead one passes into the other, as we might say in Hegelian terms. (Ricoeur 1992: 3)

Implicit, then, in this notion of the self, is a thing that is dynamic, and, in fact, sufficiently dynamic that it cannot exist without acknowledging the formative import-ance of its ontological, its narrative, and above all its social Others. This interdepend-ence, after all, is what has largely distinguished Continental phenomenology from the empirical focus of British–American philosophy for nearly a century. Moreover, it is also why English-speaking ("American") anthropologists regularly confuse the term "phenomenological" with the term "phenomenal"; for the former grows out of a particular sociohistorical argument about the *embedded* nature of human identity, while the latter implies more generally that we consider human identity as a thing made meaningful through its sensory and its experiential manifestations. The differ-ence may seem subtle, but it is also crucial.

Once acknowledged, however, this discrimination makes it much easier to under-stand why anthropological examples of Others' modes of thought are so compelling, and why, by contrast, we appear so parochial when we normalize the "everyday" worlds of Others – when we mistake, that is, the "phenomenal" for the "phenomenological." For, in the latter of these, we are not merely trying to say that other cultures have essential features that we may not have. Quite the contrary, we are saying that other modes of thought that define the self through its capacity to assimilate are *always* going to offer more creative versions of how one grows and is transformed through social encounters than do those notions of self that survive by eliminating the outside. Indeed, by this simple discrimination one can nearly measure the confidence of any social group about the sovereignty of its borders, and, at the same time, produce an inventory of cultural settings in which self and other differ dramatically from the version we today see in, say, "magic bullet" medicine, or in "precision bombing."

This assimilative notion of a body's terrain is, thus, more important than it may at first appear, because it has its own built-in mechanism for revising stereotypes. In allowing for productive mutations, *la terrain* distinguishes itself from a cathartic model of self that expels difference from what phenomenologists refer to as its regional ontology – in this case its body image boundary. It is not at all difficult, then, to see how a notion of selfhood based on the elimination of difference will be much more likely to reify stereotypes of the Other, and, by extension, to promote an incommensurable relationship between "the self and its behavioral world," to recall Hallowell (1955). In recognizing and eliminating non-self (that is, in immunology), there is little stimulus for interaction, because the goal of interacting is to neutralize

Otherness. Is it any wonder, then, that ethnic minorities who grow up abroad have so frequently voiced the opinion that they never feel so much the alienation of being a minority than upon returning to the United States – even, I might add, upon returning from countries better known than America for their racism?

I have, in other words, used French popular "culture" as an example here – rather than, say, something ethnographically "exotic" – because it would clearly be wrong to claim that the mere act of noting a proliferation of homeopaths in France is itself an act of exoticizing difference. Nor am I choosing this example because I would want anyone to think that all people with French passports value *la terrain*. The reason this concept is being noted is because an awareness of *la terrain* encourages a tendency toward *assimilation*, which is different than a tendency toward *elimination* (see Low, this volume; Napier 2002). Likewise, the famous examples that I described earlier in this chapter were also chosen for their assimilative capacities, for their articulation of the complexities of human interaction as a baseline condition, rather than as a thing thought up after modernism. They are not, in other words, unusual examples called up only to incite the suspicion of postmodernists!

The problem, then, with neutralizing difference by eliminating it, or even by reducing it to a subset of the normal, is that the outcome of this endeavor is much more damaging than might at first appear to be the case; for, in ruling out the thrill of the unknown, we also rule out any prospect for creative mutation. To put it another way, if the "other" that one engages is believed only to be a reflexive extension of an isolated self, there can, by definition, be no mutual transformation. If there is no social and reciprocal abandonment of an authoritarian "self," there can be no changing of anything; if there is no risk of self-loss, there is also no catalyst for growth.

"Honk if I'm Polish"; or, A Selfish Argument for Abandoning Postmodernism

Thus far in this essay I have used the notion of culture as a broad rubric for the assumed collectivities of which individuals (rightly or wrongly) consider themselves to be a part, or against which they define themselves as outsiders. In so doing, I have steered clear of the debate over whether one can rightly speak at all of the identity of a group of others, or of the identity that any self may assume others to share. The onset of reflexive ideas in social anthropology introduced a near complete ban on speaking or writing about collectivities, even those produced as the imaginative constructs, or even as the fantasies, of a lucid ego. So, permit me, now, to outline my reasons for framing my discussion in ways that have openly ignored postmodernism, and in so doing to illustrate why I have here, and elsewhere, characterized postmodern theory as ideologically reactionary.

The postmodern view of self is not a-structural but anti-structural

One of the greatest weaknesses of the postmodern view of self is its assumption that structuralism ossifies or ignores the phenomenal domain of individual experience. Though, as we have seen, Durkheim may certainly have pointed us in that direction by banning individual psychology from the examination of collective ideology, what he almost certainly understood as the function of social categories was rather different from how we now view them in hindsight. In fact, there is even a postmodern view of Durkheim that acknowledges the need to assess him less dogmatically (Mestrovic 1992). Without discussing this at length, one must understand here that Durkheim's quibble with psychology was in large measure the result of his belief that the examination of modes of thought could go forward in safety only so long as we restricted our inquiry to collective interactions among those who shared domains of language and thought. As long as we were not examining how those categories were judged psychologically by individual actors, we need not attach value to – or, in so doing, state a hierarchical preference for – one system over another. Whether we called these domains cultural categories or experiential tropes mattered less than the fact that culture was constituted of broadly shared metaphors within which were embedded the explanatory networks that allowed for human agreement.

Metaphors do demonstrably convey viscerally shared, and often covert, ways of organizing experience (Napier 2002). This is something that is not difficult to demonstrate, but it does require a certain critical distance from the white noise of the local networks we are attuned to. One only has to see how metaphors mutate in what used to be called "traditional" societies – that is, to experience having been poisoned – to understand why the structural straw man of postmodernism gets torched each year at Burning Man.

Looked at bluntly, nobody ever said that cultures were fixed and immutable, except perhaps for some few postmodernists who haven't the courage to be moved by genuine difference. Instead, they use the word "exotic" to describe everything that is potentially different – which, of course, is necessary if one is petrified about being changed by encounters with the unknown. In this sense postmodernism is highly dilettantish, because if one is a smart enough dresser (or under-dresser), it is possible to ward off challenges to one's identity by flirting in professional settings with artificial danger.

Postmodernists are not selfish enough

The postmodernist is scared by the possibility of losing the fragile professional edifice he has worked so hard to construct, in part because the indeterminacy of postmodernism creates uncertainty that, itself, leads to personal insecurity and a lack of conviction. So, when he looks locally, the postmodernist wants us to concentrate on each private neologism that gives what he says a novel appearance. At the same time, he cannot structure his sensations because he is anti-structuralist.

Because he lacks local empathic order, he must project his sensitivities globally. Postmodernists, therefore, talk about very *big* things much of the time because the smaller things don't really interest them – unless, of course, they can reflexively gain favorable interest on their otherwise deep feelings of neglect by glamorizing local things with invented, Latin-like words. Whether they openly do not want to be wanted I cannot say. What I can say is that they need some coaching. Touching oneself is a start; but being touched by another is much better because it not only informs you intimately about the lived world of the person touching you, but it also invites you to acknowledge how touch itself is a vehicle for empathic transference.

Prejudicing the intellect, furthermore, severely skews our ability to sense how shared domains of understanding get creatively manipulated either individually or in group rites (see White, this volume), because such prejudicing limits our awareness of how each of our senses contributes its own unique forms of social awareness. Occasionally, someone is able to sneak such an idea into print (I am thinking especially of Stoller's (1989b, 1997) work on taste; more often our academic inquisitionists prohibit such considerations from seeing the light of day. A "taste" of what I am referring to may be read online (where peer reviews do not silence the unusual), though unmonitored talk has a tendency to get "out of hand," as we say. At the same time, simply enjoying oneself makes an excellent beginning.

Postmodernists like psychoanalysis (and I don't just mean Lacan)

No one ever said that traditions are static, except for those who have never been transformed by collective catharsis. But postmodernists for the most part like psychoanalysis because it pledges to offer developmental stability, and it privileges a version of individuality with which Westerners are most familiar (Ortner 1995). One reason why postmodernists fail to recognize the flexibility of the self in traditional life is because the word "tradition" also connotes stability. If you spend too much time reading, and not enough time running naked, you will surely believe that stability is a "static" idea that you may not know at all, but that, whatever it is, it cannot be what you wish you could become – for becoming *should* be destabilizing.

The problem here stems from never having dirtied oneself in any group rite. If, in fact, one had done so, it would become immediately apparent that meaningful transformation has nothing to do with navel gazing, and probably nothing very much to do with a Protestant–Buddhist "nonself," either. This is why the *structure* of change worldwide is so stable – that is, why most "premodern" peoples have not jettisoned the idea that rites of passage affect people profoundly. Psychological instability is ameliorated by structural stability because change is a very dangerous thing. People don't become better integrated by thinking about being different. They become better integrated by laying down their modern and postmodern firearms and allowing themselves to dissociate in the presence of another human being. Van Gennep realized this in 1909. We just haven't bothered to read him. Nor have we bothered to recognize that ritual is, for those immersed within it, anything but the repetitive domain that laboratory behaviorists would have us think.

Humans don't get transformed through psychotherapy; they get transformed through selective dissociation. You don't, that is, get healed of your obsession with the self by becoming more obsessed with the self. Postmodernism has something very wrong here, and the evidence is made even clearer by what postmodernism takes to be distinctive about contemporary life.

Postmodernists covertly (and sometimes overtly) believe in evolution

Modernism is a reaction to tradition, and postmodernism is, as its name indicates, a reaction to modernism. Being reactionary, it requires some faith in historical continuity – in the evolving nature of social change. The world of postmodernism is not, in other words, the nonsense world of DADA, but the surrealist's world of psychological novelty. Though it may claim to be a-historical, its "newness" is necessarily measured against what it is meant to replace. I have never heard a postmodernist say that his or her ideas were old and unimportant.

If postmodernists cannot assure themselves that life has evolved from states of continuity to those of discontinuity (from determinacy to indeterminacy, from dull order to cute chaos), they cannot offer any new higher order theory about why things today just seem so jumbled up all the time. But whoever said that the living of life was anything other than chaotic? Where are all of the voices from the past that show life to have once been only dull and unexciting? Well, I can tell you where they are. They are in the postmodern novel itself, which is perhaps the only place I know where *ennui* is elevated to a major virtue.

But, at the level of collective ideas, there can be no such thing as evolutionary continuity. The word "culture" becomes more or less important depending on the human need for identifying with others. When times are flush, we allow ourselves to believe that our lives are controlled by how far we can network worldwide as a metaphorical McDonald's hamburger. And in the security of our homes, we feel good about feeling alone. We even write books about our alienation from the warmth of our institutional offices (Goffman 1963), or, as Pollock (1996) has cleverly shown, from the halls of our professional schools where the lament over a loss of traditional authority get reconstructed into self-indulged heroic epic. We even believe that culture has been replaced by a global order, only to find that in moments of crisis we rush home to touch up the paint on the fading coats of arms that have been relegated to the closets of virtual neglect.

Moments of *instability* do induce interdependence, which is why historically we find culture most dynamically articulated in instances such as those claimed by postmodernists to be uniquely new. This is not to say that there is nothing new, but that, in the words of Lemert's (1997) book title, "postmodernism is not what you think." What Lemert means by this is that, if postmodernism exists at all, it is not about the act of thinking, but about other things that we do today. However, because postmodernism is also a narrative "about the extent to which the world has changed" (Lemert 1997: 53), it requires some deeper acceptance that something like a "real" world has existed. This is the way in which postmodernism sees itself as radical, as Baudrillard's "hyperreality in which simulation of reality is more real than the thing itself" (Lemert 1997: 27) – where "Disneyworld replications of a mythical America are the real American thing – more real than any actual American village" (Lemert 1997: 28; Fjellman 1992). Without begging the question of just what "radical" can mean here, it is clear that, whatever is going on, there are some big claims being made about earlier times that can evoke Poussin's images of Arcadia, or Rousseau's noble savage, as much as Mickey Mouse and Ronald McDonald.

Of course, the attraction of believing in social evolution is that there must have at one time been groups of people who were less self-consciously aware of the possibility of once having been less aware. But to think that this "newness" is evidenced in the unique mutability of contemporary life – in the trope by which a presumably less mutable life has now become mutable – is simply, as Lemert illustrates, wrongheaded. Though time does create unique notions of what has happened, or is happening, around us, culture was probably no more immutable in the past than it is today –

even if anthropologists have been traditionally attracted to domains where apparent stasis allows for the more easy management of one's own presumptions. Psychologically, of course, other societies may well have been, if anything, more mutable in terms of identity change than we are today. Ancient Greeks, modern Balinese, and even at times "enlightened" Europeans have all displayed global and transnational tendencies, even if the more physically mobile reality of life today means that these events take place with greater frequency than before (Friedman 1990; Napier 1992; Ohnuki-Tierney 2001; Wikan 1996). Culture is, in this line of thinking,

> always *in motion* – becoming, reproducing itself even when disintegrating at the "core" and transforming, in a constant ebb and flow . . . as a result of the dialectic between internal developments, global and other external forces, and social agents, who are almost always cosmopolitan. (Ohnuki-Tierney 2001: 244)

The very notion of a culture as something hermetic is predicated upon the assumption that "there once were cultures, each boxed in a territorial unit, whose territorial boundaries suddenly burst open" (Ohnuki-Tierney 2001: 242), and that these changes are by and large the outcome of the New Global Order. So, aside from the deeply disappointing idea that our own era may lack the importance we wish for it, what makes today different? To answer this question we must make one additional claim about self and other in postmodernity.

Postmodernists advance as truth a view of world change that cannot be sustained

In a popular account of what he takes to be American hypocrisy, Shapiro lists page after page of the disjunction between what Americans believe of themselves and the world, and what research shows, in fact, to be the case. Americans are number one in percentage of students who say they are good in math, but last in the percentage of students who actually are good in math (Shapiro 1992: 64). We're number one in the percentage of people who believe it is necessary to be able to read a map, and number one in ignorance of geography among young people (Shapiro 1992: 68). We're number one in membership in human rights groups, and number one in not ratifying international human rights treaties (Shapiro 1992: 114). We're number one in percentage of population that believes that the commandment "Thou shalt not steal" still applies today, and number one in robberies and thieves per capita (Shapiro 1992: 132). The lists offered by Shapiro actually fill an entire paperback, but the above-cited examples are sufficient to paint a picture of a modern world whose professed values are very much at odds with the actual behavior of its citizenry.

Now, the most common postmodern explanation claims that the flow of people, of images, and of resources in the contemporary era creates a kind of "Creole" world, where West Africans now make printed kente-cloth baseball caps rather than caps made of high quality woven kente in order to compete with Koreans in New Jersey who were producing cheap baseball caps made of printed kente. Why baseball caps? Because once African Americans had exploited the use of kente strips as college graduation attire, there remained few marketing options for Ghanaian merchants eager to sell ethnicity to African-American customers, and everyone in

America (and now around the world) wants to wear a baseball cap – even American football players. Here, the cosmopolitan flow of images and practices defies any kind of traditional cultural attribution. Balinese make African sculpture for sale to Westerners and then, themselves, collect their imitations in imitation of those who buy their imitations. In such settings it becomes all but necessary to reject the idea that these artifacts are the outcome of hermetic practices in fixed locations; rather, they devolve from practices that by any definition are borderless.

However, as Harvey points out:

> The shifting social construction of space and time, creates severe problems of identity: To what space do I as an individual belong? Do I express my idea of citizenship in my neighborhood, city, region, nation, or world? These are the sorts of questions that are being at least partially addressed within the postmodern rhetoric, even when the answers (the passive acceptance of fragmentation, for example) are patently false. (Harvey 1991: 77)

For socialists, Harvey included, these conditions are created by the endless search for profit and the geographic mobility on which capitalists thrive. Part of the "flexibility" that results has been understood, from Gramsci onwards, as a function of what sociologists see as the classical disjunction between normative and emergent domains of experience. In this view, not only social life, but also individual identity, is enough uprooted from its setting to make possible – even to encourage – an emergent set of values that are much removed from, and even contradict, other coextensively held principles. Hindus in India wear leather jackets against naked chests in home-grown gangster movies, even though they are prohibited by caste to associate with such polluted substances, and they keep pets and go to restaurants with roughly equal degrees of uneasiness and enthusiasm.

In such a world, it is argued, the only way that the contradictions existing between normative and emergent values can be justified is by flexible identities that enable the postmodern individual to inhabit diverse spaces (e.g., Martin 1994). When you are at home, you are Korean; when at work, a capitalist; when traveling locally, an American, when abroad, a tourist, a cultural ambassador, an ethnographer, and so on. This is the reality that writers such as Appadurai (1996) and Gupta and Ferguson (1992, 1997a, 1997b) have explored so insightfully.

But is the apparent chaos and rapidity of contemporary life the symptom of postmodernity or merely the sign of something else? No one would argue that the disjunctions aren't there; but if they have as profound an effect on each of us as those who write about postmodernity claim, then we, least of all, are in any position to possess or to use the intellectual skills necessary to explain them. Fortunately, however, such disjunctions also existed abundantly in the past, and do still continue to occur in non-cosmopolitan settings worldwide; it is only, I would argue, that we now seem so determined to ignore the easy solutions to settling our anxieties about the act of exploring what can and cannot be known. This unwillingness is, perhaps, the most insidious feature of the so-called postmodern condition – insidious because its remedy is as obvious as it is unacknowledged; obvious because it is, well, age old. It merely awaits reinvention – awaits an awakening, that is, in a new, more pleasurable form.

"Lived worlds" of the Living Dead

As a student of phenomenology in the early 1970s it was my habit to spend my one-month spring break each year in Spain. The sunny, arid climate could not have been more different than the gray dampness of Belgium. Moreover, at that time it was so inexpensive that getting there and staying for the month was actually less costly than sitting in my college rooms in Leuven. In fact, I would set off for the train station with my student travel card and little more than 100 dollars; usually, I would return weeks later, perhaps a bit thinner than when I left, with some spare change still in pocket.

On the first such trip, I was accompanied by a friend with whom I split rooming costs. Upon reaching Madrid we decided one evening to take in a movie. Scanning the newspaper he noticed that the cult American film *Night of the Living Dead* was playing in one of the suburban theaters. It would take some doing to get there, but he really wanted to see the film, and I had more than a passing interest in it.

You see, as a Pittsburgh native, one couldn't help but know of it. Before becoming a cult film, it had played for years as the last film of the night at many neighborhood drive-in theaters. I also had other reasons for wanting to see it myself, the principal one being that it had been made by the boyfriend of a good friend's sister. Though neither my high school buddy nor I had much use for his older sister or her friends, when it came time for soliciting bodies for the zombie scenes all of my friends volunteered. Ironically, neither my best friend nor I were among the stand-ins. His mom had insisted that he pay his own way since the age of 16, which meant he had to work late nights and most weekends at the local dairy, and my parents had insisted that the best way to grow up involved working whenever possible. When I wasn't delivering papers (starting as a 7-year-old) or working at loading and unloading trucks of unpleasant chemicals at my father's water purification company, I was usually saddled with house painting, lawn mowing, or whatever else needed to be done on weekends. So, now, years later in Madrid, I would finally get to see my friends on film.

Well, I suppose this event may have qualified as an early precursor to what today would be labeled a "postmodern" experience. Seconds after the film began, it became clear to me that it had not been subtitled. Rather, I soon realized, I would be treated to seeing my old high school buddies walking through the fields not far from our home speaking the most lovely Castilian Spanish. To make matters funnier still, we were all of us very bad students of Spanish in high school, because none of us was terribly focused academically then, and everyone knew that Spanish was the easiest way to fulfill our school's language requirement. I can still hear one of my classmates answer a question posed to him in Spanish with the words "No lo understando." To hear them speaking in dubbed voices was odd enough; to hear them speaking as native speakers in a movie about Western Pennsylvania was truly weird.

For some time after this event, I couldn't quite come to terms with what I had experienced. After all, despite the film's small budget – or rather because of it – the superficial manipulation of the "real" world made, if anything, a more disturbing scene than anything out of Hollywood. Included in the drama were not only my friends who shuffled around our local fields past the Vacuform spiders that had been placed on the sides of trees to enhance the viewer's uneasiness; but also there were the local news announcers and other celebrities I had grown up with, all speaking to one another in the finest Spanish about the munching of plastic body parts by the crazed zombies that my friends were impersonating.

And all of this in the midst of the final days of our first TV war – the broadcasting of the tragic events of Vietnam that had preoccupied this very group of friends. As one of the lucky ones, I was now studying abroad as a college student. But my buddies had more difficult choices because they came from families that basically assumed that once you were out of high school, you were on your own. Of the guys I associated with after school and at work, one was a quiet Korean American who was way too serious (he did five tours of duty); one was my pool-sharking partner (he came back addicted to heroin); one went to Canada; one joined the Peace Corps; one ended up in an asylum, and on and on. The list could run to pages, but seeing my friends transformed into proper Spanish zombies in a cheap local movie that was an actual part of our daily living at the time made the notion of hyperreality seem trivial many years before the idea of postmodernism ever entered anthropological discourse. Knowing how heavily Vietnam had weighed on the hearts of those now-Castilian zombies made me come to wonder which foreign war my friends were now true veterans of.

I raise this episode, then, not only because it so easily could be construed as a "lived experience" of the postmodern sort, but also because watching this classic horror film again, I am moved by just how compressed time becomes in moments of deep psychological stress, as well as how the noncommittal nature of the flexible postmodern identity is further deadened by the zombie-like responses of immature or atrophied senses. Why, I also wondered, were so many postmodern anxieties related to the viral-like invasion of alien personae, as if somehow we were stuck as a society in the middle of some rite of passage – stuck, that is, exactly at the transformational moment when the old person is being bid farewell, but the new one has yet to identify itself fully (Turner 1977: 107)? Why, too, I wondered, was our dominant form of possession not that of love – of merging and being creatively changed through the assimilation of another enhancing life force – but of finding oneself the object of a hostile takeover that left no room for subtlety? Why were our dominant forms of possession so much more like those of psychosis and multiple personality disorder than like the assimilative possession of love in which irony makes possible the "play" of difference?

Was it inevitable that our neglecting of the senses should leave us with only the radical forms of difference to accept? Could it be possible that we would only, then, view genuine Others as we had our own internal others – as, for example, when Native Americans (alas, even in films made by Native Americans) become characterized as either noble anachronisms or as savage reactionaries (Edgerton 1994)? And did the absence of any genuine structure to our stresses mean that we would almost never recognize that anxieties could be life-enhancing? Did the absence of collective rites, in other words, lead us to think that stress could only be negative – where the stimulus for engaging the Other is replaced by our seeing Otherness in only its most extreme and threatening forms?

These are the kinds of questions that come to me time and again, as if we could only allow ourselves to assimilate the stresses that the Other causes – to use our senses to change and grow on account of the presence of that now-assimilated different thing. Was it, then, our avulsion of the senses, and our unwillingness to *structure* them in the subtle and uncertain space between Self and Other, that made us so reticent about risking real change? Worse still, was it our lack of any collective management of stress (our lack of transformational rites) that deluded us into thinking that we actually are the inhabitants of a rapidly changing world? Maybe, we all were actually possessed, but possessed by a delusion in which we saw our world as moving quickly, rather than as fading slowly from its center.

"AMODERNITY": THE PERSON REANIMATED

> Hollywood couldn't have done it better. (Response of American hostage of Taliban to the behavior of her liberators)

> Don't worry; be happy.

In his provocative early study of television, former advertising executive Jerry Mander notes the consistency in "the terms people used in ordinary conversation to describe how they felt about television." Citing the 15 phrases he most frequently recorded, he asks the reader to think observantly, in ways, in fact, that we might call anthropological:

> If you could somehow drop all preconception of television and read this list as though people were describing some instrument you'd never seen yourself, I think the picture you would obtain is of a machine that invades, controls, and deadens the people who view it. It is not unlike the alien-operated "influencing machine" of the psychopathic fantasy.

1989	"I feel hypnotized when I watch television."
1990	"Television sucks my energy."
1991	"I feel like it's brainwashing me."
1992	"I feel like a vegetable when I'm stuck there at the tube."
1993	"Television spaces me out."
1994	"Television is an addiction and I'm an addict."
1995	"My kids look like zombies when they're watching."
1996	"TV is destroying my mind."
1997	"My kids walk around like they're in a dream because of it."
1998	"Television is making people stupid."
1999	"Television is turning my mind to mush."
2000	"If a television is on, I just can't keep my eyes off it."
2001	"I feel mesmerized by it."
2002	"TV is colonizing my brain."
2003	"How can I get my kids off it and back into life?" (Mander 1978: 157–158)

After noting how his own son claimed that the television "makes me watch it" (1978: 158), Mander characterized his own reaction as "antilife,"

> as though I'd been drained in some way, or I'd been used. I came away feeling a kind of internal deadening, as if my whole physical being had gone dormant, the victim of a

vague soft assault. The longer I'd watch, the worse I'd feel. Afterward, there was nearly always the desire to go outdoors or go to sleep, to recover my strength and my feelings. Another thing. After watching television, I'd always be aware of a kind of glowing inside my head: the images! They'd remain in there even after the set was off, like an aftertaste. Against my will, I'd find them returning to my awareness hours later. (Mander 1978: 159)

In part, I have quoted these passages at length because they are so familiar, so often said, so much of the corpus of what contemporary theorists feel separates the modern person from an earlier one who routinely spent time with others in verbal, social, and physical intercourse. But I also quote this passage because the author, uniquely I think, records the feelings of others in terms they chose and then himself characterizes this ethnographic data as not just surreal, but as "antilife" – as the lived experience, if you will, of our Castilian zombies.

"After a while," he concludes,

I came to realize that people were describing concrete physical symptoms that neither they nor anyone else actually believed were real. The people who would tell me that television was controlling their minds would then laugh about it. Or they would say they were addicted to it, or felt like vegetables while watching, and then they'd laugh at that.

People were saying they were being hypnotized, controlled, drugged, deadened, but they would not assign validity to their own experience. (Mander 1978: 159–160)

For Mander, in other words, the effects of television were less that people thought that Disneyworld America was more real than the America they inhabited, but that the experience was characterized by concrete descriptions to which individuals assigned no validity – an activity, we might add, that otherwise is associated with life on stage – a reality TV for thespian zombies.

There are, as we well know, various explanations that account for this confusion, all of which claim that modern life is chaotic and that chaos is disturbing. The modernist view, as we have noted, argues that this unstable outcome is the result of a disjunction between normative and emergent domains of experience – that people become more uncertain about what they are doing, or why they are doing what they do, in any period of human history when their expectations of change are not validated, or when that validation leads to contradicting principles. The faster history unfolds, the more confused we get. The wider the gap between normative (literally that which can be "measured") and emergent (that which is in flux), the more things appear to be changing, even when they actually become more static. Likewise, socialists argue that the rapidity of postmodern life fuels networks of power by which it becomes wholly possible to maintain "highly centralized control through decentralizing tactics" (Harvey 1989: 73). Here, networking makes possible the control of others when networkers enlist and coerce new allies more rapidly than do those with whom they compete (e.g., Latour 1987).

In such views of contemporary life, those who control and win out do so through exploiting these disjunctions. Indeed, the body itself becomes similarly envisioned as a site of disintegration and refabrication (Haraway 1991). A global network in the merchandizing of body parts allows, quite literally, for the reassembling of an individual person out of transnationally bartered bits and pieces (see Lock, this volume; Lock 2002; Lock and Honde 1990; Ohnuki-Tierney 1994; Scheper-Hughes 2000). Here again, the faster one is able to mobilize networks and exploit them, the smaller likelihood that any of us will find it possible to understand what role a sense of self might play in social encounters.

Naturally, these disjunctions will always appear greatest to us when they are happening, and especially when they create instability in our own lives, for no uncertainty moves us so much as the existential one we call living. This is why institutional living promotes in the name of "seriousness" a deeply morbid version of empathy, and why, as a homeless friend of mine argues, "if you enjoy happiness, pleasure, and hedonism, you are in big trouble!"

So, what I have to offer here is not, I think, a call of the wild, but merely a call for revisiting some forms of knowledge that those with dirtier hands than yours or mine have devoted considerable empathic energies to embodying meaningfully. For the disjunction we today experience cannot, at the level of having those experiences, seem anything but unsettling unless we are able to visit those events with both enthusiasm and a sense of enjoyment – with both humoral richness and with a sense of humor, if you will.

To my colleagues, therefore, who use the words "not serious" as a criticism levied in academic circles to describe those who prefer their liminal freedom to the dehumanizing tedium of institutional networking, I can only hope that at some point each of us may willfully achieve such a distinction. Clearly, once one is willing to examine the effects of social disjunction on the sense of self, it becomes easier to see why the self frets so intensely – why, that is, we are made to feel lonely in institutions of higher whatever, and, concomitantly, why we seem so incapable of seeing stress as anything but harmful (see Ewing, this volume).

There's no reason, except for a fear of change itself, that we should be so determined to misunderstand the often beneficial nature of stress. Though we may recognize in the abstract that stress is the primary catalyst for creative, as well as destructive, transformation, we will rarely sense its positive potential where life becomes characterized by an absence of collective encounters in which the presence of another leads to some creative mutation of self (Napier 2002, in press a, in press b). And, in the absence of such collective moments, it becomes obvious why feeling like an outsider may be our most predominantly shared sensibility. In developmental terms, then, it may as easily be the case that things in the postmodern world are actually *slowing down*, that entropy reigns when we turn a blind eye to the *frisson* – the excitement – of the exotic.

Considered in this light, it may actually be the case that the self, in fact, *changes less* in this condition of "amodernity" than it might have when the structural inversions characteristic of collective rites of passage encouraged us to think more positively about the outcome of stressful encounters. This is, perhaps, the most unsettling of conclusions that postmodernity begs – that in our forgoing the interpersonal merging of self and other in orchestrated moments of danger we may now find ourselves not only wholly incapable of change, but also wholly capable of believing that we are constantly changing. Here, the consequence of so neglecting the body's senses may well be that we refuse even to consider the all-too-real probability that our self-induced love of alienation is part of the morbid outcome of taking oneself far too seriously.

REFERENCES

Appadurai, Arjun, 1996 *Modernity at Large: Cultural Dimensions of Globalization*. Minneapolis: University of Minnesota Press.

Bourdieu, Pierre, 1977 [1972] *Outline of a Theory of Practice*. Cambridge: Cambridge University Press.

Carrithers, Michael, with Steven Collins and Steven Lukes, eds., 1985 *The Category of the Person: Anthropology, Philosophy, History*. Cambridge: Cambridge University Press.

Csordas, Thomas, 1994 *The Sacred Self: A Cultural Phenomenology of Charismatic Healing*. Berkeley: University of California Press.

Durkheim, Émile, 1898 "Représentations individuelles et représentations collectives." *Revue de Métaphysique et de Morale* 6: 273–302.

— 1915 *The Elementary Forms of Religious Life*. J. W. Swain, trans. London: George Allen and Unwin.

Durkheim, Émile, and Marcel Mauss, 1903 De Quelques formes primitives de classification: contribution à l'etude des représentations collectives. *Année Sociologique* 6: 1–72.

Edgerton, Gary, 1994 "A Breed Apart". Hollywood, Racial Stereotyping, and the Promise of Revisionism in *The Last of the Mohicans*. *Journal of American Culture: Studies of a Civilization* 17 (2): 1–20.

Edgerton, Robert, 1967 *The Cloak of Competence: Stigma in the Lives of the Mentally Retarded*. Berkeley: University of California Press.

Fjellman, Stephen M., 1992 *Vinyl Leaves: Walt Disney World and America*. Boulder, CO: Westview Press.

Foucault, Michel, 1997 Technologies of the Self. In *Essential Works of Foucault, 1954–84, Vol. 1: Ethics: Subjectivity and Truth*. Paul Rabinow, ed. Robert Hurley et al., trans. Pp. 223–251. New York: New Press.

Fraser, Steven, ed., 1995 *The Bell Curve Wars: Race, Intelligence, and the Future of America*. New York: Basic Books.

Friedman, J., 1990 Being in the World: Globalization and Localization. *Theory, Culture and Society* 7 (2–3): 311–328.

Goffman, Irving, 1963 *Stigma: Notes on the Management of Spoiled Identity*. New York: Simon and Schuster.

Goldman, Irving, 1975 *The Mouth of Heaven: An Introduction to Kwakiutl Religious Thought*. New York: John Wiley.

Gupta, Akhil, and James Ferguson, 1992 Beyond "Culture": Space, Identity, and the Politics of Difference. *Cultural Anthropology* 7 (1): 6–24.

— eds., 1997a *Anthropological Locations: Boundaries and Grounds of a Field of Science*. Berkeley: University of California Press.

— eds., 1997b *Culture, Power, Place: Explorations in Critical Anthropology*. Durham, NC: Duke University Press.

Hallowell, A. Irving, 1955 *Culture and Experience*. Philadelphia: University of Pennsylvania Press.

Haraway, Donna, 1991 *Simians, Cyborgs, and Women: The Reinvention of Nature*. New York: Routledge.

Harvey, David, 1989 *The Condition of Postmodernity: An Enquiry into the Origins of Social Change*. Oxford: Blackwell.

— 1991 Flexibility: Threat or Opportunity? *Socialist Review* 21 (1): 65–77.

Hegel, G. W. F., 1977 [1807] *Phenomenology of Spirit*. Oxford: Oxford University Press.

Herrnstein, Richard, and Charles Murray, 1994 *The Bell Curve: Intelligence and Class Structure in American Life*. New York: Free Press.

Jackson, Michael, 1983a Knowledge of the Body. *Man* 18: 327–345.

— 1983b Thinking Through the Body: An Essay on Understanding Metaphor. *Social Analysis* 14: 127–149.

— 1989 *Paths Towards a Clearing: Radical Empiricism and Ethnographic Inquiry.* Bloomington: Indiana University Press.

Kenny, Michael G., 1981 Multiple Personality and Spirit Possession. *Psychiatry* 44: 337–358.

Latour, Bruno, 1987 *Science in Action: How to Follow Scientists and Engineers Through Society.* Cambridge, MA: Harvard University Press.

— 1991 *We Have Never Been Modern.* Catherine Porter, trans. Cambridge, MA: Harvard University Press.

— 1996 Petite réflexion sur le culte moderne des dieux faitiches. Paris: Synthélabo Groupe.

Leenhardt, Maurice, 1932 Documents Néo-Calédoniens. Universite de Paris. L'Institut d'Ethnologie. Travaux et Mémoires IX. Paris: Institut d'Ethnologie.

— 1937 *Gens de la grande terre.* Paris: Gallimard.

— 1970 [1942] La Structure de la personne en Mélanésie. Milan: STOA.

Lemert, Charles, 1997 *Postmodernism Is Not What You Think.* Oxford: Blackwell.

Lock, Margaret, 2002 *Twice Dead: The Circulation of Body Parts and Remembrance of Persons.* Berkeley: University of California Press.

Lock, Margaret, and C. Honde, 1990 Reaching Consensus about Death: Heart Transplants and Cultural Identity in Japan. In *Social Science Look at Medical Ethics.* G. Weisz, ed. Pp. 99–119. Dordrecht: Kluwer Academic.

Mander, Jerry, 1978 *Four Arguments for the Elimination of Television.* New York: William Morrow.

Martin, Emily, 1994 *Flexible Bodies: Tracking Immunity in American Culture – From the Days of Polio to the Age of AIDS.* Boston, MA: Beacon Press.

Massey, Irving, 1969 *The Gaping Pig: Literature and Metamorphosis.* Berkeley: University of California Press.

Mauss, Marcel, 1938 Une Catégorie de l'esprit humain: la notion de personne, celle de "moi." Huxley Memorial Lecture, *JRAI* 68: 263–281.

— 1973 [1935] Techniques of the Body. Ben Brewster, trans. *Economy and Society* 2: 70–88.

Mestrovic, Stjepan G., 1992 *Durkheim and Postmodern Culture.* New York: Aldine de Gruyter.

Napier, A. David, 1986 *Masks, Transformation, and Paradox.* Berkeley: University of California Press.

— 1992 *Foreign Bodies: Performance, Art, and Symbolic Anthropology.* Berkeley: University of California Press.

— 2002 *The Age of Immunology.* Chicago: University of Chicago Press.

— In press (a) Dressed to Kill. In *Social and Cultural Lives of Immune Systems.* James M. Wilce, Jr., ed. London: Routledge.

— In press (b) The Writing of Passage. In *The Wounded Ethnographer.* Susan DiGiacomo, ed. London: Routledge.

Needham, Rodney, 1972 *Belief, Language, and Experience.* Oxford: Blackwell.

Ohnuki-Tierney, Emiko, 1994 Brain Death and Organ Transplantation: Cultural Bases of Medical Technology. *Current Anthropology* 35 (3): 233–254.

— 2001 Historicization of the Culture Concept. *History and Anthropology* 12 (3): 213–254.

Ortner, Sherry B., 1984 Theory in Anthropology since the Sixties. *Comparative Studies in Society and History* 26 (1): 126–166.

— 1995 Resistance and the Problem of Ethnographic Refusal. *Comparative Studies in Society and History* 37 (1): 173–193.

Payer, Lynn, 1988 *Medicine and Culture: Varieties of Treatment in the United States, England, West Germany, and France.* New York: Henry Holt.

Perry, John, ed., 1975 *Personal Identity.* Berkeley: University of California Press.

Phillips, Adam, 1994 *On Flirtation*. Cambridge, MA: Harvard University Press.

Pollock, Donald, 1996 Training Tales: US Medical Autobiography. *Cultural Anthropology* 11 (3): 339–361.

Ricoeur, Paul, 1992 *Oneself as Another*. Kathleen Blamey, trans. Chicago: University of Chicago Press.

Rodseth, Lars, 1998 Distributive Models of Culture: A Sapirian Alternative to Essentialism. *American Anthropologist* 100 (1): 55–65.

Scheper-Hughes, Nancy, 2000 The Global Traffic in Human Organs (with comments). *Current Anthropology* 41 (2): 191–224.

Shapiro, Andrew, 1992 *We're Number One: Where America Stands – and Falls – in the New World Order*. New York: Random House.

Spencer, Jonathan, 1989 Anthropology as a Kind of Writing. *Man* 24: 145–164.

Stoller, Paul, 1989a *Fusion of the Worlds: An Ethnography of Possession Among the Songhay of Niger*. Chicago: University of Chicago Press.

— 1989b *The Taste of Ethnographic Things: The Senses in Anthropology*. Philadelphia: University of Pennsylvania Press.

— 1997 *Sensuous Scholarship*. Philadelphia: University of Pennsylvania Press.

Taussig, Michael, 1992 *The Nervous System*. London: Routledge.

— 1993 *Mimesis and Alterity: A Particular History of the Senses*. London: Routledge.

Turner, Victor, 1977 [1969] *The Ritual Process: Structure and Anti-Structure*. Ithaca, NY: Cornell University Press.

van Gennep, Arnold, 1960 [1909] *The Rites of Passage*. Monika Vizedom and Gabrielle Caffee, trans. Chicago: University of Chicago Press.

Weck, Wolfgang, 1976 [1937] *Heilkunde und Volkstum auf Bali*. Jakarta: P. T. Bap Bali and P. T. Intermasa.

Wikan, Unni, 1996 The Nun's Story: Reflections on an Age-Old, Postmodern Dilemma. *American Anthropologist* 98 (2): 279–289.

CHAPTER 12 Immigrant Identities and Emotion

Katherine Pratt Ewing

No matter what the circumstances, migration is a stressful, emotionally charged experience of discontinuity and rupture difficult to imagine for those who have not been through it. Americans live with an ambivalent national myth of immigration, replete with images of those who disembarked at Ellis Island, knowing they would perhaps never see their distant homeland or relatives again. Many of those whose families arrived in the first half of the twentieth century face a familial amnesia, produced by the first generation's efforts to obliterate evidence of their foreignness in the "melting pot" of America in a political and social environment where assimilation was the prerequisite for acceptance. Even within Europe, migrants, though they may have covered shorter distances, often crossed political borders and experienced barriers to communication and pressures for assimilation that increased the social distance from home. But migration in today's post-Cold War world is usually quite a different phenomenon. Migrants often arrive by airplane, after a crossing that takes hours rather than days or weeks. When they arrive, many can readily pick up the phone and call home, or fly back for visits during the holidays. And instead of a melting pot, migrants are now more likely to face a new society that, at least ostensibly, values "multiculturalism" and the preservation of ethnic identity.

Despite these changing conditions and a changing discourse surrounding cultural difference, migrants, whether they move for economic reasons or as political refugees, inevitably face cultural, social, and political dislocation. And even when a rhetoric of multiculturalism pervades public discourse, the institutions that migrants must deal with in everyday life may not recognize or tolerate cultural difference, often penalizing or pathologizing lack of conformity to mainstream values and practices. Their situation, shaped as it is by political and economic conditions, as well as the sheer force of dislocation, offers a particular challenge to the anthropology of emotions, a sub-discipline in which issues such as those faced by immigrants have often been relegated to the background.

The anthropology of emotions has been grounded in a tension between two fundamentally different approaches. One major strand, until recently the dominant one in American cultural anthropology, is cultural relativism, which in its most extreme form posits that all human experience, including emotion, is culturally and socially constituted and can only be understood with reference to the unique cultural matrix in which it emerges, an approach that leaves little place for considering those who fall between cultures. On the other side are universalist and comparative approaches that attempt to see beyond cultural variation to universal aspects of emotion or that seek to compare cultures along specific, objectively measurable dimensions that are observable across societies, such as manifestations of rage or the sense of autonomy, but that rarely extend their gaze beyond the psychobiological and, the matrix of the family (see Lindholm, this volume; Lutz and White 1986; Leavitt 1996).

In this chapter I ask how we can think about emotion and culture in such situations of radical dislocation in a way that is not hampered by these dichotomies that have traditionally plagued the anthropology of emotions and that make it difficult to focus on the in-betweenness of migration. I argue that migration is an affectively highly charged and fluid situation, which makes particularly visible the role that social and interpretive practices play in producing specific manifestations and experiences of emotion. After briefly discussing what the divergent approaches predominant in emotion theory tend to foreground and what they can contribute to the study of migrant emotion, I focus on a setting in which specific configurations of emotion, subjectivity, and identity are produced. This is the medical clinic, where many migrants seek help in managing the stresses of migration. The clinic may be seen as an example, along with the media, of what White (this volume) calls "the proximal zones of everyday experience" or social contexts in which, he argues, people interpret, discuss, and recreate emotions in their own lives. I look at how the discursive practices in clinical settings may foster miscommunication and position the migrant in relations of authority and power in ways that contribute to new articulations of emotional experience and identity formation in the new home. I then focus on the emotional structuring of memories of one's old home, which is also influenced by the historical circumstances of migration. I consider the role such memories play in migrant identity formation and in the shaping of relationships between first and second generation migrants. These relationships, in turn, play an important role in the temporal transmission of emotional structures and identity.

THE CULTURAL CONSTRUCTION OF EMOTION

Cultural constructionists focus on emotional displays as culturally constituted expressions of meaning and on culturally specific markers of social position and forms of social action. Most arguments concerning the cultural construction of emotion, including the American anthropological tradition, as well as the Foucauldian tradition, posit a notion of culture as sufficiently systemic, coherent, and hegemonic to distinctively shape the person or self, including the organization and expression of emotion: "The individual is the site, but not the source, of emotional events," and "the learned feelings that individuals express are consonant with the ambient social order, its norms, its ideals, its structures of authority" (Reddy 1999: 259). This has been a prominent strand both in the anthropology of emotions and related studies of self and identity. Drawing on the work of anthropologists such as Unni Wikan and Jean Briggs, who have questioned cultural relativism in their own ethnographic work, Lindholm (this volume) foregrounds several of the limitations of cultural constructionism, which has tended to overemphasize the cultural, cognitive articulation of emotional experience at the expense of unconscious processes, emotional conflict, and those aspects of affective experience that are not elaborated or overtly recognized within a particular cultural tradition. (Robert Levy coined the term "hypocognized" to refer to emotional states that are not verbally recognized or elaborated within a particular cultural tradition.)

There is a tendency for studies of cultural systems to focus on informants' articulated cultural understandings of emotion and to ignore what may be unarticulated contours of emotion, thereby overemphasizing the verbal dimensions of emotional communication. This bias, however, has been addressed by anthropologists who have examined the non-verbal dimensions of affective communication (e.g., Feld 1982, 1995; Irvine 1990; Urban 1988), describing in detail the observable properties of cultural practices such as ritual wailing, in order to identify the elements that make such practices identifiable to an outside observer. Such approaches provide tools for identifying expressions of culturally shaped emotional expression without relying solely on a culture's verbally articulated discursive practices. Because these contours of emotion are unarticulated, it may be expected that such implicit practices (including those of the "host" society as well as of the immigrant's society of origin) may be focal points of experiences of miscommunication for migrants.

Cultural constructionism has illuminated many of the social aspects of emotional experience and expression. There have been studies that focus on relations of power and authority in the shaping of emotion within particular societies (Myers 1979; Keeler 1983). Some of these studies observe how power flows through emotional performance (Gerber 1985; Trawick 1990; Rosaldo 1980), so that feeling is understood to be a physical expression of culturally shaped authority and resistance (see Lindholm, this volume; Rosaldo 1984: 143). Issues of power and authority and their cultural dimensions are central in migrant experience, since many migrants find themselves at the bottom of the social hierarchy. But how to frame these issues from within a culturally relativist position continues to be problematic. Theorists who focus on how culturally constituted affective styles and displays within social communities may be shaped by class identification and social position often argue these can only be understood within specific social contexts that cannot be generalized across cultures without losing the significance of a particular configuration of meaning (Besnier 1995: 435). As a theoretical starting point, a cultural constructionist approach such as this poses particular difficulty when inquiry is focused on people who are between cultures and thus not clearly shaped by a single hegemonic culture.

Aside from these theoretical limitations, strict cultural constructionism, because of its emphasis on cultural difference, may cast the issues facing the immigrant into dichotomies that have practical consequences for the position of migrants. For example, the culture of origin may be seen to shape the structures of feeling out of which emerge emotional reactions to the new place, and/or the culture of the receiving society is expected to mold newcomers, or at least their children, creating sharp discontinuities between generations. By identifying incommensurable cultures that constitute incommensurable structures of feeling, this approach foregrounds rupture and may even exaggerate discontinuities such as the one between first and second generations. By seeing the culture of origin as constituting these foreigners as alien and absolutely different, cultural relativism may encourage and legitimize the misrecognition of basic emotions and their force, thereby dehumanizing others (see Lindholm's discussion of Renato Rosaldo's work, this volume). In my discussion of the experiences of immigrants in distress who seek clinical help, I will demonstrate instances of such misrecognition that can have specific effects not only on the treatment of these immigrants, but also on their social positioning and identity.

A political consequence of the model of culture as a system of meaning that shapes individuals even to the extent of constituting their emotional responses is that social scientists and those developing social policy often operationalize such models of radical cultural difference to justify pressuring migrant groups to "assimilate" in the form of giving up one's culture of origin in order to take on a new national–cultural identity. Making the opposite argument, advocates of multiculturalism argue minorities must be allowed (and in some cases even forced) to maintain their "traditions," as if cultures are static wholes that must be preserved intact.

UNIVERSALIST AND COMPARATIVE APPROACHES

Studies that focus on the universals of emotional experience may set aside the issue of culture altogether as they seek to discover common patterns based on physiological reactions to stimuli underlying overtly different cultural practices (see Lindholm, White, this volume). Psychoanalysis and early psychoanalytic anthropology, taking a universalist approach, posited that the human psyche is grounded in conflict between biologically based drives and defenses against these drives. Though anthropologists have rightly objected that this type of psychoanalytic approach reduced culture to little more than a collective defense mechanism against socially unacceptable wishes, later psychoanalytic theory has focused on the constitution of the self through a universal developmental process of identification (Hartmann 1964; Kohut 1977), turning away from a focus on primal drives that cannot be directly observed to a focus on identifications that have culturally specific contents. This literature has been useful for anthropologists concerned with examining phenomena such as the psychodynamics of authority relations and power (Hall 1997; Ewing 2004) and the role of fantasy in these relations (Zizek 1995; Navaro-Yashin 2002). These approaches have relevance for understanding many of the conflicts that migrants experience when they find themselves at the bottom of the social hierarchy and disempowered, their sense of self and competence challenged by their experience of being culturally and socially novice in a new environment. A strength of psychoanalytically informed approaches is that they go beyond explicitly articulated and rationally motivated aspects of social interaction and experience to implicit and unrecognized dimensions of often unconscious conflicts that may profoundly and overtly shape interactions.

The social psychology and cultural psychology literatures approach emotion from a comparative perspective, focusing on the ways that universal emotions are shaped by specific features of the cultural environment to produce specific emotional orientations (e.g., Kagitçibasi 1996; Markus and Kitayama 1991; Shweder 1991). The focus, however, is not on specifying how each culture may produce a unique configuration of emotions, but rather on identifying dichotomous dimensions of difference such as "independent vs. interdependent" and "individual vs. sociocentric." By challenging the universality of a Western model of the self, this literature makes an important contribution to our understanding of what can be profound differences that shape migrant experience. Nevertheless, there is a tendency to dichotomize such self-orientations, characterizing general differences between Western and non-Western societies rather than dimensions that may vary independently (see Kagitçibasi 1996). Much of the psychology and social psychology literature has a strong normative component in which a model for optimal human development is presented. Such approaches may strongly color perspectives on migrants, by casting the "problems" of assimilation in terms of dichotomies that result in the attribution to migrants of non-modern views of personhood and emotional orientation. For example, a key problem for the immigrant may be presumed to be one of making a transition from a sociocentric family and community to a society in which people are expected to function as autonomous individuals.

In sum, cultural and social psychologists are generally concerned with finding accurate ways of diagnostically measuring emotional states that are comparable from one culture, community, or minority group to another, while psychoanalytic anthropologists tend to focus on psychodynamic processes that are associated with universal aspects of social interaction.

MIGRANTS AND EMOTION

A fruitful place to begin an anthropology of migrant emotion that escapes the dichotomy between cultural construction and biological universalism is with a focus on the experience of dislocation and how it is managed, highlighting how cultural differences are negotiated both by migrants themselves and by the receiving society, while taking into consideration power and structures of authority that migrants must negotiate and basic (universal) psychological strategies, such as the defensive linkage of certain emotions like grief and anger.

With the disruption of the notion of culture as cohesive and bounded have come anthropologists such as Renato Rosaldo (1993) who, while rejecting the clinical roots and focus of many psychological anthropologists, have recognized the universal "force" of emotions and the linkages between emotions, such as grief and anger, that transcend particular cultures. Rosaldo has focused on borders and cultural crossings, and he has been among those anthropologists who have recast the concept of culture to mean a fluid process rather than a static system. His efforts at establishing a different stance from which to view emotion and culture, by looking at people at the interstices of cultures, offer an approach especially relevant to the study of migrants and the emotional significance of their border crossings, and one that seeks to transcend the dichotomy between cultural particularity and human universals.

There are also useful models for this endeavor in the anthropological turn to issues of trauma and violence. Scheper-Hughes (1992), for instance, looks at the cultural factors and ideologies, as well as economic forces, at state and local levels that constitute a situation of everyday violence for many Brazilian shantytown mothers. She has demonstrated that the emotional attachment of these mothers to their children is blunted by the precariousness of the children's survival, so that mothers actually engage in practices that reduce the chances of survival for their weaker children even further. Instead of assuming that fixed cultural meanings shape these women's behaviors, one can see the cultural practices of these mothers emerging and developing out of dire necessity and powerlessness. Among migrants, we can also expect to see new cultural practices emerging in emotionally stressful situations generated by existing structures of power and inequality.

Also important are efforts by "historians of emotion" such as William Reddy to envisage historical change in the expression of emotions within a society by close examination of the politics of emotion. Reddy draws on Raymond Williams's concept of "structures of feeling," which arise out of the forces and relations of production characteristic of a historical era and particular location. For Williams, a structure of feeling is a hegemonic cultural configuration that justifies and organizes these relations (Williams 1973; Reddy 1999: 257). Williams emphasizes that these structures are never static, thereby allowing us to take into account even radical discontinuities such as those associated with migration. Reddy has taken up Williams's model as a starting point in his effort to develop a theory of emotion that foregrounds the question of whether and how feelings change over time in tandem with changing political conditions and associated projects of cultural hegemony or liberation. I find both Williams's and Reddy's concerns useful for considering "structures of feeling" among migrants because the situation of migration is characterized above all by change and is so profoundly constituted by the forces and changing relations of production on a global scale, with migrants being the vanguard of this globalization process.

Though it would be inaccurate to make sweeping generalizations applicable to all immigrants, there are certain common material conditions and social relations in the situations that virtually all immigrants face. There is, for example, the confrontation with sheer cultural and linguistic difference, which forces first generation immigrants to devise strategies for adaptation and to navigate the specifics of their particular situations. And there is the challenge of the discontinuities between pre- and post-migration identities, as well as between the first and second generations. These discontinuities create the experience of watching one's children grow up with a different sense of place and home and with a cultural competence in the new setting that, even in childhood, often surpasses that of their parents. On the other hand, the cultural practices and interpretive strategies that migrants bring with them shape the experience of and responses to these changing relationships.

Are there distinctive structures of feeling, associated with new and changing cultural practices, that are characteristic of immigrants? For example, immigrants today face a historically particular ideology of cultural pluralism that may generate ways of managing cultural difference and emotional expression that are very different from the expectations of total assimilation that were hegemonic in an earlier era, when in the United States the identity of America as a "melting pot" prevailed and when the nationalist project in most countries included the goal of creating a national identity in citizens that included the creation of powerful nationalist sentiments and emotional structures. I will argue below that certain kinds of nostalgia associated with a "myth of return" and its inverse, the abjection of one's homeland, are additional components of such structures of feeling that characterize migrant experience under specific conditions that are shaped by the historical relationship between the societies that the migrant is moving between and by a hegemonic discourse that serves the interests of the host society.

Given these historically particular circumstances, what sites can we identify as shaping the emotional responses of migrants to their experience of migration and its discontinuities? One everyday site that shapes immigrants' self-experience is the healthcare system. I shall turn first to clinical literature focused on immigrants who have sought help in managing the stresses of living in a diasporic situation, foregrounding the cultural practices and exercise of power and authority within the clinical situation itself and on how these are experienced by immigrants. It is in such settings that a rhetoric of multiculturalism gives way to the everyday deployment of hegemonic cultural models of illness and pathology that migrants face as they renegotiate their identities in a new social environment.

MISCOMMUNICATION IN CLINICAL SETTINGS

Clinical literature includes a range of detailed case studies of migrants who have experienced difficulties and manifest some form of symptomatic complaint. Participants in such studies are not necessarily representative of the migrant communities to which they belong, since most migrants do not actually seek help for emotional distress. But these studies, when read against the grain, do reveal the contours of one of the key structures of authority that the immigrant to a Western country is likely to experience: the healthcare system and the hegemonic cultural practices that sustain the authority of doctors and researchers to diagnose and treat. These experiences of authoritative cultural practices are likely to shape immigrant understandings of their own emotions and are a significant aspect of cultural negotiation and socialization into the new society. By reading against the grain of these studies, I mean to suggest a focus, not so much on a study's diagnostic conclusions, which are usually based on Western diagnostic categories that are assumed to be universally applicable, but on the rough spots in the clinical encounter as clinical researchers struggled with language barriers, miscommunications, and the reticence and silences of interviewees. Though there are many clinical studies in which these "rough spots" are seen as a function of the inabilities of migrant patients to communicate their distress adequately because of their cultural backwardness, I focus here on studies in which the researchers have themselves foregrounded the problem of cultural difference and question aspects of hegemonic medical discourse and practice that reinforce miscommunication.

A salient characteristic of most clinical literature is how it authorizes the medicalized discourse of the dominant "host" culture as modern scientific truth and not just as an aspect of a particular culture, and how this discourse interprets the practices and emotional discourse of the migrant as "traditional" and wrong, so that the patient in a clinical setting is often rendered unwilling to articulate or acknowledge what have been labeled "traditional" practices. Much of this literature, which includes a diagnostic component, is conceptually organized in terms of a series of dichotomies that rearticulate the migrant's structure of emotions in a clinical setting. In addition to the modern–traditional dichotomy, these dichotomies include a characterization of societies as creating either individualistic or sociocentric orientations, in terms of which the migrant is often considered to lack a strong sense of individuality by comparison with the Western subject (a distinction prominent in the social psychology literature).

Another dichotomy often imposed on patients is that between the body and the psyche. It can be humiliating or bewildering for a patient when he or she is told that complaints that are expressed and experienced as physical are really psychological and then the patient is referred to a psychotherapist. Each of these dichotomies may create or exacerbate a cultural gap in the clinical situation.

There is a pervasive dichotomy between "modern" medical and psychiatric diagnostic and treatment strategies on the one hand, and "traditional" beliefs and treatment approaches on the other. Not only is cultural difference often seen by clinicians in these hierarchically ordered terms, but also those migrants who seek treatment are likely to have experienced a similar dichotomy between modernity and backward tradition back home, and overtly concur with this judgment. Nevertheless, a person may covertly experience and understand their distress in terms of the cultural practices that prevailed in their natal families and local community, even if he or she maintains a "modern" identity and feels that they must hide what they actually think.

In specific case histories we may see individuals who disrupt these categories. For example, Streit et al. (1998) have published a culturally sensitive psychiatric case history of an unmarried middle-aged Moroccan woman who sought treatment for depression five months after migrating to Canada. She projected an identity as a modern, cosmopolitan woman who had worked as a flight attendant out of Casablanca for nearly a decade before migrating. Nevertheless, she had grown up in a small, conservative Moroccan town: she was of the first generation in her family to attend school, and her mother, herself married at the age of nine, had arranged her engagement to a cousin (which was later broken off). Despite her modern self-presentation and identity, she retained an emotional life that was powerfully shaped by this cultural background, but it does not easily correspond to the dichotomies commonly used in social psychology.

In early therapeutic sessions, she reported difficulties in her current social interactions that she attributed to cultural difference (Streit et al. 1998: 450). But as the investigators came to know her history, her descriptions of her relationships prior to migration revealed similar difficulties, including efforts to maintain "independence" and a fear of trust that predated even her move to Casablanca from the "traditional" area where she grew up. Far from "independence" being a trait she had acquired or struggled to achieve as a consequence of migration, it seemed to have been a trait for which her mother, who had been divorced by her husband after he took a second wife, had been the role model.

At the same time, this Moroccan woman is a clear instance of someone with an overtly modern identity that coexists with what have been characterized as "traditional" beliefs and practices carefully hidden in the Western clinical setting. This aspect of her emotional life emerged during the course of psychotherapy only with great difficulty and in the presence of an Arabic-speaking psychotherapist. After many weeks of psychotherapy she revealed a previously disavowed motive for her migration to Canada: the move had been an attempt to escape "sorcellerie," magical acts committed against her by her father and aunt. But far from being an enactment of an underlying, private paranoia, as might be assumed in most Western clinical settings, her migration had been a decision made on the advice of her mother's family and thus had been quite openly discussed in that context. The hegemonic cultural models that prevail in Western clinical settings make it very difficult for such a patient to admit these beliefs. In this case, they only emerged because of the unusual circumstance of the availability of a therapist who shared her language and elements of her cultural background.

During the course of my own research in Pakistan, I knew an urban family that saw themselves as being quite "modern" in orientation. All of the grown children were highly educated, and the family maintained a reformist orientation toward Islam, rejecting what they regarded as "superstitious" practices such as praying at the tombs of Sufi saints in times of need or removing evil influences by giving donations to the poor. Yet when facing distress, various family members often resorted to such practices (see Ewing 1997). I thus found a surprising disjunction between their public identity as a modern family, which was maintained through their ideological positions and overt practices in conversations with their friends, neighbors, and the visiting anthropologist, and their covert practices when in distress. This disjunction affected family dynamics, creating silences even within the family during some of their most emotionally charged situations. For those family members who subsequently migrated to the United States, this pattern of overt ideology and silence was intensified, and the therapeutic value of these stigmatized practices was further disavowed.

A study of somatizing Turkish women in Sweden by Bäärnhielm and Ekblad (2000) demonstrates the communication gap that the medical dichotomy between the psychological and the physical can generate. The women studied were labor migrants who had come originally from a group of villages in central Anatolia, and who had an average of six years of education. The authors point out that the women did not share a static, coherent system of illness beliefs and were all involved in actively internalizing new ideas and methods based in part on their encounters with the Swedish medical system. For instance, though the heart is an important idiom in Turkish for expressing emotional distress, several women described avoiding talking about the heart to Swedish caregivers because they thought they would be misunderstood. For them, psychiatric disorders were connected with a shameful loss of control and unpleasant behavior toward others (Bäärnhielm and Ekblad 2000: 440). With respect to a modern façade overlying a covert adherence to what they construed to be backwards in the Swedish clinical environment, several of the women revealed in the context of the research study that they had visited *hocas* (Turkish religious/folk healers) as well as Swedish healthcare givers, but felt that they could not discuss such visits with clinicians because they would not accept this practice or understand it. They thus hid their own participation in "traditional" cultural practices. Furthermore, because the researchers had arranged to have translations from Turkish to Swedish independently verified, the study discovered that the participants' emotional language had not always been correctly translated. The researchers concluded that such mistranslations may further contribute to clinicians' incorrect assessment of patients as somatizing psychological and social distress (Bäärnhielm and Ekblad 2000: 447).

A similar point was made in a study of elderly Korean migrants in the US (Pang 1998). Pang argued these migrants' references to physical manifestations of distress are often not, strictly speaking, somatizations at all. American clinicians, presuming cultural difference, did not recognize culturally patterned metaphorical expressions for specific forms of emotional distress. Pang, though taking as a starting point the "psychologization–somatization continuum," in which more self-directed people tend to psychologize while more other-directed people somatize, makes the important point that what may sound like somatization to a Western diagnostic ear may actually be something quite different: "With Koreans, human organs are often used as metaphors to represent emotions" (Pang 1998: 97). Pang notes, for instance, that expressions of emotion such as "clings to my heart" are stated as if these emotions had form, structure, and energy. Thus, cultural practices of naming emotions may shape the communication of distress in ways that lead Western clinicians and researchers to take literally expressions intended as metaphors, thereby exaggerating cultural difference at a diagnostic level.

Medical discourse has the power to shape these patients' experiences of themselves at the most intimate level. Diagnosis and treatment may constitute the immigrant in an alien identity – as one who is, for example, traditional, superstitious, overly dependent on others, as having "mental" problems, as helpless and incompetent, even child-like. Though not all migrants go through the mental healthcare system, virtually everyone passes through the medical system for physical ailments or routine healthcare. Even in these situations, the sense of alienation from one's old cultural practices and homeland, the potential for miscommunication, and the possibility of negative identity formation vis-à-vis the hegemonic culture are likely.

NOSTALGIA, ABJECTION, AND THE MYTH OF RETURN

Another key element shaping the experience of migration and emotional responses to it is the significance of the act of migration to the people who choose to make such a major change in their lives. The significance of migration is shaped by the socio-political, economic, and cultural context in which it occurs. Many migrants take this step as part of a larger movement in which neighbors and relatives have also chosen to migrate, and there are often specific myths of migration that are shaped both by its cultural significance and by the historical circumstances of the migration. These myths in turn shape individuals' expectations, plans, and identities. For instance, in recent years, as a result of civil war and economic crisis, young Somali men have sought to migrate as refugees. But these dramatic political and economic circumstances, though they provide the impetus for migration, are incorporated into a structure of feeling that is shaped by a Somali cultural model. Rousseau et al. (1998) describe a collective dream shared by young Somali migrants that gives the anticipation of migration a particular significance that is ritually enacted in the months of waiting for authorization to travel and powerfully shapes the experience of migration. They argue that "pastoralism predisposes the Somali to value travel as a way of maturing [and] that age-based peer groups create a special migratory dynamics" (Rousseau et al. 1998: 385). In the long liminal period between the decision to leave and the actual opportunity, these young man engage in a drug-linked ritual in which they talk about and live in a state of dream travel. The arrival in the new country creates a potentially harsh juxtaposition between the socially constituted self of dream travel and the actual situation of being marginalized at the bottom of the social hierarchy.

Just as significant for the situation and identity of the migrant is how he or she thinks of the relationship to the natal home after the move. It is here that the contours of emotion, or structures of feeling, can best be understood as a point of conjunction between desires and defenses of the individual, understood in situational and psychodynamic terms, on the one hand, and historically constituted structures of feeling on the other. In certain situations this conjunction may produce a polarized relationship to one's homeland that is characterized by either nostalgia or abjection.

The experience of nostalgia is a historically constituted structure of feeling, shaped by political and cultural factors, a major one being the relationship between the two societies that the migrant moves between. For example, rural Turks who began migrating to Germany and other parts of northern Europe in the 1960s and 1970s were labeled "guestworkers" by the host country, and they correspondingly saw their own migration as temporary. There was a clear expectation that they would return to Turkey after having saved enough money to improve the family situation back home. Most of these guestworkers thus shared a nostalgic "myth of return" – the expectation that they would eventually move back to Turkey permanently. This "myth of return" was largely fostered by the identity of "guestworker" that the Germans bestowed on them and by concrete immigration policies, which encouraged the temporary migration of men from rural areas with little education and forced them to leave their families behind. It, in turn, powerfully shaped their identities and adaptations to Germany.

But the emotional power of the nostalgic myth of return can also be understood at least in part in psychodynamic terms as a manifestation of a defensive response to the stresses of migration. Psychoanalysts have looked at the nostalgia that migrants often feel toward their "mother country" and explained it in psychodynamic terms. The psychoanalytic literature seeks to identify specific defensive strategies that people characteristically resort to when confronted with stressful situations such as migration. Evidence for the defensive strategies and conflicts that are identified can be found in the discursive structure of narratives produced in the clinical procedures of psychoanalysis and long-term psychotherapy.

According to Akhtar (1999), nostalgia helps the immigrant defend against the rage that would otherwise be experienced in the face of the frustrations and strangeness of everyday life in the new situation. This rage and frustration can be potentially overwhelming, particularly for migrants who experience a significant drop in status and constant social discrimination in the host country (see Fassbinder 1989). Nostalgia may also foster a psychological splitting, in which ambivalence about the experience of migration is managed by nostalgically creating a memory of one's homeland as "all good" and the new country as "all bad" (Mirsky 1991: 620; Nathan 1988). Though the particular cultural content of the "good" and the "bad" will be specific to the cultural background of the migrant and the characteristics of the new environment, this nostalgic splitting appears to be a common reaction. Nostalgia may generate specific responses that can make the process of integration into the host society more difficult. For instance, fear of the dangerous influences of the strange culture that are likely to corrupt one's children is made all the more threatening because it is experienced in sharp contrast to an idealized homeland, a fear that may make immigrant parents overprotective of their children, preventing them from fully entering into a social life with school friends (see Baser 1986). In other circumstances, the splitting process may actually create a relationship with the homeland that is the inverse of nostalgia, so that one's old life and culture are abjected (rejected with horror and disgust; Kristeva 1982) and the newness fully embraced, creating a kind of repression through a rejection of one's old attachments. This reaction may occur when the migrant moves to a globally dominant country such as the United States from one that has been marginalized in the global order. Fanon describes an element of this process in *Black Skin, White Masks* in his analysis of the relationship between a colonial power and the colonized subject: "let us go to welcome one of those who are coming home [to the Antilles after a stay in France]. The 'newcomer' reveals himself at once; he answers only in French, and he often no longer understands Creole [his native tongue]" (Fanon 1967: 23). Fanon's book examines what he calls a "self-division" that is generated within the colonized subject, who disavows his or her natal culture and self. A similar division can be produced in the migrant who recognizes and embraces the cultural hegemony of the country to which he or she moves. This process of abjection of one's homeland is vividly articulated in the statement of another young man, a Somali refugee who had migrated to North America: "I don't deny the existence of my native culture, but everything to do with it disgusts me" (quoted in Rousseau et al. 1998: 407).

The process of splitting and abjection, however, may be difficult for some migrants to maintain, or it may create silences or disturbances that can echo through the next generation. Rousseau et al. summarize the case of a 34-year-old Somali who had been diagnosed as a paranoid schizophrenic: "He willingly spoke about his symptoms, his diagnosis, and his medication. He became very defensive, however, when his past life was mentioned. He said that he had changed his name, converted to Christianity, and given up his Somali citizenship" (Rousseau et al. 1998: 405). It is as though a Western disease was an easier identity to accept than that of being a Somali. Among refugees, especially those who have gone through traumatic violence before migrating, splitting and silence are a common response (see, for example, Binder-Brynes et al. 1996). Children of such survivors often experience disturbances in their own lives because of these effects of trauma on their parents (Waxman 2000). Though these are extreme examples, they reflect one possible response to the stress of migration that may affect even migrant families who have not experienced severe trauma.

THE SECOND GENERATION

The myths generated through the process of migration may become transformed over time, dramatically reshaping the migrant's social positioning and identities. The myth of return among Turks living in Germany continued to shape orientations to Germany even as government policies changed and workers were allowed to bring their families during the 1980s. But now it has contributed to considerable emotional upheaval in many families, as the second generation has moved into adolescence and young adulthood.

The myth contributes to the disjunctions between the first generation's perceptions of life in Germany and the perspectives of their children who have grown up in Germany and do not see Turkey as their home. In many cases, their children have been the forces that have led them to finally give up the dream of returning. Giving up this myth has led to a cascade of changes in the orientation of these families. A common source of tension and emotional strife within such families had been the overprotectiveness of parents who perceived German society as alien and threatening. Daughters were the particular focus of parental constraint, as parents tried to maintain rural Turkish cultural practices in which daughters were closely protected and married off to a relative at an early age. As long as the first generation retained the dream of returning to Turkey, they felt that it was important to educate and train their children to be able to make the transition to living in a society that the children had participated in only during summer holidays. In the early years many also tried to minimize the formal education of their daughters. But these children did attend German schools, and most lacked sufficient formal training in Turkish to be able to adapt easily to life in Turkey. This problem was aggravated by the fact that conditions in Turkey had also changed during their prolonged absence: education in rural areas had become much more widespread and was increasingly a job requirement. Local cultural practices in Turkey had changed as migrants in Germany clung to remembered ways that had become obsolete – even the language had changed considerably.

The relinquishment of the myth of return appears to be a shift of orientation within the entire community, as each family's decision is influenced by those of their neighbors and friends, generating a new, culturally shaped structure of feeling. This decision has many repercussions. To give the example of one family: shortly after making the decision never to move back to Turkey, they replaced their old, second-hand furniture with new fancy furniture, including a large leather couch and marble coffee table. Where the oldest children had taken Turkish as their second language in school, the younger children enrolled in English. They applied for German citizenship and, finally, decided to purchase an apartment. (Families planning to return to Turkey typically invest their savings in real estate – apartments and houses – in Turkey). Along with these changes comes a new identity in relation to place. This shift is also likely to have political ramifications, as migrants focus on establishing institutions in the place that they now recognize as home.

The relinquishment of the myth of return may make nostalgia for one's homeland all the more intense. But the experience of such nostalgia is not unique to those who migrate. As a part of his exploration of structures of feeling, Raymond Williams examined the feeling of nostalgia that was associated with the passage from rural to urban life and observed that much of its power comes from its association with childhood:

> We have seen how often an idea of the country is an idea of childhood: not only the local memories, or the ideally shared communal memory, but the feel of childhood: of delighted absorption in our own world, from which, eventually, in the course of growing up, we are distanced and separated, so that it and the world become things we observe . . . But what is interesting now is that we have enough stories and memories of urban childhoods to perceive the same pattern. The old urban working-class community; the

delights of corner-shops, gas lamps, horsecabs, trams, and piestalls: all gone, it seems in successive generations. These urban ways and objects seem to have, in the literature, the same real emotional substance as the brooks, commons, hedges, cottages, and festivals of the rural scene. (Williams 1973: 292)

This is a temporal rather than a spatial nostalgia, and one that we all may partake of. The second generation of Turks in Germany have their own nostalgic memories of childhood – for the Berlin flat they spent their earliest years in, for a shop that went out of business years ago. And the second generation may also encompass a similar nostalgia for Turkey, such as the memory of a beautiful summer spent in the Anatolian hills. These memories may create an emotional bridge between parent and child. But as long as the parents' nostalgia is attached to a myth of return, it is a spatialized nostalgia that their children simply cannot share. Those who do return to Turkey and try to pick up their old lives often experience disillusionment. Migrants who are now grandparents realize that the relatives they originally left behind in Turkey are no longer as important to them as they once were, and they realize that all of their roots are really back in Germany – in the form of their own children and grandchildren.

Conclusion

Migration is at a fundamental level a dislocation that forces the migrant to adapt to a new social environment and to take up new identities associated with the fact of having moved. The taking up of new identities is a cultural process in which even the stresses of dislocation are given meaning, not only through local cultural practices and the institutions with which migrants interact, but also by broad forces such as the historical relationship and relative status of the countries between which the migrant moves. These forces can create emotional stances, shared structures of feeling, such as nostalgia for or abjection of one's former identities and homeland, that become vehicles for the expression and management of basic affects such as rage and desire and the emotional conflicts associated with managing these physiologically linked states. These structures of feeling, in turn, shape the relationship between the generations within the immigrant family and become the ground on which new identities rest.

REFERENCES

Akhtar, S., 1999 The Immigrant, the Exile, and the Experience of Nostalgia. *Journal of Applied Psychoanalytic Studies* 1: 123–130.

Bäärnhielm, Sofie, and Solvig Ekblad, 2000 Turkish Migrant Women Encountering Healthcare in Stockholm: A Qualitative Study of Somatization and Illness Meaning. *Culture, Medicine, and Psychiatry* 24: 431–452.

Baser, Tevfik, 1986 *40m2 Deutschland*. T. Baser, Director. Hamburg.

Besnier, Niko, 1995 *Literacy, Emotion, and Authority: Reading and Writing on a Polynesian Atoll*. Cambridge: Cambridge University Press.

Binder-Brynes, K., with A. Elkin, B. Kahana, J. Schmeidler, S. M. Southwick, and R. Yehuda, 1996 Dissociation in Aging Holocaust Survivors. *American Journal of Psychiatry* 153: 935–940.

Ekman, Paul, 1974 Universal Facial Expressions of Emotion. In *Culture and Personality: Contemporary Readings*. R. A. LeVine, ed. Pp. 8–15. Chicago: Aldine.

Ewing, Katherine Pratt, 1997 *Arguing Sainthood: Modernity, Psychoanalysis, and Islam*. Durham NC: Duke University Press.

— 2004 Migration, Identity Negotiation, and Self-Experience. In *Worlds on the Move: Globalization, Migration and Cultural Security*. J. Friedman, and S. Randeria, eds. London: Taurus.

Fanon, Frantz, 1967 *Black Skin, White Masks*. C. L. Markmann, trans. New York: Grove Press.

Fassbinder, Rainer Werner, dir., 1989 *Angst Essen Seele Auf* (*Fear eats the soul*). New York: New Yorker Video.

Feld, Steven, 1982 *Sound and Sentiment: Birds, Weeping, Poetics, and Song in Kaluli Expression*. Philadelphia: University of Pennsylvania Press.

— 1995 Wept Thoughts: The Voicing of Kaluli Memories. In *South Pacific Oral Traditions*. R. Finnegan and M. Orbell, eds. Bloomington: Indiana University Press.

Gerber, Eleanor, 1985 Rage and Obligation: Samoan Emotion in Conflict. In *Person, Self, and Experience: Exploring Pacific Ethnopsychologies*. G. M. White and J. Kirkpatrick, eds. Pp. 121–167. Berkeley: University of California Press.

Hall, Stuart, 1997 Introduction: Who Needs Identity? In *Questions of Cultural Identity*. Stuart Hall, ed. Pp. 1–17. London: Sage.

Hartmann, Heinz, 1964 *Essays on Ego Psychology: Selected Problems in Psychoanalytic Theory*. New York: International Universities Press.

Irvine, Judith T., 1990 Registering Affect: Heteroglossia in the Linguistic Expression of Emotion. In *Language and the Politics of Emotion*. Catherine Lutz and Lila Abu-Lughod, eds. Pp. 126–161. Cambridge: Cambridge University Press.

Kagitçibasi, Çigdem, 1996 The Autonomous-Relational Self: A New Synthesis. *European Psychologist* 1 (3): 180–186.

Keeler, Ward, 1983 Shame and Stage Fright in Java. *Ethos* 11: 152–165.

Kohut, Heinz, 1977 *The Restoration of the Self*. New York: International Universities Press.

Kristeva, Julia, 1982 *Powers of Horror: An Essay on Abjection*. New York: Columbia University Press.

Leavitt, John, 1996 Meaning and Feeling in the Anthropology of Emotions. *American Ethnologist* 23 (3): 514–539.

Lutz, Catherine A., and Geoffrey M. White, 1986 The Anthropology of Emotion. *Annual Reviews in Anthropology* 15: 405–436.

Markus, Hazel Rose, and Shinobu Kitayama, 1991 Culture and the Self: Implications for Cognition, Emotion, and Motivation. *Psychological Review* 98 (2): 224–253.

Mirsky, J., 1991 Language in Migration: Separation–Individuation Conflicts in Relation to the Mother Tongue and the New Language. *Psychotherapy* 28: 618–624.

Myers, Fred R., 1979 Emotions and the Self: A Theory of Personhood and Political Order among Pintupi Aborigines. *Ethos* 7: 343–370.

Nathan, T., 1988 La Migration des ames. *Nouvelle revue d'éthnospsychiatrie* 11: 25–42.

Navaro-Yashin, Yael, 2002 *Faces of the State: Secularism and Public Life in Turkey*. Princeton, NJ: Princeton University Press.

Pang, Keum Young Chung, 1998 Symptoms of Depression in Elderly Korean Immigrants: Narration and the Healing Process. *Culture, Medicine, and Psychiatry* 22: 93–122.

Reddy, William M., 1999 Emotional Liberty: Politics and History in the Anthropology of Emotions. *Cultural Anthropology* 14 (2): 256–288.

Rosaldo, Michelle Z., 1980 *Knowledge and Passion: Ilongot Notions of Self and Social Life.* Cambridge: Cambridge University Press.

— 1984 Toward an Anthropology of Self and Feeling. In *Culture Theory.* Richard A. Shweder and Robert A. LeVine, eds. Cambridge: Cambridge University Press.

Rosaldo, Renato, 1993 [1989] *Culture and Truth: The Remaking of Social Analysis.* Boston, MA: Beacon Press.

Rousseau, Cécile, with Taher M. Said, Marie-Josée Gagné, and Gilles Bibeau, 1998 Between Myth and Madness: The Premigration Dream of Leaving among Young Somali Refugees. *Culture, Medicine, and Psychiatry* 22: 385–411.

Scheper-Hughes, Nancy, 1992 *Death Without Weeping: The Violence of Everday Life in Brazil.* Berkeley: University of California Press.

Shweder, Richard A., 1991 *Thinking Through Cultures: Expeditions in Cultural Psychology.* Cambridge, MA: Harvard University Press.

Streit, Ursala, Jean LeBlanc, and Abdelwahed Mekki-Berrada, 1998 A Moroccan Woman Suffering from Depression: Migration as an Attampt to Escape Sorcellerie. *Culture, Medicine, and Psychiatry* 22: 445–463.

Trawick, Margaret, 1990 The Ideology of Love in a Tamil Family. In *Divine Passions: The Social Construction of Emotion In India.* Owen M. Lynch, ed. Pp. 37–63. Berkeley: University of California Press.

Urban, Greg, 1988 Ritual Wailing in Amerindian Brazil. *American Anthropologist* 90: 385–400.

Waxman, Mayer, 2000 Traumatic Hand-Me-Downs: The Holocaust, Where Does It End? *Families in Society: The Journal of Contemporary Human Services* 81 (1): 59–64.

Williams, Raymond, 1973 *The Country and the City.* Oxford: Oxford University Press.

Žižek, Slavoj, 1995 *The Sublime Object of Ideology.* London: Verso.

CHAPTER 13

Emotive Institutions

Geoffrey M. White

When writing the first draft of this chapter less than one month following the September 11 attacks, it was impossible to think about the problem of emotion without reference to the severe disturbance in American national consciousness, with grief, vengeful patriotism, and fearful anticipation rippling through people's daily lives. As that moment takes its place in world history, it nonetheless provides a powerful reminder of the social forces that elicit and shape emotions – forces that we urgently need to understand from cultural and global perspectives. One goal of developing the idea of "emotive institutions" is to do some conceptual bridge-work, however tentative, between realms of social theory that are often separated by disciplinary specializations.

All of us who were caught up in the mass-mediated images and stories of September 11 are aware of the strong influence of American media in making news out of personal stories of tragedy and heroism. Consider the special publication issued by *Time* magazine, dated September 11, which circulated a photographic montage of images of the moments of destruction and its immediate aftermath, including a two-page photo of people plunging to their death from the upper floors of the World Trade Center. In the weeks following, the media filled our electronic spaces with the imagery of grieving families, funerals, and memorials, on the one hand, and preparations for war on the other. How do such images, fleeting and partial as they may be, affect emotions and subjectivity, especially *national* subjectivity?

Adding to the discussion of emotion in other chapters in this volume, this chapter emphasizes the distinctly social character of emotion and, by implication, the role of specifically ethnographic research in understanding its meaning and force in everyday life. The chapter begins with a brief reflection on the ways the disciplines of psychology and anthropology have approached the social dimensions of emotion. I argue that longstanding (Western) models of the person as a bounded individual, and of the mind as a wellspring of natural impulses, tend to privilege psychobiological determinants of emotional experience, relegating the role of language, cognition, and social context to marginal status. The idea of "emotive institution" presumes that physiological, cognitive, and social relational factors converge in jointly producing emotional experience. The chapter then briefly considers some examples of emotive institutions as a way of illustrating its usefulness in focusing attention on the role of social context and social relational factors in constituting emotional experience.

Historically, anthropology, working in small communities, has had much to say about the ways ritual and ceremony bind emotions and identities. Yet the discipline has only recently given serious attention to the recurrent, socially organized emotions of everyday life in more complex societies. Media studies and cultural studies give attention to the electronic images and fast-moving culture flows that affect the national imagination, but there is almost no work on the social contexts within which people interpret, discuss, and recreate those emotions in their own lives. Funerals and memorial ceremonies that have recently been the subject of news reporting are good examples of institutionalized activities that evoke, define, and transform emotion. Yet what is their significance for people who participate as viewers? How do we interpolate our own experience with screen images – a subject more familiar to film theory than the anthropology of emotion? The current state of emotion theory, riven with dichotomies that separate affective experience from social and interpretive practices, has little to say about the ways emotions are produced in the proximal zones of everyday experience.

The history of emotion theory is largely one of oscillation between binaries of mind–body or nature–culture. One of the primary contributions of anthropological theory has been to strengthen the case for the salience of social and cultural factors in these oppositions. At the same time (and often in reaction to these relativizing moves), the field has been concerned to demonstrate the basis for universal, biologically based core emotions. Yet approaches to emotion across this spectrum often remain firmly anchored in individual-centered paradigms. Evolutionary theories have reinforced individual-centered models of emotion by speculating that emotions have become individualized through a historical process of increasing individuation. In this view, modern emotion is more a matter of individual experience because the modern (read *Western*) person is more autonomous, more free of the bonds of tradition or communal societies. For example:

> Moving from simple, to complex traditional, to modern communities, there is a progressive shifting of emphasis from control through shared coherent interpretations, that is through the shared definitions of reality which are possible in small isolated communities, to control through powerful externally provided symbolic forms in large, complex traditional communities, and, finally, to the complex relatively autonomous psychodynamic self-controls of modern society. (Lewis 1992: 23)

Even studies of cultural formations of emotion frequently reduce to the specification of cognitive models *about* emotions conceptualized as given, or primary, or basic. Some of the most detailed comparative studies of emotion have focused on the cognitive organization of commonsense representations of emotion, often in the form of "scripts." This chapter reflects on some of the limitations of methodological individualism and sketches the concept of emotive institution as a way to think about the mutual influences of psychology, culture, and discourse (the things that people say and do in everyday life). By focusing on the patterned contexts of emotional experience, it is possible to recognize that emotions are also located within wider spheres of ideology and political structure.

Raymond Williams's felicitous phrase "structures of feeling" provides a useful start-ing point for discussing emotive institutions. Although Williams was more interested in disrupting Marxist concepts of "structure" than expanding our thinking about "feeling," the phrase is useful precisely because it transgresses the separation of fixed, visible social "structure" and more inchoate psychological "feeling." Williams notes the "separation of the social from the personal" is a "powerful and directive cultural mode"(1977: 128). He goes on to argue institutions and traditions (the kinds of macro-formations studied by sociologists and political scientists) "become social con-sciousness only when they are lived, actively, in real relationships"(1977: 130–131).

Williams's suggestion that cultural analysis entails the study of personal and social forms as they are "actually lived" reflects the importance of practice in his theory of culture. The idea of "structures of feeling" suggests that in order to understand the meanings of emotions we need to look at the scenes and activities within which they are expressed or represented. By the same token, the flip side of Williams's connection of emotion and practice is that emotions are at the same time embedded in larger structures of ideology and political structure.

What, then, are some examples of "emotive institutions" that might illustrate this duality or dialectic of emotion – at once intensely situated in the communicative immediacy of daily life, yet also part of larger structural formations? In my own work on emotion, I have been interested in widely different means through which emo-tional meaning is created in specific forms of representation or discourse – as diverse as village meetings in Pacific Island societies and national war memorials in the United States. Across this spectrum, I have been struck by the significant role played by socially organized activities in facilitating (and creating) culturally meaningful forms of emotion. These are more than "settings" for the expression of preexisting emotions. They are culturally constituted *activities* within which understandings of self as well as social identities and relations are enacted and defined. In the process of enactment, cultural models, social identities, and emotional dispositions all become real, in the sense put forward by Raymond Williams. At the same time, they are also "at risk" of being redefined or transformed as they are manifest in communicative routines and practices.

Conflict discourse, therapeutic transactions, and memorial ceremonies are all examples of institutionalized forms of interaction rich in expressions and significa-tions of emotion. Such activities presuppose an event structure bounded loosely in time and space, as well as culturally specified subject positions and communicative practices. Participants make use of their knowledge of such contexts to craft emo-tional realities in the moment-to-moment negotiations of everyday life. As a result, these kinds of socially organized situations constitute local ecologies of emotion that organize the play of emotions emerging in recurrent frames of interaction.

Having said this, the term "institution" is liable to reintroduce an overly structured and bounded sense of social structure into the study of emotion (the very thing that Williams was concerned to get rid of decades ago). However, at this juncture, when dominant views regard emotions as things that spring from the genetically programmed neural pathways of individual physiology, the risk is probably worth taking.

EMOTIONS AND THE INDIVIDUAL: DISCIPLINARY APPROACHES

Social context has always been a dimension of emotion theory, but usually as an arena for the expression of preformed affects or cognitive scripts that encode emotional process. Earlier work in "culture and personality" also took seriously linkages between exterior and interior worlds of the individual. But most of that work assumed a greater degree of stability or solidity in concepts of social structure and cultural system than would be the case today. Similar assumptions are evident in many of the approaches from social psychology that regard social context as secondary to the primary physiological and cognitive determinants of emotion. Underlying these views of the social are individual-centered paradigms that locate emotional process in the brain, with other more public interpretive or social factors providing a subsequent layer of definition or management.

From the classic work of Tomkins (1962) and Schachter and Singer (1962) onward, much of the social psychology of emotion has focused on interpretive aspects of emotion, such as evaluations or appraisals that process information about social relations and situations. While there is a great deal of good work in this area, much of it is limited by the assumption that the relevant aspects of social context are internalized in a person's knowledge or perceptions of social interaction – in emotion schemas and the like. These approaches tend to miss the constitutive function of communicative practices that operate in culturally defined, socially organized activities. In short, the social scenes and discursive practices that define and shape emotional experience in everyday life remain a residual element in many psychological approaches.

Theorists who offer *sociological* theories of emotion, attempting to widen the lens to include social relational factors, also tend to relocate the social in cognition or dichotomize social "context" from individual affect. Theodore Kemper, for example, writes:

> The groups and group categories that matter for the production of emotions include social class; occupation, gender, and racial/ethnic groups; and peer groups, families, communities, crowds, audiences, and nations. Each of these memberships provides the individual with identity, motives, goals, roles, and interaction partners.
>
> Given that the individual is the locus of emotion – we can measure emotion nowhere but in the individual – the containment of the individual in the social matrix determines *which emotions are likely to be expressed when and where, on what grounds and for what reasons, by what modes of expression, by whom.* (Kemper 2000: 45; emphasis in original)

This separation of emotion and context is also evident in writing on the influence of social groups on the "encoding" and "decoding" of emotion. In this line of reasoning, social groups only become relevant as a fixed element of individual identity. So, for example, the members of a social group that perceives itself in a subordinate position will be more likely to respond to a violation with "sadness" than with "anger" (Hess and Kirouac 2000: 370).

Psychological approaches interested in examining the social and cultural dimensions of emotion have begun to articulate a more complicated view of emotions as located in the socially organized contexts of daily life. Kitayama and Markus, editors of a volume of studies of emotion from psychology, linguistics, and anthropology, note that a number of authors "address how emotions are constructed and experienced within a social and cultural context" and that this approach "assumes that emotions are best seen as an assortment of socially shared scripts made up of physiological, subjective, and behavioral processes . . . many of which are intermental, afforded or enabled in interpersonal communications and interactions" (1994: 10). This is a promising move toward socializing the emotions. But the analysis of these social dimensions still largely reduces to the specification of cognitive schemata that are about social interaction, such as "appraisal patterns associated with the current situation" (1994: 12).

Another way in which psychologists have pushed the boundaries of the psychological "skin" of emotion is through the idea of "focal emotion events" (de Mesquita 1993). This idea calls attention to relations between socially situated scenes of emotion and script-like cognitive schemata that represent such scenes. So, for example, a culturally significant emotion in a particular society, one that is "hypercognized" in terms described by Levy (1973), may be represented as an event category that "represents a number of appraisals, bodily reactions, and action tendencies packaged densely into a relatively coherent whole"(Kitayama and Markus 1994: 11). These ideas point to the utility of examining the operation of emotions, and talk of emotions, in actual social situations or, in other words, the ethnography of emotion.

A related approach to focal emotions is evident in Menon and Shweder's (1994) analysis of the Indian concept of *lajya*, which they describe as a kind of shame that functions to regulate women's uncontrollable, although morally justifiable, rage. Based on an analysis of narratives elicited in interviews, the authors assess the social organization of knowledge of *lajya* in terms of underlying emotion scripts. This study's attempt to locate a culturally specific emotion within its broader societal context addresses the social functions of emotion in Oriya social life. Although this study's reliance on data elicited in interview situations limits analysis to cultural ideals, the authors show clearly some of the ideological uses of emotion in articulating social problems such as issues of power and control in gender relations.

In our earlier overview of the anthropology of emotions, Catherine Lutz and I proposed a shift in emphasis in the comparative study of emotion away from discrete biopsychological affects or cultural categories of emotion to greater consideration of the social psychological work that emotions do for people in and through social life (Lutz and White 1986). As we put it then, "Emphasis is shifted away from the question of whether a somehow decontextualized emotional experience is 'the same' or 'different' across cultures to that of how people make sense of life's *events* [emphasis added]. What needs to be explored are the particular ways in which cultural meaning and social structure relate to these general characterizations" (1986: 428). We then offered several paths for such an exploration, searching for frameworks of comparison that allow an expansion of context in the analysis of emotional meaning.

THE DISCURSIVE TURN

Recent studies in anthropology, linguistics, and discursive psychology reflect broad interest in the pragmatic work done by emotion in social life (Desjarlais and O'Nell 2000; Edwards 1997; Palmer and Occhi 1999). This interest in pragmatics acknowledges the importance of language and communicative practice for the formation of emotional meaning. The methodological implications of these developments, as stated by Abu-Lughod and Lutz, entail "a turn to detailed, empirical studies of conversation, poetics, rhetoric, and argument about and with emotional content" (1990: 10).

Interest in theorizing emotion discourse, in all of the ways that the term is used, reflects growing awareness of the limitations of strictly psychological or symbolic approaches to emotion. Two books that appeared about the same time over a decade ago promoted the analysis of emotion as embedded in discourse and social context. The volume *Language and the Politics of Emotion* (Lutz and Abu-Lughod 1990) presented ethnographic studies that jointly argued for the study of emotion in the public and externalized performances of ordinary language, where emotions emerge in the communicative practice of interested actors. At the same time, *Disentangling: Conflict Discourse in Pacific Societies* (Watson-Gegeo and White 1990) brought together a range of studies using various kinds of discourse analysis to examine local practices used to solve or transform social conflicts. Although not defined initially as a study of emotions, emotions proved to be a recurrent topic in *Disentangling*. Through the comparative study of emotion in social context, those studies demonstrated that discourses of emotion are widely used to form and reform social realities.

Theory in linguistic anthropology, with its historical interest in matters of "context" and event-centered analysis, has much to offer in thinking through emotive institutions. A great deal of work in sociolinguistics has drawn attention to the mutual, contingent relations between language and context. Just as word selection, inflection, code-switching, and other kinds of linguistic variation can serve to define a social situation (as formal or informal, intimate or distant, and so forth), so expressions of emotion function as indexical signs with powerful context-defining potential. In this approach, neither "emotion" nor "identity" provides a fixed referent (Besnier 1990). To the contrary, discourse approaches view emotion as emergent in the course of social interaction. Such a perspective affords a "more complex view of the multiple, shifting, and contested meanings possible in emotional utterances" (Abu-Lughod and Lutz 1990: 11).

In his book *Discourse and Cognition*, Derek Edwards (1997) contrasts cognitivist approaches with discourse-centered approaches to emotion. He underscores the performative value or pragmatic force of emotions and emotion language in conversation, arguing that, in contrast with lexical or semantic approaches such as that of Anna Wierzbicka (1992), "the discursive approach examines samples of talk and text for how various kinds of functional, social interactional business are attended to (such as blamings, reasons, excuses, accounts, etc.), and looks for how emotion words, and even their roles in scripted sequences or scenarios, figure in those discursive activities" (1997: 179). For Edwards, a defining feature of emotion is its realization in narrative and "situated rhetoric." In his view, "Emotion categories are not graspable merely as individual feelings or expressions [nor as] a kind of detached, cognitive sensemaking. They are discursive phenomena and need to be studied as such, as part of how talk performs social actions" (1997: 187).

Discourse-centered approaches see emotions as cultural tools rather than (or in addition to) lexical entries or schematic models. In other words, an analysis of emotions as discourse does not limit itself to semantic representation, but asks what emotions, and talk about emotions, do in situated uses of language, including conversation, narrative, rhetoric, media texts, and so forth. In this way, analysis focuses directly on relations between emotions and their social and psychological significance within culturally defined contexts. So, for example, in the work of Capps and Ochs (1995) on panic disorder, they note important connections between narrative practices, especially "collaborative storytelling," and the "co-construction" of emotions and identities among family members. "In this way storytelling interactions simultaneously shape the physical and psychological spaces members have inhabited and those they will inhabit in the future" (1995: 151).

Whereas narrow readings of "discourse" refer specifically to language use or performative actions, a wider sense of discourse refers to institutionalized practices that create regimes of truth and structure social relations. When applied to emotions, this broader reading of discourse points to the ideological force of emotions and the role of emotions and emotion rhetoric in reproducing social structural arrangements. In particular, emotions and emotional expressions play important roles in (re)producing relations of power, and in defining or asserting the social identities and relations from which people speak and feel. In other words, socially significant emotions always entail a moral imperative, an impulse toward altering or redefining social worlds.

Situating Emotional Practice

Given these various developments in the study of emotion in discourse, how might we conceptualize "emotive institutions"? There is, of course, a long tradition of work in anthropology on institutionalized contexts for the expression and transformation of emotion. Much of this has been concerned with ritualized activities such as healing, initiation, and so forth. As noted by Levy and Wellenkamp (1989: 23), "Such cultural institutions as healing practices and symbolic productions (e.g., ritual, myth, folk tales, poetry, drama, etc.) are important areas of investigation for their possible functions in expressing or deflecting or defending against emotions which may not be normally expressed in other ordinary, everyday arenas."

The concept of emotive institution includes things like rituals and myths, but to be most useful should not be limited to fixed or bounded events. While ceremonial activities are important paradigmatic cases for the social expression and formation of emotion, they represent a specialized instance of practices that are more widespread and flexible, evident in all kinds of recurring scenes in everyday life, from the quasi-scripted encounters between flight attendants and airline passengers studied by Arlie Hochschild (1983) to TV news. Such interactions, although less formalized in time and space, situate emotions in recurrent frames fixed by social positions and activities as well as conventions of language. Just as the "emotion work" of flight attendants to maintain the scripts of polite customer relations indexes social identities, so the social milieu of airplanes establishes a range of culturally defined emotions. However momentary or contested they may be, such "fixings" are integral to the expression and transformation of emotion in everyday life. The key point is that emotions and identities are linked in mutually constitutive relations. The contingent relations between emotions and social identities or positions have been most thoroughly discussed in work on relations between gender and emotion (Hochschild 1983; Abu-Lughod 1987; Lutz 1990).

Emotive institutions, then, consist of socially situated discursive practices that variously evoke, represent, and transform emotional experience. In such activities, emotional and social meaning make each other up. In other words, emotive institutions are not simply institutionalized occasions for the expression of scripted emotions, but rather constitute points of *articulation* between embodied feeling, cultural models of emotion, and socially organized activities where emotions and emotion talk do specific kinds of pragmatic work. Since emotion scripts generally presuppose specific social identities and relations, emotive institutions are doubly social: they generate discourse *about* social relations, at the same time as they enable the *enactment* or *embodiment* of identities in ongoing interaction.

The notion of emotive institution pushes for closer attention to the properties of situations, contexts, and institutionalized activities in which emotions obtain social meaning and force. At the most basic level, we may ask how, when, where, by whom, and toward what culturally defined end(s) are emotions enacted in discourse. Each question represents a dimension of potential "fixing," of framing which, in turn, may be used to fix or define others. Such questions provide some useful heuristics for investigating the social ecology and pragmatic organization of emotions, but should not be mistaken for a list of necessary features of emotive institutions. To inquire about the extent to which emotion discourse is organized in recurrent, socially situated practices, we may ask whether those practices involve:

1   Culturally defined purpose(s)
2   Temporal event structure
3   Spatial location
4   Key identities and relations
5   Focal emotion schema(s)
6   Specific communicative practices

So, for example, family dinners constitute a recurrent scene for the production of emotions within middle-class American families. Obviously, the social and ritual aspects of family dinners vary widely from one household to the next. Yet, for any one family, the temporal, spatial, and social dimensions of these activities very often create consistent contexts for the production of social emotional meanings characteristic of family relations.

Consider two other widely disparate examples of emotive institutions: village meetings in a Pacific Island community and commemorative practices at a United States war memorial (White 1990, 2000). The social, political, and economic contexts of these two types of activity are obviously very different. But in both cases expressions of emotion index and define the activities at hand. In the village meetings, participants gather together to talk about "bad feelings" associated with social conflicts in the community. And at America's national memorial to the World War II attack on Pearl Harbor, the site is often said to be a place of "intense emotion" as visitors find personal meaning there.

Despite differences, both types of activity involve the (re-)narration of emotions and identities. Both are concerned to one degree or another with problematic emotions of "anger" and sentiments of moral conflict associated with past events. And both find much of their power in situated activities that support public representations and enactments that variously reimagine and re-emotionalize the histories they work to represent.

In the village meetings as well as the war memorial, emotions are more of a social achievement than a presumptive state of underlying feeling. In the case of the village meetings, participants co-narrate accounts of past events in order to re-present the significance of troublesome conflicts. But the possibility for failure is ever present, as people who should speak may remain silent or even refuse to attend, and as narrative accounts obtain varying degrees of force or persuasiveness. Quite different risks surround the war memorial. Insofar as the Pearl Harbor memorial also functions as a tourist attraction in one of the world's busiest tourist economies, those who manage the site work actively to create the context of a national cemetery and memorial rather than a "Disneyland" theme park for holiday goers. In the face of visitors who arrive at the memorial to enjoy a free movie and boat ride on a day of Hawai'i sightseeing, interpretive guides work to create a context of mournful (and patriotic) reflection. In both cases, the task of sustaining a desired social emotional reality is never final or complete.

The studies of various "disentangling" practices used by Pacific Island communities to manage or resolve social conflicts reveal a number of differences between local definitions of these events and Western categories of "conflict resolution," "therapy," "court," and so forth (Watson-Gegeo and White 1990). Recognizing these problems of translation and interpretation, the authors decided to refer to these activities with the metaphor of "disentangling," an image commonly used in Austronesian languages for such activities. The expression and management of emotions, especially through narrative, proved to be a significant dimension of many of these activities.

Disentangling practices as varied as gossip sessions and village meetings commonly involve narrative representations of contested interactions and emotional responses. In the case of village meetings, many of the institutionalized aspects of these activities follow from their significance as *culturally defined* events that entail a number of distinct, locating parameters, including:

1   Purpose: "disentangling" (conflict resolution)
2   Temporal organization: a scheduled meeting, indeterminate duration
3   Spatial location: village house
4   Social identities: kin and co-residents
5   Focal emotions: "sadness" (*di'a nagnafa*), "shame" (*mamaja*)
6   Communicative practices: narrative storytelling

Set out in these terms, the idea of emotive institution has much in common with the concept of "communicative event" as described initially by Dell Hymes (1964) and elaborated in subsequent work on "speech events" in sociolinguistics. An early interest in the emotive dimensions of speech events identified by Roman Jacobson has become an important element in this line of research (Ochs 1986; Schieffelin 1990).

As always, the social and cultural conditions of small communities allow forms of social interaction that presuppose densely shared local knowledge. Participants not only share knowledge of local histories and events, they also share the communicative competence necessary for the co-production of disentangling activities. Disentangling meetings may take many forms, large and small. A large meeting will take place in a darkened house at night, with no visible center. People speak from the margins in no obvious predetermined sequence. These events are collectively orchestrated through the artful performance of narrative talk – talk that marks beginnings and endings, as well as sequencing of topics and speakers. The definition of the situation, and the fit between particular kinds of discursive practice and social knowledge, allow participants to jointly produce narrative accounts that reconceptualize and recontextualize problematic events and the feelings that go with them.

It is the possibility of "disentangling" as a culturally constituted activity that enables the performative production of (new) emotional meanings. In particular, "disentangling" practices are particularly good at the rhetorical production of sentiments of "sadness" and "shame" (White 1990). As an emotive institution, "disentangling" condenses a set of social and cultural conditions enabling certain kinds of emotion work. The co-presence of closely related people, gathered together to talk through past conflicts with preferred modes of talk, makes it possible to represent and rework specific emotional meanings. It is also possible that the narrative invocations of "sadness" and "shame" in these contexts work to displace disruptive and threatening feelings of "anger." (Note that this chapter is unable to address the translation issues marked by these English terms.)

Seen in historical context, the larger, village-level forms of disentangling evident at mid-century have given way to a number of Christian practices, including confessional prayer and smaller family-level meetings. Whereas the latter do some of the emotion work once done in village meetings (still concerned to "disentangle" conflicts through narratives of sadness and shame), they are structured differently, with changed social identities and discourse organization (family discussion, led by a priest). The concept of emotive institution, then, makes it possible to raise questions about historical shifts in the institutional frameworks for emotion talk.

In contrast to the small-scale, bounded appearance of village meetings, the Pearl Harbor memorial is an intensely busy and complex site. Managed by the National Park Service, the USS *Arizona* Memorial is built over a sunken battleship in the middle of an active U.S. Navy base. Nearly 4,000 people visit the memorial each day. Visitors move through a space laden with significant images and texts, especially those represented in a museum and film that must be viewed before boarding a boat to visit the memorial (built over the sunken ship with its entombed crew). The space is both open-ended and directive. People may wander around the visitor center, take in parts of the museum, buy souvenirs in a gift shop, and generally gaze over today's naval base. However, one's actual visit to the memorial/shrine is highly coded by a required film and an audio program that narrate the history of Pearl Harbor just prior to setting foot on the memorial.

Here, too, it is possible to see a configuration of spatial, temporal, and discursive factors that coalesce in the cultural production of emotional meaning:

1 *Purpose(s)*: "remember," learn history, memorialize, mourn, tourist fun . . .
2 *Temporal organization*: 75-minute tour plus informal time
3 *Spatial location*: shrine site and visitor center
4 *Social identities*: nationalities, regional identities, ethnicity, "tourist" . . .
5 *Focal emotions*: sadness, grief, pride
6 *Communicative practices*: film and audio narration, museum exhibits, talks

Despite the checklist format, these factors should not be construed as some kind of finite list of discrete features or conditions of the memorial as an emotive institution. Rather, these factors identify conditions and practices that jointly organize the production of specific kinds of emotional meaning, still allowing for wide social and individual variation as people interact with these various means of representation. As was the case for village disentangling activities, the memorial is a public space for reimagining key identities and emotions. In this case, the identities are national identities and the emotions are emotions of loss associated with historic tragedy.

In comparison to disentangling activities, the memorial is less structured by specific social relations, allowing for an experience which is both personal (individual) yet sharing in avowedly collective (especially national) emotions. Individual experience here is extensively guided by diverse discursive practices, including interpretive talks, film, audio programming, and viewing the "silent" memorial in the company of others. In other words, a variety of semiotic means and social practices are available for imagining one's own place in history. In this regard, the film is especially effective in using metacommunicative strategies to suture the "I" of the viewer into the subject position of national remembrance. At the end of the film, following its documentary account of the Pearl Harbor attack, the film concludes by depicting visitors to the memorial engaged in acts of ritual remembrance. At that point the film's narrator asks, "How shall we remember them . . ." (White 1997).

As in the case of disentangling meetings, the memorial makes extensive use of narrative to craft emotional meaning. Given the diversity of visitors to the memorial, however, the effects of particular practices for any one person's understanding vary widely. (For example, in assessing generational differences in responses to the memorial's film, I have found that older Americans, especially the World War II generation, report greater degrees of emotionality than younger Americans.) Nonetheless, the managers of the memorial recognize that the narrative tools they employ to create emotional meaning work to direct and influence people's responses.

Ten years ago the memorial's Park Service managers concluded that the film being shown at the time was out of step with the purpose of the memorial. In their judgment, the film, which had been made by the US Navy, was too "aggressive." It tended to generate a sense of national pride in military victory, rather than create a reflective mood appropriate to a "cemetery." The solution was to produce a new film that would engender a different set of meanings more in harmony with shifting definitions of the site and its focal emotions. The change of films at the memorial illustrates one way in which the memorial site, as an emotive institution, creates a context and set of activities that shape desired forms of emotional meaning. In both examples it is possible to see not only the historical contingency of emotion discourse, but also the utility of the concept of emotive institution for connecting emotions with wider forces of social historical change.

Asking about emotions in the context of activities such as "disentangling" and memorial remembrance illustrates the degree to which emotions are embedded in social relations, activities, and practices. While it has long been observed that emotion concepts frequently take the form of event schemas, scenarios, dramas, and the like, these have generally been studied as cognitive structures with only secondary reference to situated activities. The concept of emotive institution attempts to make connections to the social explicit by locating emotion in recurrent culturally constituted activities, which in turn entail social positions and practices embedded in wider institutional arrangements of power, ideology, and politics.

The focus on articulations between psychological–cognitive and social–pragmatic dimensions of emotion addresses longstanding difficulties of relating cognitive models to the social and political aspects of everyday life. Capps and Ochs (1995) noted this problem in their discussion of the limitations of therapeutic practices that attempt to work primarily through ideational or cognitive interventions. They comment on the difficulties faced by narrative therapies that attempt to reformulate or re-narrate a client's subjective understanding without attending to the contexts and activities within which those understandings are used. Critiquing standard approaches to narrative therapy (e.g., White and Epston 1990), Capps and Ochs (1995: 179) ask:

> To what extent can we change our life stories (and our lives) without accessing their formation – the rudimentary linguistic tools that we use to construct them? Substituting narratives of success for problem-saturated narratives may alleviate distress, and substitute versions that provide a positive model for the interpretation of ongoing experience. Yet sufferers may not be able to sustain these models in their future lives when they tell stories to themselves and others. A missing piece of this therapeutic enterprise may well be apprenticeship into a "grammar of success."

Even more significant than the "grammar of success" and its discursive means is the social milieu within which participants co-construct social realities. If treatment remains in a symbolic plane, without specific connections to the social and interactive contexts in which clients and (significant) others create emotional meaning, new narratives are unlikely to obtain pragmatic value and force. The force of narrative models must in some way derive from their articulation with other aspects of a client's life where social meanings emerge through interactions with others.

One of the methodological implications of this critique is the need for ethnographic approaches capable of researching situated expressions of emotion. The call for ethnographies of emotion in practice directs attention to language use and the significance of emotion and emotion talk in performative contexts of everyday life. For anthropologists, this is certainly not new. For example, in their review of anthropological methods for the study of emotion, Levy and Wellenkamp (1989) note the field's preference for "techniques of observation and inquiry which are responsive to an emerging understanding of local forms" and for "detailed accounts of 'natural' settings." But as a strategy for the comparative study of emotion, the call for ethnographic work on emotive institutions does entail closer attention to the mutual, contingent relations between affect, cognitive models, and performative constructions of emotion in the recurrent scenes of everyday life.

These strategies also suggest ways of linking the narrow and broad senses of the term "discourse." At one level, emotive institutions constitute recurrent scenes and activities where focal emotions and identities emerge in everyday interaction. Here, discourse may be studied as communicative practice with methods of linguistics, psychology, and anthropology. At another level, however, emotive institutions participate in wider institutional complexes that play a role in reproducing political and ideological formations. Here, the study of emotive institutions edges into the fields of political science, sociology, and history (among others) and offers a way of looking at historical transformations, such as shifting forms of conflict resolution or the production of emotions associated with national memory. In the process, it should be possible to build further linkages between often-disconnected realms of social theory.

REFERENCES

Abu-Lughod, Lila, 1987 *Veiled Sentiments: Honor and Poetry in a Bedouin Society*. Berkeley: University of California Press.

Abu-Lughod, Lila, and Catherine Lutz, 1990 Introduction: Emotion, Discourse, and the Politics of Everyday Life. In *Language and the Politics of Emotion*. Lila Abu-Lughod and Catherine Lutz, eds. Pp. 1–23. Cambridge: Cambridge University Press.

Besnier, Nikio, 1990 Language and Affect. *Annual Review of Anthropology* 19: 419–451.

Capps, Lisa, and Elinor Ochs, 1995 *Constructing Panic: The Discourse of Agoraphobia*. Cambridge, MA: Harvard University Press.

de Mesquita, B. G., 1993 Cultural Variations in Emotions: A Comparative Study of Dutch, Surinamese and Turkish People in the Netherlands. Ph.D. dissertation. University of Amsterdam.

Desjarlais, Robert, and Theresa O'Nell, 2000 The Pragmatic Turn in Psychological Anthropology. *Ethos*, Special Issue 27 (4).

Edwards, Derek, 1997 Emotion. In *Discourse and Cognition*. Pp. 170–201. London: Sage.

Hess, U., and G. Kirouac, 2000 Emotion Expression in Groups. In *The Handbook of Emotions*. M. Lewis and J. Haviland, eds. Pp. 368–381. New York: Guilford Press.

Hochschild, Arlie Russell, 1983 *The Managed Heart: Commercialization of Human Feeling*. Berkeley: University of California Press.

Hymes, Dell, 1964 Introduction: Toward Ethnographies of Communication. In *The Ethnography of Communication*. John Gumperz and Dell Hymes, eds. *American Anthropologist*, Special Issue: 1–34.

Kemper, Theodore, 2000 The Sociology of Emotions. In *The Handbook of Emotions*. M. Lewis and J. Haviland, eds. New York: Guilford Press.

Kitayama, Shinobu, and Hazel Markus, 1994 Introduction to Cultural Psychology and Emotion Research. In *Emotion and Culture: Empirical Studies of Mutual Influence*. Shinobu Kitayama and Hazel Markus, eds. Pp. 1–19. Washington, DC: American Psychological Association.

Levy, Robert, 1973 *Tahitians: Mind and Experience in the Society Islands*. Chicago: University of Chicago Press.

Levy, Robert, and Jane Wellenkamp, 1989 Methodology in the Anthropological Study of Emotion. In *Emotion: Theory, Research, and Experience, Vol. 4: The Measurement of Emotions*. Robert Plutchik and Henry Kellerman, eds. New York: Academic Press.

Lewis, Michael, 1992 *Shame: The Exposed Self*. New York: Free Press.

Lutz, Catherine, 1990 Engendered Emotion: Gender, Power and the Rhetoric of Emotional Control in American Life. In *Language and the Politics of Emotion*. Lila Abu-Lughod and Catherine Lutz, eds. Pp. 69–91. Cambridge: Cambridge University Press.

Lutz, Catherine, and Lila Abu-Lughod, eds., 1990 *Language and the Politics of Emotion*. Cambridge: Cambridge University Press.

Lutz, Catherine, and Geoffrey White, 1986 The Anthropology of Emotions. *Annual Review of Anthropology* 15: 405–436.

Menon, U., and Richard Shweder, 1994 Kali's Tongue: Cultural Psychology and the Power of Shame in Orissa, India. In *Emotion and Culture: Empirical Studies of Mutual Influence*. Shinobu Kitayama and Hazel Markus, eds. Pp. 241–282. Washington, DC: American Psychological Association.

Ochs, Elinor, 1986 From Feelings to Grammar: A Samoan Case Study. In *Language Socialization Across Cultures*. Bambi B. Schieffelin and Elinor Ochs, eds. Cambridge: Cambridge University Press.

Palmer, Gary B., and Debra J. Occhi, 1999 *Languages of Sentiment: Cultural Constructions of Emotional Substrates*. Philadelphia, PA: J. Benjamins.

Schachter, Steven, and Jerome Singer, 1962 Cognitive, Social, and Physiological Determinants of Emotional State. *Psychological Review* 63: 379–399.

Schieffelin, Bambi, 1990 *The Give and Take of Everyday Life*. Cambridge: Cambridge University Press.

Tomkins, Silvan S., 1962 *Affect, Imagery, and Consciousness, Vol. 1: The Positive Effects*. New York: Springer.

Watson-Gegeo, Karen Ann, and Geoffrey M. White, eds., 1990 *Disentangling: Conflict Discourse in Pacific Societies*. Stanford, CA: Stanford University Press.

White, Geoffrey M., 1990 Emotion Talk and Social Inference: Disentangling in Santa Isabel, Solomon Islands. In *Disentangling: Conflict Discourse in Pacific Societies*. Karen Ann Watson-Gegeo and Geoffrey M. White, eds. Pp. 53–121. Stanford, CA: Stanford University Press.

— 1997 Moving History: The Pearl Harbor Film(s). *Positions: East-Asia Cultural Critique* 5 (3): 709–744.

— 2000 Emotional Remembering: The Pragmatics of National Memory. *Ethos* 27 (4): 505–529.

White, Michael, and David Epston, 1990 *Narrative Means to Therapeutic Ends*. New York: Norton.

Wierzbicka, Anna, 1992 *Semantics, Culture, and Cognition*. Oxford: Oxford University Press.

Williams, Raymond, 1977 *Marxism and Literature*. Oxford: Oxford University Press.

SUGGESTED FURTHER READING

Bateson, Gregory, 1958 *Naven*. Stanford, CA: Stanford University Press.

Benedict, Ruth, 1934 *Patterns of Culture*. Boston, MA: Houghton-Mifflin.

Leavitt, J., 1996 Meaning and Feeling in the Anthropology of Emotions. *American Ethnologist* 23 (3): 514–539.

Lynch, O. M., 1990 *Divine Passions: The Social Construction of Emotion in India*. Berkeley: University of California Press.

O'Nell, Theresa D., 1996 *Disciplined Hearts: History, Identity, and Depression in an American Indian Community*. Berkeley: University of California Press.

Rosaldo, Michelle, 1980 *Knowledge and Passion: Ilongot Notions of Self and Social Life*. Cambridge: Cambridge University Press.

Rosaldo, Renato, 1984 Grief and a Headhunter's Rage. In *Text, Play, and Story: The Construction and Reconstruction of Self and Society*. Stuart Plattner and Edward Bruner, eds. Pp. 178–195. Washington, DC: American Ethnological Society.

Wikan, Unni, 1990 *Managing Turbulent Hearts: A Balinese Formula for Living*. Chicago: University of Chicago Press.

CHAPTER 14
Urban Fear of Crime and Violence in Gated Communities

Setha M. Low

INTRODUCTION

According to Lynn Lofland (1998), urban fear of crime and violence is based on the possible invasion by strangers of one's private space. The rich deal with this concern by evolving separate zones within the city (Tuan 1979) or by the use of restrictive land covenants (Higley 1995). The creation of "defended neighborhoods" characterized by a homogeneous social group exerting dominance within its boundaries "in order to segregate themselves from danger, insult, and the impairment of status claims" (Flusty 1997: 57) is a newer strategy. Interestingly, the middle-class and upper-middle class strategies of avoidance through suburban segregation and defended neighborhoods seem to work in the sense that crime rates are much lower in the suburbs. These observations raise the question of how to make sense of suburban gated community residents' extraordinary discourse of urban fear about crime and violence (Low 1997, 2001).

A number of studies provide clues into alternative and underlying meanings for urban fear of crime. Davina Cooper (1998) argues all discourses of disaster, emergency, and panic reproduce existing forms of political hegemony. Wesley Skogan links racism and fear of crime to demonstrate that "residential segregation calms white fear, while interracial crime exacerbates it." Surveys confirm that residential proximity to Blacks is related to Whites' fear of crime, and that Whites who are racially prejudiced are even more fearful (Skogan 1995: 66, 59). This evidence compels us to consider the underlying social motives of racism, cultural dominance, and class-based exclusion embedded in the discourse of urban fear.

In my previous work I developed a model of the co-production of the built environment (Low 2000). Based on an ethnographic study of public space and power in Latin America, I demonstrated that the interaction of social production – the social, economic, ideological, and technological factors involved in the physical creation of the material setting – and the social construction – the phenomenological and symbolic experience of the setting – determine the meaning and form of architectural design (Low 1996). In other words, a built environment is co-produced through a complex interplay of sociopolitical forces, individual experiences, and cultural interpretations: it is the combination of social production and social construction that creates a site. This theory provides a way to move from unidirectional thinking about fear of crime and built environment (Newman 1972, 1980) to a more complex understanding of the relationship between architectural and planning design, emotion, and social life.

The gated community provides an excellent exemplar for expanding the co-production model by adding a psychological dimension based on the analysis of discourse to get at underlying and latent (and this case, socially unacceptable) meanings of the built environment. Residents' social constructions of why they are moving to gated communities focus on fear of violence and crime and the search for security. At the same time, many aspects of the social environment are improving, and both property crime and violent crime victimization rates are declining. The people living in these communities are not likely to experience violent crime, yet marketing advertisements that originally emphasized exclusivity and amenity, now focus on security and surveillance as significant amenities. These contradictions suggest that other feelings and social relations encoded in the built form are being justified, even hidden, by the discourse of fear.

Living in a gated community represents a new version of the middle-class American dream precisely because it temporarily suppresses and masks, even denies and fuses, the inherent anxieties and conflicting social values of modern urban and suburban life. It transforms Americans' dilemma of how to protect themselves, their children, and their families from danger, crime, and unknown others, and still perpetuate open, friendly neighborhoods and comfortable, safe homes. It reinforces the norms of a middle-class lifestyle in a historical period in which everyday events and news media exacerbate fears of violence and terrorism. Thus, residents cite their "need" of gated communities to provide a safe and secure home in the face of a lack of other societal alternatives.

Gated residential communities, however, intensify social segregation, racism, and exclusionary land use practices already in place in most of the United States, and raise a number of values conflicts for residents. For instance, residents acknowledge their misgivings about the possible false security provided by the gates and guards, but at the same time it satisfies their desire for emotional security associated with childhood and neighborhoods where they grew up. Living in a gated development contributes to residents' sense of well-being, but it is acquired at the price of maintaining private guards, gates, and amenities, as well as conforming to extensive homeowners association rules and regulations. Individual freedom and ease of access for residents must be limited to achieve greater privacy and social control for the community as a whole. These contradictions in what residents think, feel, and talk about provide an opportunity to understand the psychological and social meaning-making processes Americans use to order their lives.

This chapter uncovers some of the underlying motivations of moving into a residential gated community by exploring how the discourse of fear of violence and crime and the search for a secure community legitimates and rationalizes class-based exclusion strategies and residential segregation embodied in the walls, gates, guards, and surveillance technology of these built environments. I am concerned these physical changes in suburban design and planning will become normative and ultimately encode fear in a relatively open, suburban landscape. Secondarily, I am interested in untangling the relationship of emotion and environment; however, this chapter can only begin to address this larger question (Low 2000, 2002, 2003).

BACKGROUND

I define "gated community" as a residential development surrounded by walls with a secured entrance. In this chapter I focus on developments where houses, streets, sidewalks, and sometimes other amenities are physically enclosed by walls and an entrance gate is operated by a guard, key, or electronic identity card. These sorts of communities restrict access not just to residents' homes, but also to the use of public spaces – roads, parks, and open space – contained within the walls. In special cases these amenities – a beach, a pond, or farmland – have been preserved for public use, but become privatized *de facto* because only residents can enter the community.

Estimates of the number of people who currently live in gated communities within the United States vary from 4 million (Stark 1990) to 8 million (Architectural Record 1997a) or 16 million (Egan 2001), depending on the source. Some 28 million more live in tightly controlled condominiums and cooperatives. One-third of all new homes built in the United States in recent years are in gated residential developments (Blakely and Snyder 1997), and in areas such as Tampa, Florida, where crime is a high profile problem, gated communities account for four out of five home sales of $300,000 or more (Fischler 1998). A market survey found that 65 percent of callers to a 900 number responded "yes" to the question of whether they would live in a gated community, while only 35 percent responded "no" (Architectural Record 1997b), and a survey in southern California indicated that 54 percent of home shoppers wanted gated and walled developments (Starnes 1998).

Systems of walls and class division were deeply ingrained in historic England as a way for people of means to protect themselves from the local population (Turner 1999; Blakely and Snyder 1997). In the United States these design forms were not without precedent, as the colonial settlements of Roanoke and Jamestown and Spanish fort towns were walled and defended. But with the virtual elimination of the indigenous population, the need for defensive walls ceased to exist (King 1990). The domestic architectural history of open squares in New England towns, the row house-lined public streets of the urban Northeast, and most recently, the fenceless landscapes of suburban America, represent the antithesis of walls and fortifications.

At the turn of the twentieth century, secured and gated communities in the United States were built mainly to protect family estates and wealthy citizens, exemplified by New York's Tuxedo Park or the private streets of St. Louis. By the late 1960s and 1970s, planned retirement communities such as Leisure World in California were the first places where middle-class Americans could wall themselves off. Gates then spread to resorts and country club developments, and finally to middle-class suburban developments. In the 1980s, real estate speculation accelerated the building of gated communities around golf courses designed for exclusivity, prestige, and leisure. Magazine articles about white, middle-class people retreating to new, walled private communities (Guterson 1992), and radio talk shows on National Public Radio (1995), television talk shows such as Phil Donahue (1993), and feature articles in the *New York Times* (Fischler 1998), reported on this emerging social phenomenon.

The first centers of construction activity were the Sunbelt states focusing on retirees in California and Florida during the 1970s, followed by Texas and Arizona in the 1980s. Since the late 1980s, gates have become ubiquitous, and by the 1990s have become common even in the Northeast (Blakely and Snyder 1997). Newspaper advertisements and promotional brochures at first did not focus on security, but on exclusivity and comfort. But as more communities were built, security became a more central feature of the marketing strategy.

The recent expansion of gated urban and suburban developments has targeted a much broader market, including families with children. These new consumers use public schools, transportation, and accessible shopping, and then retreat to locked neighborhoods of homes with private open space and other amenities. This retreat to secured enclaves with walls, gates and guards, materially and symbolically contradicts US middle-class ethos and values, threatens democratic spatial practices such as public access to open space, and creates yet another barrier to social interaction, the building of social networks, and increasing tolerance among diverse cultural/racial/social groups.

Coincidentally, the growth in the number of gated communities has been paralleled by a dramatic increase in another kind of walled community: prison building also is increasing at a rapid rate, while at the same time crime is actually declining (Robinson 2002; Colvard 1997). Crime has declined in New York City since 1991–2 and in California since 1984. Violent crime – homicide, robbery, sexual assault, and aggravated assault – fell 12 percent nationally between 1994 and 1995, while property crime – burglary, theft, and auto theft – declined 9 percent (Brennan and Zelinka 1997). Yet the fear of crime remains high, particularly in the suburbs (Judd 1995; Stone 1996), and thus may be used to justify other fears – of strangers, of ethnic and class differences, and of cultural diversity.

Intrigued by these observations, in 1994 I began a comparative study of residents who live in upper-middle to middle-income gated communities on the edge of two large, culturally diverse cities: New York City and San Antonio, Texas. Blakely and Snyder (1997) had defined three kinds of single family residential gated communities: (1) lifestyle (retirement and resort communities), (2) prestige (upscale properties with large houses), and (3) security zone (urban neighborhoods adding fences and walls). These ideal types broke down when I tried to locate field sites, and the two communities I selected were a combination of types 1 and 2, with many of the concerns of type 3.

Four general themes – community, investment, status, and safety/security – emerged from a content analysis of ten interviews from the gated community outside of New York City. I found that, just as in other studies (Wilson 1995; Blakely and Snyder 1997), residents were retreating from their community and civic responsibilities. Many of them said that they knew they were trading a sense of community for security, but that they were not interested in making new friends. Most residents wanted to lived in a controlled, well maintained environment enforced by strictly imposed rules and covenants that would protect their financial and social investment. Some residents wanted to move up in socioeconomic status and felt that their new house in a gated community represented having arrived. Residents felt safe in their new homes and neighborhoods in contrast to where they lived before (Low 1997).

In a second content analysis of the ten interviews from New York and ten interviews from San Antonio, I found that a majority of residents reported either a recent personal crime experience or an increase in crime in their neighborhoods before moving to a gated community. Eighteen of the twenty interviews included discussions of the residents' search for a greater sense of safety and security in their choice of a gated community, and their relief at finding that they did, in fact, feel safer and more secure behind gates, walls, and guards.

In the New York suburb, residents were fleeing deteriorating neighborhoods with increased ethnic diversity and petty crimes, concluding that the neighborhood is "just not what it used to be." The New Yorkers cited changes in the local stores, problems with parking and securing a car, and frequent robberies of cars and bicycles. In San Antonio there is a similar pattern, but here the emphasis was on a fear of kidnapping and of illegal Mexican workers. Residents cited newspaper stories of children being kidnapped, drive-by shootings, and neighbors being burglarized, and talked about the large number of "break-ins." In both cities, residents moved to gated communities based on what one interviewee called "fear flight," the desire to protect oneself, family, and property from dangers perceived as overwhelming. Whether it is kidnapping or bike snatching, Mexican laborers or "ethnic changes," the message was the same: residents were using the walls, entry gates, and guards in an effort to keep the perceived dangers outside of their homes, neighborhoods, and social world. It was as if they no longer saw the world as full of disciplined citizens who shared their values and norms. The physical closeness between them and the "others" was sufficient to incite fear and concern, and in response they were selecting exclusive, private residential developments where they hoped they could keep other people out with guards and gates. The walls were making visible the systems of exclusion that were already there, now constructed in concrete (Low 1997).

Interview data from San Antonio indicate that living behind gates and walls also has an impact on children and their relationship to other people and environments. Children growing up in these new communities depend on walls and gates for their sense of security and safety from the violence they perceive outside. Robert Lang and Karen Danielson (1997) and Amitai Etzoni (1995) comment that they are concerned about the impact on children of passing through gates on a daily basis. This growing sense of comfort from and dependency on gating suggests that walls and gates could become a standard architectural feature of any upper-middle class or middle-class home.

These analyses suggested additional methodological approaches were necessary to get at the underlying motivations of residents. Even though the interview data confirmed previous findings that fear of crime, and a desire for a secure community, social control of the environment, stable house values, and increased socioeconomic status motivated these residents (Wilson 1995; Blakely and Snyder 1997; Low 1997), the analysis did not uncover underlying psychological motivations and social values.

All of the research to date has focused on what people say is their motivation for moving to a gated community – in most cases "fear of crime and violence" – without an analysis of how this discourse of fear of crime is being used to further other social ends. Blakely and Snyder (1997: 144–160) make an unsubstantiated leap from their survey data to the conclusion that "fear of crime" and gating encodes other social, class-based concerns, while Peter Marcuse's (1997) concept of the walled and gated "citadel" and Mike Davis's (1992) "fortress city" rely on theoretical discussions and selective historical examples. In order to explore the underlying social and psychological messages of moving to a walled, gated, and secured residential community, a critical discourse analysis (a method that has been used to study covert racism) is applied to get at class-based exclusionary practices.

LITERATURE REVIEW

The history of the recent increase in the number of gated communities suggests that this urban design and planning strategy is a response to late-twentieth century changes in urban and suburban North America. The economic restructuring of the 1970s and 1980s produced a number of social and political changes as a consequence of the "uneven development" resulting from the rapid relocation of capital (Harvey 1990). These changes are the same as those that residents cite when they talk about their reasons for moving to gated communities: the increase in crime, particularly in cities, but also spreading into suburban and small town communities; the increase in immigration, particularly of people of color, and their dispersion outside of urban ethnic ghettos; the increase in socioeconomic disparities; and the development of a two class system of "haves" and "have-nots" based on structural readjustments of this new form of late capitalism (Mollenkopf and Castells 1991).

The resulting cracks in the effectiveness of self-disciplinary social control mechanisms and their associated institutions (Foucault 1975; Merry 1998) are well documented. Prison riots signaled the inability of the penal system to adequately provide for inmates (Schlosser 1998). Mental hospitals were attacked as human storage vaults, and patients were released, but without adequate community services and social support (Susser 1996). Schools in poor neighborhoods were overwhelmed by the growing numbers and lack of local resources (Devine 1996). Increased numbers of immigrants also meant more people with their own sets of cultural rules, and it became difficult to integrate these diverse cultural systems into the highly bureaucratized educational system (Fine 1991). The resulting increase in school violence has justified militarization of school environments with metal detectors, guards, and police surveillance – strategies not unlike those of gated communities.

Thus, in the United States, economic restructuring due to deindustrialization and the globalization of flexible capital and labor transformed social relations, contributing to the breakdown of traditional institutions of social control such as schools, mental hospitals, prisons, and local neighborhoods. This breakdown of the social order has polarized relations between haves and have-nots, "Whites" and people of color, and between immigrants and native-born citizens, and has resulted in people employing new techniques of social control – such as the building of gated residential communities.

Mike Davis (1990, 1992) argues this creation of new gated communities, and the addition of guardhouses, walls, and entrance gates to established neighborhoods, is an integral part of the building of the "fortress city," a social control technique based on the so-called "militarization" of the city. The political and economic democratic practices that mediated some forms of class separation in the built environment are breaking down, necessitating the production of the secured enclaves and walled architecture previously found in São Paulo, Brazil (Caldeira 1996; Carvalho et al. 1997), other parts of Latin America (Low 1996), and Africa (Western 1981).

However, the processes which produce urban and suburban segregation in the United States have a long history based on racism and racial segregation. According to Massey and Denton (1988), the high level of residential segregation experienced by Blacks in American cities since the 1964 Civil Rights Act was enacted continues to be based on discriminatory real estate practices and mortgage structures designed to insulate Whites from Blacks. Nancy Denton (1994) argues that since the 1980s there has been a pattern of hyper segregation in the suburbs, reinforced by patterns of residential mobility by race, in that Blacks are less likely to move to the suburbs and more likely to return to the city (South and Crowder 1997). And according to David Harvey (1989) the suburban mode of consumption plays a vital role in residential segregation, but even more importantly in the perpetuation of the class structure.

Residential segregation based on racism and class structure is socially and materially reinforced by the logic of development projects that form "contours which structure social relations, causing commonalities of gender, sexual orientation, race, ethnicity, and class to assume spatial identities. Social groups, in turn, imprint themselves physically on the urban structure through the formation of communities, competition for territory, and segregation – in other words, through clustering, the erection of boundaries, and establishing distance" (Fainstein 1994: 1). At the local level, middle-class and upper-middle class urban neighborhoods are marked by an increasing pattern of building fences, cutting off relationships with neighbors, and moving out in response to problems and conflicts. At the same time, "government has expanded its regulatory role . . . Zoning laws, local police departments, ordinances about dogs, quiet laws, laws against domestic and interpersonal violence, all provide new forms of regulation of family and neighborhood life" (Merry 1993: 87). Thus, residential segregation is created by racial prejudice and socioeconomic disparities, but reinforced by planning practices and policing, implemented by zoning laws and regulations, and subsidized by businesses and banks.

Suburbanization, in particular, has created and maintained patterns of racial segregation that have directly contributed to the development of gated communities. Historical research points to the evolution of the suburb as a basically exclusionary enclave (McKenzie 1994). From its earliest beginnings, the suburb was an "anti-urban" community where first upper-class followed by middle-class residents search for sameness, status, and security in an ideal "new town" or "green oasis" (Langdon 1994). Land speculation beginning with the streetcar suburbs of Philadelphia accelerated the growth of these new middle-class enclaves (Jackson 1985).

The expanding suburbs of the 1950s, 1960s, and 1970s generated what was called "white flight" from densely populated, heterogeneous cities, and the development of common interest developments (CIDs) provided the legal framework for the consolidation of this form of segregation (Judd 1995). CID describes "a community in which the residents own or control common areas or shared amenities," and that "carries with it reciprocal rights and obligations enforced by a private governing body" (Louv 1985: 85, as cited in Judd 1995: 155). Specialized covenants, contracts, and deed restrictions (CC&Rs) create new forms of collective private land tenure and new forms of private government called "homeowner associations" (McKenzie 1994). The development of the "pod" and "enclave" suburban designs further refined the ability of land use planners, designers, and developers to produce suburban environments where people of different income groups – even in the same development – would have no contact with one another (Langdon 1994). Resident behavior, house type, and "taste culture" are regulated by more subtle means of control (Bourdieu 1984). Nancy and James Duncan (1997) demonstrate how landscape aesthetics function as a suburban politics of exclusion, and McKenzie (1994) documents the growing number of legal proceedings in California courts as residents attempt to deregulate their rigidly controlled environments.

The psychological lure of defended space becomes more enticing with increased media coverage and national hysteria about violent crime (Judd 1995). News stories chronicle daily murders, rapes, drive-by shootings, drug busts, and kidnappings. An ever growing proportion of people fear that they will be victimized, such that the fear of crime has increased since the mid-1960s, even though there has been a decline in all violent crime since the 1980s (Judd 1995; Stone 1996). Thus, the fear of crime has become an important leitmotif in the appeal of gated communities.

There has been considerable research that links fear of crime to the physical environment, and although none of it focuses specifically on gated communities, it suggests how communities and individuals deal with their fear within the context of a local neighborhood. Ethnographies suggest that familiarity, avoidance, and surveillance play important roles in allaying these fears. Sally Merry (1982) documents the interactions and perceptions of Black, White, and Chinese residents in a high rise, low income project in a large Midwestern city, and concludes that lack of familiarity plays an important role in the perception of danger. Elijah Anderson (1990) documents avoidance as a coping strategy in his study of "streetwise" behavior of Philadelphians, in which residents cross the street when faced with oncoming young Black males. Loic Wacquant portrays how institutional avoidance of young Black males can create a "hyperghetto" of isolated families in Chicago's Black Belt, where the streets are deserted and no longer patrolled by police; and Philippe Bourgois (1995) dramatizes the fear and sense of vulnerability experienced by residents of El Barrio and depicts their strategies of avoidance and surveillance used to deal with street crime. These ethnographies describe how fear is spatially managed in various contexts, and how avoidance and streetwise behavior are used by low to middle income people to mitigate their fears, while abandonment of the inner city by police and local institutions exacerbates these residents' sense of fear and isolation.

Environmental design studies also connect crime with the built environment, beginning with Jane Jacobs' (1961) three recommendations for creating safer streets and neighborhoods. But it was Oscar Newman (1972) who brought the relationship of crime and the physical environment to the attention of the public. He argued that the reason high rise buildings are considered dangerous is that the people who live in them cannot defend – see, own, or identify – their territory. Newman proposes that gating city streets can promote greater safety and higher house values as long as the percentage of minority residents is kept within strict limits (Newman 1980). Timothy Crowe (1991), a criminologist who coined the phrase "crime prevention through environmental design" (CPTED), has instituted a widespread CPTED program that involves all local agencies – police, fire, public works, traffic, and administration – as well as planners in the formulation and review of neighborhood plans and designs implementing Newman's defensive space concepts.

These diverse studies depict a social world in which there is a breakdown of institutions of social control and increasing reliance on urban fortification, policing, and racial and class segregation. A number of legal solutions have emerged, such as common interest developments and homeowners associations, planning solutions such as pod and enclave development, design solutions such as crime prevention through environmental design, and behavioral solutions such as avoidance and surveillance of the street. Gated communities respond to middle-class and upper-middle class individuals' concern with social control, satisfy their desire for community and intimacy, and facilitate avoidance, separation, and surveillance. It brings individual preferences, social forces, and the physical environment together in an architectural reality and cultural metaphor.

METHODOLOGY

Setting

New York and San Antonio were selected for the research study. Both have large, culturally diverse, urban populations and publicized incidents of urban crime. The two cities have increasing socioeconomic disparities, a history of residential segregation, and a documented movement of middle-class residents moving to an ever widening outer ring of exclusive suburbs. They also provide excellent comparative cases, however, because of differences among them in population size and density, history of gated community development, scale and design of the gated communities, legal and governmental structure, political climate, crime rates for the region, and cultural context and norms of behavior.

San Antonio is a medium-large city with many new suburbs and a recent downtown renovation. It was in San Antonio that I first gained entrance to a number of homes located within a locked, gated, and walled community on the outskirts of the city, and found young, white, middle-class teenagers discussing their fear of "Mexicans" who live nearby. New York City is a global East Coast city representing a different set of design concerns and a distinct cultural and industrial history. Although the gated community of Seagate in Brooklyn offers a historical example of the changing meanings of gating and policing over a hundred year time span, there are only a limited number of new gated communities in the city and surrounding suburbs.

New suburban housing developments with surrounding walls and restrictive gates located approximately 30–45 minutes' drive from their respective downtown city halls were selected. Single family house prices ranged from $650,000 to $880,000 in New York, and $350,000 to $650,000 in San Antonio. The disparity in prices reflects the considerable differences in the housing markets rather than any substantive differences in socioeconomic status and quality of life of the residents. Each gated community has its own regional style and distinctive design features, but all are enclosed by a 5–6 foot masonry wall broken only by the entry gates and monitored in person by a guard (New York) or by video camera from a central guardhouse (San Antonio).

The New York development is situated on an old estate with the original manor house retained as a community center. The individual houses are large, mostly two-story structures, built in a variety of traditional styles: Hampton Cottage, Nantucket Village, Mid-Atlantic Colonial, and Western Ranch. Houses are organized along a winding thoroughfare with dead-end streets branching off, leading to groups of houses clustered quite close together on small lots of less than a quarter acre. The remaining property is landscaped to create a park-like atmosphere. Since the community was developed as a community interest development, the homeowner association maintains all of the common grounds. The final community will contain 141 houses, tennis courts, a swimming pool, and a clubhouse. All the lots have been purchased, although many houses are still being built.

The San Antonio gated community is part of a much larger northern San Antonio development centered on a private golf and tennis club with swimming pools, a restaurant, and a clubhouse. The subdivision studied includes 120 lots, a few fronting one section of the golf course, surrounded by a 6-foot masonry wall. The main entrance is controlled by a counter-weighted gate that opens electronically by means of a hand transmitter or by a guard who is contacted by an intercom and video camera connection. The broad entrance road divides into two sections leading to a series of short streets ending in cul-de-sacs. The houses are mostly large two-story brick Colonials or stucco Scottsdale designs, with a few one-story brick Ranch-style houses. At the time of writing more than half of the houses had been built, while the remaining lots were currently under construction.

Methods

For the research, I utilized family contacts and interested real estate agents to gain entry to these communities; nonetheless, obtaining interviews was a slow and difficult process. Once having gained permission to interview residents, the research team, made up of myself, Elena Danaila, and Andrew Kirby (graduate students in Environmental Psychology) in New York City, and working alone in San Antonio, employed a "snowballing" sampling technique, using each interview respondent to lead to the next. In some cases a key informant referred us to others who might be willing to speak to us.

The interview was organized around a semi-structured residential history that lasted between 1–2 hours. Leisurely walks with respondents on weekends have provided one way to meet neighbors informally and helped gain acceptance in otherwise aggressively private spaces.

The open-ended, unstructured interviews were conducted in the home, with the wife, husband, or husband and wife together. The majority of the interviewees were European Americans and native born; however, three interviews were in households in which one spouse was born in Latin America, one interviewee was born in the South Pacific, and one interviewee's spouse was born in the Middle East. Interviewees were aged 27 through 75; all husbands were either professionals such as doctors or lawyers, businessmen, or retired from these same pursuits. In most cases the wives remained at home while the husband commuted to his place of work. A few women worked part time.

ANALYSIS

The critical discourse analysis of the interviews and fieldnotes was used to identify covert concerns with social order, social control, xenophobia, ethnocentrism, class consciousness and status anxiety, social mobility, and racism, as well as fear of crime and violence. Following Fairclough (1995), critical discourse analysis assumes that language is a form of social practice that is historically situated and dialectical to the social context; that is, language is both socially shaped and socially shaping. Drawing upon the work of Gramsci, political power of the dominant class is based on a combination of domination through state power, repression and coercion of other social groups, and through hegemony by intellectual and moral leadership. Discourse is a sphere of cultural hegemony: "the hegemony of a class or group over the whole society or over particular sections of it . . . is in part a matter of its capacity to shape discursive practices and order of discourse" (Fairclough 1995: 95) and to render them "natural."

Since language is widely misperceived as transparent, it is difficult to see how language produces, reproduces, and transforms social structures and social relations. Yet it is through texts that social control and social domination are exercised – through the everyday social action of language. Thus, it is necessary to establish a "critical language awareness" (Fairclough 1995: 209) to uncover the social and political goals of everyday discourse. Critical discourse analysis, through the analysis of context, analysis of processes of text production and interpretation (in this case the interview), and the analysis of the text, can problematize traditional models of interview analysis. For instance, in Fairclough's theory, fear of crime and violence is a discursive practice used to "naturalize" social and physical exclusionary practices. The application of critical discourse begins the process of uncovering the naturalized hegemonic basis of this discourse.

Each interview was transcribed in full according to the rules of transcription presented in Dixon and Reicher (1997). Next, I read through the interview transcripts and systematically noted all instances in which the above concepts (and others yet to be identified) were discussed or alluded to. This process yielded the body of the data set. In the final stage, I identified the different strategies used to talk about living in a gated community. The details of the linguistic constructions with their immediate functions produced an outline of the ideological structure of the conversation. The goal was not to quantify the occurrence of particular themes or rhetorical strategies, but, more importantly, to illustrate their situated effects (Dixon and Reicher 1997: 368).

FINDINGS

New York

Nine of the ten interviewees in New York mention urban crime as a major reason for selecting a gated community. The tenth interviewee, although she says that crime and safety had no bearing on why they moved, mentions that in her old neighborhood her car had been stolen from outside her door.

Nine of the ten interviewees are from the local area and moved from New York City or a nearby Long Island urban center. Many are quite vocal about the changes that they experienced in their original neighborhoods. For instance, Sharon is willing to "give up community convenience for safety." She says that increased local political corruption and neighborhood deterioration left her feeling uncomfortable in the house where she had lived for over 25 years. Even though she knew everyone in her old neighborhood and enjoyed walking to the corner store,

> when Bloomingdale's moved out and Kmart moved in, it just brought in a different group of people . . . and it wasn't the safe place that it was . . . I think it's safer having a gated community . . . They are not going to steal my car in the garage . . . [In the old neighborhood] every time we heard an alarm we were looking out the window. My daughter and son-in-law lived next door and their car was stolen twice.

Barbara and her husband Alvin express it differently:

Alvin: [Our old neighborhood was] a very, very educated community. You know, so every one goes on to college, and it stressed the role of family, and you know, it's just a wonderful community. But it is changing, it's undergoing internal transformations.
Barbara: It's ethnic changes.
Alvin: Yeah, ethnic changes, that's a very good way of putting it.
Elena: And is this something that started to happen more recently?
Barbara: In the last, probably, seven to eight years . . .

Cynthia also is concerned about staying in her old neighborhood. At first, she did not want to live in a house at all, since she would feel afraid being alone. She had grown up in Queens and would never live in a house there, because they had been robbed. Her childhood home had been in a nice neighborhood where thieves know they could find valuable things to steal:

Cynthia: And then I have a lot of friends who live in a neighborhood in Queens, and there's been more than 48 robberies there in the last year and a half. And I said to myself those are homes with security and dogs and this and that . . .
Elena: And are they gated?
Cynthia: No, they're not gated. They had alarms, and they were getting robbed because they were cutting the alarms, the phone wires outside. So I'm saying to myself, all this is in my mind, and I'm saying . . . I can get robbed. That's why I moved . . .

Sally also feels that the neighborhood where she lived was changing: she was having problems finding a place to park, and people were going through her trash at night. Her bicycle was stolen off of her terrace, and her friend's car was stolen. Her husband began to travel a lot, and she could not accompany him on his trips because she was worried about being robbed. They loved their old neighborhood, but it no longer offered safety and comfort. So they decided to move to a gated community that would provide the security that she felt they now needed. Once having made the decision and completed the move she said that she loved her newly found freedom from house responsibilities and parking problems. As she put it:

> I got to feel like I was a prisoner in the house . . . You didn't park on the street too long because you are afraid your car is going to be missing something when you get out, or the whole car is missing . . . So there's a lot of things we have the freedom here to do that we didn't do before . . .

Helen comments that it was "very nice at night to come in . . . and to have a gate and there's only one entrance to the property, so I think that makes for possibly less robberies . . ." For her, safety is

> not a main concern, but a concern. Otherwise, if I bought something . . . on two acres of land, I would have been very uncomfortable there . . . no children around . . . just being alone now in the dark . . . and my husband would get home later. I just didn't want to be surrounded by two acres of land.

She has friends in the old neighborhood who were burglarized and had become more distressed. She thinks the guards at the entrance are not careful, but it is still difficult for thieves to escape. Her mother and her children also live in gated communities.

San Antonio

Nine of the interviewees in San Antonio mention crime and a fear of "others" as a reason for moving. Stay-at-home mothers like Felicia and Donna worry about threats to their children.

Felicia states her feelings about her fear of crime and other people very clearly:

Setha: . . . has it changed how you feel about being in the gated community?
Felicia: Yes. It allows a lot more freedom for my daughter to go outside and play. We're in San Antonio, and I believe the whole country knows how many child kidnappings we've had . . . And I believe that my husband would not ever allow her outside to play without direct adult supervision unless we were gated. It allows us freedom to walk at night, if we choose to. It has, you know, it does have a flip side.
Setha: What flip side?
Felicia: Several things. First of all, it's a false sense of safety if you think about it, because our security people are not "Johnny-on-the-spot," so to speak, and anybody who wants to jump the gate could jump the gate . . . There's a perception of safety that may not be real, that could potentially leave one more vulnerable if there was ever an attack.

***

Setha: Who lives in your community?
Felicia: People who are retired and don't want to maintain large yards . . . People who want to raise families in a more protected environment [long pause].
Setha: What do you mean by that?

Felicia: There are a lot of families who have, in the last couple of years, after we built, as the crime rate, or the reporting of that crime rate, has become such a prominent part of the news of the community, there's been a lot of "fear flight." I've mentioned that people who were building or going to build based on wanting to get out of the very exclusive subdivisions without a gate, solely for the gate.

Setha: Really. There has been?

Felicia: Oh, yeah. I was telling you about a family that was shopping [for a house in Felicia's gated community] because they had been randomly robbed many times.

* * *

Felicia: When I leave the area entirely and go downtown [little laugh], I feel quite threatened, just being out in normal urban areas, unrestricted urban areas . . . Please let me explain. The north central part of this city, by and large, is middle class to upper middle class. Period. There are very few pockets of poverty. Very few. And therefore if you go to any store, you will look around and most of the clientele will be middle class as you are yourself. So you are somewhat insulated. But if you go downtown, which is much more mixed, where everybody goes, I feel much more threatened.

Setha: Okay.

Felicia: My daughter feels very threatened when she sees poor people.

Setha: How do you explain that?

Felicia: She hasn't had enough exposure. We were driving next to a truck with some day laborers and equipment in the back, and we were parked beside them at the light. She wanted to move because she was afraid those people were going to come and get her. They looked scary to her. I explained that they were workmen, they're the "backbone of our country," they're coming from work, you know, but . . .

Donna's concerns with safety also focus on her child, and his reactions to the city. She, like Felicia, is aware a false sense of security develops living inside the gates, putting her and her children in greater danger:

Donna: You know, he's always so scared . . . It has made a world of difference in him since we've been out here.

Setha: Really?

Donna: A world of difference. And it is that sense of security that they don't think people are roaming the neighborhoods and the streets and that there's people out there that can hurt him.

Setha: Ah . . . that's incredible.

Donna: . . . That's what's been most important to my husband, to get the children out here where they can feel safe, and we feel safe if they could go out in the streets and not worry that someone is going to grab them . . . we feel so secure and maybe that's wrong too.

Setha: In what sense?

Donna: You know, we've got workers out here, and we still think "oh, they're safe out here." . . . In the other neighborhood I never let him get out of my sight for a minute. Of course they were a little bit younger too, but I just, would never, you know, think of letting them go to the next street over. It would have scared me to death, because you didn't know. There was so much traffic coming in and out, you never knew who was cruising the street and how fast they can grab a child. And I don't feel that way in our area at all . . . ever.

Other San Antonio interviewees are less dramatic in expressing their concerns with safety, and concentrate more on taxation and the quality of the security system and guards. Harry and his wife feel that the biggest difference with gating is "not just anyone can come by." They are more upset about the way that the government treats private gated communities in terms of taxation.

Karen was not even looking for a place in a secured area:

Karen: It was just by accident that it was [gated] . . . But after living here, if we moved it would be different.
Setha: And why is that?
Karen: Because after seeing . . . this is a very nice neighborhood and after seeing that there are so many beautiful neighborhoods here and in other parts of the country that are not in a secure area, that's where burglary and murders take place, not here, because it's an open door [there] . . . come on [in]. Why should they try to do anything here when they can go somewhere else first. It's a strong deterrent, needless to say.

Other residents are not so sure that the gates are an adequate deterrent. Edith talks about her problems with the security guards who supposedly patrol at night and monitor the gates with security cameras. She feels the guards do not do their job. Another interviewee points out that with any gate monitored by a security camera and a guard in a remote station two cars can enter at the same time, creating an unsafe situation.

There seems to be no end to residents' concern with safety and security. In both New York and San Antonio most residents have burglar alarms they keep armed even when home during the day.

CRITICAL DISCOURSE ANALYSIS FINDINGS

In order to get at underlying social values, I selected sections of the interviews that refer to "others" (see Felicia and Barbara and Alvin excerpts presented above). I am trying to get at what Michael Billig calls "the dialogic unconscious," a concept by which the processes of repression can be studied discursively (1997: 139). I assume that some of the evidence I am looking for is "repressed"; that it is hidden not only from the interviewer, because it is socially unacceptable to talk about class and race, but from the interviewee as well, because these concerns are also psychologic-ally unacceptable. According to Billig (1997), conversational interaction can have repressive functions as well as expressive ones, so what is said can be used to get at what is not said.

Using Dixon and Reicher's (1997) article as a model, I focus on the rhetorical dimension of intergroup contact to elicit narratives about maintaining, justifying, or challenging racist (or elitist) practices (1997: 368–369). For instance, Dixon and Reicher identify a number of "disclaiming statements" about their interviewees' racist attitudes they were able to elicit by asking their respondents about their new Black neighbors in a legalized squatter settlement in South Africa. In the interviews, similar questions were asked about "Mexican laborers" in San Antonio or "recent immigrants" in New York, to produce disclaiming statements and lead to a better understanding of the social categories used by gated community residents.

For instance, after a long discussion identifying middle-class spaces in the city, Felicia tells a story about her daughter feeling threatened by day laborers. She ends the story with a disclaiming statement, explaining to her daughter in the story (and indirectly to me) that they are "workmen," the "backbone of our country." Her disclaiming statement highlights her acute understanding of social categories, and how she uses those categories to legitimate her discursive goals.

Another example of disclaiming occurs when the husband and wife in New York begin talking about the deterioration of their urban neighborhood. Barbara offers "it's ethnic changes" to Alvin, who is trying to articulate what happened that made them leave. He then repeats her term, "ethnic changes," to characterize the more elusive transformations that he was trying to convey.

In a recent presentation, Colette Daiute (pers. comm.) suggests there are five ways to interrogate a narrative: (1) as reporting an event; (2) as evaluating the event; (3) as constructing the meaning of the event; (4) as a critique of the event; and (5) as socially positioning the speaker. I have found her method helpful in identifying otherwise unarticulated discursive goals of the interviewees. For instance, Cynthia reports that there were more than 48 robberies in her neighborhood in Queens last year. She then evaluates those robberies by pointing out that they were of homes with security and dogs, but they were not gated. She then uses the logic of these two statements to construct the meaning of her move to a gated community. Finally, she critiques her own understanding: "so I'm saying to myself, all this in my mind, and I'm saying . . . I can get robbed," and positions herself with people inside the gated community (the smart ones), rather than with those living outside (those who are vulnerable to robberies.)

CONCLUSION

This chapter explores middle-class and upper-middle class residents' discourse of urban fear of violence and crime and their "fear flight" into gated communities. The research explores the complex interconnections between a discourse of fear of violence and increasing class dominance and separation by identifying class strategies of building exclusive communities, development of private neighborhoods and open space, and implementation of restrictive covenants and zoning laws. I am concerned that the walls, gates, guards, and forms of social control created by gated communities produce a suburban landscape of exclusion that encodes class dominance, and residential (race/class/ethnic) segregation permanently in the built environment. Understanding how this landscape is legitimized by feelings of urban fear uncovers how inequality is rhetorically and materially maintained and reinforced by this newly designed form.

There has been a dramatic shift in forms of ordering within modern society, including the move to more spatialized systems of control such as gated communities. These communities threaten American values of democracy, diversity, and racial integration. Gated communities are only one of the many ways that American public space – streets, parks, schools, and government – is being privatized. Identifying how these communities are legitimized by a discourse of fear will also contribute to our understanding of other discourses of fear, disaster, and emergency that contribute to the growing "moral panic" used to undermine liberal notions of civil society and social order. Understanding the rhetorical and political basis of moral panics about fear of crime will provide a partial basis for decisions about the future of public space, and whether the landscape will continue to reflect/support democratic practices (Katz 2001).

This research also contributes to the growing literature on the importance of spatial analyses for uncovering the material basis for social relations encoded in the built environment. Specifically, the research on gated communities adds a psychological and motivational dimension to the co-production model of the built environment and incorporates critical discourse analysis into the methodology of decoding meanings of new social and spatial forms. It provides new insights into the meaning of urban fear by treating these feelings as a discourse that can be understood in a broader social and political context.

REFERENCES

Anderson, Elijah, 1990 *Streetwise: Race, Class, and Change in an Urban Community.* Chicago: University of Chicago Press.
Architectural Record, 1997a To Gate or Not to Gate. *Record News, Architectural Press Roundup* April 24: 45.
Architectural Record, 1997b Record Readers Were Asked: Do Gated Communities Have Value? *Dialogue, Pulse* June: 24.
Billig, Michael, 1997 The Dialogic Unconscious. *British Journal of Social Psychology* 36: 139–159.
Blakely Edward, and Mary G. Snyder, 1997 *Fortress America.* Washington, DC: Brookings Institute.
Bourdieu, Pierre, 1984 *Distinction.* London: Routledge and Kegan Paul.
Bourgois, Phillipe, 1995 *In Search of Respect: Selling Crack in El Barrio.* New York: Cambridge University Press.
Boyle, T. Corrigan, 1995 *The Tortilla Curtain.* New York: Viking.
Brennan, D., and A. Zelinka, 1997 Safe and Sound. *Planning* August: 4–10.
Bullard, Robert D., and Charles Lee, 1994 Racism and American Apartheid. In *Residential Apartheid.* Robert D. Bullard, J. Eugene Grigsby III, and Charles Lee, eds. Pp. 1–16. Los Angeles: Center of Afro-American Studies.
Caldeira, Theresa, 1996 Fortified Enclaves: The New Urban Segregation. *Public Culture* 8: 303–328.
Carvalho, M., R. V. George, and K. H. Anthony, 1997 Residential Satisfaction in Condominios Exclusivos in Brazil. *Environment and Behavior* 29 (6): 734–768.
Colvard, Karen, 1997 Crime is Down? Don't Confuse Us with the Facts. *HFG Review* 2 (1): 19–26.
Cooper, D., 1998 *Governing Out of Order.* London: Rivers Oram Press.
Crowe, Timothy, 1991 *Crime Prevention Through Environmental Design.* Stoneham, MA: Butterworth-Heinemann.
Davis, Mike, 1990 *City of Quartz: Excavating the Future in Los Angeles.* London: Verso.
— 1992 Fortress Los Angeles: The Militarization of Urban Space. In *Variations on a Theme Park.* M. Sorkin, ed. Pp. 154–180. New York: Noonday Press.

Denton, Nancy A., 1994 Are African Americans Still Hypersegregated? In *Residential Apartheid.* Robert D. Bullard, J. Eugene Grigsby III, and Charles Lee, eds. Pp. 49–81. Los Angeles: Center for Afro-American Studies.

Devine, John, 1996 *Maximum Security.* Chicago: University of Chicago Press.

Dixon, J. A., and S. Reicher, 1997 Intergroup Contact and Desegregation in the New South Africa. *British Journal of Social Psychology* 36: 361–381.

Donahue, Phil, 1993 Town Builds Fence to Keep People Out. Transcript of television show aired December 2.

Duncan, Nancy G., and James S. Duncan, 1997 Deep Suburban Irony. In *Visions of Suburbia.* Roger Silverstone, ed. Pp. 161–179. London: Routledge.

Egan, Timothy, 2001 Las Vegas Bet on Growth but Doesn't Love Payoff. *New York Times* January 26: A1, A13.

Etzoni, A. 1995 *Rights and the Common Good.* New York: St. Martin's Press.

Fainstein, Susan, 1994 *City Builders.* Oxford: Blackwell.

Fairclough, Norman, 1995 *Critical Discourse Analysis: The Critical Study of Language.* London: Longman.

Fine, Michelle, 1991 *Framing Dropouts: Notes on the Politics of an Urban Public High School.* Albany: State University of New York Press.

Fischler, Michael S., 1998 Security the Draw at Gated Communities. *New York Times* August 16: 14LI, 6.

Flusty, Steven, 1997 Building Paranoia. In *Architecture of Fear.* N. Ellin, ed. Pp. 47–60. New York: Princeton Architectural Press.

Foucault, Michel, 1975 *Discipline and Punish.* New York: Vintage Books.

Guterson, D. 1992 No Place Like Home. *Harper's Magazine* 285 (1710), November: 35–64.

Harvey, David, 1989 *The Urban Experience.* Baltimore, MD: Johns Hopkins University Press.

— 1990 *The Condition of Postmodernity.* Oxford: Blackwell.

Higley, Steven R., 1995 *Privilege, Power, and Place.* London: Rowman and Littlefield.

Jackson, Kenneth T., 1985 *Crabgrass Frontier.* Oxford: Oxford University Press.

Jacobs, Jane, 1961 *The Death and Life of Great American Cities.* New York: Vintage Books.

Judd, D. 1995 The Rise of New Walled Cities. In *Spatial Practices.* Helen Ligget and David C. Perry, eds. Pp. 144–165. Thousand Oaks, CA: Sage.

Katz, C. 2001 The State Goes Home: Local Hypervigilance of Children and the Global Retreat from Social Reproduction. *Working Papers in Local Governance and Democracy.*

King, Anthony, 1990 *Urbanism, Colonialism, and the World Economy.* New York: Routledge.

Lang, R. E., and K. A. Danielson, 1997 Gated Communities in America. *Housing Policy Debate* 8 (4): 867–899.

Langdon, Philip, 1994 *A Better Place to Live.* Amherst: University of Massachusetts Press.

Lofland, Lyn H., 1998 *The Public Realm: Exploring the City's Quintessential Social Territory.* New York: Aldine de Gruyter.

Low, Setha M., 1996 A Response to Castells: An Anthropology of the City. *Critique of Anthropology* 16: 57–62.

— 1997 Urban Fear. *City and Society Annual Review*: 52–72.

— 2000 *On the Plaza: The Politics of Public Space and Culture.* Austin: University of Texas Press.

— 2001 The Edge of the Center: Gated Communities and the Discourse of Urban Fear. *American Anthropologist* 103 (1): 45–58.

— 2002 Communities of Exclusion. *Horizontes Antropologicos.*

— 2003 *Life, Security and the Pursuit of Happiness in Fortress America.* New York: Routledge.

McKenzie, Evan, 1994 *Privatopia: Homeowner Associations and the Rise of Residential Private Government.* New Haven, CT: Yale University Press.

Marcuse, P., 1997 The Enclave, the Citadel, and the Ghetto. *Urban Affairs Review* 33 (2): 228–264.

Massey, D. S., and Nancy A. Denton, 1988 Suburbanization and Segregation. *American Journal of Sociology* 94 (3): 592–626.

Merry, Sally, 1982 *Urban Danger*. Philadelphia, PA: Temple University Press.

— 1993 Mending Walls and Building Fences: Constructing the Private Neighborhood. *Journal of Legal Pluralism* 33: 71–90.

— 1998 The Kapu on Women Going Out to Ships: Spatial Governmentality on the Fringes of Empire. Paper presented at the Centre for Criminology at the University of Toronto and at the Law and Society Meetings, Aspen, CO.

Mishler, Eliot G., 1986 *Research Interviewing: Context and Narrative*. Cambridge, MA: Harvard University Press.

Mollenkopf, John, and Manuel Castells, 1991 *The Dual City*. New York: Russell Sage.

Newman, Oscar, 1972 *Defensible Space*. New York: Macmillan.

— 1980 *Community of Interest*. Garden City, NY: Anchor Press.

Robinson, Stuart, 2002 The Privatization and Fortification of Public Space. Paper presented at the International Conference on Private Urban Governance. Institute of Geography, Johannes Gutenberg Universitat, Mainz, Germany, June 5–9.

Schlosser, E. 1998 The Prison–Industrial Complex. *Atlantic Monthly* December: 51–77.

Sibley, David, 1995 *Geographies of Exclusion: Society and Difference in the West*. London: Routledge.

Silverman, David, 1993. *Interpreting Qualitative Data: Methods for Analyzing Talk, Text, and Interaction*. London: Sage.

Skogan, W. G., 1995 Crime and the Racial Fears of White Americans. *Annals of the American Academy of Political and Social Science* 539 (1): 59–72.

South, S., and K. D. Crowder, 1997 Residential Mobility Between Cities and Suburbs: Race, Suburbanization, and Back-to-the-City Moves. *Demography* 34 (4): 525–538.

Stark, Alister, 1990 *The Mind of South Africa*. New York: Knopf.

Starnes, E. M., 1998 Review of Blakely and Snyder, Fortress America. H-Net, Urban History discussion list.

Stone, Christopher, 1996 Crime and the City. In *Breaking Away: The Future of Cities*. Julia Vitullo-Martin, ed. Pp. 98–103. New York: Twentieth Century Fund Press.

Susser, Ida, 1996 The Construction of Poverty and Homelessness in US Cities. *Annual Review of Anthropology* 411–435.

Tuan, Yi-fu, 1979 *Landscapes of Fear*. New York: Pantheon Books.

Turner, E. S., 1999 Gilder Drainpipes. *London Review of Books* June 10: 31–32.

Western, John, 1981 *Outcast Cape Town*. Minneapolis: University of Minnesota Press.

Wilson, Georgeanna J., 1995 The Fortressing of Residential Life. Ph.D. dissertation, University of California, Irvine.

CHAPTER **15** # Race: Local Biology and Culture in Mind

Atwood D. Gaines

In this chapter, I consider concepts of "race" from several perspectives. I view "race(s)" through the lenses of cultural and psychological anthropology, psychoanalysis, medical anthropology, and the cultural studies of science. The latter also encompasses the study of biomedical research, theory, and practice. It is germane to include in this discussion medical and scientific conceptions from the United States for, as a preeminent world nation, its social categories, including "racial" ideologies, are often exported in part or in whole to other countries as elements of portable scientific and medical knowledge, inscription devices, theories, and practices.

While researchers have demonstrated the lack of empirical bases for any biological conception of "race," it remains a paramount, albeit declining, cultural, medical, and scientific reality in the United States (American Anthropological Association 1998; American Association of Physical Anthropologists 1996; Gaines 2004a). Examples of the exportation of science, its conceptions and its devices, are many. They range from the export of measurement devices (Biagioli 1999), to the movement of the laboratory to the "outside" (Latour 1999), to an entire field of (English) psychiatry exported to Greece (Blue 1992). German psychiatry was exported to the United States along with notions of the biological bases of mental disorder (Gaines 1992a; Young 1991), showing that disease notions also travel as with neurasthenia (see Kleinman 1988) and Alzheimer Disease (Whitehouse et al. 2000). Life transitions may also be borrowed, as with menopause being borrowed by Japan from the United States (Lock 1993).

Botanical classifications diffused from Europe to the world, eliding their local social and gendered assumptions (Schiebinger 1993), while statistical analyses in medicine came to the United States from France (Cassedy 1984). Statistics used constitutively in the study of "race" were exported from England to the United States and elsewhere (Gould 1981, 1996). By way of Germany and England, general notions of the biological bases of differences among humans have been exported to the

United States (Barkan 1992; Gaines 1995, 2004a; Gilman 1985, 1988). As we shall see, this latter idea of a biological basis for human physical and cultural differences is a key element in the cultural psychology of "race" in parts of the West, which we will consider in the context of the transdisciplinary field of the cultural studies of science that increasingly includes anthropology, especially the more theoretical forms of medical anthropology (see Gaines 1998a for an analysis of this trend; see also Fujimura 1996; Hahn 1995; Kleinman and Good 1985; Young 1995). The cultural studies of science (Rouse 1999) bridges and redefines disciplines, bringing history and religious and cultural studies into the field of science and placing it in dialogue and in common intellectual spaces with traditionally defined social sciences.

ON LOCAL BIOLOGY: WHEN BIOLOGY IS CULTURE AND CULTURE IS BIOLOGY

Science exhibits a "trust in numbers" (Cassedy 1984; Porter 1995), a trust that is wedded to this culture's mistrust of difference, even that which is manifestly falsified (Duster 1990; Fausto-Sterling 1992; Gilman 1985; Gould 1995). Differences are arranged hierarchically (Shweder and Bourne 1982). Because of these two central cultural tendencies of the dominant culture in the United States (it is incorrect to say that it is the "majority" culture: see below), both physicians and lay people believe that life careers and illness courses and outcomes differ for reasons of nature/ biology in the form of "race." Progress is seen in medicine when it advocates specific treatment/therapies for specific "races," as in the fields of cardiovascular medicine and psychiatry (Gaines 2004a).

Science and popular culture ignore social factors, leaving only the biological as explanations of difference (DeVos and Wagatsuma 1966; Kleinman 1986). The social factors bear the mark of the oppressors, a group that includes the researchers and clinicians (Devereux 1958). As well, social factors militate against the supremacy and autonomy of the biogenetic models of biomedicine.

The scientific use of "race" is part of the cultural conversation that creates and recreates in mind a *local biology* of "race"; it fashions a discursive formation into an apparent natural, empirical, and biological reality (Duster 1990; Gilman 1985, 1988; Gaines 1987, 1992a, 1992b, n.d.; Harding 1993). Because it is a thing of the mind, the semantic meaning of "race" differs from place to place and time to time even in the same place. Where (and when) such concepts are biological (some notions of "race" are cultural), they constitute a key component of local biology, the local cultural construction of human biology taken to be real, natural, and universal.

Because "race(s)" as categories of mind have a history, it is important to consider the historical construction of these social categories. I shall not segregate (pun intended) the discussions of these enterprises, local and scientific, as their "racial" discourses interpenetrate; separation into discrete realms would falsify their cultural conceptions, wrongly suggesting that elites foist ideas onto an unsuspecting laity when it is clear that laity and medical scientific elites share many racial beliefs (Gaines 1992a, 1992c; Young 1995).

"Race" is a psychocultural construct that intersects with other identity constructs, such as gender and age, to define spaces of action and constraint (Andersen and

Collins 1995; Butler 1993; Devereux 1970; Rothenberg 1998). Here, I am primarily concerned with cultural history and with the psychocultural construction of "race," and its implications and uses in societies, sciences, and medicines.

MEANING RACE: BODIES IN MIND, IDEAL REALITIES

First, we recognize that concepts of "race" are not peculiar to the West, nor are they universal. We find "racial" beliefs in a variety of cultures around the world. However, the meaning of the term is not the same in those places and, of course, did not and does not exist in the majority of extinct or extant cultures. The meaning of "race" also varies among the cultures of Western Europe. This variation exists despite common assertions about a "Western view" of "race" as a rationalist product of some allegedly culturally unitary expansionist enterprise (e.g., Gregory and Sanjek 1999). Such economic explanations, in fact, tend to give "racial" thinking a veneer of rationality (and therefore, respectability in the West) that analyses demonstrate it lacks. Rather, we see cultural historical mental patterns adapting to change rather than rational responses to it. And we see that such mental phenomena are preeminently local or (re)localized even when transplanted.

The views of "race" of the Latin and the Germanic traditions of Western Europe are fundamentally distinctive. The differing conceptions are the results of profoundly different cultural historical processes that have imprinted each tradition with a distinctive cultural logic (Gaines 1992b, 1992c).

In the United States, "race" is a central popular conception that derives not from the Latin traditions of Western Europe, but from the Germanic tradition, a tradition altered through its transmission to the United States through England. This folk conception of the biological bases of human differences is, in the United States, also central to a variety of scientific enterprises, including clinical, bench, and population biomedical sciences. Notions of "race" are evident in the application of biomedical theory, whether to populations as in public health or in genetics, clinical therapy, and in the newer therapies such as the allocation of resources in organ transplantation (Duster 1990; Gaines 1992a, 1992b, Larson 1995). The notion of "race" is likewise enshrined in the use of codes to indicate the research populations of NIH-sponsored activities. There we find a "minority" code (and a code for the scientific acceptability, or lack thereof, of the inclusion or exclusion of such populations). As I note below, the concept of "minority" has meaning only in the context of a "racial" ideology that defines group affiliation. We find ideas of "race" in the social and psychological sciences, as well as in the popular cultures that constitute its psychocultural contexts.

THE MINORITY MAJORITY

In the United States, an allegedly majority group, variously called "white" or "Caucasian," is distinguished in research not only as a biogenetic group, but also as a distinct culture. The "majority" cultural group definition creates other groups as "minorities." However, this usage manifests an implicit "racial" classificatory system and a leap in logic from there. That is, people assume that "race" is culture. Hence, in science and society, individuals refer to something called the "majority," "mainstream," or "dominant culture" borne by "white" or "Caucasian" people.

The subsumption of people of European ancestry in the United States under a single cultural label is without basis (other than in "racial" ideology). In ethnic, religious, or cultural terms, there exists no majority culture in the United States; everyone in the United States belongs to an ethnic or cultural minority group. One minority group does bear the dominant culture. I refer to this tradition as the Northern European Protestant Tradition (for it excludes many of the Protestant groups in the United States such as Baptists, Pentecostals, Mormons, and Evangelicals), otherwise known as Anglo-Saxon Protestants. It is a minority group, as are all other ethnic groups in the United States. Other traditions are those that derive from the Mediterranean culture area (including France) (Gaines 1985; Gaines and Farmer 1986).

"Race" as Local Biology

The system of social classification based upon cultural notions of "race" greatly affects life chances in the United States and in other societies that hold "racial" beliefs, such as Japan (e.g., DeVos and Wagatsuma 1966; Myrdal 1954). The fact of local constructions of human differences at a biological level suggests that we recognize that there are distinctive notions of biology in the world. That which is biological is by no means universal, as biomedicine asserts (Mishler 1981; Gaines 1992b, 2004a). Hence, one must pluralize and speak of "biologies," not biology (Gaines 1987, n.d.), and acknowledge the distinct biological constructs and processes we find in local popular and scientific contexts.

I subsume these distinct notions under the general rubric of "local biology" (Gaines 1992c, 1995, 1998a). Elements of various local biologies may include not only notions of "race," but also distinctive biologies of gender and social class (Carlson 2001; Fausto-Sterling 1992, 2000; Gaines 1998a, 2004a, n.d.; Gould 1996; Haraway 1991; Laqueur 1990; Lock 1993; Pernick 1985). Such alleged biological identities often entail putative moral and intellectual, as well as cultural differences (Carlson 2001; DeVos and Wagatsuma 1966; Gaines 1992a, 1992c; Gould 1996; Lamont 2003).

"Race" is equally important in the development of anthropology as a discipline, largely because it is within this field that there arose the first attacks on scientific racism in the West as well as some early scientific characterizations of "race." The initiator of the struggle against scientific racism was the founder of anthropology in the United States, Franz Boas (see his *Race, Language and Culture*, 1940, with essays dating from 1910 and earlier; Stocking 1968). It is here that we find some of the major critiques of the concept of "race" being used for the first time.

With respect to the several societies that hold biological "racial" beliefs, such as the United States, Germany, and Japan, we find that they do not share the same classificatory systems, nor do they share physiognomic stereotypes or characterological imputations. Though all systems of "racial" beliefs are cultural constructions, they may form paramount social realities in a given culture. These conceptions are examples of "culture in mind," to use Bradd Shore's felicitous phrase (1996), in the form of local biology. In societies adhering to beliefs about biological bases of various human groups, we find that differences having to do with achievement, wealth, intelligence, morality, and other indices of success and well-being, are presumed to derive from biology. This deterministic view is (re)asserted in that paean to the "natural" virtues of inequality, *The Bell Curve* (Herrnstein and Murray 1994) (see also Carlson 2001; Cohen 1998). Such works typically ignore the rather obvious social (and cultural) contexts and constraints on life status and achievement.

CLASSIFICATION AS PSYCHOLOGICAL DEFENSE

Beliefs in the natural inequality of peoples classed as "races" have been used historically as justification for domination, exploitation, and extermination (Gilman 1985; Gould 1995, 1996; Gregory and Sanjek 1999; Weber 1992). The psychological processes are rather clear. The victim is dehumanized such that their suffering carries no moral implication or responsibility for the agent(s) of their suffering (Gaines 1992a; Lamont 2003).

We can observe today the dramatic results of difference in definitions of the humanity, or lack thereof, of a subject people in the Americas. Whereas the Spanish crown determined that Native Americans were people in the early seventeenth century (and therefore to be converted, not slaughtered), the British and their descendent colonialists in the United States did not (Takaki 1993; Weber 1992). As a direct result, today there are many millions of Native Americans in Latin America but scarcely one half million remaining in the United States.

In this way, the concept of "race" serves as a culturally constituted defense mechanism, as Spiro (1970) outlined some time ago with respect to Burmese religious roles. Hence, as I discuss below, it is resilient and continues in the face of telling refutations of the concept by social experience, as well as genetic and social science research findings.

MENTAL CATEGORIES, CLASSIFIED BODIES

While many, perhaps most, cultures of the world past and present did not and do not hold "racial" theories, such theories are important to consider in discussions of science and society, especially in the United States and, by extension, the Western world. "Race" is one of a number of popular cultural conceptions about human difference. The Western concept was developed in its present scientific and related lay versions largely in the nineteenth century (Barkan 1992; Gossett 1965; Naroll and Naroll 1973; Stocking 1968). It was not a result of scientific progress. In classical and pre-classical times, people recognized differences in physical appearance, but such differences were irrelevant or read primarily in the aesthetic domain (Kuriyama 1993; Sherwin-White 1967). Language differences were noteworthy in these times, as well as differences in customs and morals (MacIntyre 1966). However, differences among human groups were nowhere perceived as reflections of inhering and immutable biological distinctiveness expressed as culture.

Because early civilizations comprised a number of physical types and cultural or ethnic groups in varying levels of assimilation (Sherwin-White 1967), it would have been difficult to usefully assert a notion of biologically determined morals or behaviors specific to one people or "race." The moral component of group membership became, in the West, a significant feature of "racial" attribution, one that continues to affect the foci and data (mis)interpretation in US medical research and practice (Adebimpe 1981; Brandt 1978, 1985; Carlson 2001; Duster 1990; Gaines 1992a, 1992c, 1998a, 2004a; Gilman 1985; Osborne and Feit 1992).

The idea of "race" emerged slowly in parts of the West and it did so in very different terms in different locations. An important step in the development of the notion of "race" that is believed to signify membership in a particular human biological population comes in the eighteenth century in the work of the Swedish botanist and taxonomist Carol Linnaeus (1707–78). His work built upon earlier notions of "species." Species were distinct animal populations that naturalists thought formed discontinuous groups. These distinct groups were sufficiently different that, naturalists thought, they could not interbreed. In addition to his classification of plants and other things, Linnaeus proposed a classification of human beings. He distinguished six human "groups," exemplars of most of which he had never seen. He labeled the six "groups," not "races."

Any notion that the human groups were distinct species (as the term was then used) already had been contradicted by the interbreeding of Europeans, such as the French and the Spanish in the New World, with native populations. However, such obvious realities would be ignored in subsequent periods (Carlson 2001; Gilman 1985; Gould 1996).

The French naturalist Georges Louis Leclerc Comte de Buffon (1707–88) introduced the term "race" into the biological literature in 1749. His term did not refer to distinct human groups as having separate origins or biologies, however, as he did not view them as distinct species (Montagu 1964). Buffon and Linnaeus's early reflections on human group differences saw these as representing variations of a single species.

In the eighteenth and nineteenth centuries, English and German philosophy and science began the construction of ideas of fundamental, incommensurate, biological differences that distinguished human groups (Barkan 1992; Boas 1940; Gould 1996). Nineteenth-century theories in the West were largely alike in expressing racist sentiments that incorporated a Spencerian "survival of the fittest" ideology (Gould 1996). Such sentiments rather explicitly justified colonialism and genocide.

English historians of the nineteenth century repeatedly referred to such "racial traits" as "rationality" and "freedom loving," traits said to be found among the English (the result of the merging of the German tribes of the Angles and Saxons in Britain, and later the Danes) and their ancestors, the Germans (Barkan 1992; Gossett 1965). In National Socialist "race science," which included medical sciences, most people commonly regarded in the United States as belonging to a "white race" were excluded. Thus, Italian, Slavic, and Irish Americans and others belonged to separate and inferior "races," as did Africans and Asians. The so-called "master race" was the mythical "German race," not a generalized European or "white race" as is now assumed in the United States.

A central figure in the shrouding of "racial" ideology in scientific terms congenial to the colonial mind in Western Europe was Sir Francis Galton (1822–1911). Called the "father of statistics," he lent both his ideas of the reality *and* inequality of "races," as well as methods allegedly useful in their determination. Scientists saw his statistical methods as the epitome of science, as the "trust in numbers" took hold as secular gospel. He coined the term "eugenics," conceiving of his new "science" as a program for "racial improvement" (Gould 1996).

The notion of the need for watchfulness over the genetic patrimony of a dominant group was widely found in the West, in science and politics as well as social policy (Brandt 1985; Carlson 2001; Gould 1996). The Nazis carried eugenics to its ultimate extreme in science and medicine, but its ideas were well entrenched in US science (e.g., Barkan 1992; Brandt 1985; Kater 1989).

Contemporary claims of innate differences, for example in IQ, continue to be made by people on the political right. *The Bell Curve* showed the affinity of the ideas of racism, sexism, and elitism in the United States that has been apparent in English science. Most important, from a psychological anthropological viewpoint, is the relationship to one another of the variety of forms of communalism. That is, those who believe in innate "racial" differences are likely to believe in innate differences between the sexes (beyond mere sexual dimorphism) and even the social classes (e.g., the assumption that the wealthy are "better people" who are deserving and hard working) (Gould 1996; Lamont 2003).

BIOLOGICAL ESSENTIALISM

We may view this position as a particular "thought model" in Devereux's (1958) terms. This model views human differences as derived from biology (or genetics) and is a construction that I have referred to as biological essentialism (Gaines 1992a). Thus, racism and sexism appear as two sides of the same conceptual coin of biological essentialism.

Biological essentialism is in fact a folk idea that science adopted and veiled in its discursive mantel. There the concept directs research and colors interpretations of results. For example, in research, in medical and social spheres in the United States, comparison groups are selected to provide a basis for determining "difference." These groups are usually "racial" groups (now sometimes called "ethnic" groups) employed as units of comparison for which researchers assume differences will be found (Osborne and Feit 1992).

MINDING RACE

Researchers biologize people's psychologies as well. This biologization is most apparent in studies of IQ and mental disorders. Most notorious in psychological research was England's dean of educational psychology for most of the twentieth century. Sir Cyril Burt (1883–1971) conducted a large number of twin studies conclusively showing the heritability of IQ, or so UK psychologists (and educational policy makers) assumed. After his death, researchers found that most of his twin studies, purporting to show the genetic and unchangeable basis of IQ, were fraudulent, but by this time they had already made an impact on English notions of "breeding." In the United States, Burt's elitist, biological essentialist arguments were converted into racist (and sexist) theories by his students, most especially psychologists Hans Eysenck (1990) and Arthur Jensen (see Gould 1995; Fausto-Sterling 1992). Jensen's work on the heritability of measured IQ is built on the same false assumptions as those asserted by the authors of *The Bell Curve*, Herrnstein and Murray (1994), who wrongly assumed that IQ can be measured with a simple number, then ranked and used as an unchangeable, universal standard (Gould 1996; Fausto-Sterling 1992).

Murray built upon and defended Jensen's position in a 1971 article that was without documentation. He then went on to provide with Herrnstein (often false and/or distorted) documentation in *The Bell Curve*. Jensen himself has tried to defend the "legacy," such as it is, of Burt (e.g., Jensen 1992), an important defense since the entire heritability argument is fundamentally grounded in Burt's fraudulent results.

The research course in the United States articulated its key notion of difference, "race," in the stead of England's (biological) notion of class distinctiveness. While their statistics might be hard to challenge, one can easily falsify the social categories on which the statistics related to IQ were and are collected. First, researchers mistakenly and steadfastly presume that the social categories represent distinctive genetic groups. Second, they presume that genetics determines IQ. Third, they presume that social experience and expectation does not influence performance on tests. However, the Human Genome Project has demonstrated the central impossibility of all attempts to classify groups on the basis of distinctive genomes, for humans share some 99.95 percent of their genes.

The genetic approach is also a psychological defense of intellectualization, for it is a way for researchers, policy analysts, and lay persons to exclude the obvious differences in opportunity that result in great differences in education, wealth, and health. The genetic approach often allows a seemingly scientific approach to mirror racist (or classist and/or sexist) beliefs and assumptions. Such work also facilitates a blame-the-victim approach in science.

A dominant idea since 1980 in US psychiatry is that mental illnesses are biological (Gaines 1992a, 1992c; Luhrmann 2000). This position is a version of biological essentialism that was borrowed from German psychiatry, which in turn borrowed it from German philosophy. German philosophy itself had internalized the concept from German popular culture (Gaines 1992c; Young 1991). This gives the United States a genealogy of an ostensibly scientific conception. The ideas serve cultural, social, and personal psychological interests. That is, members of the elite or dominant group comfort themselves with notions of superiority and just desserts (Gaines 1992a; Lamont 2003; Rowan 1995).

THE CRITIQUE OF SCIENTIFIC RACISM

Evolutionists of the nineteenth century explained the increasing knowledge of human diversity in biological terms (Barkan 1992; Boas 1940; Gossett 1965). They proposed that different "levels" or stages of societies, typically evaluated by measures of material culture, signified inborn abilities. As a consequence, "history" meant European history. Racist evolutionist ideas, and many that were not evolutionist, permeated much of medicine, psychology, biology, and other sciences in both Europe and the United States. Among the first to lead a concentrated and protracted attack on scientific racism was Franz Boas (1858–1942).

A German immigrant and the founder of US anthropology, Boas was among the first to challenge the homogenized notions of "race" in science at a time when people inside and outside of anthropology were quite comfortable with them. He showed the malleability of the human form. His findings flatly contradicted assumptions about the conservative biological nature (and culture) of "races." We now see the differences among populations as less and less significant. These differences have been produced by human biology so plastic that all its variations have developed from a common group (in Africa) in something less than 120,000 years.

However, most importantly, Boas showed that biology was not related to culture. He demonstrated that groups said to be "races" do not have "race-specific" languages, religions, or other cultural practices. As he demonstrated, members of the same "race" spoke different languages, held different religious beliefs, and otherwise exhibited distinct cultures. Thus, "race" (or biology) cannot determine forms of human behavior (Boas 1940; Stocking 1968). Many of the positions advanced by Boas remain the most powerful anti-racist arguments. It is remarkable that he began his assault on scientific racism before 1910, when blatantly racist statements were common in science and popular culture, including Teddy Roosevelt, who worried about "race suicide" (see Brandt 1985).

By the late nineteenth century, scholars saw evolutionary schemes as being based on biased conjecture. There were no empirical bases for the evolutionary stages of Marx, Spencer, Tylor, or any of the other evolutionary theorists. Diffusionism replaced evolutionism in the United States (functionalism in Europe) with its still-important ideas of relativism and the unrankable differences among cultures.

We may see here an analogy with psychology. Whereas anthropology recognized cultures in the place of Culture, psychology yet maintains the idea that there is a universal "g," or general human intelligence, that can be measured. Different cultural beliefs and values become, in this view, noise interfering with the reading of the underlying, universal psychological reality. Anthropology has shifted, in a parallel fashion to Boas's use of cultures rather than Culture, in recognizing cultural psychologies, not a universal psychology (Shore 1996; Shweder 1990).

Evolutionists rank people and cultures from low to high, worst to best. Implicit in evolutionist thinking is the idea of progress, the idea that things are changing for the better. The two ideas, evolution and progress, are unrelated and must be kept separate. Evolutionary change is simply descent with modification; there is no implication of improvement, superiority, or progress of later social or biological forms over earlier ones. A counter to the linking of evolution and progress is Boas's notion of "cultural relativism."

The relativist thrust within anthropology was further enriched by Geertz's (1973) concern with people's understandings of their own experiences, rather than with "experience-distant" *explanations* of human behavior. Further developments have shown that individuals may contest notions or beliefs in their cultures and that one's vantage point in society affects one's view of it (i.e., Shweder's "view from somewhere"). We see cultures and their psychologies more as organized diversity than replicated uniformity, as Wallace (1961) suggested long ago.

Biomedical and social sciences often evidence not the relativism of Boas but the hierarchical, evaluative thinking indicative of evolutionism (Shweder and Bourne 1982). An implicit ranking system appeared in medicine and persists in notions of defects afflicting groups of people. Historians of medicine show that this idea was disseminated through medicine's depiction of specific illness states that employed representations of specific ethnic groups (called "races") and/or women or members of lower classes (Carlson 2001; Chesler 1972; Gilman 1985; Pernick 1985). These attempts show but one technique used to pathologize differences, which themselves are often created rather than observed. Ideas are impressed upon the body and recast it. Today, in the waning days of the "age of the gene," embodied differences/deficits are cast in genetic terms rather than in terms of blood or bodies (see Terry and Urla 1995).

Seeing Difference

An implicit age, gender, and ethnic standard and vantage point exists in medical and psychiatric thought. It is a Protestant (European Protestant), Anglo, male, and adult (Gaines 1992a) perspective that determines "difference" in medical and psychiatric thought. Difference is then represented as problematic, dangerous, pathological, defective, weak, vulnerable, and/or requiring "special" treatment (Carlson 2001; Duster 1990; Gaines 1992a; Gilman 1985; Osborne and Feit 1992). People afflicted with differences were "unfit" in the eugenics ideology and, hence, disposable (Carlson 2001; Duster 1990). Ultimately, the idea that is communicated is that culturally defined "others" such as non-European ethnics, women, and children are simply, and inherently, "not normal' (Gaines 1992a; Gilman 1985). In US psychiatry, we see the gradual pathologization of the entirety of women's lives, calendrical and biographical (Gaines 1992a). The gender- and economically dominant individuals, the voice in which psychiatric classification is written, then take emotional and psychological solace in their implied normality.

Making Up "Races"

The naturalness of "racial" groups used as comparison groups, as above, is problematic for another reason: the precise number of them has never been agreed upon. Throughout the last century and a half, enumerations of groups said to constitute "races" differ from author to author. Indeed, the number of racial groups is still changing. A recent example is the creation, starting in the early 1980s, of a "Hispanic race" in the United States and even more recently a "Middle Eastern race."

The delineation of a "race" is all the more striking because *la raza*, the Latino "race," is known to be composed of the descendents of West Africa, Western Europe, and Native America. People in the United States often ignore history to create a "race" out of an obviously heterogeneous (genotypically, phenotypically, and culturally) population. Here we see that rationality takes a back seat to cultural categories and the ways of perceiving and understanding difference they provide. Like gender, "racial" bodies exhibit an immateriality and shifting boundaries (see Butler 1993).

In 1991, taking note of the increasing interest (and conflict) of the United States with people of the Middle East, I argued then that people of this region were being constructed as a "race" (Gaines 1991). Increasingly, after that date, medical papers appeared wherein people from the Middle East were compared to other groups. Since the events of September 11, 2001, we see the fluorescence of this conceptualization. The "racialization" of a group has now advanced to where profiling is defended as "just," a reaction to "evil doers," in the words of the current vocabulary-challenged president (2003). The problem, however, is that the people of the Middle East and North Africa have always been classified as "Caucasian" or "white." Still, the process is not complete, for we note that no one has actually come up with a name for the "race" that is being created in order to be profiled. The term used in the media is typically "people of Middle Eastern descent" or even more ambiguously, "Middle Eastern-looking" people. Technically speaking, if logic and reason had any role, all classificatory "whites" should be subject to profiling by United States security forces. The lack of fixed criteria for differentiation is also noteworthy in the changes over time in "racial" labels of individuals in modern health statistical records (Hahn 1992).

THE HETEROGENEITY OF "RACE"

Analyses of biogenetic differences of human groups lead to the recognition of a great variety of characteristics, most of which are shared in various proportions. Local configurations of traits (height, color, etc.) produce a huge number of distinguishable groups. On the African continent, there are about 1,000 biologically distinguishable groups (Hiernaux 1970). Indeed, since genetic distinctiveness derives from the time separated from other groups, and since the first human populations lived in Africa, we can demonstrate that there is more variation of human groups in Africa than among the populations of the rest of the world (Gould 1996).

The central problem for any "racial" classification is that there exist no intrinsically salient human characteristics upon which one might base such a system of classification. Whether or not variations in hair form or skin color or height or weight are important depends upon the culture and the fashion of the moment. For example, a body on which effort has been inscribed (in the form of muscles and toning) is now fashionable in the United States, but was not a few decades earlier. In the 1800s, in fact, it was seen as physically dangerous for women to engage in "physical culture" (i.e., exercise) (Vertinsky 1990). European-American woman were gentle and delicate to a fault (Russett 1989). But other, "minority" and low status immigrant women were assumed to tolerate physical stress and pain (Pernick 1985; Vertinsky and Captain 1998). Today, myths of supernormal strength persist with respect to African Americans, but this view is advanced with respect to black females as a common (literary) "compensating construction" (see Harris 1995).

The deleterious effect of racism on perception and cognition is obvious. Misrepresentations appear in scientific research as well as in the popular media. The two – research and media – engage in a kind of cultural conversation that confirms the reality of "race." An objective look at the ancestry of members of the major groups in the United States reveals "race" as a fatally flawed conceptual problem in popular domains, as well as in public health and medical research.

I will briefly summarize some general information about the ancestry of putatively distinct "racial" groups in the United States. We find that in the United States, most people labeled by self and others as Native Americans are biologically part European; in many cases, they are largely so. Many such individuals also have West African ancestry. In addition, in another seemingly distinct group, we find that virtually all American "blacks," or African Americans, are biologically part European. In many if not most cases, more of their ancestry comes from Europe than from West Africa. Quite commonly, African Americans also have Native American ancestry (Blu 1980; Domínguez 1986; Hallowell 1976; Katz 1987; Naroll and Naroll 1973).

It is germane to point out that physical anthropology suggests that classificatory "whites" claiming multigenerational descent in the South all have West African ancestry and, very likely, Native American ancestry as well (Domínguez 1986; Hallowell 1976; Naroll and Naroll 1973). This should not be surprising, since most of the soldiers and colonists, first Spanish and then English, who came to the US South were single males (Takaki 1993; Weber 1992). The relatively few unmarried females were lower status and in long-term bond service. Without Native American and African women, European males in the Southwest and South could not reproduce.

In the move West, into what was northern Mexico where the Spanish settled among Native Americans more than a century before the first English (and their Celtic slaves) came to the East Coast, one finds again that those "Americans" who went into the area were primarily males from the South and East. For this reason, the descendants of these early settlers in the West (settlers who were themselves illegal immigrants because this was northern Mexico) are today of "mixed" ancestry, whether or not this is publicly known (Josephy 1991; Katz 1987; Limón 1998; Meier and Rivera 1972; Takaki 1993).

Another distortion relates directly to Latinos. Mexicans, and other groups of "Hispanics," are descendants of western European, Native American, and West African peoples. This mixture is what the term *la raza* means, a "race" born of a mixture of elements. Because many Mexicans are Native American or partly so, the difference between Native Americans (many of whom are Spanish speaking) and Latinos is often only nationality, a matter of socio-legal definition, not ancestry. In other instances, Latinos have no Native-American ancestry, but do have West African ancestry in addition to West European ancestry. In many Latino groups, West African ancestry is virtually universal (e.g., Venezuela, Dominican Republic, Brazil, Puerto Rico, etc.). However, among those with West African ancestry, we find that the history of intermingling of different West African ethnic groups in the Americas has produced populations genetically distinct from any found in Africa. Despite this complicated history of interchange, US biomedical research and practice routinely treat Latinos as a distinct, homogeneous biogenetic population. Despite the very definition of Latino as people of mixed cultural and biological ancestry, medical science has homogenized this language group and, in the 1990s, it became a "race" (Gaines 1992b).

In reality, the groups seen as discrete in the United States – white, African American, Native American, and Latino – are not at all biologically distinct. Indeed, individuals in any of the categories may embody the same mixed ancestry as individuals in another or others. Thus, the seemingly immutable categories overlay a reality in which virtually anyone could be a member of any classificatory "race." The classification depends upon sociocultural context, not biology (or genetics), although such is used to support the classificatory discriminations. Here we see again the importance of *conceptions* about social reality over and above that social reality. We also see the lack of a coherent logic in mind with respect to "racial" classification and certainly not an aspect of human nature (e.g., Williams 1999).

Because racism clearly influences cognition, perception, and affect (emotion), it could well appear in psychiatric classifications as a specific disorder (Gaines 1992a). Rather than as a condition of professional psychiatric concern, racism and its twin – sexism – instead appear as significant implicit elements *in* medical and psychiatric (mis)diagnosis and (mis)treatment (Adebimpe 1981; Chesler 1972; Gaines 1992a; 1995; Good 1993; Osborne and Feit 1992).

The views of "race" found in the United States encode several distinct ideas, all of which have been falsified. They are: (1) a fixed number of distinct biological populations, or "races," exist in nature; (2) races have distinctive physical, mental, and behavioral characteristics; (3) "racial" characteristics (physical and behavioral) are naturally reproduced over time; and (4) specific group characteristics – physical, mental, and often moral – are hierarchically ranked; that is, some groups are superior to others (Boas 1940; Gould 1981; Lamont 2003; Stocking 1968; Montagu 1964). These assumptions, however, are not the only extant "racial" views of human difference.

In the United States, responses to "racial" categorization and the discriminatory practices related to its conceptual systems have been widely noted. These include negative self-concepts, aggression ("Black Rage" in the book by Grier and Cobbs), self-defeating behaviors, and ego defense mechanisms of denial, intellectualization, displacement and splitting, as well as deleterious representations of gendered bodies, whether that of the submissive or the superhuman (hooks 1981; Morton 1991; Vertinsky and Captain 1998). However, novel responses may be noted as well. These include the construction of a parallel psychological universe among African-American psychological writers who have taken their cue from W. E. B. DuBois, who developed the notion of "dual consciousness" in his classic work, *The Souls of Black Folk*.

As a direct descendent of his work, we find studies of dual consciousness as well as newer notions of ethnic psychopathology such as "mammyism" and "John Henryism" (Harris 1995). These and others are extensively developed in the African-American professional psychological literature. While one might easily show that these forms of psychopathology are well established in the nosology of the dominant group by other terms, the fact of the existence of this parallel psychological universe demonstrates the wide gulf created by "racial" thinking.

MORE FROM BEYOND THE UNITED STATES

Some writers have argued that capitalism, with a need for cheap labor and for justifying expropriation of land and resources, provided the political context and motivation that drove science to create a defensible basis in biology for immoral acts such as slavery and genocide (e.g., Rex and Mason 1988). Certainly, Europeans' encounters with Native Americans and imported West Africans affected their con-structions of human difference (Gossett 1965). However, with an understanding that culture is not conscious it appears more likely that "racial" views are a form of local biology (Gaines 1992a, 1998a). These ideas may sometimes serve economic interests, but it is clear that such classificatory fictions predate capitalism in the West. As well, cultures without any expansionist leanings may exhibit "racial" classifica-tions. Also, the various capitalist countries exhibit distinctive notions of "race," not just one. These notions result in very different treatments of those designated as belonging to particular "races."

Race in Europe

The German "racial" conception is a kind of ancient kinship theory, a theory of a coherent, related descent group (Gaines 1992a) that later merged with evolutionist ideas. Since it is much like a kinship system, it is much narrower than US notions. It determines social identity as well as citizenship and suitability to hold political office, for non-Germans cannot hold any political office or become citizens. In this system, the idiom of *Blut* or blood is central and is the forerunner of biogenetic notions.

The same system of social classification is found in Alsace, the culturally Germanic (or better, Teutonic) northeastern province of France. The biological Germanic system (Gaines 2002) exists alongside a very different, French, cultural system that determines ethnic identity by other means. It accords in-group identity to those sharing French civilization and culture. Membership is based primarily on language, not appearance or place of birth (Gaines 1992a). The term "race" in France thus refers to people who share a particular language and civilization, both of which can be acquired, but the latter only by means of the former (Lamont 2003). The so-called "racist" groups of France associated with Le Pen may be seen more as "culturalists"; their targets are not immigrant "races" but culturally distinct groups, such as unassimilated Muslims.

"Race" in Japan and South Africa

In the modern industrial societies of Japan, a conception of human "races" exists that differs from that found in the United States. Japanese sciences and medicine hold, and offer evidence to support, that the Japanese are a "race" distinct from Koreans, Chinese, the indigenous Ainu people, and the outcast Eta group (DeVos and Wagatsuma 1966; Harris 1995). By contrast, in the United States, science and social groups often consider all people from the East ("Asian") as constituting a single biological "race."

In South Africa, there exists yet another system that classifies "racial groups." There, before the collapse of apartheid, a socio-legal system was in place that dis-tinguished four groups: black, white, Asian, and colored. All people with ancestry in more than one of the first three groups were categorized as colored. Chinese were Asian, but at times, Japanese were white. Each group historically has had different rights and privileges (see Swartz, in Gaines 1992b).

In the United States, virtually all people called black or African American (a term coined by anthropologist Melville Herskovits) would be classified in South Africa as colored because of their mixed ancestry (West African, western European, Native American). Indeed, all US residents who claim long lines of US antecedents would be classified likewise because they, too, have mixed ancestry. The same would hold true for most Native Americans and Latinos. Ironically, the major US "racial" groups, those with major antipathies and conflicts enduring over centuries based on their "racial differences," would all be classified in South Africa as belonging to the same "racial" group: colored.

BIOMEDICAL RESEARCH AND PRACTICE: RECREATING POPULAR WISDOM

The ideas of "race" enumerated above underlie almost all medical and psychiatric research in the United States that pertains to group differences other than age or sex (Gaines 1992b; Hahn 1992; Osborne and Feit 1992). We find that in the medical sciences, research, theory, and practice often play a culturally supportive role in US society by serving as "scientific" justifications for the persistence of popular conceptions of "race" and of "racial" differences (Brandt 1985; Gilman 1985). Indeed, we find that new avenues of medical research, such as genetic studies of disease, lead US researchers back to old "racial" ideas and the (re)creation of notions of defective groups (see especially, Carlson 2001; Duster 1990; Graves 2001).

Because "racial" groups are mental constructs, they cannot evidence medical conditions, behavioral propensities, moral or aesthetic sensibilities, and the like. Yet "one of the most common methodological blunders in scientific studies of the significance of racial differences in the United States is the tacit acceptance of this phantasmic notion of race as the basis for establishing research samples" (Harris 1968: 264).

THE MYTH OF "RACE-SPECIFIC" DISEASE: (RE)"RACING" THE GLOBE

In biological or psychological research, science is used to reach conclusions that are in fact *a priori* assumptions. In case after case, we see that "prejudice not documentation, dictates conclusions" (Gould 1981: 80). In today's medical and scientific community, expressed ideas concerning ethnic and gender inferiority are largely implicit. They have been replaced in the medical literature by vague assertions such as vulnerability, susceptibility, tendency, increased risk, and just plain difference. One aspect of this discourse that constructs and maintains "racial" difference is "race-specific diseases."

At the beginning of the twentieth century, Dr. Herrick found sickle cell anemia originally through laboratory analysis rather than physical examination of the patient and his or her symptoms. This was the first time in US medicine that laboratory results superseded physicians' diagnostic gaze. Herrick examined the blood of five patients. Two of the patients were European Americans, two were called "mulattos" (in the parlance of the time, persons of mixed European and West African ancestry, but very largely the former), and one "Negro" (who, doubtless, was also part European, as is ubiquitous). Herrick reported his findings in the medical literature as a condition found only in "Negroes" (Wailoo 1991). He thereby established nearly a century of misdiagnoses. This was the beginning of the history of the association of sickle cell anemia, one of several hemoglobinopathies, with African Americans – a condition that has existed in many world populations, including Mediterraneans, Middle Easterners, South Asians, Filipinos, and South Americans. Instructively, the condition is not found among people in East, South, or Central Africa, but only in West Africa, the ancestral area of most people in the Americas with African ancestry. The condition is not a "racial disease" but rather a condition of specific local populations.

The notion of "race-specific" disorders is part of the US discourse aimed at (re)creating racial groups and asserting their dissimilarity. The fictions of "race-specific diseases" express racism from the medical community in a discourse believed to be beyond culture. The notion of "race" has no biological reality, thus no disease or condition can be "race specific." Another example of a so-called "race-specific disease" is that of Tay-Sachs disease, said to be a "Jewish disease." Here again we see the category fallacy wherein members of a social category are assumed to share a common biology, despite the fact that the name of this category is a religion! In reality, this is a disorder found in a specific local population of the eastern Mediterranean from which some Jews, as well as Arabs, came. Jews not from this area and not descended from people who were, have no risk of developing the disorder. The disorder is a local, not a "Jewish" disease.

The same can be said of BRAC 1 and BRAC 2. These two genes confer increased risk of breast cancer on the carrier. This is reported as another "Jewish disease." In fact, the mutations are local (eastern Mediterranean) genetic phenomena that can appear in any person from the region, whether secular, Moslem, or Jewish.

The fiction of "racial diseases" is maintained through a number of techniques, including part-for-whole thinking. A recent example in psychiatry demonstrates this (il)logic: a clinical finding that (East) Indians in Britain required lower therapeutic levels of certain psychotropic medications became the basis for research comparing "Asians" and "Caucasians," as well as other ethnic groups. These comparisons ultimately led to the development of a field referred to as "ethno-psychopharmacology" (Lin et al. 1986; Lin et al. 1990). The premise of this "cutting edge" field is that specific ethnic groups have distinctive therapeutic levels for psychotropic medications, based on the assumption that ethnic groups share some biogenetic distinctiveness. The field presents in glaring terms the confusion of ethnicity and "race."

Common to intentional and unintentional discriminatory motivations is the unstated theory that ancestry in non-white groups "taints" the individual, not only determining identity but also causing disease. This is the implicit pathologization of perceived "difference" typical in research on high blood pressure and diabetes, as well as a variety of other conditions (Cowie et al. 1989; Jones and Mitchell 1987). Considering the study of diabetes in African Americans more closely, it is found that while no risk factors and few cases of diabetes exist in West Africa, individuals classified as African American are still commonly said to be at "high risk" for developing the disease because of their "racial/ethnic ancestry." The presence of diabetes in these populations has other probable causes that are normally overlooked, including the European genetic background of African Americans, poverty and related poor nutrition caused by discrimination, and the high carbohydrate and animal-fat content of the dominant northern European diet.

Research on the treatments of choice and treatment recommendations in US bio-medicine demonstrates that medical and psychiatric diagnoses and therapeutic choices are often made on the basis of patients' social identity, be it "race," class, or gender, rather than objective need (Brandt 1985; Gilman 1985; Good 1993; Lindenbaum and Lock 1993; Osborne and Feit 1992). This once included the differential use of anesthesia (Pernick 1985).

Interventions in psychiatry (for example, pharmacotherapy and psychotherapy) are today heavily dependent on "racial" and/or sexual stereotypes (see Gaines 1982, 1992a, 1992b; Littlewood 1982; Nuckolls 1998). Blacks and Hispanics are often seen as belonging to that group of patients termed "psychologically unsophisticated" or "not psychologically minded" and may be couched in evolutionist terms (Leff 1981). Psychopharmacotherapy is seen as more "appropriate" for such patients.

US psychiatry in the nineteenth century "found" that a psychiatric disorder explained why black slaves would "unaccountably" run away from their masters: a psychiatric disease, called "draeptomania." This is a historical version of a biological psychiatry that posits that all conditions are biological and will ultimately yield to somatic interventions. In medical research, as in popular culture, behavior is related to "race." Medical researchers often choose topics implicative of immoral or incautious behavior when dealing with minority populations. Examples are research efforts focused on sexual experience, unwed motherhood, and drug addiction (Gaines 1985; Osborne and Feit 1992). In this way, medical research also becomes moral research and supports "blame-the-victim" thinking.

In the West, emotions are believed to be natural, universal, and distinct from cognition. But anthropological research shows that specific emotions are neither uni-versal nor naturally distinct from cognitive or bodily states and functions (see Lutz 1985; Obeyesekere 1985). While highly valued in a very few cultures, psychologization of distress is not "natural," but rather a learned, shared, and transmitted cultural approach (Kleinman 1988). Psychologization is not found in many areas of Europe itself; for example, the Mediterranean and Eastern Europe (Gaines 1992a; Gaines and Farmer 1986), or in China, Japan, and India (Kleinman and Good 1985; Leslie and Young 1992).

Research on "racial" differences provides the scientific bases for the maintenance of popular and scientific "racial" ideology. This ideology clearly leads to differential evaluation of social actors in medical and non-medical contexts. As such, biomedical theory and practice contributes to the social problems caused by racism. These problems include unequal access to medicine and poor medical outcomes. The use of "racial" categories in biomedicine, then, may be seen in and of itself as a breach of the medical profession's own primary ethical injunction to "do no harm" (Gaines 2004a).

LOCATING EVIL: GENES, "RACE," AND VIOLENCE

Biomedicine conceives of its domain as the discovery and manipulation of a con-structed Nature (see Gordon 1988). Its wider culture perceives nature as something to be dominated and controlled (Pike 1992). Ideas of nature, as well as those of differ-ence and inferiority that are encoded in "racial" and gender identities, greatly affect practice and research in US biomedical sciences, as noted above. Classes of people believed to be closer to nature are seen as requiring control and guidance, even domination. Such people are, in the United States, rather widely believed to be emotional, and therefore dangerous, unpredictable, and wild. Comments about "natural abilities" (intuitive, musical, irrational, fierce, shrewd) or characteristics of particular groups indicate their closeness to nature; they, like animals, are "dominated" by instinct and irrationality, not by "reason," a European cultural and masculine virtue (Chesler 1972; Fausto-Sterling 1992; Gaines 1995; see also Lutz 1985; Pike 1992).

The imputation of wildness, impulsivity, and irrationality is doubtless a culturally constituted defensive projection of aggression that actually exists in the dominant group (Gilman 1985; Pike 1992). It is used to justify control, domination, and even extermination, as with Africans and Native Americans in the United States and non-German ethnics and the mentally and physically disabled in World War II Germany.

A similar logic appears in contemporary US society. Urban violence, born of repression, discrimination, violence, and poverty, is recast as "predispositions to violence or criminality" (Lamont 2003), especially after periods of civil unrest. However, rather obvious examples of genetic predispositions toward criminality and violence in the dominant group are regularly ignored.

It appears that violence and criminality are possible genetic predispositions only when they appear in individuals belonging to specific low status "racial" or class groups (see Carlson 2001; Duster 1990). This appears to be much like Evans-Pritchard's (1937) classic account of witchcraft among the Azande. This stratified society tolerated intraclass witchcraft accusations among the royal class and commoner class and it accepted accusations from the royal class toward commoners. But accusations from commoners about royals were manifestly not credible.

That "racial" groups are considered unequally in US biomedical science and society is clearly demonstrated by the infamous and tragic Tuskegee Syphilis Study. It was reported in the medical literature for over four decades, but aroused no ethical or legal concerns about the informed consent of these human subjects, or the government conspiracy to withhold efficacious treatments (Brandt 1978, 1985; Jones 1993).

Aside from specific research projects that indicate differential concern for specific groups in the United States, "minorities" in day-to-day medical settings are often under-diagnosed for problems that could be treated (e.g., heart disease) and over-diagnosed for others (e.g., schizophrenia). These misdiagnoses lead to confinement and inappropriate pharmacological regimens. Loss of freedom and improper use of powerful psychotropic medications may themselves lead to chronicity in the illnesses that are left untreated (i.e., the very illnesses that led the patient to the attention of health professionals) (see Adebimpe 1981; Good 1993). Biomedical treatments may create the chronicity of particular disorders as well as increase the reported incidence of them in specific populations. The circular logic is completed by the subsequent tendency to over-diagnose disorders in individuals who belong to specific categories in whom particular conditions are reported as "common."

CONCLUSIONS

It is important for a full understanding of the place of "racial" classifications in culture to consider their use and function within science and medicine as well as popular culture. "Race" in the US, and in a few other cultures, represents versions of human biology. As such, they are forms of local biology. This form of local biology assumes that social categories – "races" – are reflections of nature rather than culture. However, as we have seen, nature is itself quite various. Because of notions of biology and nature found in a culture, biomedical and other scientific work, public healthcare as well as social life are conducted and interpreted in these terms. In clinical practice in US medicine, every patient record begins with what are regarded as three critical elements of information: age, "race," and gender (e.g., "A 37-year-old black female presented with . . ."). This usage is a significant part of the discourse of medicine that reconfirms the cultural conceptions that "race," age, and sex are natural and empirical realities that make a difference. Science, government, and biomedicine subsequently validate these folk conceptions (Duster 1990; Harding 1993). Even though contemporary institutional usage often exchanges "racial" terms for ethnic ones, the problems of the notion of a biological basis for human differences persists. The error is simple: the confusion of ethnicity, which has a cultural referent, and "race," which has a putatively biological one. The two terms are incommensurate and cannot be used interchangeably.

Intentionally or unintentionally, science, as in genetics and biomedicine, conserves and disseminates "racial" (and gender-biased) conceptions in its theories and practices. Such actions derive *both* from habit (i.e., tradition in the Weberian sense) and nefarious intent. The result is often a reflexive creation of a parallel psychological and biological universe. Circular thinking further supports the illusion of "race." Support for the harmony of illusions about "race" also comes from the well-intentioned who are struggling against the "racial divide" or the "color line" (e.g., Gilroy 2000), for the discourse about "divides" and "lines" is precisely what (re)creates difference in mind.

REFERENCES

Adebimpe, V. R., 1981 Overview: White Norms and Psychiatric Diagnosis of Black Patients. *American Journal of Psychiatry* 138: 279–285.

American Anthropological Association (AAA), 1998 Statement on "Race." www.aaanet.org/stmts/racepp.htm.

American Association of Physical Anthropologists (AAPA), 1996 AAPA Statement on Biological Aspects of Race. *American Journal of Physical Anthropology* 101: 569–570.

Andersen, Margaret L., and Patricia Hill Collins, eds., 1995 *Race, Class, and Gender*. Belmont, CA: Wadsworth.

Barkan, Elazar, 1992 *The Retreat of Scientific Racism*. Cambridge: Cambridge University Press.

Biagioli, Mario, ed., 1999 *The Science Studies Reader*. New York: Routledge.

Blu, Karen, 1980 *The Lumbee Problem*. Cambridge: Cambridge University Press.

Blue, Amy V., 1992 The Rise of Greek Professional Ethnopsychiatry. In *Ethnopsychiatry*. Atwood D. Gaines, ed. Albany: State University of New York Press.

Boas, Franz, 1940 *Race, Language, and Culture*. New York: Free Press.

Brandt, Allan, 1978 Racism and Research: The Case of the Tuskegee Syphilis Study. *Hastings Center Report*. December: 21–29.

— 1985 *No Magic Bullet: A Social History of Venereal Disease in the United States since 1880*. Oxford: Oxford University Press.

Butler, Judith, 1993 *Bodies That Matter*. New York: Routledge.

Carlson, Elof Axel, 2001 *The Unfit: A History of a Bad Idea*. Cold Spring Harbor, NY: Cold Spring Harbor Laboratory Press.

Cassedy, James, 1984 *American Medicine and Statistical Thinking: 1800–1860*. Cambridge, MA: Harvard University Press.

Chesler, Phyllis, 1972 *Women and Madness*. New York: Harcourt, Brace, Jovanovich.

Cohen, Mark Nathan, 1998 *Culture of Intolerance: Chauvinism, Class, and Racism in the United States*. New Haven, CT: Yale University Press.

Cowie, C., et al., 1989 Disparities in Incidence of Diabetic End-Stage Renal Disease According to Race and Type of Diabetes. *New England Journal of Medicine* 321: 1074–1079.

Devereux, George, 1958 Cultural Thought Models in Primitive and Modern Psychiatry. *Psychiatry* 21: 359–374.

— 1970 Ethnic Identity: Its Logical Foundations and its Dysfunctions. In *Ethnic Identity: Cultural Continuity and Change*. George DeVos and Lola Romanucci-Ross, eds. Palo Alto, CA: Mayfield.

DeVos, George, and Hiroshi Wagatsuma, 1966 *Japan's Invisible Race: Caste in Culture and Personality*. Berkeley: University of California Press.

Domínguez, Virginia, 1986 *White by Definition*. New Brunswick, NJ: Rutgers University Press.

Duster, Troy, 1990 *Backdoor to Eugenics*. New York: Routledge.

Evans-Pritchard, E. E., 1937 *Witchcraft, Oracles and Magic Among the Azande*. Oxford: Clarendon Press.

Eysenck, Hans, 1990 *Rebel with a Cause*. London: W. H. Allen.

Fausto-Sterling, Anne, 1992 *Myths of Gender: Biological Theories about Women and Men*, 2nd edn. New York: Basic Books.

— 2000 *Sexing the Body: Gender Politics and the Construction of Sexuality*. New York: Basic Books.

Fujimura, Joan, 1996 *Crafting Science: A Socio-History of the Quest for the Genetics of Cancer*. Cambridge: Cambridge University Press.

Gaines, Atwood D., 1982 Cultural Definitions, Behavior and the Person in American Psychiatry. In *Cultural Conceptions of Mental Health and Therapy*. Anthony Marsella and Geoffrey White, eds. Dordrecht: D. Reidel.

— 1985 Faith, Fashion, and Family: Religion, Aesthetics, Identity, and Social Organization in Strasbourg. *Anthropological Quarterly* 58 (2): 47–62.

— 1987 Cultures, Biologies, and Dysphorias. *Transcultural Psychiatric Research Review* 24 (1): 31–57.

— 1991 Biomedicine and Folk Biology: "Race" and Racism in American Medical Theory and Practice. Paper presented in the symposium "Is Culturalism an Improvement on Racism?" American Ethnological Society Meeting. March, Charleston, SC.

— 1992a From DSM-I to III-R; Voices of Self, Mastery and the Other: A Cultural Constructivist Reading of US Psychiatric Classification. *Social Science and Medicine* 35 (1): 3–24.

— ed., 1992b *Ethnopsychiatry: The Cultural Construction of Professional and Folk Psychiatries*. Albany: State University of New York Press.

— 1992c Medical/Psychiatric Knowledge in France and the United States: Culture and Sickness in History and Biology. In *Ethnopsychiatry: The Cultural Construction of Professional and Folk Psychiatries*. Atwood D. Gaines, ed. Albany: State University of New York Press.

— 1995 Race and Racism. In *Encyclopedia of Bioethics*. Warren T. Reich, ed. New York: Macmillan.

— 1998a From Margin to Center: From Medical Anthropology to the Cultural Studies of Science. *American Anthropologist* 100 (1): 101–194.

— 2002 Alsatians. In *Encyclopedia of World Cultures Supplement*. Carol R. Ember, Melvin Ember, and Ian Skoggard, eds. New York: Macmillan.

— 2004a Race and Racism. In *Encyclopedia of Bioethics*, 3rd edn. Stephen G. Post, ed. New York: Macmillan.

— 2004b Mental Illness II: Cultural Perspectives. In *Encyclopedia of Bioethics*, 3rd edn. Stephen G. Post, ed. New York: Macmillan.

— 2004c Masculinities and Race(s). In *Encyclopedia of Men and Masculinities*. Michael Kimmel, ed. Santa Barbara, CA: ABC-CLIO Press.

— n.d. *Figures of Speech: Local Biology, Bodies and "Race" in Millennial Medical Anthropology.*

Gaines, Atwood D., and Paul Farmer, 1986 Visible Saints: Social Cynosures and Dysphoria in the Mediterranean Tradition. *Culture, Medicine and Psychiatry* 10 (4): 295–330.

Geertz, Clifford, 1973 *The Interpretation of Cultures*. New York: Basic Books.

Gilman, Sander L., 1985 *Difference and Pathology: Stereotypes of Sexuality, Race, and Madness*. Ithaca, NY: Cornell University Press.

— 1988 *Disease and Representation: Images of Illness from Madness to AIDS*. Ithaca, NY: Cornell University Press.

Gilroy, Paul, 2000 *Against Race*. Cambridge, MA: Belknap/Harvard University Press.

Good, Byron J., 1993 Culture, Diagnosis and Comorbidity. *Culture, Medicine and Psychiatry* 16: 427–446.

Gordon, Deborah, 1988 Tenacious Assumptions in Western Medicine. In *Biomedicine Examined*. Margaret Lock and Deborah Gordon, eds. Dordrecht: Kluwer Academic.

Gossett, Thomas F., 1965 *Race: The History of an Idea in America*. New York: Schocken.

Gould, Stephen J., 1981 *The Mismeasure of Man*. New York: W. W. Norton.

— 1995 Mismeasure by Any Measure. In *The Bell Curve Debate: History, Documents, Opinions*. Russell Jacoby and Naomi Glauberman, eds. New York: Times Books/Random House.

— 1996 *The Mismeasure of Man*, 15th anniversary edn. New York: W. W. Norton.

Graves, Joseph L., 2001 *The Emperor's New Clothes: Biological Theories of Race at the Millennium*. New Brunswick, NJ: Rutgers University Press.

Gregory, Steven, and Roger Sanjek, eds., 1999 *Race*. New Brunswick, NJ: Rutgers University Press.

Hahn, Robert A., 1992 The State of Federal Health Statistics on Racial and Ethnic Groups. *Journal of the American Medical Association* 267 (2): 268–273.

— 1995 *Sickness and Healing*. New Haven, CT: Yale University Press.

Hallowell, A. I., 1976 *Contributions to Anthropology: Selected Papers of A. Irving Hallowell*. Chicago: University of Chicago Press.

Haraway, Donna, 1991 *Simians, Cyborgs and Women: The Reinvention of Nature*. New York: Routledge.

Harding, Sandra, ed., 1993 *The Racial Economy of Science: Toward a Democratic Future. Race, Gender and Science*. Bloomington: University of Indiana Press.

Harris, Marvin, 1968 Race. *International Encyclopedia of the Social Sciences*. New York: Macmillan.

Harris, Trudier, 1995 This Disease Called Strength: Some Observations on the Compensating Construction of Black Female Character. *Literature and Medicine* 14 (1): 109–126.

Hearnshaw, Leslie, 1979 *Cyril Burt, Psychologist*. Ithaca, NY: Cornell University Press.

Herrnstein, Richard, and Charles Murray, 1994 *The Bell Curve: The Reshaping of American Life by Difference in Intelligence*. New York: Free Press.

Hiernaux, Jean, 1970 The Concept of Race and the Taxonomy of Mankind. In *The Concept of Race*. Ashley Montagu, ed. New York: Macmillan.

hooks, bell, 1981 *Ain't I a Woman? Black Women and Feminism*. Boston, MA: South End Press.

— 1990 *Yearning: Race, Gender, and Cultural Politics*. Boston, MA: South End Press.

Jensen, Arthur R., 1992 Scientific Fraud or False Accusations? The Case of Cyril Burt. In *Research Fraud in the Behavioural and Biomedical Sciences*. D. F. Miller and M. Hersen, eds. New York: John Wiley.

Jones, W., and R. Mitchell, eds., 1987 *Healthcare Issues in Black America*. New York: Greenwood Press.

Jones, J., 1993 *Bad Blood: The Tuskegee Syphilis Experiment*. New York: Free Press.

Josephy, Jr., Alvin M., 1991 *The Indian Heritage of America*. Boston, MA: Houghton-Mifflin.

Kater, Michael H., 1989 *Doctors Under Hitler*. Chapel Hill: University of North Carolina Press.

Katz, William L., 1987 *The Black West*, 3rd edn. Seattle, WA: Open Hand Publishing.

Kleinman, Arthur, 1986 *Social Origins of Distress and Disease: Depression, Neurasthenia, and Pain in Modern China*. New Haven, CT: Yale University Press.

— 1988 *Rethinking Psychiatry*. New York: Free Press.

Kleinman, Arthur, and Byron Good, eds., 1985 *Culture and Depression: Studies in the Anthropology and Cross-Cultural Psychiatry of Affect and Disorder*. Berkeley: University of California Press.

Kuriyama, Shigehisa, 1992 Between Mind and Eye. In *Paths to Asian Medical Knowledge*. Charles Leslie and Allan Young, eds. Berkeley: University of California Press.

— 1993 On Winds and Airs. Paper presented at the conference "Local Biologies." Atwood D. Gaines and Carol Worthman, Orgs. Center for Behavioral Sciences. Palo Alto, CA.

Lamont, Michèle, 2003 Who Counts as "Them?": Racism and Virtue in the United States and France. *Contexts* 2 (4): 36–41.

Laqueur, Thomas, 1990 *Making Sex: Body and Gender From the Greeks to Freud*. Cambridge, MA: Harvard University Press.

Larson, Edward J., 1995 *Sex, Race, and Science: Eugenics in the Deep South*. Baltimore, MD: Johns Hopkins University Press.

Latour, Bruno, 1999 Give Me a Laboratory and I Will Raise the World. In *The Science Studies Reader*. Mario Biagioli, ed. New York: Routledge.

Leff, Julian, 1981 *Psychiatry Around the Globe: A Transcultural View*. New York: Marcel Dekker.

Leslie, Charles, and Allan Young, eds., 1992 *Paths to Asian Medical Knowledge*. Berkeley: University of California Press.

Limón, José, 1998 American Encounters: Greater Mexico, the United States, and the Erotics of Culture. Boston, MA: Beacon Press.

Lin, K. M., R. Poland, and C. Chien, 1990 Ethnicity and Psychopharmacology: Recent Findings and Future Research Directions. In *Family, Culture, and Psychobiology*. New York: Legas.

Lin, K. M., with R. Poland and I. Lesser, 1986 Ethnicity and Psychopharmacology. *Culture, Medicine, and Psychiatry* 10 (2): 151–165.

Lindenbaum, Shirley, and Margaret Lock, eds., 1993 *Knowledge, Power, and Practice*. Berkeley: University of California Press.

Littlewood, Roland, 1982 *Aliens and Alienists: Ethnic Minorities and Psychiatry*. London: Penguin Books.

Lock, Margaret, 1993 *Encounters with Aging*. Berkeley: University of California Press.

Luhrmann, Tanya, 2000 *Of Two Minds: The Growing Disorder in American Psychiatry*. New York: Alfred Knopf.

Lutz, Catherine, 1985 Depression and the Translation of Emotional Worlds. In *Culture and Depression*. Arthur Kleinman and Byron Good, eds. Berkeley: University of California Press.

MacIntyre, Alasdair, 1966 *A Short History of Ethics*. New York: Collier/Macmillan.

Meier, Matt S., and Feliciano Rivera, 1972 *The Chicanos*. New York: Hill and Wang.

Mishler, Elliott, 1981 Viewpoint: Critical Perspectives on the Biomedical Model. In *Social Contexts of Health, Illness, and Patient Care*. E. Mishler, L. R. Amara Singham, S. Hauser, R. Liem, S. Osherson, and N. Waxler, eds. Cambridge: Cambridge University Press.

Montagu, Ashley, 1964 *Man's Most Dangerous Myth: The Fallacy of Race*. Cleveland, OH: World Publishing.

Morton, Patricia, 1991 *Disfigured Images: The Historical Assault on Afro-American Women*. Westport, CT: Greenwood Press.

Myrdal, Gunnar, 1954 [1944] *An American Dilemma*. New York: Harper and Row.

Naroll, R., and F. Naroll, eds., 1973 *Main Currents in Cultural Anthropology*. New York: Appleton-Century-Crofts.

Nuckolls, Charles W., 1998 *Culture: A Problem that Cannot be Solved*. Madison: University of Wisconsin Press.

Obeyesekere, Gananath, 1985 Depression, Buddhism, and the Work of Culture in Sri Lanka. In *Culture and Depression*. Arthur Kleinman and Byron Good, eds. Berkeley: University of California Press.

Osborne, Newton G., and Marvin D. Feit, 1992 The Status of Race in Medical Research. *Journal of the American Medical Association* 267 (2): 275–279.

Pernick, Martin, 1985 *A Calculus of Suffering*. New York: Columbia University Press.

Pike, Fredrick B., 1992 *The United States and Latin America: Myths and Stereotypes of Civilization and Nature*. Austin: University of Texas Press.

Porter, Theodore, 1995 *Trust in Numbers: The Pursuit of Objectivity in Science and Public Life*. Princeton, NJ: Princeton University Press.

Rex, John, and David Mason, eds., 1988 *Theories of Race and Ethnic Relations*. Cambridge: Cambridge University Press.

Rothenberg, Paula S., ed., 1998 *Race, Class, and Gender*. New York: St. Martin's Press.

Rouse, Joseph, 1999 Understanding Scientific Practices: Cultural Studies of Science as a Philosophical Program. In *The Science Studies Reader*. Mario Biagioli, ed. New York: Routledge.

Rowan, Carl, 1995 Blood Simple. In *The Bell Curve Debate: History, Documents, Opinions*. Russell Jacoby and Naomi Glauberman, eds. New York: Times Books/Random House.

Russett, Cynthia Eagle, 1989 *Sexual Science: The Victorian Construction of Womanhood*. Cambridge, MA: Harvard University Press.

Schiebinger, Londa, 1993 *Nature's Body*. Boston, MA: Beacon Press.

Sherwin-White, A. N., 1967 *Racial Prejudice in Imperial Rome*. Cambridge: Cambridge University Press.

Shore, Bradd, 1996 *Culture in Mind*. Oxford: Oxford University Press.

Shweder, Richard, 1990 Cultural Psychology – What Is It? In *Cultural Psychology: Essays on Comparative Human Development*. James W. Stigler, Richard Shweder, and Gilbert Herdt, eds. Cambridge: Cambridge University Press.

Shweder, Richard, and Peter Bourne, 1982 Do Conceptions of the Person Vary Cross-Culturally? In *Cultural Conceptions of Mental Health and Therapy*. Anthony Marsella and Geoffrey White, eds. Dordrecht: D. Reidel.

Spiro, Melford, 1970 *Buddhism and Society*. New York: Harper and Row.

Stocking, George W., Jr., 1968 *Race, Culture, and Evolution: Essays in the History of Anthropology*. New York: Free Press.

Swartz, Leslie, 1992 Professional Ethnopsychiatry in South Africa: The Question of Relativism. In *Ethnopsychiatry*. Atwood D. Gaines, ed. Albany: State University of New York Press.

Takaki, Ronald, 1993 *A Different Mirror: A History of Multicultural America*. Boston, MA: Little, Brown.

Terry, Jennifer, and Jacqueline Urla, eds., 1995 *Deviant Bodies*. Bloomington: Indiana University Press.

UNESCO, 1969 *Race and Science.* New York: Columbia University Press.

Vertinsky, Patricia, 1990 *The Eternally Wounded Woman: Women, Doctors, and Exercise in the Late Nineteenth Century.* Manchester: Manchester University Press.

Vertinsky, Patricia, and Gwendolyn Captain, 1998 More Myth than History: American Culture and Representations of the Black Female's Athletic Ability. *Journal of Sport History* 25 (3): 532–561.

Wailoo, Keith, 1991 A Disease sui generis: The Origins of Sickle Cell Anemia and the Emergence of Modern Clinical Research 1904–1924. *Bulletin of the History of Medicine* 65 (2): 185–208.

Wallace, Anthony F. C., 1961 *Culture and Personality.* New York: Random House.

Weber, David J., 1992 *The Spanish Frontier in North America.* New Haven, CT: Yale University Press.

Whitehouse, P. J., with Konrad Mauer and Jesse F. Ballenger, eds., 2000 *Concepts of Alzheimer Disease: Biological, Clinical, and Cultural Perspectives.* Baltimore, MD: Johns Hopkins University Press.

Williams, Melvin D., 1999 *Race for Theory and Biophobia Hypothesis.* Westport, CT: Praeger.

Young, Allan, 1991 Emil Kraepelin and the Origins of American Psychiatric Diagnosis. In *Anthropologies of Medicine.* Beatrix Pfleiderer and Gilles Bibeau, eds. Wiesbaden: Vieweg.

— 1995 *The Harmony of Illusions: Inventing Post-Traumatic Stress Disorder.* Princeton, NJ: Princeton University Press.

16 Unbound
Subjectivities and
New Biomedical
Technologies

Margaret Lock

Subjectivity is a creation of the early nineteenth century, a modern concept, conveying the idea of a consciousness of one's own inner state or feelings. From the
outset the idea raised more confusion than it settled, in large part because of its
close association with a second, messy concept: "subjective." Writers of the day,
notwithstanding Hume's assertion that reason should be the slave of passion, equated
subjectivity with being subjective and so with egoism and being dominated by
or absorbed in one's own personal feelings. It was argued that subjectivity clouds
the eyes, cripples invention, rests in the mind only, and mars efforts to be rational
and objective. Almost without exception subjectivity is rendered negatively in the
nineteenth century, although Coleridge takes an altogether different position, one
that is not judgmental, when he makes the observation "in the object, we infer our
own existence and subjectivity" (1821, cited in the *Oxford English Dictionary*).
Coleridge's social and semiotic approach to the creation of the interiority of human
subjects is one with which anthropologists will feel intuitively comfortable.

Consciousness of self is widely recognized today by most social scientists as
socially informed, indeed some would argue, fully socially constructed. But such
an approach is severely criticized by psychoanalysts such as Chodorow (1999) when
they insist on the priority of the "intrapsychic," with its peculiarly personal and
individualistic attributes that permit untrammeled self-construction and creativity
without interference from the world at large.

Of course, if subjectivity is socially produced and intimately associated with everyday
awareness, then experiences about which we have no recollection – the unconscious
of psychoanalytic language – cannot contribute to subjectivity. Obeyesekere (1981)
has gone to some lengths to try to overcome this dilemma. He criticizes the unhelpful
distinction made by social anthropologists in the middle of the last century between

public and private symbols, and makes use of subjectification as a bridging concept. For Obeyesekere, subjectification is "the process whereby cultural patterns and symbol systems are put back into the melting pot of consciousness and refashioned to create a culturally tolerated set of images." The resultant images constitute individual, "subjective imagery" which may then come to function creatively through public airing to become "proto culture" or "culture in the making," although by no means do all forms of subjective imagery end up as part of culture. Subjective imagery, that which is based on "objective culture," has the *potential* for group acceptance, but this depends in large part upon social and economic conditions. Obeyesekere (1981: 169) argues subjective imagery is not the same as individual fantasy and similar musings, which are closely associated with the unconscious, and have no prior cultural underpinnings.

Today, most anthropologists would probably avoid such a clear demarcation between public and private imaginary as does Obeyesekere, but even so oppositional tensions proliferate in debates about the mind and subjectivity. Part of the difficulty arises because mind is so often conceptualized unproblematically as a discrete entity encased inside the brain where, it is assumed, subjectification takes place. Competing protagonists follow for the most part one of three lines of argument. For many basic scientists, including some anthropologists, mind is biologically programmed and culture is simply the icing on the cake, so that subjectivity is constituted largely through chemistry, in particular by the biologically based emotions (passions in a strait-jacket). Alternatively, followers of psychoanalytic theory concentrate on the importance of creation of "mindfulness" – an enlightened subjectivity – that can be attained by bringing a suppressed past into conscious awareness through analysis or meditation.

The third line of argument is set out by Geertz when he writes that the human brain is "thoroughly dependent on cultural resources for its very operation, and those resources are, consequently, not adjuncts to, but constituents of mental activity" (1973: 76). For the most part, these tensions are of the nature/nurture, individual/culture kind – chicken and egg questions – in which few of the adversaries totally deny that biology, culture, or even the unconscious are inevitably involved – but weight their relative importance quite differently, and point causal arrows in different directions. The difficulty with these arguments, whether they set out from biology, the psyche, or culture as the prime driving force, is that mind and subjectivity are typically understood as thingified end products and mind–body and nature–culture dichotomies are left largely intact – a point to which I will return.

A second difficulty of long standing in connection with subjectivity is a concern about whether subjective assessments can be judged as ethical or not. If subjectivity is associated with the passions, then surely subjectively based opinions function irrationally and out of self-interest. As Lutz (1988) has noted when discussing emotions, subjectivity is inevitably associated with bias in the minds of many. But when subjectivity becomes tangled with other concepts and values such as individual rights, rights to privacy, individual autonomy, and so on, then we reach an impasse, for surely individuals must be the best judges of what is rightfully in their own interest; of what is ethical? Anthropologists, being inclined to cultural relativity and concerned primarily with social relations, and less so with individual dilemmas, have rarely faced up to this impasse. It is to Michel Foucault and to certain contemporary sociologists that we must turn for assistance here.

Nikolas Rose, following Foucault, has proposed a "genealogy of subjectification" (1996: 128). By this he means, not a history of ideas, nor an exploration of how the concept came to be, but rather an investigation of practices, techniques, and thoughts associated with the idea of subjectivity. He is concerned with the concept as it functions in a localized space and time frame, namely the current era in the "Western" world, where persons are equipped with an inner domain – a "psychology" – "structured by the interaction of biographical experience with certain laws or processes characteristic of human psychology." A genealogy of subjectification takes as its object of investigation the individualized, interiorized, and psychologized understanding of what it is to be human. Rose does not assume that this modern "regime of the self" is the product of a gradual process of enlightenment; rather, it is contingent upon various practices and processes, which by no means cohere into a grand design. He is interested in the way in which "the self" functions as a regulatory idea in so many aspects of contemporary forms of life and, above all, with "our relation to ourselves" as Foucault put it (1981: 135).

Rose does not deny that such relations can be understood in part through an examination of their historical emergence, but he does not want subjectivity explained in terms of modernity, late modernity, or "risk society," nor in terms of a history of the rise of the individual and individualism. Subjectivity should not be examined, he argues, as derivative of vast social transformations over time, nor conceptualized as a product of a major epistemic break from premodern thinking. Rose suggests a genealogy of subjectification will focus directly on the practices within which human beings have been located "in particular 'regimes of the person'" (1996: 131) and therefore an examination of the government of self by others as well as an examination of "technologies of the self" are in order.

The challenge, Rose recognizes, is to avoid an assumption of a metapsychology that drives behavior and practices. He eschews psychoanalytic theory and also debates in which a final appeal is made to the human being as a subject of rights, freedom, or autonomy, on the grounds that such knowledge and concepts are themselves products of nineteenth-century thinking. He self-consciously sets aside a worry common among feminists: that without appropriate theorization to account for agency and resistance, individuals are set up as passive; mere objects swept along by larger historical forces. Rose disagrees. He wants to dispose of any concept of an essential interiority, and draws instead on the idea of a "fold" or "pleat" first suggested by Deleuze, in which it is argued that whatever is "inside" is merely an infolding of an exterior. Rose argues these infoldings are partially stabilized, in that people imagine themselves as subjects of a biography and draw on memory to hold things securely in place. Body boundaries become fluid in such an approach:

> The human being is emplaced, enacted through a regime of devices, gazes, techniques which extend beyond the limits of the flesh into spaces and assemblies . . . and in each of these spaces, repertoires of conduct are activated that are not bounded by the enclosure formed by the human skin or carried in a stable form in the interior of an individual. (Rose 1996: 143–144)

One of Rose's objectives in elaborating this approach is to destabilize the idea of a unified personality that in his opinion circumscribes the horizon of the thinkable today. He is also working towards a critical analysis of the new ethical vocabularies focused on responsible self-advancement which at the same time de-politicize pathologies and inequities, transforming them into individual problems. In addition, Rose is concerned about the marketing of new subjectivities: the making of selves through consumption and by resort to new technologies. These are contemporary strategies for the "conduct of conduct" that the social sciences would do well to investigate, he suggests.

A genealogy of subjectification avoids assumptions of history as progress, cultures as essentialized, and persons as psychologized. But it does not tackle the question of biology and its relation to subjectivity. Similar to Foucault, Rose leaves the body essentially black-boxed. For Foucault, the body of modernity, as is well known, is at once productive and subjected; doubly disciplined through power and self, but Foucault never made it clear as to where he stands with respect to the malleability of the natural body. His position is not one of universalism (and here he parts company from his teacher Merleau-Ponty). What he terms the "validity" of his concept of micro-physics of power is situated somewhere between the institutions and apparatuses of power and "the bodies themselves with their materiality and their forces" (Foucault 1979: 26). Materiality remains obdurate for Foucault, but it is at this critical juncture that anthropologists and feminists have made major contributions. It is not simply the bounded, psychologized person that must be deconstructed, but also the bounded, material body.

Anthropology, Subjectivities, and Everyday Life

When researching the relationship of the senses, ritual, violence, and government to bodily experience and practices and to subjectivity and its narration, several of the strategies suggested by Rose have been put into practice by a good number of anthropologists for more than a decade now (see, for example, Anagnost 1997; Das 1997, 2000; Farquhar 1994; Feldman 1991; Kleinman 2000; Lutz 1988; Seremetakis 1991, 1994). The strength of Rose's project is his rigorous exposure of the psychologized, interiorized self as a construction of and integral to modernity. Anthropological studies, although they rarely resort to an uncritical use of psychologized language, do not focus on the production of this particular discourse and its relation to subjectivity. Instead, anthropologists usually highlight the experience and expression of social forces as individuals situated in specific historical and cultural contexts enact and talk about them. Eliciting narrative accounts and observing bodily behavior and rituals (most often those performed in the public domain) are the usual analytic tools yielding results that must then be situated in time and place.

Seremetakis, for example, examines the construction of power by Inner Maniat women as a complex ritualized process carried out through improvised mourning songs, dreaming, and exhumation of the dead. She argues explicitly that mourning ceremonies are not merely expressive performances but are transformative in which material forces such as pain, the body, and ritual pollution "creatively interact with women's experience in the economic and domestic spheres of life" (1991: 2). For Seremetakis, understanding death rituals is inseparable from understanding the Inner Maniat cultural imagination; these performances are not only individuated psychological or literary artifacts, but also ongoing social processes. Bifurcation between public and private is avoided entirely, and the relationship of not only mind but also the material body to the production of the social and the individual is handled with exquisite care.

Veena Das, in a contribution to a book she co-edited entitled *Violence and Subjectivity*, asks how the violations "inscribed on the female body (both literally and figuratively) and the discursive formations around these violations made visible the imagination of the nation as a *masculine* nation" (2000: 205). What did this experience do, Das asks, to the subjectivity of women? Subjugation is crucial, but Das argues women's subject positions are not fully determined by acts of violence. Through complex public transactions Punjabi women are able "both to *voice* and to *show* the hurt done to them" and, further, to provide witness to the harm done to the whole social fabric (2000: 205). Making extensive use of one contextualized case study, Das is able to critique what she understands as rather crude models of power/resistance and reveals the "delicate" work of self-recreation with its manifold social and political ramifications (2000: 222).

The subjectivity discussed in these essays is not that associated with Euro-American modernity, leading inevitably to an implicit critique of modernization theory itself. The Maniat women live in Greece, but nevertheless they constitute a European periphery, where their daily life was one relatively untouched by the trappings of modernity at the time Seremetakis was writing. In the case of the Punjabi women it is the effects of hostilities associated with ethnic difference, a situation exacerbated by a postcolonial, modernizing environment, that is discussed by Das. Research of this kind, although it often owes a debt to Foucault, at the same time exposes the limitations of his thesis. Above all, it is clear that we must recognize that a genealogy of subjectification is top-heavy and limited in scope if it fails to take into account a plurality of possible subjectivities and their relationship to society at large and even to globalization.

In writing about violence in Northern Ireland, Feldman argues "the very act of violence invests the body with agency" and inevitably "struggles will occur over competing transcriptions" of same and different bodies. The body as an "organic," "natural" object is thus fractured, resulting in different forms of subjectification (1991: 7).

I want to add another dimension to anthropological contributions of the kind just cited by considering the effects certain biomedical technologies have on both subjectification and subjectivity. Using three specific examples – organ transplants, the artificial ventilator, and immortalized cell lines – I argue these technologies permit the creation of entirely new forms of self-knowing. Moreover, because fragmentation of bodies takes place, followed, with technological assistance, by their reconstitution as new forms of life, the body and body parts must be understood as both self and other and, further, as commodities, or as potential commodities. Technologically fashioned bodies have profound implications, not only for subjectification and subjectivity, but also for society at large; one of the most obvious being the emergence of competing arguments about what actually constitutes a subjectivity that is in part or wholly technologically constituted.

EMBODYING A NEW SUBJECTIVITY

Before the removal of organs from donors and their preparation as living substitutes can come about, the necessary technology must be accessible. Furthermore, human organs have to be understood as fungible, and donors must be designated as dead before dissection takes place. A tacit agreement must also exist that the body will not be violated through organ removal, and to this end conceptualization of organs as objects is enabling. However, organs for transplant are, by definition, alive; although objectified, they cannot be reduced to mere things, even in the minds of involved physicians, and retain, therefore, a hybrid status.

Mixed metaphors associated with human organs encourage confusion about their worth. On the one hand the language of medicine insists human body parts are material entities, devoid entirely of identity, whether located in donors or recipients. On the other hand, in order to promote donation, organs are animated with a life force that can be gifted, and donor families are not discouraged from interpreting their agreement to these acts as permitting their relatives to "live on" in the bodies of recipients. Organ donation is very often understood as creating meaning out of a senseless, accidental, horrifying death – a technological path to transcendence, although the enforced anonymity of the donor family ensures that no earthly ties of solidarity between donors and recipients can be formed except on rare occasions.

Despite this enforced cloak of anonymity – this subjectification – it has been shown on many occasions that large numbers of recipients experience a frustrated sense of obligation about the need to repay the family of the donor for the extraordinary act of benevolence that has brought them back from the brink of death (Fox and Swazey 1978, 1992; Simmons et al. 1987; Sharp 1995). The "tyranny of the gift" has been well documented in the transplant world (Fox 1978: 1168), but it is not merely a desire to try to settle accounts that is at work when people desire to know more about the donor. It is abundantly clear that donated organs very often represent much more than mere biological body parts; the life with which they are animated is experienced by recipients as personified, an agency that manifests itself in some surprising ways and profoundly influences subjectivity.

A conversation I had a few years ago with a heart transplant surgeon was most revealing in this respect. This surgeon was responding to stories that have been circulating for some time now about a debate taking place in several of the American states as to whether prisoners on death row should have the option of donating their organs for transplant before they are put to death. The argument is that prisoners should be given the choice of making a "gift" to society just before their lives are extinguished. Perhaps those among the prisoners who are believers may even go straight to heaven.

This surgeon was uncomfortable about the idea of organ donations made by death row prisoners, not so much because he was concerned about the highly questionable ethics (can one make an "informed choice" in such circumstances?), but about receiving a heart that had been taken out of the body of a murderer. He said to me, with some embarrassment, "I wouldn't like to have a murderer's heart put into my body," then added hastily, glancing at my tape recorder and trying to make a joke out of the situation, "I might find myself starting to change."

A good number of organ recipients worry about the gender, ethnicity, skin color, personality, and the social status of their donors, and many believe that their mode of being-in-the-world is radically changed after a transplant, thanks to the power and vitality diffusing from the organ they have received. That certain of their surgeons also think this way suggests that fetishism is doubly at work, even in the materially oriented world of biomedicine. Both the fetishism of objectification postulated by Marx and the fetishism noted by Marcel Mauss, in which gifts (including, we assume, human body parts) remain infused with a personal essence even on entering systems of exchange, can be detected. Contradictions are rife. Once transplanted into a recipient, if she attributes this "life-saving" organ with animistic qualities, she is severely reprimanded, even thought of as exhibiting pathology (Sharp 1995). Human organs are "promiscuous," as Nicholas Thomas suggests with respect to commodified objects in general: both things-in-themselves, and at the same time diffused with a life force and an agency that is manifestly social.

Interviews that I carried out in 1996 with 30 transplant recipients living in Montréal reveal that just under half are very matter-of-fact about the organs they have received (Lock 2002). These people insist that after an interim period of a few months they ceased to be concerned about the source of the new organ encased in their bodies and resumed their lives as best they could, unchanged in any profound way despite a massive daily medication regime. The responses of the remaining recipients were different: they produced emotionally charged accounts about their donors (whom in reality they knew very little about), the particular organ they had received, and often about their transformed subjectivity.

Forty-one-year-old Stefan Rivet falls into the first group. He is a kidney recipient, doing well when interviewed five years after the transplant. He says:

> "I heard about the donor, even though I wasn't supposed to. It was a woman between 20 and 25. She was in a car accident. You know, don't you, that you can't meet the family because the doctors think it would be too emotional? But I wrote a letter to them, it must have been a terrible time for them, and I wanted to thank them."
>
> "Did you find it hard to write that letter?" I asked.
>
> "No, no, it wasn't hard for me. Like saying 'thank you' to someone if they do something for you, that's just the way it was."
>
> "Did you feel at all strange because it was a woman's kidney?"
>
> "No. At first you wonder how could a female kidney work in a man. You think about it. But once the doctor tells you that it works exactly the same in men and women you don't question things any more. It doesn't bug me. I have my kidney, and I can live, that's all you really worry about.
>
> "When I first woke up in hospital I was worried. Of course, I didn't know whose kidney it was then, all you know is that there's a strange organ in there and you hope that it works; you don't want anything to go wrong. After a while though, you adapt and you stop thinking about it, except that it's really important to take the pills. I just say now that it's my second life."

In contrast to recipients such as Stefan Rivet, many others undergo a rather dramatic transformative experience (see also Sharp 1995). One such was Katherine White, who first received a kidney transplant in 1982, and then, in 1994 after that kidney failed and her own liver was also in jeopardy, she received a double transplant of liver and kidney. Six months after the second surgery she had this to say:

> I have no idea who the donor was, all I know is that both the kidney and liver came from one person because you can't survive if they put organs from two different people into you at once – your body would never be able to deal with it. I wrote a thank-you note right away that I gave to the nurse. But they don't like you to know who it is; sometimes people feel that their child has been reborn in you and they want to make close contact. That could lead to problems. I still think of it as a different person inside me – yes I do, still. It's not all of me, and it's not all this person either. Actually, I might like some contact with the donor family . . .
>
> You know, I never liked cheese and stuff like that, and some people think I'm joking, but all of a sudden I couldn't stop eating Kraft slices – that was after the first kidney. This time around, the first thing I did was to eat chocolate. I have a craving for chocolate and now I eat some every day. It's driving me crazy because I'm not a chocolate fanatic. So maybe this person who gave me the liver was a chocoholic! It's funny like that, and some of the doctors say it's the drugs that do things to you. I'm certainly moody these days. You do change whether you like it or not. I can't say that I'm the same person I was, but in a way I think that I'm a better person.
>
> You know, sometimes I feel as if I'm pregnant, as if I'm giving birth to somebody. I don't know what it is really, but there's another life inside of me, and I'm actually storing this life, and it makes me feel fantastic. It's weird, I constantly think of that other person, the donor . . . but I know a lot of people who receive organs don't think about the donors at all.
>
> A while ago I saw a TV program about Russia and it seemed as though they were actually killing children in orphanages to take out their eyes and other organs. This disturbed me no end. I hope to God it's not really like that. My parents and my uncles all thought I shouldn't have a transplant, they said you can't be sure that the patient is really dead. Brain dead is not death, they said. But I know that's not right. I had a friend a few years back who had a bad fall off a bicycle and her husband donated her organs. Once you're brain dead that's it.

"What do you think happens when people die?" I asked.

> I hope I go to heaven! I don't believe in resurrection but I do believe in a heaven and hell and an in-between, you know? I think there's a person up there who knows that I'm carrying a part of her around with me. I always think there's somebody watching me . . . but you know, I don't really believe in religion . . . I really don't. In a way I wish I could have a pig's liver or kidney – it would be much simpler then.

Despite the power of the medical profession working against animation of donated organs by patients, and their flat rejection of the possibility of any transformation in subjectivity, it is clear from numerous interviews carried out independently by Leslie Sharp and myself that a large number of patients, at least in Canada and the United States, believe themselves to be "reborn" after a transplant. These patients often form affiliations with other transplant recipients, but this group identity is only the visible part of a more substantial transformation; many recipients undergo a second more intimate change, and experience embodiment in a radically different way after a transplant. Such experiences challenge the idea of subjectivity as constituted solely by mind; an entity essentially independent of the body. Further, as biomedical technologies become increasingly sophisticated it is evident that, with the literal fragmentation and reconstitution of bodies, concepts of self and other, even though they are in part constituted through bodies, are no longer bound or confined to bodies. We have entered an era of a confusion of subjectivities.

THE GLOBALIZATION OF SUBJECTIVITY

In Japan, only in 1997 was it agreed that the bodies of brain dead donors could be commodified for use in transplants, with the result that a very high proportion of patients receive what are known as "living related organ donations" in that country, that is, organs are usually procured from living relatives. One exception was Naka Yoshitomo, a retired school principal, 63 years of age when the kidney taken from a 70-year-old American brain dead donor was sewn into his body. The transplant took place between 60 and 70 hours after the kidney was first procured, having traveled half way across the world and then languished in a cooler while people disputed for and against its use. Exactly one year later, in 1996, when I interviewed him, Naka was experiencing mild rejection, but since that time, by all reports, he has done exceptionally well:

> "I've become ten years younger since I had the transplant. I was on dialysis for 13 years, every Tuesday, Thursday, and Saturday, afternoons and evenings."
> "How did you feel about having a kidney from such an old donor?"
> "My wife was opposed, partly because of the cost. But my son agreed as soon as he understood that I was keen. I felt really lucky to be right at the top of the list of waiting people just because I happened to be the best match. I didn't want to lose this chance – this seemed really to be a 'gift of love and health' [*ai to kenkô no okurimono*], finally, after all the waiting."

In the event, once the operation was completed, it took only five days before the kidney started its work. In the United States this kidney would have been thrown out as defective because of its extended existence outside a human body. One morning, shortly after the operation, Naka was completely taken aback when he noticed in the street below the sounds of one of the oppressively noisy military-like vehicles used by the extreme right wing in Japan to stir up nationalistic sentiment. As it crawled back and forth outside the hospital he gradually became aware of the message being screamed into the loudspeakers: "Bad doctors have taken part in a cover-up. Importation of defective kidneys." On and on they droned, strident and abusive. Lying in his hospital bed, shocked, Naka was plagued by serious doubts and began to believe that in his haste to get a transplant he had done something wrong. He had been told that the chances of success for the transplant were about 80 percent, but now he wondered whom he should believe.

Naka reported to me that he lives daily with thoughts about his donor: "Hopefully, I will understand how he felt one day. We must change our ideas in Japan [and be more generous about donation], and that is why I wrote the book." "Did you write a letter to the donor's family?" I asked.

Oh yes! I was happy to send that letter. I sent a copy of my book to UNOS as well. Now I'm working hard on cultural exchange between my hometown and our sister town in America. I go to America all the time arranging visits and events. I can't think of a better way to thank that family for what they did for me.

Naka and other Japanese in his situation have been targeted by a few of their bellicose countrymen as being unpatriotic. Both the recognition of brain death and carrying out organ transplants making use of brain dead donors, whether Japanese or foreign, have caused hostile reactions from the extreme right as "unnatural" acts in which Japan should not participate. After his first shock, Naka had no trouble in the end in ignoring the hostility directed primarily at his doctors, but also at himself. He believes that as a result of his travails and their resolution he is able now to transcend the boundaries of his former self and become a global citizen where transnational cooperation is the order of the day.

BRAIN DEATH AND SUBJECTIVITY

Most human organs for transplant are procured from brain dead donors. This new death located in the brain was legally recognized in North America two decades ago. In Japan, brain death was officially recognized only three years ago, and then under very specific circumscribed conditions. Brain dead patients who do not wish to donate organs retain the rights associated with other patients, and are treated in Japan as though living. Those few people who wish to become donors, with family agreement, can be legally taken off the ventilator and the procurement then goes ahead. Although essentially the same technologies, basic scientific knowledge, and clinical expertise are present in North America and Japan, transition from an embodied living patient to a living cadaver from which organs can be procured is remarkably different in these two locations. In one location the living cadaver is unequivocally recognized as dead, whereas in the other it is alive but can be counted as dead if the family so wishes.

There is unanimous agreement among physicians working in intensive care units in both Japan and North America that the clinical criteria for whole brain death are infallible *if* the tests are performed correctly. It is also agreed that whole brain death, properly diagnosed, is an irreversible state, from which no one has ever recovered. At the same time a unanimous sentiment exists that the organs and cells of the body remain alive, thanks to the artificial brain stem supplied by the ventilator. Indeed, if organs are to be transplanted, then they *must* be kept alive and functioning as close to "normal" as is possible. Intensivists (medical specialists who work in intensive care units) are aware that infants have been delivered from brain dead bodies. It is not possible to disregard the fact that the brain dead are warm and usually retain a good color, that digestion, metabolism, and excretion continue, and some intensivists know that the hair and nails continue to grow. Further, clusters of cells in the brain often remain active after brain death has been declared, and endocrine and other types of physiological activity continue for some time.

For by far the majority of North American intensivists, although biological death has clearly not occurred, a diagnosis of brain death indicates that the patient has entered into a *second* irreversible state, in that the "person" and/or "spirit" is no longer present in the body.

The body has assumed a hybrid status – that of a dead-person-in-a-living-body, about which confusion is evident. However, rather than dwell on ambiguities or engage in extended discussion over conceptual ideas about death, most clinical practitioners are, not surprisingly, interested first and foremost in accuracy and certainty. In order to convey their certainty that an irreversible biological condition has set in, in addition to explaining about tests and examinations to families, they emphasize that the "person" is no longer present, even though the appearance of the entity lying in front of them gives little visual support to this argument.

When interviewed, intensivists stated that they say things to families at the bedside such as: "the things that make her *her* are not there any more," or, "he's not going to recover. Death is inevitable." One doctor, who in common with many of his colleagues, chooses not to say simply that the patient is dead, because for him personally this is not the case, tells the family firmly that the patient is "brain dead" but that there is "absolutely no doubt but that things will get worse." Another physician pointed out that it is difficult to assess what is best to say to the family, because in most cases one does not know if they have religious beliefs or not:

> I believe that a "humanistic" death happens at the same time as brain death. If I didn't believe this, then I couldn't take care of these patients and permit them to become organ donors. For me, the child has gone to heaven or wherever, and I'm dealing with an organism, respectfully, of course, but that child's soul, or whatever you want to call it, is no longer there. I don't know, of course, whether the family believes in souls or not, although sometimes I can make a good guess. So I simply have to say that "Johnny" is no longer here.

One of the intensivists thinks of the brain dead body as a vessel, and tells the family that what is left of their relative is only an empty container, because the "person has gone." For a doctor born in Latin America, the "essence" of the patient has gone, and this is what he tells the family. All the intensivists except one agreed that the departure of the person is evident *because* of the diagnosis of an irreversible loss of brain function, thus establishing a permanent lack of consciousness, no awareness, and no sensation of pain. In other words, a sensate, suffering individual has ceased to exist because their mind no longer functions. When mind is finished, so too is subjectivity.

It is essential that the doctor takes control "a bit," argued one interviewee when discussing brain death. Families, she insisted, often find it difficult to accept that there is no chance of a reversal, and this is where the doctor cannot afford to appear diffident or equivocating. One doctor stated: "You can't go back to the family and say that their relative is brain dead, you've *got* to say that they are dead – you could be arrested for messing up on this." He recalled that during his training he had described a patient as "basically dead" to his supervisor, who had responded abruptly by insisting: "He's dead. That's what you mean, basically." The task for intensivists then is to convince the family that, even though their relative appears to be sleeping, they are in fact no longer *essentially* alive; what remains is an organism or vessel that has suffered a mortal blow.

It is clear that intensivists have few second thoughts about reversibility, but it is also evident that many of them nevertheless harbor some doubts about the condition of a recently declared brain dead patient, and it is often those with the longest experience who exhibit the most misgivings. An intensivist with over 15 years of experience said that he often lies in bed at night after sending a brain dead body for organ procurement and asks himself, "Was that patient *really* dead? It is irreversible – I know that, and the clinical tests are infallible. My rational mind is sure, but some nagging, irrational doubt seeps in." This doctor and the majority of other intensivists interviewed take some consolation from their belief that to remain in a severely vegetative state is much worse than to be dead. *If* a mistake has been made, and a patient is diagnosed prematurely, or treated as though brain dead when this is not the case, then it is assumed that either the patient would have become brain dead shortly thereafter, or permanent unconsciousness would have been their lot. But doubts continue to fester away at some people.

One intensivist who came to North America from India as an immigrant when a child stated that for him a brain dead body is "an in-between thing. It's neither a cadaver, nor a person, but then again, there is still somebody's precious child in front of me. The child is legally brain dead, has no awareness or connection with the world around him, but he's still a child, deserving of respect. I've done my tests, but there's still a child there." When asked by families, as he often is, if the patient has any consciousness or feels pain, this intensivist has no difficulty in reassuring them that their child is dead, and is no longer suffering. He noted that it is especially hard for relatives when they take the hand of their child and sometimes the hand seems to respond and grasp back. This reflex response was noted by several of the intensivists and nurses as very disconcerting, especially when one is trying to convince families that the patient is no longer alive.

One doctor professed to a belief in a spirit or soul that takes leave of the body at death. For her, if brain damage is involved, this happens when the patient's brain is irreversibly damaged, at the moment of trauma or shortly thereafter. Another intensivist insisted at first, as did many of the individuals interviewed, that he had no difficulty with the idea of brain death: "It seems pretty straightforward to me. Do the tests, allow a certain amount of time; a flat EEG and you're dead." Then, ten minutes later he said: "I guess I equate the death of a person with the death of the spirit because I don't really know about anything else, like a hereafter. I'm not sure anyway, if a hereafter makes a difference or not." When asked what he meant by the word "spirit," this intensivist replied:

I guess one would have to take it as meaning that part of a person which is different, sort of not in the physical realm . . . outside the physical realm. It's not just the brain, or the mind, but something more than that. I don't really know. But anyway, a brain dead patient, someone's loved one, won't ever be the person they used to know. Sure their nails can grow and their hair can grow, but that's not the essence.

A senior doctor, struggling to express his feelings, imbued the physical body with a will: "The body *wants* to die, you can sense that when it becomes difficult to keep the blood pressure stable and so on." This intensivist, although he accepts that brain death is the end of meaningful life, revealed considerable irresolution in going on to talk about the procurement of organs: "We don't want this patient to expire before we can harvest the organs, so it's important to keep them stable and alive, and that's why we keep up the same treatment after brain death." Yet another interviewee acknowledged that "real" death happens when the heart stops: "The patient dies two deaths." For these physicians, an organ donor is by definition biologically alive, or at least "partially" biologically alive, when sent to the operating room for organ retrieval, because there can be no argument about the liveliness of the principal body organs, aside from the brain. But the patient has no subjectivity.

Perhaps most revealing of some confusion and occasional doubts in connection with the status of a brain dead individual is that, among the 32 doctors interviewed, only 6 had signed their donor cards or left other forms of advanced directives, and one other wasn't sure whether he had done so or not. When I pressed for reasons as to why people appeared hesitant, I was not given any very convincing reasons. Doctors said that their family would know what to do, or that they just didn't feel quite right about donation or, alternatively, that they supposed they should get it sorted out.

Despite the routinization of organ procurement from brain dead bodies, rendering these entities as cadaver-like and as non-persons, even though it is agreed that they are entirely lacking in subjectivity, has never been beyond dispute. Use of the concept of brain death is currently being subjected to a new round of debate, and several influential dissenters have emerged in North America who insist that a massive public lie has in effect been perpetrated by making brain death equivalent to the end of human life (Lock 2002).

In Japan, where the debate about brain death has continued non-stop for 30 years, a total of only 10 organ procurements have been made from brain dead bodies. It has proved very difficult to overcome the profound hesitation that many Japanese feel, including many doctors, about cutting up entities that they believe are not-quite-dead. It is also clear from interviews with medical professionals and among the Japanese public that subjectivity is by no means always located in mind. Even though not everyone adheres to the idea, commonly, a life force that circulates throughout the body is understood as partly or even wholly constituting subjectivity.

Even more important, a semiotic self and subjectivity is widely entertained, in which it is recognized that only through meditation-like activities or engaged social interactions can one's inner feelings be brought to awareness (Kondo 1990; Lock 1993; Plath 1980; Rohlen 1978). Widely publicized doubtful activities on the part of some Japanese physicians in connection with organ procurement, oppositional rhetoric laced with nationalistic sentiment, together with stone-walling on the part of the legal profession, have all worked against the public recognition of brain death in Japan. Even so, it is doubtful if this weighty opposition could have been so effective as to completely ignore the plight of patients dying for want of organs had not culturally constructed pervasive arguments about subjectivity also been brought into play.

Embodiment and disembodiment, the presence or absence of subjectivity and its constitution, have their own histories. Body boundaries are fluid and self–other, mind–body dichotomies do not stand up to scrutiny. Without the invention of the artificial ventilator early in the twentieth century, or its technological equivalent, brain dead bodies could not exist; medical technologies such as the ventilator make boundary marking between life and death highly problematic, and closely related concepts, often assumed to be natural facts, are destabilized.

Mind, body, subjectification, and subjectivity all have genealogies that vary considerably, not only in time but also through space. For more than a century, and increasingly in the global era, these genealogies themselves have leaky boundaries, leading to disputes about the parts played by nature and culture in the formation of mind, body, and subjectivity. But a nature–culture dichotomy holds fast in "the West" even in the face of entities such as brain dead bodies that radically challenge it. We have to invoke spirits and souls, or else psychologized selves, to patch up the cracks that are opened up between ICU practices and permanently comatose patients and the discourse about them. Despite well over a century of exposure to the psychologized self of the West, in Japan, it is the naturalized social body that takes priority, creating different types of internal disputes about bodies and subjectivity.

IMMORTALIZED CELL LINES AND SUBJECTIVITY

Many thousands of human cell lines are maintained in hundreds of laboratories around the world today. Their source is from patients, healthy research subjects, and cadavers. Every one of us is a potential source of these "biologicals" (a term coined in the early 1980s; Landecker 1999: 204) and practices that create cells lines "make it increasingly difficult to say where the body is bounded in time, space, or form" (Landecker 1999: 221). The most famous of these cell lines is known as HeLa, named after the African American Henrietta Lacks, from whom the virulent cancer cells were obtained. These cells have been cloned and stored in laboratories around the world so that, in the words of Anne Enright, "there is more of her [Henrietta Lacks] now, in terms of biomass, than there ever was when she was alive" (2000: 8).

Some cell lines are patented and others are not, with remarkably different consequences (Landecker 1999). Those that are patented make it particularly difficult to separate out their use value in terms of the goals of scientific inquiry, progress, and profit, from their status as "gifts" made by donors without whom no cell lines would exist. In order to procure patents on biologicals it must be shown that through the "process of their production" the "natural" object has been transformed into an "invention" (Cambrosio and Keating 1995). Even though a human/non-human hybrid, a discontinuity between the human source and the biological invention must be established; in other words, reification of the cells as solely a technological creation is integral to patent claims.

Attempts to set the Human Genome Diversity Project in motion, a project designed primarily to map the migration of human populations through time, that will rely heavily on the production of immortalized cell lines, have run into numerous, as yet unsolved political problems. Anthropologists and others involved in designing the HGDP insist that they will not patent the cell lines that result from this project. However, given the way that access to cell lines is set up at present, third parties may procure such lines from their storage sites for a small fee and take out patents on products created out of them.

The present impasse can be understood in large part as a dispute over concepts of subjectivity and self. In effect, the HGDP conceptualizes "exotic" bodies as a scarce resource, the essence of which can be extracted in the form of DNA to create immortalized cell lines that will transcend time and space, and join the never ending circulation of commodities integral to late modernity. Concerns of individuals from whom the cells are slated to be taken are primarily about a perceived continued indifference on the part of the capitalist world order to their condition.

The political activist Aroha Te Pareake Mead, Foreign Policy Convenor and Deputy Convenor of the Maori Congress in Aotearoa, has responded to this indifference with insightful barbs. She says all human genetic research must be viewed in the context of colonial imperialistic history. "Human genes are being treated by science in the same way that indigenous 'artifacts' were gathered by museums; collected, stored, immortalized, reproduced, engineered – all for the sake of humanity and public education, or so we were asked to believe" (1996: 46). Mead insists that a gene and combinations of genes are not the sole property of individuals: "They are part of the heritage of families, communities, clans, tribes, and entire indigenous nations" (1996: 48). She adds that the survival of marginalized cultures will not come about through gene banks, but through an observance of fundamental human rights. As far as Mead is concerned, patenting is not a tool of humanitarian research. Mead claims, moreover, that talk of ethics is simply deception; "informed" consent among peoples such as the largely non-literate Hagahai of New Guinea was probably obtained originally through sign language, she argues. She insists that the burden of proof should be on HGDP planners and other researchers to demonstrate how their project will benefit communities. Mead notes that the HGDP assumes that knowledge is "by nature" empowering to all, but her blunt response is that this is not so. She adds that the issue for her is not one of "anti-science," but rather that "most indigenous peoples of her acquaintance" do not consider the HGDP to be "good" or "sustainable" science, nor do they wish to know what it might purportedly tell them about their origins. It is questionable, of course, whom exactly Mead represents when making these assertions. Cavalier claims on behalf of "indigenous" peoples are increasingly common, and paternalism is not limited to descendents of former colonists.

In commenting on some of the difficulties posed by the HGDP, Haraway notes that the majority of targeted peoples clearly do not consider themselves as a "biodiversity resource." The problem is one of "what may count as modern knowledge and who will count as producers of that knowledge" (1997: 249). Commodification of body tissues is contested, and the potential for the accumulation of scientific knowledge from the creation of immortalized cell lines, together with the enormous profit incentive associated with it, is weighed against inalienable possessions and subjectivities. Body cells and tissues represent history, genealogy, and even the survival or demise of entire groups of people. But disentangling who speaks for whom, who represents what interests, and what value blood samples have to the involved parties is like walking in a hall of distorting mirrors.

How can regulation of the procurement of genetic material be monitored and enforced, and at whose expense, particularly when so much research is initiated by the private sector? Who "owns" genetic material? Individuals? Communities or tribal groups? Corporate organizations? Or humankind? Representatives of indigenous groups for the most part exhibit a preference for group ownership (Shelton n.d.), whereas United States property law upholds individual ownership provided that body parts are not separated from the body in question. Other people argue DNA cannot belong to anyone, or alternatively, that it belongs to us all, and yet others claim that ownership through patenting of body tissues and cells is essential if scientific research is to remain competitive (see, for example, Eisenberg 1992). Contracts drawn up in connection with genetic research focus on entitlement, patenting, access, distribution, and uses to which genetic material may be put. In hammering out the terms of agreement of such contracts, radically different ontological perspectives about the human body, the location of subjectivity, and the uses to which body parts may be put can readily be discerned.

Above all, it is questions of stigmatization, discrimination, and eugenics associated with investigations into genetic diversity that are the greatest source of anxiety, and clearly some of those spearheading the opposition also experience a threat to their individual integrity. This political skirmish about the HGDP has made the idea of genes as armament for a self-conscious politicized discourse visible. At the same time, genes have become "real" entities for peoples everywhere that are made use of to constitute new forms of subjectivity. The boundaries of self, subjectivity, and ethnicity are hardening into new, exclusionary biosocialities (Rabinow 1996) – biologized subjectivities – even as new biomedical technologies enable us to dissolve such boundaries and reconstitute them in remarkable ways.

REFERENCES

Anagnost, Ann, 1997 *National Past-Times: Narrative, Representation, and Power in Modern China*. Durham, NC: Duke University Press.

Cambrosio, Alberto, and Peter Keating, 1995 *Exquisite Specificity: The Monoclonal Antibody Revolution*. Oxford: Oxford University Press.

Chodorow, Nancy J., 1999 *The Power of Feelings: Personal Meaning in Psychoanalysis, Gender, and Culture*. New Haven, CT: Yale University Press.

Das, Veena, 1997 Language and Body: Transactions in the Construction of Pain. In *Social Suffering*. Arthur Kleinman, Veena Das, and Margaret Lock, eds. Berkeley: University of California Press.

— 2000 The Act of Witnessing Violence: Poisonous Knowledge and Subjectivity. In *Violence and Subjectivity*. Veena Das, Arthur Kleinman, Mamphela Ramphele, and Pamela Reynolds, eds. Pp. 205–225. Berkeley: University of California Press.

Eisenberg, R., 1992 Genes, Patents, and Product Development. *Science* 257: 903.

Enright, Anne, 2000 What's Left of Henrietta Lacks? *London Review of Books*, April 13: 8–10.

Farquhar, Judith, 1994 *Knowing Practice: The Clinical Encounter of Chinese Medicine*. Oxford: Westview Press.

Feldman, Allen, 1991 *Formations of Violence: The Narrative of the Body and Political Terror in Northern Ireland*. Chicago: University of Chicago Press.

Foucault, Michel, 1979 *Discipline and Punish: The Birth of the Prison*. London: Perigrin Books.

— 1981 *The History of Sexuality*. Trans. Robert Hurley. New York: Pantheon Books.

— 1991 Governmentality. In *The Foucault Effect: Studies in Governmentality*. G. Burchell, C. Gordon, and P. Miller, eds. Pp. 87–104. Hemel Hempstead: Harvester Wheatsheaf.

Fox, Renee, 1978 Organ Transplantation: Sociocultural Aspects. In *Encyclopedia of Bioethics*, Vol. 3. W. T. Reich, ed. Pp. 1166–1169. New York: Free Press.

Fox, Renee, and Judith P. Swazey, 1978 *The Courage to Fail: A Social View of Organ Transplants and Dialysis*. Chicago: University of Chicago Press.

— 1992 *Spare Parts: Organ Replacement in American Society*. Oxford: Oxford University Press.

Geertz, Clifford, 1973 *Person, Time, and Conduct in Bali: The Interpretation of Culture.* New York: Basic Books.

Haraway, Donna, 1997 *Modest_Witness@Second_Millenium: FemaleMan_Meets_Oncomouse.* New York: Routledge.

Kleinman, Arthur, 2000 The Violence of Everyday Life: The Multiple Forms and Dynamics of Social Violence. In *Violence and Subjectivity.* Veena Das, Arthur Kleinman, Mamphela Ramphele, and Pamela Reynolds, eds. Pp. 226–241. Berkeley: University of California Press.

Kondo, Dorinne, 1990 *Crafting Selves: Power, Gender, and Discourses of Identity in a Japanese Workplace.* Chicago: University of Chicago Press.

Landecker, Hannah, 1999 Between Beneficence and Chattel: The Human Biological in Law and Science. *Science in Context* 12 (1): 203–225.

Lock, Margaret, 1993 *Encounters with Aging: Mythologies of Menopause in Japan and North America.* Berkeley: University of California Press.

— 2002 *Twice Dead: The Circulation of Body Parts and Remembrance of Persons.* Berkeley: University of California Press.

Lutz, Catherine A., 1988 *Unnatural Emotions: Everyday Sentiments on a Micronesian Atoll and Their Challenge to Western Theory.* Chicago: University of Chicago Press.

Mead, Aroha Te Pareake, 1996 Genealogy, Sacredness, and the Commodities Market. *Cultural Survival Quarterly* (summer): 46–51.

Obeyesekere, Gananath, 1981 *Medusa's Hair: An Essay on Personal Symbols and Religious Experience.* Chicago: University of Chicago Press.

Plath, David, 1980 *Long Engagements.* Stanford, CA: Stanford University Press.

Rabinow, Paul, 1996 *Essays on the Anthropology of Reason.* Princeton, NJ: Princeton University Press.

Rohlen, Thomas, 1978 The Promise of Adulthood in Japanese Spiritualism. In *Adulthood.* Erik Erikson, ed. Pp. 125–143. New York: Norton.

Rose, Nicolas, 1996 Identity, Genealogy, History. In *Questions of Cultural Identity.* Stuart Hall and Paul du Gay, eds. Pp. 128–150. London: Sage.

Seremetakis, C. Nadia, 1991 *The Last Word: Women, Death, and Divination in Inner Mani.* Chicago: University of Chicago Press.

— 1994 *The Senses Still: Perception and Memory as Material Culture in Modernity.* Chicago: University of Chicago Press.

Sharp, Lesley A., 1995 Organ Transplantation as a Transformative Experience: Anthropological Insights into the Restructuring of the Self. *Medical Anthropology Quarterly* 9 (3): 357–389.

Shelton, Brett Lee, n.d. Genetic Research and Native Peoples. Unpublished MS.

Simmons, Roberta G., with Susan K. Marine and Richard L. Simmons, 1987 *Gift of Life: The Effect of Organ Transplantation on Individual, Family, and Societal Dynamics.* New Brunswick, NJ: Transaction Books.

CHAPTER 17

Globalization, Childhood, and Psychological Anthropology

*Thomas S. Weisner and
Edward D. Lowe*

The anthropology of childhood and adolescence documents and accounts for the marvelous variety of childhoods found around the world. The psychocultural anthropology of childhood asks how children and adolescents around the world acquire, transform, share, integrate, and transmit cultural knowledge. This scientific project is central to the study of globalization and its impacts on children, adolescents, and youth. Globalization processes impact all parts of the world through immigration, market economics, and politics, and it changes the roles of children and youth as well. Hence, globalization *demands* a pluralistic, cross-cultural view of childhood and adolescence. Psychological anthropology and the cross-cultural study of childhood have *always* had such a view. Since the psychological anthropology of human development specializes in the intensive study of the developing person and family life in local contexts and populations, psychological anthropology is uniquely able to understand those varying local forms of, and responses to, globalization. The field is especially suited to provide empirical, evidence-based research and policy recommendations regarding children, families, and globalization in the twenty-first century.

Strong as psychological anthropology is, it is fair to say that there is not a consensus theory of how local and global cultural communities socialize children and adolescents. Rather, there are many competing ways of conceptualizing and measuring cultural contexts and how they influence young people, and there are different views concerning which features of the human mind matter most for the acquisition, internalization, transformation, and enactment of cultural practices, especially under conditions of global change. Although there may not be one common theory of culture or mind, the great advantage of the field is that it always focuses on concrete, measurable features of cultural context (specific beliefs, material and social resources, kinds of interactional styles, sociolinguistic and communication styles, child age differences) and tries to measure these. The other great advantage is that the field *does* take seriously the mechanisms of the mind, and how these develop in childhood and adolescence (learning styles, memory processes, scripts and schematized knowledge, self and identity theory, psychodynamic mechanisms, sensitive periods in development, evolved capacities at different ages, etc.). These are great advantages for the study of globalization and childhood. No matter how differently globalization shapes the lives of young people, *some* version of these theories of context and mind are going to help to understand globalization and its impacts. The psychological anthropology of childhood does not (and should not) simply revert to generic and ungrounded notions of "discourses" to account for variations in childhoods. Nor does (or should) the field concentrate on exclusively moral evaluations focused only on negative impacts of globalization, since the evidence shows all kinds of impacts, some clearly positive or negative, and some very mixed.

An ecological–cultural (ecocultural) perspective on human development, though certainly not a consensus theory in the field, is one that has widespread support (LeVine et al. 1994; Super and Harkness 1997; Whiting and Edwards 1988; Weisner 1997). Ecocultural theories recognize evolved capacities and individual differences among children (Small 1998), focusing on the local sociocultural contexts and cultural ecology of particular communities. The features of cultural ecology that seem to be particularly important for children's development around the world include: the subsistence and work cycles of the family and community; health and demographic characteristics; threats to safety; the nature of the division of labor by age and sex; children's tasks and work, including domestic, childcare, and school work; roles of fathers and older siblings; children's play and play groups; roles of women and girls in the community and supports for them; the varied sources of cultural influence and information available; and the extent of community heterogeneity in models of care and child activities (Weisner 1984). Many of these features are precisely the ones impacted by globalization (e.g., the explosion in varied sources of information; greater community heterogeneity and overlapping communities; new work; demographic and mortality changes; changing status of women and girls).

Every cultural community provides developmental *pathways* for children within a local ecocultural context. Cultural pathways are made up of everyday routines of life, and routines are made up of cultural activities (bedtime; playing video games; homework; watching TV; cooking dinner; soccer practice; visiting grandma; babysitting for money). Activities are useful units for cultural analysis because they are obvious, meaningful units for parents and children to understand, and they are amenable to ethnographic fieldwork and systematic observation and interviewing methods. Activities are a recognized unit that often can be compared across cultures, they are an event or context that children and parents experience, and they crystallize many of the important aspects of culture. Activities are made up of values and *goals*; *resources* needed to make the activity happen; *people* in relationships; the *tasks* the activity is there to accomplish; *emotions* and feelings of those engaged in the activity; and a *script* defining the appropriate, normative way we expect to do that activity. Imagine cultural pathways as made up of cultural activities we "step" into – engage in – react to, and walk alongside throughout life. A key question then becomes how are children's pathways and activities, and their experiences in those pathways, changing due to global processes (Weisner 2002)?

Ecocultural theory assumes our behavior is organized by a local, ecologically and culturally situated rationality (D'Andrade 1986; Shore 1996; Shweder 1991; Strauss and Quinn 1997). The "local situation" consists of the everyday routines and activities of a cultural community. Parents and children use connected, schematized, shared knowledge of the cultural community to adapt and make complex decisions. This is why there is a focus on *locally* rational decisions, in context. Culture is the pre-eminent tool that children learn to use for adaptation to life. The scripts, plans, and intentions of the parents and children in any cultural community are important in understanding the patterns of behavior and actions that result. These scripts are learned through everyday sociolinguistic communication and apprenticeship (Schieffelin and Ochs 1987; Rogoff 1990). Rational choice and cost-benefit theories in economics and other fields are models of the mind used to account for the effects of globalization in those fields. The models of the mind and of the human inferences leading to action in psychological anthropology and human development are much more complex and multi-determined. Human behavior is shaped, in this view, by many cognitive processes, including psychodynamic, social inference, meaning-centered, and a variety of memory processes, and the events and scripts stored in mind and available for directing action (Garro 2001; Mattingly and Garro 2000; Nisbett and Ross 1980; Schacter 1999).

GLOBALIZATION, ECONOMIC DEVELOPMENT, AND CHILDREN'S DEVELOPMENT

Globalization includes the rapid spread of materials and products, ideas, images, capital flows, and people across spaces and borders (national or otherwise) that formerly were far more difficult if not impossible to connect. Fundamentally, globalization

> is the closer integration of the countries and peoples of the world which has been brought about by the enormous reduction of costs of transportation and communication, and the breaking down of artificial barriers to the flows of goods, services, capital, knowledge, and (to a lesser extent) people across borders. (Stiglitz 2002: 9)

Stiglitz suggests the world is more "integrated" because of this process. However, the economic impact of globalization not only concentrates wealth, it also often (though certainly not always) puts that wealth in the hands of a particular ethnic community. Chua points out what often results:

> Contrary to what its proponents assume, free markets outside the West do not spread wealth evenly and enrich entire developing societies. Instead, they tend to concentrate glaring wealth in the hands of an "outsider" minority, generating ethnic envy and hatred among frustrated, impoverished majorities.
>
> ... In countries with a market-dominant minority, democratization, rather than reinforcing the market's efficiency and wealth-producing effects, leads to powerful ethnonationalist, anti-market pressures and routinely results in confiscation, instability, authoritarian backlash, and violence.

...the United States should not be exporting markets in the unrestrained, laissez-faire form that the West itself has repudiated, just as it should not be promoting unrestrained, overnight majority rule – a form of democracy that the West has repudiated. (Chua 2004: 16–17)

Hence globalization can lead to the disintegration of local communities, and the fragmentation of social ties that connect economic classes and ethnic communities, families, religions, and so forth.

At the same time, within-group boundaries are often expanded, and made more permeable through processes of globalization. Improved global communication and transportation have strengthened transnational communities and enhanced connections between receiving and sending countries and diasporic groups around the world (Sutton and Chaney 1987). Non-economic causes of migration (migration shaped by the values, beliefs, and feelings which hold social structures, families, and regions together) are clearly more relevant because of the ease of communication and connections (Jobes et al. 1992).

Often, children play an important role in the production and maintenance of the diaspora and its connection to the home community. For example, the term "parachute children" describes adolescents and youth who are sent by affluent parents in non-Western countries to go to school in the West, and while there, make contacts for their families, who remain behind in the natal country. On the other hand, when entire families immigrate, children often act as linguistic and cultural translators for their parents and work for their families in other significant ways in the new country (Suarez-Orozco 2001; Weisner 2001b).

Globalization is not the same thing as economic development, although those with a view of markets as free-floating, non-social forces might falsely confound the two. First of all, economic systems and markets are social systems. Economic systems are comprised of people living out *cultural* careers, as well as economic ones, who try to make economic life fit their goals, motives, capacities, and cultural models of the world (Weisner 2000). In the best case model, economic development, unlike globalization, is "about transforming societies, improving the lives of the poor, enabling everyone to have a chance at success and access to healthcare and education" (Stiglitz 2002: 252). The United Nations assessment of the state of the world's children, using the nation-state as the unit of analysis, and relying on general indicators of development, applies this concept to its definition of "human development":

Human development is . . . about creating an environment in which people can develop their full potential and lead productive, creative lives in accord with their needs and interests . . . It is thus about much more than economic growth, which is only a means . . . of enlarging people's choices. Fundamental to enlarging these choices is building human capabilities – the range of things people can do or be in life. The most basic capabilities for human development are to lead long and healthy lives, to be knowledgeable, to have access to the resources needed for a decent standard of living and to be able to participate in the life of the community. Without these, many choices are simply not available, and many opportunities in life remain inaccessible. (United Nations Development Program, 2001: 9)

While global processes actually have helped many families and children attain these economic and social goals, they have certainly not everywhere led to greater social integration or economic and personal security, at least not for families and children. Ted Lewellen's definition emphasizes this "push back" – the local and deeply *personal* transformation of global flows:

> Contemporary globalization is the increasing flow of trade, finance, culture, ideas, and people brought about by the sophisticated technology of communications and travel and by the worldwide spread of neoliberal capitalism, and it is the local and regional adaptations and resistances against these flows. (Lewellen 2002: 7–8)

> Because globalization expands the scale and reach of change, it has multiple pathways of impact (media, work, capital flows, immigration, artifacts), that lead to increased homogeneity or heterogeneity across and within nations and continents. Some argue that global messages and markets are created and controlled by elites. Some sense its omnipresence and totalization across all domains in life. Some attribute a growing market oriented view of children, and new definitions of childhood itself, to global processes. (Stephens 1995a)

The accompanying feeling is that globalization penetrates the very sense of personhood and self. The role of the Internet, cell phones, and media are central to such global penetration. Increased migration makes such global forces not only present in imagined, distant worlds, but also in real contacts from people children and parents *know* who have moved to such places. Globalization extends the ability to not only imagine and identify with people and places across former boundaries, but also to *engage* them in new, more direct, personal, and intimate ways. This is true even though the vast majority of the world's children are going to grow up and live fairly near their places of birth, in their current nations.

Globalization is more than an intensification of patterns of global commerce established through the emergence of Western capitalism and the industrial revolution centuries ago. It is a dramatic shift in the organization of global capitalism in place at the end of World War II (Harvey 1990). Before the 1960s, the world economy was based on mass production and consumption and strong centralized controls (economies of scale). Today, it is moving to an economy based on "flexible accumulation" (Harvey 1990: 147), where global production and the control of finances is decentralized and based more on "economies of scope." This shift has had profound implications for the organization of labor markets, both within and between nation-states, and led to fast-paced developments of technologies of information and communication. Global processes paradoxically encourage both corporate mergers as well as the rapid proliferation of small artisanal and family owned enterprises. The economies in the United States and the United Kingdom, among others, now are driven more by "financialization" and capital allocation. When we discuss the lives of children and adolescents in the era of globalization, it is this historical period with these kinds of broad changes that we have in mind.

Whatever the extent or uniqueness of global change (and reflecting on the changes, for good or ill, that have utterly transformed, or destroyed, communities throughout history, it is difficult to view globalization as uniquely more wrenching, or vastly better or worse, than many of those), the evidence is that national, local, and institutional patterns of life remain deeply important in the lives of children, adolescents, and their families. Psychological anthropology is in the position, both theoretically and methodologically, to understand such diversity. First, evidence from broad surveys of the state of the world's children and families suggests that local, cultural, and population-specific variations in the impacts of globalization are found everywhere. Psychocultural studies of childhood provide just this kind of intensive, local, holistic understanding of the lives of young people and their families. Second, psychological anthropologists focus on topics in development that both impact and are impacted by globalization: identity, self, trust and attachments, cognition and memory, acquisition and sharing of cultural knowledge (for example, parenting, childhood stages, child health), social behavior, personality, and character. Studies of globalization often overlook such topics altogether, or do not provide the depth of ethnographic evidence needed to study them.

Anthropology also has a point of view regarding what promotes a good childhood or adolescence and what defines a good parent. For anthropology, well-being is more than physical health, or the attainment of skills and competence or of successful subsequent reproduction, important as these outcomes are. It is surely important to systematically measure such outcomes in the study of the impacts of globalization on children, using standard indicators that are widely available (Hauser et al. 1997). But these kinds of assessments are not sufficient. Well-being within a local family and community context (and this remains the context in which children experience the world and acquire well-being) is the capacity of a child for engaged participation in the activities that a cultural community deems desirable, and the psychological experiences that go along with that participation. Hence, well-being includes the production of cultural well-being in children, adolescents, and youth. Understanding the impacts of globalization on the well-being of young people is an outcome that matters for children seen as whole persons. This is a central topic in the psychological anthropology of childhood.

GLOBALIZATION, PSYCHOCULTURAL WELL-BEING, AND THE DEVELOPING CHILD

It is useful to distinguish between the universal requirements for social supports and opportunities that all children and their families and caregivers need, and the locally variable ways in which communities live and how they want to raise their children. The basic, universal conditions all children and families need are important because without basic health, food, and physical security, and reasonable stability in communities, no child would be in the *position* to follow the promise of successful pathways for development in globalizing world contexts.

In considering general indicators of child development, it is impossible to separate changes associated with globalization from the effects of population growth, or from the sheer intensification of longstanding economic and subsistence pressures, environmental degradation, or the loss of land or other resources. Furthermore, we should be wary of the assumption that local cultural adaptations used to be better, and have only recently been degraded by globalization or intensification or population pressures brought to communities by the rise of or disintegration of modern nation-states (Edgerton 2000). The situation for children may be very different today, but it may or may not have been better, by one or another criterion, in the past. The point is that changes in indicators of child and family well-being – whether improvements or not – do not necessarily show that globalization is the cause of such changes.

Without assuming that global processes have directly caused indicators of well-being, have the basic levels of health and well-being improved for children, adolescents, and youth around the world in the past few decades as globalization becomes more ubiquitous? Global processes seem to have been associated with absolute improvements in the universal requirements for child health and well-being for many, while also leading to growing inequalities in child health and well-being. The answer also depends on which regions one is talking about and at what level of analysis. For example, there have been dramatic gains in economic growth, involvement in formal education, and basic indicators of health and well-being at the national and world regional level. However, regions remain impoverished relative to others, most notably parts of sub-Saharan Africa (the "except for" continent as Roe, 1999, phrased it) and those states that once made up the former Soviet bloc. Large numbers of children and adolescents live in war-torn or economically marginalized places (Stephens 1995b).

Presumably, if per capita GDP increases, families and children should benefit. Between 1970 and 1999 worldwide, per capita GDP grew by 1.3 percent annually on average. Much of this growth was concentrated in East and South Asia, where GDP growth ranged from 2.3 percent to 6 percent annually. Arab states, Latin America, and the Caribbean experienced more modest growth, between 0.3 percent and 0.6 percent annually on average during the 1970–1999 period. Sub-Saharan Africa experienced an overall 1 percent decline in GDP annually during this 30-year period. Moreover, in the decade from 1990 to 1999, the states of Eastern Europe and other former states of the Soviet Union actually faced a dramatic 3.4 percent average annual decline in per capita GDP (UNDP 2001).

There is growing income inequality between the wealthiest regions and all others, even for the regions of East Asia, the Pacific, and South Asia, which demonstrated the highest income growth between 1970 and 1999. For example, the income disparity in per capita GDP between East Asia and the Pacific (excluding Japan and South Korea) and the wealthiest industrial nations (including Japan) was about $6,000 in 1960; but it grew to $13,000 in 1998 even after adjusting for inflation and local cost of living differences (UNDP 2001: 17). Moreover, it appears that for most nations, income inequality grew between the mid-1980s and the late 1990s (UNDP 2001: 19).

As per capita income has grown, so have improvements in children's access to basic education and basic health. For example, there has been general improvement in the rates of primary school enrollment worldwide in the past few decades. UNICEF (2002) estimates that by the end of the 1990s 82 percent of the world's children were enrolled in primary school. However, millions of children in low-income communities receive a poor quality education and many in developing nations stop attending after the first few primary grades (UNDP 2001). Some 190 million working children between the ages of 10 and 14 do not have access to basic education (UNICEF 2002). The gender gap that exists in many countries between girls and boys enrolled in primary school has narrowed or disappeared in recent years for all world regions except sub-Saharan Africa, where 4 percent fewer girls, on average, are enrolled than boys (UNDP 2001).

The under-5 mortality rate also improved worldwide by 58 percent between 1960 and 2000: from 198 per 100,000 in 1960 to 83 per 100,000 in 2000 (UNICEF 2002). Every country for which there are data showed improvement in its under-5 mortality rate during this period. Generally, the rates of improvement are better than 50 percent for all world regions except for sub-Saharan Africa, where the under-5 mortality rate "only" improved 31 percent. These improvements in mortality are striking and have a large impact because of the huge differences in the age–sex structure of developed and developing nations. *There are seven times more children and youth in developing countries than in the developed nations* (URL: kidscount.org). "Within a framework of general improvement [in child mortality] the level of international inequality has actually grown considerably" (Sutcliffe 2001: chart 37). In many African countries, rates of malnutrition actually increased between 1990 and 1999, a trend that is opposite to that of the rest of the world regions, where (in aggregate) malnutrition and food insecurity declined (UNICEF 2002). *Hunger and Shame* provides a vivid and close-up ethnographic account of child hunger and inequality among the Chagga of Tanzania (Howard and Millard 1997). The current AIDS pandemic in sub-Saharan Africa, where it was estimated in 1999 that over 1 million children between the ages of zero and 14 are infected (UNDP 2001), will only make this disparity worse in the near term.

As the basic indicators of physical health and well-being for children and adolescents have improved in recent decades, national indicators of mental health have worsened, particularly for adolescents and youth (World Health Organization 2002a). The number of children and adolescents living as refugees, who participate in armed conflict, who are undomiciled/homeless, or who leave school before legal leaving age has increased dramatically in the past few decades, particularly for children in low-income countries or in low-income communities within countries (Desjarlais et al. 1995; Panter-Brick 2002). Many of these problems are associated with rapid urbanization and high poverty levels within cities in developing countries and in areas of urban decay in wealthier industrial countries. Children who live as refugees under conditions of war or in the squalor of urban ghettos have much higher rates of under-5 mortality, malnutrition, and lower access to and/or attendance in quality educational settings. They experience a profoundly different childhood and adolescence than children in more stable, peaceful, and wealthier circumstances in their own countries, much less in comparison to children in the industrialized world (Desjarlais et al. 1995).

Children and adolescents in impoverished developmental settings are at risk for a number of developmental and mental health problems. For younger children, inadequate consumption of healthy foods and inadequate levels of emotional support and cognitive stimulation can lead to developmental attrition, or the consistent failure to reach developmental milestones over time (Desjarlais et al. 1995). If these developmental milestones occur during sensitive periods of early childhood development, a child's failure to develop adequately can lead to life-long impairment (Schore 1994). For adolescents and youth who have lived much of their lives on the streets of over-crowded cities, refugee camps, or as parties in armed conflict, heavy involvement in unsupervised peer cultures can lead to social–behavioral problems like aggression, substance abuse, and associated mood disorders.

PLURALISTIC CHILDHOOD PATHWAYS ARE ASSOCIATED WITH GLOBALIZATION

Many researchers outside of psychological anthropology certainly appreciate the importance of local and regional variations in cultural communities in shaping global-ization. They are finding evidence of such variety, and calling for changes in their own disciplines to study them (Wozniak 1993). A recent issue of *Human Development* (2002 45, 4) is devoted to the question, "How can we study cultural aspects of human development?" A recent special issue of the *Journal of Research on Adolescence* focused entirely on globalization, societal change, and new technology. The authors, coming from psychology and sociology and based in Western nations, recognize that a "new, more global, and pluralistic view of adolescence" is emerging. They remark that the idea of adolescence as a special, stressful stage was a Western invention and that the notion is ironically now appearing in some other parts of the world, while it is disappearing elsewhere (Larson 2002: 2). There are many new "adolescences," "refracted through distinct circumstances and cultural systems," forming around the world, not a single world youth culture (Larson 2002: 2). At the same time, they point out that these plural developmental pathways are shaped by some common demographic and institutional forms (e.g., expanded schooling, delayed employment, later marriage, urbanization, girls' increased participation in schooling, and common exposure to mass media).

These pluralistic child and adolescent pathways are found among modern, indus-trial nation-states as well. Shwalb and Shwalb (1996) review two generations of developmental research in Japan, much of it done by anthropologists, which tracks the unique influence of Japanese cultural beliefs and institutions in the midst of a modern nation-state. Rothbaum et al. (2000), Shimizu and LeVine (2001), and White (1993) show the remarkable impacts of Japanese culture on children's develop-ment. Moral reasoning, mother–child relationships, "symbiotic relational harmony" as a goal for developmental pathways and self-development (vs. "generative tension"), school and peer worlds, material culture, and adolescent experience are all at variance with US and European patterns.

Analogous variations are found all over the world. Yan (1999) shows the remark-able transformations that impact contemporary Chinese youth. Seymour (1999) documents uniquely Indian responses to global change across three generations of girls and mothers in Orissa. Tudge and colleagues (1999) looked at parents and chil-dren in four industrialized, urban, literate cities (Greensboro, USA; Obninsk, Russia; Tartu, Estonia; and Suwon, Korea). They showed that socioeconomic heterogeneity within each site was important for parental beliefs about self-direction and children's own initiation of activities. In each city, they compared working-class and middle-class families. Parents in all sites valued self-direction in their children, but middle-class parents did so more than working-class parents in each city. The point is that heterogeneity may be found among different groups of parents and children in local communities (ethnic, class, neighborhood, occupational), even under seemingly similar global influences in addition to cross-national differences. This message that national and cultural variations are still powerful influences also is clear in recent studies of youth in the West. Even if we focus on the United States, Canada, and Europe – those parts of the world most clearly exemplifying all the features of globalization and its various mechanisms – the evidence for heterogeneity of child and youth experience is considerable.

One way to explore this empirically is to see if there is in fact a youth and young adult world of beliefs and attitudes and practices that is very different from those of older people. If global processes have already had an overwhelming influence on youth in the West, then measures of youth attitudes and practices *across* as well as within nations should show that youth are similar to each other, and different from their parents' and grandparents' cohorts (both within and across nations). Such a convergence of a world youth culture should be most visible with regard to attitudes and practices which reflect a more liberal and tolerant set of political and social attitudes, or that include concerns about the environment, for example (Inglehart 1990).

But data from the World Values Survey (WVS) show that much more than this kind of straightforward convergence is going on. There are clear "cultural zones" that also shape social values, political institutions, and economic growth, controlling for the levels of economic wealth (GNP/capita) that vary so dramatically around the world (Inglehart 2000). James Tilley (2002) used the WVS to compare generational differences in attitudes (political ideology and participation; religion and the role of family; work and overall life satisfaction) across 32 national samples. Tilley finds that cultural regions shape the attitudes and practices of the young compared to older respondents, more than does age for most items, and that gender differences are also striking in beliefs about religion (women are more religious), women's roles, and other attitudes.

> . . . apart from political activity . . . membership [in one of the six regional/national groups] has a greater effect [on attitudes] than does age group . . . Although all age-group effects are significant (apart from life satisfaction), they are generally dwarfed by the much larger effects of nationality. The young worldwide do not appear to be a coherent grouping with a common base of values . . . aside from life satisfaction and religious beliefs (which are dominated by [regional national group differences]), gender differences are of comparable magnitude, as well. (Tilley 2002: 252–253)

Weisner (2001c) found a similar pattern of intergenerational continuity and gender differences in an 18-year longitudinal study of children born to non-conventional and counter-cultural families in California. Mothers' values orientations (sex egalitarianism, importance of materialism, skepticism about authority, humanism/tolerance) measured at their child's birth, were correlated with adolescents' values (and mothers' own values) 18 years later. But the specific value or attitude we measured mattered as to whether adolescents were relatively higher or lower on each value compared to parents. For example, there is a secular trend for youth to be more materialistic than their parents in this particular sample (counter-cultural parents are relatively non-materialistic). Youth are relatively more trusting of social authority and leaders than the more skeptical and questioning parents in this sample. But girls *and* their mothers are substantially more committed to gender equity relative to either boys or fathers.

Harkness and Super (1996) point out significant variations in parental beliefs and infant and childcare comparing Dutch and US parents. Dutch parents favor a calmer, more regulated daily routine and time schedule for children. They have babies who sleep longer and have more regular schedules than US babies have. LeVine et al. (1988) report similar variations in their work on parental belief systems.

Youth experiences continue to be strongly influenced by local and national cultural traditions instantiated in very different institutions and policies (Breen and Buchmann 2002). Consider the transitions from adolescence to young adulthood in Italy, Sweden, Germany, and the United States (Cook and Furstenberg 2002). Common changes are occurring in all these places (and many others around the world): expansion of education for secondary and higher levels; increased gender equity in schooling and jobs; higher unemployment rates for youth and more part-time work; more cohabitation, later marriage and childbearing ages, and lower birthrates.

But between 15 and 35 each country shows often substantial variations in how youth reach adulthood. The Italian story of youth development is influenced by a weaker state support system, small businesses driving the economy, more family engagement with children, and by adolescents and youth continuing to live with their parents for many years before forming a separate household. Sweden encourages a period of experimentation and tolerance among teenagers before cohabitation, marriage, and jobs become settled. The Swedish state, industries, and unions all provide some institutional paths to guide youth. German youth start on either a university or an apprenticeship-training track early, but German guild institutions cannot match up jobs with these youth's training, so work is often part-time and uncertain. The United States has fewer state family supports, yet offers more diverse pathways to education and jobs. The US cultural and political economic ideal is one of individualistic choice, but poverty and race and ethnic barriers lead many youth who are not on the education track to flounder in the United States. Hence, the meaning of marriage, work, children, and even age itself varies across these countries, all of which would otherwise be grouped as similarly global, postmodern, affluent, industrialized, Western nations. In other words it depends on the levels of analysis, time scale, and sample as to whether one could conclude that common changes due to globalization are occurring in children and youth's developmental pathways, even among the highly economically developed European nations and the US.

Mass schooling of children and youth is surely the most dramatic and sustained global change in children's lives and experiences of the last half of the twentieth century. As we pointed out earlier, secular trends around the world reveal gains in years of schooling for boys and girls, with far greater rates of increase for girls. Yet the forms schools take depend on local beliefs about development, parental and teacher concerns, and national institutional variations. Preschool routines and activities, and their moral significance, also vary enormously (Tobin et al. 1989), and parental beliefs about the values of literacy and school success both motivate and divide communities, exacerbate tensions between boys and girls, and frustrate children who work hard at school, but without economic benefit to them or their families (Stambach 2000). Schooling in Zambia has changed children's "life-ways" (their whole intellectual and moral development) in local communities, sometimes in harmony with local life-ways, but more often not (Serpell 1993). Schooling is a worldwide change which has had similar consequences specific to classroom education (increased literacy and numeracy, learning common national curriculum content, new peer learning situations), yet widely divergent consequences *beyond* the classroom in the lives of children, both positive and negative. For example, schools can divide communities into elites and marginalized youth.

For instance, there is a widely replicated finding that more schooling of girls subsequently reduces fertility and child mortality, independent of husband's schooling and SES, virtually everywhere in the world. But why does this happen – what are the mechanisms in particular communities around the world that produce such a change? Do these mechanisms vary? LeVine and colleagues (LeVine and LeVine, 2001; LeVine et al. 2001) identified four pathways that could be involved, separately or jointly, in how schooling changes subsequent practices: new status aspirations of women; changes in identity and sense of empowerment; new skills; and the learning and incorporation of new models of learning and teaching. LeVine and his team then went out to study the local variations in quality and years of girls' schooling and childrearing around the world: in Nepal (where only 15 percent of adult women have attended school), Venezuela, Mexico (in both rural and urban settings), and Zambia. Multiple methods (ethnography, institutional observations in each community, behavioral observation, interviews, and child and maternal cognitive and language assessments) were all used to understand the meaning of schools and the impacts of education on subsequent behaviors. This is a complex story, in which all four postulated pathways have some impacts in some situations in different countries. As we have already seen is so often true, local communities influenced the ways schooling mattered for mothers and children. However, a central finding emerged: a common effect of new language and communicative practices:

> Schools are training grounds for participation in bureaucratic organizations and . . . their training is in the communicative code of such bureaucracies [e.g., decontextualized language or synoptic communication] . . . which enables a woman to use bureaucratic health and contraceptive services more effectively. (LeVine and LeVine 2001: 267)

This research program is a model for the systematic study of globalizing institutions (schools, classrooms, child health clinics, nutritional changes, child labor) and the quite variable ways they have impacts on children at local levels. The "same" global institution (schools teaching literacy) may have a broadly similar impact in childhood and somewhat similar consequences *later* in development (better youth and child health; lower fertility). However, this happens through *varying* pathways and mechanisms (socio-linguistic; self-efficacy and worth; new goals and status; different interactional scripts and schemas for understanding) in different communities.

If substantial variations in the values and developmental pathways of children, adolescents, and youth exist even in Europe and North America, and are essential to understand the consequences of mass schooling around the world, such variations are vastly greater in the rest of the world and for other kinds of child outcomes. Leis and Hollos (1995), for example, compare two Ijo communities in the Niger Delta studied before Nigerian independence and again 25 years later. One community was relatively unacculturated to Western influences. Would intergenerational continuity from adolescence to adulthood (greater consistency between expectations for behavior of children and adults) be stronger in the less acculturated community during the 25 years of rapid change? After all, in the less acculturated community, adults and children had been more homogeneous, and had had more shared intergenerational beliefs and practices 25 years earlier. In fact, the opposite happened. The initially more slowly changing, less developed community had adolescents with greater discontinuity at follow-up. *Relative* changes (and feelings of relative deprivation) in wealth and modernity within the community *felt* greater in the initially less acculturated villages. Hollos and Leis (2001) went on to consider models of the self and person-hood among Ijo. Self-identity continues to be defined by interdependence with kin and ancestors, but the sense of independence and self-reliance is also very strong – made possible by diverse community supports and individual patrons. Although "the post-modern tendency to view the future of anthropological studies as being the study of globalization and third-world underdevelopment has made a concern with kinship seem somewhat irrelevant," a multidimensional model of self and identity (global, local community, and individual) which includes kinship, fits their data more closely (Hollos and Leis 2001: 384).

Consider another example: contemporary concerns over girls in the United States losing their "voice," or their autonomous sense of self, concerns over various forms of abuse of girls, and girls' worries over body image, and high rates of anorexia/bulimia. Anderson-Fye (2001) describes how adolescent girls in San Andres, a tourist-economy caye in Belize, have negotiated two ideas drawn from global media – child abuse and slender body image. Far from the notion of girls losing their selves and voices at adolescence, Belizean high school girls strive to "never leave yourself." This widely shared local ethnopsy-chological construct of a true and honest self is activated in times of crises, obstacles, or temptations in life. Contrary to the wide-spread and heterogeneous experiences of domestic violence in previous generations in Belize, abuse of girls today is increasingly rejected in that community by females. Anderson-Fye traces several reasons for these changes. Specific abuse practices are now part of a more homogeneous schema of abuse/violence among Belizean adolescents. The very naming and identification of abuse in media (TV talk shows; magazines) brought some girls to the understanding that their experiences *were* abusive by hearing about other communities around the world. Western-style body types and eating disorders also appear in TV and magazine images, but Belizean girls are satisfied with their bodies and feel attractive compared with girls around the world. Hence, few eating disorders appear in the Belizean data. Protecting "your self" meant not depriving the body of food, and resting enough. Local beliefs and shared schemas, like "never leave yourself," illustrate how global media and tourism influences are mediated by ethnopsychological beliefs about the self. Such beliefs assist Belizean girls to choose paths which both local and Western standards would call "healthy."

The importance of assessing the fit between global and local traditions is true for changes in children's social behavior and parental beliefs and goals for children (Weisner 2000). In Kenya and much of sub-Saharan African, children are cared for through socially distributed systems, as opposed to exclusively parental or conjug-ally organized care. Older siblings care for younger, and children are sometimes fostered, adopted, or loaned for periods to other kin, or apprenticed. Adults other than parents also care for children. This pattern can continue, become transformed, or be lost entirely due to migration, economic dislocation, parental deaths from HIV, and the dislocations of war and conflicts. The meanings, purposes, and forms of socially distributed care are changed, but the practices continue. The traits parents want to establish in their children's character that will lead to success also show this blend (Whiting 1996). Parents identify traits useful for the school and market (confidence, inquisitiveness, cleverness, bravery, independence), but also continue to train their children for traits such as good-heartedness, respect (for parents and elders) obedience, and generosity to kin, which come from their agrarian, kin-based local world. Moral discourse about kinship and family investment shows a similar balance between respect for family authority and investments in one's own future (Weisner et al. 1997).

Suicide is another example of a global trend (suicide rates are increasing) with highly local and specific variations and implications for children and youth. For example, the World Health Organization (2002a) reports that there has been a substantial increase in suicide rates for males in the period 1950 to 1995, but a more modest increase in suicide rates for females. These rates have trended younger between 1950 and 1995. The proportion of suicides committed by those between the ages of 5 and 45 had grown from 44 percent in 1950 to 53 percent in 1995 (WHO 2002b). Much of this growth has occurred among late adolescents and youth between the ages of 15 and 29. Suicide is currently among the top three leading causes of death for youth and young adults between the ages of 15 and 34 in many countries (WHO 2001).

The risk for suicide, social delinquency, homicide, and substance abuse has increased dramatically for adolescents and youth in many regions of the world (Desjarlais et al. 1995). In many places, different sub-groups of youth are most at risk for different problems. For example, older African-American boys and young men in the United States are at an extremely high risk for being victims of violent crime and firearm related homicide (United States Center for Disease Control 2001). Older girls and young women in rural China, among Fijian Indians, and in (Western) Samoa are at unusually high risk for suicide, with rates higher than the rates for older boys and young men (Booth 1999; Phillips et al. 1999). Yet in the Pacific Islands of Pohnpei and Chuuk (formerly Truk), located in the Federated States of Micronesia (FSM), young men seem to be at an unusually high risk for family disturbances, substance abuse, and suicide, while young women are at an unusually low risk for these problems (Hezel 1987; Lowe 2002).

Given the apparent variation within and between communities, these health risks cannot be directly attributed to globalization and related social changes common to youth in many regions of the world. Rather, a determining factor is the degree to which the changes associated with the processes of globalization (e.g., increasing access to formal education, wage markets, opportunities for migration to urban centers, and mass produced goods) promote or obstruct a "fit" between youth in their local contexts of everyday social life. It appears that where the fit is relatively positive, local effects of globalization on children and youth can be positive; where the fit is poor, effects can be negative with regard to impacts on child and adolescent health and well-being (Lowe 2003).

The suicide epidemic that has ravaged youth in parts of Micronesia for the past few decades illustrates the selective, negative consequences of global change on boys. By 1994–6, the suicide rates for adolescents and youth were 14 times higher for 15 to 19 year olds and 7 times higher for 20 to 24 year olds than they were in 1964–6 (Lowe 2002). The rates have been extremely high even by international standards. For example, the suicide rate for 15 to 19 year olds in the FSM in 1994–6 was

78.5 per 100,000 (Lowe 2002). As a comparison, the suicide rate for 15 to 19 year old Native Americans in 1999, who have the highest suicide rates among any ethnic group in the United States, was about 22 per 100,000 (United States Center for Disease Control 2001).

In the FSM State of Chuuk, the dramatic rise in suicide has been concentrated among older boys and young men. For example, of the 173 cases of suicide reported for Chuuk between 1970 and 1985, only 11 (6 percent) were female suicides (Hezel 1987). Although males commit suicide more than females worldwide, a male to female ratio of 15 to 1 is extraordinary. The sharp increase in suicide among male youth in Chuuk is also associated with reported increased substance abuse, diagnosed mental illnesses, aggression, and delinquency (Hezel 1987; Marshall 1987; Micronesian Seminar 1997).

The people of Chuuk went through a century of tremendous social change as a result of colonial activities in the area and local manifestations of the global flows of people, goods, and capital between industrial nations and those in the periphery (Hezel 1983, 2001). Social change and globalization have impacted male and female youth similarly in their access to Western media (e.g., videos), American style education, and various aspects of Western youth culture (e.g., styles of dress and music). But these changes altered the daily routines and social relational worlds of male and female youth in fundamentally different ways. Male youth in particular have intensified their participation in the unsupervised peer group, often at the expense of family obligations. Female youth, on the other hand, have intensified their participation in *family* activities, such that their daily chores are a significant part of their daily routines, often at the expense of their participation in peer-related activities.

A youth's interests in these various settings come into conflict. Conflicts between the family and the peer group appear to be most intense (Hezel 1987; Lowe 2003; Marshall 1979), and are strongest for male youth because the activities that matter most for building status in the peer group often run counter to those activities that are important for maintaining their family relationships (Marshall 1979). Older girls and young women who spend time among their peers engage in peer-related activities of much greater social acceptability.

There are also important differences in the social supports for male and female youth. Older girls' daily routines afford them more opportunities to foster emotionally supportive social relationships within the family and among adult kin. Older boys, on the other hand, who are encouraged to avoid their sisters and their homes post-puberty, generally have fewer opportunities to foster emotionally supportive relationships among their family and kin (Rubinstein 1995).

The combination of increased potential for conflict between the various interests of male youth and poorer levels of social support place boys at greater risk for substance abuse and suicide in Chuuk (Lowe 2003). Thus, social changes associated with globalization in Chuuk have produced poorer "fit" or coherence, across the multiple social contexts in the everyday lives of male youth, whereas a reasonable degree of fit has been maintained in the everyday lives of female youth. These differences in the fit between male and female youth and their everyday social contexts are probably responsible for the differential rates of social problems between them.

ENDURING QUESTIONS IN THE STUDY OF YOUNG PEOPLE AND GLOBALIZATION

Anthropology has focused on how cultural knowledge is *acquired* by children throughout development; how families and communities *socialize* children and engage (or fail to engage) children in meaningful and necessary activities and practices; and what knowledge is *shared* and to what extent. Our view is that these enduring concerns continue to matter to children and families, and to the scientific study of childhoods around the world. The child developmental topics important in the field for much of the past century remain important today. These include the development and meaning of gender differences; trust and attachment; cognitive development; emotions and their meaning and expression; disability and deviance; cultural competencies (social appropriacy, family obligation and task skills, literacy and numeracy) and how these are acquired and vary; the development of social behaviors such as nurturance, responsibility, aggression/dominance, and sociability; the development of self and identity throughout childhood; and others. How globalization alters these contexts, ways of thought and feeling, and outcomes later in life, are the empirical questions.

ENDURING CONCERNS: CHILDREN'S VOICES AND EFFECTS ON THE POOR AND MARGINALIZED

Anthropology has been concerned with minorities, the poor and non-literate, and those, including children, adolescents, and youth, so often powerless and marginal. To the extent that anthropological research focuses on the impoverished and marginalized, this tradition of research, like the central developmental topics, will continue to be relevant.

We read the evidence to say that basic health, food, and physical security have improved for most children, adolescents, and youth globally, though inequality within and between communities, nations, and regions has dramatically increased at the same time. Life remains difficult – sometimes horrifically difficult – for children and parents affected by major global disruptions and by growing relative inequality. Many children and their parents suffer in the midst of global increasing affluence. More and more nations in a globalizing world economy now *could* provide the basic conditions for health, food security, safety, and other supports and opportunities to the impoverished and marginalized – *yet they do not*. Perhaps in past historical periods there was neither the potential nor the mechanisms available for global responses to suffering. But as barriers to the flow of information and goods fall, then more people can see what might be done. This has led psychological anthropologists to the study of power relationships and global processes, and the moral conditions that produce such inequality. Psychological anthropology attempts to broaden the research problem beyond inequality of incomes or resources alone, important as such inequality is, to an understanding of the often glaring differences in the *capabilities* of families and children to function and achieve their goals in their local communities (Sen 1992).

Scheper-Hughes (1992a, 1992b) describes child mortality in the northeast of Brazil with its deep poverty and the sheer inability of parents to provide for children.

She describes *nervos* (a Brazilian illness construct which includes feelings of weakness, irritability, headaches, angry weeping, and paralysis) as "caused by" (or simply a transformed form of) hunger and uncertainty regarding basic survival. She describes *nervos* as a response to poverty and an oppressive social system that should be resisted as a social fact, not glossed as a medical diagnosis. "My illness is really just my own life," as one mother says. Howard and Millard (1997) vividly describe food insecurity and malnutrition among Chagga children in Tanzania. Government, missionaries, and others have ineffectively intervened, even exacerbated these problems, for several generations. Howard and Millard point out the complexity of cultural and historical factors that produced malnutrition, the changing class and kin hierarchies involved, and the role of wage labor migration in dividing families and communities.

Psychological anthropology has contributed to studies of other risks and afflictions of childhood and adolescence that are impacted by globalization, but which are hardly new. For instance, anthropological studies of childhood disability and deviance show somewhat improved services, greater acceptance and social integration of children with physical and cognitive disabilities in many communities. A concern for tolerance and inclusion and services for children with disabilities is gradually diffusing, in highly variable ways, around the world (Ingstad and Whyte 1995).

Anthropologists are concerned with children at risk around the globe, including (for example) children under stress from academic examinations in Japan and Korea, immigrant children, street children, and children in the squatter settlements growing in cities around the world (Reynolds 1989; Stephens 1995b; Kilbride et al. 2000). Anthropologists also are concerned with the rights of children and adolescents in smaller indigenous and native cultures, and the lack of provision of basic protections for children in those communities (*Cultural Survival Quarterly*, 2000).

The sexual and physical abuse of young people around the world is a concern for anthropologists. Cultural beliefs and practices regarding appropriate discipline and treatment of children clearly do vary widely, and Western definitions of abuse are not universal. Goldstein (1998), for example, frankly describes the life world of Graca, a poor Brazilian woman in a *favela* of Rio, who uses harsh physical punishment and verbal abuse to try to discipline her children to survive in a world filled with gangs, drugs, and violence. Child discipline and punishment are abusive by Western legal definition and norms, but fit into the stark socialization Goldstein and Graca see as required for survival. Childhood, she says, "is a privilege of the rich" (1998: 393). However, repeated and unchecked physical aggression, or intrafamilial sexual relations between close kin and children, are nowhere defined as normative and acceptable (Korbin 1981). To the extent that globalization exacerbates and changes the scope and scale of war, children, adolescents, and youth are not only disproportionately the victims of such wars and conflicts, they are also sometimes combatants in those wars (Leavitt and Fox 1993).

Many remarkable strengths of children can be seen amid the difficult conditions of immigration, poverty, and dislocation. For example, children are often the mediators and translators of languages and cultural traditions in new immigrant communities in the United States and elsewhere, and often prove to be remarkably resilient in these roles (Orellana et al. 2001; Suarez-Orozco and Suarez-Orozco 1995). Children's adaptive strengths and enthusiasms in their countries of origin, as well as in the receiving communities to which they migrate, are remarkable (Greenfield and

Cocking 1994). Moroccan adolescents, for example, selectively use Islamic tradition (such as the importance of "social sense" or contextual sensitivity) to bridge old traditions, along with their dreams for material affluence, by using global connections through the Internet (Davis and Davis 1989).

The opportunities are stunning for new research and applied knowledge about children and global processes, based on the tradition of child and family research in local communities in psychological anthropology. After all, the children are the ones who are going to be carrying the burdens and opportunities of globalization, as well as our cultural traditions, into the future.

REFERENCES

Anderson-Fye, Eileen, 2001 Adolescent Girls' Experiences of Abuse and Globalization in Belize. Society for Psychological Anthropology Biennial Meeting, Atlanta, GA.

Booth, H., 1999 Pacific Island Suicide in Comparative Perspective. *Journal of Biosocial Science* 31: 433–448.

Breen, R., and M. Buchmann 2002 Institutional Variation and the Position of Young People: A Comparative Perspective. In *Early Adulthood in Cross-National Perspective*, Vol. 580, March. *Annals of the American Academy of Political and Social Science*. Frank Furstenberg, ed. Pp. 288–305. Thousand Oaks, CA: Sage.

Chua, Amy, 2004 *World on Fire: How Exporting Free Market Democracy Breeds Ethnic Hatred and Global Insecurity*. New York: Anchor Books.

Cook, T. D., and F. Furstenberg, 2002 Explaining Aspects of the Transition to Adulthood in Italy, Sweden, Germany, and the United States: A Cross-Disciplinary, Case Synthesis Approach. In *Early Adulthood in Cross-National Perspective*, Vol. 580, March. *Annals of the American Academy of Political and Social Science*. Frank Furstenberg, ed. Pp. 288–305. Thousand Oaks, CA: Sage.

Cultural Survival Quarterly, 2000 Rethinking Childhood: Perspectives on Children's Rights, 24 (2).

D'Andrade, Roy, 1986 Afterward. In *Human Motives and Cultural Models*. Roy D'Andrade and Claudia Strauss, eds. Pp. 225–232. Cambridge: Cambridge University Press.

Davis, S. S., and D. A. Davis, 1989 *Adolescence in a Moroccan Town*. New Brunswick, NJ: Rutgers University Press.

Desjarlais, Robert, L. Eisenberg, Byron Good, and Arthur Kleinman, 1995 *World Mental Health: Problems and Priorities in Low-Income Countries*. New York: Oxford University Press.

Edgerton, Robert B., 2000 Traditional Beliefs and Practices – Are Some Better Than Others? In *Culture Matters: How Values Shape Human Progress*. L. E. Harrison and S. P. Huntington, eds. Pp. 126–140. New York: Basic Books.

Garro, Linda C., 2001 The Remembered Past in a Culturally Meaningful Life: Remembering as Cultural, Social, and Cognitive Process. In *The Psychology of Cultural Experience*. C. C. Moore and H. F. Mathew, eds. Pp. 105–147. Cambridge: Cambridge University Press.

Goldstein, D. M., 1998 Nothing Bad Intended: Child Discipline, Punishment, and Survival in a Shantytown in Rio De Janeiro, Brazil. In *Small Wars: The Cultural Politics of Childhood*. N. Scheper-Hughes and C. Sargent, eds. Pp. 389–415. Berkeley: University of California Press.

Greenfield, Patricia M., and Rodney R. Cocking, eds., 1994 *Cross-Cultural Roots of Minority Child Development*. Hillsdale, NJ: Erlbaum.

Harkness, Sara, and C. M. Super, eds., 1996 *Parents' Cultural Belief Systems*. New York: Guilford Press.

Harvey, David, 1990 *The Condition of Postmodernity*. Oxford: Blackwell.

Hauser, R. M., B. V. Brown, and W. R. Prosser, eds., 1997 *Indicators of Children's Well-Being*. New York: Russell Sage Foundation.

Hezel, F. X., 1983 *The First Taint of Civilization: A History of the Caroline and Marshall Islands in Pre-Colonial Days. Pacific Islands Monograph Series*, Vol. 1. Pp. 1521–1885. Honolulu: University of Hawaii Press.

— 1987 Truk Suicide Epidemic and Social Change. *Human Organization* 46: 283–291.

— 2001 *The New Shape of Old Island Cultures: A Half Century of Social Change in Micronesia*. Honolulu: University of Hawaii Press.

Hollos, M., and P. E. Leis, 2001 Remodeling Concepts of the Self: An Ijo Example. *Ethos* 29 (3): 371–387.

Howard, M., and A. V. Millard, 1997 *Hunger and Shame: Poverty and Child Malnutrition on Mount Kilimanjaro*. New York: Routledge.

Human Development, 2002 Vol. 45 (4).

Inglehart, R., 1990 *Culture Shift in Advanced Industrial Society*. Princeton, NJ: Princeton University Press.

— 2000 Culture and Democracy. In *Culture Matters: How Values Shape Human Progress*. L. Harrison and S. Huntington, eds. Pp. 80–97. New York: Basic Books.

Ingstad, Benedicte, and Susan R. Whyte, 1995 *Disability and Culture*. Berkeley: University of California Press.

Jobes, P. C., W. F. Stinner, and J. M. Wardwell, eds., 1992 *Community, Society, and Migration: Non-Economic Migration in America*. Lanham, MD: University Press of America.

Kilbride, Phillip, C. Suda, and E. Njeru, 2000 *Street Children in Kenya*. Westport, CT: Bergin and Garvey.

Korbin, Jill E., ed., 1981 *Child Abuse and Neglect: Cross-Cultural Perspectives*. Berkeley: University of California Press.

Larson, R. W., 2002 Globalization, Societal Change, and New Technologies: What They Mean for the Future of Adolescence. *Journal of Research on Adolescence* 12 (1): 1–30.

Leavitt, L. A., and N. A. Fox, eds., 1993 *The Psychological Effects of War and Violence on Children*. Hillsdale, NJ: Erlbaum.

Leis, P. E., and M. Hollos, 1995 Intergenerational Discontinuities in Nigeria. *Ethos* 23 (1): 103–118.

LeVine, R. A., A. S. Dixon, S. LeVine, A. Richman, P. H. Leiderman, C. H. Keefer, and T. B. Brazelton, eds., 1994 *Child Care and Culture: Lessons from Africa*. Cambridge: Cambridge University Press.

LeVine, R. A., and S. E. LeVine, 2001 The Schooling of Women: Maternal Behavior and Child Environments. *Ethos* 29 (3): 259–270.

LeVine, R. A., S. E. LeVine, and B. Schnell, 2001 "Improve the Women": Mass Schooling, Female Literacy, and Worldwide Social Change. *Harvard Educational Review* 17 (3): 459–496.

LeVine, R. A., P. Miller, and M. West, eds., 1988 *Parental Behavior in Diverse Societies*. San Francisco, CA: Jossey-Bass.

Lewellen, Ted C., 2002 *The Anthropology of Globalization: Cultural Anthropology Enters the Twenty-First Century*. Westport, CT: Bergin and Garvey.

Lowe, Edward D., 2002 The Relationship of Globalization to Adolescent Suicide in the Pacific: An Analysis of Materials from the Micronesian Society of Chuuk. Presented at the Biennial Meetings of the Society for Research on Adolescence, April, New Orleans, LA.

— 2003 Identity, Activity, and the Well-Being of Adolescents and Youth: Lessons from Young People in a Micronesian Society. *Culture, Medicine, and Psychiatry* 27: 187–219.

Marshall, Mac, 1979 *Weekend Warriors: Alcohol in a Micronesian Culture*. Palo Alto, CA: Mayfield Press.

— 1987 "Young Men's Work': Alcohol Use in the Contemporary Pacific. In *Contemporary Issues in Mental Health Research in the Pacific Islands*. A. B. Robillard and A. J. Marsella, eds. Pp. 72–93. Honolulu: SSRI, University of Hawaii Press.

Mattingly, Cheryl, and Linda C. Garro, eds., 2000 *Narrative and the Cultural Construction of Illness and Healing*. Berkeley: University of California Press.

Micronesian Seminar, 1997 Alcohol in the FSM: An Assessment of the Problem with Implications for Prevention and Treatment. Pohnpei, Federated States of Micronesia: Micronesian Seminar Report.

Milanovic, B., 2000 *True World Income Distribution, 1988 and 1993: First Calculation Based on Household Surveys Alone*. Washington, DC: World Bank.

Nisbett, R. E., and L. Ross, 1980 *Human Inference: Strategies and Shortcomings of Social Judgment*. Englewood Cliffs, NJ: Prentice-Hall.

Orellana, M. F., B. Thorne, A. Chee, and W. S. E. Lam, 2001 Transnational Childhoods: The Participation of Children in Processes of Family Migration. *Social Problems* 48 (4): 572–591.

Panter-Brick, Catherine, 2002 Street Children, Human Rights, and Public Health: A Critique and Future Directions. *Annual Review of Anthropology* 31: 147–171.

Phillips, Michael R., Huaqing Liu, and Yanping Zhang, 1999 Suicide and Social Change in China. *Culture, Medicine, and Psychiatry* 23: 25–50.

Reynolds, Pamela, 1989 *Childhood in Crossroads: Cognition and Society in South Africa*. Grand Rapids, MI: William B. Eerdmans.

Roe, E., 1999 *Except-Africa: Remaking Development, Rethinking Power*. New Brunswick, NJ: Transaction Books.

Rogoff, Barbara, 1990 *Apprenticeship in Thinking: Cognitive Development in Social Context*. New York: Oxford University Press.

Rothbaum, F., M. Pott, H. Azuma, K. Miyake, and J. Weisz, 2000 The Development of Close Relationships in Japan and the United States: Paths of Symbiotic Harmony and Generative Tension. *Child Development* 71 (5): 1121–1142.

Rubinstein, D. H. 1995 Love and Suffering: Adolescent Socialization and Suicide in Micronesia. *Contemporary Pacific* 7: 21–53.

Schacter, D. L., 1999 The Seven Sins of Memory: Insights from Psychology and Cognitive Neuroscience. *American Psychologist* 54 (3): 182–203.

Scheper-Hughes, Nancy, 1992a *Death Without Weeping: The Violence of Everyday Life in Brazil*. Berkeley: University of California Press.

— 1992b Hungry Bodies, Medicine, and the State: Toward a Critical Psychological Anthropology. In *New Directions in Psychological Anthropology*. Ted Schwartz, Geoffrey M. White, and Catherine A. Lutz, eds. Pp. 221–247. New York: Cambridge University Press.

Schieffelin, Bambi B., and Elinor Ochs, eds., 1987 *Language Socialization Across Cultures*. Cambridge: Cambridge University Press.

Schore, A. N., 1994 *Affect Regulation and the Origin of the Self*. Hillsdale, NJ: Erlbaum.

Sen, A., 1992 *Inequality Reexamined*. New York: Russell Sage Foundation.

Serpell, R., 1993 *The Significance of Schooling: Life-Journeys in an African Society*. Cambridge: Cambridge University Press.

Seymour, Susan C., 1999 *Women, Family, and Child Care in India: A World in Transition*. Cambridge: Cambridge University Press.

Shimizu, H., and Robert A. LeVine, 2001 *Japanese Frames of Mind: Cultural Perspectives on Human Development*. Cambridge: Cambridge University Press.

Shore, Bradd, 1996 *Culture in Mind: Cognition, Culture, and the Problem of Meaning*. New York: Oxford University Press.

Shwalb, D. W., and B. J. Shwalb, eds., 1996 *Japanese Childrearing*. New York: Guilford Press.

Shweder, Richard A., 1991 Cultural Psychology: What is It? In *Thinking Through Cultures: Expeditions in Cultural Psychology*. Richard Shweder, ed. Pp. 73–112. Cambridge, MA: Harvard University Press.

Small, M., 1998 *Our Babies, Ourselves: How Biology and Culture Shape the Way We Parent*. New York: Anchor Books.

Stambach, A., 2000 *Lessons from Mount Kilimanjaro: Schooling, Community, and Gender in East Africa*. New York: Routledge.

Stephens, Sharon, 1995a Children and the Politics of Culture in "Late Capitalism." In *Children and the Politics of Culture*. Sharon Stephens, ed. Pp. 3–48. Princeton, NJ: Princeton University Press.

— 1995b *Children and the Politics of Culture*. Princeton, NJ: Princeton University Press.

Stiglitz, Joseph E., 2002 *Globalization and Its Discontents*. New York: W. W. Norton.

Strauss, Claudia, and Naomi Quinn, 1997 *A Cognitive Theory of Cultural Meaning*. Cambridge: Cambridge University Press.

Suárez-Orozco, Marcelo, 2001 *Children of Immigration*. Cambridge, MA: Harvard University Press.

Suárez-Orozco, C., and Marcelo Suárez-Orozco, 1995 *Transformations: Migration, Family Life, and Achievement Motivation Among Latino Adolescents*. Stanford, CA: Stanford University Press.

Super, C. M., and Sara Harkness, 1997 The Cultural Structuring of Child Development. In *Handbook of Cross-Cultural Psychology*, Vol. 2. J. Berry, P. R. Dasen, and T. S. Saraswathi, eds. Pp. 3–29. Boston, MA: Allyn and Bacon.

Sutcliffe, Bob, 2001 *100 Ways of Seeing an Unequal World*. London: Zed Books.

Sutton, C. R., and E. M. Chaney, eds., 1987 *Caribbean Life in New York City: Sociocultural Dimensions*. New York: Center for Migration Studies of New York.

Tilley, J., 2002 Is Youth a Better Predictor of Sociopolitical Values Than is Nationality? In *Early Adulthood in Cross-National Perspective*, Vol. 580. *Annals of the American Academy of Political and Social Science*. F. Furstenberg, ed. Pp. 226–256. Thousand Oaks, CA: Sage.

Tobin, J., D. Wu, and D. Davidson, 1989 *Preschool in Three Cultures: Japan, China, and the United States*. New Haven, CT: Yale University Press.

Tudge, J., D. Hogan, S. Lee, M. M. Tammeveski, N. Kulakova, I. Snezhkova, and S. Putnam, 1999 Cultural Heterogeneity: Parental Values and Beliefs and Their Preschoolers' Activities in the United States, South Korea, Russia, and Estonia. In *Children's Engagement in the World*. A. Goncu, ed. Pp. 62–96. Cambridge: Cambridge University Press.

UC Atlas of Global Inequality, 2002 http://www2.ucsc.edu/atlas/. Accessed October 4, 2002.

UNICEF, 2002 *The State of the World's Children 2002*. New York: UNICEF.

United Nations Development Program (UNDP), 2001 *Making New Technologies Work for Human Development: Human Development Report 2001*. New York: Oxford University Press.

United States Center for Disease Control, 2001 *National Vital Statistics Report,* Vol. 49 (11).

Weisner, Thomas S., 1984 Ecocultural Niches of Middle Childhood: A Cross-Cultural Perspective. In *Development During Middle Childhood: The Years from Six to Twelve*. W. A. Collins, ed. Pp. 335–369. Washington, DC: National Academy of Sciences Press.

— 1997 The Ecocultural Project of Human Development: Why Ethnography and Its Findings Matter. *Ethos* 25 (2): 177–190.

— 2000 Culture, Childhood, and Progress in Sub-Saharan Africa. In *Culture Matters: How Values Shape Human Progress*. L. E. Harrison and S. P. Huntington, eds. Pp. 141–157. New York: Basic Books.

— 2001a Anthropological Aspects of Childhood. In *The International Encyclopedia of the Social Sciences*, Vol. 3. Pp. 1697–1701. Oxford: Elsevier Science.

— 2001b Children Investing in Their Families: The Importance of Child Obligation in Successful Development. In Family Obligation and Assistance During Adolescence: Contextual Variations and Developmental Implications. A. Fuligni, ed. *New Directions in Child Development* 94 (winter): 77–83.

— 2001c The American Dependency Conflict: Continuities and Discontinuities in Behavior and Values of Countercultural Parents and Their Children. *Ethos* 29 (3): 271–295.

— 2002 Ecocultural Understanding of Children's Developmental Pathways. *Human Development* 174: 275–281.

Weisner, Thomas S., C. Bradley, and Phillip Kilbride, eds., 1997 *African Families and the Crisis of Social Change*. Westport, CT: Bergin and Garvey.

White, M., 1993 *The Material Child: Coming of Age in Japan and America*. Berkeley: University of California Press.

Whiting, Beatrice, 1996 The Effect of Social Change on Concepts of the Good Child and Good Mothering: A Study of Families in Kenya. *Ethos* 24 (1): 3–35.

Whiting, Beatrice, and C. Edwards, 1988 *Children of Different Worlds: The Formation of Social Behavior*. Cambridge, MA: Harvard University Press.

World Health Organization (WHO), 2001 *World Health Report 2001: Mental Health: New Understanding, New Hope*. Geneva: World Health Organization.

— 2002a Evolution 1950–1995 of Global Suicide Rates (per 100,000). www5.who.int/mental_health/main.cfm?p=0000000147.

— 2002b Changes in Age Distribution of Cases of Suicide Between 1950 and 1995. www5.who.int/mental_health/main.cfm?p=0000000148.

Wozniak, R. H., 1993 *Worlds of Childhood Reader*. New York: Harper Collins.

Yan, Y., 1999 Rural Youth and Youth Culture in North China. *Culture, Medicine, and Psychiatry* 23: 75–97.

CHAPTER 18 Drugs and Modernization

Michael Winkelman and
Keith Bletzer

INTRODUCTION

The human drive to alter consciousness through use of psychoactive plants is found throughout human history and existed far back in prehistory. Anthropological perspectives provide several vantage points from which to address this impetus for the use of consciousness altering substances, general cross-cultural variation in their patterns of use, and subsequent technological transformations and evolution into disfavor as illicit drugs. A major contribution is in understanding the interaction of cultural and biological factors, specifically how cultural assumptions and practices affect societal attitudes towards alteration of consciousness, how use patterns change across time, and how cultures vary in response to the psychobiological dynamics of the addictive potential of substances that alter consciousness. Anthropology's cross-cultural perspectives reveal the different values that are placed upon drug substances affect their patterns of use and their effects upon users.

Cultures differ considerably in the attention and support that they give to the induction of altered states of consciousness (ASC), including drug induced ASC. All cultures have practices that utilize some process to obtain ASC (Laughlin et al. 1992; Winkelman 1992). Since ASC reflect biologically based structures of consciousness, a latent human potential that Winkelman (2000) refers to as "integrative consciousness", they continue to be manifested in some form within society, even when there is cultural repression of ASC. However, the concept of these consciousness altering substances as harmful drugs, instead of sacraments and medicines, developed during the processes of modernization.

Dramatic changes in views and uses of various substances that occurred during modernization transformed the constructive uses of sacred substances for enhancing communal integration and psychosocial therapy and made them obsessive addictions. Worldwide dissemination of contemporary prevalent drugs resulted from colonization processes of modernization. Massive dependence on drugs, ranging from licit substances such as tobacco and alcohol to the illicit substances of cocaine and the opiates, reflects changes in psychosocial conditions, technology, and commercialization produced by modernization. The addictive properties of contemporary drugs are outgrowths of the technologies that permitted purification, concentration, and synthetic production, coupled with social changes that insulated their use from communal and spiritual traditions.

This chapter characterizes drug modernization from baseline perspectives on their premodern uses. The approach is largely psychohistorical, cultural, and psychodynamic, rather than physiological. It focuses primarily on the United States and the countries of Europe. Substances and historical processes from other parts of the world are primarily considered where they have implications for understanding their roles in the United States. Major drugs and categories of effects that are addressed in this chapter include hallucinogens or "psychointegrators," that is, serotonin-reuptake inhibitors (Winkelman 1996, 2001a); stimulants, namely, cocaine, nicotine, and the so-called food drugs (coffee and tea); and depressants or inebriants, namely, alcohol and opioids.

One aspect of the modernization of drugs involves prohibition and the political response exemplified in the "war on drugs," an exercise in the power of the modern state that has controlled and protected various drugs, and opposed others, in an effort to meet political and economic objectives (Musto 1999). The conclusions of this chapter address the "postmodernization" of drug attitudes, an approach that questions modern attitudes and attempts to redress their detrimental effects. Postmodern trends reject addictive drug use patterns and oppressive control, reconsidering their roles as spiritual substances and their relationship to human consciousness.

THE PREHISTORY OF PSYCHOINTEGRATOR SUBSTANCES

Early humans found a variety of psychoactive plant substances to be of startling significance, and they built cultural institutions around them. In prehistoric, ancient, and premodern cultures, plants with names meaning "plants of the gods," "food of the gods," "saintly children," and "voices of the gods" were considered sacraments, an embodiment of god, the mystical and the spiritual (Furst 1976; Schultes and Hofmann 1992). These substances were used to increase sacred or spiritual awareness. McKenna (1992) documents worldwide prehistoric practices using hallucinogenic mushrooms as part of a cultural ethos relating to the earth and mysteries of nature. Cross-culturally, these plants were believed to be powerful spiritual forces with religious and therapeutic applications (Winkelman 1996). Substances contained in these plants provoke enhanced self-awareness and contact with a "Transcendent Other," reflecting the sentience and intelligence of nature, an intimate interconnectedness with nature and the earth, an awareness of our symbiotic relationship with nature and the universe (McKenna 1992). Common effects of these plants include a personal relationship and sense of connectedness with the supernatural world; participation in a mythical world with spiritual relationships with animals; power enhancement through strengthening of self-identification; ego dissolution that often is conceived as resurrection and spiritual transformation; treatment of a variety of diseases and illnesses; and enhancement of social integration (Winkelman 1996). These substances are used for both physical and psychological conditions (Winkelman 2001a).

The term "psychointegrator" (Winkelman 1996, 2001a) better characterizes substances that are labeled hallucinogens, psychedelics, and entheogens ("evoking the god within"). Psychointegrator reflects neurologically induced changes produced by particular substances that enhance serotonin availability. Enhanced serotonin facilitates neuromodulation of other transmitter systems and evokes synchronized theta brain waves that produce physiological integration of cognitive, emotional, and behavioral levels of the brain. Psychointegrators have been considered the source of religious traditions and the bases of civilizations around the world. McKenna (1992) proposes these substances played an important role in the evolution of human consciousness, producing a sense of interconnectedness and balance with nature. La Barre (1972) noted that their potential to stimulate visions and spiritual experiences led many ancient cultures to attribute to them the source of their religious traditions.

Psychointegrators were central to many shamanic practices. Shamanism is manifested worldwide in hunter-gatherer societies, as an adaptation to psychobiological structures of human consciousness (Winkelman 2000). Training of shamanistic healers often incorporated these substances for inducing altered states of consciousness and establishing contact with the spirit world. Shamanism used psychointegrators because they produce profound effects upon consciousness and create a sense of connectedness with community and nature. These plants were used in rites of initiation and resocialization ordained by elders, which often were collective forms of puberty rites that marked an individual's transition to adult status (Grob and Dobkin de Rios 1992).

Premodern transformations

This panhuman religious and spiritual heritage involving an integrated community ethos and harmony with nature was lost with sociocultural evolution. Climatic changes driving populations to new areas limited access to previous substances, which became less central in agricultural systems that favored alcoholic beverages for altering consciousness. With the premodern and early modern loss of psychointegrators, Western cultures lost access to these forms of gnosis (knowing) and community integration (McKenna 1992). The last vestiges of this panhuman religious substrate in European cultures may have been the mysteries of Eleusis (Sherratt 1991) and European fertility practices that were mis-labeled as "witchcraft" (Harner 1973). Western thought has produced an ethos that denied and repressed the sacred qualities of nature and the feminine that is associated with the psychointegrators. These community-based ritual systems were brutally repressed by agricultural states and their socio-religious systems of patrilineal authority and class power, sky gods, and the cults of alcohol. The prior communal religious systems were persecuted and transformed into personifications of the devil and witchcraft (Fuller 2000).

Cross-cultural differences in use of psychointegrators indicate their decline was part of the early development of complex hierarchical societies. Societies with higher levels of political complexity typically restrict use of psychointegrator plants (Dobkin de Rios and Smith 1997). Their ritual use is negatively correlated with levels of political integration (Winkelman 1991), reflecting inherent conflicts of the psychosocial and cognitive dynamics produced by these substances with the needs of hierarchical politically integrated societies. The use of these psychointegrator plants is typically repressed in complex societies. Their use is opposed by those who hold political power because they are used in *local* social contexts that play powerful roles in interpretations of these spiritual experiences. Consequently, they threaten the ideology of those who hold social and religious power.

ALCOHOL PREHISTORY AND HISTORY

Alcohol is one of humanity's most ancient consciousness altering substances. Extensive use required ready sources of foods with high sugar content necessary for fermentation, which made extensive alcohol consumption dependent upon agriculture. The wide diffusion of alcohol during selected prehistoric periods (particularly the Neolithic) was part of the spread of a drinking complex that occurred during periods of rapid sociocultural and economic change (Rudgley 1993). Central to these new political structures were elite male warrior cults, whose use of alcohol is well attested to in the drinking vessels found in their graves.

Alcohol consumption was a central feature of the ritual, political, and communal life of one of the later prehistoric periods (Iron Age) in Europe. Alcohol has its roots in religious practice but was transformed into a key element of ritual processes of establishing and maintaining social relationships of patrons with their supporters (Arnold 1999). Alcohol was a social lubricant in the context of intergroup and intragroup competition, power, and patronage. Warrior nobles gathered with their drinking patrons to solidify friendships and formalize commitments to militarily defend their benefactor. This is exemplified in the Celtic culture of the British Isles, where the king provided feasts that expressed values of open-handed generosity and friendship, liberally enhanced by libations of alcoholic beverages. This consumption was part of trade connections with the Mediterranean world that provided a storable commodity, namely wine, that replaced perishable beer. This enhanced the power of "aggrandizers" and their political influence, because wine allowed communities to stockpile supplies which was not possible with beer. Alcohol's political role was based in its longstanding importance in religious and social life, in feasts that constituted ostentatious public demonstrations. Banquets were contexts for judicial and public business, establishing a hierarchy among supporters, extracting public declarations of loyalty, and making symbolic statements of dependence and dominance that were used to form alliances.

Alcohol was such a core element of pre-Christian European religiosity that it survived as a central sacrament of Christianity. The early Christian ethos had wine as a central feature for altering mood, gladdening the heart, and bringing joy to life as an integral element of family, as well as communal and ritual, celebrations (Fuller 2000). This reflected continuity with earlier Jewish uses of wine in religious celebrations and as a means of creating spiritual connections and community solidarity. Wine as a Christian tradition was reinforced in Christ's drinking of wine at his Last Supper, equating it with his own blood and asking the disciples to drink it "in remembrance of me."

Anthropological studies have contributed to the perspective that alcohol effects are part of a cultural and community dynamic that dramatically mediates consequences of alcohol consumption. This contributes to psychocultural rather than physiological views of alcohol effects. Anthropological studies have found a widespread use of alcohol in premodern societies, with anxiety and social relations as significant predictors of the extent to which drunkenness occurs (for a review, see Baer et al. 1997). Prominent features of premodern alcohol consumption involved its use in communal settings as a social lubricant, for production of euphoric feelings, and for relief from work and anxiety. Alcohol's ritual use to facilitate group integration and interpersonal rapport is widely noted. Heath's (1994) examination of rural Bolivia, for example, characterizes traditional alcohol use patterns as integrated with multi-day rituals and festivals that reinforce community solidarity, social cohesion and rapport, and internal hierarchy.

McKenna (1992) suggests that during the shift from premodern to modern societies alcohol came to play a central role in "dominator–exploiter" cultures through empowering the ego and loosening social boundaries. These initial effects are followed by a diminishing awareness and reduced ability to respond to social cues. McKenna links alcohol to male–female relations, noting its role in wife abuse. Alcohol use is linked to ego obsession and immediate gratification, an anxiety-laden response reflecting alienation from the matrix of the feminine mother nature. Alcohol is central to repressive opposition to other consciousness altering substances in spite of the enormous evidence of the numerous deleterious effects of alcohol.

The transition from communal to state societies during the shift from premodern to modern was accompanied by a shift to alcohol as the drug of choice among Western civilizations. This shift was exploited in the modernization of the mercantile nation-state and, subsequently, capitalism. Production of distilled alcohol was a central feature of colonial enterprises in the Americas and played a fundamental role in the demand for and trade in African slaves to produce the sugar required for fermentation (Rudgley 1993).

CANNABIS (MARIJUANA): THE PREMODERN BACKGROUND

Cannabis was introduced into Europe during the process of modernization and brought with it a reputation derived from traditional lore in other parts of the world. Rätsch's overview of premodern cannabis use documents its medicinal and ritual applications as "one of the oldest and best known of humankind's healing plants" (2001: xiv). Shamanic roots also remained embedded in the medicinal lore that surrounds marijuana. Cannabis was a spiritual plant for establishing relationships with the gods, a source of nutrients, a treatment for wounds, sores, and physical diseases, and a remedy for depression and sexual dysfunction. The importance of marijuana in these cultures is shown by epitaphs such as "milk of the gods," "plant of the love goddess," "giver of delight," and "food of Kundalini." Shamanic practices of hunter-gatherer societies that incorporated marijuana as a means of altering consciousness persisted in horticultural societies. Typical use was by healers for divination and establishing contact with the spirit world. It also was smoked or ingested as a drink by patients. The Scythians, for example, engaged in the communal use of cannabis as "incense" in sweat baths that produced jubilation in a form of "family shamanism" for establishing relations with ancestors and providing a sense of immortality of the soul and purification of the body.

Cannabis use was found in complex societies. For example, it was associated with the Nepalese god Shiva, known as "Lord of Hemp." Chinese medicine also considered cannabis a sacred plant and a central ingredient in elixirs of immortality. Cannabis was also used for rheumatism, gout, menstrual conditions, constipation, and as an anesthetic and antiseptic. Ayurvedic medicine of India used buds, leaves, resins, and the seeds of cannabis in a wide range of medicines for physical ailments of virtually every part and system of the body, particularly for ulcers, migraines, and sexual disorders, as well as sedation. Cannabis beverages had shamanic functions in permitting one to "fly" and acquire other magical powers (*siddhis*), serving as a "cosmic intercessor" and assisting in concentration during meditation. Cannabis also was used to treat emotional disorders, rejuvenate the body, and stimulate sexual desire and love.

Tibetan medicine has roots in shamanic practices where cannabis was viewed as a sacred plant and used to obtain mystical experience. Cannabis was used in Tibet for physical (e.g., respiratory, rheumatism, inflammation) and psychological (e.g., epilepsy, pain, sexual rejuvenation) conditions. There is a long history of socially accepted cannabis use in Arabic and Islamic medicinal traditions, where it is known as hashish. Hashish was used as a universal antidote for physical and psychological ailments, but was typically associated with the mystical order of the Sufis and their dervish dances, ecstatic music, and meditation. Indo-European cultures used cannabis in antiquity, associating it with the goddess of love, fertility, and life (Germany), and cannabis was recognized in Europe and became a part of its botany, alchemy, folk medicine, and homeopathy. Rätsch (2001) documents its association with the "witches" who were persecuted during the Christian Inquisition.

Cannabis and modernization

Arabic traders introduced marijuana from India into Europe, and European colonization and warfare expanded contact with cultures where cannabis was used as a social and spiritual drug. Cannabis use encountered in Africa involved important social occasions, including festivals and treaties. Cannabis was used for its unifying effects and as a social lubricant: "the men would gather at the main squares of the villages every evening for a common ceremonial smoke" (Rätsch 2001: 128). Cannabis became a part of European medical practice in the 1600s, but its use was infrequent. Colonization introduced cannabis to other cultures as Spain transported it to the Americas during the conquest.

Cannabis was adopted into the medicinal and spiritual practices of Native Americans, where it was combined in smoking mixtures. Cannabis became widely diffused among indigenous and mestizo cultures of Latin America, where it acquired a role in revolutionary resistance, in addition to its use as a pacifier and relaxant. East Indian immigration into the Caribbean extended marijuana's diffusion. Marijuana became an adjunct to jazz, blues, and reggae music of the Americas in the modern period, as well as similar musical traditions in the Middle East (Rätsch 2001). Marijuana entered the United States in the eighteenth century largely as a patent medicine that was used for insomnia, cramps, and as a cough suppressant. Cautions similar to those that were raised about the opiates (see below) began to accrue in the latter half of the 1800s, but its populist appeal grew by reputation among the common folk who used it for medicinal purposes. Early marijuana smoking in the United States occurred among "fringe groups," but became widely diffused in the United States in the early twentieth century through several routes, notably Turkish smoking parlors in the late 1800s and Mexican immigrants in the Southwest. During alcohol prohibition in the 1920s and 1930s, marijuana became widely adopted as a recreational intoxicant. It continued to grow in popularity with a broad cultural acceptance during the 1960s as part of a counter-cultural (hippie) and anti-war movement in the United States and Europe.

OPIUM AND MODERNIZATION'S CONSEQUENCES: MORPHINE AND HEROIN

Opium (*Papaver somniferum*) is one of humanity's most important medicinal plants, with evidence dating its domestication to the sixth millennium BC or earlier (Rudgley 1993). Early use included religious applications. Opium was important in the ancient pharmacies of Greeks, Romans, Egyptians, and Arabs, who had a sophisticated understanding of its cultivation, harvest, and use, as well as its benefits and dangers (Scarborough 1995). Alexander the Great distributed opium to his troops to combat fatigue and pain and to make them fearless warriors. Opium primarily was used for pain, as a medicine to combat a wide variety of diseases, and to induce sleep. Opium was generally consumed in mixtures with other psychoactive substances, particularly in liquid form as infusions in wine. Opium was globalized to a limited extent in premodern eras as Arab traders spread opium over trade routes to Persia, India and China, and the Roman Empire (Courtwright 2001). The Mohammedan Conquest of Europe in the tenth and eleventh centuries, for example, and the return of the Crusaders, introduced opium into Europe. By the 1500s, opium was established in Western European medicine, and by the 1800s it was particularly popular among country people in Britain, who were more common users of opium than people in British cities (Berridge 1999).

European nations and companies gained tremendously from the cultivation and distribution of opium, although its production took place outside of Europe (Janin 1999). Opium was central to British trade with China and led to the nineteenth-century "Opium wars" that sought to assure China's continued acceptance of Britain's opium supply from crops grown in India. Taxation and tariff levies brought monies to European treasuries. English merchants and investors in London (especially the Levant Company chartered by Elizabeth I) and French investors and organizers in Marseilles controlled European opium trade (Janin 1999). Opium brokers (wholesalers) in London supplied the "corner shop" in local communities, which became the principal source of opium medication that was prescribed for ailments ranging from fatigue and sore muscles in adults, to insomnia in children. Opium had an early status akin to the psychointegrators, as a means to reach mystical union, rapture, and spiritual experience.

Modernization of opiates transformed them into the most powerful sources of addiction. Opium refinement through the extraction of key ingredients, which was a technological outgrowth of modernization, transformed the nature of its use. Morphine was the first active ingredient isolated from opium, occurring at the beginning of the 1800s; it became a commercial product shortly thereafter. Heroin followed in 1874, marketed by Bayer. Development of the hypodermic syringe at the beginning of the second half of the 1800s provided the means for quick assimilation into the body and further assured globalization of morphine and heroin. Modernization's methods of administration based on injection supplanted the patterns of nasal inhalation (smoking and powdered inhalation) that characterized traditional opium use.

Spiritualist traditions of nineteenth-century Europe were influenced by the mind expanding properties of opium. Development of opiate use in the United States was unrelated to religion. Its use occurred more as a byproduct of the Civil War, where morphine was used for the care of the wounded. In the 1800s all social classes were present among persons addicted to morphine and opium, from physicians, who had ready access, to prostitutes, who had regular need to blunt their pain. It has been said that the typical opiate addict in the nineteenth-century United States was a middle-aged rural white woman who obtained it through patent medicines available in catalogues (Musto 1999). Throughout the early 1800s and into the early 1900s, physicians raised concerns and recommended cautions on dosage owing to morphine's use as a medicinal prescription. A number of individuals became addicted and continued using the product.

STIMULANTS: PREMODERN TO MODERN

Humans have probably always sought plants with stimulating properties. Among the first were those that could be chewed, which included kwat (also known as *qat*) (*Catha edulis*) and betel (made from the seed of the *Areca* palm, combined with slaked lime and a leaf from *Piper betel*). Major stimulants were derived from plants that usually were prepared as a beverage, such as coffee (*Café* sp.) and coca (*Erythroxylon coca*), and those that usually were smoked, such as tobacco (*Nicotiana* sp.) (Rudgley 1993; Marshall 1993). Early stimulant use was associated with ritual and religious uses and sacred interpretations (e.g., use of tea in Buddhist practices in Japan, coffee in the Sufi Muslim mystical practices, and coca in South America). Later, the stimulants acquired secular and communal functions. Sacred use of coffee in the Arabic world became secularized in coffee houses and as part of a change in the moral and political atmosphere that reflected social adaptations to the enhanced importance of extra-familial social organization. Enhancement of social interaction by use of stimulants is attested to, for example, in use of kwat in Northeast Africa. Kwat consumption occurred on a daily basis throughout the Middle East in recognizable patterns of social interaction that enhanced a sense of communal connectedness that was derived from increases in communication and the sense of harmony among males. Betel use in the Pacific Islands (Marshall 1993) is an expression of good will and hospitality, friendliness and peaceful relations, and was used to enhance work, social activity, and personal enjoyment. Chewing of betel induces an alteration of consciousness that is personal as well as social. Stimulants generally provide mechanisms for enhancing social interaction and signaling of social status by attesting to economic resources of the users and their connections for acquiring consciousness altering substances from distant places.

Widespread use of stimulants globally (particularly coffee) developed during the colonization period. Stimulants in modern Europe were introduced as a colonial export in the form of packaged coffee, tea, and cacao (with sugar because of their bitter properties) that partially replaced a traditional reliance upon non-distilled alcoholic beverages. In Europe during the Enlightenment, coffee became the drink of the intelligentsia, merchants, and scientists of the newly emerging middle class.

Tobacco

Although tobacco is a "New World" American plant, other species of *Nicotiana* have been used around the world. During the prehistoric era, tobacco was the most widespread sacred plant of the Americas. Tobacco was virtually universal in its use among indigenous North Americans, and was acquired through trade far beyond its area of production. Tobacco was considered a sacred substance and used in shamanistic rituals. Its typical use was not the modern habit of chronic smoking. Tobacco often was mixed with powerful psychoactive plants (e.g., *Datura*). In some cultures, it was imbibed through the nose as a liquid extract in doses powerful enough to produce intense hallucinatory experiences. This procedure generally involved *Nicotiana rustica*, a stronger species than contemporary tobacco. Premodern use of tobacco was intimately integrated with both shamanistic and communal rituals (Wilbert 1987), and it typically was not used in a pattern of secular addiction.

Europeans were introduced to tobacco in the 1500s through colonial contact with the Americas. Tobacco's medicinal qualities were emphasized as a "panacea" and "holy herb," and inhalation of tobacco smoke served as a remedy for many ailments. Although it was cultivated as a crop for personal use, Native Americans were not compelled to grow tobacco for European export. Europeans thus used indentured servants to grow tobacco, but this arrangement proved unsatisfactory, leading to the importation of African slaves for the colonial tobacco production. The British dominated tobacco production, building upon the American colonial foundation of Jamestown, Virginia, "the colony built upon smoke," in creating a global production and distribution network by the late 1800s. Investors in London expanded production through initial plantations in the Caribbean islands and the Virginia Company in the southeastern colonies. Tobacco was used by all social classes and reached proportions of mass consumption by the turn of the eighteenth century in Europe. For most of the late 1600s and 1700s, European importation of tobacco exceeded demand, and tobacco was re-exported to numerous destinations, including Asia and Africa (Goodman 1993). Eventually tobacco use, particularly as cigarettes, spread throughout most of the world. Cigarette smoking was adopted by a majority of male adults in some nations, and often included women among its users.

Coca and cocaine

Coca has a 6,000-year history of use in the Andes as a tea and chewed substance. Used in both ritual and secular contexts, it was considered a "food of the gods." Although its existence was recognized early in the colonization period, coca was not developed and marketed until the 1800s. Its byproduct, cocaine, was isolated in the second half of the nineteenth century, when commercial production of cocaine hydrochloride first took place in Germany by the Merck Company in 1862. By the 1880s, several countries in Europe were importing its products. Endorsement by researchers and physicians such as Sigmund Freud expanded its demand, but criticism of cocaine's addictive effects led German authorities to legislate pharmaceutical controls in 1872. Increasing regulation occurred in the 1890s and into the 1900s, culminating with its designation as a schedule drug with the passage of the Harrison Act in 1914. Medical efforts to find an appropriate use for cocaine emphasized how it was capable of increasing physical endurance and alleviating fatigue. Eventually, the cocaine alkaloid was discovered to be an anesthetic, and it gained medical acceptance. Early cocaine use was primarily from physician prescription, but it became popular as a recreational drug among those who first had taken it for medicinal reasons (Gootenberg 1999).

Cocaine appeared in the United States in wines in the 1880s. During this period, pharmacies sold both pure cocaine, in its powder form, and products containing cocaine such as lozenges, typically without instructions on appropriate use. One who had prior experience (family, neighbor, friend) provided suggestions for its use. Cocaine was added to a variety of foods, especially drinks (the most famous was Coca-Cola), to make people energetic and relieve their headaches, fatigue, and boredom. By the 1890s, cocaine was popular in both Europe and the United States. Physicians and the middle class were the most frequent consumers of cocaine. Rural women more than rural men became addicted, unknowingly, by consuming cocaine in patent medicines. The temperance movement that spearheaded alcohol prohibition advocated the use of cocaine to lace their drinks and in the patent medicines they recommended as family remedies. Cocaine was given to African-American dock and warehouse workers to increase work productivity. The prohibition of alcohol and opiate use by African Americans contributed to their early adoption of cocaine as a recreational drug.

MODERNIZATION AND THE EMERGENCE OF "DRUGS": COLONIAL PRODUCTION, GLOBAL COMMODITIES

Modernization produced changes in work, residence, and politics by fracturing traditional ties of family, kinship, and community (Lyon 1999). Modernity undermined identity, communalism, and face-to-face personal relations in producing a segregation of spheres of life. Workers experienced an alienation from humanity, a social fragmentation and isolation that caused a loss of self-identity with group. The loss of social purpose in a series of pluralized life worlds led to individualism and isolation.

Modernity's forces of factory, bureaucracy, and state changed economy and day-to-day life, increasing work demands and producing stress and dislocation, increasing the needs for drugs as "chemical comforters." Work encouraged stimulant use (particularly caffeine, tobacco, and cocaine) to enhance productivity. Depressants (primarily alcohol for the popular classes, opium for selected groups villanized by society) provided for after-work relaxation. Modernity's emphasis on reason and replacement of religion by science and materialism (Lyon 1999) transformed sacraments and medicines into commodities to alleviate the negative aspects of work and to enhance pleasure. A disruption of community ended communal patterns of substance use that reinforced social solidarity. Capitalism induced a drive for acquisition, particularly of prestige-signaling commodities in drugs such as tobacco, caffeine, and alcohol. Modernization occurred in a broader political context in which capitalism and the military state became the dominant powers in the macro-level political economy. Integral to modernization was the commercialization of drugs as an economic basis for the colonies, as well as a source of taxation revenues for emerging European states, and a visible symbol consumed by the emerging commercial elites of Europe. Modernization made drugs widely available, enabling the development of the concept of addiction and processes of dependence.

Mood-altering consumable commodities, the so-called "food drugs," are those that best characterize modernization's take-off phase of capitalism: coffee, distilled alcohol (rum), tea, tobacco, cacao, and sugar (Mintz 1985). These substances became available for mass consumption as products of colonial enterprises created by the new mercantile class of Europe. These substances entered European consciousness largely as medicines rather than food, beverages, or recreational entertainment (Matthee 1995). These substances were central sources of commercial development during colonization and quickly became common commodities around the world. Except for alcohol, and to a lesser extent tobacco in recent decades, there never was a concerted effort to ban these substances. Nonetheless, since the earliest periods, various forms of regulation, control, and taxation existed. Early modern states developed infrastructures of regulation and control over production, importation, and exportation of these substances to generate revenues through taxation.

These substances were initially scarce and expensive, limiting their consumption to sailors and soldiers, who acquired them directly, and the relatively wealthy, who could afford them. Use of these substances became part of self-definition and a public image among the emerging entrepreneurial elites of Europe and played a role in defining separations based upon class and gender. As supplies increased, their prices fell, making them accessible for mass consumption. European consumption of sugar and chocolate, as the sweetest of "the sweet," and coffee and tea, as "time markers," eventually became low-cost substitutes for a nutritious diet among the common folk in Europe (Mintz 1985). To provide these commodities, European companies developed plantation economies in their colonies for growing sugar cane, cacao, coffee, and tea.

Sugar was readily accepted in Europe, and its consumption was even encouraged by colonial administrations. This reflects its use as "energy" for the human machine within colonial and capitalist enterprises. Coffee became the antithesis of alcohol as a marker of temporal entry into the world of work (morning), with alcohol consumption as the marker of after-work (evening) (Gusfield 1987). Tobacco and alcohol provided relief and alleviated the sense of drudgery in monotonous wage labor, and their use often was encouraged. The commercial production of tobacco was state-subsidized at times, and alcohol often was included as "part-pay" (wages) in several parts of the world (Baer et al. 1997; Goodman 1993).

Prohibition: A modern response

In the late nineteenth and early twentieth centuries, a major differentiation occurred in the conceptualization of substance use that turned them into drugs of abuse. The American response to them, however, differed from that of other industrialized countries. Alcohol and tobacco, while "demonized" medically and socially, remained legally accepted. But cannabis, coca, and opium, and their respective derivatives, became illegal. The fate of coca and opium was due to their metamorphosis in form and mode of administration, which was a result of their technological transformation: from coca to cocaine hydrochloride to crack-cocaine, and from opium to morphine and heroin. These substances with origins outside the United States underwent a process of revision that transformed them from a "medical good" to a "social evil."

The American acceptance of alcohol and tobacco was a result of the deep cultural roots of these substances. Popular attitudes and official US policies towards drugs were strongly shaped by a cultural history that has affected views of mind altering substances. The establishment of the American colonies by Puritans who based their economy upon trade in tobacco and alcohol normalized these substances and produced cultural blinders to their adverse effects. Treating alcohol and tobacco as normal commodities became a part of early American culture, producing a legacy in which we still distinguish them from "drugs," including a limited legal use and a disinclination to call habitual users of alcohol and tobacco "drug addicts." These two food-drugs, combined with coffee and tea stimulants and acquired through colonization and trade, played a central role in the development of modern mentalities and coping mechanisms. The modern industrial society encouraged stimulants to enhance productivity and depressants to counteract their effects and produce leisure time and compensatory pleasure.

Although generally considered appropriate for consumption in moderation, the licit substances of alcohol, coffee, sugar, cacao, tea, and tobacco underwent divergent trajectories during the rise of capitalism. Consumption of coffee, rum, tea, and tobacco at one time was mildly controlled or taxed by the state (e.g., the Tea Tax that spawned the American Revolution). Some substances, such as tobacco and alcohol, were officially discouraged and occasionally considered "illegal" (Baer et al. 1997; Carlson 1996).

Drug prohibition has roots in early nineteenth-century temperance movements that developed in response to widespread excesses and the debilitating effects of distilled spirits (hard liquor). Prohibition sentiments in the United States were stimulated by a Protestant religious revivalism and reaction against Catholic immigrants (Irish, German, Italian), whose respective cultures supported alcohol use. The National Prohibition Act became the 18th Amendment in 1920, making alcohol illegal in the United States. Prohibition produced a market for organized crime activities in supplying alcohol, leading to lawlessness that eventually prompted the repeal of prohibition in 1933.

As the process of individualization of the members of society accompanied the rise of the modern state, the right of individuals to do with their bodies as they wanted was restricted (Berridge 1999; Rudgley 1993). This contributed to the perception of certain substances, specifically heroin and cocaine, as "illicit drugs" that required control and regulation, or as "licit substances" (e.g., alcohol and tobacco) that were prohibited to minors and minorities. These licit substances later required state-sanctioned warnings on appropriate use. The modern era is characterized by citizen-influenced legal initiatives, state-directed police actions, and religion-sanctioned moral campaigns that sought to control and regulate the use of designated substances. Sale and use of opium and its derivatives was unregulated in Great Britain until prescription was limited to physicians through the Pharmacy Act of 1868. US seizure of the Philippines in 1898 brought religious missionaries who were stunned by the massive opiate addiction there and in China. These Puritan missionaries fomented international political action, led by the United States, to make opium and its derivatives illegal. This led directly to significant anti-drug legislation in the Harrison Act of 1914 (US) and the Defense of the Realm Act in 1916 (Britain). These legislative acts were the outgrowth of international concerns, as well as nation-specific efforts and professional testimony. Although there was an international climate of concern over a number of substances, the United States led the world in legislation and control of the "drug problem." This reflected its Puritanical foundations wherein pleasure was a sin, and a growing awareness of the devastating effects of addiction to the newly refined extracts.

The US Constitution was an impediment to the national control of drugs, as recognized in the temperance movement (alcohol prohibition required a constitutional amendment). Control of opiates was achieved by relegating their use to the exclusive domain of physicians, the last segment of society allowed control over distribution of morphine and cocaine (Musto 1999). Use of opiates to enhance health and wellness was transformed into an immoral behavior. They could be used in the due course of medical treatment, but not to maintain addicts. The initial provisions of the Harrison Act of 1914 emphasized professional responsibility for keeping records of the distribution of substances that were deemed potentially harmful. The Act focused primarily upon substances originating outside of the United States, which were the consequence of European technological transformations (cocaine, morphine, and heroin). These substances ultimately became associated with minorities (Page 1999). Opium was "Orientalized" through its association with Chinese immigrants (Musto 1999) and disaffected native-born Westerners (Berridge 1999). It was the first substance to be racialized as its medical potential fell into disfavor. The Chinese in the United States were prohibited from using opium, before broader laws were enacted that affected populations other than Chinese. A racist mentality was central to an ideology that promoted a national ban on cocaine. Prohibition of cocaine was tied to the perception that it was largely a drug of African Americans, and it was responsible for violent attacks against white Americans in the South. Early local laws prohibited cocaine use by African Americans, but not their inclusion in patent medicines consumed by the white population.

Although marijuana was not technologically transformed as occurred with opium and coca leaves, it nonetheless came under scrutiny. Opposition to marijuana use was organized by Randolph Hearst, the publisher, and supported by Harry J. Anslinger, who was Chief of the Bureau of Narcotics. Marijuana was demonized through gross distortions of its effects in the media (such as in the well-known film *Reefer Madness*) and through its association with Mexican nationals in the southwestern United States. When employment became scarce in the 1930s Depression, migrant workers of Mexican origins were perceived as a threat in the Southwest. Their use of marijuana was noted as a means of enflaming public fears, which eventually led to congressional action with the passage of the Marijuana Tax Act of 1937. Lacking constitutional authority to ban its use, Congress established a "stamp tax" for legal possession, but the stamps generally were made unavailable. Federal provisions were used to justify the deportation of Mexicans during the Depression.

POSTMODERN PERSPECTIVES ON DRUGS

The late twentieth century encountered an increase in many aspects of drug use. Increasing illegal drug use during a period of national crisis in the United States in the 1960s led to a powerful modern response, the "War on Drugs." Drug violence grew nationally and internationally as a new global prohibition spawned criminal organizations and massive illegal economies that challenged the powerful nation-states.

The late modern period (late twentieth century) produced a variety of responses to drugs that have challenged modern attitudes. A notable development was the inclusion within the category of "drugs" of some substances previously considered "non-drugs" (e.g., tobacco and alcohol). Alcohol was eventually transformed from a common beverage into a substance used by those whose inner being was "morally bankrupt," to one where the psychosocial self was deemed to be "ill" (Bennett and Cook 1996). Tobacco became associated with persons thwarted (e.g., women and minorities) or delayed (e.g., youth) in passage into the next social status (Baer et al. 1997). In response to the "drug war," an "anti-war" movement focused on the repeal of drug laws that were created by oppressive state powers.

The technologies of modernization also spawned new drugs such as the meth-amphetamines that stimulated the blitzkrieg of Hitler's Panzer divisions. They became popular because they supported work habits and were substituted for the more expensive cocaine. Cocaine became a major drug of abuse, gaining popularity during the 1970s disco era. Widespread addiction occurred as cocaine became the drug of choice of the elite and the entertainment industry (Adler 1993). Cocaine caused financial ruin for its middle-class addicts, and a slide into violent crime, engagement in the sex trade, and incarceration for thousands of inner-city poor who fell victim to its smokeable form, namely, "crack" (Bourgois 1995). Drugs of abuse expanded as new chemical derivatives entered the popular market and became a part of public consciousness (e.g., "designer drugs") (Beck 2000), exemplified by MDMA or "ecstasy." Ecstasy use occurred primarily in "raves," which was a popular movement that involved large groups of people in social activities that generally were clandestine parties (often hidden in abandoned warehouses) that played techno music and lasted from dusk to dawn. These counter-culture forces challenged conventional drug attitudes and cultural preferences of modernization.

Marijuana as drug postmodernization

The twentieth-century manifestations of marijuana in popular youth cultures of the United States and Europe have a decidedly "postmodern" attitude, one of resistance to a dominant rationalist orientation and materialist values. The application of cannabis as a medicine is associated with gay culture, having been used as an appetite stimulant to combat the wasting syndromes and appetite suppression associated with AIDS. Cannabis is used for a variety of ailments: asthma, tension syndromes, epilepsy, labor, and many more physical and psychological conditions. But the dominant use of cannabis remains one of alteration of consciousness and mood. To many, it stands as a symbol of rebellious protest against the establishment. The medicinal applications of cannabis have acquired considerable scientific support in spite of broad prohibitions on the clinical study of its effects and its classification by the Food and Drug

Administration as a Schedule I drug, without accepted medicinal applications. This inaccuracy is attested to by the long clinical history of cannabis use by many contemporary regional and cosmopolitan medical systems (Rätsch 2001) and a growing body of clinical and laboratory research. This indicates applicability as an analgesic and sedative, and for migraines, ulcers and psychoneurological problems, rheumatic conditions, cancers, and delivery and post-partum treatments. Marijuana generally remains a stand-alone substance outside professional discussions of "addiction," despite the fact that its potential for dependence is widely recognized.

Psychointegrator use as a postmodern reaction

The plants with psychointegrator effects had a late-modern impact upon Westerners; the early twentieth-century impacts of peyote and mushrooms of the genus *Psilocybe* were minimal compared to the eventual impact of the synthetic ergot alkaloid LSD (lysergic acid diethylamide). There was, however, a range of other plants used in non-Western cultures which became significant forces affecting modern attitudes towards primarily illicit drugs. Findings from studies of psychointegrator uses suggest that they facilitate psychosocial adaptations to rapid social transformation and psychosocial changes (Andritzky 1989; Aberle 1966; Winkelman 1996). Psychointegrators facilitate mediation between conceptual systems. The genus *Banisteriopsis*, for example, is widely used in the Amazonian basin in collective rituals that strengthen social cohesion and group identity, and assist in the management of acculturation problems by mediating the indigenous worldview and imposed European systems. These substances evoke powerful emotional images that symbolically represent social conflicts between traditional systems and modern systems; in general, they facilitate psychosocial adjustment (Andritzky 1989). The Navajo adoption of the peyote use in the Native American Church (NAC) is another example of a plant substance with consciousness altering properties that nicely illustrates this role in psychosocial adjustment. Early Navajo adherents were primarily those who experienced the greatest relative deprivation in society (Aberle 1966). The NAC facilitated an adjustment of Navajo values, emphasizing collectivism in contrast to the broader societal emphasis on individualism, resisting colonizing influences, while maintaining socially valued community and religious experiences (Calabrese 1997; Wiedman 1990). The NAC assisted in stimulating religious and cultural renewal in disintegrating cultures and produced stable and adaptive communal and psychological relations. The societal dynamics of the use of and reaction to these substances in the 1960s reflects both of these patterns: their use to facilitate adjustment during rampant social change, and the repressive legislation enacted against them by what was the hierarchy of an industrial–military system that sought to control threats to the established political–economic structures and cosmological orders of American culture.

Perspectives on these substances as psychointegrators exemplify a postmodern approach to drugs that challenges a modernist rationalist perspective. This was exemplified by Timothy Leary's approach to LSD, which he advocated for pursuit of religious and spiritual life. The use of psychointegrators among late modern populations has been resistant to modern consciousness. A prominent manifestation is the "rave" scene, where contemporary youth reenact shamanic dynamics of altered consciousness with all-night dancing and music. These dynamics at a "rave" are enhanced by use of similar substances in recent designer drugs (especially "ecstasy"). The return to spirituality, harmony with nature, and a community ethos has exemplified the psychointegrator-inspired ideology that emphasizes a continued evolution of human consciousness through the guiding influences of these substances. The therapeutic applications of these consciousness altering substances continue to be found in traditional ethnomedical systems (Winkelman and Andritzky 1996; Heggenhougen 1997) and similar Western medical practices (Mangini 1998; Winkelman 2001b).

Postmodern considerations have included a natural theology and neuro-theology approach that conceptualizes their neurotransmitter properties as producing innate forms of spiritual consciousness. The observation that these plants combine therapeutic as well as religious and spiritual roles has important implications for understanding human consciousness and mystical experiences (Smith 2000; Grof, 1992; Winkelman 2000). Their ability to produce spiritual experiences, even under laboratory settings (e.g., see Strassman 2001), has made them a cutting-edge tool in forming an uncomfortable link between spirituality and science, particularly consciousness research (Winkelman 2001a). The failure of society to address the spiritual and communal dimensions in a constructive manner has made psychointegrators the most rapidly increasing category of drug that is used among contemporary youth and has elevated discussion of their applicability as a central issue in religious and cognitive freedom. These substances have come to test the limits of American religious freedom; state and Supreme Courts, for example, have ruled that NAC members do not have freedom from prosecution or punishment for the use of classified substances.

ANTHROPOLOGICAL CONTRIBUTIONS TO THE STUDY OF ADDICTION

Anthropological contributions to our knowledge of biocultural processes and cross-cultural differences have been significant in increasing our understanding of drug use and drug addiction. Anthropology expands the medical model that forms the basis of the biology of addiction into an understanding of the evolutionary biology of addiction (Smith 1999). What were the adaptive reasons that selected for a human biological propensity to seek out certain substances and become dependent upon them? Addictive potentials may be an evolutionary byproduct and a general dopamine mechanism (Smith 1999) that produces feelings of euphoria and well-being. These propensities to addiction involve the same brain mechanisms as those producing ASC, suggesting a common basis in the innate drive to seek ASC (Siegal 1990; Winkelman 2000, 2001a, 2001b) and the inevitable complication of becoming addicted. The common biological dynamics that underlie drug induced ASC and other forms of alterations of consciousness illustrate the importance of assessing Western patterns of drug use and dependence in the context of cross-cultural patterns of ASC. The universal distribution of institutionalized practices of ASC and its use for rites of healing (Bourguignon 1973; Winkelman 1986, 1992) reflects a mode of integrative consciousness that is biologically based (Winkelman 2000). This biological basis indicates that all cultures must make some adaptation to an innate quest, and perhaps human need, to induce ASC.

Cultures differ in how they relate institutionally and personally to the experiences and potentials of ASC. While the dominant cultural ethos of Indo-European societies accepted alcohol, nicotine, and caffeine induced alterations of consciousness (along with a range of pharmaceutical anti-depressants and tranquilizers), society has generally ignored expansive forms of consciousness, or subjected those who seek them to pathologization, social marginalization, and persecution. Historically, indigenous Western practices for inducing ASC through plants were persecuted by dominant religious and political groups through accusations of witchcraft (Harner 1973). While religion is the primary context for the institutionalization of ASC in most cultures, dominant churches and denominations of the United States do not utilize ASC, which are primarily manifested in marginal sects and foreign origin cults that practice (clandestinely) in American society. Contemporary Indo-European societies lack central, legitimate institutionalized procedures for accessing ASC. Nonetheless, many forms of ASC are both sought and utilized in contemporary US society, often through harmful or illegal means (e.g., alcohol, tobacco, marijuana, opiates, cocaine, sedatives). Because of an underlying psychobiological basis and need for ASC, when societies fail to sanction or provide legitimate procedures for accessing these states of consciousness, they are sought through other means.

Puritan influences marginalized the acceptance of various forms of ASC in society, demonizing these spiritual and consciousness altering traditions. Puritanical values opposed pleasure and fantasy, contributing to cultural evaluations of drug use as a reflection of moral weakness and deviance. Class relations that entailed the differential use of drugs were changed by the medicalization of society that gradually began in the nineteenth century and accelerated in the early twentieth century. These changes shifted perceptions of drug use from nondescript people who behaved in certain ways (i.e., drug use as a descriptor) to people with specific (generic) identities. These included not only the new category of "addict," but also an increased "racialization" of those who used drugs. The process of racialization characterized drug use problems as a product of groups of people (e.g., Chinese, Blacks, Mexicans) rather than the substances themselves. This trend was extended in a medical–social process of producing pathological deviants out of the users, moving social perceptions from the dangers of foreign substances to strategic concerns about the addict as a social problem. Heggenhougen (1997) points out that one of the problems that conventional rehabilitation programs face is an imposition of these Puritanical cultural values in treating addicts. The view of drug use as sinful and evil has justified a dehumanizing treatment of addicts in rehabilitation programs. Such treatment reinforces a negative self-concept and a psychodynamic that contributes to a continuation of addiction in a process of recovery and relapse.

A contrast to hostile Western attitudes toward most drug induced ASC is found in the view that many cultures have of hallucinogens as "sacred plants" (e.g., see Schultes and Hofmann 1992; Winkelman and Andritzky 1996). Metzner (1994) contrasts Eastern and Western psychospiritual traditions in their approach to addiction recovery, wherein the Western tradition parallels Dante's classic "Descent into Hell," while the Eastern traditions focus on progressive detachment that leads to liberation and transcendence through spiritual practices that enable one to transcend conflicts and reality.

Addiction researchers have suggested that drug abuse and addiction be viewed in the context of a universal human desire to achieve ASC. McPeake et al. (1991) suggest that recovery and prevention of relapse could be enhanced by teaching a recovering individual to experience non-substance induced ASC. These changes in consciousness are considered central to the spiritual awakening that is deemed essential in the Alcoholics Anonymous recovery process, which has been adapted as a central dimension of most drug rehabilitation programs. The incorporation of non-drug practices to deliberately induce ASC could be useful both as a prophylactic against drug abuse, as well as a potential treatment for addiction (Winkelman 2001b). There are many roles for alternative therapies in substance abuse treatment and rehabilitation. These include an alternative to the drug in order to achieve transcendence, a smoother transition to the path of recovery, a social support group, and a set of activities to occupy the addict's time and energies. Any of these aspects can facilitate recovery by easing the physical longing and mental anguish of abstinence, providing a series of productive and supportive activities for the recovering addict, creating a social reference group to modulate affect and support a sense of the self as worthy, which is central to the self-transformation that is essential to recovery. Some alternative substance abuse therapies are based upon the use of psychointegrators (Winkelman 2001b; Sanchez-Ramos and Mash 1996).

The cross-cultural investigation of drug use has had significant influences upon the broader society. The postmodern resurgence of psychointegrators as "entheogens" is an approach inspired by the perspectives of other cultures. The cultural views of plants as sacred substances were an ideological foundation for the LSD movement of the 1960s. Anthropology's data and perspectives on ASC inspired a broader openness towards and tolerance of these drug induced altered states, reversing their characterization as demonic influences and reestablishing their roles as spiritual and consciousness transforming agents. Ethnographic and experiential data on drug and ASC traditions have revealed a great complexity of human self-awareness, expanding our models of human nature and characteristics of personality. The potential for these substances to serve as therapeutic agents has been accelerated by perspectives of medical anthropology and a recognition that these agents have significant therapeutic applications (Winkelman and Andritzky 1996; Winkelman 2001b).

CONCLUSION: DRUG MODERNIZATION

The introduction of drugs into European society typically occurred through direct agents of colonization: sailors, military personnel, and entrepreneurs. The emergence of a new drug combination that often was used jointly or in tandem, namely, a stimulant (e.g., coffee, tea, cocaine) and a depressant (e.g., alcohol and opiates), occurred in a secular context that was increasingly individualizing rather than communal. The importance of drugs expanded in the modern era, creating massive economies in both legal substances (alcohol, coffee, and tobacco) and illegal substances (marijuana, heroin, cocaine, amphetamines, and psychointegrators). The role of substances that alter consciousness underwent dramatic changes in the process of transformation from premodern traditional societies with communitarian cultures to modern anomic society that is concentrated in cosmopolitan (urban) centers. This process involved a transformation of substances that had important sacred, ritual, and secular functions in other cultures, into secular and addictive patterns of use that predate the modernization of European societies. The process of modernization produced a loss of spiritual and communal patterns of the use of these substances for expansion of consciousness. Decontextualization of these drugs from their traditional ceremonial patterns, combined with the technological transformation of their effects through the refinement of their modes of administration, changed them from consciousness raising and community enhancing sacraments to addictive drugs. Human demand for these substances has created an illegal infrastructure within informal economies that challenges legitimate political systems. Legitimate and illegitimate uses constitute public health problems of a magnitude that ranks among the leading causes of death in modern industrialized societies, particularly in high rates of mortality from long-term use of tobacco and alcohol related automobile fatalities. Social prohibitions have not eliminated the natural drive to alter consciousness. The form in which people and communities seek consciousness alteration has generated an industry and a culture of risk reduction education and harm reduction approaches to managing drugs and their consequences.

REFERENCES

Aberle, David, 1966 *The Peyote Religion Among the Navaho*. Chicago: Aldine.

Adler, Patricia, 1993 *Wheeling and Dealing: An Ethnography of an Upper-Level Drug Dealing and Smuggling Community*. New York: Columbia University Press.

Andritzky, Walter, 1989 Sociopsychotherapeutic Functions of Ayahuasca Healing in Amazonia. *Journal of Psychoactive Drugs* 21 (1): 77–89.

Arnold, Bettina, 1999 "Drinking the Feast": Alcohol and the Legitimization of Power in Celtic Europe. *Cambridge Archaeological Journal* 9 (1): 71–93.

Baer, Hans, A. Merrill Singer, and Ida Susser, 1997 *Medical Anthropology and the World System: A Critical Perspective*. Westport, CT: Bergin and Garvey.

Beck, J., 2000 MDMA in the USA: An Epidemiological Overview. *Yearbook for Ethnomedicine and the Study of Consciousness 1997/1998* 6 (7): 127–136.

Bennett, Linda, and Paul W. Cook, Jr. 1996 Alcohol and Drug Studies. In *Medical Anthropology: Contemporary Theory and Method*. Carolyn F. Sargent and Thomas M. Johnson, eds. Pp. 235–251. Westport, CT: Praeger.

Berridge, Virginia, 1999 *Opium and the People: Opiate Use and Drug Control Policy in Nineteenth and Early Twentieth Century England*. New York: Free Association Books.

Bourgois, Philippe, 1995 *In Search of Respect: Selling Crack in El Barrio*. Cambridge: Cambridge University Press.

Bourguignon, Erika, 1973 Introduction: A Framework for the Comparative Study of Altered States of Consciousness. In *Religion, Altered States of Consciousness, and Social Change*. Erika Bourguignon, ed. Pp. 3–35. Columbus: Ohio State University Press.

Calabrese, Joseph D., II, 1997 Spiritual Healing and Human Development in the Native American Church: Toward a Cultural Psychiatry of Peyote. *Psychoanalytic Review* 84 (2): 237–255.

Carlson, Robert G., 1996 The Political Economy of AIDS among Drug Users in the United States: Beyond Blaming the Victim or Powerful Others. *American Anthropologist* 98: 266–278.

Courtwright, David T., 2001 *Dark Paradise: A History of Opiate Addiction in America*. Cambridge, MA: Harvard University Press.

Dobkin de Rios, Marlene, 1984 *Hallucinogens: Cross-Cultural Perspectives*. Albuquerque: University of New Mexico Press.

Dobkin de Rios, Marlene, and David E. Smith, 1977 Drug Use and Abuse in Cross-Cultural Perspective. *Human Organization* 36 (1): 14–21.

Friman, Richard, and Peter Andreas, eds., 1999 *The Illicit Global Economy and State Power.* Lanham, MD: Rowman and Littlefield.

Fuller, Robert, C. 2000 *Stairways to Heaven: Drugs in American Religious History.* Boulder, CO: Westview Press.

Furst, Peter, T. ed., 1976 *Hallucinogens and Culture.* San Francisco: Chandler and Sharp.

Goodman, Jordan, 1993 *Tobacco in History: The Cultures of Dependence.* London: Routledge.

Gootenberg, Paul (ed.), 1999 *Cocaine: Global Histories.* London: Routledge.

Grob, Charles, and Marlene Dobkin de Rios, 1992 Adolescent Drug Use in Cross-Cultural Perspective. *Journal of Drug Issues* 22 (1): 121–138.

Grof, Stanislav, 1992 *The Holotropic Mind.* San Francisco: Harper Collins.

Gusfield, Joseph R., 1987 Passage to Play: Rituals of Drinking Time in American Society. In *Constructive Drinking.* Mary Douglas, ed. Pp. 73–90. Cambridge: Cambridge University Press.

Harner, Michael (ed.), 1973 *Hallucinogens and Shamanism.* New York: Oxford University Press.

Heath, Dwight B., 1994 Agricultural Changes and Drinking Among the Bolivian Camba *Human Organization* 53 (4): 357–360.

Heggenhougen, Kris, 1997 *Reaching New Highs: Alternative Therapies for Drug Addicts.* Northvale, NJ: Jason Aronson.

Janin, Hunt, 1999 *The India–China Opium Trade in the Nineteenth Century.* Jefferson, NC: McFarland.

La Barre, Weston, 1972 Hallucinogens and the Shamanic Origins of Religion. In *Flesh of the Gods.* Peter Furst, ed. Pp. 261–278. New York: Praeger.

Laughlin, Charles D. Jr., McManus, John, and d'Aquili, Eugene E., 1992 *Brain, Symbol and Experience: Toward a Neurophenomenology of Consciousness.* Boston, MA: Shambhala. Reprinted by Columbia University Press.

Lyon, David, 1999 *Postmodernity.* Minneapolis: University of Minnesota Press.

McKenna, Terence, 1992 *Food of the Gods: The Search for the Original Tree of Knowledge: A Radical History of Plants, Drugs, and Human Evolution.* New York: Bantam Books.

McPeake, John D., Kennedy, Bruce P., and Gordon, Sharon M., 1991 Altered States of Consciousness Therapy: A Missing Component in Alcohol and Drug Rehabilitation Treatment. *Journal of Substance Abuse Treatment* 8: 75–82.

Mangini, Mariavittoria, 1998 Treatment of Alcoholism Using Psychedelic Drugs: A Review of the Program of Research. *Journal of Psychoactive Drugs* 30 (4): 381–418.

Marshall, Mac, 1993 A Pacific Haze: Alcohol and Drugs in Oceania. In *Contemporary Pacific Societies.* Victoria S. Lockwood and Thomas G. Harding, eds. Pp. 260–272. New York: Prentice-Hall.

Matthee, Rudi, 1995 Exotic Substances: The Introduction and Global Spread of Tobacco, Cocoa, Tea and Distilled Liquor, Sixteenth to Eighteenth Centuries. In *Drugs and Narcotics in History.* Roy Porter and Mikulás Teich, eds. Pp. 24–51. Cambridge: Cambridge University Press, 1995.

Metzner, Ralph, 1994 Addiction and Transcendence as Altered States of Consciousness. *Journal of Transpersonal Psychology* 26 (1): 1–17.

Mintz, Sidney, 1985 *Sweetness and Power.* New York: Penguin Books.

Musto, David, F., 1999 *The American Disease: Origins of Narcotic Control.* New York: Oxford University Press.

Page, J., Bryan, 1999 Historical Overview of Other Abusable Drugs. In *Prevention and Societal Impact of Drug and Alcohol Abuse.* Robert T. Ammerman, Peggy J. Ott, and Ralph E. Tarter, eds. Pp. 47–63. Mahweh, NJ: Erlbaum.

Rätsch, Christian, 2001 *Marijuana Medicine: A World Tour of the Healing and Visionary Powers of Cannabis*. Rochester, VT: Healing Arts Press.

Rudgley, Richard, 1993 *The Alchemy of Culture: Intoxicants in Society*. London: British Museum Press.

Sanchez-Ramos, Juan, and Deborah Mash, 1996 Pharmacotherapy of Drug Dependence with Ibogain. In *Yearbook of Cross-Cultural Medicine, Vol. 5: Sacred Plants, Consciousness and Healing*. Michael Winkelman and Walter Andritzky, eds. Pp. 353–367. Berlin: Verlag.

Scarborough, John, 1995 The Opium Poppy in Hellenistic and Roman Medicine. In *Drugs and Narcotics in History*. Roy Porter and Mikulás Teich eds. Pp. 4–23. Cambridge: Cambridge University Press.

Schultes, Richard Evans, and Albert Hofmann, 1992 [1979] *Plants of the Gods*: Origins of Hallucinogenic use. Rochester, VT: Healing Arts Press.

Sherratt, Andrew, 1991 Sacred and Profane Substances: The Ritual Use of Narcotics in Later Neolithic Europe. In *Sacred and Profane*. Paul Garwood, David Jennings, Robin Skeates, and Judith Toms, eds. Pp. 50–64. Oxford: Oxbow Books.

Siegel, Ronald K., 1990 *Intoxication: Life in Pursuit of Artificial Paradise*. New York: Dutton.

Smith, Euclid O., 1999 Evolution, Substance Abuse, and Addiction. In *Evolutionary Medicine*. Wenda R. Trevathan, Euclid O., Smith, and James J. McKenna, eds. Pp. 375–405. New York: Oxford University Press.

Smith, Huston, 2000 *Cleansing the Doors of Perception: The Religious Significance of Entheogenic Plants and Chemicals*. New York: J. P. Tarcher.

Strassman, Rich, 2001 *DMT: The Spirit Molecule*. Rochester, VT: Park Street Press.

Wiedman, Dennis, 1990 Big and Little Moon Peyotism as Health Care Delivery Systems. *Medical Anthropology* 12: 371–387.

Wilbert, Johannes, 1987 *Tobacco and Shamanism in South America*. New Haven, CT: Yale University Press.

Winkelman, Michael, 1986 Magico-religious Practitioner Types and Socioeconomic Conditions. *Behavior Science Research* 20 (1–4): 17–46.

— 1991 Physiological, Social, and Functional Aspects of Drug and Non-Drug Altered States of Consciousness. In *Yearbook of Cross-Cultural Medicine and Psychotherapy*, Vol. 1. Pp.183–198. Berlin: Verlag.

— 1992 Shamans, Priests, and Witches: A Cross-Cultural Study of Magico-Religious Practitioners. Tempe, AZ: Anthropological Research Papers 44.

— 1996 Psychointegrator Plants: Their Roles in Human Culture and Health. In *Yearbook of Cross-Cultural Medicine and Psychotherapy, Vol. 5: Sacred Plants, Consciousness, and Healing*. Michael Winkelman and Walter Andritzky, eds. Pp. 9–53. Berlin: Verlag.

— 2000 *Shamanism: The Neural Ecology of Consciousness and Healing*. Westport, CT: Bergin and Garvey.

— 2001a Psychointegrators: Multidisciplinary Perspectives on the Therapeutic Effects of Hallucinogens. *Complementary Health Practice Review* 6 (3): 219–237.

— 2001b Alternative and Complementary Medicine Approaches to Substance Abuse: A Shamanic Perspective. *International Journal of Drug Policy* 12: 337–351.

Winkelman, Michael, and Walter Andritzky, eds., 1996 *Yearbook of Cross-Cultural Medicine and Psychotherapy, Vol. 5: Sacred Plants, Consciousness, and Healing*. Berlin: Verlag.

CHAPTER 19

Ritual Practice and Its Discontents

Don Seeman

Religious ritual has not always fared well in social theory. It has been metaphorized, pathologized, in some cases even demonized (Frankfurter 2002), but rarely taken seriously on its own terms. Even anthropology, which certainly has been the most sympathetic of the academic disciplines, has in practice often helped to reproduce misleading cultural biases concerning ritual activity. It is not entirely surprising, as Asad (1993) points out, that the popular dichotomy in the Western intellectual tradition between authentic, "spontaneous" experience and the imposed quality of ritual sentiment has been taken up in social analysis. Nor is it any wonder, given the specific religious history of the modern West, that ritual modes of being-in-the-world have tended to be collapsed into accounts of disembodied symbolism and discursive meaning, the flesh become word. Overwhelmingly, ritual practice has been portrayed as a burden of *other* cultures or of other times. Psychology and anthropology both have deployed ritual as an icon for the primitive Barbaric or Arcadian realms through which they staked (and continue to stake) their overlapping and competing claims to expert knowledge of human affairs (Kuper 1988; Lucas and Barrett 1995). It is impossible, in fact, to describe the current situation of psychocultural anthropology without returning to the analysis of ritual practice with which its two constitutive parent disciplines – psychology and anthropology – each effectively began.

DECIPHERING RITUAL

"I am certainly not the first," Sigmund Freud wrote in 1907, "to be struck by the resemblance between what are called obsessive acts in neurotics and those religious observances by means of which the faithful give expression to their piety" (Freud 1963: 17). In this one sentence, Freud gave voice to a persistent suspicion that ritual practice and neurotic behavior share a similar if not common etiology, and that similar hermeneutic tools can therefore be applied to their interpretation. This was merely the opening frame in a set of arguments that Freud was to develop at length over the course of his later works, but my interest here is less in Freud's own intellectual history than in the legacy of his analytical style for future psychocultural research. Freud's belief that ritual practice must be deciphered as a *symptom* of hidden psychic realities continues to exercise its influence in a variety of ways today. In some cases, religious ritual is still treated as literally a symptom of disorder, but I have in mind also the much more subtle belief that ritual activity derives primarily from intrapsychic processes that take place unobserved and deep within the self, and that this is where analysis should begin.

For Freud, evidence for the similarity or even identity of religious ritual and neurotic behavior was prima facie. Both kinds of activity were characterized by seemingly meaningless repetition and by a powerful inner sense of compulsion or guilt which he attributed to the incomplete suppression of instinctual drives, especially incestuous sexual desire. According to Freud's "hydraulic" conception, neurosis expressed the powerful resistance of problematic memories or instinctual drives that individuals sought to suppress, but which therefore welled up in symbolic form. A girl whose neurosis involved endless hand washing might, for instance, be suppressing a sexual desire or memory that required cleansing. Psychoanalysis taught that neuroses such as these could be deprived of their powerful eruptive capacity in human affairs only once their sources had been revealed. Psychoanalysis became a kind of therapeutic archaeology through which patient and healer cooperated in the retrieval of a vanished past.

Drawing on the work of nineteenth-century theorists like Charles Darwin and W. Robertson Smith, Freud would eventually come to construct an elaborate theory of ritual phenomena, but in 1907 his comparisons between ritual and neurotic behavior were all the more forceful for their bluntness. He viewed neurosis as "the pathological counterpart to the formation of a religion" (i.e., "a private religious system") and described religion as a "universal . . . neurosis" (Freud 1963: 25). While interpreters have argued over whether Freud necessarily meant to imply that ritual is always therefore pathogenic (Bell 1997: 15), one thing at least is clear. The analogy between collective ritual and private neurosis means that rituals do not have *interpretations* for Freud so much as they have etiologies in the clinical sense, stories of (pathological) causality that can be projected backwards in time to a primary antecedent. Since psychoanalysis promised to explain the origins of ritual in this sense, it was also perforce a theory of human culture, and it was perhaps the first such theory to explicitly link illness, ritual, and the roots of human subjectivity within a single analytical frame.

Between 1912 and 1913, Freud delivered the lectures that would become the basis for *Totem and Taboo*, in which he first laid out his complete theory of human psychic prehistory. He showed relatively little interest in Darwin's influential work on the *physical* origin of species, but he did adopt a single Darwinian speculation according to which early humans might have lived in small bands dominated by a single reproductive male, not unlike certain contemporary primates. By itself, this speculation might not have proven overly suggestive, but Freud linked it with a set of assumptions about *social* evolution which he had derived from his reading of evolutionary anthropology, including Robertson Smith's 1889 book *Religion of the Semites*. Some twenty years before *Totem and Taboo* was written, Smith had marshaled linguistic and ethnological evidence for his argument that ancient Semitic societies had at one time passed through a so-called "totemic phase" of development that preceded civilization. Given Robertson Smith's evolutionary proclivities, this also meant by implication that *all* human societies had passed through a totemic phase at some point. It was this account of allegedly universal human origins that would later fascinate Sigmund Freud, even though it had already lost favor by then among many evolutionists (Kuper 1988).

Nineteenth-century evolutionary anthropology had appropriated the word "totem" from the Ojibwa language, where it referred to the animal species with which different exogamous ("out-marrying") clans in Ojibwa society identified themselves. In addition to the prohibition on marriage within each clan, clan members observed a prohibition or taboo against killing and eating the totem animal (which was often described as an ancestor of the group) except on special ritual occasions. For Freud, these prohibitions suggested a symbolic reenactment of some foundational event, which he understood in psychological rather than purely historical terms. He reasoned that the dominant male of the "primal horde" in which human life began would have monopolized sexual access to all of the females in the group, and that his sons would one day have had to kill him if they wanted to mate. Seized with remorse, as well as with dread that a similar fate might befall any one of them, however, they soon banded together in a clan to share power among themselves, and renounced sexual access to the females of their own clan to avoid competition. The first incest prohibition and the first complex society thus came into being together, and they were both the result of a guilty conscience. The sons of the primal father sought "on the one hand to atone for the act of parricide," according to Freud's theory, "and on the other to consolidate the advantages it had brought" (Freud 1952: 77), and their ensuing ambivalence was literally inherited by subsequent generations.

Given this reconstruction, it is easy to see why Freud accorded such special status to totemic ritual. The totem animal from which the clan claimed to be descended clearly "stood for" the primal father, according to Freud, and so it was protected, but also occasionally ritually killed. Similar Oedipal ambivalence could be sublimated and expressed diffusely in all manner of "poetry, religion and philosophy" (1952: 77), but ritual practice was its real epicenter, to which Freud and his students continually returned. In a daring gesture for his time, Freud even went so far as to argue that the abstract father God of monotheistic religions was a kind of totemic figure writ large, and that familiar European rituals could therefore be understood, no less than "primitive" religions, on the totemic model. Christian communion could be deciphered as a kind of "totemic feast" expressing the suppressed desire of sons to kill and consume their fathers, while Jewish circumcision rites expressed the parallel desire of fathers to kill, but also to nurture their sons (Reik 1946: 10, 117).

Freud and his students showed great ingenuity in adapting different ritual expressions to psychoanalytic exegesis without necessarily belaboring the details or contexts of particular practices. Theodore Reik and Geza Róheim each published ethnological studies on ritual across cultures, offering psychoanalytic interpretations of a wide variety of different practices, but never explaining why some societies should favor certain rituals in this scheme over others (Reik 1946; Róheim 1943, 1971). Reik casually dismisses native explanations of particular ritual practices (like the assertion by members of some societies that circumcision promotes male virility, for example) and argues instead that these beliefs are psychic "defenses" which act to shield indi-viduals against the recognition of unpalatable psychological truths. Reik himself makes use of native explanations when they seem to support psychoanalytic expectations, however. He approvingly cites the view of a medieval Jewish exegete, for example, who claimed that circumcision helps to curtail the sex drive, although Reik interprets this comment as a veiled reference to fathers' ambivalence toward their sons' castration (1946: 55–56, 118). Rituals may vary, in other words, but they point to an invariant set of psychic dilemmas that can always with ingenuity be discovered.

Neither Freud nor Reik was apparently well acquainted with the work of contem-porary anthropologists like Franz Boas (Manson 1986: 72), whose relativistic notion of culture would increasingly be invoked to challenge or modify the universalistic presumptions of evolutionary anthropology. Like the evolutionists with whom he argued, Boas wanted to study the historical development of human societies, but he eschewed the claim that universal mechanisms drove social change in a single direction. "The causal conditions of cultural happenings," he wrote, "lie always in the interac-tion between individual and society, and no classificatory study of societies will solve this problem" (Boas 1940: 257). This manifesto for anthropology set it invariably at odds with social evolutionism and at least to some extent with the assumptions then prevailing in psychoanalytic theory. The problem of "interaction between individual and society" of which Boas spoke would later be taken up with great energy by some of his students under the rubric of "culture and personality" studies (more on which below). But it was Boas's insistence on detailed and holistic studies of par-ticular societies and their cultures which came above all to define the new discipline of cultural anthropology.

The divergence between psychoanalytic and cultural approaches to the study of ritual since Boas has been pronounced, even when advocates of psychoanalysis have attempted to take culture into account. Orhan M. Ozturk, a psychiatrist from Turkey, argues that the public nature of circumcision rituals in that Muslim society transforms circumcision into an important ego need for boys, despite the "castration anxiety" with which it is still inevitably associated (Ozturk 1973). While his view represents a clear departure from the narrow account of circumcision championed by Reik, it still falls short of the cultural relativism advocated by many cultural anthropologists, who tend to argue that such practices should be viewed within the context of local gender ideologies, social hierarchies, and metaphors of reproduc-tion. Ritual metaphors that have been relevant in some societies include the need to "open" or to "prune" male bodies for fruitfulness (Boddy 1989; Goldberg 1996; Seeman 1998), and this is precisely the kind of argument that Reik dismisses as a psychological "defense" in his analysis.

In one anthropological study conducted in northern Sudan, Janice Boddy (1989) found that villagers viewed male circumcision and clitoridectomy of women as parallel operations, designed to emphasize the differently gendered nature of "open" male and "closed" female bodies. But she also found that these practices could hardly be interpreted without reference to a wider *political* understanding of the place of Sudan within a global Muslim context and history of European colonialism. It is impossible to discuss the local meaning of female genital surgery, for example, with-out knowing that the British colonial government turned this practice into a mark of local resistance by trying to forcibly prevent it, and that this has made the issue especially complicated for local women's rights activists. This kind of reading does not necessarily contradict a psychoanalytic view, but it shifts attention from allegedly intrapsychic and subconscious *causes* of rituals to their rich and historically contingent *meanings* within a particular cultural frame. It may originally have been social evolutionism that helped to distinguish early psychoanalytic and cultural approaches to the study of ritual, but the distinction has survived evolutionism's demise. Simply put, it can be said that anthropologists in the spirit of Boas have attempted to *interpret* ritual like a text (even before the advent of self-consciously interpretive trends in anthropological thinking), while psychoanalytic thinkers and those anthropologists most influenced by them have attempted to *decipher* ritual like a code. It is worth spending a moment to clarify this distinction.

Freud's reliance on Robertson Smith's theory of "totemism" was problematic not just because it presumed a historical narrative that no longer seems credible to most observers, but because it viewed the meaning of ritual practice almost exclusively as an encoding of lost origins. Like historical philology, by which it was inspired, nineteenth-century anthropology sought to "recover a vanished past from vestiges unconsciously preserved in living languages, detectable only to those who could decipher the signs" (Trautmann 1987: 73). Kinship theorists like Lewis Henry Morgan scoured the terminology of supposedly primitive peoples for clues as to how those people had once organized their societies, but paid little attention to the actual uses of kinship nomenclature in contemporary social life. Thus, societies that deployed "classificatory kinship" language (i.e., societies in which all members of the ascendant generation are referred to as "mother" or "father," for example) were thought to have preserved in their language a trace of primitive "group marriage" which once made the determination of biological parenthood difficult. No one working in this research paradigm thought to ask what such usage might have meant to the people who used it in their contemporary social lives, or how it might be related integrally with other aspects of their culture.

It is important to emphasize that scholars like Lewis Henry Morgan were *not* arguing that group marriage could still be observed in the cultures that they studied, but that the *signs* of these realities were preserved like fossils in the languages that primitive peoples still used. Even more important for our purposes than the evolutionary assumptions they all shared, therefore, was the tendency of nineteenth-century scholars to interpret cultural materials reductively, and to tear language from the contexts of its use. "Semantics," writes Al-Azmeh in a related context, "thus gives way to an abstract lexicalism, and the unfounded assumption is made that the meaning of words, of terms . . . no less than of dogmas, of texts, and of statements, are univocal, and can therefore be uncovered once their origin has been exposed" (1993: 135). This is precisely analogous to the logic that Reik adopted in his study on ritual, which he took to be the most slowly changing aspect of religion and hence "an avenue of expression for underlying psychological [i.e., primitive] impulses that are only with difficulty discoverable by other means" (1946: 17–19).

Ritual was thought, in other words, to be like the kinship terminology of savages or the ceremonials of obsessive patients which provide clues as to their own origins but have no meaning at all, in a strict sense, for social actors in the here and now. This erasure of poetics – of concern with the ways in which meaning is created and deployed in different contexts by social actors – allowed Freud and Reik to collapse ritual into a rigid causal or etiological code that required deciphering. But I will argue that non-evolutionary approaches may fall into the same trap if they reduce ritual to a code for allegedly cultural categories that are in fact far removed from the social poetics of everyday life (Herzfeld 1987; Bauman and Briggs 1990). This is in fact the danger inherent to psychocultural anthropology, which promises to balance the strengths of two competing disciplines (psychology and anthropology) but always risks falling prey to the reductive tendencies that are inherent to each.

RITUAL AND THE APOTHEOSIS OF CULTURE

Despite their sometimes vociferous disagreements, early psychoanalysts and cultural anthropologists shared some basic assumptions. Theodore Reik argued that the fate of "races" was dependent on the influence of two factors, namely innate disposition of individuals and "precipitate experience" (essentially race history), which together endowed people with specific gifts and talents (1946: 20). The "culture and personality" school that grew up among the students of Boas and their contemporaries rejected "race" as a matter of principle, yet they sometimes made strikingly similar dichotomous claims. Margaret Mead (1963), for example, argued individuals are shaped by innate disposition and by "culture," which meant the repository of all the beliefs, practices, and taken-for-granted knowledge about the world that were shared by a bounded social group. Because culture is learned rather than inherited, culture and personality theorists were far more sanguine than "race scientists" about the possibilities for social engineering and reform. But "culture" in Mead's sense and "precipitate experience" in Reik's played structurally similar roles in social theory, and could be used, as Stocking (1986) has argued, to advance similarly deterministic accounts of human affairs.

A good example is the way in which some anthropologists stamped whole societies with stereotypical and practically inescapable "personality types" allegedly imposed through cultural training at a young age. Individuals appear in culture and personality texts like those authored by Margaret Mead and Ruth Benedict primarily as apotheoses of sovereign cultural ideals or as examples of social "deviance" that require explanation. If ritual was previously reduced to a lexical expression of psychic and evolutionary history, it now ran the risk of reduction to an all-encompassing cultural ethos of which it was the almost mechanical expression. Ruth Benedict famously distinguished between the stately "Apollonian" culture of the Zuni pueblos and the ecstatic "Dionysian" culture of the Kwakiutl, and it is worth noting that her account of each begins with characteristic ritual practices and the diffuse ethos they supposedly signify. In many passages, she identifies culture almost reflexively with these distinctive rituals, and with the image of unchanging, bounded unity that collective practices seem to entail. "Their culture has not disintegrated," she writes of the pueblo Zuni. "Month by month and year by year, the old dances of the gods are danced in the stone villages" (1959: 62).

The "disintegration" of culture which Benedict feared was marked, conversely, by the loss or disruption of ritual patterns, and was identified with moral dystopia and social as well as mental breakdown. No longer conceived as analogous to pathology as it had been for Freud, ritual practice was now idealized as a means to (and expression of) cultural well-being. Another way of saying this might be that ritual *worked* for writers in the culture and personality school to the extent that it helped to shore up the hegemony of culture and to increase the ability of individuals to live happily within it. As a proxy for the too abstract concept of culture adopted in early anthropology, ritual was sometimes deployed in anthropological writing as a sort of icon for the social conformity in which mental health and social integration were thought to be achieved. This is not to say that preservation of ritual practice would have seemed unimportant to pueblo Zuni struggling under the pressure of white society, or that their ability to go on "dancing in the old stone villages" cannot be viewed as an expression of cultural resilience. But because ritual was treated almost exclusively as a canonical form that worked to reproduce stable sets of inherent meanings, Benedict's approach ran the risk of lexical reduction no less than that of psychoanalysis.

It is important to emphasize that both Mead and Benedict were painfully aware of the coercive and sometimes literally "sickening" power of culture over individuals whose inherent dispositions put them at odds with accepted social norms. Mead's 1935 *Sex and Temperament* explicitly critiqued the narrow range of gender roles allowed to men and women in American culture, and went so far as to argue this narrowness would exact a cost in the mental health and well-being of individuals who could not fit in. Not incidentally, Mead was probably the first anthropologist to direct attention toward the intimate daily rituals of child rearing and to argue that these rituals were uniquely important for determining the psychological and cultural development of children. Her short ethnographic film *Baby Washing in Three Societies* compares daily rituals in Bali, New Guinea, and the United States, but it is tellingly only in the American example that Mead represents the possibility of change over time as women become influenced by more "progressive" theories of childcare. Despite the powerful critiques of their own cultures launched by Benedict and Mead, they refrained from critiquing the culture concept as such and this critique, left to their colleague Edward Sapir, has important consequences for the remainder of my argument.

Sapir was involved to a much greater degree than most of Boas's other students in the attempt to build formal disciplinary bridges between anthropology and psychology (Darnell 1986). Perhaps because of his strong psychological interests (but also partly in defiance of them) he became disturbed by the seeming inability of cultural anthropology to deal with the complexities of individual experience, by which he did not necessarily mean psychological categories. Sapir resisted the attempt to ascribe "personality types" to whole societies as Mead and Benedict had done (Handler 1986), and argued "cultures . . . are merely abstracted configurations of idea and action patterns, which have endlessly different meanings for the various individuals in the group" (Sapir 1956: 200–201). This was a radical critique (and for that reason perhaps largely ignored) because it called for a whole new approach to anthropological data.

Sapir was *not* arguing for culture-free analysis of human affairs, but he was concerned that the "distributive locus" of culture in anthropological writing tended to reify its object, and thus to distract attention from "the configuration of experience, both actual and potential, in the life of the [specific] person being appealed to" (1956: 200–201). For Sapir, who was an accomplished linguist, culture was more like a grammar than like a code, since each individual uses culture to express things that *could not have been predicted* from the grammar alone. "It is not the concept of culture which is subtly misleading," he wrote in 1932, "but the metaphysical locus to which culture is generally assigned" (Sapir 1985: 509).

It may be useful to think about the shift from evolutionary to cultural paradigms in anthropology as a shift in the kind of spatial or directional metaphors that could most usefully be employed. While evolutionary anthropologists and later psychoanalysts sought to excavate some version of the vanished past, working on a vertical or depth metaphor, cultural anthropologists traveled laterally "to the field," and almost always began their ethnographies with accounts of these professionally legitimating journeys. Recent authors have critiqued both the anthropological identification of culture with geography (Gupta and Ferguson 1992) and the notion of discrete, bounded, and impermeable cultures which this identification seems to entail.

Building on this critique for psychocultural research, Gilles Bibeau (1997) recently called for a new research agenda in cultural psychiatry that will better be attuned to the "creolizing" of cultures in a modern, globalizing world. But even Bibeau's useful set of suggestions fall short of Sapir's more radical claim that the idea of culture has *always* been an abstraction and that the proper locus of anthropological study has always been the human actors in whose lives cultural significance appears. Still poised uneasily between lateral and depth approaches to the study of human beings, psychocultural research in its various forms seems to resist rethinking along the lines that Sapir advocated.

This resistance is especially striking in the work of an anthropologist like Richard A. Shweder, whose "lateral" style of cultural reasoning (or as he puts it, "thinking through cultures") invokes Sapir at every turn. Shweder self-consciously undertakes and radicalizes the culture and personality project first undertaken by students of Boas. Culture does not merely influence psychological development, according to Shweder, as Mead or Benedict might have claimed, but actually constitutes the so-called "psyche" which psychologists have sought. Psyche, for Shweder, is simply the "intentional person" who chooses and undergoes, while "culture" is the "intentional world" in which such persons do so. Shweder has no need and finds no evidence for "deep and invariant psychological laws or processes of motivation, affect, and intellect," and no principle of psychic unity upon which cross-cultural analysis can rely (Shweder 1991: 90). He calls his approach a "polytheistic" one because it affirms that there are as many kinds of human psychology as there are human cultures, and because he insists that each of these can be understood only on its own terms.

Not surprisingly, Shweder focuses a good deal of his discussion on religious ritual as an icon of the essential *difference* that underlies various cultural ways of being human. But his emphasis is also on the ways in which different rituals express potentially universal human experiences:

> Orthodox Hindus in India . . . have, as intentional beings for thousands of years reflected on the relationship between moral action and outcome, on hierarchy . . . on sanctity and pollution. The more we try to conceive of an intentional world in their intentional terms, the more their doctrines and rituals and art forms . . . come to seem like sophisticated expressions of repressed, dormant, and potentially creative and transformative aspects of our own psyche pushed off by our intentional world to some mental fringe. (Shweder 1991: 108)

"We [Westerners] do not know quite how to acknowledge the experience of personal sanctity," continues Shweder, "yet we feel it." Hindu ritual is one powerful means of focusing that experience or casting it into sharper relief. "Personal sanctity" emerges here not as a culture-specific *concept*, as in ethnopsychology, but as a dimension of human experience energized by ritual, upon which some cultures choose to build.

One of the problems with Shweder's approach to ritual is that it tends to idealize the authorized interpretations of privileged groups. Ritual, as Geertz (1977: 112) has taught, helps to create the lived sense that some particular conception of the world is "really real" by "somehow generating" the long lasting moods and motivations that constitute religion from a cultural point of view. The notion of personal sanctity that Shweder describes may in fact draw on thousands of years of reflection by Hindus about the relation between moral action and outcome, as he suggests. But it should be clear that people in specific social positions undertook this reflection, and that the *same* practices may therefore carry rather different meanings when viewed from elsewhere in social space. Lawrence Cohen (1992) argues for instance that many lower caste Hindus actually experience the purity regime as an expression of structural violence and vulnerability vis-à-vis higher status groups. Shweder cites Sapir's 1929 comment to the effect that "the worlds in which different societies live are distinct worlds, not merely the same world with different labels attached" (Shweder 1991: 97, 155, 292, 362), but he fails simultaneously to grapple with Sapir's powerful interrogation of culture's "metaphysical locus," as Cohen does through his focus on lived experience. The result is that ritual practice emerges for Shweder primarily as an ideal form, divorced from the messy but overbearing practical relevance (Kleinman and Seeman 1998) that alone transforms it into a "social fact."

Not surprisingly, psychoanalytically oriented anthropologists have criticized Shweder for "disavowing human nature" and for reducing the psyche to "internalized cultural ideas and propositions." From John Ingham's point of view, for example, Shweder's "cultural psychology lacks a compelling story about the intrapsychic, embodied foundations of will, desire, and agency" (1996: 8), which seem intuitively irreducible to cultural forms. This is a serious argument, which brings us close to the heart of the ongoing debate between depth and lateral approaches in psychocultural research. By arguing that different cultures focus on different aspects of a universal human experiential repertoire, Shweder manages to avoid the most severe forms of cultural determinism. But it remains unclear, on his view, how human beings manage to transcend or appropriate cultural meanings in new and surprising ways, or how we can account for our intuitive sense (also borne out in the best ethnographies) that there is something in being human that transcends culture (Archer 2000). For Ingham at least, the answer is that Shweder has forgotten about the psyche.

Still, Ingham cautions against the psychological determinism of writers who view Hindu practice almost entirely through a lens of early childhood experience and oedipal trauma that fails to account for distinctive Indian kinship systems and family dynamics. "Hinduism may resonate with unconscious fantasies," Ingham writes, "but this is not all it is about and, in any case, what is more interesting is the way in which Hindu epics, lore, and practice may have rhetorical effects on socially germane unconscious motivation" (1996: 238). For Ingham, even myths and folklore that seem to express universal oedipal themes – the "phallic god" Shiva cuts off his son Ganesha's head for preventing him from entering the house where his mother is bathing – need to be understood within a local social and cultural context. The whole rhetorical position of the story may shift depending on who is doing the telling – a family patriarch, for instance, or a rebellious young wife chafing at the control exercised by her husband's kin. Yet Ingham still locates the rhetorical effects of lore and practice at the level of "unconscious motivation," and herein lies a possible dilemma.

Contra Shweder, Ingham does posit a "deep and invariant psychological law or process of motivation" that includes oedipal desire and inhibition, but he moderates that claim by emphasizing the cultural context of its expression and perhaps more importantly, the changing *rhetorical* context of its deployment in real social life. Our interest in ritual, according to Ingham, cannot be merely lexical. But this only begs the question of why we are compelled to seek or to assert a universal oedipal background to myths and rituals in the first place. Ingham's own summary of literature in the field (1996: 222–246) includes a strong critique of assertions about the oedipal basis of Hindu myths (Carstairs 1957; Kakar 1978), New Guinea initiation rites (Lidz and Lidz 1984; Herdt 1989), and worship of the Virgin Mary (Carroll 1986) that take insufficient notice, in his view, of local culture. Ingham favors works that focus on local *versions* of the intrapsychic conflicts posited by psychoanalysis, like Beidelman's (1966) account of intrapsychic tension between idealized agnatic solidarity and loyalty to uterine kin among Nuer men. But it remains unclear from this account whether there is any reason besides *a priori* or intuitive personal commitment to the categories of psychoanalysis for applying the latter to studies of myth and ritual across cultures. For those who remain agnostic, the only question would seem to be whether a "compelling story about the embodied [but not necessarily intrapsychic] foundations of will, desire, and agency," to paraphrase Ingham, can be fashioned for anthropology on any other ground.

RITUAL, SUBJECTIVITY, AND THE PROBLEM OF EFFICACY

The abiding virtue of psychocultural models – despite the limitations of both "depth" and "lateral" approaches described above – has been their attempt to locate ritual within a broad understanding of human subjectivity and personhood that transcends putative social function. Furthering that project may however require a more phenomenological approach than has been common, one that is capable of answering to Edward Sapir's early critique of anthropological reductionism, and that avoids collapsing human experience into a metaphysical quest for cultural or psychological essence. This is actually a return to a path that cultural and personality theorists glimpsed but never developed, set as they were on developing "culture" (and by extension ritual) as a realm of special expertise for their new field.

Experience oriented styles in contemporary social science vary widely, from the densely philosophical "cultural phenomenology" advocated by ethnographers like Thomas Csordas (1994) to the no-nonsense sociological "realism" advocated by Margaret Archer (2000). Yet these researchers are agreed that the "embodied foundations of will, desire, and agency" lie within the world of lived experience rather than outside of it, and that this is where attention ought to be focused. With respect to the study of ritual practice, this means that a sound research paradigm will (1) privilege the lived experience of ritual actors, (2) recognize the embodied character of all ritual activity, and (3) focus on the problem of ritual efficacy as it emerges in local settings. Together, these commitments help to turn anthropological thinking about ritual away from its earlier preoccupation with origins or with the quest for unitary cultural significance and towards the uncertain ritual *accomplishments* whose attainment or failure helps to galvanize social life.

Privileging lived experience entails attention to the ways in which rituals are taken up in specific settings in ways that may differ in whole or in part from what Sapir called "the explicit cultural table of contents" with which they are identified. Returning to circumcision, for example, Deepak Mehta (1997) shows how this operation helps boys in a community of Muslim Indian weavers to "become male" and at the same time "become Muslim" as they are graphically cut off by means of this ritual from the world of childhood and women. But circumcision also takes on other meanings in the context of antagonistic structural opposition between Hindus and Muslims, as the new *Musulmani* (circumcised Muslim) body is set apart from the bodies of Hindus who "fear to shed their blood." Some Hindus reverse these expressions by casting circumcision as a kind of castration that dehumanizes Muslim men and legitimates the visitation of pain upon male Muslim bodies. It would be easy to misread this account as a catalogue of fixed cultural ideologies (Hindus believe . . . Muslims believe . . .), but far more useful to view it as an exploration of the ways in which specific rhetorical practices come to constitute a "local structure of feeling" (Das and Kleinman 2000: 9) in which violence is made to seem almost inevitable. Cultural patterns and religious rituals certainly contribute to this local affective structure, but they do not in any simple way determine its content.

One of the great challenges of experience-oriented approaches to ritual is precisely to map the points of intersection between bodily and rhetorical practices, cultural repertoires of meaning, structures of constraint, and the crystallization of public events. Something is always at stake in the performance of rituals, but the stakes for different participants may be varied or even opposed, and the meaning of ritual is always contingent on this fact. In a religio-bureaucratic setting such as the group circumcision of Ethiopian immigrants to Israel (Seeman 2003), it may be the case that articulate discursive or symbolic meanings are less apparent than are the disciplinary powers of institutions to mold subjectivity, and Asad (1993) has argued this is true of many traditional religious settings (i.e., monasteries) as well. Yet we need to be cautious with respect to the ability of such institutions (whether state or religious) to succeed at imposing their will in this manner. In the case of the immigrants whose mass circumcision I witnessed, assent to the "official" bureaucratic narrative (that circumcision of this type signifies both ethnic authenticity and submission to religious and state authority) was moderated by cynicism, humor, or muted defiance on the part of some participants. Here it is not the ritual act per se that seems vital to parse ethnographically, so much as the larger structure of agency and constraint within which the ritual act is embedded.

The articulation of agency and constraint in ritual contexts leads directly to a consideration of ritual efficacy, or the question of whether and how rituals *work* in particular social and moral universes. Some ritualized performances are best conceived as "spectacles," in the sense that they create an appropriate model of some feature of social life (such as power relations or social hierarchy), which are thereby laid out for public acknowledgment (Handelman 1997). Other ritual practices are however transformative, in that they act (or are meant to act) to shift the social position, shape the subjectivity, or affect the material circumstances of ritual actors. These are the rituals in which agency and constraint are most forcefully brought to the fore not just of anthropological analysis but of reflection and concern on the part of those who hold vital stakes in ritual's outcome, especially in contexts of illness or of suffering and healing. It is not surprising, therefore, that illness and healing are the contexts in which phenomenological and psychocultural approaches have been most fruitfully (and urgently) brought together in both clinical and ethnographic research over the last several decades.

The power of ritual to mediate both bodily and affective states with public meaning is well attested in anthropological literature, even though the specific biosocial pathways through which this occurs are poorly understood (Kleinman 1995). Socially salient, embodied metaphor seems everywhere to play an important role in ritual practice (metaphor by definition links different realms or contexts), but this is especially true of ritual healing, in which the uncertain and sometimes contested *material* consequences of ritual practice are brought strongly to the fore (Kirmayer 1993). It is demonstrably untrue that the problem of suffering "from a religious point of view" lies only in "how to suffer" and not in how to avoid suffering, as Clifford Geertz (1973: 104) once argued, although clearly the two questions are often related in religious or ritual healing. The same metaphor of vital flow and blockage can for instance relate simultaneously to the preservation of abstract cosmic order, to the healing of individual bodies, and to the quest for an experience of effective agency despite brutal political repression and violence. All three of these levels are invoked by the Jewish mystic and communal leader Kalonymos Shapira in his writings from the Warsaw Ghetto, as a response to the ongoing genocide that eventually claimed his life (Seeman, 2004 and forthcoming). For Shapira, ritual strategies for the management of human affect were by extension strategies to manage the flow of divine vitality (*hiyyut*) into the phenomenal world, since Hasidic cosmology conceived emotion essentially as an expression of divine effulgence. Far from being an intrapsychic, private event, therefore, the ritual management of emotions – through ritualized weeping, dancing, even sacred study – offers the promise of ritual power and salvation from an untenable reality.

The efficacy of ritual strategies adopted *in extremis* can be hard to gauge, or even to properly define. In Rabbi Shapira's case, ritual strategies may well have created room for a kind of limited agency in the face of subject-extinguishing anguish among the victims of genocide, and were in this sense efficacious, at least for a time. Yet the author of these texts, his family, and the civilization he represented were all exterminated anyway, giving rise to the possibility of a cynical reading that views ritual practice as little more than a distraction from the hard business of effecting real change or recognizing its hopelessness. At the very least, we need to say with Kleinman (1995: 10) that efficacy is "complex, differentially constructed, even contested in experience and needs to be examined simultaneously on several levels." While the Warsaw Ghetto provides an extreme example of this dilemma, it is one that extends in principle to all ritual and religious healing, even if it is one typically asked by anthropological researchers only "as an afterthought" (Csordas and Lewton

1998: 493). Shapira himself openly grappled with the possibility of failure in his endeavors, which he feared might lead to the loss of his own humanity, to physical and emotional defeat, or to the destruction of the cosmos. The point is that neither cultural nor psychological arguments alone can adequately define emergent ritual efficacy outside of some contingent *experiential* context, in which healing is – or may be – achieved.

The study of ritual failure is actually a vital and neglected aspect of ritual efficacy research because it forces analysis more resolutely to confront the specific circumstances, constraints, and experiential horizons in which healing is sought, but which are often elided in traditional psychocultural accounts. This is as true of clinical as it is of anthropological accounts to the extent that the old dichotomies of culture and psyche still hold sway. The anthropological "culture concept," which was once a province of disciplinary specialists, has indeed come to inform the whole intellectual climate of our times, but often in a perfunctory or overly abstract way that recalls Sapir's initial critique. The psychiatric nosology of DSM-IV, for instance, which was released in 1994, makes greater efforts than previous versions of that standard diagnostic manual to take the cultural context of mental health and disorder into account. But as Lawrence Kirmayer (1998: 342) has commented, "a psychiatric nosology is concerned with pathological entities rather than human predicaments," so that the place of culture in DSM-IV has generally been reduced to reified "cultural beliefs" and exotic "culture-bound syndromes" (Hughes 1998) that resist phenomenological evaluation. This is an especially powerful form of reductionism, since it allows "culture" to be invoked in a strictly lexical way as a set of fixed points that require decoding into the dominant language of context free psychopathology. The basis of that language may no longer be primarily psychoanalytic as it was for Freud or Reik, but the process of linguistic collapse that this process entails is essentially the same.

Given this context, it is significant that numbers of culturally sensitive clinicians have experimented in recent years with the use of religious or ritual healing alongside of or in cooperation with standard psychodynamic and biomedical paradigms. In some cases the idea has been to strike up a therapeutic alliance with indigenous healers such as Bedouin Dervishes (Al-Krenawi et al. 1996); in others the clinicians themselves have adopted culturally authorized ritual forms (exorcisms, guided spirit journeys, etc.) in order to strike up more positive therapeutic alliances with patients (Bilu et al. 1990). The promise of such approaches, aside from their hopeful therapeutic utility, lies in the possibility that engagement with these local moral worlds will eventually encourage researchers and clinicians to develop paradigms that overcome the dualism inherent to the history of psychocultural research. They will need to locate ritual efficacy within a broad phenomenological frame that includes serious attention to the social, socioeconomic, and cultural constraints on human agency and on the ways in which ritual practice intersects with these constraints in a variety of ways. Anthropologists, meanwhile, will need to resist being cast primarily as "cultural experts" who can decode exotic ritual languages into standard psychological frames (Seeman 1999). Ritual practice, which Reik viewed as a window onto the unchanging "survival" of primitive mental forms, and which some early anthropologists took to be an expression of unchanging culture, can also help to open a privileged window onto the world of human contingency and change.

REFERENCES

Al-Azmeh, A., 1993 *Islams and Modernities*. New York: Verso.

Al-Krenawi, A., with J. Graham and B. Moaz, 1996 The Healing Significance of the Negev's Bedouin Dervish. *Social Science and Medicine* 43: 13–21.

Archer, Margaret, 2000 *Being Human: The Problem of Agency*. Cambridge: Cambridge University Press.

Asad, Talal, 1993 *Genealogies of Religion*. Baltimore, MD: Johns Hopkins University Press.

Bauman, R., and Charles L. Briggs, 1990 Poetics and Performance as Critical Perspectives on Language and Social Life. *Annual Review of Anthropology* 19: 59–88.

Beidelman, T. O., 1966 The Ox and Nuer Sacrifice: Some Freudian Hypotheses About Nuer Symbolism. *Man* 1: 453–467.

Bell, C., 1997 *Ritual: Perspectives and Dimensions*. Oxford: Oxford University Press.

Benedict, Ruth, 1959 [1934] *Patterns of Culture*. New York: Mentor Books.

Bibeau, Gilles, 1997 Cultural Psychiatry in a Creolizing World: Questions for a New Research Agenda. *Transcultural Psychiatry* 34 (1): 9–41.

Bilu, Yoram, with E. Witztum and O. Van Der Hart, 1990 Miraculous Healing in an Israeli Psychiatric Clinic. *Culture, Medicine, and Psychiatry* 14: 105–127.

Boas, Franz, 1940 *Race, Language, and Culture*. Chicago: University of Chicago Press.

Boddy, Janice, 1989 *Women and Alien Spirits*. Madison: University of Wisconsin Press.

Carroll, M. P., 1986 *The Cult of the Virgin Mary: Psychological Origins*. Princeton, NJ: Princeton University Press.

Carstairs, G. M., 1957 *The Twice-Born: A Study of a Community of High-Caste Hindus*. London: Hogarth Press.

Cohen, Lawrence, 1992 *No Aging in India*. Berkeley: University of California Press.

Csordas, Thomas, 1994 *The Sacred Self: A Cultural Phenomenology of Charismatic Healing*. Berkeley: University of California Press.

Csordas, Thomas, and E. Lewton, 1998 Practice, Performance and Experience in Ritual Healing. *Transcultural Psychiatry* 35: 435–512.

Darnell, Regna, 1986 Personality and Culture: The Fate of the Sapirian Alternative. In *Malinowski, Rivers, Benedict, and Others*. G. W. Stocking, Jr., ed. Pp. 156–183. Madison: University of Wisconsin Press.

Das, Veena, and Arthur Kleinman, 2000 Introduction. *Violence and Subjectivity*. Veena Das, Arthur Kleinman, Mamphela Ramphele and Pamela Reynolds, eds. Berkeley: University of California Press.

Frankfurter, D., 2002 Ritual as Accusation and Atrocity: Satanic Ritual Abuse, Gnostic Libertinism, and Primal Murders. *History of Religions*: 299–320.

Freud, Sigmund, 1946 [1912–13] *Totem and Taboo*. A. A. Brill, trans. New York: Vintage Books.

— 1952 [1935] *An Autobiographical Study*. James Strachey, trans. New York: W. W. Norton.

— 1963 [1907] Obsessive Acts and Religious Practices. In *Character and Culture*. P. Reiff, ed. New York: Collier.

Geertz, Clifford, 1973 *The Interpretation of Cultures*. New York: Basic Books.

Goldberg, H., 1996 Cambridge in the Land of Canaan: Descent, Alliance, Circumcision, and Instruction in the Bible. *JANES* 24: 9–34.

Gupta, Akhil, and James Ferguson, 1992 Beyond "Culture": Space, Identity, and the Politics of Difference. *Cultural Anthropology* 7: 63–79.

Handelman, D., 1997 Rituals/Spectacles. *International Social Science Journal* 49: 387–399.

Handler, R., 1986 Vigorous Male and Aspiring Female: Poetry, Personality and Culture in Edward Sapir and Ruth Benedict. In *Malinowski, Rivers, Benedict, and Others*. G. W. Stocking, Jr., ed. Pp. 127–155. Madison: University of Wisconsin Press.

Herdt, Gilbert H., 1989 Father Presence and Ritual Homosexuality. *Ethos* 17: 326–370.

Herzfeld, Michael, 1987 *Anthropology Through the Looking Glass: Critical Ethnography in the Margins of Europe.* Cambridge: Cambridge University Press.

Hughes, C., 1998 The Glossary of "Culture-Bound Syndromes" in DSM-IV: A Critique. *Transcultural Psychiatry* 35: 413–421.

Ingham, J. M., 1996 *Psychological Anthropology Reconsidered.* Cambridge: Cambridge University Press.

Kakar, S., 1978 *The Inner-World: A Psycho-Analytic Study of Childhood and Society in India.* Delhi: Oxford University Press.

Kirmayer, Lawrence J., 1993 Healing and the Invention of Metaphor: The Effectiveness of Symbols Revisited. *Culture, Medicine, and Psychiatry* 17: 161–195.

— 1998 The Fate of Culture in DSM-IV. *Transcultural Psychiatry* 35: 339–342.

Kleinman, Arthur, 1995 *Writing at the Margins.* Berkeley: University of California Press.

Kleinman, Arthur, and Don Seeman, 1998 The Politics of Moral Practice in Psychotherapy and Religious Healing. *Contributions to Indian Sociology* 32 (2): 237–252.

Kuper, Adam, 1988 *The Invention of Primitive Society.* London: Routledge.

Lidz, T., and R. W. Lidz, 1984 Oedipus in the Stone Age. *Journal of the American Psychoanalytic Association* 32: 507–527.

Lucas, Rod H., and Robert J. Barrett, 1995 Interpreting Culture and Psychopathology: Primitivist Themes in Cross-Cultural Debate. *Culture, Medicine, and Psychiatry* 19: 287–326.

Manson, W. C., 1986 Abraham Kardiner and the Neo-Freudian Alternative in Culture and Personality. In *Malinowski, Rivers, Benedict, and Others.* G. W. Stocking, Jr., ed. Madison: University of Wisconsin Press.

Mead, Margaret, 1963 [1935] *Sex and Temperament in Three Primitive Societies.* New York: Morrow Quill.

Mehta, D., 2000 Circumcision, Body, Masculinity: The Ritual Wound and Collective Violence. In *Violence and Subjectivity.* Veena Das and Arthur Kleinman, eds. Berkeley: University of California Press.

Morgan, L. H., 1973 [1877] Ancient Society. In *High Points in Anthropology.* Paul Bohannan and Mark Glazer, eds. Pp. 32–60. New York: Publisher?

Ozturk, O. M., 1973 Ritual Circumcision and Castration Anxiety. *Psychiatry* 36: 49–60.

Reik, T., 1946 *Ritual: Four Psychoanalytic Studies.* D. Bryan, trans. New York: Grove Press.

Robertson Smith, W., 1972 [1885, 1903] *Religion of the Semites: The Fundamental Institutions,* 2nd edn. Boston, MA: Beacon Press.

Róheim, G., 1943 *The Origin and Function of Culture.* New York: Nervous and Mental Disease Monographs.

— 1971 [1925] *Australian Totemism: A Psychoanalytic Study in Anthropology.* New York: Humanities Press.

Sapir, Edward, 1957 The Emergence of the Concept of Personality in the Study of Cultures. In *Culture, Language, and Personality: Selected Essays.* D. G. Mandelbaum, ed. Berkeley: University of California Press.

— 1985 [1932] Cultural Anthropology and Psychiatry. In *Selected Writings in Language, Personality, and Culture.* D. G. Mandelbaum, ed. Berkeley: University of California Press.

Seeman, Don, 1998 "Where is Sarah Your Wife": Cultural Poetics of Gender and Nationhood in the Hebrew Bible. *Harvard Theological Review* 91: 103–126.

— 1999 Subjectivity, Culture, Life-World: An Appraisal. *Transcultural Psychiatry,* 36: 437–445.

— 2003 Agency, Bureaucracy and Religious Conversion Among Ethiopian "Feleshmura" Immigrants to Israel. In *The Anthropology of Religious Conversion.* Andrew Buckser and Steven D. Glazier, eds. London: Rowman and Littlefield.

— forthcoming *Ritual, Emotion, and "Useless Suffering" in the Warsaw Ghetto*.

— 2004 Otherwise than Meaning: On the Generosity of Ritual. *Social Analysis*, 48: 53–69.

Shweder, Richard, 1991 *Thinking Through Cultures: Expeditions in Cultural Psychology*. Cambridge, MA: Harvard University Press.

Stocking, G. W., Jr., 1986 Introduction. In *Malinowski, Rivers, Benedict, and Others*. G. W. Stocking, Jr., ed. Madison: University of Wisconsin Press.

Trautmann, T. R., 1987 *Lewis Henry Morgan and the Invention of Kinship*. Berkeley: University of California Press.

CHAPTER 20 Spirit Possession

Erika Bourguignon

Beliefs in spirit possession are both very widespread in human societies and very ancient. Such beliefs are present in large portions of the contemporary world and find expression in ways that closely tie in with various aspects of cultural and social change. This includes current issues, such as physical and psychological ailments, be they AIDS or depression, economic displacements and others directly or indirectly involved with what has come to be termed globalization. They appear in many different contexts, exhibiting great adaptability and innovative potential.

In some sense, spirit possession is about identity – short or long term. In the context of change and globalization, identity, personal and collective, has become a major issue. It is manifested in many ways: in people's choices in areas ranging from clothing to house styles, food and medicine, religion, work and sports, politics and child rearing, and much else. Contact with outsiders, be they missionaries (Russell 1999) or tourists (Costa 2001), produces the observation that some people have more power than others. This power may appear as being of a supernatural nature or it may be perceived as involving access to resources. This too raises questions of identity; the question then is not only "Who am I?" but also "Who am I in relation to, or in comparison with, these others?" Globalization has affected the most intimate aspects of people's lives virtually everywhere, their sense of self and of who they are.

Of special interest are the ways in which responses to change are expressed through the relationship between spirits and humans. These responses range from resistance to change and to its human agents, from rejection of some aspects of the new to its partial acceptance. This may involve intragroup and intergroup conflict, but also illness and healing. It is a context of learning about the world, a theater where issues of power and means of coping are played out. Much of this may be expressed through the appearance of new spirits. The identity of the spirits and their often novel demands will particularly concern us here.

Here is a recent example. Casey (1999) tells of an outbreak of bizarre behavior among Muslim Hausa secondary school girls in the city of Kano, Nigeria. The schoolgirls were celebrating their success in school exams with a loud party, when an elderly woman with disheveled red hair appeared to them to complain about the noise. The girls insulted the woman, then the next day were struck by compulsive Indian dancing, and paralysis, contagious behavior that rapidly spread throughout the region, affecting, however, only girls of the Hausa group, originating in Kano. In the community these symptoms were thought to be due to possession by spirits from foreign lands, or a combination of possession and witchcraft. Contact with cultural products of distant lands brings new practices and new risks, including conflict over appropriate behavior. Note that the "globalization" here does not refer to Western influences.

In the same community, Moslem healers, in their practice of Islam, have acquired new spirit helpers, for example, Moslem spirits (*jinn*) from Lebanon. There are Lebanese communities in Nigeria, offering another foreign influence, yet one that is culturally congenial within the contexts of spirit possession.

Spirits have also played an important role in recent African wars. Behrend (1999) tells the complex story of one leading spirit medium: Alice, an Acholi woman, first medium for Lakewana, a new Christian spirit, and a healer and diviner and then also the leader of a Uganda military movement. Among her spirits were an American, a Zairean, a Korean, and various male and female Islamic spirits. She fielded an army of 7,000–10,000 men and women, but was defeated in battle.

These two recent reports illustrate the great diversity in the ways in which spirit possession works in the contemporary scene. To consider the forms spirit possession beliefs take and the rituals in which they are expressed, some background information is required. A large-scale cross-cultural study (Bourguignon 1973) found that possession beliefs existed in 70 percent of 488 sample societies. Altogether, 90 percent of sample societies had institutionalized some form of trance (altered state of consciousness) in a ritual context. That is to say, some of these societies used trance in a religious context that does not involve a belief in spirit possession. This suggests strongly not only that trancing is a universal human capacity, with its own evolutionary history, but also that human societies structure its experience, meaning, and performance. An intimate personal experience – trancing – is utilized not only for personal but also for social ends. That in turn suggests that trancing is shaped through cultural learning. It is therefore not surprising to see the transformations it has undergone in response to various aspects of change in the public as well as the intimate dimensions of people's lives. By contrast, belief in spirit possession, of whatever kind, is significantly rarer. This suggests that it is a cultural creation and has been subject to both diffusion and modification over time. Indeed, these two processes – diffusion and modification – can be observed at present; they will be the subject of much that follows.

Most, but not all, societies considered in this cross-cultural study were pre-industrial, and had been reported on by anthropologists in the course of the last 100 years. Two major types of beliefs were identified: possession trance (PT) and non-trance possession (P). The former refers to a ritual practice in which a psycho-physiological state (trance) is interpreted by participants as due to possession by a spirit entity. The latter does not involve a psychological or physiological alteration, but rather refers to changes in capacities or powers. The two types of possession beliefs may occur in separate groups in a given population, but more typically appear in different types of societies. In particular, PT is highly correlated with sub-Saharan Africa and consequently is also frequent in the African Diaspora, both in the Americas and in North Africa. In many of these societies, trance is intentionally induced, that is, the spirits are invited to participate in ritual occasions. The majority of possession trancers, as reported over and over again, are women. In some other societies, particularly in Jewish and Christian traditions, as well as those of South Asia, the spirits thought to possess individuals are seen as evil and subject to exorcism. Here, too, the majority of victims are women.

In PT, the identity of the host is displaced, temporarily, by another: the words and actions are those of this "other." Yet the behavior and speech of the possession trancer have an impact on the participants in the ritual and perhaps also on the non-ritual life of the spirit's host, and of the wider community. It is these changes that are of major interest when the redefinition of individual identities is of concern both to individuals and communities in the current world situation.

Examples of non-trance possession are also found in many parts of the world. They tend to be reported more frequently for men than for women. For instance, Evans-Pritchard (1937), in his classic work on the Azande, reports on the belief that some people, mostly men, are "witches." This means that they harbor a witchcraft being in their bodies, which causes harm to others. It acts independently of its host. Evidence for the existence of such beings is sought in autopsies of suspected witches. Evans-Pritchard observed that such evidence might consist of liver abnormalities and other such bodily features. (Hallen and Sodipo (1986) warn that this description of Azande witchcraft must not be generalized across Africa, as has been done by various authors.) Quite a different example of non-trance possession appears in North America, as among the Havasupai (Spier 1928), where a healer's powers reside in his or her body. While the Havasupai are not unique with regard to this type of possession belief, other kinds have also been reported from the Americas. For example, Harner (1962) notes that among the Jívaro of South America men acquire certain types of souls, in addition to their own, as a result of a vision quest or by killing another person. The acquisition of such a soul is said to be felt as a sudden surge of power, self-confidence, intelligence, and physical strength. It also protects its host against being killed, whether by warfare or sorcery. Under the name of "spirit intrusion," non-trance possession has also been considered to be a major explanatory theory for the presence of disease.

Belief in such non-trance possession has been found to be correlated with hunting, fishing, and gathering societies, whereas possession trance societies are more likely to have agriculture and to be structurally more complex. The Azande, incidentally, have not only non-trance possession, as noted above, but also women diviners who engage in possession trance. While possession then empowers the individual, whether positively or negatively, and often does so on a permanent basis, possession trance turns the individual, at least temporarily, into another, thus producing a change in identity. This other is likely to be more powerful than his or her host. In the following discussion, the primary concern will be with possession trance in its many contexts and forms in the contemporary world.

Possession trance is based on a conception of the human person as consisting of multiple separable elements, such as body and soul (or multiple souls), or self, mind, identity, name, and so forth. One of these elements can be replaced temporarily by a spirit or other entity. During this take-over, the soul or self of the host is in abeyance. Therefore, when the soul returns, there is no memory of the events. Such amnesia is culturally normative and is probably genuine, at least in part. (It is likely that if the altered state of consciousness during which the possessing spirit presents itself is of extended length, perhaps several hours, it will vary in depth. That is, the host may be aware of what is going on, including his or her own actions, for at least part of the time.)

Where there is a belief in non-trance possession as discussed above such a conception of the human being is not a necessary precondition, since the acquired soul or intrusive spirit does not replace the host's soul or self, but rather is conceived of as being present in addition to it.

The societies reviewed in the cross-cultural study referred to above constituted a sample drawn from those coded in the Ethnographic Atlas (Murdock 1967). The ethnographic literature on these societies on the whole represents rather static pictures of the social structure and of local beliefs and practices. The emphasis in the present discussion, by contrast, is on the dynamic nature of beliefs and practices in the contemporary world. Nevertheless, the findings of the cross-cultural study provide two important assets to this discussion. First, they show us that the beliefs under consideration are not simply products of present-day conditions, but are rooted in human history and in common psychological and biological features, while also providing information on correlations between beliefs and practices on the one hand and sociocultural features on the other. That is to say, variations among groups and regions are not random or arbitrary. Second, they provide a classification and terminology that offer a means of ordering data. The literature – at the time of this study and at present – employs diverse terminologies, often using the words "possession" and "trance" as synonymous, even in the same sentence. For example, the well-known British anthropologist Raymond Firth, in his 1959 Huxley Memorial Lecture, says:

> Spirit possession is a form of trance in which behavior actions of a person are interpreted as evidence of control of his behavior by a spirit normally external to him. Spirit mediumship is normally a form of possession in which the person is conceived as serving as an intermediary between spirits and men.

This statement ignores the possibility of spirit possession without trance and also seems to imply that there are types of possession trance in which people act but do not speak; that is, that there are contexts in which the possessed person does not serve as a mouthpiece for the spirits. Firth bases his distinctions largely on his own fieldwork in Kelantan (Malaysia) and Tikopia (Polynesia).

Moreover, many authors tend to treat their specific ethnographic cases without reference to the broader context. While individual cultures and societies are indeed likely to be unique in significant respects, this should not be assumed *a priori*, nor are they likely to be unique in all respects. A comparative perspective allows us to see the larger picture.

The literature strikingly reflects the preoccupations of the authors. This can clearly be seen if we consider the history of the study of vodou, the Afro-Catholic folk religion of Haiti, and of possession trance as a prominent feature of that religion.

We see how the shifting interests of writers and researchers, and indeed their own identities and the political as well as intellectual context of their studies, direct their orientations. Haiti is here to be taken as an exemplar, for similar histories could be written for other possession trance religions.

During the US occupation of Haiti (1915–34), numerous American authors presented a picture of vodou as savage and barbaric. At the same time, the occupation stimulated a reaction which, among Haitian intellectuals, strengthened their sense of Haiti's African roots and the role vodou played in the Haitian revolution against the French colonial power at the end of the eighteenth century. The Haitian physician J. C. Dorsainvil (1931), under the influence of French psychiatry, saw possession trance as pathological behavior, related to what he saw as the Haitians' "hereditary nervous instability," to be explained by Haiti's terrible history. For him, Haiti is a special case, with its unique history and without a larger context. This theme of pathology was taken up by Catholic as well as Protestant missionaries, who added the possibility of demonic intervention. That is, they identified the spirits of vodou with demons and the Devil. In his 1937 study of a Haitian village, the anthropologist and Africanist M. J. Herskovits speaks of possession trance as culturally normal and related to Haiti's African ancestry. He thereby gave support to the intellectual movement restoring interest in Haitian folk culture and its African background. In addition to the work of social scientists, in the 1940s and 1950s some romantic writing associating Haitian vodou with various metaphysical positions came to the fore. In the 1960s, when transcultural psychiatry developed, some American psychiatrists began to look at the role of the vodou priest as a healer, and at possession trance as prophylactic or therapeutic, thereby coming full circle from the position of Dorsainvil. On the other hand, under the dictatorship of Duvalier, father and son, vodou became intensely enmeshed in Haitian politics and has remained so.

A further word of caution needs to be introduced here. Beliefs in spirit possession of various types come to us from New Testament sources (Mark 5: 1–17; Luke 11: 14–15) and from ancient Greece. This has colored the perceptions of Western observers of non-Western peoples. That is, they have been liable to interpret unfamiliar behavior in familiar terms. The case of Haitian vodou, cited above, exemplifies this tendency. Moreover, "possession," as translation of native terms, can at best, as we shall see, involve only an approximation of local meanings and requires elaboration if serious study is to be undertaken.

The "trance" or altered state of consciousness, which is linked to possession beliefs, may take many different forms. If such a state occurs spontaneously, it may be interpreted in local terms by diviners or other diagnosticians as due to possession or intrusion by a spirit entity. In biomedical terms these spontaneous states may include such varied conditions as seizures, fugue states, even coma, as well as dissociational states. Some, but not all, of these states may be understood as pathological. Dissociation, as a psychological mechanism, may occur in the context of a major psychiatric disease such as schizophrenia. In other situations, it may be learned – even taught systematically – in the absence of psychiatric disease. Some altered states are induced by various psychoactive substances (hallucinatory drugs). However, it should be noted that these are rarely used in the context of possession rituals. They are frequently associated with other types of practices and beliefs, such as those of classic shamanism where the soul leaves the body to seek contact with the spirit world. As Fernandez (1965: 905) writes, with reference to a reformative cult among the Fang people of Gabon: "An alkaloid intoxicant, eboga (Tabernenthes eboka), is taken . . . to achieve an ecstatic state . . . The intoxicant is taken . . . 'in order to make the body light and to enable the soul to fly.' The spiritual world . . . does not, in this cult . . . come to possess the worshipper. It is rather the worshipper who must leave himself in order to make contact with the unseen." Fernandez stresses how unusual this is in Africa, where possession by spirits is a great deal more typical as ritual behavior. In fact, it is practiced, without the use of drugs, in the traditional ancestor cult among the Fang. In his study of the reformative cult of Bwiti, which seeks symbolic consensus among its members, Fernandez points to significant changes among the Fang, such as the growth of economic individualism and the abandonment among many of traditional ceremonial institutions, resulting in mutual distrust. The Bwiti cult attempts to restore (or develop) a sense of social harmony in the face of social disruption. This then is one way in which contemporary religious movements respond to social and economic change. It constitutes an example of a conscious attempt to create a better society. Wallace (1966) has termed such innovative religions revitalization movements. We shall consider other types of responses in what follows.

The date of Fernandez's research should be noted: economic individualism developed in many places during the colonial period, when European influences in parts of Africa were strong. Such influences are not limited to the current period of globalization. They have, however, been accentuated and extended to areas previously touched to a lesser degree.

Before turning to specific examples illustrating a relationship between possession trance religions and contemporary sociocultural and economic change, it will be helpful to consider three major types of ritual contexts. We may refer to these as involving three different sorts of relationships between the spirits and those they possess. These are: (1) service on the part of the human hosts and protection by the spirits; (2) illness and harassment of certain humans on the part of the spirits, but protection and healing by them once the human host offers service and meets the spirit's demands; (3) possession by evil spirits, who harm human individuals and must be exorcised by ritual specialists. We may refer to these three types of relationships between humans and spirits as "service and protection," "propitiation and alliance," and "harm and exorcism." It must however be remembered that these are rough groupings and that each sociocultural context may be expected to have its own characteristic features. In considering specific examples in each category, the effect of economic and social modernization can then be considered.

In the first category, we find various West African groups, such as the Fon of Benin and the Yoruba of Nigeria, where spirits are invited to participate in rituals. Here, possession trance is seen as desirable. This invitation is expressed by means of specific drum rhythms, songs, dance steps, and other elements of rituals. Neither drugs nor masks are used on these occasions, although drugs may be used during the initiation process. The hosts of the spirits, the majority of whom are women, are termed the spirits' "horses," and possession is referred to as "mounting." This symbolically expresses the idea that the relationship between spirit and human is one of power. This metaphorical expression of the relationship between the spirits and their human hosts has a very wide distribution in Africa and beyond. The women are also called "wives" of the spirits and possession is referred to in sexual terms. This is a theme that has even wider distribution. One aspect of this refers to the experiential dimension of possession trance as a specifically female experience. This is dramatized in some societies where men as well as women possession trancers are understood to be wives of their spirits.

A first possession trance may be induced or, more likely, occur spontaneously, to be followed by initiation rituals. Motivations for undergoing initiation vary, but often individuals are believed to be possessed by spirits who claim them as representatives of their kin group, and might expect punishment from them if they did not follow the spirit's demands. Alternatively, they are called to serve because they had attracted a spirit's attention in some way.

This is the overall pattern that we also find in the Americas, where a variety of Afro-American (or Afro-Catholic) religions flourish: vodou in Haiti, santería in Cuba, and Candomblé, Xango, Macumba, Umbanda, and others in Brazil. Many of these are now represented in the United States and in Europe as well. It should be noted that while some spirits are ancient and familiar, in many groups new spirits have made their appearance, or old spirits have acquired new functions and behaviors. An example of a novel spirit appeared among the Yoruba when a woman was possessed annually by the spirit of a sanitary inspector. In a film by Raymond Prince and Frank Speed (1964) she is seen checking out various items on a list. Prince (1964), himself a psychiatrist, saw this novel ritual, enacting a new type of spirit, as a prophylactic practice, keeping her from having recurring psychotic episodes.

In Brazil we find, in addition to spirits of various African pantheons, spirits of American Indians (*caboclos*) and of "old Blacks" (*pretos velos*). There are also *exus* (tricksters, experts in magic) and child spirits. In her study of the Umbanda religion in São Paulo, Pressel (1973) has suggested that this combination of four different categories of spirits represents the different aspects of modern Brazilian identity.

The propitiation and alliance pattern is found in Africa, as in the Bori cult among the Hausa of Northern Nigeria and Niger, or the Zar cult of Eastern Africa, which has a very wide distribution from Somalia in the South to Sudan and Egypt in the North. It appears among Moslems and Christians, and in Ethiopia also among Jews. This last group has brought the Zar cult to Israel in recent years. These are largely healing religions, to which women are drawn by physical and often reproductive complaints. The woman leader diagnoses the complaint by inducing possession trance in the patient, so that the possessing spirit can be identified and his or her demands specified. If the patient then will comply with the spirit's demands a permanent relationship is established and the spirit is turned from a harasser into an ally.

In her study of a village in the Northern Sudan, Boddy (1989) notes that among the spirits that possess the women in the local Zar cult some are foreigners, males, and prostitutes. Among the foreign spirits are several kinds of Ethiopians; large numbers of refugees from Ethiopian wars had come into the region. Some are Europeans and Americans. One such character is an "American doctor and big game hunter, who drinks prodigious amounts of whiskey . . . his prey are small antelopes . . . he is a lascivious character" (1989: 289). Boddy suggests that such spirits, caricatures of foreigners, constitute a warning against Western technology, including medicine. (The Zar spirits prohibit the use of Western medicine, a form of resistance against modernity.) One important aspect of this temporary incarnation of a variety of powerful spirits is that they behave in ways that break a whole range of taboos in this Moslem population: they drink and smoke, appear to chase women, and the female ones behave provocatively. The Ethiopians are Christians and have Christian symbols, such as crosses. As Boddy says: "A potential enemy is dealt with . . . by acknowledging His [existence and power], by inviting Him into the villagers' midst in a controlled if evanescent manner." (1989: 290). One might argue that in an altered state of consciousness these Sudanese women try out what it might be like to be a different kind of person: a man, a prostitute, a Westerner, a Christian, or a person with power.

A different example of the alliance type of relationship between women and spirits is found in the Zebola cult in the Congo. This cult originated among the rural Mongo, but has spread to the capital city of Kinshasa. Corin (1989) describes it in its urban form. There, women of different classes and ethnic groups participate. In this cult, certain illnesses experienced by women are explained as due to the malevolence of others, often due to jealousy over a woman's advantages. (This is in contrast to the Zar cult, where the illness is sent by the spirits themselves.) Here, too, diagnosis is made by inducing possession trance in the patient. It is the spirit – that of a dead Mongo woman – who identifies herself and announces demands to be fulfilled in exchange for a cure. Therapy, however, consists of controlling the presence of the invading spirit, that is, inhibiting trance. This is achieved by means of an initiation into the cult that lasts several months, during which the patient lives with other women at the healer's compound. Medications are administered and complex dance performances are taught to the patient. Through group member-ship in the cult and participation in recurring rituals, the patient then maintains a lifelong relationship with the spirit, who has been transformed into a protector. It is noteworthy that what began as a cult based on kinship and ethnic community among the Mongo has become, in the urban environment, a voluntary association of unrelated women, brought together by the need for a cure. Corin (1998: 102) concludes her lengthy analysis by noting cautiously: "It is possible that the import-ance of spirit possession in modern Central Africa . . . could provide an escape from some of the dehumanizing features of (post)-modernity and contribute to the creation of an African . . . [new] 'Person.'"

There are many examples of such religions. Only brief mention can be made here of a number of these. The Haouka of the Songhay were made famous through their portrayal in the remarkable film *Les Maîtres fous* by Jean Rouch (1954) and in more recent studies by Stoller (1995) in Niger. Because this cult began among male migrant workers to Ghana, it is primarily a men's religion. The spirits they embody are modeled after various French and British colonial authorities: the general, the colonel, the doctor, the doctor's wife, but also the train (or the train conductor), the truck driver, and so forth. They appear as caricatures or parodies of their human models, but they are also powerful and fearful. As with the Zar spirits in the Sudan, we may ask whether the behavior of the spirit-possessed trancers is a parody only in the eyes of the Western beholder. By enacting the identities and behaviors of these strangers, the hosts of these spirits are investigating what it is like to be one of them, to be this Other. The spirits and their powers are thereby made familiar and domesticated.

A more recent phenomenon, that of the Dodo spirit mediums of Niger, has been described by Masquelier (1999). These spirits cause illness in their chosen "horses" and tell them to hold ceremonies. The former patient becomes the spirit's medium, and as such, a powerful healer and diviner. The distinctive feature of these spirits is that they prohibit certain aspects of modernity, although which ones varies among them. They resist not only Westernization but also aspects of both Islam and the more ancient Bori cult that has been commercialized in the region. Prohibitions range from sexual promiscuity to charging significant fees for healing services; from the use of rubber sandals to motorized transport and literacy. As Masquelier (1999: 37) puts it:

> The conventions of Dodo mediums constitute an imaginative, yet no less pragmatic, effort to regain control over a moral order whose viability hinges on the strength of the spiritual bond rather than the power of market relations.

This pattern, with illness as possession and cure by means of possession trance, is also found in Mayotte, in the Comorro Islands. Here, too, women are the majority of the possession trancers. Lambeck (1981) sees this as due to the inhibiting effect of Islam on men, keeping most of them from accepting possession trance. He finds no evidence for the argument made by Lewis (1989) that possession is due to women's deprivation or their attempt to compensate and retaliate for this deprivation. Moreover, here "participation in possession activities by women is not so much an expression of opposition toward Islam as freedom from it" (Lewis 1989: 64). In Mayotte, as in Haiti, the relationship is a triangular one between the host, the spirit, and an interlocutor. In Mayotte this is usually the host's husband, who develops a special relationship with the spirit. The spirit and the husband can discuss family matters in a manner that is not available in the husband–wife relationship.

It should be noted that in modern or modernizing societies traditional healers may not be available, families may be reluctant to use their services or, indeed, their treatments may not be effective. Sometimes, too, family support may not exist for migrants. Under such circumstances patients may be taken to Western biomedical services and given a diagnosis and treatment consistent with that approach. The literature is not clear on how effective such treatments are. Some psychiatrists have become aware of the incongruity of the biomedical approach with the patients' and often the families' explanatory systems (cf. Witzum et al. 1996; Littlewood and Lipsedge 1989).

A third type of possession trance involves quite a different relationship between spirit and human host. In Christianity, it finds its model in several accounts in the New Testament. The spirit is seen as harmful, causing illness or bad behavior. It is defined as either demonic or as the soul of a dead sinner. Its attack may be directed at religious belief and at the community, or specifically at its host. There is no accommodation with the spirit – it has to be exorcised. In mainline Christianity, possession and exorcism had virtually disappeared in the nineteenth century. However, in the last thirty years, it has made a major comeback, both in Catholicism and in the various Protestant churches. Historically, possession and exorcism, linked to beliefs in witchcraft as well, have had a role in both American and European history. The nineteenth-century French psychiatrist J. M. Charcot and members of his school were impressed by the similarities between the behavior of their hysterical patients and such famous historical cases as that of the possessed nuns of Loudon (Certeau 2000). The best-known American case involves the witchcraft accusations and trials at Salem (Starkey 1973). Possession trance behavior requiring exorcism is to be found in Judaism and Islam as well. Islam, however, in the regions where it is the official religion, has accommodated itself to the existence of various spirit cults, some of which are based on the local pre-Islamic practices.

What we may call "negative" possession trance, requiring exorcism, may be of a collective or of a personal, individual nature. Ong (1987) describes trance epidemics among women factory workers and students in Malaysia. These are interpreted by the women and their families as possession, requiring exorcism. Exorcists explain the outbreaks as due to some form of contagion of the premises, or the result of some offense to the local spirits. Entrepreneurs see exorcism as a necessary cost of doing business. Biomedically, such epidemics have been explained as examples of collective contagious hysteria. Ong sees these cases as reflecting resistance by the women to a capitalist discipline of work, quite alien to their traditional village life style.

Negative possession exists in India, where ghost possession has been studied by Kakar (1982), a psychoanalyst and himself an Indian, and by anthropologists such as Freed and Freed (1985). Kakar describes and discusses exorcistic rites at a temple. The people treated are primarily rural young married women, and the possessing spirits are those of people who have broken moral rules. In Kakar's view (1982: 76), the ghosts are those of forbidden sexual and aggressive wishes (that is, the ghosts symbolize such wishes). The illness represents the women's "accumulated and repressed rage, their helpless anger . . . at the lack of their social emancipation." These young women are suffering in the transition from life in their family of origin to the home of their new husbands and their domination by their mothers-in-law. As for those young men who suffer from possession illness, in Kakar's view, they are those who find the responsibility of autonomy and individuation at marriage threatening.

The Freeds provide a complex, long-term psychomedical case history of a young village woman of North India, which illustrates Kakar's description. They first met Sita in 1958, and again twenty years later. During this time Sita's life changed in many ways, and so did the Freeds' anthropological perspective. In 1958 Sita was a young bride in her parents-in-law's home. The spirit she was possessed by, and who spoke through her, was that of a childhood friend. This girl had committed suicide after she became pregnant by a village boy. She was rejected by the husband to whom she had been engaged and his family when the pregnancy was discovered after the wedding. She was also rejected by her own family. Such a possession indicates the stresses Sita experienced as a new bride; it also expresses a warning to the community about what bad behavior is and how it is punished both in this world and the next.

Witnessing this first possession, the Freeds also had occasion to observe attempts at exorcism. This consisted largely of trying to question the rather uncooperative spirit, in order to discover its identity. It also involved applying pain to Sita's body. Several more exorcisms by different professional exorcists followed. She had remissions but also suffered periodic recurrences. For a number of years when these came on, she would be sent home to her natal village for a prolonged visit. The Freeds visited her and her family again in 1978. Sita now had five children and had

had a variety of illnesses. Although she was no longer possessed in the earlier manner, she now had periodic "fits" which involved loss of consciousness as well as screaming and other types of aggressive behavior. She herself attributed her fits to worries and stress.

Since 1958, a public health system has developed in India and Sita has been treated at a hospital for various ailments, including kidney stones. The Freeds take a close look at her medical history and consider how her physical health and its problems interacted with her psychological stresses so that together they offer some insight into her possessions and fits.

Although the various examples cited here differ with reference to their specificity, they have much in common. There seems to be an overall concern with the restoration – or establishment – of a moral order. This may involve an idealization of the past and a concern with a recent disruption of social relations. A great range of items is selected by the spirits – or their human stand-ins – and often in a way that may seem arbitrary to us, to represent the ancient moral order and the present-day moral decline.

The spirits with whom humans interact through possession may be ancestors or ancient nature spirits or ghosts (i.e., the souls of dead sinners) or demons. They have a symbolic dimension. Where exorcism is practiced, it may be that witchcraft has caused the victim of the evil spirit to be vulnerable to the attack. In others, as in some contemporary American Protestant cases, the victim may simply have frequented places that were haunted by ghosts of dead sinners. In the Jewish tradition, possession by a *dybbuk*, the spirit of a dead sinner, occurs because the victim has made herself vulnerable by her own sinful behavior.

Note that possession trance religions or cults are not limited to traditional or modernizing societies. Spiritualism developed in nineteenth-century America and spread to Europe and Latin America, developing a large continuing following. Most of the mediums, presenting the recent dead, were women. Channeling is a more recent form of mediumship. Most Channelers are women, while most of the spirits who speak through them are male. They are, however, entities of the distant past, whose personal characteristics are not clearly defined. Moreover, Channeling is linked to a belief in reincarnation and multiple lives (Brown 1997).

Relation with the spirits reflects a number of principal themes: power, aggression, sexuality. Possession trance and its symbolic language (horse and rider, wife and husband, container and contained, etc.) alerts us to the underlying issues. Possession by alien and powerful spirits involves identification with these entities. The phenomenon is reminiscent of what George Herbert Mead called playing the role of the other and is familiar to us from studies of child development, but of course not limited to that. Often, what we see is, in psychoanalytic terms, "identification with the aggressor." This has been referred to as mimesis and is one way of achieving mastery over fearful beings and interactions with them, a strategy (albeit an unconscious one) for gaining intimate acquaintance with strangers and the power to deal with them. Also, more generally, it is a way of learning about the world beyond the direct experience of the spirits' hosts and their communities. As suggested above, what Boddy sees as parodies may not seem such to the cult participants.

An interesting aspect of possession trance is that the hosts of the spirits are generally women who do not have the power to speak in their own voices. Possession trance involves a range of activities: acting out the characteristic behavior of the possessing spirit through dancing, singing, curing, responding to questions, making demands, and other interactions with other spirits and with an audience. This active possession trance is enacted by a human host and is represented by a passive imagery. The possession trancer is the spirit's wife, his mount, his vehicle or vessel. She is mounted, ridden, entered, indeed possessed by the spirit. She is no longer herself and for the duration of the possession becomes another. As the passive instrument of another, she achieves mastery by abdicating her own self. A more powerful being takes over her body and performs actions while residing there. In brief, the active performance is linked to a passive fantasy. The possession trancer is not responsible for any of the spirit's actions, and this is emphasized by the fact that she does not, and is not expected to, remember any of the events. This separation of the spirit from its host is so great that there is no direct communication between them. Any communication must always involve a third party. The spirit who wishes to give a message to the host must leave a message with another individual. In the Haitian phrase, the spirit says: "Tell my horse . . ." As noted above, Lambeck (1981), too, speaking of Mayotte, tells us that the relation between spirit, host, and interlocutor is a triangular one.

In possession trance, women's requirement to be obedient reaches a maximum, yet it may become a means of manipulating the woman's own life circumstances and to affect the lives of others. Lewis (1989) has argued women's possession trance is an element of a war between the sexes. He observed that, in Somalia, women who became ill and whose spirits required expensive gifts, might thereby keep a husband from marrying an additional wife in this polygynous Muslim society.

The symbolism of the relationship between humans and spirits as love, marriage, and sex is not limited to Africa and the African Diaspora. We find it, for example, in Korea and Burma. The sexual aspect of the spirit–human relationship, however, has another dimension as well. Beyond horse and rider, wife and husband, there is the metaphor of the vessel or container and that which it contains. There is an image of two in one. This applies not only to the concept of possession but also to its precondition, the image of a soul contained in a body. The model for this seems to be pregnancy. Curiously, this is confirmed in the metaphorical language used in the Jewish tradition concerning possession, where the term for possession is *ibbur*, impregnation. A number of recent accounts of possession and exorcism in the Israeli press tell stories in which the exorcist/diviner was said to have been able to see the spirit curled up, like a fetus, in the possessed woman's abdomen (Goldish 2002).

These somewhat arbitrarily chosen examples used to illustrate the suggested typology also serve to highlight the distinctive character of each of the cases. It is important to stress the diversity among them in spite of the significant features they share. Dissociation, a psychological mechanism, looms large among these common features and so a word on that subject is indicated. Dissociation occurs in pathological and non-pathological settings. It is learned and therefore can be taught. While initial spontaneous trance may, as we have seen, be of various types, induced trance, as part of ritual, is most likely to be dissociation, regardless of the specific context. Possession trance religions require the spirits' hosts to be in control, at some level, of the ritual performance. Disordered, unpredictable behavior, outside the ritual context, is generally considered dangerous and requires treatment by experts.

Individual spirits have their own characteristics, involving such matters as physical appearance, movements, music, colors, tastes, etc. Over time, these may take on the features of true secondary personalities, with memories of their own. This has led to comparisons with what has been called, in Western psychiatry, MPD (Multiple Personality Disorder) and, more recently, DID (Dissociative Identity Disorder).

In spite of the striking similarities between the spirit personalities that appear in possession trance and the alters of DID, there are also important differences. One of these is that possession trancers learn roles that have cultural meaning in their group and thereby fulfill a significant social role in our three types. One important role concerns a warning about breaches of morality. In situations of the third type, where exorcism is practiced, this is a process which is diametrically opposed to that of the psychotherapist who attempts a cure in a case of DID: the exorcist identifies the strange presence as an intrusive spirit and seeks to get rid of it. The therapist claims the alter or secondary personality as part of the patient's own and attempts to integrate what is seen as the split-off part of the personality with the rest.

Human beings have the ability to share their private experiences, be they dreams, visions, or fantasies, by means of language and other symbolic systems. Thereby, these experiences can be integrated into existing belief systems or can be used to develop and elaborate new beliefs, together with the corresponding systems of rituals. As we have seen, power and aggression, sex and reproduction are recurrent themes in the relations between humans and spirits. But so are issues of morality in interpersonal relations and how these are perceived to have been affected by ongoing social and economic changes resulting from innovations and globalization.

The main concern of this discussion has been with beliefs and states that are culturally patterned in a ritual way and that are given religious meanings. It is clear that the universal psychological and physiological raw material has been used over and over again in human history, and in the process has been culturally shaped in very particular ways which are coherent and consistent with the needs of different types of societies. Moreover, this is an ongoing process, in which new conditions create new needs; some of these are addressed in the examples cited above – and in many others as well – in ways that are a mixture of the old and the new. Other cults and religions, utilizing the themes discussed here, may be expected in the wake of further social and economic changes and the stresses they bring in their wake.

REFERENCES

Behrend, Heike, 1999 *Alice Lakwena and the Holy Spirits: War in Northern Uganda, 1986–97*. Athens: Ohio University Press.

Boddy, Janice, 1989 *Wombs and Alien Spirits: Women, Men, and the Zar Cult in Northern Sudan*. Madison: University of Wisconsin Press.

Bourguignon, Erika, ed. 1973 *Religion, Altered States of Consciousness, and Social Change*. Columbus: Ohio State University Press.

— 1976 Spirit Possession Belief and Social Structure. In *The Extra Human Realm: Ideas and Actions*. Agehananda Bharati, ed. Pp. 17–26. The Hague: Mouton.

Brown, Michael F., 1997 *The Channeling Zone: American Spirituality in an Anxious Age*. Cambridge, MA: Harvard University Press.

Casey, Conerly, 1999 "Dancing Like They Do in Indian Film": Media Images, Possession, and Evangelical Islamic Medicine in Northern Nigeria. Paper presented at the American Anthropological Association meetings, Washington, DC.

Certeau, Michel de, 2000 *The Possessions of Loudon*. M. B. Smith, trans. Chicago: University of Chicago Press.

Corin, Ellen, 1998 Refiguring the Person: Dynamics of Affect and Symbols in an African Spirit Possession Cult. In *Bodies and Persons: Comparative Perspectives from Africa and Melanesia*. Michael Lambeck and Andrew Strathern, eds. Pp. 80–102. Cambridge: Cambridge University Press.

Costa, K. A., 2001 *The Brokered Image: Material Culture and Identity in the Subaital*. Lanham, MD: University Press of America.

Dorsainvil, J. C., 1931 *Vodou et névrose*. Port-au-Prince: Imprimerie La Presse.

Evans-Pritchard, E. E., 1937 *Witchcraft, Oracles, and Magic Among the Azande*. Oxford: Clarendon Press.

Fernandez, James W., 1965 Symbolic Consensus in a Fang Reformative Cult. *American Anthropologist* 67: 902–929.

Firth, Raymond, 1959 Problem and Assumption in an Anthropological Study of Religion. *Huxley Memorial Lecture* 1959. *Journal of the Royal Anthropological Institute* 8: 129–148.

Freed, R. S., and S. A. Freed, 1985 The Psychomedical History of a Low-Caste Woman of North India. *Anthropological Papers of the American Museum of Natural History* 60: part 2.

Goldish, Matt, ed., 2002 *Spirit Possession in Judaism*. Madison: University of Wisconsin Press.

Hallen, Barry, and J. Olubi Sodipo, 1986 *Knowledge, Belief, and Witchcraft: Analytic Experiments in African Philosophy*. London: Ethnographic.

Harner, Michael, 1962 Jívaro Souls. *American Anthropologist* 64: 258–272.

Herskovits, M. J., 1937 *Life in a Haitian Valley*. New York: Knopf.

Kakar, Sudhir, 1982 *Shamans, Mystics, and Doctors: A Psychological Inquiry into India and its Healing Traditions*. New York: Knopf.

Lambeck, Michael, 1981 *Human Spirits: A Cultural Account of Trance in Mayotte*. Cambridge: Cambridge University Press.

Lewis, I .M., 1989 [1971] *Ecstatic Religion: An Anthropological Study of Spirit Possession and Shamanism*, 2nd edn. London: Routledge.

Littlewood, Roland, and Maurice Lipsedge, 1989 *Aliens and Alienists: Ethnic Minorities and Psychiatry*. London: Unwin Hyman.

Masquelier, Adeline, 1999 The Invention of Anti-Tradition: Dodo Spirits in Southern Nigeria. In *Spirit Possession: Modernity and Power in Africa*. H. Behrend and U. Luig, eds. Pp. 34–49. Madison: University of Wisconsin Press.

Murdock, G. P., 1967 *Ethnographic Atlas*. Pittsburgh, PA: University of Pittsburgh Press.

Ong, Aiwha, 1987 *Spirits of Resistance and Capitalist Work Discipline: Factory Women in Malaysia*. Albany: State University of New York Press.

Pressel, Ester, 1973 Umbanda in São Paulo: Religious Innovation in a Developing Society. In *Religion, Altered States of Consciousness, and Social Change*. Erika Bourguignon, ed. Pp. 264–318. Columbus: University of Ohio Press.

Prince, Raymond, 1964 Indigenous Yoruba Psychiatry. In *Magic, Faith, and Healing: Studies in Primitive Psychiatry Today*. Ari Kiev, ed. Pp. 84–120. New York: Free Press of Glencoe.

Rouch, Jean, 1978 Jean Rouch Talks about his Films to John Marshall. *American Anthropologist* 80: 1005–1022.

Russell, A. Sue, 1999 *Conversion, Identity, and Power: The Impact of Christianity on Power Relationships and Social Exchanges*. Lanham, MD: University Press of America.

Spier, Leslie, 1928 Havasupai Ethnography. *American Museum of Natural History Anthropological Papers* 29: 81–292.

Starkey, Marion, 1973 *The Visionary Girls*. Boston, MA: Little, Brown.

Stoller, Paul, 1995 *Embodying Colonial Memories*. New York: Routledge.
Wallace, A. F. C., 1966 *Religion: An Anthropological View*. New York: Random House.
Witzum, E., with N. Grisaru and D. Budowski, 1996 The "Zar" Possession Syndrome Among Ethiopian Immigrants to Israel: Cultural and Clinical Aspects. *British Journal of Psychiatry* 69: 207–225.

SUGGESTED FURTHER READING

Bourguignon, Erika, 1991 *Possession*. Prospect Heights, IL: Waveland.
Oesterreich, Traugott K., 1966 [1921] *Possession, Demoniacal and Other among Primitive Races in Antiquity, the Middle Ages, and Modern Times*. D. Ibberson, trans. Hyde Park, NY: University Books.

FILMS

Bateson, Gregory, and Margaret Mead, 1952 *Trance and Dance in Bali*. New York: New York University.
Prince, Raymond, and Francis Speed, 1964 *Were Ni: He is a Madman. The Management of Psychiatric Disorders by the Yoruba of Nigeria*. Town and Country Productions, UK.
Rouch, Jean, 1954 *Les Maîtres fous*. Ghana: Les Filmes de la Pleiade. With English narration, New York: McGraw-Hill.

CHAPTER 21 Witchcraft and Sorcery

René Devisch

This chapter seeks some understanding of genuine forms of lethal bewitchment. My study is primarily concerned with the captivating and often harmful intercorporeal and transactional field, mobilized between a victimized person and an aggressor's congenital capacity for fatal attack. It is my aim to avoid the ethnocentricity and moralizing that have characterized Western modernist views of "witchcraft" and "sorcery" beliefs and practices.

Before embarking on an endogenous account of bewitchment, it is useful to clarify some crucial terms and distinctions. First, we examine Africanist anthropological studies, adopting the distinctions drawn by Evans-Pritchard (1937: 9–10) between witchcraft, sorcery, and magic. These distinctions – which do not always overlap with local terms (Moore and Sanders 2001: 4) – are made with reference to various interrelated forms of occult attack and defense. Both witchcraft and sorcery use fetishes or learned occult techniques. In Evans-Pritchard's view, the sorcerer is believed to use these techniques, together with toxic substances, for maleficent aims. Thus, *sorcery* refers to learned occult techniques and the use of maleficent fetishes (occult power objects designed to ward off evil from clients, while casting evil or harm onto aggressors).

Witchcraft, like the *evil eye*, primarily refers to congenital or innate (most often unconsciously activated) offensive as well as defensive capacities of the mind. Since fetishes or occult power objects (for seeking good fortune and for defensive and aggressive ends) are extremely versatile and are often used in association with witchcraft as well as sorcery, I consider it counter-productive to stick to the culture-specific (Zande) distinction between witchcraft and sorcery. Witchcraft, like spirit possession (Bourguignon, this volume), entails a very dynamic and intercorporeal understanding of personhood: the life force that permeates the cosmos and the body is also the very substance of relations between blood relatives, the deceased and the living, spirits and human beings. Possession trance, like witchcraft, is very much engaged with the modern world as a symptom and/or treatment, articulating (each in its mode) some of the innovations, paradoxes, big questions, new inequities, and forms of propitiation or exclusion of these specific forms of alter/native modernities (Gaonkar 1999).

My study is primarily concerned with the fatal intercorporeal and transactional field in bewitchment. It focuses on the prereflective consciousness (a kind of intelligence at play in the skin, the "flesh," the senses, and the belly) stirred by interactive bodies and which is gradually consumed by a magma of "forces" (see below) of abjection, transgression, and annihilation. My analysis does not rely much on collective representations replete with fantasies of persecution by envious and nefarious witches in the family. Yet both the symbolism in the protective and vindicating fetishes, as well as the intercorporeal and intersubjective transactional dynamics mobilized by bewitchment, suggest that the maleficent witch is first and foremost a projective figuration of one's anxiety and (largely unconscious) fantasies of threat or persecution, ill luck and insecurity, or "cognitive paranoia" (an expression of Appadurai 1998: 234).

In other words, unlike sorcerers, there are no witches who, out of their own conscious will, attack their victims. Without a bewitched, there is no witch. A fatal bewitchment only comes about at the level of affect in individuals who imagine that an evildoer is responsible for their weakening or ill-fate, and who come to characterize themselves as victimized persons and possibly as counter-attackers. Whereas sorcery refers to a wrongdoer's fatal aggression by means of medicines and bad spells, the witch is the bewitched's negative image projected into the intercorporeal zone constitutive of the former's ill-feeling. The transactional field of witchcraft intertwines with primal fantasies and the intersubjective worlds of desire, corporeality, and significance. A primary idiom of witchcraft is *orality* and perverted *commensality*. Oral witchcraft perverts the vital web of commensality: collective fantasies depict the witch as "eating" or "devouring" the life-substance or vital flow taken from the body of a blood relative or kin, most readily those with whom the witch shares meals and daily physical proximity.

Bewitchment through a strong or envious *gaze* may extend beyond blood ties. Some cultures define such encroachment as the "evil eye" – the very opposite of the protective, benevolent, or watchful eye. It is close to the obscene sorts of intimacy between witch and victim (Mbembe 1992). It can hamper, destroy, or "dry up" the life substance and (re)productive potential, merely by (enviously) looking, praising, or staring at a person or object. Only diviners or divinatory oracles that display the gift to "look into the hidden" can authoritatively "see" and unmask the plot of witchcraft. It is then up to a ritual specialist ("the one who knows") to lift the spells and protect the victim.

I will advance the claim that we need to establish an *endogenous* account of the way bewitchment takes shape within an embodied, yet barely verbalized dimension, of "subjectification" (as Lock, this volume, defines it basically in line with Foucault). This account attempts to place the transactional field of bewitchment within the context of local meaning in line with a given people's very culture-specific epistemological, sociological, and ethical rationale. Throughout, I will engage with an approach to witchcraft's gnostic cosmology and anthropology, leaving aside exogenous sociological accounts of how witchcraft functions as sociopolitical power in processes such as urbanization. Within this same exogenous and sociological tenor, one can examine the role of witchcraft discourses in the collective representations and power games of the public domain vis-à-vis the moralizing "power of defining" exercised by public or postcolonial institutions (van Rinsum 2001). That power has increasingly been monopolized by economic hegemonies, Christian religion or Islam, Western-born academia, and mass media.

This chapter has basically (but not exclusively) an African focus, since it draws primarily on detailed and longstanding information that I have collected since the 1970s by way of interviews and participant observation in southwestern Congo (formerly Zaire) and Kinshasa. There is no space here to describe the manifold local variations; however, the chapter is cognizant of the related topical literature with regard to many Black African and African-American cultures, including the literature on extreme ethnic and state violence in Black Africa. Moreover, the study crosscuts, though all too superficially, with the evil eye syndrome in the circum-Mediterranean cultural zone and its extension in Latin America, as well as the Balkans and the Near East. The literature on witchcraft and the witch-hunt in both pre-industrial and contemporary Europe shows their entanglements with Judaeo-Christian, viri-centered and patriarchal discourses on secure order and malevolence. If, in the great variety of these regions, more or less vaguely expressed suspicions and confessions of occult aggression may witness to witchcraft beliefs and the use of fetishes among a very small minority of people, the great majority of people (commoners and elite alike) share a fascination and fear of the hungry and life-enhancing, jealous and protect-ing, noxious or beneficial, debauching or liberating forces of witchcraft. These quite heterogeneous practices, perceptions, and popular beliefs have no canonical scrip-tures, institutions, or systems. Together, they constitute pre-ethical, diverse, and idiosyncratic attempts at gaining access, on the far side of the enigmatic, elusive, and ambivalent, to what lies behind the intelligible, the ordered and meaningful, and the established social order.

Since my focus here is primarily on the puzzling topic of lethal witchcraft, it is important to understand the notion of maleficent fetish, which comes into play not only in the aggressive phase of bewitchment, but also in the process of unbewitchment. Witchcraft and fetishes may unleash destructive violence – introjected by those who victimize themselves – which reverts against the suspected evildoer or aggressor. Maleficent witchcraft and fetishes channel phantasmagoric "forces" (see below) from macrocosm to microcosm. Through some innate disposition, the witch is believed to attack the victim's body/self: witchcraft unleashes forces and signs in and between the various fields of existence of the victimized or bewitched and the witch. It brings into play intersubjectivity, or rather intercorporeality (see below), and feeds on a flux of forces that emerge in dream, fantasy, and in particular the "imaginary." Witchcraft is at odds with the ontological and rationalist presuppositions and foundations under-lying the dominant concerns, prisms, and discourses of modern Western science, Western bourgeois moralities, neoliberal economy, logical positivism, and political mainstreams. It is witchcraft – in particular its very irreducibility to these presup-positions and concerns – which is one of this chapter's major challenges. And at the same time, "witchcraft and occult beliefs and practices articulate differently with different trajectories of modernity" (Moore and Sanders 2001: 12).

Such processes of bewitchment are probably at work in the quasi-suicidal clinging of anorectic girls to idols such as Madonna and Jane Fonda as martyrs of aerobics. Similarly, adolescents may shape a homosexual identity by identifying with their fantasies regarding Michael Jackson or Mutant X (in US sitcoms) with such exotic names as Magneto, Store, Mystique, and Cyclops. In other words, these adolescents seem to become bewitched by their very fantasy model. Is there any commonality between such bewitching alteration and the stigmatics who, in the late European Middle Ages, "incorporated" the wounds of the crucified Christ (Maertens 1987)?

This chapter is structured as follows. First, it analyzes a number of innovative epistemological tenets in some "alter/native" metaphysics of the uncanny, as well as that of the invisible, the poetics of imagination, and transgression or abjection. Second, it discusses arguments about intercorporeality and deadly pleasure. Third, it examines the notion of dismemberment and terror. Fourth, it puts forward some positive suggestions regarding the strained social fabric.

It is important to note that my familiarization in western Congo with the topic of this study has helped me to disentangle a few paths towards a more genuine and endogenous anthropological understanding. The thematization which follows seeks to render the life of the senses, the play of tropes, the experiences of the lived body and the lived environment, the intense drives, and the tortured social fabric, as well as the researcher's post hoc self-critical reflection on his own native sociocultural setting.

The Alter/native Metaphysics of Force-Fields and Becoming: Towards an Integrative and Endogenous Focus

> We have been led . . . to take interest in the effects of forces, namely those which transcend and escape from the domain of social exchanges – letting out floating energies, not yet fixed or invested in signs and techniques . . . Through what manifestations does the force express itself? How can we conceptualize this force without sliding into the signs representing it? There has been a way out: we must cease to accord primordial attention to the meaning of signs, to their representative contents, in order to concentrate on their *practical effects*. (Gil 1985: 8–10; my translation)

During the Western expansionist era, three major perspectives – the Enlightenment view of universal rationality, the reformist civilizational project based on belief in progress, and the missionary endeavor to supplant African paganism with a salvationist Christianity – all looked down on fetish and witchcraft. They imagined witchcraft as a manifestation of the primitive and bizarre Other in the grip of phantasmagoric irrationality, superstition, and moral backwardness. Evans-Pritchard's classic study (1937) of witchcraft, sorcery, and magic among the Zande of southern Sudan offers an influential, though paradoxical, approach. It clears the way for an endogenous understanding, while it sticks to the evolutionist and rationalist presuppositions of Western science and (bourgeois) culture. Drawing on participant observation, Evans-Pritchard is keen to recognize Zande sorcery as a genuine social reality, almost a form of social engineering. And yet, from his view of science's capacity to assess "reality" in a context-independent manner, he considers the beliefs and behavior of Zande witchcraft and sorcery as bad science and void technical acts. He argues that from an objective stance, there appears to be no factual causal nexus possible between the sorcerous act and the unfortunate outcome it is intended to produce

(Evans-Pritchard 1937: 12). As part of the high-modernist discourses of "Othering" (Rutherford 1999), such a rationalist view and Eurocentric depiction of the Other in terms of lack and alterity remain tenacious. And yet, despite decades of scientific, missionary, technocratic, and educational development programs exported from the West and designed to expand Enlightenment civilization to the colony (later called the Third World and the Periphery), witchcraft/sorcery and fetish, like the evil eye syndrome, remain vigorously alive. Such phenomena confront the dominant discourse of science with its double-edged ignorance. Its reformist (high modernist) and rationalist creed in modern Western hegemonic and globalizing discourse ceaselessly leads it to impose its prejudicial views on local realities and knowledge practices, while ignoring its own Eurocentric prejudices and epistemological biases about universal rationality, transfer of knowledge and business rationale, technocratic know-how, and state crafting. The essence of the problem can be traced to the fact that anthropological studies (more particularly, Africanist ones) dealing with local practices of sorcery pursue fundamentally different perspectives (Crick 1976; de Surgy 1994).

The constructivist perspective looks at witchcraft's amazingly fertile immersion in the imaginary. In actual fact, witchcraft practices seem to celebrate life as re-immersed and re-energized in contact with people's imaginary flux of potent unconscious *forces*. These forces are thought to relate to affects, sensuality, and visceral passion entailing horror and cruelty. Witchcraft thus comprises an imaginary dimension based on a bipolar concept of *life enhancing* and *life deflating*. What witchcraft enhances or weakens are those forces that mainly come into play beyond reflective consciousness, verbal discourse, and conceptual representation. Witchcraft practices are by no means fully transparent and we as the uninitiated cannot elucidate the meanings that its experts proffer. In the constructivist perspective, the notion of witchcraft refers to this inmost or congenital endowment of forces or dispositions that allow for the gifted member of a family to shake the unconscious field of forces both in the family and its life-world. This shaking of forces occurs when the gifted person plays out the unlocalizable plots of defense or attack that escape any conventional pigeonholing and understanding. Witchcraft's plots may be submitted to a divinatory oracle's scrutiny that draws on endogenous etiological frameworks to interpret the propagation of anomalies and ills in the intercorporeal fields of the domestic, kinship, reproduction, and micropolitics. Bewitchment appears to entail the victim's deprivation of forces, as well as a violation of their personhood. Here, interpretation takes a persecuting and projective twist: the evil resides in and comes from the Other.

A second approach to understanding witchcraft is termed *cognitive*. It privileges representations and beliefs. The cognitive framework seeks out the cluster of philosophical, cosmological, and ethical assumptions that a particular social group deploys through narratives in order to grasp the meaning and vagaries of existence. These might include misfortune, illness, and death, as well as any abnormal circumstance in the human and phenomenal environment. Here, the notion of maleficent witchcraft mainly refers to anti-models, the role of which is to promote the integration of norms through extreme deviance and subsequent abhorrence. Thus, as an anti-model, maleficent witchcraft only has a repulsive characteristic able to affect some deviant pattern of behavior. That is to say, witchcraft allegations point to problematic social relations that the plot of bewitchment aims to resolve beyond formal institutional means. Inasmuch as witchcraft conjectures and accusations prove to be unsystematic, informal, and endlessly modifiable, and without a proper cosmology or public practitioners, this approach assimilates witchcraft to society's informal cognitive procedures for dealing with social symptoms and ills. Thus, when making his case for understanding witchcraft practices among the Kongo in west Congo, MacGaffey (1977, 2000: 203) offers an argument that refers to witchcraft merely as a constitutive element of people's broader cultural and cognitive system. Other scholars are committed to the same view. Crick (1976: 109–127), for example, thinks that, apart from its usage in a particular period and culture, no essential particularity lies implicit in witchcraft that might be singled out from moral or semantic configurations (associating particular evaluating ideas, person categories, rules and conceptual systems, with certain types of action and motivation). He therefore proposes an analytic obviation of the topic itself (1976: 112). He justifies this move with reference to analogous treatments of totemism by Lévi-Strauss and kinship by Needham.

The third approach to witchcraft takes us into narrow *sociological* or *sociologist* considerations. A sociologist perspective is one that largely focuses on the possible cathartic or obstetric effects of the practices and allegations of maleficent witch-craft on individual and collective health and relationships (Gillies 1976: xxvii). In this context, and in the course of an etiological examination (whether divinatory or juridical), the term witchcraft serves to qualify the illicit character of acts, since these acts appear to be devoid of any reconciliatory or obstetric effect. This perception has also been the focus of an argument by Bayart (1989), to the effect that people use the idiom of witchcraft as a popular mode for dealing with life's whims and with the savage pretence of hegemonic state machinery. Moreover, as suggested by Geschiere (1995), the leveling effect of witchcraft is rather weak in the political arena. In many African countries, such as Cameroon, Geschiere considers representations, rumors, accusations, and practices of witchcraft (*djambe*) to be more focused on people's worries about consumption and protection against their aggressors. More import-antly, it is the search for social security and survival that here most preoccupies individuals and social groups.

Unlike these accounts of witchcraft, I will suggest that witchcraft primarily per-tains to the imaginary and comprises practices whose modes and concrete effects are to be contextually understood in culture-appropriate ways. It is within the societies in which witchcraft is acknowledged as self-evident and solemnly real (Nyamnjoh 2001) that such ways – reaching beyond the mere representational level – are apprehended. Such an integrative and tentatively more endogenous approach is in line with such authors as Augé (1975), Comaroff and Comaroff (1993), Mallart Guimera (1981), and Moore and Sanders (2001). Thus, witchcraft remains a relevant topic for research, necessitating a particular anthropological approach that as far as possible entails endogenous perspectives – insofar as it is designated, for example, in the cultures of Bantu Africa by its own specific and related terms deriving from the proto-Bantu root **dog-* (Guthrie 1970: 111).

Favret-Saada's studies (see below) of the psychodynamic, social, and cosmological fields of forces interlocking with the imaginary that are mobilized and consecrated in unbewitchment in contemporary rural Brittany offer an innovative endogenous epistemology for analyzing bewitchment. Further, a fascinating intercultural debate on this topic was inaugurated in *Witchcraft Dialogues* (Bond and Ciekawy 2001), which examines the limitations of Western-bound intellectual traditions and explores new paradigms to deal with the metaphysical properties and people's lived experiences of "witchcraft" and "sorcery." This and similar postmodern anthropological encounters (Appiah 1992; Hountondji 1994; Ngugi wa Thiong'o 1986; Scott 1998; van Rinsum 2001) attempt to open up to modes of alter/native structuring of the life-world. It deeply resists the appropriation of the plurality of situated or context-specific cultural practices into the modern Western (Hellenistic) preoccupation with some mono-essentiality of life, as this is very much equated in high modernism with increasing orderliness and the logic of non-contradiction. Unlike the West, African cosmologies in particular do not recognize a strict dichotomy between the material, the measurable, and the tangible on the one hand, and the non-material on the other. Thus, such cosmologies do not cling to a view according to which only the tangible is demonstratively real, sound, and valuable. In matters of nurturing or of the weakening of life, ritual experts, as well as witches, may attribute equal efficacy to beliefs and pragmatic behaviors about that part of the life-world where existence can only be imagined and sensed (such as curse, dream, bewitchment, and ancestral presence). Their practices are therefore intended primarily to sustain the community, so as to increase the life-force of its members.

THE RIFT BETWEEN THE HYBRIDIZATION OF THE WITCH AND THE MASTER NARRATIVE OF REASON

Witchcraft's cosmology and anthropology are basically traversed by becoming, propagation by contagion, hybrid amalgamations, fickle fortunes, co-functioning forces, and the affects of a nature that is out of reach to reason (Deleuze and Guattari 1987: 233). As such, it is impervious to the master narratives of the so-called modern regimes of order and reason that associate progress with state rule and administration, the triumph of agnostic science and technocracy. Witchcraft develops beyond the rationale of any orthodoxy, whether derived from the reception of a divine ordering and unifying of things that make up the world, or from a Hegelian-like World-Spirit yielding the paths of Law and Order, or the Enlightenment dictates of Reason and Progress. It discredits the Christian world-historical truth regime of (original) sin and subsequent triumph of divine redemption or salvation. According to Eurocentric modernity, an overarching world order and well-being grow out of a readable orientation and planning in concrete space-time settings. Christianity (as a universal oriented "religion of the book"), Western science, and the modern bureaucratic state approach humankind and its environment in their *legible* and planned dimensions (Van Rinsum 2001: 2; Scott 1998). Discarding such aims, witchcraft functions in the context-specific realms of division and multiplicity, and in the pretence of untraceable or unlocalizable ubiquity. The clairvoyant witch participates in and clings to another mode of reality pertaining to the otherworldly. Through a keen sense of vision, they engage and merge with the beings therein, and tap their power, transmuting it, while creating confusion about the stirring of life and the sheer malignancy of human destructiveness.

Taken in its own right (that is, endogenously), witchcraft (as is the case in south-western Congo, in Yaka society) points to non-dichotomizing ontological premises, unconstrained by the rationalizing categories, the moralizing perceptions, values, fences, and divisions of diurnal and public community. According to its own meta-physics, witchcraft captures and channels intercorporeal, intersubjective forces, energies, fevers, vigor, and voluptuousness within and across the environment, human society, and the worlds of the living and the dead. Witchcraft relies on the particular innate ability of the witch to embody and transact to a victim the uncanniest of forces, such as the dreaded crocodile, the pounding lightning, a vulture killing its prey, con-tagious bacteria, and poisons.

In line with Edvard Hviding's (1996: 173) endogenous analysis of the alter/native epistemology of the Marovo in the Solomon Islands, I venture to say that witches incorporate and encompass simultaneously several levels of causality in people–environment and people–people relationships, surpassing and mixing up dualisms such as culture–nature, physical–non-physical, life–death, and beauty–abomination. The witches' partly unconscious meddling and capacity of interference seem to unfold beyond the grasp of the visual classificatory logic of filiated regimes and hereditary reproduction. Witches have the congenital capacity to extract or mani-pulate flows of energies or forces from the intercorporeal fields that interconnect subjectivities via reciprocal webs of consanguinity and filiation, or the sharing of meals, bodily intimacy, and experience. Witchcraft develops along the borders and passageways between the mutually transposable physical, social, and cosmic bodies (namely, the human body, the family, the life-world), the tangible world here and the otherworldly. Yet the witch relies on innate and/or special initiatory (visionary, ecstatic) capacities or methods to arouse, concentrate, and transact these forces across worlds (namely, the worlds of the living and deceased kin; of affects, emotions, body, family, and life-world).

The "grands récits" of thought's sophistication in Western high modernity concern the "non-personal" life of thought, such as science's puzzling problem of validation, fallibility, or erroneous judgment. Witchcraft, on its behalf, is basically about a very "personal," idiosyncratic, or subjective intertwinement of unrestrained affects and excessive desire (impulses, greed, lust, attraction, hunger), wild (Dionysian) sensibility, the sovereign power of the imagination and of passion (the Dionysian fusion with images and forces of the world), and with paradoxical incentives to change. Also deeply enmeshed with the imaginary, witchcraft mobilizes and unleashes, in the intercorporeal fields of forces and phantasms in which the victim is enmeshed, plots of envy and malice, buffoonery and a-social compulsions, seduction and quarrelsomeness, empathy and treason. Witchcraft's proliferating transfusions of dual (positive and negative, life-bearing and death-giving) forces into the bewitched is almost indiscriminately able to enhance or deflate the victim's vital tissue of affects and life-sharing.

THE TENSION BETWEEN BENIGN AND MALEFICENT WITCHCRAFT

As a matter of fact, when I saw this red fish, I was greatly terrified . . . its head was just like a tortoise's head, but it was as big as an elephant's head, and it had over 30 horns

and large eyes which surrounded the head. All these horns were spread out as an
umbrella. It could not walk but was only gliding on the ground like a snake and its
body was just like a bat's body and covered with long red hair like strings. It could only
fly to a short distance, and if it shouted a person who was four miles away would hear.
All the eyes which surrounded its head were closing and opening at the same time as if
a man was pressing a switch on and off. (Tutuola 1952: 79–80)

Benign or life-seeking witchcraft entails an innocent exploration of extraterritorial-
ity, the utopian and libidinal spectacle of lust and vagabond desire. Witchcraft and
fetishes become maleficent in their attack on sight, while perverting every code. This
representational pathos arouses aggressive impulses, intruding upon those weakened
by fear of dismemberment: their sense of integrity and autonomy is attacked. The
deployment of defensive fetishes or power objects and aggressive witchcraft depends
on the phenomenon of "catastrophic retroflexion" and the homoeopathic principle
present in the "floating signifier" of residue or detritus. Fetishes may at the same
time serve as a means of aggression or protection; in the latter case they take the
form of a counter-attack. Witchcraft and fetishes are thus able to depict an imaginary
order inasmuch as it assigns meaning to bivalent forces that are both morbid and
life-seeking. It is my hypothesis that bewitched persons kill themselves by introjecting
either the fatal desires of intimidating Others or the images of death channeled
through the fetishes' floating signifiers.

Utopian Imageries

In the widespread beliefs among the Yaka in southwestern Congo, as well as
among other central African peoples, witchcraft is first described in a most innocent
mood as a fantastic realm of energies, unbridled lust, and sensualism. Through folklore, mainly addressing children, people place benign witchcraft in the realm typified
by fabulous imagination and passionate acts beyond the reach of any judging gaze.
Understood in this perspective, benign witchcraft, assisted with appropriate fetishes,
seeks to disarm the misfortunes of daily life and, in particular, stave off the threat
of death. It does this basically by provoking a mood of lust and frenzy, which is a
utopian state whose depiction appears akin – as I will argue below – to that of the
collective trance and glossolalia observed in the independent healing churches of
the Holy Spirit (better called healing communes of the sacred spirit). Such a mood
is evocative of the pervasive dandy cult adopted by the young in many Black African
cities. It is generally displayed with pride and in a style of verbal relaxation and
mimicry. The frenzy mood also manifests itself in other mockingly ostentatious and
hedonistic life styles propagated by transnational mass media.

As the popular fairy tale has it, benign witchcraft is hosted within a time-space of
wonders. Only through dream, or as a result of magical power, can such a space be
made more accessible to an individual. It is a commonplace practice to look to this
world as the dwelling place of ancestors or deceased grandparents, who let blessings
flow over their offspring. Following this conception, domestic animals such as dogs
are believed to be valuable and clever companions to a hunter or traveler, as they are

capable of showing the way to man's desire and furthest utopia. The stories related
to desires and utopia are engraved in children's memories as modes of original and
dreamlike exploration. They reveal the fact that a benign witch is an enchanted person
very much like the hunter or like the "big man" (*le patron*, the boss) in the city
showing off as a playboy. Benign witchcraft celebrates a pre-objective and fantasmatic
approach to being-in-the-world, which precedes symbolic function, cogitation, or
reflective cognition (see Berry 1993). It is an astounding dreamlike journey across
the world of uncanny strangeness and beyond the familiar patterns of life and conventions. An ordinary person certainly cannot be expected to enter this wonderful,
invisible world that is normally destined to the enchanted person. Such dreamlike
wandering seems to celebrate a mood of "deterritorialization" (Deleuze and Guattari
1987), effected through an initiatory excursion or rebirth into the virtualities of an
"elsewhere" in search of primordial energies and the levers of fortune.

As it is, witchcraft points to a culture-unique topos of unboundedness, escape,
intrusion, and dislocation. It is in this topos that an enchanted individual comes to
grips with the liberating and awakening experiences of bodily affects and emotions.
These emotions and affects include desire, seduction, passion, chance, aspiration,
hunger, curiosity, avidity, and ardor. This is a level of existence beyond conscience,
beyond the usual cognitive maps of space-time limits, resemblance, contiguity, and
causality. Such vagrancy is believed to occur in the deepest night, between midnight
and the first cockcrow, when darkness enshrouds everything in an aura of dream and
enigma. Witchcraft expresses an aspiration or a yearning for people's fantastically
basic source of vitality, emotion, and gratification. All these elements extend far
beyond the sociocultural order instilled by distinction and division.

Benign witchcraft's interactions with different animate and inanimate features
of the environment follows rhizome-like tracings, co-emerging and co-fading with
nomadic movement, multi-nodal intertwinement, and transaction by contagion or
intrusion. The rhizome (Deleuze and Guattari 1987: 10–11) is a decentered, non-
hierarchical, and non-signifying system lacking an organizing memory and proper
direction. It develops at the crossroads of various and discontinuous sites. It is an
anti-genealogy, a short-term memory or anti-memory. Its mode of operation passes
through variation, expansion, conquest, capture, and offshoots. Witches sense out
emotional and sensual lines of flight to deterritorialize themselves into a line of self-
empowering (or, possibly, annihilation) maleficent witchcraft (Deleuze and Guattari
1987: 250).

This form of witchcraft, along with other modes of lustful frenzy, stands in
relation to a floating point where forces and distinctions emerge and vanish: this
is the realm of arousal by image and representation, and of the interplay between
desire and response, the animal and the human, dreaming and reflection, night and
day, death and life, evil and innocence. Witchcraft's imagery is very much at home
in these bivalent zones. On the one hand, it enjoys the utopia of uninhibited desire,
while, on the other, it constantly faces up to the consequences of inertia, void, loss,
or death in the midst of life. However, the fabulous capacity that innocuous witchcraft possesses for inventiveness resists discursive distinctions, formations, and ethical
law. More fundamentally, it is a space-time order in which the one is included in
the other, a bivalent world embracing both wonder and innocent predation, where
transgression and the poetics of intrusion hold sway.

Maleficent Witchcraft and Fetishes: Representational Pathos and Versatility

We noted earlier that sociologist approaches might well be inadequate for understanding and describing maleficent witchcraft. From my standpoint, fetishes used in maleficent witchcraft are transpersonal, imaginary, passionate, and disruptive props and plots of "raw experience" (Feldman 1997). They are indistinguishably entrenched in the intricate processes of ingestion and excretion, both life-bearing and death-giving. A careful comparison between data collected among the Yaka people and those from other people in west Congo suggests that such fetishes may include such deposits as shards collected from a tomb. They may also consist of grains of soil surreptitiously taken from below the bed of an old widow or widower suffering from rectal piles and unable to control their urination. Sometimes, maleficent fetishes are made up of a piece of cloth or leaves that a girl has used at her first menstruation. At other times, such fetishes also comprise a madman's saliva, a rooster's heart, or the so-called "sperm of lightning" (vitrified sand or the latex exuded from a lightning-torn tree). Finally, such fetishes may also contain the blood and other abominable residual substances of someone who has fallen victim to a murderous attack. Only after the ingredients have been deposited on the tomb of an irascible ancestor are they tightly wrapped up in a loincloth for the client to tie it against his or her rectum.

The question, obviously, is about the effect that such recourse to fetishes may have on the habitual and pre-adapted ways of seeing of those exposed to these plots. As a "representational pathos" (Taussig 1998) confronted with a versatile assemblage of delirious manifestations, the fetish leaks its whirligig semantic and ethical turbulence and mess into its victims. The fetish is a weird prop where meaning as determinate order collapses (Kristeva 1980). The substances amalgamated in the fetish come from people's various (inhabited, sensuous, practical, and knowledge) scenes of life. The manipulation and amalgamation of such substances deconstruct the ethical yardsticks guiding a social group and its culture-specific orders of speech. Any sure ethical foundation for human dignity, authority, and sense of belonging is attacked in the hideous and delirious signifiers amalgamated in the fetish. Imbalance, encroachment, uncanny luck, and death wishes are all intermingled with the fetish to exact hatred and vengeance (Baudrillard 1990; Parkin 1985; Ricoeur 1967).

As will become clear below, through its amalgamation of residues and floating signifiers, the fetish (like maleficent witchcraft itself) resonates with imaginary appetites and operates in a no-man's land of vertigo and fascination. The privileged site comprises foot imprints, crushed leaves, ash, and traces of blood. These residues form the realm of indeterminate contamination, and a reversal between attack and ineptness. This reversal also occurs between the voluptuousness of engendering life and inebriation in the face of death and corruption. Thus, for example, in a bewitching *do ut des* transactional logic, the parent-accomplice claims his or her rights to the booty of the next witchcraft transaction, or to magical economic gain or political power once his or her (grand)child or (classificatory) sister's or brother's child is handed over to the nocturnal witches' market for death or transformation into a mindless zombie.

The fetish and witchcraft work at the edge of cognitive and moral subjection and mastery. Like any fatal bewitchment, the fetish breaks every code or order of things so as to release more fascinating life-forces and stratagems, which feed the regenerative capabilities to the point of emptying these out. Certain forms of murderous witchcraft, especially those accompanying the fatal manipulation of fetishes steered at a victim, are cast along the lines of a process of birth in reverse. Alternatively, they are conceived as a kind of death-giving birth or anal birth-giving that is entrenched in decay. The fetish is as bivalent and versatile as witchcraft itself. The significance of such bivalence and versatility is that the fetish combines both life-bearing and harmful potencies, greed for life and the lust of predation of the attacker-intruder. It invests the libidinal energy in a sculpture or a pouch filled with bewitching residue. The fetish acts as a surrealist or fantastic support for the actions of the witch. As such, it can convey a series of imagoes of group energies dealing with death, rather than life forces. In addition, such a fetish excites more fears than it assuages. Its bivalence and versatility may arouse fear of dismemberment in the bewitched person. On the one hand, it can arouse or even undermine the sense of integrity and autonomy for that person. On the other hand, it might protect and enhance their well-being and success. As a bivalent reality, the fetish constitutes a delirious point of contamination between death and life, or between violation and restitution of the social code. It is understood that in order for the witch to capture and absorb the destructive forces of the fetish, they need to lick the fetish and apply it to their rectum for a while. The witch thereby seeks to carry annihilating forces beyond any homoeopathic possibility for reversal and redress.

Catastrophic Retroflection, Floating Signifier, and Cross-Breeding

As has been suggested above, witchcraft captures and enacts a delirious impulse and it does so in the course of changing the order of the body and things into so-called catastrophic retroflection (Kristeva 1980: 226). By this is meant the lack of differentiation that occurs between opposites (such as life and death, food and excrement). This lack turns witchcraft and the fetish into a paradoxical crucible where antithetic forces come together and in which Logos and madness find a common origin. Maleficent witchcraft, which the fetish weaves, pushes the amalgamation of these opposite forces to the point that they become untamed. Symbolism itself is twisted and reality seems to slide into the surreal. Fetishes used in lethal witchcraft are charged with potent forces, despite being no more than ashes or a mixture of charred remains ground into powder. The mixture resembles nothing in particular; that is, it offers no visible signs with which one can decipher the nature of the fetish. This sort of magma intrudes upon conventional frames of encoding. As an untraceable play of signs, the mixture dissolves difference and its modes of concoction blur origin and violence, sense and nonsense, attraction and repulsion.

At its most general, the maleficent fetish develops at the behavioral and semiological boundaries that define the relevant culture and its possibilities. On that fringe, it carries floating signifiers that resist conventional meaning, for the fetish at this point is crossbreeding the determinate and the indeterminate, the self and the other, the origin and its disintegration. There is a puzzling analogy between the floating signifier in witchcraft, the cyborg-like nature of the fetish, and the dis-individualizing of self brought about by some new biomedical technologies (see Lock, this volume). The floating signifier (Gil 1985: 24) is often bound up to a type of residue or to a hollow or bivalent sign. It is drained of its load or symbolic valence while feeding itself on impulses and psychic forces generated by the collective imaginary. Such an object serves a different purpose to its habitual use in normal circumstances. The floating signifier is severed from its conventional meaning, maximized by criteria such as smell, role, and cosmological habitat. It erodes the conventional principles of categorical identification and semantic articulation.

A clear example of how the signifier floats is embedded in the Bantu traditional belief that it is associated with an individual's doubleness. The latter involves not only his or her shadow but also his or her remains, which includes bodily secretions and excretions (i.e., saliva, sweat, nail clippings, hair, urine, menses, imprints, teeth, and any old garment). These remains are bivalent in that they form a residue carrying the mark of its origin as well as of the body from which it is detached, thus facing the ensuing loss of its original form. In this sense, a residue appears to be a volatile sign that materializes both the origin and the disintegration of things, meaningfulness and phantasmagoria.

INTERCORPOREALITY AND DEADLY PLEASURE

> In December of 1979 I set out for the town of Wanzerbe in the western region of the Republic of Niger . . . People warned me not to seek out Kassey. "She can transform herself into a vulture," they told me. "She can maim or kill you," they cautioned, "by reciting a few verses." "She'll make you disappear if she doesn't like you."
>
> Despite these warnings, I went on to Wanzerbe, and sought out the illustrious woman. Having heard through the grapevine of my imminent arrival, Kassey left town. Dejected at Kassey's refusal to meet with me, I wondered what to do. People suggested that I see Dangar, also a woman, who was Kassey's powerful associate. And so I did.
>
> . . . Our meeting was an abject failure. And so I returned to my host's house, ate dinner, and went to bed.
>
> In the middle of the night I awoke to the tatter of steps on the roof and became aware of a presence in the room. Frightened, I wanted to bolt from the house. I started to get up but could not move. I pinched my thighs and felt nothing. And then I remembered what my teacher, Adamu Jenitongo, had told me: "Whenever you feel danger, recite the *genji how*," the Songhay incantation that by harmonizing the forces of the bush protects the person reciting it. And so I recited it until I began to feel sensation in my feet and legs . . . (Stoller 1998: 239)

The best way to illustrate the ideas of intercorporeality and deadly pleasure is perhaps to refer to the familiar pattern of beliefs drawn from the Yaka of southwestern Congo. The Yaka kinship system combines patrilineal descent with uterine filiation (Devisch and Brodeur 1999: 51). Their divinatory etiology of misfortune identifies two major sources of fatal bewitchment: abusive feeding on uterine blood ties, and the visual intrusion implicating agnates.

The first model of fatal witchcraft operates along uterine lines. It is viewed as a form of "*eating* the commensal." The ability to bewitch is believed to be congenital in the sense that one normally becomes a witch when one has inherited it from birth, either by one's mother or maternal uncle. On this account, allegations of witch-craft seek to domesticate in-laws and married women as well as to sustain exogamy. It appears that when witches attack or curse, they only do so when a maternal uncle has "interfered," that is, when he has made himself an accomplice. Witches tap the vital flow from other kinsfolk. The transmission and exercise of congenital witchcraft is largely a question of the matrikin, which involves three generations of uncles as well as their sisters' children. Obviously, this occurs in a strictly exogamous sphere. The uterine lineage describes bewitchment as a form of selfish eating or feeding from the blood of a consanguine. Bewitchment is portrayed as an oral drainage of forces, in a perversion of the family's basic web of sharing and commensality.

The second model of fatal witchcraft within the agnatic line is transmitted and exploited as a form of sharp *vision*, a correlate of the elders' keen sense of vision. The agnatic life force flows from ancestor to descendant and stands out to be most powerful in the agnatic elder. This force endows the agnatic leader with clear-sightedness and a piercing gaze of supervision. Sometimes such a force turns out to be the witch-like intrusive eye, enabling the senior member of the patrikin to steer his or her junior victim. It does so by letting the aggressor penetrate the victim's thoughts, heart, motives, and dreams. In this context, the junior members of the family generally nurse some fears of the family elders. It is believed that the only way for a young family member to stem or contain the fear resulting from the elders' anger is to provide them with gifts and deference.

Generally speaking, a patriarch sees that the elder in his lineage will avenge any of his descendants who suffer from bewitchment. This means that the witch will be made to pay back for the damage they have caused. How, then, does the lineage elder come to know who bewitches his kin? We said earlier that the patriarch is generally guided by his clear-sightedness. In other words, he is deemed to have power objects that sustain his ability to detect and deflect a fatal bewitching transaction occurring among members of the lineage. Any elder's intrusive and lethal gaze, introjected by a victimized family member, can dispossess the latter from his or her selfhood and inner life force. However, among the Yaka, the elder's gaze by itself cannot kill unless there is complicity in the matriline on behalf of the mother or the mother's brother (i.e., the maternal uncle): both may "eat away" the victim's life essence or vital flow. When the bewitched person is made aware of the impending harm through an oracle, they may legitimately respond by placing a curse on the suspected culprit.

BLENDING EROS WITH THANATOS

> "That is why you ate him. I saw you last night turning yourself into a howl. I was sleeping as a caiman with an eye half-opened. I saw you. You grasped his soul into your paws. You fled to the leaves of the big kapok-tree. Other people turning themselves into howls joined you. It was a boisterous dance. You ate the skull. It is you who ate the brain before leaving the remains to your associates. It is you and only you!" roared Colonel Papa Le Bon. (Kourouma 2000: 68; my translation)

The imagery of predatory witchcraft and evil eye is widespread in many societies. It lives out a crude complaisance with the undomesticated and the transgressive in a delirious odyssey of desire and male libido. Put briefly, predatory oral witchcraft and its cannibalistic phantasms blend commensality and sexuality into a single exorbitant act of incestuous mating and cannibalistic orgy (Pouillon 1972). The indistinct affinity between incestuous sexuality (the latter defined as an act believed to "reverse the course of blood") and the "devouring" of blood relatives ("alimentary incest"), like the evil eye belief in the Balkans and the Near East, or the circum-Mediterranean cultures, with its reverberation in Latin America (Fredrikson 2000; Krohn-Hansen 1995; Taussig 1980), represent a delirious blending of *Eros* and *Thanatos.*

In a sense, the blending of communion and depletion surrenders itself to the paranoid delusion of envy and group persecution. What the evil eye does in these circumstances is to convey a powerful libidinized load of ocular rape and unconscious exhibition. In so doing, its syndrome fosters ocular aggression and voyeurism. In the hispanophone Mediterranean setting of the unconscious, the evil eye or *mirada fuerte* (strong staring) stands for the inescapably intrusive eye of the community, which arouses a pervasive sense of persecution and paranoid anxiety (Gilmore 1987: 154). Witchcraft builds on the instinctual and monstrous dialectics between the prolific pleasurable drive and forces associated with devouring cannibalism and incest.

The extent to which witchcraft pervades the collective imaginary in African countries is revealed through stories, contemporary novels, and folklore (Kourouma 2000; Sony Labu Tansi 1979; Tutuola 1952). They portray the collective fantasies according to which family heads or other accomplices, during a meeting in broad daylight, agree "to kill [poison] a descendant." The vitiated familial sharing secretly transmutes the elders into conspiring witches. By the same token, these witches engage with the destruction of the gift-economy and its virtue of binding kin: the self-serving taking of the gift of life consecrates what it destroys.

As the common beliefs hold, witches join the cannibalistic banquet by means of their invisible double. With the aid of their fetishes, witches are able to change their shape – more precisely, split themselves into two parts. This means that they project their shadow or double far beyond the physical body: witches move out of their beds and assume the form of a sinister bird or insect. They leave behind their dormant bodily sheath and travel in a way that makes it difficult for them to be spotted. The destination of their journey is the nocturnal marketplace, where they meet like-minded and naked associates in order to dance and indulge their sexual and incestuous desires.

TROPE OF THE NOCTURNAL BANQUET OF MALEFICENT WITCHES

Folklore narrates the way in which witches feed on human blood acquired through butchering and distribution following a witches' court ruling. The working of this mysterious tribunal is believed to be based on the *lex talionis*, where revenge is exacted. Such a court constitutes a particular topological understanding of both the physical and social bodies in the cannibalistic transaction. Reflecting their rank and former transactions, the participants transmit or receive one or another value-laden morsel of the victim's dismembered body: head, heart, breast, bone, mouth, hip, leg, or sexual organ. These parts are "eaten" raw that very night. Alternatively, in order to escape denunciation by the divinatory oracle or the so-called witchfinder, the witches may take their victim home and eat the meat when the victim's burial and the ensuing consultation with the oracle have taken place. In the latter case, the victim will be very weakened and languish for some time before death occurs, as they have already been drained of the life force. They eventually die from exhaustion, or their untimely death may occur as a result of a dubious accident.

The trope of the maleficent witch allows the collective imagination to affirm some basic rules for intercorporeality and intersubjectivity in the family group. Here, family members establish jointness-in-differentiation, adjust self-serving lust and life-sustaining sharing. The trope negatively depicts the social ideal that the kin-group prescribes to each member: the imperative of a smooth integration into the group via an acceptance of the incontrovertible norm of reciprocity regarding sharing of life and life-sustaining activities between co-residential family members (namely, those sharing the same house, fireplace, meals, bodily smell, intimacy of the night, conjugal bed). Through the fantasized scenes of the fatal horror of witchcraft, the familial order produces an unmistakably inverse image of itself which it is then better able to denounce. This inversion has an integrating epistemic function serving to stitch together the diverse roles, values, classificatory categories, and cultural spaces of the domestic group and intermarrying families. In popular stories and etiologies in numerous anti-witchcraft practices, the character of the witch is a living example of what the average family member should not become. They all depict what will inevitably happen to family members if they stray from the path set out by the ancestors.

Clearly, the witches' banquet negatively evokes the law of commensality and the prohibition of incest. The more the collective imagination regards the nocturnal markets as an explosion of sexual inebriety and delirious voluptuousness in a fantasized, hence fantasmatic, spectacle of rape, murder, and trade in the blood of relatives, the more the imagery of the witch spells out for the society the limits of understanding and of life, even the basis of their own survival. Denying or negating any sociality in a drastic and delirious manner, the participant in maleficent witchcraft faces abjection as a mixture of bodily affect and inner sense, piercing his or her awareness with the absolute prohibition of murder and incest set in place by the incontrovertible law of retaliation. The insane scene of incest and cannibalism allows the collective imagination – or rather that conscience which emerges in the life of a group – to transform hallucinatory perceptions and fantastic constructs of witchcraft into a depiction of the *lex talionis*. This might be phrased: "Whoever abuses the life of a member of their own group is finally turned on themselves and will consume their own flesh and self-destruct." In order to survive, an individual must acknowledge the law of blood's necessary reproduction in the ongoing familial saga, and thus the right of another to life and to a place in the kin-group as on a par with one's own.

FATAL DISMEMBERMENT AND TERROR

When dealing with the activities of witches, one faces the question of how they actually kill their victims. We can only work on the assumption that a bewitched person takes his or her own life by incarnating the mortal desires of the intimidating

Others. They can only kill themselves by introjecting delirious references to destruction and death-giving. These references are enabled and transmitted by the fetishes and phantasms involved with bewitchment. The fetish and the bewitching threat, in other words, may suffocate or empty out the body-self of the victimized, by mobilizing energies, imagoes, and/or unconscious impulses of fatal attack: their traces are engrafted in commonly shared spheres.

Following Greenwood (2000), Kapferer (1997), Moore and Sanders (2001), and Overing (1978), we venture to label these spheres – as well as the meltdown of their traces – as follows. First, we have forms of intentionality involving spaces and time horizons (such as origin, simultaneity, premonition, past, present, and future). These forms mobilize intentions and emotions between people and their life-worlds, or fix inner identities. Secondly, there are culturally shaped, sensual, kinesthetic (olfactory, aural, visual, tactile) arts, habits, and dispositions involved. These are tied in with the otherworldly, which makes it seem sensible and realistic. Thirdly, culturally shaped fantasies emerge, as well as collective anxieties and symbolic traces. The traces are carried by beliefs, stories, spells, incantations, and paraphernalia, as well as by the substances of the voluptuous, uncanny, nonsensical, void, destitute, deficient, wild, wicked, disastrous, horrifying, and the like.

Bewitching spells, like the weird assemblages in fetishes, stir affects, emotions, and bodily motions deep within the bewitched. Through contagion, and in particular through an attack on the senses and sensibility of the bewitched, they seek to transfuse to the victim the foredoom ordained by the spell and its horizon of the anomalous. The victim may waste away or be exposed to misfortune, first by changing their very self-perception while clinging fantastically to the vindictive mood mobilized by the culture-appropriate spell: such a mood is reshaped by fairy tales, for example, or is transferred by the imageries of the presumed aggressor's secret piercing of an "egg" ("meant to summon the vulture of lightning to snatch its prey"), or by the imageries of the aggressor's circular crushing of a toxic mushroom with a club or between two stones (so as to conjure the victim's mortal accident in a hunt, or while the latter is handling medicines). The power object whose nefarious use is being imagined by the victimized person entails a threshold or borderline functioning of deadly contagion. "A fiber stretches from a human to an animal, from a human or an animal to molecules, from molecules to particles, and so on to the imperceptible. Every fiber is a Universe fiber. A fiber strung across borderlines constitutes a line of flight or of deterritorialization" (Deleuze and Guattari 1987: 249).

In many an African society, similar regimes of transworld contagion and composing are also integral to the way senior office holders participate in the life of the group and its world. Such acts are potentially baneful and form an integral and indispensable part of their social position and ritual office. Such office entitles them to trust and to probe the ancestrally prescribed and inherited (hence, incorporated) paths of ritual action, which may be at odds with the commonsense course of life or activities (characteristic of the commoners). Where their conversion to Christianity and membership in a Christian or healing church forbids witchcraft and the use of fetishes, or at least any public reference to them, converts turn to prayer, benedictions, and offerings as an alternative recourse to vindictive justice-seeking and protection from persecution or the whims of life.

From the argument above, we can understand that the lethal efficacy of the fetish and of aggressive witchcraft stems from linking a series of bodily sensations (e.g., habitus, sentiment, sensation, and imagination) with the sub-symbolic imaginary order. Such an order is disrupted in a flood of unbridled energy in direct and wild interference with the physical body, the senses, and the libido. Maleficent fetishes and fatal witchcraft stir up the group imaginary's stock of floating forces and imagoes or vital signs of all sorts (regarding the uncanny, chaos, the economy of the invisible, and shocking transgression). The person surrendering to those forces finds his or her affects and bodily sensations tied in below the grip of mediating discourse or cultural signification. All this occurs far beyond the ethical order. Witchcraft, like fetishes, freely explores the many virtualities of breaking down or fragmenting and disuniting taken-for-granted and multifaceted semiological divisions, such as internal and external, self and other, human and animal, and life-giving and life-taking processes.

The plot and fetish mobilize and disfigure transpersonal body images of inter-corporeality (Feldman 1997; La Fontaine 1998; Weiss 1999; Young 1997). In particular, such a plot deconstructs the symbolic-classificatory and sociological rules of discourse and exchange (in commensality, conjugality, birth-giving, nourishing life), and the culturally defined body order. This order is about the production of person-hood *par excellence*. The disruption of society's cultural and ethical order occurs when the fetish and witchcraft severely undermine symbolic-classificatory terms and breach conventional rules of discourse and exchange. It is mainly through the disconnection of meaningful orders and the messing up of signifiers that the disruptive effects of the fetish and witchcraft set in. The fetish and witchcraft rule out any coherent pattern of boundaries and divisions proper to the body image and the moral and symbolic order of a given cultural community. To become efficacious, the fetish and witchcraft move from speech to pictograms (Aulagnier 1975). In such a movement, they close the web of the suspected aggressor and his or her victim into their disfigured selves and in a form of terror that is hard to disentangle.

The feeling of bewitchment may grow even when the victimized person remains unaware of the content of the fetish or the intent of their suspected wrongdoer. Through semi-public recourse to fetishes and spells, as well as through the narratives and suspicions regarding murderous bewitchment, the implicated sensual, symbolic, and imaginary orders are surreptitiously inscribed in people's corporeality by way of pictograms. Through people's participation in divinatory oracles and ensuing palavers, which draw on a common cosmology, witchcraft and fetishes moreover become a community's embodied experience. The taboo on witchcraft becomes densely emotional because the forces entailed cohere with, and influence, the clients' bodies in ways prefigured or pre-traced through sensuous channels, which are depicted as a serpent's successive sloughing. The efficacy of the fetish and of the supposed bewitching attack thereby relies on the culture-specific consonance (hence consubstantiation) effected in the body between the individual and the group, in particular by the moods of transition rituals venturing across various distressful and agonistic states (Das 1997). This efficacy of the fetish moreover thrives on a specific culturally shaped bodily predisposition, receptive to imagoes proper to the unconscious operating without the cognized mediation of the cultural symbolic.

It is clear that, as an effect of supposed witchcraft, victimized members of a social group are affected in their bodily self. This is especially the case if they occupy the lower sphere of society and experience such afflictions as threats, illness, and bad omens. All these afflictions are likely to lead to perpetual anxieties. In the subconscious domain of affects, the victimized person undergoes an increasingly grave and complex crisis and with time gradually abdicates their status as a subject; they believe that others are responsible for their misfortune and surrender their weakened body to the uncontrollable events surrounding them. Such "suicidal victimization" under the spell of maleficent fetishes and/or bewitchment is usually prevented through group control and the counter-attack of one's own dually charged fetishes. The victim who surrenders the center of decisions and evaluations, gradually plunges into chaos, disorientation, or despondency. Ultimately, the victim's body and life force are given over to crisis or even death. Without recognized defense by the body-self, the victim opens up to angry spirits (having no master, acting on their own behalf), inner drives, or non-conscious portions of his or her personality. And they expose themselves to the morbid desires unleashed by certain despotic relatives. The fatal desire of others (their dislike, hatred, or aggression) is incorporated by the victim, for in their bodily disposition and condition they have opened up to imagoes in which the forces of life and death, love and hatred, placebo and nocebo, intersect, and in this mingling consume the life resources of the victimized person. In brief, bewitchment erodes and undermines the victim and their bond with, or grasp on, life. The often fatal embrace of the collective imaginary realm of forces ultimately overpowers the victim in their imaginary, affects, and body.

In order for such a process of introjection to be effective it somehow needs to be reliant on perception. However, the actual locus of its operation goes far beyond the reach of recognizable order. How, then, can the victim of witchcraft escape the moorings of their supposed aggressor? The way out is obviously to consult a diviner and a therapist. The move to seek solutions to their predicament allows the victim to break the fatal embrace of forces, for they open themselves up to the symbolic and restoration of differences encoded or metaphorized in that symbolic. In other words, the victim seeks a word, scenario, or set of actors in the nebulous sphere of adversity and monstrosity that may help them to expel self-destructive inclinations – or what may be described as their suicidal victimization and self-destruction or conflagration as a victim, or a living dead (Watson 1998: 42). A culturally authorized agency of fear invades and suffocates the victim's life forces, hence the body-self. In other cases, this agency of fear may assist the individual in confronting and overcoming them. We observe here what I would term a war between the impulses of life and death, a battle between meaning and its suspension, waged within the victim.

THE STRAIN OF THE SOCIAL FABRIC

There emerges from beliefs and rumors about witchcraft an important idiom that enables people to interrelate their social predicaments (such as those connected with abusive state institutions, class inequalities, famine, sickness, and other afflictions) with the mindscapes of interpersonal intrigues (such as envy, jealousy, greed, hatred, and misogyny). The more people's interpersonal and entrepreneurial networks reach far beyond their kin, as in many urban contexts, the more the circle of fear or vulnerability and the search for new protections tie in with larger networks *ad extra*, beyond their inward looking to kin relations.

AD INTRA: THE DIVINATORY DISCOURSE OF EXCHANGE, TRANSMISSION, SHARING

British functionalists (Douglas 1963; Gluckman 1965; Marwick 1965; Middleton and Winter 1963) hold that witchcraft accusations are used in rural African societies to voice conflicts. They argue these accusations serve as a "social strain gauge" in face-to-face, closed, tight-knit communities. The accusation and scape-goating, possibly followed by ritualized exorcism, spur anger that is targeted at a particular member as an embodiment of evildoing. The action taken to expel witchcraft and demonize the opponent, turning him or her into a societal misfit, serves to recast social bonds, morality, and ethical standards.

Regarding Black Africa, one of the fundamental differences between lethal witchcraft and divination is that jealousy, contention, or aggression eschews exposure. Fetishes seek to transform signs into forces charged with affects of the body and imagoes of the imaginary register. Yet witchcraft is unable to do the inverse, a task for divination. As for the diviner's oracle, it gradually transposes the imaginary into an order of discourse; that is, it leads toward the symbolic and the order of language and social code (Devisch 1993: ch. 5; Devisch and Brodeur 1999: ch. 2). The oracle seeks to decode signs at the fringe of the collective imaginary register, and in particular at the level where a mingling contact with forces and imagoes brings about pleasure and enjoyment, fear and aggression. Here, the oracle introduces something of a demarcation line between pleasure and displeasure, between life and death, namely between the imaginary and the symbolic.

The diviner's oracle brings about the intervention of a third party. There is a place for mediation and speech to play a crucial role in addressing a crisis. The assumption is that if such a crisis is to be properly addressed, the diviner must first tame something that resists conceptualization and the social order. The diviner must follow a procedure whereby his or her word provides form for the mass of unformed bodily affects and sensations. The diviner's word makes up an anxious situation or traumatic episode paralyzing the client. Through speech, the diviner articulates the banal realities as well as the whims of the daily life of their client (the victim) and sets their predicament against the background of the epic universe of witchcraft. The diviner or the divinatory apparatus (Pemberton 2000) decodes the client's problem and suffering, systematically running through the vicissitudes of the principle of exchange in the kinship group and the particular vulnerabilities of the patient. The divinatory oracle thus reconstructs the primordial scenario of the sense of self and of the conscience (when language becomes memory of social order). But the oracle does not evoke the coming into being of communal law ethics. In other words, it is the divinatory oracle and not the afflicted person that holds the position of the subject of the enunciation with regard to the unsettling crisis.

In the particular context of uncontrolled urbanization and of the globalizing spirals of economic inflation, the discourse of maleficent witchcraft attempts to domesticate the alienating "global" forces of the state (Bayart 1989; Geschiere 1995). It also seeks to tame the domination of international structures, which includes the externally based market economy and technocracy, dysfunctional formal education and its diplomas, the mass media, and widespread afflictions such as AIDS.

AD EXTRA: THREE CASES

Witch-hunt and witchcraft imputations articulating a morality of Othering

According to de Certeau (1970), Levack (1988), Murray (1962), and Thomas (1971), the witch-hunt parallel to the exalted grandmother devotion of the Holy Anna in Western Europe between 1450 and the Reformation (in particular in adjacent German-Rhineland and southern French, Swiss, and northern Italian regions) was related to the social and moral crisis engendered by the secularization of power and the new sexual division of labor in the transition from an agrarian society to a more hierarchical, collective, and male-dominated supervision of life and labor in the growing cities. It manipulated the popular fear of the evildoing witch (on the European continent the witch is seen as devilish) so as to expel from society and people's life-world the all-embracing "evil." In this period of famine and a growing clash between agrarian and urban culture, the image of the witch is very much centered on orality, fertility, and the social position of older or barren women.

Popular beliefs in rural France and the averting of evil

> The originality of Jeanne Favret-Saada's book on witchcraft amid the Norman Bocage [or woodlands region in Brittany, France] is undoubtedly that it reckons with the usual treatment of witchcraft by classical ethnography . . . the approach being now that . . . the bewitched's discourse is taken seriously. One wonders why the bewitched uses so special a language to speak out about his or her misfortune. Why does the bewitched link the manifestations of repeated woes (whether these are related to illness or death) with forces (rather than with ordinary symbolic mediating or with the known social as well as rational causalities)? (Gil 1985: 24; my translation)

Jeanne Favret-Saada's studies of witchcraft must be read through the lens of unbewitchment in the peasant and very Catholic woodland region of Brittany (Favret-Saada 1971, 1977, 1985a, 1985b, 1986; Favret-Saada and Contreras 1981). She reminds us of Christian and modernist assumptions and of the "power of defining," also found in (post)colonial Africa. Her fieldwork, conducted in the late 1960s, bore witness to the changes which the Roman Catholic Church was undergoing after the Second Vatican Council. In that same period, engineers, veterinarians, and bank experts started to design peasants' incorporation into high-modernist development programs and the macro-economic order. This modernizing move threw suspicion on local knowledge practices, in particular in the realm of popular religion. Till then, the Catholic church in many peasant communities of France had propagated a civilization starting from and centered on the parish.

In line with its ethics, the church, in its liturgy and pastoral work prior to the 1960s, ran its worship of the Mother-Virgin and the Saints. In preparation for Easter, it also held the annual week of retreat, with sermons and confession, in order to instigate repentance and reconciliation for the entire parish community. The pastoral work and the liturgy were an attempt to mobilize a kind of socio- and psycho-drama centered on dangerous moods of fear and transgression. It also entailed a move that consisted in provisions of solidarity, gift, and sacrifice for the family. In sermons about devilish powers, purgatory and hell, heretics and sinners, the church offered a space for multiform projection and symbolization: incertitude, failure, threat, fears of possible aggression, decay, death, and evil were canalized and symbolized in the embracing and all-transcending domain of divine mercy and redemption.

The Second Vatican Council recanted on this popular pastoral of fear, the mystery and the miraculous (such as the Gregorian chants, the popular saint devotion, the pilgrimages and processions). The aim of the official church was now to clear popular belief. The believer was urged on to greater personal commitment and enlightened experience of his or her faith. It was the end of the parish-centered civilization in Western Europe. Institutionalized religion lost its credibility and its prescriptive or emancipatory power with regard to suffering, misfortune, evil, and the "dark" (greedy, libidinal, aggressive, antigenic) sides of the individual and life; to social inequalities and their origin; to religious ethics, particularly with regard to sex. The belief in Satan, hell, purgatory, sin, and confession became vague. The practice of the Christian sacraments, prayer, and fasting diminished. Many domains and aspects of society were withdrawn from the authority of church institutions and religious symbols. However, the number of agnostics *strictu sensu* is not increasing. People keep calling on the church for the major rites of passage (baptisms, confirmations, marriages, funerals), and pilgrimages remain popular.

Yet the concept of (ab)normality was meanwhile increasingly monopolized by the expert medical gaze and discourse, at the expense of the popular and ecclesiastical judgment and heed. The medical institution was still selecting its staff mainly from the male, well-to-do urban bourgeoisie. It gradually became the only legitimate authority to define and assess normality – normal and reasonable conduct, as opposed to the pathological – and this on the basis of organicist views, rationalist theories, and agnostic science. This exogenous knowledge about patients was gradually complemented by authoritative psychological insights by and into the subjects themselves and their life-worlds. Out of Sigmund Freud's revolutionary view of the psychic origin of insanity and psychosomatic ailments, multiple psychotherapeutic techniques developed within Western urban cultures to foster an intra- and intersubjective recovery of the identity and vitality of the subject. Simultaneously, endogenous views and approaches gradually managed to legitimize themselves in complementarity with medical techniques. The centuries-old folk healing techniques, such as unbewitchment and cartomancy or tarot reading, became more and more marginalized and stigmatized as an "alternative one of quacks and irrational credulity." This gap was enforced by the prestige of modern science, the medical institution, and elitist church institutions (the elitist healers of body, mind, psyche, and soul), largely co-opted by the state administration.

In the 1960s, peasant family enterprises in Brittany's Bocage region (and all over Western Europe) were the scene of a shift in technical expertise. On the one hand, medical doctors, veterinary experts, agronomists, brokers, and bankers brought in increasingly efficacious services and technical know-how for recovering or increasing the physical (re)productive capacity and economic success of the family enterprise. On the other hand, there were the traditional healers – of people and the farm's reproductive potential – whose protective and healing powers were vested in personal charisma which was only locally acknowledged. Unbewitchers and local saints were credited with a similar symbolic efficacy on the basis of their personal charisma. Their activities were heterodox with regard to the discourse and the formal function of the school, the state, and the church. Being outlawed, these practices had to withdraw from public visibility. Banished, unbewitchers withdrew to the anonymity of the urban scene and mainstream reformist-modernist culture. They are consulted in secrecy.

In the age-old perspective of Bocage folk culture, the bewitched person, family, or family enterprise can be weakened by the evil deeds of a witch from within the neighborhood, who in turn in this very intrusive act proves and re-energizes their superiority. The bewitched feels weakened and devoid of any defense to resist the aggressor. Facing the repeated misfortune and the overall weakening or leaking of one's energy and the crisis of the farm's reproductive capacity, there is no other solution – just as in modern psychotherapy – other than to turn to a "holder of forces" or unbewitcher for help. The afflicted will accept such a solution only after confidential and cautious advice from a friend who has already undergone the whole experience and now suspects witchcraft is involved. Nobody can or will declare themselves to be bewitched, since such insight and expertise would mean that one is a witch initiated in the arts of witchcraft.

Popular religion, now waning, offered a canvas of symbolic techniques to thwart misfortune and evil. It sufficed to pray the Lord's Prayer or a Hail Mary, or to make the sign of the cross, to drive away Satan. Burying the relic of a saint on the night of St. John was enough to expel a Sabbath of witches. Bullets that had rested on sacred objects were in that very act empowered for averting accidents, such as an attack by wolves or a thunderstorm caused by witches.

Witchdoctors are those "who know." Until the 1950s, the witchdoctor (witch-hunter, witch-fighter) of rural origin was a charismatic figure, contrary to the highly learned expert from the city (priest, medical doctor) whose authority was vested in his (occult) science drawn from books. The priests and medical doctors were depicted as experts who themselves no longer believed in those witch stories they had to counter. Charismatic old men or women, in particular those who were widowed and had survived an accident, were seen as blessed with a supernatural power for knowing and staving off evil or unbewitching.

In the countryside during the last century, it was mainly outsiders who were suspected of being witches. The shepherd, who lived as a nomad, unmarried and without possessions or social responsibility, was suspected of some *bons tours*, such as stopping the coach or drawing off cider from a distance. Other suspects could be reckoned from among traveling beggars, workmen, and merchants. The only strangers who nowadays come to the farm are professionals outside any sphere of charisma, disregarding in their advice issues of vital force, anxiety, and otherworldly reality. Today, neighboring farmers may be suspected and relations between aggressor and victim are direct and intemperate.

In the nineteenth century it was thought that individuals drew their secret force from "evil books baptized by Satan," namely books with magical receipts [recipes?].

Nowadays, extraordinary strength is thought to be derived from "strong blood" and charisma expressed, for example, in one's capacity to recover from cancer or a fatal accident, unmask a witch, or predict an extraordinary event. Witchcraft is somehow undergoing a desacralizing demystification: as such, Satan no longer seems to be in play. Unlike in the nineteenth century, today's witches no longer are able to make someone dance "a St. Guy's dance of utter madness." Nowadays, these disturbances are diagnosed by psychiatrists as hysteria, psychosis, or schizophrenia. Given the competence and public authority of psychiatry, witchdoctors in the Bocage have become reluctant to deal with the mentally ill.

Yet today a person's witch-power has come to apply only within the boundaries of the family domain. It is not so much an idiom to keep marginal people under control, but an idiom and practice for the entrepreneur and his wife to learn how to have a firmer hold on their enterprise, endogenously, from within its proper resources. It is Jeanne Favret-Saada's (1985a) thesis that by channeling – in practice, almost unnoticed – forces in the protagonists, the unbewitchment and tarot reading delicately promote the entrepreneur's ability to defend himself, yet mobilize the native's wife's social emancipation over against the farmer's rampant dependency on technocracy.

ANTI-WITCHCRAFT MOVEMENTS AND HEALING COMMUNES DOMESTICATING ALIENATING GLOBAL POWERS AND VALUES

In most parts of present day (non-Islamic) Africa, anti-witchcraft movements seek to domesticate or bring home the alienating "global" forces of literacy, mass media, money, technocracy, and the state. As my findings in Congo have demonstrated, the people of Kinshasa (or Kinois) have particularly become increasingly aware that their faith in liberating Westernizing modernity has quite paradoxically led to proletarization and beggary. It seems almost obvious that with extensive pillaging and uncontrollable rioting, the Kinois population has stifled the mirroring process and false hopes generated by the (post)colonial legacy of modern state institutions (Devisch 1995, 1998). The mirrors of progress and improvement helped the state to conceal the extent to which it has contributed to overall socioeconomic decline. In fact, the adaptation to the ideals of President Mobutu's Authenticity project, launched in 1973, consisted in merely recycling the Westernization endeavor. In the 1990s, the Authenticity project which contributed to the bankruptcy of the state proved to be a dead end. This is forcefully rendered by a song made popular in 1994 by pop star Pepe Kale: *Bakendeki na Poto, bakweyi na désert*, roughly meaning "Those who on their way to Poto (i.e., the outside developed world) have fallen into a desert" (see De Boeck 1996). People sense that Western or postcolonial modernization is a trap, as it marginalizes or "downsizes" them all on the national and international scene (see Stein, this volume).

Within the context of the healing communes in Kinshasa, numbering in the hundreds, one often hears the now ill-fated (post)colonial legacy of Western modernity and state-building associated with *sataani*: this local term for the Christian-imported notion of Satan connotes witchcraft's abomination. This alien moralizing notion has clearly been recycled by the discourse of the healing communes, for whom it denotes the reverse side of the Holy Spirit, along the lines of the tradition-born imaginary regarding ancestral wrath and evil as the polar opposite of ordered diurnal life. In fact, facing existential challenges, suburbanites tend to turn not so much to the Christian notion of conscience and illumination by the Holy Spirit, as to their own understanding of the sacred spirit. This associates the Holy Spirit with the ancestral spirit for the sake of healing afflicted group members.

One observes that the rural and urban cosmologies and sociologics of witchcraft are fundamentally similar, although their representational contents and devices may be expressed differently. I contend that the versatile figure of sataani has in this context become a figure of farce, irony, and mockery in the face of the idiosyncrasy and alienating characteristics of increasingly intrusive Western ways of life and religion. This usage of the term sataani versus sacred spirit by members of the healing communes reenacts and dwells upon the memory of the shadowy identity of the Congolese vis-à-vis the White Man. Throughout colonial and postcolonial times, the latter has defined himself as the universal and normative civilization hero and prototype of modern history through school education, Christian mission discourse, and international television. In contrast, the Western presence has been experienced by the populace as an arbitrary intrusion that has increasingly deprived the majority of access to employment, state power, and cash goods. As an epithet, the term sataani has surreptitiously become associated with the West and Western ways (defined as selfish and acquisitive, therefore bewitching), the missionary, the figure of Jesus, and the negative altero-definitions applied to the local Congolese and their worlds by (post)colonial and missionary discourses.

The bipolar figure of the sacred spirit-sataani has provided the healing communes with a conceptual framework for developing both a new and totaling, though manicheistic, moral economy, as well as a compelling critique of, and skepticism about, ongoing modernization, which looks more like sheer folly. Such parody has become the principal defense for local communities in their confrontations with the cleptocratic state and international structures of domination (Bayart 1989; Mbembe 1992) and in their struggles with more distant sources of problematic powers and values, such as the inequities and exclusion brought about by the import of high technology consumer goods from externally centered market economies, motorized transport, literacy, a monetary economy, formal education and its diplomas, and modern diseases, including AIDS. Witchcraft and the figure of sataani-sacred spirit both function as idioms allowing these communities to demystify, at least in part, the new world order of modernity as folly (see Ausslander 1993; Comaroff 1997; De Boeck 1996; Geschiere 1995; Masquelier 2001; Meyer 1995; Stoller and Olkes 1987). The power of the sacred spirit, as celebrated by the healing communes, is more profoundly subversive due to its capacity to animate and entrance followers corporeally, and not just touch their whitened souls. In these communes, the sacred spirit is responsible for a genuinely endogenous reenchantment of the community and the world beyond a Western or Christian evolutionist and moralizing ethos (see Comaroff and Comaroff 1991, 1993).

REFERENCES

Appadurai, Arjun, 1998 Dead Certainty: Ethnic Violence in the Era of Globalization. *Public Culture* 10 (2): 225–247.

Appiah, Kwame, 1992 *In My Father's House: Africa in the Philosophy of Culture.* Oxford: Oxford University Press.

Augé, Marc, 1975 *Théorie des pouvoirs et idéologie: étude de cas en Côte d'Ivoire.* Paris: Hermann.

Aulagnier, Piera, 1975 *La Violence de l'interprétation: du pictogramme à l'énoncé.* Paris: Presses Universitaires de France.

Ausslander, Marc, 1993 Open the Wombs!: The Symbolic Politics of Modern Ngoni Witchfinding. In *Modernity and Its Discontents.* Jean Comaroff and John Comaroff, eds. Pp. 167–192. Chicago: University of Chicago Press.

Baudrillard, Jean, 1990 *La Transparence du mal: essai sur les phénomènes extrêmes.* Paris: Galilée.

Bayart, Jean-Françoise, 1989 *L'Etat en Afrique: la politique du ventre.* Paris: Maspéro.

Berry, Nicole, 1993 *Anges et fantômes.* Toulouse: Ombres.

Bond, George, and Diane Ciekawy, eds., 2001 *Witchcraft Dialogues: Anthropological and Philosophical Dialogues.* Athens: Ohio University Center for International Studies.

Comaroff, Jean, 1997 Consuming Passions: Child Abuse, Fetishism, and the New World Order. *Culture* 17: 7–19.

Comaroff, Jean, and John Comaroff, 1991 *Of Revelation and Revolution: Christianity, Colonialism and Consciousness in South Africa.* Chicago: University of Chicago Press.

— eds., 1993 *Modernity and its Malcontents: Ritual and Power in Postcolonial Africa.* Chicago: University of Chicago Press.

Crick, Malcolm, 1976 *Explorations in Language and Meaning: Towards a Semantic Anthropology.* London: Malaby.

Das, Veena, 1997 Sufferings, Theodicies, Disciplinary Practices, Appropriations. *International Social Science Journal* 154: 563–572.

De Boeck, Filip, 1996 Postcolonialism, Power, and Identity: Local and Global Perspectives in Zaire. In *Postcolonial Identities in Africa.* Richard Werbner and Terence Ranger, eds. Pp. 75–106. London: Zed Books.

de Certeau, Michel, 1970 *La Possession de Loudun.* Paris: Julliard.

Deleuze, Gilles, and Felix Guattari, 1987 *A Thousand Plateaus.* Minneapolis: University of Minnesota Press.

de Surgy, Albert, 1994 *Nature et fonction des fétiches en Afrique noire.* Paris: Harmattan.

Devisch, René, 1993 *Weaving the Threads of Life: The Khita Gynecological Healing Cult among the Yaka.* Chicago: University of Chicago Press.

— 1995 Frenzy, Violence, and Ethical Renewal in Kinshasa. *Public Culture* 7: 593–629.

— 1996 "Pillaging Jesus": Healing Churches and the Villagization of Kinshasa. *Africa* 66: 555–586.

— 1998 La Violence à Kinshasa, ou l'institution en négatif. *Cahiers d'etudes Africaines* 38 (150–152): 441–469.

Devisch, René, and C. Brodeur, 1999 *The Law of the Life-Givers: The Domestication of Desire.* Amsterdam: Harwood Academic Publishers.

Douglas, Mary, 1963 *The Lele of the Kasai.* Oxford: Oxford University Press.

Evans-Pritchard, Edward 1937 *Witchcraft, Oracles, and Magic Among the Azande.* Oxford: Clarendon Press.

Favret-Saada, Jeanne, 1971 Le Malheur biologique et sa répétition. *Annales économies sociétés civilizations* 3–4: 873–888.

— 1977 *Les Mots, la mort, les sorts: la sorcellerie dans le Bocage.* Paris: Gallimard.

— 1985a La Thérapie sans le savoir. *Nouvelle revue de psychanalyse* 31: 223–238.

— 1985b. L'Embrayeur de violence: quelques mécanismes thérapeutiques du désorcèlement. In *Le Moi et l'autre*. Maud Mannoni, ed. Pp. 97–125. Paris: Denoël.

— 1986 L'Invention d'une thérapie: la sorcellerie Bocaine 1887–1970. *Débat* 40: 29–46.

Favret-Saada, Jeanne and Josée Contreras, 1981 *Corps pour corps: enquête sur la sorcellerie dans le Bocage*. Paris: Gallimard.

Feldman, Allen, 1997 Violence and Vision: The Prosthetics and Aesthetics of Terror. *Public Culture* 10 (1): 24–60.

Fredrikson, Charles, 2000 Quand comprendre, c'est accuser: l'analyse des contes à sorcière. *L'Homme* no. 153: 269–290.

Gaonkar, Dilip Parameshar, ed., 1999 Alter/native Modernities. Special Millenium Quartet. *Public Culture* 1.

Geschiere, Peter, 1995 *La Viande des autres: sorcellerie et politique en Afrique*. Paris: Karthala.

Gil, José, 1985 *Métamorphoses du corps*. Paris: Éditions de la Différence.

Gillies, Eva, 1976 [1937] Introduction. In E. Evans-Pritchard, *Witchcraft, Oracles, and Magic Among the Azande*. Oxford: Clarendon Press.

Gilmore, David, 1987 *Aggression and Community*. New Haven, CT: Yale University Press.

Gluckman, Max, 1965 *Politics, Law, and Ritual in Tribal Society*. Oxford: Blackwell.

Greenwood, Susan, 2000 *Magic, Witchcraft, and the Otherworld: An Anthropology*. Oxford: Berg.

Guthrie, Malcolm, 1970 *Comparative Bantu*, vol. 4. Farnborough: Gregg.

Hountondji, Paulin, ed., 1994 *Les Savoirs endogènes: pistes pour une recherche*. Paris: Karthala.

Hviding, Edvard, 1996 Nature, Culture, Magic, Science: On Meta-Languages for Comparison in Cultural Ecology. In *Nature and Society: Anthropological Perspectives*. P. Descola and G. Palsson, eds. Pp. 165–184. London: Routledge.

Kapferer, Bruce, 1997 *The Feast of the Sorcerer: Practices of Consciousness and Power*. Chicago: University of Chicago Press.

Kourouma, Ahmadou, 2000 *Allah n'est pas obligé*. Paris: Seuil.

Kristeva, Julia, 1980 *Pouvoir de l'horreur: essai sur l'abjection*. Paris: Seuil.

Krohn-Hansen, Christian, 1995 Magic, Money, and Alterity Among Dominicans. *Social Anthropology* 3 (2): 129–146.

La Fontaine, Jean, 1998 *Speak of the Devil: Tales of Satanic Abuse in Contemporary England*. Cambridge: Cambridge University Press.

Levack, Brian, 1988 *The Witch-Hunt in Early Modern Europe*. London: Longman.

MacGaffey, Wyatt, 1977 Fetishism Revisited: Kongo Nkisi in Sociological Perspective. *Africa* 47: 140–152.

— 2000 *Kongo Political Culture: The Conceptual Challenge of the Particular*. Bloomington: Indiana University Press.

Maertens, Thierry, 1987 *Ritanalyses*. Montbonnot-Saint-Martin: J. Millon.

Mallart Guimera, Louis, 1981 *Ni dos Ni Ventre: Religion, Magie et Sorcellerie Evuzok*. Paris: Société d'Ethnographie.

Marwick, Max, 1965 *Sorcery in its Social Setting: A Study of the Northern Rhodesian Cewa*. Manchester: Manchester University Press.

Masquelier, Adeline, 2001 *Prayer has Spoiled Everything: Possession, Power, and Identity in an Islamic Town of Niger*. Durham, NC: Duke University Press.

Mbembe, Achille, 1992 Provisional Notes on the Postcolony. *Africa* 62 (1): 3–37.

Meyer, Brigit, 1995 "Delivered from the Powers of Darkness": Confessions about Satanic Riches in Christian Ghana. *Africa* 65: 236–255.

Middleton, John, and E. H. Winter, eds., 1963 *Sorcery and Witchcraft in East Africa*. London: Routledge.

Moore, Henrietta, and Todd Sanders, eds., 2001 *Magical Interpretations, Material Realities: Modernity, Witchcraft, and the Occult in Postcolonial Africa*. London: Routledge.

Murray, Margaret, 1962 [1921] *The Witch-Cult in Western Europe*. Oxford: Clarendon Press.

Ngugi wa Thiong'o, 1986 *Decolonizing the Mind: The Politics of Language in African Literature*. London: James Currey.

Nyamnjoh, Francis, 2001 Delusions of Development and the Enrichment of Witchcraft Discourses in Cameroon. In *Magical Interpretations, Material Realities: Modernity, Witchcraft, and the Occult in Postcolonial Africa*. H. Moore and T. Sanders, eds. Pp. 28–49. London: Routledge.

Overing, Joanna, 1978 The Shaman as a Maker of Worlds: Nelson Goodman in the Amazon. *Man* 25: 602–619.

Parkin, David, ed., 1985 *The Anthropology of Evil*. Oxford: Blackwell.

Pemberton, John, ed., 2000 *Insight and Artistry in African Divination*. Washington, DC: Smithsonian Institution Press.

Pouillon, Jean, 1972 Manières de table, manières de lit, manières de langage. *Nouvelle revue de psychanalyse* 6: 9–26.

Ricoeur, Paul, 1967 *The Symbolism of Evil*. Boston, MA: Beacon Press.

Rutherford, Blair, 1999 To Find an African Witch: Anthropology, Modernity, and Witch-Finding in Northwest Zimbabwe. *Critique of Anthropology* 19: 89–109.

Scott, James, 1998 *Seeing Like a State. How Certain Schemes to Improve the Human Condition Have Failed*. New Haven, CT: Yale University Press.

Sony, Labu Tansi, 1979 *La Vie et demie*. Paris: Seuil.

Stoller, Paul, 1998 Rationality. In *Critical Terms for Religious Studies*. M. Taylor, ed. Pp. 239–255. Chicago: University of Chicago Press.

Stoller, Paul, and Cheryll Olkes, 1987 *In Sorcery's Shadow*. Chicago: University of Chicago Press.

Taussig, Michael, 1980 *The Devil and Commodity Fetishism in South America*. Chapel Hill: University of North Carolina Press.

— 1998 Transgression. In *Critical Terms for Religious Studies*. M. Taylor, ed. Pp. 349–364. Chicago: University of Chicago Press.

Thomas, Keith, 1971 *Religion and the Decline of Magic: Studies in Popular Beliefs in Sixteenth and Seventeenth Century England*. London: Paladin.

Tutuola, Amos, 1952 *The Palm-Wine Drinkard*. London: Faber and Faber.

van Rinsum, Henk, 2001 Slaves of Definition: In Quest of the Unbeliever and the Ignoramus. Published Ph.D. thesis, Utrecht.

Watson, Sean, 1998 The Neurobiology of Sorcery: Deleuze and Guattari's Brain. *Body and Society* 4 (4): 23–45.

Weiss, Gail, 1999 *Body Images: Embodiment as Intercorporeality*. London: Routledge.

Young, Katherine, 1997 *Presence in the Flesh: The Body in Medicine*. Cambridge, MA: Harvard University Press.

PART IV Aggression, Dominance, and Violence

Modern genocide is an element of social engineering, meant to bring about a social order conforming to the design of the perfect society.

(Bauman 2002: 120)

The colonized man finds his freedom in and through violence.

(Fanon 1963: 68)

Around the world, modernization, (de)colonization, and democratization have contributed to violence, even genocidal massacres, while stimulating many forms of historical revision and "truth-telling," most notably South Africa's Truth and Reconciliation Commission (TRC). "Transparency" has become a buzzword in political discussions about whose history is "truth," while public, often emotional confessions of wrongdoing are on the rise. These confessions, like Feldman's "telling" practices, (1997: 34) mobilize imagery and project images of embodied ethnicity, religion, and body politics, which once transcribed onto the body, play a critical role in the construction of identity and agency. Official confessional narratives about identity and agency, meant for public witnessing, concretize the perceptual and somatic bounds of what Feldman refers to as "the politically visible and the politically unseen" (1997: 35). What does it mean, for instance, that more black South Africans have confessed to violence than state-sponsored white perpetrators? What modern aspects of daily life – master-images of "civilization," state authority, social engineering, bureaucracy, hierarchical and functional divisions of labour, the substitution of technical for moral responsibility, and the use of abstract identity categories – lend themselves to violence? How shall we evaluate the violence of yesterday's victims? How is violence localized and personalized?

Contributors to part four take up the critical question of political visibility and what constitutes symbolic and physical forms of violence. Their chapters address the larger question of what stands as evidence of "truth" within the contexts of colonization, South Africa's Truth and Reconciliation Commission, Western academic empiricism, or from within the perspectives of young adults socialized by American corporations. In the aftermath of violence, what are the responsibilities of state organizations such as the TRC or of world organizations such as the United Nations? What impact do narrations of violence, based on Christian notions of confession and forgiveness, have among non-Christians? What forms of healing and social justice work in our world's diverse sociocultural communities, whose histories and memories of violence intertwine differently with global processes such as the media or telecommunications?

22 Genocide and Modernity

Alexander Laban Hinton

Modern genocide is genocide with a purpose . . . It is a means to an end . . . *The end itself is a grand vision of a better, and radically different, society . . .* This is the gardener's vision, projected upon a world-size screen . . . Some gardeners hate the weeds that spoil their design – that ugliness in the midst of beauty, litter in the midst of serene order. Some others are quite unemotional about them: just a problem to be solved, an extra job to be done. Not that it makes a difference to the weeds; both gardeners exterminate them.

Zygmunt Bauman, *Modernity and the Holocaust*

If modernity is accompanied by a set of master narratives, ranging from faith in reason to a conviction that social engineering can lead to human emancipation, genocide flows as a counter-current, creating ripples and ruptures through the surfaces of progress. Genocide is modernity's dark side, inflecting these master narratives with the specter of hundreds of millions of dead, unimaginable suffering, and an unrelenting question: *Why?* How is it possible that, in a "modern" world in which "civilization" has supposedly triumphed over "savagery," such mass murder continues to take place?

Some people find the solution in the framing of the question, portraying genocide as a brief paroxysm of the repressed, an aberrant regression back to the "primitive," a momentary confirmation of the truths embodied in modern novels like *Lord of the Flies* or *Heart of Darkness*. Genocide seemingly emerges from modernity's id, the manifestations of which must be quickly diagnosed, contained, and, ultimately, repressed once more. The latest incarnation of these modernist myths of genocide could be seen in Rwanda, where "primitive" black bodies were portrayed as engaging in a carnage that again seemed to affirm the latent threat of civilization's underbelly – that primordial cauldron of seething primitive hatreds. "We" could take solace in the fact that such events happen to a "less developed" group, not in our "advanced" society. Maybe, we lament, we could have done more. For, "modern" societies often view themselves as having a moral obligation to lend a helping (and armed) hand to "less enlightened" peoples, restoring "order" and helping to institute the modern elixirs of "civil society" and "the rule of law" – though these ideals have failed to provoke much preventive action in the case of genocide (Power 2002).

Yet another way to examine the question, however, is to look at modernity itself. Perhaps, scholars like Zygmunt Bauman (1989) argue, genocide is, at least in part, the Janus face of modernity, a manifestation of modernity's lethal potentialities. As opposed to viewing genocide as a lower stage in the teleological march of progress, then, we might view genocide as something that is envisioned by this very master narrative, as modernist architects attempt to revamp society so that people who are classified in particular sorts of ways (as human and non-human, racial types, savage and civilized, citizen and non-citizen) will be enabled to enjoy the benefits of a certain sort of ("developed," with its capitalist connotations) being. These projects of social engineering are just one dimension of genocide, a complex phenomenon involving an array of factors and requiring an examination of various levels of analysis. This chapter takes the position that genocide and modernity are closely interwoven, a warp and woof not easily unraveled. While other fabrics of understanding are possible, we ignore this warp and woof at our own peril, as the engines of modernity continue to churn, often leaving suffering, destruction, and dead bodies in their wake.

Broadly, this chapter calls for greater anthropological dialogue about the issue of genocide. Prior to the last two decades or so, anthropologists, often content to remain focused on local level processes in small-scale societies and perhaps stymied by their commitment to cultural relativism, largely ignored the issue of genocide, as illustrated by the discipline's almost complete silence on the Armenian genocide and the Holocaust. While anthropologists have more recently begun to address the issues of political violence and, less frequently, genocide (see Hinton 2002b, 2002c), much work remains to be done. More indirectly, this chapter calls for psychological anthropologists to engage with broader socioeconomic and political processes like modernity and globalization, which they have tended to overlook due to their tendency to focus on the individual. Scholars of modernity and globalization, in turn, who tend to invoke psychological concepts like "identity," "subjectivity," "sentiment," "imagination," and "being," have much to gain from the work of psychological anthropologists, who have developed nuanced analyses of such ideas. To illustrate how such an engagement might proceed, I move back and forth between genocide and modernity, drawing on a range of cases, including Cambodia, the fieldsite where I conducted my ethnographic research (Hinton 2005).

THE MODERNITY OF GENOCIDE

In the present Convention, genocide means any of the following acts committed with intent to destroy, in whole or in part, a national, ethnical, racial, or religious group, as such:

(a) Killing members of the group;
(b) Causing serious bodily or mental harm to members of the group;

(c)   Deliberately inflicting on the group conditions of life calculated to bring about its physical destruction in whole or in part;
(d)   Imposing measures intended to prevent births within the group;
(e)   Forcibly transferring children of the group to another group.
(Article II, 1948 United Nations Genocide Convention)

To select a date is to stain the fabric of history. Certain times, peoples, and places are colored into the foreground, while others fade into the background or simply disappear from view. For the analyst, given moments are more amenable to the die the scholar wishes to cast, though others would no doubt sketch the events with different shades and tones. For my purposes, 1946 stands as a year that highlights a number of interconnections between modernity and genocide, as the "civilized" world attempted to make sense of the horrors of World War II – the mass death and destruction wrought by modern industrial warfare, by the atomic bomb, and by genocide as epitomized by the Holocaust. Instead of taking a long hard look at this dark side of modernity, many people in the modern world chose instead to project it onto imagined "primitive" others, who could be safely placed into abstract categories of concept and type. Such moves, however, bring both the contours and the shadows of modernity into sight.

United Nations, 1946
On December 11, 1946, the United Nations General Assembly, which had been established just the year before, passed the following resolution on genocide and encouraged the enactment of legislation to make genocide a crime:

> Genocide is a denial of the right of existence of entire human groups, as homicide is the denial of the right to live of individual human beings; such denial of the right of existence shocks the conscience of mankind, results in great losses to humanity in the form of cultural and other contributions represented by those groups, and is contrary to moral law and to the spirit and aims of the United Nations. Many instances of such crimes of genocide have occurred, when racial, religious, political and other groups have been destroyed, entirely or in part. The punishment of the crime of genocide is a matter of international concern.
> The General Assembly therefore, affirms that genocide is a crime under international law that the civilized world condemns, and for the commission of which principals and accomplices – whether private individuals, public officials or statesmen, and whether the crime is committed on religious, racial, political or any other grounds – are punishable.

The emergence of this resolution is striking given the fact that the term "genocide" had been coined only a couple of years earlier by the Polish jurist Raphaël Lemkin (1944) from "the ancient Greek word *genos* (race, tribe) and the Latin *cide* (killing)." In 1945, the year after the publication of Lemkin's groundbreaking book *Axis Rule in Occupied Europe*, genocide was included among the indictments at the Nuremberg War Trials.

When, after passage of the 1946 resolution, various UN committees began debating the wording of the UN Convention, however, a number of controversies ensued. Leo Kuper (1981) notes five main issues that structured the debate (Andreopoulos

1994; Fein 1990; Hinton 2002b: 4–5, 6–7, 8; Kuper 1981). First, committee members disagreed over which groups should be protected. Led by the Soviet bloc, which may well have feared being indicted for its domestic treatment of political and class "enemies," several representatives argued that the inclusion of more "mutable" group identities, such as political affiliation, would "weaken" the Convention because of the difficulty of defining membership. As a result, only "national, ethnical, racial or religious" groups were protected in the final version of the Genocide Convention. Second, problems arose over the issue of intent. For, if genocide involves the "intent to destroy" a group "as such," then it becomes possible for perpetrators to dispute their culpability for the "inadvertent" destruction of domestic groups, particularly indigenous peoples. Thus, when Paraguay was accused of being complicit in the destruction of the Aché Indians in 1974, the government tried to refute the charge through a simple denial of intent (see Arens 1976).

Third, the representatives argued about the types of actions that should be characterized as "genocide." Lemkin had originally proposed a very broad range of genocidal "techniques," including the destruction of a group's cultural way of life. Countries with a history of domestic and international colonization were particularly worried about being indicted on this charge, however, so "cultural genocide" was ultimately dropped from the Convention. (Drawing on another term proposed by Lemkin, scholars now often refer to cultural genocide as "ethnocide.") Fourth, committee members had to confront the problem of numbers. How does one quantify genocide? How many people have to be annihilated before massacre becomes genocide? The final version of the UN Convention did not provide an answer to this question, vaguely referring to the intent to destroy a group "in whole or in part."

Finally, there is the difficulty of enforcement. While few countries have a problem indicting genocidal leaders who have fallen from power, many are resistant to passing legislation that could compromise their sovereignty. As opposed to establishing an international tribunal with unrestricted powers of enforcement, the UN Convention ultimately left prosecution to the states themselves, creating a paradoxical situation in which regnant genocidal regimes would effectively be responsible for trying themselves. Nevertheless, it took the United States Congress almost forty years to overcome its fear of indictment and ratify the Convention, which became international law in 1951 (see LeBlanc 1991).

At a conference in Rome in July 1998, a UN Statute for the establishment of an international criminal court was passed by a vote of 120 to 7; the United States, fearing the indictment of US troops in foreign operations, joined Iran, Iraq, China, Libya, Algeria, and Sudan in opposing the Statute. Only two weeks before he left office in January 2001, President Clinton finally signed the treaty, though Senate confirmation remained in doubt. The following year, President Bush announced that his administration would not only not send the treaty to the Senate for ratification, but also intended to take the almost unprecedented step of removing their signature from the treaty (Crossette 2002). Moreover, the administration declared that the United States would not assist with the new international criminal court, which began to operate on July 1, 2002. While complicated, the Bush administration's decision was largely based on the fear that the treaty would infringe upon US sovereignty by giving an international prosecutor the power to indict US officials and military personnel (Lewis 2002). . . .

As this brief discussion suggests, the concept and practice of genocide are intimately bound up with modernity (Bauman 1989; Giddens 1990; Hall et al. 1995; Hinton 1998; Kaye and Strath 2000b; Scott 1998; Toulmin 1990). Politically, discussions of genocide assume a world of modern nation-states with fixed territorial boundaries, centralized control of force, claims to legitimacy, and populations subject to their laws and policies (see Giddens 1985; Held 1995). Since the 1648 Treaty of Westphalia that ended the Thirty Years War, states had been regarded as sovereign entities, responsible for their own internal legal and administrative affairs. The principle of sovereignty, however, created a tension at the heart of modernity. For, if each state would ideally rule in a "humane" fashion, this idea could be interpreted in very different ways. Thus, the annihilation of indigenous peoples during the Age of Conquest and colonial era could be legitimated in the name of Enlightenment discourses about reason, progress, and emancipation. (The genocides perpetrated against indigenous peoples were also fueled by another engine of modernity, monetarized exchange and the capitalist search for resources and profit.)

If the annihilation of indigenous "savages" was readily overlooked, the 1915 Armenian genocide, perpetrated against a group of Christians in the midst of World War I while the world watched, foregrounded the sovereignty problem (see Power 2002: 8). While many people later forgot about this annihilation of roughly 1 million Armenians (in 1939, when contemplating genocide, Hitler famously remarked: "Who today still speaks of the massacre of the Armenians?"), others, like Lemkin, did not. In 1933, at the Fifth International Conference for the Unification of Penal Law in Madrid, Lemkin (unsuccessfully) proposed the promulgation of a new international law that would criminalize "barbarity," or the "oppression and destruction" of national, religious, and racial groups (see Lemkin 1944: 91). For the next fifteen years, Lemkin continued to lobby for the enactment of such an international law that would undermine that ability of a state to use sovereignty as an excuse to commit mass murder (Kuper 1981; Power 2002).

Lemkin's word choice is suggestive about modernity and genocide. As early as 1933, he was attempting to criminalize the destruction of national, religious, and racial groups, a phrase that, in modified form, was incorporated into the UN Convention definition. Genocide is a crime perpetrated against groups of people, not individuals per se. As Lemkin stated: "Genocide is directed against a national group as an entity and the attack on individuals is only secondary to the annihilation of the national group to which they belong" (1945: 39). This emphasis on categorization and classification is a hallmark of modernity, stemming in part from the Enlightenment preoccupation with abstract reason, universal law, science, classification, and human nature, from the nation-state's desire to better control and monitor its population, and from contact with "others" during the Age of Exploration and colonial era. All of these factors contributed to the rise of anthropology, which in many ways can be seen as modernity's discipline of difference, with its traditional "scientific" project of studying, sorting, and recording diverse cultural others in the world.

Categorization inevitably strips individuals of their personal histories, identifying them primarily on the basis of their imagined membership in an abstract, socially constructed grouping. In and of itself, categorization is benign. Categorization becomes dangerous and even lethal when coupled with modern notions of social engineering, biological race, and Social Darwinism. The notion of biological race has certainly been a key trope in many twentieth-century genocides, ranging from the Nazi invocation of racial purity to the Hutu Power Movement's obsession with the Hamitic Hypothesis. In almost every genocidal ideology, metaphors of purity and contamination combine with essentialized notions of belonging to legitimate the forced removal, destruction, or annihilation of a group. The notion of genocidal "intent" – as manifest in Lemkin's writings and the UN Convention phrase "intent to destroy" – implies the existence of abstract classifications that serve as the basis for projects of social engineering. Such projects are, ironically, frequently justified in the name of scientific humanism, that perpetually incomplete modern goal of bettering the human condition through application of "science" and "reason." Emancipation and "progress" are pursued at the cost of thousands, tens of thousands, hundreds of thousands, or sometimes even millions of lives.

The modernity of genocide, however, has often been glossed over by associated discourses about barbarism (Bauman 1989; Kaye and Strath 2000b). In such con-texts, genocide serves as a container for and representation of the barbaric, a sort of twentieth-century stage theory of mass violence in which "barbaric" acts of violence are linked to modes of being antithetical to and lower than "civilization." This con-ception is evident in Lemkin's writings, as illustrated by the fact that he originally proposed calling genocidal acts "crimes of *barbarity*" (Lemkin 1944, italics his). Lemkin's search for a neologism was inspired, in part, by speech in which Churchill proclaimed: "We are in the presence of a crime without a name" (quoted in Power 2002: 29). In one of his unpublished notebooks, Lemkin drew a line connecting "THE WORD" to "MORAL JUDGMENT;" elsewhere he stated that the new term would serve as an "index of civilization" (Power 2002: 42). In other words, his signifier would index a certain type of "modern" morality – and a type of "civil" society governed by international law – by marking its binary opposite. Through its association with barbarity, "genocide," the signifier that Lemkin ultimately selected, implicitly diverted attention away from the possibility that something all-too-modern was involved in this mass violence.

This type of discourse about genocide was also prevalent in UN documents and discussions. The 1946 UN General Assembly resolution quoted above, for example, linked genocide and barbarity through such phrases as: "shocks the conscience of mankind," "results in great losses to humanity," "is contrary to moral law," and "which the civilized world condemns." Similar language was incorporated into the final text of the 1948 UN Convention, which included the following clauses in its preamble:

> *Recognizing* that at all periods of history genocide has inflicted great losses on humanity; and *being convinced* that, in order to liberate mankind from such an odious scourge, international cooperation is required . . .

Leaving aside the question of how appropriate it is to use a thoroughly modern concept to characterize acts committed in the ancient past or in radically different societies (which raises further questions about how global discourses about genocide are localized), we should note that such language depicts genocide as a "primitive" regression into "the barbaric" that is to be contained through modern law. By casting "genocide" into the timeless past, it could also be constructed in terms of favored metanarratives of modernity, such as the tropes of progress and human emancipation. Through the enlightenment of international law, "mankind" would be "liberated" from an "odious scourge" that had throughout history impeded its march of progress (see Kaye and Strath 2000a: 25). Genocide thereby becomes a symbolic container: it conceptually cordons off and stigmatizes a "them" that commits the deed, from "us," the civilized world that watches and judges.

My point here is not to deconstruct and dismiss the criminalization of genocide, which I support and which has the potential to help save millions of lives. Instead, I want to highlight how, through its association with discourses about "civilization" and "barbarity," genocide is often portrayed as an aberration, a momentary regression to a lower, barbaric state of being, with the associated primordial connotations. To do so may lead one to overlook the many ways in which acts of genocide are intimately linked to modernity and to explain away such mass atrocities as a momentary eruption of ancient, primitive sentiments, a line of thinking that was used to legitimate international inaction in Bosnia and Rwanda. . . .

While scholars like Horkheimer and Adorno (1944) and Arendt (1963) made important early contributions to our understanding of the relationship between modernity and the Holocaust, Zygmunt Bauman (1989, 2000) has perhaps made this argument most forcefully – though this line of analysis can easily be extended to other genocides (see Hinton 2002a; Kaye and Strath 2000b). Modernity, Bauman argues, is a necessary (but not sufficient) condition that made the Holocaust possible: if it did not "cause" the Holocaust, modernity contained potentialities that made it possible. To more fully comprehend the Holocaust, scholars must therefore take into account a tragic coalescence of various aspects of modernity.

Abstract categorization, for example, was at the core of Nazi ideology (Bauman 1989). With the emergence of Enlightenment ideals of equality, the uniform citizen, and human nature, biological race emerged as a new way of differentiating human beings. Science was enlisted in the effort to create a new hierarchy of the human and not fully human, on top of which the Aryan race stood supreme. Difference was biologized into an immutable essence; each human being could be assigned a place in this new order based on their race, an abstract category that superseded and rendered insignificant complex personal backgrounds and identities (Bauman 1989; see also Kaye and Strath 2000b). Elsewhere, I have referred to this general process as "manufacturing difference" (Hinton 2000, 2005), one component of which is the "crystallization of difference," whereby genocidal regimes construct, essentialize, and propagate sociopolitical categories of difference, crystallizing what are normally much more complex, fluid, and contextually variable forms of identity. Germans are distinguished from Jews, Hutus from Tutsis, Turks from Armenians, Bosnian Serbs from Muslims, Cambodian "old people" from "new people" and ethnic incorrigibles, the "civilized" from indigenous "savages," and so forth. This is a hallmark of genocide: each person is assessed not on their individual characteristics, but in terms of their membership in an abstract group category that is essentialized and stigmatized (this "marking of difference" is a second component of manufacturing difference).

As difference is essentialized and marked and individuals are sorted into their "proper" group categories, genocidal regimes use modern institutions, modes of organization, and instrumental goals to achieve their lethal goals. The modern nation-state is distinct in its centralization of power and control, which gives it enormous power to discipline and punish its subjects (Foucault 1979). In genocidal situations, a regime may institute various institutional, legal, and political changes that transform the conditions under which perpetrators and their newly marked victims live and, ultimately, perish. The structural changes that underlie this "organization of difference," a third process involved in "manufacturing difference," create mechanisms, disciplines, and social spaces for distinguishing, dividing, confining, and regulating the target group, such as the Nazi Nuremberg Laws, racial courts, ghettos and concentration camps, propaganda outlets, and secret police. An analogous process of organizing difference can be seen in other genocides: the death marches of Armenians into the desert, the extensive Khmer Rouge prison system, Bosnian concentration camps, and Hutu roadblocks.

Science and technology, particularly technologies of death, make the power of the nation-state all the more potentially lethal. "Experts" may be brought in to make the killing process more efficient, a pattern taken to the extreme by the Nazi doctors, technicians, and scientists who worked relentlessly to create ever better and more efficient ways of killing Jews – gas chambers, the production and use of Zyklon-B, crematoriums, cyanide, injections of Phenol, gas vans, and medical experiments (see Bauman 1989; Lifton 1986; Hilberg 1985).

Bureaucracy, another mode of organization associated with modernity, may also be used to facilitate the production of mass death (Bauman 1989). To optimize "efficiency," work tasks are increasingly specialized and divided, culminating in impersonal bureaucracies that substitute technical proficiency for moral responsibility. As the division of labor is specialized, each bureaucrat becomes another step removed from the task that is ultimately performed. "Distanciation," in turn, facilitates dehumanization, as the human beings whose lives are affected by the task lose their distinctiveness, becoming objects often referred to in euphemistic language (Bauman 1989). In Nazi Germany, the result was a bureaucrat like Eichmann, who efficiently carried out his tasks, unconcerned about the dehumanized individuals he was helping to annihilate. While bureaucracy is not inherently genocidal, Bauman argues, it has the potential to facilitate lethal projects of social engineering, particularly when other moral safeguards break down. This is precisely what happened in Nazi Germany, as religious leaders, politicians, and intellectuals stood by – or even applauded or helped out – while Hitler's government annihilated Jews and other "contaminating" groups.

If modern technology, bureaucracy, state authority, moral blindness, and abstract categorization all have the potential to foment the genocidal process, they ultimately require a vision to guide them toward this end. Genocide is almost always associated with that thoroughly modern project of social engineering, as the state classifies, marks, reorganizes, and remakes a population of abstract categorical "units" (Bauman 1989; Scott 1998). If some of these groups need to be moved to promote the "larger social good" (as defined by a perpetrator regime's social blueprint for a "better" world), relocations may ensue. If some of these groups threaten to "contaminate" and "destroy" the country, ethnic cleansing and mass annihilation may be required. Thus, the Nazi regime set out to reshape the social landscape by systematically and efficiently destroying the human weeds (Jews, Gypsies, "lives not worth living") that threatened to ruin this rational "garden" of Aryan purity – to use Bauman's metaphor in the passage I quoted at the beginning of this chapter. More than 200,000 severely disabled or mentally ill people, classified by German physicians as "lives not worth living," were murdered in the name of eugenics and euthanasia. Similarly, the Nazis executed up to 6 million Jews who were ideologically portrayed as a "disease," as "bacilli," and as "parasites" that threatened to poison the German national body and contaminate the purity of German blood (Koenigsberg 1975; Linke 1999).

MODERNITY, GENOCIDE, AND PSYCHOLOGICAL ANTHROPOLOGY

Bauman's analysis of the relationship of modernity and the Holocaust is crucial to our understanding of genocide and demands a reconsideration of primordialist arguments. In his relentless quest to force us to look at the dark side of modernity, however, Bauman at times overstates his case. From the perspective of anthropology in general, and psychological anthropology in particular, such an argument about the relationship of genocide and modernity needs to be complicated in at least two further ways to take account of local knowledge and individual agency, motivation, and meaning.

The locality of modernity

Given that Bauman's work is centered on modernity and the Holocaust, it is not surprising that he does not explicitly address the question of how modernity is linked to genocide in general. His argument is certainly suggestive in this regard, as elements of modernity have been a factor in genocides ranging from the destruction of indigenous peoples to Rwanda (Hinton 2002b, 2002c; Kaye and Strath 2000b). Unfortunately, Bauman's attack on the notion that the Holocaust was an aberration leads him to be wary of explanations that explain genocide in local terms:

> Yet the exercise in focusing on the *Germanness* of the crime as on that aspect in which the explanation of the crime must lie is simultaneously an exercise in exonerating every-one else, and particularly *everything* else. The implication that the perpetrators of the Holocaust were a wound or a malady of our civilization – rather than its horrifying, yet legitimate product – rests not only in the moral comfort of self-exculpation, but also in the dire threat of moral and political disarmament. It all happened "out there" – in another time, another place. The more "they" are to blame, the more the rest of "us" are safe, and the less we have to do to defend this safety. (Bauman 1989: xii)

Not surprisingly, Bauman (2000) is extremely critical of Daniel Goldhagen's (1996) work, since it not only stresses the "Germanness" of the Holocaust, but also focuses predominantly upon one dimension of that Germanness ("eliminationist anti-semitism") (see Hinton 1998).

While Bauman has reason to be critical of such arguments, he generally down-plays the ways in which "the local" may play a role in genocide – despite the fact that his own analysis of the Holocaust could be read as an example of how modernity is "localized" in a particular genocidal context, Nazi Germany. As anthropologists and other scholars have shown, modernity is not a singular phenomenon – it is localized in different ways in various historical and sociopolitical situations. To approach modernity in this manner does not explain it away as a completely local

phenomenon, but treats modernity as a set of a dynamic processes that have particular manifestations (including their incarnations in genocides), yet retain a family
resemblance. Each of the variables associated with modernity that Bauman discusses
– ranging from abstract categorization, to technology, to bureaucratic organization
– is mediated by local cultural understandings that have distinct meanings, entailments,
and motivational consequences.

Khmer Rouge ideology, for example, was strongly influenced by the spirit of
modernity (Hinton n.d.). The Khmer Rouge leaders believed the "science" of Marxist-
Leninism provided them with the analytical tools to "resolve" Cambodia's problems
and help initiate a "super great leap forward" toward a communist utopia. This progress would be achieved through a project of social engineering that would create a
society composed of new social institutions and revolutionary beings with a proper
consciousness. Those who opposed the regime or failed to transform themselves
would be "cleaned up" (*boas sam'at*). Such people were often told: "To keep you is
no gain; to destroy you is no loss."

Nevertheless, the Khmer Rouge version of Marxist Leninism involved a blend of
the old and the new, particularly given that these ideas had to be translated in terms
that the rural masses could comprehend. And local cadres frequently did a retransla-
tion of the leadership's ideological translations, further localizing on-the-ground
understandings. Ironically, despite its assault and ban on Buddhism, the Khmer Rouge
often used Buddhist terms to translate key ideological concepts such as "dialectical
materialism" (*sâmapheareah bâdechchâsâmobbat*), which used the Khmer Buddhist
term for dependent origination (*bâdechchâsâmobbat*). Such translations could have
important consequences. The word for dependent origination, for example, carried
ontologically resonant connotations of impermanence and change that helped generate an atmosphere of deep suspicion and paranoia (Hinton 2005).

Such ideological amalgams can also influence the patterning of violence, including
the "bodily inscription of violence," a fourth dimension of manufacturing difference.
Given that there is often enormous uncertainty about identity during genocide
(as the realities on the ground fail to match the crystallization of difference that
genocidal regimes assert), perpetrators may use forms of violence that (re)produce
the identity of victim groups (see Appadurai 1996; Feldman 1991; Taussig 1987).
In Rwanda, for example, Hutu and Tutsi identity was transformed into abstract
categories of difference, buttressed by notions of race (particularly through the Hamitic
Hypothesis, which has its origins in colonial rule) and the institutionalization of
identity (through mechanisms like the census and identity cards). Nevertheless,
enormous uncertainty often existed about the identity of a person during the Rwandan
genocide. Christopher Taylor (1999) has argued that many of the forms of violence
used by Rwandan perpetrators, ranging from stuffing people into latrines to cutting
their Achilles' tendons at militia roadblocks, were patterned by local conceptions
of bodily flow and blockage (for example, a Tutsi who was stuffed into a latrine
became an icon of "blockage," an impure state of being reflecting the Tutsis' status
as impure beings).

Similarly, Michael Taussig (1984, 1987) has explored how the bodily inscription
of difference was articulated in a radically different genocidal context – the horrible
abuses perpetrated by rubber traders against Indians living along the Putumayo river
in Columbia at the turn of the twentieth century, as reported by Roger Casement.

Taussig argues this "space of death" was pervaded by enormous fear and uncertainty, which was heightened by a disjointed mixing of Western and local images. It was precisely within such sites of what Taussig calls "epistemic murk" that terror took on cultural forms, as both perpetrator and victim, colonizer and colonized, attempted to make sense of their encounter with this terrifying and mysterious "other" onto whom their fantasies were projected. For the rubber traders on the Putumayo, Taussig argues, Indians, who they associated with the wild, savagery, ignorance, and cannibalism, were transformed into the very images they were supposed to signify through acts of terror, brutality, and violence: rites of degradation confirming the inhuman status of the Indians; the burning or inverted crucifixion of the "infidels"; the rape or sexual enslavement of the "lascivious" group's women; the confinement of these inhabitants of "the wild" in cages and stockades; and the murder and dismemberment of "cannibalistic" savages. Through their depictions of such acts, even observers like Casement affirmed the very cultural images that were patterning the violence.

Genocide and psychological dimensions of modernity

While it would be unfair to say that Bauman dismisses psychologically oriented explanations, he tends to regard them as largely irrelevant to his argument about the modernity of the Holocaust. This perspective is in part grounded in a wariness of psychological reductionism, which can reposition the Holocaust as a regression – a momentary eruption of "primitive" emotions or unconscious processes – that stands in contrast to the "normal" state of affairs in "civilized" society. Ultimately, Bauman argues, it does not matter that much whether Nazi perpetrators hated their victims, since they were part of a larger bureaucratic project of scientific engineering that called for the extermination of the "weeds" that were spoiling the design of the social "garden" that the Nazis wanted to create, to use Bauman's metaphor. In many ways, Bauman's argument can be read as a more developed extension of Arendt's insights about the "banality of evil," as exemplified by Eichmann, the paradigmatic Nazi bureaucrat.

This perspective stands in contrast to Goldhagen's argument that it was precisely the strong emotions associated with "eliminationist antisemitism" that motivated Nazis to brutalize and kill Jews. Bauman replies: "for every villain of Goldhagen's book, for every German and non-German who killed his victims with pleasure and enthusiasm, there were dozens and hundreds of Germans and non-Germans who contributed to the mass murder no less effectively without feeling anything about their victims and about the nature of the actions involved" (2000: 52). For Bauman, the key insight about the modernity of the Holocaust, which psychologically oriented perspectives tend to ignore, is that modern society enables "ordinary folks, 'just good workers,' to contribute to the killing – and to make that killing cleaner, morally antiseptic and efficient as never before" (2000: 55).

Unfortunately, Bauman overstates his case, leading him to take a somewhat unidimensional approach to the Holocaust. Even as he makes a sociological argument, psychological concepts and issues slip into his discussion. The very notion of abstract categorization, for example, presupposes questions about human cognition, including the psychological processes that predispose human beings to sort, label, and categorize things in their environment, including other human beings, in certain sorts of ways (see Allport 1979; Bruner 1957; Hirschfeld 1996).

Elsewhere, in a discussion of "Genocide as Order-Building," Bauman (2000: 38–40), drawing on the work of Ulrich Beck, notes that, through its future-oriented quest for progress and the betterment of the human condition, modernity is characterized by an incompleteness and dissatisfaction. New social visions lead to new social orders, which quickly become "old" and must be transcended by still newer visions of human emancipation and progress that lead to yet another new social order. This tension in modernity creates an experience of being that is "unnerving," "disturbing," and "anxiety generating." In such situations, Bauman argues, people crave greater security and certainty, which are sometimes precariously achieved by visions of "law and order" that seek control over the uncertain. Such feelings can help drive genocide when they are displaced onto disordering and threatening "others."

More broadly, Bauman is touching upon a dimension of modernity that a number of scholars have discussed, the generation of an existential state of anxiety, despair, and meaninglessness. The theoretical genealogy of this idea is impressive, including Nietzsche's concept of nihilism, Marx's alienation, Durkheim's anomie, Simmel's metropolis, and Weber's "iron cage" and "polar night of icy darkness." If the structures of modern societies – for example, capitalism, bureaucracy, atomization, the division of labor, urbanism – help produce such states of being, a sense of meaninglessness and anxiety is also fostered through ideological dimensions of modernity, particularly the Enlightenment obsession with science, rationality, and secularism. Science and rationality began to supplant myth and superstition, including religious belief, leading to Nietzsche's proclamation that "God is Dead." At the same time modernity promises "progress," then, it contains a destructive impulse that undercuts "traditional" norms, ideas, morals, and values that had provided human beings with a more certain sense of meaning. The problem is that it is difficult to replace religious understandings with scientific laws and mathematical formulas (though both contain a common faith in the truth of what they assert). Quintessentially "modern" individuals are left with a series of fairly sterile abstractions that are largely devoid of deeper meaning – and thus unable to adequately deal with the feelings of existential anxiety, anomie, and dread associated with modernity.

All of this suggests that modernity tends to generate certain psychological modes of being that may play an important role in modern genocides, which almost always have a strong ideological dimension and arise in a context of socioeconomic and/or political upheaval. Modernity cleaves apart preexisting meanings. Upheaval exacerbates existential anxiety and meaninglessness, and increases the appeal of more simplified schemas for thought and behavior (what I have elsewhere called "cognitive constriction": Hinton 2005). Ideology, often in the name of progress and social engineering, promises renewal. Anthropologists will recognize the millenarian overtones of this sequence (Wallace 1956), as genocide is legitimated in the name of social transformations that will lead to a new and more satisfactory way of life – including the elimination of specific elements of the population that threaten this revitalization. Charismatic leaders are often central to this process, as they espouse a certainty and purpose to which their followers are drawn and with which they want and need to identify. Not all modern genocides are full-fledged revitalization movements, but all contain the notion that the annihilation of a threatening or impure group will help create the preconditions for a better and more fulfilling way of life.

Nazi Germany and Cambodia constitute perhaps the clearest examples of genocidal regimes that came to power as revitalization movements. The Nazis, for example, rose to power in the wake of socioeconomic upheaval caused by World War I, the Treaty of Versailles, and worldwide depression (Connor 1989). Led by the charismatic Hitler (Lindholm 1990), the Nazis promised to lead the country out of this dismal condition through the creation of a German folk community (*volkgemeinschaft*) of pure Aryans. The annihilation of Jews and other "impure" groups was justified as necessary to ensure the health of this community. In *Mein Kampf* and in later speeches, for example, Hitler repeatedly described Jews as "vermin," "alien bodies," "eternal bloodsuckers," "parasites," "bacteria," "a disease," "an infection," and "a plague" that threatened to destroy the German body politic (see Koenigsberg 1975). The following passage of Hitler's is typical: "[The Jew] is and remains the typical parasite, a sponger who like a noxious bacillus keeps spreading as soon as a favorable medium invites him. And the effect of his existence is also like that of spongers: wherever he appears, the host people dies out after a shorter or longer period" (Hitler 1971: 305).

A roughly similar process unfolded in Cambodia, which was rocked by the Vietnam War and crises that emerged from its wake – civil war, economic collapse, intensive bombing, death and destruction, foreign invasion, and the breakdown in state control and order (Hinton 1999, 2005). This upheaval helped the Khmer Rouge gain recruits, who were drawn to the movement's promise to establish a "clean and just" utopian society that would be free of economic exploitation and oppression. After coming to power, the Khmer Rouge embarked upon a radical project of social engineering in which the elimination of certain "impure" groups was legitimated in the name of the larger social good. While the details vary, elements of this process of genocidal "revitalization" can also be seen in places like Idi Amin's Uganda, Habyarimana's Rwanda, and Milosovic's Yugoslavia.

Yet another psychological dimension of modernity that Bauman leaves underexplored is the intimacy between perpetrator and victim. For Bauman, abstract categorization, bureaucracy, and technology all have the effect of increasing the distance between perpetrator and victim, creating an Eichmann effect, or a banal and emotionally uninvested participation in genocide. There are at least two problems with such a perspective. First, during the Holocaust, there was a great deal of killing that involved face-to-face interactions, such as the *Einsatzgruppen* and Police Battalions (Browning 1992; Goldhagen 1996). A similar point could be made about the killing of familiars in other genocides, ranging from friends and neighbors to family members in Cambodia, Bosnia, and Rwanda. Most genocides involve a range of contexts that vary in the degree of distance between perpetrator and victim, and the dynamics involved in these situations may differ from the Eichmann effect accordingly (see Vetlesen 2000).

Second, and relatedly, there is often a degree of intimacy and emotional investment involved in the most bureaucratic and "distanced" forms of killing. Even as it generates feelings of meaninglessness and despair, modernity provides abstract categories that may become receptacles for these feelings. Writing as World War II was coming to an end, Horkheimer and Adorno (1944) made an interesting argument along these lines, asserting that Jews served as abstract containers for the projection of the Nazi's feelings of existential dread, fear, and uncertainty (see also Fromm 1941; Schmidt 2000). If a bureaucrat like Eichmann may have engaged in such projections to a moderate extent, perpetrators who violate their victims in an even more proximate manner – ranging from torture, to rape, to bodily mutilation – are likely to do so to an even greater degree. At times, this bodily inscription of difference may be an attempt by the perpetrator to assert their sense of being through the domination of others, inflating their sense of self as they penetrate, mutilate, and even eradicate the bodies of "enemies" who reflect back their fears. To annihilate an "other" in this manner is in a sense an attempt to annihilate one's own fear of nothingness. Jean Améry (1980) has provided a gripping account of how such a dynamic seemed to be driving his Nazi torturers. . . .

In conclusion, I want to reiterate that genocide, as it was originally conceptualized and practiced in the twentieth century, cannot be fully explained without taking account of the crucial ways in which modernity has laid important foundations for such mass annihilation. At the same time, an analysis that focuses predominantly on modernity, such as Bauman's *Modernity and the Holocaust*, has limitations, particularly insofar as it ignores questions of the local and individual motivation. Gardeners may desire to destroy the weeds that spoil their design, but the "gardens" within which genocide unfolds are local ones, and the gardeners themselves are complex individuals with complex motivations.

With its stress on the local and the individual, psychological anthropology stands ideally poised to enter into such debates about genocide in particular, and modernity in general. To do so, however, psychological anthropologists must begin to more fully engage with the macro-level structures and dynamics that constrain and inform the worlds in which individuals act. Bauman's important work on the Holocaust illustrates the significance of adequately dealing with such phenomena. As I have suggested, however, such work can be greatly augmented by key concepts in psychological anthropology, such as revitalization, identity, the self, emotion, projection, existential being, and subjectivity. These notions also provide a possible bridge between Bauman's insights about modernity and Goldhagen's assertion that an explanation of the Holocaust must account for the extreme brutality and hatred of so many Nazis.

Before ending, I should briefly note that parts of this analysis could be extended to a discussion of the relationship of modernity, globalization, and genocide. In many ways, globalization involves an acceleration of many of the processes associated with modernity, as people, ideas, images, capital, and technology flow more rapidly throughout the world (Appadurai 1996; Inda and Rosaldo 2002). This "intensification of global interconnectedness" has the potential to generate an increasing sense of fragmentation, uncertainty, and ambivalence, as time and space are compressed and people are increasingly exposed to alternatives modes of being that undercut the seeming certainty of their traditional ways of life (Giddens 1990, 1991; Harvey 1989). Globalization, then, potentially intensifies the crisis of meaning and existential despair that modernity tends to generate. Under such conditions, large numbers of people are likely to be attracted to totalizing ideologies that offer a new sense of identity, meaning, and renewal. Perhaps, this suggests, the world will continue to be plagued by genocide in the twenty-first century, as anomic individuals are drawn to visions of "progress" that are predicated on the need to annihilate abstract categories of beings, who serve as icons of their feelings of existential dread and nothingness.

REFERENCES

Allport, Gordon W., 1979 *The Nature of Prejudice*, 25th anniversary edn. Reading, MA: Addison-Wesley.

Améry, Jean, 1980 *At the Mind's Limits: Contemplations by a Survivor on Auschwitz and Its Realities*. Bloomington: Indiana University Press.

Andreopoulos, George J., ed., 1994 *Genocide: Conceptual and Historical Issues*. Philadelphia: University of Pennsylvania Press.

Appadurai, Arjun, 1996 *Modernity at Large: Cultural Dimensions of Globalization*. Minneapolis: University of Minnesota Press.

Arendt, Hannah, 1963 *Eichmann in Jerusalem: A Report on the Banality of Evil*. New York: Viking Penguin.

Arens, Richard, ed., 1976 *Genocide in Paraguay*. Philadelphia, PA: Temple University Press.

Bauman, Zygmunt, 1989 *Modernity and the Holocaust*. Ithaca, NY: Cornell University Press.

— 2000 The Duty to Remember – But What? In *Enlightenment and Genocide, Contradictions of Modernity*. James Kaye and Bo Strath, eds. Pp. 31–57. Brussels: PIE–Peter Lang.

Bodley, John H., 1999 *Victims of Progress*. Mountain View, CA: Mayfield.

Browning, Christopher R., 1992 *Ordinary Men: Reserve Police Battalion 101 and the Final Solution in Poland*. New York: Harper Collins.

Bruner, Jerome S., 1957 On Perceptual Readiness. *Psychological Review* 64: 123–151.

Connor, John W., 1989 From Ghost Dance to Death Camps: Nazi Germany as a Crisis Cult. *Ethos* 17 (3): 259–288.

Crossette, Barbara, 2002 War Crimes Tribunal Becomes Reality, Without US Role. *New York Times* April 12: A3.

Fein, Helen, 1990 Genocide: A Sociological Perspective. *Current Sociology* 38 (1): v–126.

Feldman, Allen, 1991 *Formations of Violence: The Narrative of the Body and Political Terror in Northern Ireland*. Chicago: University of Chicago Press.

Foucault, Michel, 1979 *Discipline and Punish: The Birth of the Prison*. Alan Sheridan, trans. New York: Vintage Books.

Fromm, Erich, 1941 *Escape from Freedom*. New York: Rinehart.

Giddens, Anthony, 1985 *The Nation-State and Violence*. Berkeley: University of California Press.

— 1990 *The Consequences of Modernity*. Stanford, CA: Stanford University Press.

— 1991 *Modernity and Self-Identity*. Cambridge: Polity Press.

Goldhagen, Daniel Jonah, 1996 *Hitler's Willing Executioners: Ordinary Germans and the Holocaust*. New York: Knopf.

Hall, Stuart, with David Held, Don Hubert, and Kenneth Thompson, eds., 1995 *Modernity: An Introduction to Modern Societies*. Cambridge: Polity Press.

Harvey, David, 1989 *The Condition of Postmodernity*. Oxford: Blackwell.

Held, David, 1995 The Development of the Modern State. In *Modernity: An Introduction to Modern Societies*. Stuart Hall, David Held, Don Hubert, and Kenneth Thompson, eds. Pp. 56–89. Cambridge: Polity Press.

Hilberg, Raul, 1985 *The Destruction of the European Jews*. New York: Holmes and Meier.

Hinton, Alexander Laban, 1998 Why did the Nazis Kill? Anthropology, Genocide, and the Goldhagen Controversy. *Anthropology Today* 14 (3): 9–15.

— 1999 Revitalization and Genocide. Paper presented at the biennial meeting of the Society for Psychological Anthropology. Albuquerque, NM, September 22.

— 2000 Under the Shade of Pol Pot's Umbrella: Mandala, Myth, and Politics in the Cambodian Genocide. In *The Vision Thing: Myth, Politics, and Psyche in the World*. Thomas Singer, ed. Pp. 170–204. New York: Routledge.

— 2002a Introduction: Genocide and Anthropology. In *Genocide: An Anthropological Reader*. Alexander Laban Hinton, ed. Pp. 1–23. Oxford: Blackwell.

— ed. 2002b *Genocide: An Anthropological Reader*. Oxford: Blackwell.

— 2002c *Annihilating Difference: The Anthropology of Genocide*. Berkeley: University of California Press.

— 2005 *Why Did They Kill? Cambodia in the Shadow of Genocide*. Berkeley: University of California Press.

Hirschfeld, Lawrence A., 1996 *Race in the Making: Cognition, Culture, and the Child's Construction of Human Kinds*. Cambridge, MA: MIT Press.

Hitler, Adolf, 1971 *Mein Kampf*. Ralph Manheim, trans. Boston, MA: Houghton-Mifflin.

Horkheimer, Max, and Theodor W. Adorno, 1944 *Dialectic of Enlightenment*. John Cumming, trans. New York: Continuum.

Inda, Jonathan Xavier, and Renato Rosaldo, eds., 2002 *The Anthropology of Globalization: A Reader*. Oxford: Blackwell.

Kaye, James, and Bo Strath, 2000a Introduction. In *Enlightenment and Genocide, Contradictions of Modernity*. James Kaye and Bo Strath, eds. Pp. 11–29. Brussels: PIE–Peter Lang.

Kaye, James, and Bo Strath, eds., 2000b *Enlightenment and Genocide, Contradictions of Modernity*. Brussels: PIE–Peter Lang.

Koenigsberg, Richard A., 1975 *Hitler's Ideology: A Study in Psychoanalytic Sociology*. New York: Library of Social Science.

Kuper, Leo, 1981 *Genocide: Its Political Use in the Twentieth Century*. New Haven, CT: Yale University Press.

LeBlanc, Lawrence J., 1991 *The United States and the Genocide Convention*. Durham, NC: Duke University Press.

Lemkin, Raphaël, 1944 *Axis Rule in Occupied Europe*. Washington, DC: Carnegie Endowment for International Peace.

— 1945 Genocide – A Modern Crime. *Free World* 9 (4): 39–43.

Lewis, Neil A., 2002 US Rejects All Support for New Court on Atrocities. *New York Times* May 7: A11.

Lifton, Robert Jay, 1986 *The Nazi Doctors: Medical Killing and the Psychology of Genocide*. New York: Basic Books.

Lindholm, Charles, 1990 *Charisma*. Oxford: Blackwell.

Linke, Uli, 1999 *Blood and Nation: The European Aesthetics of Race*. Philadelphia: University of Pennsylvania Press.

Power, Samantha, 2002 *"A Problem from Hell": America and the Age of Genocide*. New York: Basic Books.

Schmidt, James, 2000 Genocide and the Limits of Enlightenment: Horkheimer and Adorno Revisted. In *Enlightenment and Genocide, Contradictions of Modernity*. James Kaye and Bo Strath, eds. Pp. 81–102. Brussels: PIE–Peter Lang.

Scott, James C., 1998 *Seeing Like a State: How Certain Schemes to Improve the Human Condition Have Failed*. New Haven, CT: Yale University Press.

Taussig, Michael, 1984 Culture of Terror – Space of Death: Roger Casement's Putumayo Report and the Explanation of Torture. *Comparative Studies in Society and History* 26 (3): 467–97.

— 1987 *Shamanism, Colonialism, and the Wild Man: A Study in Terror and Healing*. Chicago: University of Chicago Press.

Taylor, Christopher C., 1999 *Sacrifice as Terror: The Rwandan Genocide of 1994*. Oxford: Berg.

Toulmin, Stephen, 1990 *Cosmopolis: The Hidden Agenda of Modernity.* Chicago: University of Chicago Press.

Vetlesen, Arne Johan, 2000 Yugoslavia, Genocide, and Modernity. In *Enlightenment and Genocide, Contradictions of Modernity.* James Kaye and Bo Strath, eds. Pp. 151–183. Brussels: PIE–Peter Lang.

Wallace, Anthony F. C., 1956 Revitalization Movements. *American Anthropologist* 58: 264–281.

CHAPTER 23 Corporate Violence

Howard F. Stein

It's not the big things that are important to me, but the everyday life of tyranny, which gets forgotten. A thousand mosquito bites are worse than a blow to the head. I observe, note down the mosquito bites.

Victor Klemperer, I Will Bear Witness

DOWNSIZING AND THE TASK OF PSYCHOLOGICAL ANTHROPOLOGY

This chapter approaches the understanding of downsizing (and cognate or related terms) from two complementary perspectives. The first is the modernizing context of corporate and wider American culture – and its globalization – during the period from the mid-1980s through the present. The second is the context(s) variously called the human condition, human nature, and species-specific human biology. What makes this second viewpoint a contribution to psychological anthropology is the fact that human thought and emotion, often unconscious, are part of our condition, nature, and biology. In this chapter, I ask two related questions. In the first place, "What kind of companies, or Americans, do downsizing?" Here, downsizing becomes both manifestation and symptom of American modernization. I also ask a broader question to situate this local study in the project of psychological anthropology: "What (and who) is the human animal that does something called 'downsizing'?" The "corporate condition," the "American condition," and the "human condition" are all expressions of the human animal (La Barre 1954, 1972).

I begin briefly with the "corporate" and "American" conditions. As a business strategy, downsizing can be understood (at least) two ways. In the popular view, companies drastically fire large numbers of workers in order to increase *profits* markedly and quickly. In the corporate view (which partially overlaps with the lay view), the goal of drastic payroll reduction is to quickly raise the *stock price* (Lurie 1998). The latter is a specific use and situation for which downsizing is the frequent, virtually automatic solution: to create short-term optimization of stockholder (shareholder) value. In a sense, the shareholder becomes the only constituency (stakeholder) who ultimately matters and to whom the company feels accountable.

The cruel paradox, as Jonathan Lurie (1998) says, is that "downsizing raises the perceived value of the firm but lowers the actual value." In countless instances, the stock price soars, but the company then becomes crippled by its success. Perhaps the greatest irony is that the period of the early through nearly late 1990s was simultaneously the time of the most relentless downsizing and the time of a flourishing economy (low unemployment, high profits and productivity).

One of the key characteristics, or distinctive features, is the embeddedness of downsizing in irony and paradox. The very subject matter of this chapter even makes a quick and immediate identification and definition of terms problematic! Things are not what they are supposed to seem. "Downsizing" and its cognate terms are part of a larger gestalt of cultural mystification. My point of departure is linguistic, and in many respects the exploration and demystification is psycholinguistic and sociolinguistic. The work of downsizing occurs in the idiom of euphemism.

I shall argue that downsizing is at once a cultural metaphor about business and about life, a social form, a cultural problem solving mode, and is a symbolic as well as economic process. I shall explore both the experience of downsizing and the causes of downsizing, and I shall suggest that they are linked. Specifically, I shall argue that the destructive "motive(s)" for downsizing are a clue to the experience and consequences of downsizing. Further, the "automatic," obligatory nature of downsizing as a solution suggests its status as obsession and compulsion rather than based on an assessment of reality. Finally, I shall suggest that death anxiety rather than strictly business considerations is a powerful force in "driving" the choice of downsizing as a dominant culture-wide solution.

Consider, next, the practice and experience of downsizing in relation to several core concepts and interests in anthropology that help to understand the *human* condition. Anthropologists are interested in biological and cultural *adaptation*, including what is called *preadaptation*. That is, we humans both adapt *to* new environments, and we adapt to them *with* tools, beliefs, feelings, attitudes, and values we bring from before. People who have been fired from often career-long jobs take their experience of sudden disposability, and the emotions unleashed by rejection and abandonment, into their next jobs and working relationships. They often keep new working relationships at arm's length, and are more indifferent than loyal to their new employers. The experience and emotional response to downsizing shapes experience and culture in the new workplace to which one (pre)adapts.

Anthropologists have long contrasted *instrumental* and *expressive activities* to distinguish between practical, reality oriented practices and symbolic ones. Ostensibly, the firing of tens of thousands of people from their jobs is purely an objective, business decision; that is, an instrumental act. Yet it is highly influenced and contaminated by brutality, sadism, indifference to suffering, and the magical thinking that mass firings can turn around years (if not decades) of poor decisions.

Anthropologists have long applied the concept of *culture* to tribal, ethnic, and national groups and units into which they are born and of which they become members. The term is used both to designate that people "have" a culture, and "are" a culture. The phenomenon of corporate downsizing raises the question of corporate workplaces as cultures, their relation to national culture, and the effect of tumultuous, ongoing change on both – while never reifying any of these units into entities outside real people's experiences.

Finally, anthropologists (together with linguists) have studied people's *language* use as part of a wider effort to understand human communication. In corporate downsizing, euphemism plays a key role as language's contribution to large-scale deception and self-deception, manipulation, and destruction. In short, the study of downsizing and of other forms of "managed social change" contributes simultaneously to understanding workplace life in the United States and many core concepts in general, as well as psychological anthropology.

Let me situate myself in this study. I did not set out to study downsizing. I am a psychoanalytically oriented clinical anthropologist who teaches family medicine residents (apprentice physicians). I "specialize" in the doctor–patient relationship, including its wide social parameters. Over the past fifteen years, however, it has become clear that corporate language, thinking, sentiment, and social structure is coming to regulate the outpatient clinic and hospital and teaching facility just as it has in virtually every other "industry." Downsizing and other forms of "managed social change" have become a part of everyday clinical and academic life. Not only did I study my own work settings, but also as an organizational consultant, I was invited to assist other organizational settings in "humanizing" their own downsizing process. I worked as an applied anthropologist in action oriented projects. I was also the target of downsizing efforts for nearly a decade. A byproduct of this work was a number of publications on downsizing (Stein 1994, 1997, 1998a, 1998b, 2001; Allcorn et al. 1996). The study is ongoing.

THE TWO LANGUAGES OF DOWNSIZING

If downsizing is so rational, objective, dispassionate, and strictly economic an organizational procedure, why is it so often *also* described in the language of unbridled physical force and assault? The imagery and metaphors of downsizing offer crucial data about what lies behind the slogan, "Nothing Personal, Just Business." The discourse of downsizing is steeped in imagery of war and death. Executives' scenarios are intimidating, inspiring terror and historical memory of calamity. I have heard many executives, managers, and workers speak of downsizing (and its cognate terms) in the Holocaust language of selections, queues awaiting terrible fate, and trains destined for death camps. What, then, are we to make of downsizing?

Were an observant traveler such as Alexis de Tocqueville or Max Weber to visit the United States between the middle 1980s and the present, he or she would be certain to encounter – and likely be baffled by – a constellation of terms that are further subsumed under the category of "managed social change." Although these terms are separate and certainly can be "operationally" defined independently of one another, in actual use and practice, they all imply one another and are all members of a cultural ethos or worldview.

Downsizing per se is one member of an official semantic web of interchangeable terms that includes reduction in force (and the acronym RIFing), rightsizing, surplusing, and redundancy (a British term). All these terms are interchangeable. They are all attempts to describe induced change in the language of impersonal, abstract, organizational engineering, and avoid human or personal connotation. As part of an official cultural language matrix, there are cognate (that is, closely related, but not identical) terms as well: outsourcing, reengineering, restructuring, deskilling, managed healthcare, among others. Although all these are denotatively corporate, workplace terms, they have come connotatively to be the official signposts of a national cultural ethos.

Significantly, one can observe historically the continued effort to further disguise the disguises, suggesting displacement and rationalization, as well as denial. Downsizing and reduction in force were supplemented, and to a degree supplanted, by the acronym RIF, which takes multiple forms as noun, verb, and present participle. The term rightsize(-ing) is a yet further attempt to obscure the destructiveness and aggression, an effort aided by the processes of undoing and further intellectualization. To use my own words: *tearing down* is transmuted into *setting right*. Throughout this process, one puts increasing emotional distance between the motivation, the deed, and the word.

Corporate executives and managers adamantly distinguish downsizing from "firing," "laying off," "cutting," and "terminating" employees. In the latter schemes, actions are to be construed as something *directly* done to workers, while in the former, official scheme, the riddance of people as employees is an unfortunate *indirect* consequence of the perceived need to make the organization more efficiently productive and profitable by making "it" smaller. Motivation is deceptively obscured, hidden, and kept secret, even from decision-makers themselves. Workplace and organization come to be reified, separated from the people who constitute and work in them. Euphemism becomes a major governing force, not only of the workplace, but also of modernizing and globalizing society.

Collectively, these "human engineering" terms serve the stated goal of ensuring that "the bottom line" of profit and profitability stays or can be quickly turned "into the black" (that is, into profit rather than loss). The "bottom line" becomes the supreme value, the *summum bonum*, of our cultural era – and one of its chief metaphors. To know the full meaning of the "bottom line" is to know the current variation on the American ethos. In bottom line thinking, the time line is radically foreshortened in the service of producing quarterly statements that show (more) profit to trustees, boards of directors, and shareholders. For all participants, time anxiety is intense. In sum, the constellation of "economic" terms has in common the character of euphemism: they reveal by concealing; they direct attention to one set of images and feelings by directing attention away from another set.

This second set of terms is an *unofficial* cultural language matrix, one heard more in office break rooms and in hallway conversation than in formal boardroom meetings. Abstractly speaking, the first language – its speakers, spokespersons, and enforcers – disavows the second language. The second language draws terms, images, and feelings from the Holocaust, from the Vietnam War, from meat butchering and body mutilation. The second language arose, so to speak, in people's efforts to find images and metaphors that could contain and articulate the anxiety, fragmentation, demoralization, rage, and grief that they were feeling in the wake of experiences that upper management explained as "just business."

Consider the term "gooks." In the Vietnam War, the memory of which still haunts us nearly thirty years later, we Americans did not know who was friend or foe. All Vietnamese became potentially dangerous "gooks" – things, not people – depersonalized menaces. Today, in our American hospitals, corporations, banks, research and development institutions, industries, universities, and government, we do not know from one day to the next who is ally or enemy. Many upper management have said to me: "The person or board whose firings I execute today could fire me tomorrow, no matter how productive or loyal an employee I have been." The living are all potentially disposable waste.

Although downsizing and cognate terms are conventionally understood to be principally business or economics terms, I hope to show that in fact they are primarily cultural and secondarily, or derivatively, economic. That is, I shall situate "business" *within* "culture" rather than argue that business is American culture's driving force. And although I shall focus on downsizing as a social form, all the other terms (and their processes) are implied in its study. Downsizing and its related language can be characterized as *euphemism in the guise of reality.* The deeper significance of downsizing can be found in the psychology – the meanings, feelings, and motivated behavior – that underlies it. Beginning as a study of corporate language and life, the exploration of downsizing takes us to the heart of the experience of being an American at the end of the twentieth century and the beginning of the twenty-first.

CULTURAL "EPIDEMIOLOGY" OF DOWNSIZING

What corroborative data are available to support this position and claim? In this section I attempt to answer that question both quantitatively and qualitatively. At issue is the *magnitude* of downsizing in all senses of the word. The scale of destructiveness is overwhelming, as a 1995 Department of Human Services announcement describes:

> If the 1980s are remembered as the decade of mergers and acquisitions, the legacy of the 1990s will be the decade of downsizing and reorganization . . . It has been estimated that two-thirds of all large firms in the United States – more than 5,000 employers – reduced their workforces in the latter half of the 1980s. From 1983 to 1988, approximately 4.6 million US workers were displaced, with 2.7 million (57.8 percent) resulting from plant closings. (US Department of Health and Human Services 1995: 3)

In a 1996 review of literature on managed social change, Allcorn et al. note that, "of the *Fortune* 1000 companies, 85 percent report downsizing between 1987 and 1991 with 50 percent downsizing in 1990 (Mishra and Mishra 1994). Of the companies that downsize once, 65 percent will often do it again the following year, and multiple downsizings are not uncommon" (Allcorn et al. 1996: 3).

Uchitelle (2001) writes that American companies announced, in the first half of 2001 alone, plans to eliminate some 777,362 jobs, compared with 613,960 in all of the previous year. Summarizing a six-part, March 1996 *New York Times* series on "The Downsizing of America," the Benchmark Study Report on downsizing writes that "more than 43 million jobs have been lost in the United States since 1979, affecting nearly one-third of all households" (US Government 1997). For those who have been downsized, the next job is likely to have a lower wage or salary, fewer or no benefits, and little or no job security. Not only have many people been downsized more than once, but also it is also virtually impossible not to know someone, or their family, whose life has not been shaken by downsizing. A telling marker – and metaphor – of the consequences of downsizing is the fact that in the mid-1980s the largest private employer in the US was General Motors, while in the mid-1990s it became Manpower Inc., a temporary employment agency (cf. Uchitelle 1996).

Downsizing continues to be rampant and is far from only an artifact of the 1990s. Long before the waves of firings that followed the September 11, 2001 attacks on the World Trade Center and the Pentagon, downsizing served as a robust mode of solving organizational problems affected by economic downturn and poor corporate decision-making. The July 9, 2001 issue of *Fortune*, for instance, reported that 378,305 people had been laid off between January and June 2001. Likewise, the cover story of the *Wall Street Journal*, July 9, 2001, was titled: "Corporate Dieting Is Far From Over" (Hilsenrath 2001). The dread of "Could I Be Next?" (Kauffman 2001) haunts those who are passed over in the most recent downsizing episode.

Downsizing affects both private (corporate) and public (government) sector employees, even though the official rationale is different for each. Private sector groups strive to reduce costs in order to be competitive, profitable, and productive in a global economy, and to maximize shareholder value over the shortest possible time. Public sector groups reduce costs through budget reductions and technological improvement. Different political–economic ideologies have identical effects. In both instances, fewer workers are asked to do increasing amounts of work and in shorter times. Likewise, in both instances, downsizing is the main means of "reinventing" government (Osborne and Goebler 1993) and "redesigning" or "reengineering" corporate workplaces (Hammer 1990; Hammer and Champy 1993).

The timing of both private and public sector reinvention is identical. The bestseller *Reinventing Government: How the Entrepreneurial Spirit is Transforming the Public Sector* (Osborne and Goebler 1993) became something of a Malinowskian cultural "charter" for reforming the public sector, as did Michael Hammer and James Champy's bestseller of the same era, *Reengineering the Corporation: A Manifesto for Business Revolution* (1993). Here, as elsewhere in this chapter, attention to the language of discourse pays interpretive dividends!

In public and private sectors alike, not only is smallness expected to produce greater efficiency of operation, it is also expected to "revitalize" workplace and even national life (Wallace 1956). Part of the price of this corporate rebirth is death, albeit symbolic, from the sacrifice of those "redundant" workers. Paradoxically, instead of diminishing the sense of free-floating death anxiety, both forms of downsizing only increase it, resulting in an even more vulnerable and vigilant workforce.

Based on a wide variety of experiences, theories, and independent data sets, an increasing number of organizational theorists, consultants, and journalists are coming to question the wisdom behind, and assumptions governing, the many forms of managed social change. Many writers are recognizing that these forms are rife with magical, lockstep thinking. Beginning on March 3, 1996, the *New York Times* published a six-part series on "The Downsizing of America: A National Heartache." Authors Uchitelle and Kleinfield supply abundant organizational demographics and vignettes to support their argument that downsizing and its cognate terms (RIFing, rightsizing, etc.) have produced demoralization more than they have rejuvenated workplaces.

The 1997 US Government Benchmarking Study Report, noted above, writes that productivity, morale, customer service, and product quality often suffer in the wake of downsizing. "A leading human resource consulting company survey of restructuring practices among 531 large companies, conducted in 1993, revealed that although well over half of the companies surveyed achieved their goal of reducing costs and expenses, less than half achieved their goals of increased profitability, productivity, and consumer satisfaction" (US Government 1997: 4).

In a *Washington Post* essay, Grimsley (1995) describes "The Downside of Downsizing: What's Good for the Bottom Line Isn't Necessarily Good for Business." Byrne (1994) writes of "The Pain of Downsizing" in the cover story of *Business Week*. Gertz, a vice-president of Mercer Management Consulting Inc. (Boston), writes of the consequences of downsizing: "The best managers and workers, tired of the turmoil, begin to jump ship, while the remaining employees, disheartened and distracted, become ever less productive. Ultimately, downsizers find that they've cut the muscle from their companies, not just the fat" (1996: 11A; see also Gertz and Baptista 1995).

Downsizing often fails to deliver on its vast expectations. Productivity, trust, and morale, among others, often suffer with downsizing. The anticipated reduction of expenses and dramatic increase in profit are far from universal (Cameron 1994). Downsizing and its related forms of social change have virtually redefined work and employment. What Levinson (1962) called the "psychological contract" (which is a profoundly social one) between employer and employee, even between executive and company, has been unilaterally and summarily cancelled (Uchitelle and Kleinfield 1996), and a cascade of downward mobility – real and feared – is the result.

The cover story of *Newsweek*'s February 26, 1996 issue is titled "Corporate Killers." A large hatchet-head accompanies the article's listing in the table of contents. Indeed, images of axes, hatchets, and guillotines have been commonly drawn by editorial cartoonists over the past decade to depict the experience of downsizing, managed care, reengineering, and restructuring. The *Wall Street Journal* and the *Washington Post* now regularly publish articles that question the claims of managed social change.

Micklethwait and Wooldridge (2000) argue in *A Future Perfect* that the long-term advantages of economic globalization far outweigh the temporary destruction of jobs. By contrast, William Adler (2000) closely examines the disrupted lives of three women whose assembly-line jobs – and the company – move from New Jersey to rural Mississippi and to Matamoros, Mexico, across the border from Brownsville, Texas, in search of productivity and profit through globalization. In *The Working Life: The Promise and Betrayal of Modern Work*, ethicist Joanne Ciulla (2000) describes how organizations cultivate and exploit workers' loyalty, only to discard them by the thousands with no sense of reciprocal obligation. The work ethic of intimidation and fear induces only the pressure to work harder for a future that is always in question.

Psychologist Jacalyn Hughes conducted ethnographic research on downsizing in a public agency. Employees characterized the process of firing as coming without forewarning, impersonal and invalidating, and creating distrust and feelings of betrayal (2000: 260). Emotional and physical reactions included multiple losses, feelings of anger and blame, depression, stress and anxiety, physical illness, and both physical and emotional avoidance, including denial. The "survivor syndrome" was present among the remaining employees.

In *Stiffed: The Betrayal of the American Man*, journalist Susan Faludi (1999) explores the consequences of downsizing and reengineering. Faludi documents how these induce vulnerability, anxiety over loss, and dread of futurelessness that derive from American workers' shared social predicament and mutual identification. The social production of meaninglessness and rage is the outcome of the assault of the prevailing American business ethic on masculinity. One wonders what quiet despair or volatile rages, what disappointments, what impenetrable silences and sullenness, their children witness and unconsciously identify with – even among the most out-wardly adaptive and resilient parents. The future envisaged by those who bear the brunt of globalization and its many strategies is far from "perfect."

POPULAR CULTURE AND DOWNSIZING

At least in some respects, popular culture in the US is ahead of scholarship in realizing the brutality of downsizing, both in motivation and consequence. Business slogans or mottoes, for instance, condense the death-obsession and future-drivenness of our culture: time is money; time is short; and time is up. Here, the dread is that, irrespective of how hard one works, organizational death is still inevitable.

The popularity of cartoonist Scott Adams's Dilbert cartoons is one measure (Stein 1998a, 1998b). Disguising terror through biting humor, the Dilbert cartoon char-acters and workplace scenarios appear in newspaper cartoons, in books, and in a television show. The United Feature Syndicate character and ruthlessness of decision-making style is distilled literally into an art form. CEO Dilbert, his consulting partner Ratbert, the Evil Human Relations Director Catbert, and others are relentlessly, sadistically inventive in ways to get rid of people, to get them to destroy themselves, to torment and torture them, to distort and distend their workers' very bodies. A few examples must suffice to illustrate the genre.

In a 1995 Dilbert cartoon, Dogbert, acting as a downsizing consultant, demon-strates how to notify employees that their jobs will be outsourced by having his consulting partner, Ratbert, bend over. At the edge of a desktop, Dogbert kicks Ratbert in the buttocks into the trashcan. In the final scene, the "Pointy-Haired Boss" asked Dobgert, "How do I get them all stooped over?" Dogbert recommends "a program of very bad ergonomics."

In a 1996 cartoon, one of HR Director Catbert's strategies for downsizing is to get stressed-out employee Wally and others to start smoking, and thereby "have frequent company-sanctioned breaks throughout the day." In another of Catbert's policies, he orders all employees to wear shoes one size smaller than their feet: "We must do this to be competitive." The practice is called "footsizing" (1996 cartoon, parody on downsizing). Recurrent themes in Adams's Dilbert business cartoons are brutality, indifference to suffering, the pleasure in inducing pain, and the writing off of large numbers of people for dead.

As something of a cartoon-folklore variant of Dilbert, consider a widely syndicated "Rubes" cartoon by Leigh Rubin in a February 21, 1999 newspaper. It depicts a scantily clad, smiling tribal shaman holding his victim by the loincloth at the end of a stick at the summit of a steep volcano. The shaman says: "On behalf of myself and the rest of the tribe, I'd like to thank you for appeasing the volcano god and ensuring us another year of good health." The victim looks bulge-eyed over the edge of the precipice. The caption at the bottom of the cartoon reads: "How certain tribes pay their annual health insurance premium." One is reminded how primitive are managed care, downsizing, and reengineering at their motivational core (at their implicit, in contrast with their explicit, level).

An iconographic or "folk" variant on the hatchet/axe theme ("Cut-slash-chop") in cartoons and business advertisements about downsizing and corporate survival, is the imagery of a carnivorous animal or fish chasing another, mouth open wide, teeth showing, about to devour its opponent. The image is usually associated with a caption about locating oneself or one's corporation on the "food chain," and determining in this competitive world whether one will "eat" or "be eaten." Here, castration and death anxiety fuse with imagery of oral aggression (one's own, and projected) and annihilation. The message of Social Darwinism is explicit.

Attention to language in popular culture uncovers the sadistic destructiveness behind the aura of rationality in corporate business practice. Popular fantasy and folklore have created the sobriquet "Neutron Jack" for Jack Welch, head of General Electric, who is seen as eliminating people and leaving only buildings and their contents standing. Likewise, "Chainsaw Al" is assigned to Albert J. Dunlap, head of Scott Paper and later Sunbeam, who is seen as brutally turning companies around by mass firings. Sometimes even official business culture taps into fantasy language. Michael Hammer's ("father of reengineering") celebrated article in the 1990 *Harvard Business Review* was titled "Reengineering Work: Don't Automate, Obliterate." His language deserves to be taken seriously, even literally. Human mechanization, commoditization, and dehumanization work in grim tandem. Popular culture tells us informally what we cannot (even must not) say or even know formally. A widespread cultural – not only "organizational" – category is that of "violence in the workplace." It refers to the use of guns, knives, and bombs against co-workers and workplaces. But how do we go about conceptualizing the workplace itself as a form of violence (albeit "psychological" violence)?

AN APPETITE FOR DOWNSIZING: CREATING THE "LEAN AND MEAN" WORKPLACE VIA "ORGANIZATIONAL ANOREXIA"

In workplaces, the media, and popular culture alike, organizations become anthropomorphized into living, biological, human organisms. They are experienced as having distinct lives of their own, including body morphology and disease. Since the mid-1980s, shareholders, executives, boards of directors, and much of the public have come to view large workplace organizations as fat, bloated, and lazy, in need of radical surgery by axes and hatchets, or alternatively, radical weight reduction regimens. The surgery (downsizing) must cut off "dead meat" and "fat," sometimes must "cut muscle," even "cut down to the bone." The "deep cuts" are essential in order to "save the organization" (organism) by making it into a "lean, mean, fighting machine." The corporate "body" is at war for survival, at worst, and conquest, at best (military metaphor).

Organizational anorexia is simultaneously a survival strategy and a disease. The corporation or agency must cast off unnecessary "dead weight," undertake a crash diet to lose more and more weight (through multiple downsizings), and exercise relentlessly in order to make it vital and competitive in the marketplace. The "self-starving" is necessary for a radical reduction. Often, the reduction cannot stop and becomes self-starving. The organization (organism) has a "distorted body image," namely that it is far fatter than it is (or ever was), and that it must continue to lose weight even if it means starvation to death. The business strategy of "cutting" and "dieting" becomes an obsession, an end in itself, removed from the initial and ostensible business goals. These twin metaphors govern much explicit and implicit organizational thinking and decision-making that lead to one or many downsizings.

One gains an understanding of the motivation for (repeated) downsizing if one pursues the metaphors. What does the fear, the dread, of being fat represent (Wilson et al. 1983)? Why do its adherents believe in it, even when the organization is thriving? Intolerable fantasies, feelings and wishes over greed, insatiability, ferocious oral aggression, relentless anxiety over separateness and identity, and the courtship of death as a solution to the conviction of fatness are at once a part of the "disease" and of the "organizational disease." Corporate anorexia is organizational sacrifice through the ritual sacrifice (riddance) of large numbers of its members. Yet the solution perpetuates the problem. The attempt to rid oneself of death only brings one nearer to it. Or, in the alternative metaphor, cutting to the bone is also a form of suicide.

A further key to understanding the cultural plausibility and "choice" of the cutting and anorexia nervosa metaphors is the *delusional* self-image of the (corporate, organizational) body as always fat, too fat, and ugly, no matter how much cutting and dieting one does. It cannot be emphasized too strongly or too often that these draconian organizational strategies and measures were designed and implemented during economically flourishing times.

A culturally clinical formula comes into play: "We are fat" and "We are dying" is the diagnosis; "Sacrifice" is the treatment. If *we* feel we are obese and dying, *infected* with death (as introject), then, under the pull of regression and the catastrophic dread of annihilation (Devereux 1955), *we* initiate the sacrifice of *them* as a sacred ritual of purification in order to restore *us* to life, to enable *us* to be reborn as a group, by expelling and *killing* death. Through sacrifice, *we* bring order (life) out of the chaos (death), purity out of impurity (and its danger), strength out of weakness – a familiar formula for nationalist and religious revolutions. Sacrifice is the designated means toward this end. To draw on one metaphor, the identification, segregation, and elimination of metaphoric Jews from the workplace is the symbolic action by which organizations expect to be magically renewed, cleansed, and born again by the casting out of death (that is, symbolically putting one's own death into another, and then eliminating them, as in scape-goating).

The 1980s' era of "Reaganomics," with its social policies of deregulation and elimination of programs, set the stage for intense corporate competitivism, mergers, takeovers, and collapses. The "managed social change" that followed in the 1990s built on the same restoration-by-sacrifice imagery and policies. The end of the Cold War deprived the US of the "evil empire" as a "focus of evil." Intense free-floating anxiety, targetless aggression, and domestic "wars" arose in the wake of the absence of a reliable, permanent enemy. Symbolic war, death, and sacrifice came home.

NOTES FROM THE FIELD

What holds at the macro-level occurs at the local, micro-levels as well. The local, everyday experience of work-life both enacts and mirrors what takes place at meetings of corporate shareholders and executives. They are, in fact, both facets of the identical cultural process. What downsizing and other forms of "managed social change" feel like are conveyed in countless settings. The ethnographer must, above all, be prepared to recognize what is in front of his or her eyes. Four vignettes illustrate this perspective of the individual *experiencing* downsizing and related forms of managed social change.

Vignette 1: The threat at a Christmas party
The example that follows illustrates the nationwide (and increasingly global) psychological terrorizing of managers and workforce into capitulation and dependency upon decision-makers. The process affects blue collar and white collar workers alike Consider the following scenario.

At one Great Plains hospital's mid-1990s Christmas party, the invited speaker, a physician–administrator, admonished his largely healthcare professional audience to accept managed care as the inexorable wave of the future. He told the group to make up their minds that it was simply a matter of altering their thinking to conform to the changes. To make his point, he showed a cartoon depicting a steamroller smashing down one doctor in the asphalt, while another wisely sidestepped his destruction. The caption read: "You can become part of the solution or part of the pavement." Uncharacteristic of prairie decorum, several physicians got up in the middle of the talk and walked out in disgust.

A week later, a physician colleague who had been in the audience wrote to me: "Does this [cartoon, attitude] not instill a sense of helplessness? A sort of ultimatum? This doesn't smack of fascism, does it?" What he inquires in the negative, he affirms in the act of asking. It is as if what is not supposed to be happening is in fact happening. It is a matter of trusting – and mistrusting – one's senses.

Vignette 2: Believe it or not
What downsizing is supposed to produce, and what it in fact does produce, often diverge widely. The following example illustrates this divergence. A mid-level manager at a large telecommunications corporation described her experience of the aftermath of a buyout by another corporation, followed by several waves of downsizing and restructuring of the remaining employees. Although her experience is not quantitatively typical, it is nonetheless characteristic. She speaks with eloquence and precision (quoted with permission).

> It is so difficult to reconcile the upbeat messages we get from senior management about "improving the bottom line" with our own very personal and daily experiences of what that actually means to us employees as human beings. The thing that strikes me in all of this is that we end up stripped of our autonomy and of our dignity, while at the same time we are asked to "rise to the occasion" for the good of the company.

Furthermore, it is difficult to know how to negotiate relationships with co-workers in this [ever-shifting] context. It is difficult to establish trust and friendship, which are important factors in effective teamwork, when we all know that our neighbor might be gone tomorrow.

Later that day, she said to me:

This has been quite a journey for me. Four days after I returned from my month on vacation last fall, the very project for which I had been kept on because I was "essential" was cancelled. Besides that, all my staff [subordinates] were gone ... (80 of the group were laid off). It has been a fairly depressing state of affairs, actually.

Since November [it was now April] I have "made up" work to keep occupied, some of which has been interesting, and most of which has been dull beyond belief. A major problem has been that since no one knows what pieces of the business will survive, no one can take on long-term plans. So we are all just doing the best we can with an eye to the very short term.

In this quotation, an articulate corporate manager interweaves (and condenses, as in a dream) the experience of work, of self, of time, of relationships between supervisors and co-workers, of abruptly redefined reality, of loss, of sham, and of feeling depressed. She describes a sense of futurelessness and the inner experience and outer shape of adaptation to the dehumanization that pervades the redefinition of work.

Vignette 3: Symbolic Jews and Nazis

The vignette to follow illustrates the invocation of Holocaust imagery and metaphors to make emotional sense of organizational downsizing. At one large urban health sciences center that consisted of a confederation of a dozen specialty hospitals, it was widely rumored in late 1994 that some 400 people would soon be fired from the hospital system, and 400 additional unfilled hospital staff positions (clinical and administrative) would be eliminated. One entire hospital building was to be closed, and position transfers to other hospitals would not be permitted. The campus learned of this decision through the local newspaper in mid-January 1995. I was invited by upper management to work with the department of human relations, the personnel department, and nursing administration of the hospital system to assist a task force prepare the campus for this process and to help them deal with the extended aftermath.

During an initial two-hour planning committee meeting in late January 1995, I made field notes while I served as consultant. Among my notes appear a number of stark phrases spoken by staff members:

I'm planning a funeral for somebody who's going to die but doesn't know they're going to die ... As a manager I feel it's like World War II. The Nazis have come in and tell us "Point out all the Jewish people" so we can get rid of them. Then tell us "Bring the Gypsies, then the Poles ..." That's what it feels like ... We're asked to plan a funeral and we don't know who's going to be attending ... This is my home (the hospitals; spoken with tears in her eyes)! They are my family! ... Nursing is nurturing and difficult to let people go. So how does a nurse tell another nurse she's fired? I'm a manager. How do I work with a shorter staff (and still be nurturing)? If I survive this time around, how do I know I'll be here the next cutback? . . . I have vast concerns that I will not be employed here long, and I'm one of the people in charge of the program for the people who are being fired now.

Vignette 4: The finger in the waterbowl

For my final vignette, I offer what might seem to be a tiny, discountable incident – but one that turns out to take us to the heart of downsizing and its wake. In 1999, following a presentation I had made about downsizing and reengineering, I spoke with a secretary who had worked for many years for a multinational petrochemical firm that had undergone several waves of downsizing. First thanking me for validating her own experience during my lecture, she said that she wanted to offer an example of what I had been talking about. A new mid-level manager had arrived and was eager to make his mark on the organization. At a meeting of his supervisees, he admonished them: "We have a lot of work to get done here. Don't think for a minute that you're essential to this corporation. Everyone here is dispensable. There are a hundred people out there hungry for your job. And if you leave, your absence will be as noticed like a finger taken out of a bowl of water. They won't even know that you'd been here."

She and I both shuddered. We briefly mused on its effect for worker morale: inducing, perhaps, identification with the aggressor, and feverish productivity, accompanied by chronic terror, indifference, and deep rage at such humiliation. We also wondered about the new manager's own sense of expendability, and about the kind of childhood that might have set the stage for such drivenness. Does the conviction of inner worthlessness cultivate worthlessness – and hopelessness – in others? Here, a third managerial philosophy – terror – supplements the traditional distinction between "carrot" and "stick." What, in the workplace, does the threat of homicide look and sound like?

As an organizational ethnographer, I attempt to describe, evoke, portray, and interpret the cultural world of workplace organizations. The image of murder – even if it is "only" symbolic – is not hyperbole. Our language requires some way to do justice to the degradation of, and the assault on, human dignity, one that is never merely symbolic. Our cultural category of "violence in the workplace" does injustice to the scope and range of workplace destructiveness when we turn a blind eye and deaf ear to everything that *precedes* and often *provokes* the use of guns, knives, and bombs against people and property. To say that no one is murdered until someone is physically killed helps set the stage for physical violence at work – and is itself an act of brutality. An assault on the human spirit is an attack on a person's existence. Only our mind–body split gives us the comforting illusion that it is not.

CONCLUSIONS: DOWNSIZING AND THE PSYCHOLOGICAL ANTHROPOLOGY OF COLLECTIVE HUMAN BRUTALITY

In this chapter, I have described, evoked, and offered interpretations of downsizing. I have explored some of its psychodynamic motivations and consequences. I have discussed the many paradoxes and ironies of the modernizing strategy of downsizing, especially the self-destructiveness – as well as the destructiveness – in the guise of survival and revival. I have suggested that downsizing, as a corporate and wider metaphor, exemplifies "culture against man" (Henry 1963) and "sick societies" (Edgerton 1992). I have suggested that attention to symbols, metaphors, and their unconscious dynamics often takes us to the core of the experience and meanings in a society, and not merely the periphery. Downsizing turns out not to be pure business, but brutality in the guise and idiom of business. In its deliberate destruction of relationship and meaning (if I may be permitted to reify downsizing for rhetorical purposes), its most uniform "product" is demoralization. The image of modernity that downsizing reveals is not the one it advertises. The face of death is the bottom line everywhere.

I have attempted both to portray an intensive ethnographic study and to trace out some of its ethnological implications – especially for a psychologically informed anthropology. In particular, specifically, a constellation of attitudes and strategies emerges from single and repeated downsizings, reengineerings, restructurings, outsourcings, deskillings, and the like. A subterranean language of catastrophism attempts to wrest meaning, feeling, and psychic reality out of an official world enshrouded in the language of euphemism. These in turn can be variously construed as preadaptive, adaptive, and maladaptive in new employment contexts – not to mention family, religious, neighborhood, and community settings as well. The betrayal of trust and loyalty, the abrupt severing of the psychological/social contract, the utter discounting of human relatedness, the chronic condition of disposability, leads to self-protective measures, often unconscious, among workers and managers alike, among those fired and among the survivors.

Among these self-protections are defensive narcissism, refusal to commit one's vulnerable self to any organization, privatism, withdrawal into narrow "self" interest, dropping out and entrepreneurialism, competitivism, and so on. These work-related feelings, fantasies, attitudes, and styles follow people into new organizations and to new roles in their old organizations. Viewed from the long-term interest of the workplace organization, such preadaptations are maladaptive. A terrorized workforce that gives its skills but not its "heart" ultimately withholds skills as well. Skills and their associated tasks are profoundly interpersonal – even group – enterprises, and are never entirely a matter of technological prowess.

The new organizational culture(s) are heir to the unconscious wishes and defenses, attitudes, values, hopes, expectations, and disappointments that derive from (mal-, pre-) adaptation to "managed social change." Just as expressive culture permeated and shaped instrumental culture in the design and implementation of downsizing and its social engineering relatives, likewise does it pervade and give form to the surviving organization and to those who took other large organizational jobs, became entrepreneurs, or simply dropped out of sight.

A terrible cultural irony and paradox emerges. Downsizing and the reduction of ultimate value to "shareholder value" work in tandem with the degradation of work, workplace, and the "work ethic" itself. Shareholders become the only legitimate "stakeholders" and reference group. The hope for meaning and security through paid employment is eroded if not dashed, and becomes supplemented, if not supplanted, by investment in mutual funds and the stock market as the place in which one invests one's hope for "real" earnings, and "real" security in retirement. Death anxiety becomes focused on the workings of the stock market. "Work" is increasingly felt to be incapable of earning a worker (and the worker's family) a livelihood – or a future. Unwittingly, workers also participate in the degradation of work and in the short-termist shareholder mentality through participating in mutual funds and in pension funds rooted in mutual funds (Sievers 2001). Moreover, instead of the stock market being a place for slow, gradual growth and long-term income, it becomes the place where short-term relief of death anxiety prevails (Becker 1973; Sievers 2001). The result is a culture turned against itself (Henry 1963), the social destruction of meaning in the name of ultimate economic meaning, and the creation of death as a secular means of salvation from death.

In sum, if I have succeeded in showing downsizing to be a manifestation of late twentieth and early twenty-first century American culture, and a manifestation of how humans create and deal with persecutory and death anxiety, my aim will have been accomplished.

POSTSCRIPT

In the aftermath of the terrible events of September 11, 2001 – the destruction of the World Trade Center in New York City, and the attack on the Pentagon in Washington, DC – the temptation for Americans is to direct attention entirely to "what *they* (evil people) did and might still do to *us.*" It is tempting to divert or displace attention from "what *we* (Americans) do and still might do to *ourselves.*" Josef Stalin and his supporters "successfully" did the same kind of thing through what Soviets came to call the Great Patriotic War against Hitler. Remembering and forgetting are always linked.

What Americans do with the fact of downsizing and modernism will be as important as what Americans do with international terrorism. Part of our measure and stature will be the acknowledgment – or lack – of what, in the name of short-term profit and stock value, we have done to our own for a decade and a half. We often say that the enemy "has no value for human life." As I have said in this chapter, one lesson of downsizing is that the same observation, sadly, applies at least in part to us as Americans.

REFERENCES

Adler, William M., 2000 *Mollie's Job: A Story of Life and Work on the Global Assembly Line.* New York: Scribner.

Allcorn, Seth, with H. S. Baum, M. A. Diamond, and Howard F. Stein, 1996 *The Human Cost of a Management Failure: Organizational Downsizing at General Hospital.* Westport, CT: Quorum Books.

Becker, Ernest, 1973 *The Denial of Death.* New York: Free Press.

Byrne, J., 1994 The Pain of Downsizing. *Business Week* 3370 (1): 60–68.

Cameron, K., 1994 Strategies for Successful Organizational Downsizing. *Human Resource Management* 33 (2): 189–211.

Caudron, S., 2001 Stakeholders Revolt. *Business Finance* (January): 57–60.

Ciulla, Joanne B., 2000 *The Working Life: The Promise and Betrayal of Modern Work*. New York: Times Books.

Devereux, George, 1955 Charismatic Leadership and Crisis. *Psychoanalysis and the Social Sciences* 4: 145–157.

Edgerton, Robert B., 1992 *Sick Societies: Challenging the Myth of Primitive Harmony*. New York: Free Press.

Faludi, Susan, 1999 *Stiffed: The Betrayal of the American Man*. New York: William Morrow.

Gertz, Dwight, 1996 Growth, Not Downsizing, Leads to Greatness. *USA Today* February 7: 11A.

Gertz, Dwight, and Baptista, Joao P. A., 1995 *Grow to Be Great: Breaking the Downsizing Cycle*. New York: Free Press.

Grimsley, K. D., 1995 The Downside of Downsizing: What's Good for the Bottom Line Isn't Necessarily Good for Business. *Washington Post National Edition* November 13–19: A16–17.

Hammer, Michael, 1990 Reengineering Work: Don't Automate, Obliterate. *Harvard Business Review* 68: 104–113.

Hammer, Michael, and James Champy, 1993 *Reengineering the Corporation: A Manifesto for Business Revolution*. New York: Harper Business.

Henry, Jules, 1963 *Culture Against Man*. New York: Random House.

Hilsenrath, J. E., 2001 Corporate Dieting Is Far From Over. *Wall Street Journal* July 9: A1.

Hughes, J. L., 2000 Avoidance of Emotional Pain During Downsizing in a Public Agency. *Consulting Psychology Journal: Practice and Research* 52 (4): 256–268.

Kauffman, K., 2001 Could I Be Next?: Seeing Others Get Dismissed Creates Feelings of Anger, Relief, and Fear for Co-workers Who Stay. *Dallas Morning News* November 6: 1C, 2C.

Klemperer, Victor, 1999 *I Will Bear Witness: 1942–1945, A Diary of the Nazi Years*. Martin Chalmers, trans. New York: Modern Library/Random House.

La Barre, W., 1954 *The Human Animal*. Chicago: University of Chicago Press.

— 1972 *The Ghost Dance: The Origins of Religion*. New York: Dell.

Levinson, Harry, 1962 *Men, Management, and Mental Health*. Cambridge, MA: Harvard University Press.

Lurie, J., 1998 Downsizing. Ph.D. dissertation, Princeton University. http://geocities.com/WallStreet/Exchange/4280.

Micklethwait, John, and Adrian Wooldridge, A., 2000 *A Future Perfect: The Essentials of Globalization*. New York: Crown Business.

Mishra, A., and K. Mishra, 1994 The Role of Mutual Trust in Effective Downsizing Strategies. *Human Resource Management* 33 (2): 261–279.

Osborne, David E., and Ted Goebler, 1993 [1992] *Reinventing Government: How the Entrepreneurial Spirit is Transforming the Public Sector*. New York: Plume.

Sievers, B., 2001 Your Money or Your Life: Psychotic Implications of the Pension Fund System: Towards a Socio-Analysis of the Financial Services Revolution. Paper presented at the International Society for the Psychoanalytic Study of Organizations, Paris, June 22–24.

Stein, Howard F., 1994 *Listening Deeply: An Approach to Understanding and Consulting in Organizational Culture*. Boulder, CO: Westview Press.

— 1997 Death Imagery and the Experience of Organizational Downsizing: Or, Is Your Name on Schindler's List? *Administration and Society* 29 (2): 222–247.

— 1998a *Euphemism, Spin, and the Crisis in Organizational Life*. Westport, CT: Quorum Books.

— 1998b Organizational Euphemism and the Cultural Mystification of Evil. *Administrative Theory and Praxis* 20 (3): 346–357.

— 2001 *Nothing Personal, Just Business: A Guided Journey into Organizational Darkness.* Westport, CT: Quorum Books.

Uchitelle, L., 1996 More Downsized Workers are Returning as Rentals. *New York Times* December 8: A1.

— 2001 As Job Cuts Spread, Tears Replace Anger. *New York Times* (email August 4, 2001): 1–8. http://email.nytimes.com/email/email.jsp?eta5.

Uchitelle L., and Kleinfield, N. R., 1996 On the Battlefields of Business, Millions of Casualties. *New York Times* March 3: A1: 26–29.

US Department of Health and Human Services, Public Health Service, Centers for Disease Control, National Institute for Occupational Health, 1995 Prevention of Stress and Health Consequences of Workplace Downsizing and Reorganization. Announcement Number 572. Atlanta, GA.

US Government, 1997 Serving the American Public: Best Practices in Downsizing – Benchmarking Study Report. National Performance Review, Al Gore. September. http://www.npr.gov/library/papers/benchmark/downsize.html.

Wallace, A. F. C., 1956 Revitalization Movements. *American Anthropologist* 58: 264–281.

Wilson, C. Philip, with Charles C. Hogan, and Ira L. Mintz, eds., 1983 *Fear of Being Fat: Treatment of Anorexia Nervosa and Bulimia.* New York: Jason Aronson.

CHAPTER 24

Political Violence

Christopher J. Colvin

POLITICAL VIOLENCE AND THE MEMORIAL IMPERATIVE

If it is true that ethnographers, despite their best-laid plans, always end up studying what those around them want to talk about, the terms of my project on political violence in South Africa were spelled out for me several months into fieldwork on a trip to a rural community outside of Cape Town. This community had been prominent in the anti-apartheid struggle and was subsequently the focus of a large number of historians, anthropologists, social workers, and journalists. I first visited this township as a volunteer for Khulumani, a victim support and advocacy group that wanted to recruit new members in the rural areas. I asked to be introduced only as a volunteer for Khulumani and for the Trauma Centre, a Cape Town NGO that provides trauma counseling to victims of violence.

Our first visit was with Nothemba Dludlu, a long-time activist and victim of apartheid-era political violence. She had told her story to the Truth and Reconciliation Commission (TRC), been interviewed by journalists, and participated in interviews and group meetings with a number of anthropologists and psychologists. Introductions were made, but before Khulumani members could explain their visit, Nothemba began a loud complaint in the local language about how angry she was at people who kept asking for her "story," taking her words and leaving her nothing and never, despite their predictable promises, sharing any of the fruits of their research. Assuming, incorrectly, that I didn't understand her, she mentioned me and said she had dealt with the Trauma Centre and foreign researchers before and telling her story had done her no good. All this transpired without any prior mention of my research topic or any intention to interview her.

Before I could explain that I had not come for her story, she turned to me, smiled, and asked in English if I had my pen and paper ready, as she was ready to tell her story. A bit shocked, I replied that her story was neither the reason for our visit nor the focus of my research. She seemed quite relieved and the meeting began. As we were preparing to leave an hour later, though, she pulled me aside and presented a tattered, manila envelope from which she produced pension and reparation applications, newspaper clippings about her TRC testimony, and letters from researchers, NGOs, and local politicians promising assistance. Adding her ID book (the "Book of Life") to the pile, she told me I was free to photocopy these materials if I returned them safely. Not having solicited them, I asked if she needed me to do something specific for her. She said she didn't know what I could do, but she didn't want me to forget her. She said if there was any help available "out there," I must remember her and "keep [her] story safe."

Nothemba's complicated relationship to the work of storytelling was not unusual. When I began research with Khulumani, I found myself confronted with anxious stories from many directions. A short recitation of their "story" (always in the singular) was standard when introduced to a victim. Some of my formal interviews consist of a simple warm-up question followed by two unbroken hours of autobiography. This apparent "need" to talk about suffering, though, was usually accompanied by a fear that storytelling would not make any long-term difference. In the middle of these frequent, unsolicited stories, group members paradoxically complained that telling their stories "does no good." They have told their stories to doctors, psychologists, journalists, researchers, priests, and government officials, but, they say, they are still poor, sick, and without hope for the future. That many members don't trust the practical efficacy of storytelling, however, has not prevented it from continuing as a kind of anxious pursuit. It remains a part of their post-apartheid way of life, a form of individual self-awareness and self-presentation as well as, increasingly, a mode of social and political practice.

What came across most strongly during these first few months of fieldwork was the memorial imperative, or the demand for memory, that victims of political violence labor under in South Africa. This demand comes from many quarters. Journalists and researchers urge victims to "break their silence" and "give voice" to other victims by bringing their story forward. Psychologists remind them that only through talking through the trauma can they be released from its pathological effects. Priests tell victims that confronting and forgiving perpetrators is the only way to avoid being consumed by hatred. The TRC asked victims (and perpetrators) to contribute to nation-building by testifying (often on a public stage in front of TV cameras) to the violations they experienced. Victims heard from all directions that only through this kind of storytelling would they be healed and future violence prevented.

By encouraging these painful performances of storytelling and confession and by choreographing emotional encounters between victims and perpetrators, the TRC sought to link the "inner" worlds of victims and perpetrators (their memories, motivations, ideologies, and perceptions) to the "outer" worlds of social, political, cultural, and economic processes. In its own way, it developed a local psychological anthropology of political violence. The TRC, however, was first and foremost a vehicle of nation-building and political legitimation for the new government. Its linking of the inner and the outer realities of political violence is conditioned by these concerns. In this chapter, I explore what a psychologically informed anthropology might have to tell us about the causes and effects of political violence, not only in South Africa, but also in a globalizing world more broadly.

WHAT IS "POLITICAL VIOLENCE"?

Before we can ask what a psychological anthropology of political violence has been or should be in the future, we must confront what exactly we mean by "political violence." I have described Khulumani members as victims of political violence. The support group was originally a product of the Trauma Centre's "Torture Project" and called itself the Ex-political Prisoners Group. Torture victims and political prisoners can usually make unproblematic claims to be victims of political violence. Khulumani members, however, have never been exclusively, or even predominantly, victims of imprisonment or torture. Most of the members or their families have been victimized directly by apartheid security forces, but the violations range from police harassment, loss of property, and arson, to illegal detention, torture, and assassination.

At a recent commemoration of International Torture Day, Khulumani members critiqued the conventional definitions of torture, arguing that living in poverty, losing educational opportunities, and being denied their dignity through discrimination was just as much "torture" as what had happened in the police cells. "Torture" became a metaphor for all kinds of political oppression, not because members see no difference between prejudice and electric shocks, but because they recognize that both kinds of violations are linked and sustained through the same forms of power. Their attempt to widen the scope of what is labeled "torture" or "political violence" also speaks to the currency the "political" has over the merely "criminal" or "domestic."

Defining the "political" in political violence is also an issue of considerable concern for perpetrators. Nancy Scheper-Hughes's chapter (this volume) describes two prominent attacks (against the St. James church and against Amy Biehl) carried out in 1993 by anti-apartheid liberation groups against largely white, "civilian" South Africans and Americans. Negotiations between the government and these liberation groups had been underway for some time and the attacks were considered by some to be particularly unjustified. In their amnesty applications, the perpetrators argued that their violence was "political," since it was committed with the broad purpose of ensuring the final collapse of apartheid. Lawyers protesting the amnesty applications argued that this violence was better described as "mob," "criminal," or "terrorist" violence, that it was performed with no reasonable political purpose (given the developing negotiations), and that the civilian nature of the targets disqualified the attacks as political.

In these cases, the concept of political violence came under pressure in several ways. Can political violence be determined by the perpetrator's intention and/or by the victim's interpretation? Can political violence only be recognized against targets that are expressly "political?" Can violence be *both* political and criminal? Political and religious? Political and domestic? Does the rage and violence born of political oppression but expressed without an explicit political framework still qualify as political?

Part of the problem lies with the many modifiers available for violence. Some attempt to be purely descriptive (individual, collective, organized, group). Others focus on the agents (state, gang, terrorist, domestic), the "causes" (political, religious, criminal), or the instruments and effects of violence (spiritual, symbolic, emotional, physical, genocidal). Still others emphasize broader analytic perspectives (structural, everyday, epistemic). All of these terms overlap with many of the others, none of them can be defined unproblematically, and all carry (and often hide) their ideological content.

It is not clear, either, what the word "political" itself means. Recent critical theories of power have greatly (and constructively) expanded the scope of this term. Politics, these days, is not just about the formal organization of power and decision-making, but something that pervades our language, our relationships, even our bodies. If the personal and the everyday are increasingly seen as political, in what ways could domestic and everyday forms of violence also be understood as political violence?

The problems are not simply conceptual, though. Most definitions of political violence incorporate an idea of the motivation of perpetrators. The first difficulty is epistemological and concerns the old question of how "we" (as analysts, victims, bystanders, or even perpetrators) can come to confidently "know" the motivations behind violence. The second difficulty is ethical. Political violence is often seen as more justified (even if in a limited sense) than criminal violence. As Scheper-Hughes (1997) has pointed out elsewhere, many South Africans wanted to label Amy Biehl's killing an act of criminal violence, arguing that since things were "getting better," there was no justification for political violence. Calling her killing "criminal" denied the perpetrators' contradictory position that the political situation had indeed not changed.

None of this is to say that there are no discernible qualities that might usefully distinguish political violence from other kinds of violence. We might ask, following Hinton's analysis of genocide (this volume), if political violence could be interpreted as a characteristically modern form of violence. Political violence almost always involves the state (as either target, perpetrator, or antagonist) and mobilizes discourses of freedom, equality, ethnic identity, progress, and/or rationality. It is often carried out through modern, institutional forms of organization, frequently utilizes high technology, and is conditioned by the demands and responsiveness of the global media.

As Robben and Suárez-Orozco (2000: 6) have noted of organized violence more generally, political violence is usually "guided by an intellectual framework," something that is not characteristic of criminal, everyday, or structural forms of violence. They have also pointed out that organized forms of violence target "social bonds and cultural practices" explicitly and publicly (2000: 10). Though other forms of violence certainly have their corrosive effects on social and cultural (not to mention psychological and economic) circumstances, political violence often openly announces these as its targets.

Political violence, like related forms of organized state violence, also often seeks to justify and prove itself rational by separating the instrumental and affective dimensions of violence. Robben and Suárez-Orozco have described how fighter pilots are encouraged to show pride in accomplishing the technical feats of destruction but have been censored when they display the thrill of the kill (2000: 32). Those in the armed struggle against apartheid also often defended their acts of violence as rational and instrumental. It has only been in private that I have heard the rush and satisfaction of military success described by some of these men and women.

It is impossible to imagine popular images of political violence (freedom struggles, terrorism, ethnic violence, rioting, civil wars, rebellions) without the modern state, its monopoly claim on violence, and its languages of rationality, nationalism, self-determination, democracy, and equality. Though the state defines itself through its rational commitments to its citizens, many anthropologists have shown that the ties between state and citizen are anything but coolly logical or technical (Taussig 1987; Mahmood 1996). The state relies on its subjects' feelings and fantasies as much as it does on the notions of the social contract and bureaucratic reason to produce (and reproduce) its presence and power (Aretxaga 2001).

Though modernity may mold the forms, justifications, and instruments of political violence, its own discourses of freedom and reason are not enough to explain the energies that continue to animate political violence throughout the world. Psychological anthropology, with its concern for relating "inner" experiences, perceptions, and motivations to "external" social and political processes, is in a good position to examine how political violence grows out of the feelings and fantasies of individuals in ways that are shaped by both local and global processes.

Theory Responds to a Century of Violence

The instability of the analytic concept of political violence makes it difficult to identify a coherent thread of theory or research under the heading of the "psychological anthropology of political violence." Compounding this is the general neglect of forms of mass violence in all branches of anthropology (LeVine 2000). Though violence and its polysemous cousin "suffering" have recently been the subject of considerable anthropological interest (Antze and Lambek 1996; Daniel 1996; Nordstrom and Martin 1992), a survey of recent syllabuses posted by the Society for Psychological Anthropology reveals a continued lack of attention to the problems of large-scale violence. Nonetheless, there has been useful work in anthropology and related fields during the last century that integrates individual and social levels in the analysis of political violence.

Though the early relationship between anthropology and psychoanalysis was more concerned with issues of mental illness, oedipal complexes, and childrearing than with the origins and consequences of group violence (Robben and Suárez-Orozco 2000: 3), psychoanalysis has posed a number of useful questions about violence. First and foremost, it asked about the psychic origin of the aggressive impulse and was generally divided into "innate" and "reactive" theories of violence. Innate theories held that aggression is an essential and universal psychological feature, whereas reactive theories suggested that aggression is a response to external stimuli such as extreme frustration, mourning, or threats to identity (Fromm 1941; Klein and Riviere 1964).

These theories generally located the primary causes and effects of aggression in psychic conflict. Aggression, whether innate or reactive, was understood to be *triggered* by social and material conflict, with culture simply providing the particular local modes of its expression. The development of the "culture and personality" school of psychological anthropology was partly a response to the universalizing, internalizing tendencies of early psychoanalysis. It was also part of a war effort to understand the enemies Allied forces faced in World War II. Margaret Mead and Ruth Benedict both produced "national character studies" that were part of a larger attempt to understand the cultural patterns that lay behind the military behavior of Axis nations. Benedict's study of Japanese culture and personality, *The Chrysanthemum and the Sword* (1946), is probably the best known of these studies of "culture at a distance."

Culture and personality approaches asked how cultural values, social structures, and local practices like childrearing, etc., combine to generate an archetypal personality within a given culture that may be prone to specific kinds of (violent) behavior. In South Africa, for example, they might have asked if there is something about Afrikaner culture that produced particularly authoritarian or aggressive personality traits. Unlike psychoanalysis, which would have looked for the answer in the (universal) psychic conflicts of individuals, culture and personality looked to local "culture" for the answer.

Though culture and personality played relativist to psychoanalysis' universalism, it suffered from similar reductive tendencies. Whereas culture was sidelined in the psychic drives, conflicts, and repressions of psychoanalysis, culture and personality marginalized sociocultural conflict and individual agency, meaning, and motivation. There is little attention in either to the possibility of mutually constituting relationships between individual and group processes and little incorporation of structural or historical perspectives. Mead and Benedict were also concerned about the manipulation of their relativist theories to support racist ideologies. Their mental maps of culture and psyche became, in other hands, biological maps of race and psyche.

It would be a psychoanalyst, albeit a very unusual one, who would further develop these questions of race, political violence, and the psychological. Frantz Fanon, a French-trained Algerian psychiatrist writing during the emerging, violent, anti-colonial wars of the 1950s and 1960s, examined the effect of colonial oppression on the production and experience of political violence (Fanon 1967). He investigated the effect of colonialism's brutality on the psychic lives of its subjects and how this in turn produced its own violent and, ultimately, liberating reaction. Though Fanon drew extensively from psychoanalysis and structuralism, his early linking of psychodynamics, macropolitical processes, and political violence was largely ignored in mainstream anthropology. His work was important in South Africa, however, as the developing anti-apartheid (and especially Black Consciousness) groups used his theories to explain the terrorizing psychological effects of apartheid and justify the armed resistance.

In anthropology, by contrast, the cognitive and linguistic turns were in full swing. Structuralism, for example, asserted the cognitive and linguistic roots of culture, interpreting the diversity of the world's cultures as a set of permutations of universal contrasts and mythic elements and procedures. If it had been tempted to analyze political violence (which it rarely if ever was), it might have considered how binary oppositional thinking or mythic operators could condition the perpetration and experience of violence. In South Africa there were a number of psychoanalytic accounts of political violence that mobilized structuralist theory to ask why the racial contrasts of black and white wield such power in this country (Bulhan 1993). More recently, others have asked if the demise of apartheid has created a crisis in the "adversarial [oppositional] imagination" and a subsequent anxious search for new enemies, new contrasts, and new oppositions (Nixon 1998; E. Harper pers. comm.).

Symbolic anthropology tried to counter the psychological reductionism of structuralism in the same way culture and personality did – by looking to culture. Symbolic anthropological approaches were less concerned with rendering cultural differences in terms of personality or other psychological concepts. It looked to symbols, language, and discourse and sought to characterize cultures and explain their behavior according to that culture's own unique configuration of values, ideas, symbols, beliefs, etc. Given its emphasis on mental representations as the key explanatory variable, it typically understood political violence as either the product of a particular symbolic universe or as the result of conflict between two or more contradictory worldviews. In his famous explanation of the killing of Captain Cook in 1779 by the inhabitants of Hawaii, for example, Marshall Sahlins (1995) argues that the local Hawaiians interpreted the arrival of Captain Cook and his fleet in terms of their own mythico-historical belief system and considered Cook to be the deity Lono. Cook's subsequent strange behavior (returning to Hawaii after a storm, contrary to mythic predictions) confounded their expectations and his killing was the product of this cosmological conflict.

In a similar vein, we might try to understand the political violence of apartheid as a product of conflicting symbols, beliefs, and ideologies. Ideologies of race compete with ideologies of ethnicity. Liberal humanism and *ubuntu* ("African" humanism) compete with beliefs in racial separation and superiority. Intervening in political conflict would then involve translating between, coordinating, or changing outright the conflicting symbolic universes of antagonists. Indeed, the TRC was based on the idea that crafting a new, shared set of symbols, values, and beliefs would reconcile former enemies.

Structuralism, like psychoanalysis, suffers from a universalizing impulse, and symbolic anthropology, like its cousin culture and personality, tends to reduce historical change, social stratification, and cultural contradictions to overly coherent and stable portraits of symbolic order. Both also seem to have made cognition do too much of the work of motivation. Though the conventional division between perception, cognition, and motivation is overly simplistic, any theory that adequately incorporates psychological insights cannot allow cognitive processes to replace the functions and effects of other psychic phenomena (whether these are labeled drives, emotions, desires, or something else).

Other theories in fashion around this time, though, pay little or no attention to the psychological world of individuals at all. Functionalism could only understand political violence as something that either contributes to or detracts from the stability of the social system. Materialism might interpret political violence as the consequence of competition over scarce resources and explain violent ideologies as the simple product of this conflict over resources. Neither attaches much importance to the inner lives of individuals.

This by-now familiar summary and critique of anthropology in the 1950s and 1960s, however, should not blind us to the usefulness of these approaches. Certainly, it would be foolish to interpret the extreme nature of apartheid violence without giving due weight to the intractable power of binary (and especially racial) oppositions. Efforts to reconcile after violence without adequate attention to the conflicting symbols, values, and discourses of former enemies would be dangerously incomplete. Building on Taussig's (1987) insights into the productive capacity of terror, one could argue that political violence in South Africa has been at times conducive to the functioning of the apartheid order and at other times a reflection of the decay of that order. Finally, considering South African history without reference to the vexed (and still vexing) issues of competition over land, gold, diamond, and labor resources would ignore one of the main vehicles of historical change in Southern Africa.

If anthropology did not fully engage with the problems of political violence during this period, there is one strand of social and psychological theory that did consider group and individual violence more closely. These approaches to group violence concentrate on the idea of "unfinished mourning" wherein a group that has experienced a defeat, tragedy, or humiliation has been prevented (or prevented itself) from properly "mourning" this loss. Vamik Volkan (1997) has probably taken this theory the furthest in his notion of the "chosen trauma" experienced by a group. The group, unable to "digest" or mourn this trauma properly, unconsciously passes down this humiliation and hatred to successive generations. This "chosen trauma" forms the basis of group identity and all imaginations of and relationships with the Other are mediated by this group dynamic of unfinished mourning. Other studies have examined similar psychosocial dynamics in US–Soviet relations (Stein 1989). Some have wondered if the violence of apartheid reflects the unfinished nature of Afrikaners' relationship to their defeat at the beginning of the century in the Anglo-Boer War (Mamdani, quoted in Krog 1998: 113).

If the anti-colonial movements of the 1950s and 1960s weren't enough to move the problem of political violence firmly into the mainstream of anthropology, the war in Vietnam proved more than capable of doing so. Though the number of civilian casualties of political conflict had been steadily rising since World War I, it was Vietnam that first brought this reality into American and European homes through TV, radio, and photography. A range of new critical theories came to the fore in anthropology and one of their goals was to account for the prevalence of political violence throughout the world. These new theories highlighted power, inequality, and oppressive forms of economic organization as perpetuating violence in the postcolonial world (Scott 1985). Poststructural theorists broadened the notion of violence to include the "epistemic violences" of colonialism, while historically minded anthropologists emphasized the experiences and perspectives of those who suffered these multiple violences of colonialism (Asad 1973; Spivak 1988). Though many of these theoretical innovations were just as (if not more) universalizing than their predecessors, they made it possible to consider the problems of political violence in a much more explicit and productive manner.

These "critical" theories strove to uncover the often hidden relationships between power and violence in various forms of sociopolitical organization. Whether it is Marx's class conflict, Foucault's liberal power, Fanon's colonial oppression, or the semiotic violence of poststructuralism, all theorize violence, in one way or another, as a consequence of the constitution and practice of power. Violence here is not (only) produced through breakdowns of psychic or social structures, failures of communication and translation, or the scarcity of natural resources. Rather, these theorists emphasized the ways that the political violence in blossom around the world was part of the warp and woof of modernity (see Hinton's chapter in this volume for a similar discussion of the modernity of genocide).

Analyses of political violence in South Africa at the time refocused attention on the class struggle at the heart of apartheid and investigated the bureaucratic languages and procedures of disciplinary power that kept apartheid in place. This work argued apartheid was less a physically violent form of power (though this was one of its faces) and more an administrative, disciplinary, legal, linguistic, and individually practiced form of modern power (Butchart 1998).

As Hinton points out, however, these theories are often overly generalizing. They leave little room for local culture and practice or for individual meaning, motivation, and action. They have been challenged over time from a number of angles. Postmodernism has questioned their universal claims and has emphasized the local, the individual, and the creative aspects of power (Lyotard 1984). Practice and performance theory have highlighted how the seemingly monolithic structures and processes described by Marx and Foucault require constant local reproduction. They argue that state power is just as much the product of the daily activity, imagination, and emotion of citizens as it is the product of laws, guns, and butter (Beeman 1986; Bourdieu 1991). Identity theory, struggling to account for the violent wave of ethnic nationalism after the Cold War, incorporated individual and group identity and emotions of vengeance, love, and loyalty into analyses of nationalist and racist forms of violence (Hintjens 2001). Finally, feminism has criticized the lack of attention to gender in all of these theories (di Leonardo 1991; Mohanty 1994). The recent emergence of female Palestinian suicide bombers seems surprising, but is not without precedent. The chairperson of Khulumani was a well educated, white, middle-class nurse and social worker before she became a commander in the armed wing of the African National Congress. These cases highlight the need to examine the intersections of violence and gender more critically.

Some of the more recent approaches in psychological anthropology have looked less to psychoanalysis in broadening their accounts of motivation. Roy D'Andrade (1992) has integrated motivation into theories of cognitive schema and demonstrated how cognitive frameworks can directly inspire action. Catherine Lutz has made a similar move by incorporating the performative dimension into symbolic accounts of emotion, arguing that emotions are not simply felt or conceived in culturally specific ways, but need to be performed and "externalized" within (often changing) sociopolitical contexts to come fully into existence and realize their power (Lutz and White 1986). Stephen Leavitt (1995) has integrated individuals' sociopolitical strategies into analyses of their narrative accounts of suffering. His work reflects the growing importance of "pragmatics" in psychological anthropology (O'Nell 2000). These anthropologists have also studied more closely the ways emotions, for example, are used, shaped, and channeled by sociopolitical ideologies and institutions. The TRC, the Trauma Centre, and Khulumani are each model examples of how the performance of emotion is channeled and put to various social, political, legal, and medical ends. These institutions, and the performances they engender, in turn shape the range and variety of emotional expression of those caught up in their structures.

Anthropologists, working within the sub-disciplines of psychological anthropology and critical medical anthropology, have reached beyond critical theories, arguing firstly that critical theories often posit an "empty" and ungendered subject at the mercy of regimes of truth and, secondly, that they can not account for the excesses of violence that occur in the modern world (Aretxaga 2001). Violence certainly has its productive dimension, but it never fully determines the subject and the social. Likewise, surpluses of violence beyond what is instrumentally "necessary" have always occurred and need to be explained. Apartheid failed in the end to create the docile subjects imagined by Foucault and its violence was often in excess of its instrumental requirements.

Allan Young's (1995) work on post-traumatic stress disorder is another prominent example of critical perspectives in the psychological anthropology of political violence. His research examined how the psychiatric discourse of trauma that developed out of the experiences of Vietnam War veterans came to operate as a moral and political language of self, suffering, and recovery. He argued that veterans, faced with a contradiction between the emotional consequences of their war experiences and the sociopolitical context back home, looked to the medical language of trauma to explain and express both their psychological distress and their political frustration. Likewise, in South Africa, the theory and treatment of trauma are tied to the broader political processes of reconciliation. The medical discourse of trauma provides victims with a new language of complaint and the government with a new language of control.

Joshua Breslau (2000) has described how the practice of trauma debriefing teaches political lessons to survivors of violence and disasters about the importance of self-reliance, the value of expert psychiatric knowledge, and the need to "move on" and begin recovery. In societies trying to pull themselves out of years of political violence, the use of psychiatric knowledge and practice to treat the effects of political violence might seem welcome. This discourse of trauma can be empowering to people whose suffering has been hidden. The scientific legitimacy that the label "trauma" brings can be helpful and validating. On the other hand, victims of political violence often face difficulty being treated as fully active cultural, moral, and political agents when their feelings and actions are too quickly captured, reduced, and made safe by the psychiatric discourse of trauma.

STORYTELLING BETWEEN THE LOCAL AND THE GLOBAL

Breslau's concern with both the ambivalent power of the trauma discourse as well as its globalizing dimension has resonances in the storytelling work of victims of apartheid violence described earlier. To understand what storytelling means for victims of political violence and why it has become such an industry in South Africa, we must examine how global forces are realigning social, cultural, political, and economic values and relationships. Previous theoretical tools are still very relevant, but they were not designed to account for the myriad ways the flow of people, money, images, and ideas has upset conventional notions of the individual, the social, the cultural, and the political.

One of the earliest salvos in the debate about globalization and political violence was delivered by Baudrillard (1995) in his claim that the Gulf War "did not take place" in any real sense of the word for most viewers of this highly televised, and thus, for some, "simulated," war. The role of the media in shaping the meanings and experiences of political violence should not be underestimated. The recent violence between Israelis and Palestinians, for example, is significantly influenced by TV coverage, especially through its circulation of images of dead or dying children.

The storytelling work of Khulumani members is created and/or conditioned by globalization in several ways. First, storytelling is an important component of

TRC-style conflict resolution interventions promoted throughout the world for "post-conflict" societies. An international network of conflict resolution experts, peace-keepers, and diplomats promotes and implements these interventions, which have become the most legitimate forms of post-conflict reconciliation. Truth commissions are most often organized around the idea of "truth-telling" and demand that both victims and perpetrators undergo a process of revealing and confessing.

Khulumani's storytelling is also part of the globalization of psychiatric knowledge and the discourse of trauma. Khulumani and the Trauma Centre are very much the products of global flows of funding for, experts in, ideas about, and images of the trauma of political violence. A visiting psychologist at the Trauma Centre described a saying from the Balkans that after the "black angels" of international military and diplomatic intervention, come the "white angels" of mental health. These angels bring a particular style of psychiatric reasoning in understanding and "treating" victims of violence. The Trauma Centre applies this discourse in its work and receives international funding, researchers, and expertise in the process. Khulumani's recognition by the Trauma Centre and access to its resources are related to the degree members directly engage with this transnational language and practice of trauma therapy.

One of the global forces that has most directly affected storytelling has been the expanding web of researchers and journalists writing about political violence. These individuals produce knowledge and circulate images and narratives of violence throughout the world. Khulumani members' anxious relationship to storytelling is partly a response to (and reaction against) this type of investigation. The production and circulation of these narratives also entails the creation of new kinds of social relationships between researcher and "subject." Some Khulumani members have extensive postal contact with journalists and researchers in the US, Canada, Europe, Asia, and Latin America. One member boasted that he had "friends" in every academic field in most European countries and encouraged me to test him by picking a field or country at random.

The situation, however, isn't only of outside forces impinging on Khulumani. Through the global flow of activists, money, and information, Khulumani has become part of a network of victim advocates. This linking is not yet stable or sustained, but it is important within the group. Members increasingly relate their experiences and struggles to those of other groups and individuals. Whether they are hosting members of victim support groups from Northern Ireland or sending representatives to Germany to fight for reparations, they are increasingly caught up in the globalizing flow of activist energy, images, ideas, and individuals. This marks a significantly new form of political agency, organization, and meaning-making. The speed and power of communication technologies are making local political action (no matter how "grassroots") always already part of the global.

Khulumani members face another global political dynamic in that they are acting in relation to a state that is managing an "emerging" market and is promoting a neoliberal political subjectivity. Accordingly, Khulumani is finding that much of the rhetoric and strategy of the anti-apartheid struggle (often derived from Cold War discourses of capitalism versus communism) are increasingly less relevant and effective. Their fight for reparations, for example, has needed to be tailored to a political environment more concerned with human (individual) rights, legal rationalism, foreign direct investment, and economic growth.

Finally, the growing number of refugees and immigrants from other parts of Africa also forms part of the shifting political geography of suffering Khulumani confronts. Many in Khulumani perceive these "outsiders" as undeservedly taking both the material resources and the symbolic capital associated with those who have suffered. The wide "transnational flows of traumatized individuals" export the consequences of political violence throughout the world (Suárez-Orozco 2000). In the process, these individuals create new social and political tensions, introduce added economic pressures, and bring the personal effects of political violence into the heart of those societies often thought to be the most distant from political violence.

EXPANDING VIOLENCE

Globalization means that action, motivation, culture, society, politics, agency, perception, symbols, resources, repression, and economy – the conceptual building blocks of our many theories – must all be (re)conceived in terms of the ways information technology, transnational commerce, and displaced populations bring the local and the global into anxious contact. It has already forced revision of many core concepts of anthropological theory. This final section will consider how the analytic concept of violence might be fruitfully expanded in response to a changing global context.

The recent development of notions of "everyday violence" and "social suffering" has expanded the horizons of theories of violence of all kinds. Inevitably, these attempts to consider violence more holistically, in a way that integrates social, cultural, economic, political, and individual levels of explanation, make it more difficult to work with narrow concepts like "political" violence. Nonetheless, this move towards expanding and complicating our concepts of violence is crucial. The notion of everyday violence has highlighted the "implicit, legitimate, organized, and routinized violence of particular social–political state formations" among the poorest of the world's peoples (Scheper-Hughes 1997: 471). Kleinman has suggested that this notion be expanded to embrace the *violences* of everyday life by identifying violence among different social classes and by emphasizing how routinized violence is a feature of all societies and social positions (Das et al. 2000: 238).

The recent series of three edited volumes on "social suffering" has attempted to reintroduce (without reducing) the subject into the question of violence (Kleinman et al. 1997; Das et al. 2000, 2001). These ethnographic accounts of suffering attempt to integrate structural and critical perspectives, as well as theories of self and subjectivity, with the increasing influence of the global on the local. They argue for a more integrated approach to the problems of violence and suffering, calling into question "established distinctions between war and civil violence on the one hand, and times of peace and times of violence on the other" (Das et al. 2000: 16). They do this by examining the interrelationships between self, suffering, and community at individual, local, state, and global levels of practice and experience.

Following on from this useful work, I want to suggest that we focus more attention on the everydayness of what is labeled "political violence." I do not want to suggest that everyday violence and political violence are substantially the same. The theory of everyday violence emphasizes the hidden and/or accepted aspects of the violence that pervades particular social and moral orders. When social theorists or journalists speak of *political* violence, they are almost always referring to public attacks on these social and moral orders. One of the biggest mistakes, however, when considering violence that is not "everyday" is to exceptionalize it, to make it seem an aberration, an unusual or exceptional "event" or as the unintended consequence of "non-violent" local or global processes. Violence that is an explicit and "illegitimate" attack on a sociopolitical arrangement is thus different from "everyday violence," but the causes and effects of this public violence are very much "everyday" in that they are grounded in a local, day-to-day, practiced social world. We should highlight the connections between "political violence" and the violence of everyday life rather than compartmentalize different "types" and theories of violence.

Expanding and integrating our various definitions of violence provides the opportunity for development in other areas. Broadening our adult-centered theories of violence enables the discussion of young victims of political violence, but also, crucially, young perpetrators of political violence. Africa, in particular, has suffered from the scourge of child soldiers. Like the female suicide bombers, children who kill are very difficult to make sense of in terms of conventional theories of violence.

Adult perpetrators, however, are not necessarily any easier to understand. Images of the "perpetrator," whether in popular media discourses or in our own analyses, too often entail the "typing" of perpetrators along the lines of one's favorite explanatory framework. A strong tendency exists to reduce the perpetration of violence to ultimate types and causes and to classify perpetrators in relation to these causes (religious zealot, Marxist guerilla, tribal warrior, criminal gang member). Paraphrasing Geoffrey White, we should not ask "what type of person would do this," or even "what are the indigenous labels applied to perpetrators of this type," but "what kinds of cultural and political dynamics had to come into play to make this type of person necessary or thinkable?" (White 1992).

Violence, its causes, its commission, and its consequences, are the product of multiple, interacting fields of force that include biological, linguistic, cognitive, structural, embodied, economic, political, social, and cultural elements. Khulumani members' experiences with political violence and their subsequent attempts to make some sense out of their suffering reveal the limitations of popular approaches to political violence which reduce the experience of violence and recovery and restrict the expressive and political strategies they have available. As long as a concept of violence is reified, medicalized, and managed within institutions of expert knowledge and practice, our understanding of violence will always run the risk of being reduced.

The misrecognition of political violence as unusual, unexpected, or pathological is dangerous and serves to make invisible the very ordinariness, socialness, and interconnectedness of all kinds of violence. This is not to say that individual approaches (whether psychoanalysis, neuropsychology, or cognitive or developmental psychology) have nothing to say about violence. Rather, their answers are insufficient without the integration of other modes of explanation (social, economic, and political structures, contingent, historical, or "critical events," cultural representations and symbols, the embodied, practiced, and developmental aspects of individuals, linguistics, the environment, etc.). "Trauma" is not a mysterious kind of unrepresentable experience that leaves meaning destroyed in its wake. It is a disturbingly familiar experience for much of the world's population, one that challenges without destroying meaning, often forcing people to creatively reshape their perspectives. Nor is the perpetration of violence ever "unthinkable" or "senseless." This is not to excuse it or to propose a "natural history of violence" as a kind of inevitable feature of all human life. It is simply to say that violence is never without a multitude of interacting reasons and that these reasons are always rooted in particular lived experiences and social and cultural worlds. This is a useful perspective to keep in mind in a globalizing world that is creating new, unfamiliar geographies and ecologies of violence, while exposing the violent traces and fault lines of older forms of domination and (dis)order.

REFERENCES

Antze, Paul, and Michael Lambek, eds., 1996 *Tense Past: Cultural Essays in Trauma and Memory.* New York: Routledge.

Aretxaga, Begona, 2001 The Sexual Games of the Body Politic: Fantasy and State Violence in Northern Ireland. *Culture, Medicine, and Psychiatry* 25 (1): 1–27.

Asad, Talal, 1973 *Anthropology and the Colonial Encounter.* Atlantic Highlands, NJ: Humanities Press.

Baudrillard, Jean, 1995 *The Gulf War Did Not Take Place.* Bloomington: Indiana University Press.

Beeman, William O., 1986 *Language, Status, and Power in Iran.* Bloomington: Indiana University Press.

Benedict, Ruth, 1946 *The Chrysanthemum and the Sword: Patterns of Japanese Culture.* Boston, MA: Houghton-Mifflin.

Bourdieu, Pierre, 1991 *Language and Symbolic Power.* Cambridge, MA: Harvard University Press.

Bresleau, Joshua, 2000 Globalizing Disaster Trauma: Psychiatry, Science, and Culture after the Kobe Earthquake. *Ethos* 28 (2): 174–197.

Bulhan, Hussein, 1993 Imperialism in Studies of the Psyche: A Critique of African Psychological Research. In *Psychology and Oppression: Critiques and Proposals.* L. Nicholas, ed. Pp. 1–34. Johannesburg: Skotaville.

Butchart, Alexander, 1998 *The Anatomy of Power: European Constructions of the African Body.* Pretoria: UNISA Press.

D'Andrade, Roy, 1992 Schemas and Motivation. In *Human Motives and Cultural Models.* Roy D'Andrade and Claudia Strauss, eds. Pp. 23–44. Cambridge: Cambridge University Press.

Daniel, E. Valentine, 1996 *Charred Lullabies: Chapters in an Anthropography of Violence.* Princeton, NJ: Princeton University Press.

Das, Veena, with Arthur Kleinman, Margaret Lock, Michelle Ramphele, and Pamela Reynolds, eds., 2001 *Remaking a World: Violence, Social Suffering, and Recovery.* Berkeley: University of California Press.

Das, Veena, with Arthur Kleinman, Michelle Ramphele, and Pamela Reynolds, eds., 2000 *Violence and Subjectivity.* Berkeley: University of California Press.

di Leonardo, Micaela, ed., 1991 *Gender at the Crossroads of Knowledge: Feminist Anthropology in the Postmodern Era.* Berkeley: University of California Press.

Fanon, Frantz, 1967 [1952] *Black Skins, White Masks.* New York: Grove Press.

Fromm, Eric, 1941 *Escape from Freedom.* New York: Farrar and Rinehart.

Hintjens, H., 2001 When Identity Becomes a Knife. *Ethnicities* 1 (1): 25–55.

Klein, Melanie, and Joan Riviere, 1964 *Love, Hate, and Reparation.* New York: Norton.

Kleinman, Arthur, with Veena Das, and Margaret Lock, eds., 1997 *Social Suffering.* Berkeley: University of California Press.

Krog, Antjie, 1998 *Country of My Skull.* Johannesburg: Random House.

Leavitt, S., 1995 Suppressed Meanings in Narratives of Suffering. *Anthropology and Humanism* 20 (2): 133–152.

LeVine, Robert, 2000 Epilogue. In *Cultures Under Siege: Collective Violence and Trauma.* Antonius Robben and Marcelo Suárez-Orozco, eds. Pp. 272–275. Cambridge: Cambridge University Press.

Lutz, Catherine, and Geoffrey M. White, 1986 The Anthropology of Emotions. *Annual Review of Anthropology* 15: 405–436.

Lyotard, Jean, 1984 *The Postmodern Condition.* Minneapolis: University of Minnesota Press.

Mahmood, Cynthia, 1996 *Fighting for Faith and Nation: Dialogues with Sikh Militants.* Philadelphia: University of Pennsylvania Press.

Mohanty, Chandra, 1994 Under Western Eyes: Feminist Scholarship and Colonial Discourse. In *Colonial Discourse and Postcolonial Theory: A Reader.* Patrick Williams and Laura Chrisman, eds. Pp. 196–220. New York: Columbia University Press.

Nixon, R., 1998 Aftermaths. *Transitions* 72.

Nordstrom, Carolyn, and JoAnn Martin, eds., 1992 *The Paths to Domination, Resistance, and Terror.* Berkeley: University of California Press.

O'Nell, Theresa, 2000 "Coming Home" among Northern Plains Vietnam Veterans: Psychological Transformations in Pragmatic Perspective. *Ethos* 27 (4): 441–465.

Robben, Antonius, and Marcelo Suárez-Orozco, 2000 Interdisciplinary Perspectives on Violence and Trauma. In *Cultures Under Siege: Collective Violence and Trauma.* Antonius Robben and Marcelo Suárez-Orozco, eds. Pp. 1–41. Cambridge: Cambridge University Press.

Sahlins, Marshall, 1995 *Islands of History.* Chicago: University of Chicago Press.

Scheper-Hughes, Nancy, 1997 Specificities: Peace-Time Crimes. *Social Identities* 3 (3): 471–497.

Scott, James C., 1985 *Weapons of the Weak: Everyday Forms of Peasant Resistance.* New Haven, CT: Yale University Press.

Spivak, Gayatri, 1988 Can the Subaltern Speak? In *Marxism and the Interpretation of Culture.* C. Nelson and Lawrence Grossberg, eds. Pp. 271–313. Urbana: University of Illinois Press.

Stein, Howard F., 1989 The Indispensable Enemy and American–Soviet Relations. *Ethos* 17 (4): 480–503.

Suárez-Orozco, Marcelo, 2000 Identities Under Siege: Immigration Stress and Social Mirroring Among the Children of Immigrants. In *Cultures Under Siege: Collective Violence and Trauma.* Antonius Robben and Marcelo Suárez-Orozco, eds. Pp. 194–227. Cambridge: Cambridge University Press.

Taussig, Michael, 1987 *Shamanism, Colonialism, and the Wild Man: A Study in Terror and Healing.* Chicago: University of Chicago Press.

Volkan, Vamik, 1997 *Bloodlines: From Ethnic Pride to Ethnic Terrorism.* New York: Farrar, Straus, and Giroux.

White, Geoffrey, 1992 Ethnopsychology. In *New Directions in Psychological Anthropology.* Ted Schwartz, Geoffrey White, and Catherine Lutz, eds. Pp. 21–46. Cambridge: Cambridge University Press.

Young, Alan, 1995 *The Harmony of Illusions: Inventing Post-Traumatic Stress Disorder.* Princeton, NJ: Princeton University Press.

SUGGESTED FURTHER READING

Borneman, John, 1997 *Settling Accounts: Violence, Justice, and Accountability in Post-Socialist Europe.* Princeton, NJ: Princeton University Press.

Feldman, Allen, 1991 *Formations of Violence: The Narrative of the Body and Political Terror in Northern Ireland.* Chicago: University of Chicago Press.

Good, Mary-Jo, and Byron Good, 1988 Ritual, the State, and the Transformation of Emotional Discourse in Iranian Society. *Culture, Medicine, and Psychiatry* 12: 43–63.

Nordstrom, Carolyn, and Anthony Robben, eds., 1995 *Fieldwork Under Fire: Contemporary Studies of Violence and Survival.* Berkeley: University of California Press.

Rejali, Darius, 1994 *Torture and Modernity: Self, Society, and State in Modern Iran.* Boulder, CO: Westview Press.

Tambiah, Stanley, 1986 *Sri Lanka: Ethnic Fratricide and the Dismantling of Democracy.* Chicago: University of Chicago Press.

25 The Politics of Remorse

Nancy Scheper-Hughes

There is therefore a poetics of blood. It is a poetics of tragedy and pain, for blood is never happy.

Gaston Bachelard

For the purposes of this volume, I am taking on the politically and morally ambiguous task of telling the story of political violence and recovery in South Africa through the experiences, narratives, and points of view of a small number of white South Africans, drawn from across the social class and political spectrum. It should be taken as a psychological anthropologically informed reflection on suffering, remorse, and reconciliation among a small number of white South Africans who were historically and existentially "thrown" into a political drama where they were cast as either active collaborators, passive beneficiaries, or revolutionary "race traitors" vis-à-vis the old apartheid state. Today, they are trying to make sense of their country's violent history and of their role in that history, to undo past wrongs, and to mend spoiled identities, and to resume interrupted lives. Obviously, due to the history of apartheid, "black," "colored," and "white" South Africans inhabit vastly different spatial, social, psychological, and moral worlds. As a consequence, they have experienced the transition to democracy and the formal processes of social healing through the independent Truth and Reconciliation Commission (TRC) with very different emotions, meanings, and agendas.

STILL WAITING

I went to the Cape of Good Hope in 1993 in a fit of post-partum depression following the publication of *Death without Weeping* (1992), which concluded more than twenty years of intermittent research on hunger and death among impoverished sugar plantation workers and their families in northeast Brazil. I went to lose my grieving anthropological self in a new "field site." This time I wanted to be somewhere when something good and beautiful and hopeful was about to happen. The first demo-cratic elections in South Africa were surely a beacon in an otherwise increasingly dark and chaotic world. Temporarily assuming a senior position at the University of Cape Town, I hoped that during my tenure I could document some aspect of the radical changes that were occurring and to be as it were an ethnographer of the (democratic) transition.

I thought of revisiting the small, "picturesque" Western Cape fruit and wine pro-ducing village of Wyndal (actually Franschhoek), which was the ethnographic setting for Vincent Crapanzano's brilliant and controversial book *Waiting: The Whites of South Africa* (1985). In his deceptively simple, open-ended conversations with some forty white villagers, Crapanzano produced a devastating portrait of South African whites. As a skillful pathologist of the human condition, he deftly sliced away at the diseased tissues of the social body, exposing the soft underbelly of race apartheid in the dark, airless, occasionally soulless narratives of a tiny sample of affluent whites during the early 1980s. This was at a time when the anti-apartheid struggle was gathering its greatest momentum, strength, and moral conviction amid heightened police and state repression.

According to Crapanzano, the response of the white villagers of Wyndal/Franschhoek to the political storm clouds gathering over their heads was to retreat all the deeper into a kind of paranoid, isolated domesticity. Others sought redemp-tion through participation in a charismatic, Evangelical Christian Renewal move-ment that was sweeping white rural villages and towns in the Western Cape, even reaching cosmopolitan Cape Town. He portrayed the whites of Wyndal as comfort-able, self-absorbed racists trapped in a passive mode, a "dead time" of suspended animation, "waiting" in fear and dread for the inevitable future to somehow miracu-lously pass over them and leave them alone. Since the protagonists lacked any critical self-awareness, what could have been tragic was simply pathetic, little more than a story of self-indulgence, cowardice, and bad faith. For the whites of Wyndal, "waiting" implied a bunker or a citadel mentality, a stubborn waiting-it-out. Meanwhile, black South Africans were also waiting, of course, but their waiting was illuminated by hope and poised for action. Perhaps waiting was a more accurate metaphor to describe the Black and Coloured experience in South Africa. Theirs was a watchful waiting, endowed with the certainty that time, history, and God were on their side.

Waiting was heatedly contested by white South African anthropologists and by other South African intellectuals who saw in the portraits a caricature of the region's far more complex white spectrum. The book was unfair and "biased," local critics charged, a blow beneath the belt. Above all, they felt that it was self-serving, pro-jecting an image of white South African "extreme": racists to ease the guilt of American whites. According to his South African critics, Crapanzano had betrayed his hosts at the university and in the gracious farm homes of Wyndal/Franschhoek where he had been "fed and kindly received." "Don't Crapanzano us!" white South Africans often warned me during the early months of my own fieldwork in Franschhoek. Had they known more about my own complex relations with those whom I have studied, they might have just as easily said: "Don't Scheper-Hughes us!" Indeed, the problems of subject–object relations in the field do not go away when anthropologists study people who are very much like themselves.

Still, I wondered what could be learned by revisiting the Wyndal/Franschhoek farm community more than a decade after Crapanzano's original fieldwork and just as the nation was on the cusp of its democratic revolution. By the time I arrived in Cape Town in July 1993, official apartheid was over. Radical movements and oppositional political parties were unbanned, and Nelson Mandela had been recently released from his last prison, where he had been held, under a complicated form of house arrest, in a suburban stucco ranch house on the grounds of Victor Verster prison, just a few miles from the village of Wyndal/Franschhoek.

Although I did go to Franschhoek for four successive periods of intensive fieldwork between 1993 and 1999 (focusing on all three populations, – white, black, and colored – living there), political events in South Africa interrupted my original plans on conducting a post-apartheid ethnography of that community. The approaching elections that would sweep Mr. Mandela and the ANC into power in a glorious display of popular victory in April 1994 were preceded by a final, desperate attempt of the National Party government's internal security forces to disrupt the transition. Meanwhile, the Pan Africanist Congress (PAC) and its military wing, the Azanian Peoples Liberation Army (APLA), and other radical factions on the extreme right and left of South African politics, were dissatisfied with the terms of the negotiated settlement being hammered out in Kempton Park and they had stepped up the militant struggle.

The assassination in spring 1993 of Chris Hani, hero and intellectual mentor to the politicized youth of the townships, spurred riots and other acts of township resistance. The leaders of PASO, the Pan African Student Association, launched "Operation Vala" (close down) and then "Operation Barcelona," a campaign of anti-government burnings and stonings by township youths. The latter campaign took its name from the Olympic games in Barcelona and its symbolism from the "torches" carried by lead athletes and runners. But here the torches would be used to clear out all suspected government agents and to prevent "white" motorists from entering the townships, which were declared as "no go" zones to all outsiders during this period. The violence peaked in government orchestrated "Third Force" attacks of bombs, bullets, stones, and sticks designed to block the coming elections. And so 1993 was the most violent year in more than a decade of undeclared civil war in South Africa; in all 3,794 people died in political violence that year.

BLOOD IN THE GARDEN

The day after we arrived in Cape Town on July 25, 1993, three young men dressed in overalls and head scarves burst into the evening service of the St. James Evangelical Christian Church in the white suburb of Kenilworth, bordering the University of Cape Town (UCT) community where my family and I had just settled into a faculty–student dorm on Main Road. The young men – one was a boy of 17 years – opened several rounds of ammunition and tossed nail-spiked hand grenades into the congregation of more than 400 worshippers while they were singing the opening hymn, "Come to the Garden." In seconds – for that is just how long such an attack takes – eleven people were dead and more than fifty others were seriously wounded and maimed. Some would lose their arms and legs. Even more might have died in the "St. James Church Massacre," as it came to be called, if a young white parishioner had not pulled out a gun and fired back at the assailants, who turned and fled from the church. They escaped in a getaway car that had been stolen earlier that day in Khayalitsha, a sprawling black township containing nearly a million refugees from former apartheid designated homelands.

Less than a month later, during the anti-government strike called "Operation Barcelona," American Fulbright student Amy Biehl was dragged from her car as it approached the entrance to Guguletu township in Cape Town and she was stoned and stabbed to death by a few PAC ring-leaders as they were egged on by a cheering crowd of "toyi-toying" high school students. The driver of the car was identified as a "white," "a settler" (a non-African), and therefore as an enemy of the people of Guguletu. The murder of Amy Biehl was a watershed in the final months of the anti-apartheid struggle; her death was invoked to explain, depending on the speaker's political views, why the elections *must* go forward or why the elections must *never* go forward.

Then, on New Year's Day 1994, a nondescript tavern in the student "bohemian" quarter of Observatory in Cape Town was attacked by PAC revolutionaries and four people were killed, two of them UCT students, one white and one brown. A third victim was an acquaintance of ours, the owner of a Portuguese seafood restaurant, Machados, where we often went to "*matar saudades*" (kill our homesickness) of Brazil. The fourth victim was a young, mixed race ("colored") woman, a grade school teacher. Two of our young adult children were down the street at another student hangout when the Heidelberg Pub Massacre took place. Indeed, everyone – black, white, and colored – was suspected of harboring some sort of violent sentiments during the final phase of the anti-apartheid struggle. The Heidelberg tavern massacre, though modest in its carnage, stayed with me the longest, along with the images of the frozen, startled faces of the four victims for I accompanied the state pathologist to the Salt River Mortuary in Cape Town for the autopsies and identifications (Scheper-Hughes 1994). Their random deaths over-determined my research on democracy and violence.

Of course, these much-publicized incidents of "black-on-white" violence were exceptions to the general rule of official and sanctioned "white-on-black" violence. Some of the attacks on whites were carried out by paid or intimidated black collaborators. So overwhelming were the daily "stats" on township deaths that year that both black and white newspapers recorded them only as "body counts." "Another 40 bodies found on the East Rand"; "Dozen bodies removed from Guguletu in weekend casualties"; "Nine bodies found in two shacks gutted by fires in Khayalitsha," and so on. Violent political deaths were the legacy of black South Africans.

Still, the democratic elections prevailed and a celebratory mood bathed all South Africans momentarily in a luxurious sea of good will. A sense of humor and vitality appeared and the intensely private, claustrophobic worlds of long hibernating white Capetonians opened up to a newly fashioned public space. Indeed, there was much to celebrate in this land of terrible beauty. But the legacy of the violence remains. The scars are deep and etched into the gutted and destroyed landscapes left by the apartheid state, in the empty spaces left by those who died in the political violence, and in the wounded bodies of those who survived the violence and chaos, but just barely. The following entry from my field notes in February 1994 should suffice:

You cannot avoid them for they are present at every political event. Father Michael Lapsley with the startling metal hooks where his hands should be . . . There he is mischievously lighting a young woman's cigarette (a magician's trick!). Or, over there, skillfully holding the stem of a wine glass raised in a defiant toast . . . And over there, with his back carelessly turned to the door, stands Albie Sachs with his handsomely lined face and his resonant soothing voice, the agnostics' theologian, dressed in his priestly robes, his bright and bold dashiki . . . with its freely waving sleeve, Albie's sweet banner of liberty . . . Of thee, I sing, Albie.

My new research questions were ready-made. During the phase of national recuperation and moral – as well as economic and social – reconstruction, how were new social self-identities being fashioned in a crucible in which all racial identities had been "spoiled" by the perverse history of apartheid's insane bureaucratic system of classification? What narratives of self, personhood, identity, suffering, and recovery were being told? How did people emerging from a past characterized by competing and contradictory histories begin to build a new sense of nationhood and belonging based on a negotiated version of that same history?

First, in isolating the experiences of "white" South Africans from those of the "black" and "colored" majority of South Africans, I realize that I run the risk of highlighting the experiences and the "suffering" (if that word is even permissible in this fraught social and political context) of one social group, those generally identified as either the perpetrators or the passive beneficiaries of race apartheid, at the expense of other social groups – black and colored South Africans – generally seen as the victims of that same genocidal system.

Second, the exercise continues to circulate and thereby reinvent the scandalous categories of apartheid, which so many South Africans of good will and conscience – across the color spectrum – are trying to destabilize. Third, in mixing and combining the narratives of "white" South Africans who suffered violence and death as the anonymous and incidental "soft targets" of late stage PAC terrorist attacks with the narratives of radicalized whites who suffered strategic attacks on their lives as the specific targets and known political enemies of the apartheid government, I risk perpetuating a basic "category fallacy." For the only things that these "white" South Africans had in common, up to the point of their wounding, was the color of their skin and arbitrary birth in a nation obsessed with "race" and ancestry. To be "white" in South Africa was, and is, an unbearably "heavy" and fraught condition. Indeed, I had originally subtitled this chapter: 'The Unbearable Whiteness of Being'.

The old apartheid state constructed and enforced, often with violence, a set of often highly arbitrary racial categories and group identities (Boonzaier and Sharp 1989). Over time, it revised and "updated" the official system of classification and the official discourses on race, ethnicity, community, tribe, nation, citizenship, progress and development, violence and public security, which the white police state used to define and control South African political and social realities *and* individual and group subjectivities.

One of the deepest injuries left by the old apartheid state is the legacy of spoiled identities. Erving Goffman (1963) identified the social dynamics of "spoiled identity" resulting from the stigmas of physical difference, ethnicity, and tribe, to which I would add the stigmas of history and place. Indeed, in these terms, South Africa today is a land of "spoiled identities." But if the history of apartheid spoiled all cultural and racial identities, some are more spoiled than others: Zulu identity, because of its identification with the right-wing Inkatha Freedom Party and that party's collusions with the apartheid government; "colored" identity because it was a fictive category, an "invention" of apartheid (Scheper-Hughes 2004); black "youth," once the courageous "Young Lions" of the anti-apartheid struggle, re-labeled a "lost generation" once the official struggle was over (Scheper-Hughes 1995). The "stigma" of whiteness will be discussed below.

Of course, a strong counter-culture of political resistance sought to free South Africans from the legacy of racist thinking by constructing alternative identities in terms of political commitment to the anti-apartheid struggle and to the process of building a democratic and pluralistic state. Most South Africans are keenly aware of how socially invented categories of "race," "color," "tribe," "ethnicity," and "culture" were defined and used to implement apartheid. Today, South Africans from all communities have their hands raised and fingers flexed, ready to supply the necessary "air quotes" that question and destabilize the race terms and the social fictions that the old state wanted South Africans to accept as plain facts and as part of the natural, given world.

South Africa today is something of a terminological land mine. One must be painfully conscious of the contested nature of almost every social category – from Xhosa to gay to Zionist Christian to Cape colored to Boer. One refers politely, for example, to "so-called" coloreds or even more awkwardly to "those people who were formerly classified as colored." Sometimes one offers a double qualifier: simultaneously making the sign for quotation and referring to the "so-called," as in referring to an "Indian [supply air quotes] so-called colored person." The indeterminacy of racial labels signifies both language and identity in motion, and represents a fierce reaction against the ways that ethnicity and race had been frozen in essentialist discourse. Still, some South African social identities are understood as "more real" (or less questionable) than others. Rarely does one hear reference to "so-called whites," for example. It remains an unmarked and uncontested category.

"WHITE" IN SOUTH AFRICA

> We are betrayed by what is false within.
>
> George Meredith

> And that, my friend, is why I ran away. I ran away because I was scared of the coming changes, and scared of the consequences of not changing. I ran because I wouldn't carry a gun for apartheid, and because I wouldn't carry a gun against it. I ran away because I hated Afrikaners [white Afrikaans-speakers] and loved blacks. I ran away because I was an Afrikaner and feared blacks. You could say, I suppose, that I ran away from the paradox.
>
> Rian Malan, *My Traitor's Heart*

There is, of course, no easy way to be "white" in South Africa, even in the "new" non-racial South Africa. In the old South Africa the horns of the dilemma were cast in terms of the following double-binding injunction: leave the country and you are a coward ("You should have stayed and fought it out with the rest"). Stay behind and you will be viewed as secretly complicit, enjoying white privilege and riding on the coattails of apartheid. Virtually all South African whites – English or Afrikaner speaking, Jewish, gay, or Marxist – found themselves suspect during the struggle years unless they could prove their political credentials – often physically and graphically on their very bodies (see Sachs 2000). What were you doing during the struggle years? Where were you? How did your life, your family, your home, your choices, your work, your profession, figure into the struggle?

Rian Milan, the author of the problematic and politically incorrect but powerful testimonial *My Traitor's Heart* (1990), traces his family roots through a genealogy of colonialism and apartheid going back to Jacques Malan, who had fled religious oppression in France to arrive as a "settler" to the Western Cape. Before fleeing into exile himself, the younger Milan struggled with his inherited history and imposed race identity. He posed the question raised by a hybrid "Boer reggae" song: "How do I live in this strange place?" Initially, he tried to escape his whiteness by becoming a communist, experimenting with drugs, taking a black lover, espousing violence, espousing non-violence, smoking daccha (dope), growing his hair long, cutting it short, spray painting American Black Power slogans on the walls of white monuments in the white suburbs of Johannesburg: "I'm black and I'm Proud." And then, in confusion, he simply ran away.

Milan returned for the transition to African rule, but still he was "caught." What does whiteness mean for those descendants of Afrikaner "settlers" and farmers who can neither leave the land (for they, unlike English-speaking South Africans, have no options) nor (in a moral sense) inherit it? Can the South African "Boer" identity, which once meant simply Dutch/Huguenot "farmer," be reclaimed and reconstituted today?

Michael Lapsley, a naturalized South African from New Zealand, and a chaplain to the ANC, reflected on his "whiteness" for the first time when he arrived as a young Anglican priest in South Africa and experienced his white skin as a mark of Cain, a stigma. He told me: "Whiteness became for me like leprosy, something that wouldn't wash off. Although I knew a lot about apartheid before I came, I never understood what it would mean, really, to be seen as an oppressor . . . So my decision to join the struggle for liberation was actually a struggle for the recovery of my own humanity." From my own experience as a white civil rights worker in Selma, Alabama (1966–1967) during the transition to Black Power, I knew exactly what he meant.

UNDOING

Undoing seems to be an appropriate metaphor in looking at the present context of national recovery in South Africa. The word is part of a semantic network that includes "getting over", with its Biblical images of safe passage, and "overcoming". But, just what needs to be undone or "gotten over" if South Africa and South Africans are to get safely to the other side? Is reconciliation possible without some kind of powerful, transcendental faith? Joe Slovo, the self-designated "believing unbeliever", offered one model. Surely, as many have argued, a first step in the politics of reconciliation and forgiveness is knowledge seeking, learning exactly what happened to whom, by whom, and why. What could the state level terrorists have been thinking?

"I sometimes wonder," said Father Lapsley, "who that man or woman was who typed my name on the envelope that was supposed to kill me. I wonder what did they tell their spouses or children that night at suppertime about what they did in the office that day? Either they are so dehumanized that they don't care or else they have learned to live comfortably with their guilt . . . I don't want vengeance, but I think that the names and faces of these people should be known."

The official vehicle to facilitate individual and collective "getting over" and liberating South Africa of the ghosts of its past was South Africa's Truth and Reconciliation Commission (TRC), described by Colvin (this volume). In hundreds of hearings around the country, more than 2,000 victims of apartheid-era brutality told their stories to the independent Human Rights Violations Committee. A smaller number of perpetrators of the violence have come forward to confess the details of their attacks on civilians in exchange for political amnesty.

Indeed, those seeking truth in South Africa today do not want the partial, indeterminate, shifting "truths" of the postmodernist, which resemble the dissembling, "complex" truths and realities promoted by the old apartheid state. Instead, they desire the single, sweet, "objective" truth of the moralist, and with it a restored sense of wholeness and a taste of justice. But, as Albie Sachs has noted, South Africans are willing to settle for an agreed upon, a "good enough" truth – a narrative that will at least place black and white South Africans, Afrikaners and English speakers, Xhosas and Zulus, ANC and PAC members, on the same map rather than in different countries across the road from one another.

There have been many critics (as well as hagiographers) of the TRC (see, for example, Boraine 2000; Hamber and Wilson 2002; Ignatieff 1997; James and Vande Vijver 2000; Jeffrey 1999; Nuttall and Coetzee 1998; and Ross 2003). Some worried about the focus on the "exceptional," the "extreme," and on the "gross" acts of human rights violation which ran the risk of obscuring, or worse, of normalizing the ordinary, daily, routine acts of apartheid's structural violence: the legal, medical, economic, bureaucratic, and commercial violations of human rights that alienated millions of South Africans from their property, their homes, their families, their labor, their citizenship, and even from their own bodies.

Others worried about the dangers of 'numbing' via over-exposure to media coverage of the TRC's routinized public rituals of confession, remorse and coerced forgiveness. I recall a chilling scene evoked by anthropologist Michael Taussig (personal communication) when several years ago, he was visiting a town in an unnamed South American country during a period of official truth and soul searching. He was directed to a local municipal office where those who had been tortured during the previous regime were filing documents. Taussig described the petty bureaucrats as seated along a bench behind a very long table. In front of each official stood a long line of ordinary, and some very poor and sandaled, people waiting their turn to testify to the suffering they had endured. They were asked to do so following the official form and set formula of questions. Each petitioner was given three or four minutes to answer the questions: When were you abducted? Where were you taken? Were you beaten? Tortured? On which parts of your body? What tools were used? What questions were you asked? How did you reply? The officers might have been tax collectors. And so the original torture was mimetically reproduced by a new structure of indifferent state interrogators.

MAKING SENSE OF SUFFERING

The first step in the politics of reconciliation and forgiveness is knowledge seeking, learning just what happened to whom and why. In recent years an anthropology of suffering (see Das et al. 2000; Kleinman, Das and Lock 1997; Das et al. 2001) has emerged as a new kind of theodicy, a cultural inquiry into the ways that people attempt to explain the presence of pain, affliction, and evil in the world. At times of crisis, moments of intense suffering, people every-where demand an answer to the existential question: "Why me, oh God? (Of all people?) Why now?" The quest for meaning may be poised to vindicate an indifferent God, to quell one's self-doubt, to restore one's faith in an orderly and righteous world. The one thing humans seem unable to accept is the idea of the world as deficient in meaning.

Accounting for one's own suffering is one thing. Making sense of the suffering of the other is quite another and fraught with ethical quandaries, according to Levinas (1988). This distinction becomes explicit following any collective tragedy – whether "natural" or "political" – when the "Why me?" question becomes the "Why *not* me? Why was *I* spared?" as survivors try to account for their exemption, their saving grace.

Although the St. James congregation is extremely faithful in its attendance, some regular worshippers did, of course, miss the Sunday service on that rainy evening in late July, 1993. A clerical worker had car trouble; a teacher was down with the flu; a university student grew impatient waiting in the rain for a friend to arrive, and she went home rather than disrupt the Sunday evening service after it had begun. Each one shared their thoughts with me about why God had chosen to spare them on that night, along with their doubts about whether it was a good or a bad thing to have been spared. "You see," said Nadja, "God was speaking very directly to us at that moment." And for those present during the 90 second attack that changed their lives and transformed their understanding of the world forever, the challenge remained to make sense of the checkerboard pattern that killed some, injured so many others, and left the others physically unscathed.

Dawie Ackerman, who lost his wife in the massacre, has played over and over in his mind the moment that he walked into the church a few minutes after his wife and rather than disrupt Marita and the woman with whom she was sitting and chatting in the front left-hand side pew, he quietly took his place several pews behind her. During a painful interview in February of 1998 he said:

> Now why didn't I take my seat next to my wife? Why didn't I interrupt the conversation and smiling, take her by the arm to sit beside me where she might have been safe? But I left her, instead, in the front line of the attack, surely one of the first to be killed . . . My nature is to act quickly, so that when the attack happened I would have thought that I would have been one of the first up there to try and stop it. But, obviously, I had no gun . . . and well, I just fell down and hid like everyone else . . . and those are the sorts of things that were always going through my mind at first. You would try to sleep and it would get to you . . . But I realize now, afterwards, that there was a reason why I did not die. I was protected through God's intervention. The two hand grenades that were thrown into the congregation just missed me. One exploded only 3 meters away and the other was about 6 meters from me. That is very close. People all around me

were hurt, hit by shrapnel; some were sprayed with rifle bullets, and stray bullets killed some people sitting just behind me. A man sitting on one side of me lost both his arms and his legs. I had to walk over several dead and wounded bodies to get to my wife. But neither the grenades nor the bullets caused me any damage. Not a bit of the shrapnel hit me. I was spared. Why? I believe I had been spared to take care of my three children . . . Also, I believe that in the grand scheme of things there was another reason. I had to ask why it was I, a leader Elder of the Church, who was spared? Later on, when I started unpacking all of this, I had to accept that God had both chosen our church [for the attack] and He had chosen the individuals who survived to give testimony that would bring honor to Him. And, since the first moment of the attack, that has been the desire of my heart, to do that. *That* is the grander mission.

Two weeks after the St. James attack I joined a few dozen church members at the large tea room above the auditorium following Sunday evening service. The massacre was still, of course, uppermost in everyone's mind. Their pastor, Bishop Reteif, had been leading them through a series of theological reflections on the meaning of suffering. But their own independent interpretations were, paradoxically, both more mystical and more embodied than the smart and intellectualized sermon "Where was God?" they had just heard their pastor deliver. Instead, they spoke among themselves with intensity of a "secret message" encoded in the attack. If only they knew what it was. "We know God was trying to tell us something," said Marlene Sidreic. "Only, the true meaning hasn't been revealed to us yet." Most agreed, citing the inscrutability of God's ways, but Cynthia had a more direct interpretation: "I believe God's message to us was that life is given, life is taken away. Live life fully, day to day. Be kind to those you love, cherish them now, for you never know if they will all be wiped out tomorrow."

Barely a week after the Heidelberg tavern massacre (see Scheper-Hughes 1994), I attended two post-trauma therapy and healing sessions for several survivors held at the Anglican church sponsored Center for Victims of Torture and Political Violence in Cape Town. All the survivors were, naturally, preoccupied with having so narrowly escaped death. "I was in Cape Town," said an older woman, "to celebrate my daughter's wedding. I almost celebrated her funeral instead." But despite the heavy media coverage and the informed political commentary surrounding what was immediately labeled a "senseless," "meaningless" attack on "innocent" soft targets during the late and extremely optimistic stages of political negotiations, all these survivors understood the attack as strategically and politically motivated. "This is South Africa," said a white, former soldier. "We knew something like this was going to happen sooner or later."

Another survivor, a young mixed race "colored" man, said: "I live in a township and I understand the rage that lies behind this attack, and the feelings some young people have that the negotiations aren't going right, that things are not going to change their lives for the better." A local hospital worker who lost a friend in the attack agreed. "Every day I see the wounds of the townships that come into the emergency room. And I think to myself, 'how long can things go on like this?'" While attributing a larger political meaning and purpose to the attack, all saw themselves as misplaced, misidentified, if you will, targets. "Why did they go for us?" "People of all colors come to this pub." And they doubted, even as they hung onto the hope that, as one participant put it, "Some good might come out of this in the end."

The ability to turn bad into good is a sign of resilience, necessary for healing, and is immeasurably aided by strong religious faith and/or equally strong political convictions. Father Michael Lapsley, who received a letter bomb in 1990 (posing as a religious epistle) from some still unknown officials employed by the old South African government, has been able to say that he is a victor and not a victim of the apartheid state that tried to kill him. Each day, just by living, he defeats evil and death. Like some of the St. James Church survivors (albeit survivors of a very different sort of violence), Father Lapsley believes he was never closer to God than in the almost transcendent moment of the evil blast that took away an eye and his hands: "I sensed the presence of the Holy Spirit accompanying me and sustaining me," he said to me in 1994. During a visit to Harlem's Canaan Baptist Church of Christ on 116th Street in Harlem less than three years after the bomb, he addressed the congregation:

> I stand before you as a sign of what apartheid has done, of the physical ruptures it has caused . . . But I also stand before you as a sign of the power of God to heal, the power of love, of gentleness, of compassion. The power of light is stronger than the power of darkness, and in the power of God we shall be victorious.

SACRED WOUNDS

The wounded body often becomes a template of individual and collective memory, both a map and a moral charter. In the St. James Church tea room, Mrs. K., one of the wounded, rolled back her turtle neck to reveal a large and inflamed wound covering her neck and shoulder where shrapnel was removed. "Do you know what this means?" she asked me. I shook my head dumbly. "This means I belong to Jesus. I am His. This wound is precious to me. It has removed all my fears. Nothing can ever hurt me again. Let them return. I am ready for them for His mark is upon me. He owns me and what is left of my life is in His hands." The woman's intensity frightens me. Suddenly, I want to change the subject, even though, presumably, this is my subject.

The quest to "make sense" of suffering and premature, chaotic death is as old as Job, and as fraught with moral ambiguity. This is as true for the anthropologist/ witness as for the companions of Job. It is so for whoever demands a reason, an explanation for suffering, usually one that is compatible with one's convictions, religious or political. Just as the companions of Job taunt him to elicit an explanation for his suffering ("You must have sinned against God"), the friends and relatives of those blameless people kidnapped and tortured during the Argentine "Dirty War" insisted: "You must have been into something." Similarly, at the memorial service at the University of the Western Cape the day after Amy Biehl was stoned, her grieving friends and colleagues whispered conspiratorially among themselves: "We don't want to blame her, but Amy of all people should have known better!" What was she doing driving her comrades home into Guguletu, a no-go zone, a war zone during those tense days?

But Job righteously and steadfastly refuses the temptation to self-blame, insisting that he was a just man. Albie Sachs, who lost an arm to the anti-apartheid struggle, insists he and his ANC comrades suffered and died "because we were good, not because we were bad." So, too, Amy Biehl refused the judgment of her attackers and she approached their raised arms (smiling, even, I was told) saying: "No, stop. You are mistaken. I am not a settler. I'm Amy, a comrade." Amy's naive and possibly even presumptuous claim coming from her large, white, smiling face may have enraged the angry young men even further. But, later, her words came back to haunt those who were ultimately convicted of her murder. At his TRC amnesty hearing, Ntobeko Peni ended his testimony with the following ambivalent statement of remorse:

> I feel sorry and very down-hearted, especially today [when I see that] I took part in a killing of someone who was on our side, someone we could have used to achieve our aims. Amy was one of those people who, in an international sense, could have worked for the country.

And so, Ntobeko did finally come to accept that Amy was a comrade, as she said.

The danger, Immanuel Levinas (1988) notes, of all theodicies, of all attempts to make meaningful the suffering of others, is the risk of normalizing and accepting the suffering and death of the other. In all theodicies – theological, philosophical, psychological, political, and anthropological – the arbitrary character of suffering and death is hidden. The companions of Job return to goad the hurt, the disappeared, the maimed, the dying: "You must have been into something"; "You must have neglected your religious [or political] obligations"; "You yourself must have really wanted to suffer or die"; "Your death will serve as a lesson for the living"; "Your wounds will serve as a sign, a beacon." The endless search for meaning, the attempt to make sense of suffering, has allowed people, Levinas writes, to blame sufferers for their own pain, to value suffering as penance for past sins or as a means to an end or as the price of sensitivity and consciousness, or, especially within the Christian tradition, as the path of saints and martyrs.

The grieving mother of Amy Biehl, for example, whispered to me during a break in the trial of Amy's alleged killers in Cape Town: "Don't you think there was something destined about Amy's death? Don't you think that for some reason, perhaps not known to us here and now, why Amy had to die?" Later, during a break in the trial, I asked Linda Biehl to explain further what she had meant. She replied over a cup of Roibos tea:

> There is something you need to know about Amy. She was so dedicated, an incredible high achiever, but in the end something always happened to check her, to trip her up. Perhaps she was ambivalent about her success. So I wasn't really surprised when I heard that she was murdered on the day before she was to leave South Africa . . . In a way I was even prepared for it . . . The very last photo I have of her is a newspaper clipping showing Amy just as she came through the finish line in a [Cape Town] marathon. Her face is full of ecstasy, pain, exhaustion, and relief. I like to think that this is how Amy looked when she died in Guguletu – as if she was just breaking through another, her most difficult, finish line.

Mrs. Jeannette Fourie, who lost her daughter in the Heidelberg Pub Massacre, said that she thought – though her husband Johan (she cautioned me) must never know her thoughts – that Lindy-Anne would have been proud to have given her life for the New South Africa. "Even," I asked, "in such an absurd and meaningless attack?" "Yes," she replied calmly. "Even so. I really believe this."

One can only sympathize with Linda Biehl's desire to substitute an image of beauty and light for the brutal photos attached to Amy's autopsy reports. And it must have summoned all of her faith to refer to Amy as a "martyr" in the tradition of Saint Stephen, whose life was also taken in a battery of stones. It is a painful sort of accommodationist "maternal thinking" that allows a mother – Linda Biehl or Jeanette Fourie – to accept the suffering and death of their own child as over-determined, as meaningful, and even as necessary. But these sentiments are redeemed, as it were, by their life-saving refusal to condemn their children's youthful killers and to see them, as one survivor put it, "as children just like our own, children who under normal circumstances would have led ordinary lives."

Linda Biehl's faith in the idea of meaningful suffering allowed her to approach and to embrace the mother of one of her daughter's killers and at the TRC hearings to publicly forgive the young men who murdered her daughter and to refuse to stand in the way of their being granted political amnesty. Linda Biehl, along with a multitude of mothers, sisters, and wives in South Africa who are being called on to do the same, summoned her own and family's tragedy to serve the larger cause of national reconciliation and healing.

Of course, these individuals are exemplary figures and do not represent the majority of white South Africans, who for the most part have not acknowledged their history of passive complicity with the apartheid state. Most failed to get the point behind the TRC. A great many ordinary South African whites I spoke with in malls and shopping centers, in tea rooms and in public gardens, in office buildings and in hospitals, in private homes and large farm estates throughout the western Cape, worried that the TRC was an exercise in "witch-hunting, scape-goating, and perse-cution of whites." Time and again I was told that if General Malan or Eugene de Kock (see Gobodo-Madikizela 2003) had ordered tortures or massacres it was be-cause he had to do so for the sake of national security. Those who were detained, tortured, and killed were not merely "activists," they said, but "terrorists" and "communists" who were part of an international conspiracy to take over all of southern Africa. And these statements were made after the fall of the Soviet Union.

FAILURES OF REMORSE

I am a South African. My skin color is irrelevant.

F. W. De Klerk, 1996

As for those who played a part in the defense of apartheid, the majority has yet to acknowledge the evil that this entailed. Rather than admitting to abuses and atrocities committed, they defended their innocence, thus leaving the amnesty commissioners perplexed. If there was no violation of human rights, no crime, no atrocity, there could be no pardon, no amnesty. Why had this person bothered to appear? For example, the police who detained the Black Consciousness leader Steven Biko continued to maintain before the Amnesty panel that Biko had caused his own death, that he had gotten aggressive and banged his head against the prison wall. If that was the truth then the police actions were in self-defense and there was no reason for them to look for amnesty. Amnesty was denied and the Biko killers could still be tried for their crime. "We discovered in the course of the Commission's investigations," Archbishop Tutu observed, "that the supporters of apartheid were willing to lie at the drop of a hat . . . they lied as if it were going out of fashion, brazenly and with considerable conviction." He did not reflect on whether this cast doubt on the entire process.

The refusals of the TRC process by the old apartheid and National Party government and security forces are well documented. In March 1996 I had an hour-long, open-ended interview with then Deputy President F. W. De Klerk at his parliamentary offices in Cape Town. It was just a few days before he stepped down from the Government of National Unity. Toward the end of the long and rambling interview (see Scheper-Hughes 1996), I broached the question of the TRC and the role of the National Party in gross human rights violations. De Klerk replied:

> Political violence from the side of government forces is wrong. But political violence from the side of the so-called liberation forces where innocent civilians have been killed is equally wrong. There must be even-handed treatment of this violence by the TRC. I fought for that essential principle.

In response to my objections that revolutionary and state violence could not be equated, he replied:

> It is a fallacy that the National Party state behaved as it did just to suppress people. It is also a fallacy that everything was done just to promote apartheid . . . I'm not saying that when security force people went beyond what is internationally acceptable in fighting terrorism in our country that it was right. I don't want to whitewash it at all . . . There are international norms. But what do you do when you are fighting revolutionary forces aiming to overthrow the state in an unlawful manner when that state is internationally recognized, as ours was?

Do you have regrets about *anything*? I persisted.

> If I . . . with all the advantage of hindsight had to do everything all over again, none of my major decisions would have been taken any differently.
>   How would you like to be remembered?
>   As someone who made a positive difference . . . who had the guts to take very fundamental decisions when the time was ripe.

A few years later, in 1998, I interviewed Mr. Wynand Breytenbach, a former Deputy Defense Minister who served in the Ministry of Defense under both Presidents Botha and De Klerk. Today, Mr. Breytenbach is very comfortably retired on a government pension and living out the remainder of his days as a recovering heart transplant patient in a luxurious and securely gated community in Sun Valley, outside Cape Town. I asked Breytenbach his opinion of the TRC and the Amnesty Hearings in particular. He himself, like most of his colleagues in the Defense Forces, had not applied for amnesty. He explained:

> I just don't think this TRC is the right thing to do. Instead of reconciling us, it is making the divisions even larger. It is becoming a witch-hunt. What we must be doing now is to join people together. Most people – even I, as an official in the Secretary of Defense – were completely unaware of what was going on. I was shocked out of my mind to hear of the . . . well, let's just call them atrocities and that sort of thing.

I asked Mr. Breytenbach if he watched the televised summaries of the TRC. He replied:

I watch it with disgust, yah. But I tell you that I sat in at all the top executive meetings where all these decisions were taken. There was Magnus Malan, the whole Defense Council, generals, all the so on, and myself and I swear to you never were these sorts of things discussed. OK, we said that we must experiment with some things in this area [i.e., torture] to try to get stability for the country. But some of these characters went out and slaughtered people like cattle . . . it was like . . . well; if you read the *Sword and the Swastika* you can see what the Germans did to the Jews . . . it was sickening; I walked around the house for days after I read it . . . There, too, in Germany, in Europe you can find the same things as happened here. It all boils down to a few bad individuals, a few rotten apples, and small people sitting in big jobs who think that they can play God. Chaps thinking that they can just "remove" certain people. But nowhere and at no time were these things ever discussed during our executive meetings.

I asked, "So security had broken down and De Klerk and Botha had no idea what was happening within their own forces?"

No, they must have known something because when I was a member of the Security Committee we kept asking for money for arms and such to take care of the problems. It was a case of people looking you in the eye and saying one thing while doing another.

"You are opposed to amnesty then?" I inquired.

No, amnesty is a good thing. If a man has something on his chest, he should come out and confess it and get amnesty for it.
  What has most shocked you coming out of the TRC?
  [Deep sigh!] Ach! So many things. That [Eugene] De Kock chap . . . he's a real monster. That shocked me. And the Biko thing. And this Kondile case that is going on now [at the Cape Town TRC Amnesty Hearings]. The burnings of the bodies and all that. It is just terrible . . . But again, I go back to the Nazi era when pretty much the same thing happened. People lost all sense of humanity. If you really want to talk about atrocities, when I was stationed in Kenya during the Mau Mau massacres I used to fly and do observations from the air . . . I saw farmers, cattle, and small babies . . . all of them slaughtered. You can't sleep for months after seeing something like that. And, even today into KwaZulu-Natal you will find massacres still going on – blacks killing the blacks. So, this whole business is not so clear-cut. *All* the races are to blame, and there is more to this than just politics.
  What else is at stake?
  What really concerns me now is that there is no more law and order in the country. When my four grown sons see these so-called disadvantaged people marching in the streets, breaking things, and stealing whatever they want, they become very negative and cynical. They think that there is no good policing any more. And they think that if these people can get away with this, whites can too. But I tell them never to lower their standards, not to become like the bad eggs who are destroying what is left of our poor country.

In this extraordinary interview, the former Deputy Minister of Defense managed to simultaneously deny and assert his own role in police atrocities, to attribute blame to those both above and below him, to reassure himself that the atrocities committed by the apartheid state were not unique and even took place in a civilized place like Germany, let alone in Kenya during the Mau Mau era. In the end, Breytenbach identifies the real bad guys as poor and black South Africans who have "no respect" for law and order and who are corrupting the morals of his own sons. Like a great many South African whites I have met and interviewed since 1993, Mr. Breytenbach fails to see the enormous grace by which he, his sons, and all white South Africans have been spared. And, of course, Mr. Breytenbach never gave any thought to applying for amnesty under the TRC for any gross human rights violations in which his own ministry was involved.

Most amnesty petitions came not from the higher ranks of apartheid leaders like Mr. Breytenbach but from their small fry operatives, often black police collaborators whose admissions of guilt and complicity with the white state were met with rage and hate by their neighbors and kin. Amnesty petitions also came from PAC militants, like the Biehl killers and those convicted in the tavern and church massacres who were already in jail and had the most to gain from public confession.

One amnesty case made by a white South African captured international attention: the testimony of Sergeant Jeffrey Benzien, who demonstrated before TV cameras the use of his specialty – the wet bag torture. When asked by one of his victims, Tony Yengeni, how it felt when the sergeant put a wet bag around his head causing him to suffocate, Benzien broke down and he started to cry. But he then took refuge (through the testimony of his clinical psychologist) in a psychiatric defense – that he was suffering from PTSD, Post-Traumatic Stress Disorder. Like so many of his colleagues in the security forces, Benzien claimed to be confused, anxious, sleepless and, above all, amnesiac. Like Adolf Eichmann, he was a good police officer forced to take the rap for his superiors. He was being publicly humiliated for what were systematic and thoroughly institutionalized violations.

As Allan Young (1995) noted with respect to the Vietnam Vets at the Mei Lai massacre, there is something morally troubling about a medical exemption that can fall as easily on the perpetrator of violence as on the victim. Benzien was awarded amnesty and he is still working for the South African police, though he has been downgraded to a low profile job at the Cape Town airport. An attempt to interview Benzien led me to a rundown little bungalow in a white working-class suburb of Cape Town. Weeds had overtaken what was once a garden. The curtains were tightly drawn. Several loud raps on the door finally brought out a timid, pale faced little girl of perhaps eight years, who on encountering a stranger with a foreign accent, shook her head and quickly slammed the door, bolting it fast from inside. *Her* fear and shame were palpable.

REPARATIONS

Throughout, a key question has remained: Would the long-suffering, impoverished, and land hungry populations of the former homelands and the townships be satisfied with the proceedings? How would their righteous demands for material and economic reconstruction be dealt with? In the early stages of its operation, the Reparations and Rehabilitation (R&R) Committee was reduced to dehumanizing deliberations about the monetary value of a missing person, a missing arm, a life interrupted, or the mental anguish of forced collaboration extracted through torture.

To South Africans of means, like Albie Sachs, now a Justice in the Constitutional Court of South Africa, the idea of any monetary compensation for the loss of his arm and the sight of one eye was morally repulsive:

> How much do you think my arm is worth? Five thousand? Five million? You can't put a price tag on something that is an integral part of your entire existence! You are trivializing my body. Worse, you are saying that there is no human experience, no part of the self that cannot be quantified. You are putting the ideals that guided my life as a political activist into the market.

This is the primary route that the R&R committee took in promoting symbolic reparations, which included exhumations and re-burials, issuing death certificates, erecting headstones, clearing criminal records, resolving outstanding legal matters related to the violations, providing emergency medical care, wheelchairs and prostheses, special schooling and college scholarships, renaming streets and facilities, and dedicating memorial parks and local monuments to those who died during the struggle as terrorists and public enemies of the apartheid state. Public rituals to restore the "good names" of ANC and PAC militants, many of them deceased, who were falsely accused of collaboration with the South African police, were one of the most important restorative functions of the TRC.

Yet, for the thousands of impoverished black South Africans who related their personal stories of torture, shack burnings, and political kidnapping before the TRC, the idea of monetary compensation was neither repulsive nor degrading. Traditional law among Xhosas and Zulus usually demanded some material reparations (gifts of cattle, for example) to restore a sense of justice to the injured party. While in public, black South African survivors often felt compelled to ask only for acknowledgment and an apology; in private, many requested material compensation in the form of land or a home or help setting up a small business.

In April 2003, following earlier recommendations made by the reparations committee of the TRC, the ANC government of Thabo Mbeki awarded each officially recognized victim of gross apartheid abuses a one time cash payment of 30,000 South African rands. Meanwhile, broader and more basic "reparations" in the form of land, farm, and corporate expropriations to correct past injustices (as demanded, for example, by PAC) were never even considered.

MULTIPLE TRUTHS AND CHEAP FORGIVENESS

The structure of the TRC pitted victims and perpetrators in a battle over memory and truth. From the start, the TRC had to grapple with what definitions of truth it would employ. Justice Sachs distinguished among four levels of truth: (1) *legal truth* in which the field is limited to only that which can be verified through hypothesis testing and hard evidence: (2) *logical truth* in which truth is deduced from logical propositions; (3) *experiential truth*, or that which is phenomenologically, subjectively, and personally experienced as "true" while not necessarily historically or scientifically "true"; (4) *dialogical truth*, truth that is "negotiated out of a vibrant context of multiple voices contesting, combating, sharing, and sometimes drowning each other out." It is *dialogical* truth (Sachs concluded) that the TRC was most able to produce.

While admirable from the point of view of the dramatist or playwright, many ordinary people who came to the TRC seeking "truth" left disappointed. Instead of the single, objective, sweet truth of the moralist, they had to make do with a compromise, settling for a negotiated "good enough" truth – something analogous to the AIDS "names project," a crazy quilt of competing narratives, losses, sorrows, and contested truths.

Father Michael Lapsley sharply criticized the TRC for implementing a cheap theology of forgiveness. Although he accepted the conditional amnesty process on principle for the sake of the "greater good" of South Africa, he expressed deep resentment toward those who expected him to show a spirit of uncomplicated, unconditional "Christian" forgiveness. He commented on how often his speeches were misheard by white South Africans and white Americans who come up to thank him for being "so forgiving" toward the apartheid operatives who tried to kill him, when he never once even mentioned forgiveness.

Albie Sachs often tells the story of his own refusal to embrace the new national ethos of reconciliation and forgiveness, which has since become a kind of civic duty. Soon after returning from exile in Mozambique, Albie was enjoying an evening out at a jazz bar, "Rosie's and all that Jazz," on Cape Town's beautiful waterfront. He was approached by a heavy set white man who asked in thickly Afrikaner-accented English: "Are you Albie Sachs?" "I am," Albie replied brusquely, and tried to move past him. But the large man blocked his way in the crowded room. "Verskoon my" – Forgive me, he said huskily in Afrikaans, staring at Albie's empty sleeve. His voice was almost drowned out by the drummers. Sachs said nothing. The man repeated more loudly, "Forgive me." Albie brushed him aside, saying in a broken Afrikaans mixed with English and Portuguese: "This lovely club is your forgiveness." And they parted company, both dissatisfied. Later, Albie thought of the things he might have said, "Don't ask *me* for forgiveness. I was a volunteer in the struggle. I chose my fate. What about the millions of black South Africans who had no choice but to suffer and die under apartheid? Why not ask *them* for forgiveness?" Still later, when I met with Albie in 1998, he conceded: "What I probably *should* have done was to put my one good arm around the man, give him a half-bear hug, and to accept his forgiveness. But I just wasn't ready to do that" (see also Sachs 2000).

Failures to forgive are easy to understand. The remorselessness of so many deeply implicated white South Africans is more difficult to accept. In observing the amnesty proceedings in Cape Town during our winter of 1998, I was struck by the dry, banal, legalistic questioning and the emotionally and morally stunted testimonies given by the tanned, relaxed, pensioned, and legally well-defended South African police officers, like those involved in the kidnapping, torture, murder, and burning of comrade Kondile, a young ANC militant. Adding insult to injury, the four colluding police officers seeking pardon for the murder of Kondile, described the young man, in the presence of his grieving family members, as having been easily turned into a double-agent, albeit not a very useful one, whom they quickly dispatched, once he was no longer of any use to them.

There were moments during these hearings when the bloodless recitation of the tortures devised by former security police to rid the country of its "black terrorists" seemed only to rub salt in the wounds of the survivors who were accorded places of honor in front row seats marked "Family Members." As the police told of having a barbecue around the sizzling bonfire that was later lit under Kondile's body, the victim's mother, borne up on either side by her surviving adult children, walked unsteadily out of the hearings. "I will *never* forgive them," she said.

BYSTANDERS: WHITE APATHY AND INDIFFERENCE

In the end, the huge gamble of the TRC will stand or fall on the extent to which it has been able to create a shared history and collective narrative, one capable of putting white, black, and brown South Africans on the same map, sharing the same country. A huge obstacle to that, it seems to me, is the role of the ordinary white South African bystander, English speaking as well as Afrikaner, both Jews and Christians, those who were enriched and enabled by the systematic violence against black South Africans.

Among them is a lovely and gentle man, Jack Swart, Nelson Mandela's cook at Victor Verster in Paarl, Madiba's last prison where he was kept under a kind of house arrest. An Afrikaner prison guard who enjoyed cooking, Jack was assigned the role of personal attendant to the future president. His duties included instructing Mr. Mandela in how to dress, how to swim a minimally acceptable dog-paddle in the small private pool attached to the ranch house in a secluded part of the prison grounds, and how to use such innovations as the computer, to operate a remote control TV, and to use the microwave oven. The stiff but amiable prison guard reminisced with me about Paarl's most celebrated prisoner and how much Nelson Mandela liked brown rice and lasagna, which were novelties to him. But Mr. Swart clearly had an agenda and toward the end of my first visit to his neat little home on the grounds of Victor Verster prison, during which I had taken down a few of Madiba's favorite recipes, including one for a creamy chicken and mushroom pasta, Jack asked if I might want to work as his literary agent. He hoped there might be a market – and some royalties to be had – in peddling a collection of recipes under the title, proposed without a hint of irony, "The Nelson Mandela Prison Cook Book."

There is one extraordinary moment, however, in the TRC document, one described as intriguing, when an unnamed Indian woman applied for amnesty for what she describes as "apathy," based on her recognition that all individuals "can and should be held accountable by history for our lack of necessary action in times of crisis . . . in exercising apathy rather than commitment we allow(ed) others to sacrifice their lives for the sake of our freedom and an increase in our standard of living." This heart-felt petition was turned down by the Commission as falling outside the brief of the TRC. Apathy, the commissioners concluded, had no clear political motivation. And so a crucial opportunity was lost to confront the real litmus test of social and self-transformation.

RECONCILIATION

Albie Sachs once said to me that he wished there could be more "felt emotion," more remorse, expressed by the perpetrators of political violence. He referred, specifically, to those like Botha, Winnie Mandela, and F. W. De Klerk who have refused the new history, and who remain frozen in the past. I reminded Albie of his own "failure" to embrace the remorse of the Afrikaner stranger who appeared unbidden before him at Rosie's café. He smiled ruefully. Albie's own day of final reckoning, brought about by the larger machinations of the TRC, did finally come about. In February of 1999, Albie received a call in his chambers in Johannesburg. "Judge Sachs, a man named Henry is here to see you. He says he was involved in an assassination attempt and would you be willing to see him?" Albie continues:

> So, I went out to the reception area and there standing next to my secretary was Henry, a little man, shorter than myself. Younger, leaner, I looked at him; he looked at me. We walked together down the hall to my chambers – he with a tight, military gait, me with my looser judicial ambulatory style. Henry told me that he had come from a very decent family, God-fearing. He joined the army at a young age and had advanced through the ranks rapidly. He was quite proud of that. Then he was chosen for an elite corps involved with planning the logistics for commando-like attacks on enemy targets, of which I had been one. He had photographed my car, planned where the bomb should be placed. The initial plan had been postponed and then he had a falling out with his superior and he read about the attack he had planned in the newspapers. He was involved in many other operations in Mozambique designed to create mayhem. Botha finally called it off eventually. I was curious to know more, but I wanted to leave all the questioning to the TRC.
>
> We talked and talked. Henry told about his life since leaving the army. He was full of grievance and complaint. He had been asked to leave the army and was given a golden handshake of R150,000 (about $30,000), which he considered to be grossly inadequate, and which he had invested in some arms importation deal that had gone bankrupt. He said that he, too, had been injured in his foot and he remarked at how unfair the world was. Here I was now [the terrorist] sitting in [the high] Court, honored and respected and with a handsome salary, and here was he, so faithful to the old government, who had fought so hard to preserve what he was told was justice and civilized values, discarded, unemployed, and left out in the cold. He expressed his anger at the generals and the other higher ups who had used him. He was, unbelievably, looking to *me* for sympathy and for some validation of his view that life was terribly unfair. And I looked at him, wondering who this man was who had tried to kill me. He didn't know me. He didn't seem to hate me, then or now. At the time of the bombing the one thing I could not stand was the idea that someone who did not know me at all was willing to extinguish me. There was no connection, no relation; I was simply in the way. Perhaps he was thinking along similar lines about me. We were reluctant to end the conversation.
>
> "Henry," I said. "Normally when people leave my chambers I shake hands with them." I resisted making a cheap joke: "But you *know* why I can't shake hands with you." Instead I said: "I can't shake hands with you *now*, but if you go to the TRC and if you tell them everything that you know perhaps afterwards we can meet again and I will shake your hand." Henry walked away; this time, he didn't have that smart soldier stride, and instead he looked like a soldier in defeat – his shoulders hunched over, defeated, downhearted, disconsolate.

Then, a year later at an end of the year party given by the producer of a bold and gritty South African soap opera, Albie heard his name being called: "Albie!" Then louder: "Albie!" Albie turned to see a familiar face: "Henry! It's you!" "Yes." They went to a corner of the room, where Henry started talking very rapidly. "I wrote to the TRC," he said. "I told them everything I knew. And then Bobby, Sue, and Farouk came to question me." "These were *my* ANC friends," said Albie, "I was in exile with them – and now they were *his* friends, and he was on a first name basis with them! I could tell by his face that he had told the truth. So I repeated to him my promise and I shook his hand and he went away elated. There was a new bounce in his walk. But I nearly fainted."

Like Albie, Dawie Ackerman also had to confront, finally, the young men who killed his wife in the church massacre, when he appeared at the TRC intending initially to contest their petition for amnesty. But toward the very end of the amnesty proceedings, Dawie was transformed. In making a final statement before the panel, Dawie directly confronted the young men who killed his wife. He told the four young men how he had to step over the dead bodies to get to Marita, his wife of more than twenty years, who was still sitting upright in her front row pew, and how all the while he was hoping against hope, that Marita might just be shell-shocked but still alive, until he finally crossed that endless expanse of space and reached for her, but just as he touched her back, her body rolled over and fell with a dull thud to the floor, her special Sunday clothes splattered with blood. Dawie continued, his composure broken, his voice cracking with the tears that have been, he said, a very long time, five years, in fact, in coming:

> I never cried since I lost my wife other than to have silent cries. I've never had an emotional outburst till now. When . . . when Mr. Makoma here [the young man who was 17 at the time he took part in the church attack] was testifying, he talked about his own tortures in prison, and that he was suicidal at times, but that he never once cried. I thought to myself – and I passed you [a TRC counselor] a note, asking you to please bring your cross-examination to an end. Because . . . what are we doing here? The truth . . . the truth . . . yes. But when I looked at the way Mr. Makoma answered and saw all his anger . . . I thought, what on earth are we doing? *He* cannot be reconciled.

At this point in his statement, weeping and emotionally overwrought, Dawie Ackerman asked the three young amnesty applicants to turn their heads and face him directly. Amazingly, their heads (which had been bowed to the floor) snapped up to attention and they looked directly at Dawie, who said: "This is the first opportunity we have had to look each other in the eye while talking. I want to ask Mr. Makoma, who actually entered the church, a question . . . My . . . my wife was sitting at the door when you came in. [Dawie weeps and the words seem to be dragged from the roots of his shaking body.] She was wearing a long blue coat. Please, can you remember if you shot her?"

Makoma looks up at Dawie, terrified, as though seeing Hamlet's father's ghost. He bites his lower lip and slowly shakes his head. No, he cannot remember, neither Marita nor her long blue coat. But all three young men apologized to Dawie. Makoma is naturally the most affected and he says: "We are truly sorry for what we have done. But it was not intentional . . . Although people died, we did not do that out of our own will. It was the situation in South Africa we were living under. And now we are asking you please, do forgive us."

Dawie Ackerman did so, at least officially, and he withdrew his carefully prepared legal objections to the amnesty process. After the hearing, Dawie and several other survivors, including Bishop Reteif, withdrew to a smaller room where they met in private with the young militants, each of whom walked around the table addressing each survivor in turn, shaking their hands, and whispering messages of condolence. Brian Smart, a survivor of St. James, was impressed by the ages of the young militants: "They were only 17 years old, and I could relate to that. When I was 18 I was in the South Africa Air Force and sent out in defense of the realm, if you like. The only difference between them and myself was that I was operating under controlled military orders. So a massacre [like this one] would not have happened. In their case the command structure was very weak and, unfortunately, they had the normal soldier's ability to kill, just as I had."

Bishop Reteif, who was not in the church until moments after the attack took place, and who subsequently suffered a great deal of pastoral survivor guilt, originally opposed the granting of amnesty to "terrorists." His initial response to the massacre was to heroine the South African police and to demonize the PAC youth as "instruments" of evil forces. After the TRC hearings the bishop was contrite and mindful of the "blindness" of his evangelical church to the suffering caused by apartheid, and indirectly by a large wealthy church that had benefited from the suffering of the majority population. He told me: "Now, I finally understand why it [the TRC] was necessary."

As for Linda and Peter Biehl, their extraordinary faith in their daughter's "meaningful" death allowed them to "move forward," as Peter (who died in March 2002) put it in his US Midwestern down to earth style. For them, this has meant not only facing, but also embracing, their daughter's killers and devoting their lives to the townships within and outside Cape Town, especially Guguletu, where three of the young militants convicted of their daughter's death – Easy Nofemela, Mangesi, and Ntbeko Peni – have returned to live since the TRC amnesty panel released them from Pollsmor prison. In accepting amnesty for the killers, the Biehls, Ginn Fourie, and Dawie Ackerman – along with a multitude of black South Africans called upon to do the same – allowed their own personal tragedies to serve as a symbol of national healing and reconciliation. Their ability to find some transcendent purpose, some beauty even, in the death of their loved ones was a stepping stone in "getting over" the past in order to reach the other side.

Some critics of the TRC have suggested that the structure of public confession, apology, and reconciliation comprises externally imposed Christian, indeed Anglican, rituals that have little resonance with the majority of black South Africans. But collective rituals of truth telling and face-to-face apologies are an essential feature of traditional cultures in the former homelands of South Africans, and of popular justice in their townships. To be sure, among those who have participated in amnesty seeking before the TRC are those, like young Makoma, who remain bitter and unreconciled, who feel abandoned by their paramilitary command structure and humiliated before their comrades. Indeed, the very structure of the TRC both pathologized and individualized the experience of the anti-apartheid struggle, turning all those who participated in the proceedings into victims or perpetrators. What got written out of the whole process was the act of political resistance itself.

After his TRC hearing, Makoma, then serving a 20-year sentence for his part in the St. James Church Massacre, returned to Polsmor prison to await the result of his amnesty petition, which he was eventually granted. But while Dawie Ackerman, Bishop Reteif, and other church members seem to have experienced a catharsis through the TRC process, Makoma did not immediately find any such relief. During a prison visit between Makoma and Dawie Ackerman's daughter, Leisel Ackerman asked Makoma how he *felt* on being shown at the amnesty hearings the graphic police photos "of all the people and all the blood" of those he had killed. Makoma replied to the girl whose mother he had killed:

> Yah, I remember seeing that . . . and I had bad feelings then. It *was* bad. But, no matter how I feel now, at this time, or at this moment, about what I did then was bad, there is nothing, which I can do. The people are dead. Why ask me how I feel about that? How I feel cannot change anything, cannot bring them back to life.

A "disciplined" PAC revolutionary, Makoma feels that these emotional demands and ritual performances are unseemly and beside the point. Dead is dead and what happened cannot be undone.

Ntbeko Peni and Easy Nofemela, who petitioned for and received amnesty for their role in the killing of Amy Biehl, feel differently about the TRC. After arranging with great difficulty an initial meeting with the young men in their concrete "shacks" in a rundown section of Guguletu in July 1999, I faced a wall of seething silence. After a while, Ntbeko explained that he did not believe in or trust the TRC, which he described as an arm of the ANC, no friend of his organization (PAC). But, he said, he decided to "confess" anyway because of the "heaviness" in his heart. But it had not helped, and since being granted amnesty and returning to live in Guguletu, his days were very dark. He could not sleep. He could not have a girlfriend. He could not take up work. He could not study. He hid from people. Above all, he was full of shame. He said:

> I thought to myself that there might be one thing that could make me better. I wanted to tell that Mr. Biehl that I did not take the death of his daughter lightly. That this thing has weighed so heavily on me. And I wanted him to know that he is a hero father to me. So I thought, if you could help me, if you could just get that Peter Biehl to listen to me and to really forgive me – that would be as good as bread.

That arranged meeting, held a few weeks later, again in the home of Ntbeko Peni, led to a strange and wonderful association. After an initially painful emotional standoff between Peter Biehl, Ntbeko, Easy Nofemela, and several of their comrades, the boys tried their best to explain their political position to Peter along with their sense of sadness over a death, they now say, that should never have happened at all. They told Peter about the youth group they had started in Gugs and they showed us photos of the hikes they took with the young people up and around Table Mountain.

Peter was impressed and he invited the two boys to work for the Amy Biehl Foundation, which, after shaking their heads in disbelief, they accepted. In the last two years they have apprenticed as welders and helped Peter Biehl organize the distribution and sale of "Amy's Bread" out of the large communal bakery the Biehls helped to establish in the community. Linda Biehl told me that she is proud that Easy and Ntbeko now shyly call her "Mama," a term of respect used by Xhosa youth for respected mature women, and that Ntbeko refers to Peter as his "hero father." Not only Ntbeko, but Linda, too, refers to the "great weight" that has now been lifted from her, even if it still does not fill the permanent void and sadness she still feels.

HOPE AND OPTIMISM IN SPITE OF PRESENT DIFFICULTIES

The TRC process opened up new social spaces where conversations and interactions that were once unthinkable have taken place. The unlikely encounters between perpetrators and victims able to empathize with each other's situation are a case in point. But even those who now try to deny or minimize their support for the old apartheid regime have added something to the new South Africa. Even those disgruntled white South Africans who had to get up from their easy chairs to switch the channel from the weekly summaries of the TRC hearings back to Sunday evening sports, represent a small moral victory for the new dispensation.

The South African TRC was a hybrid institution, neither a court of law nor guerilla theater, while sharing aspects of both. It was like no other truth commission. It was videotaped and televised. There was almost complete transparency in the proceedings. There were experiments and innovations – witnesses and survivors of human rights atrocities were provided with "comforters" who served like traditional "doulas" to the laboring mother. Unlike court hearings, strong emotions were elicited and displayed openly, led by Archbishop Tutu, who set an example to a country that thought it had lost the ability to feel anything anymore. The TRC provided a National Theater on a large stage where dialogue, difference, and dignity were displayed and celebrated. Consequently, the moral as well as the political climate of South Africa has been changed. The transformation of knowledge into personal acknowledgment locates what has been revealed in a meaningful, moral universe. I am suggesting that a political economy of affect, of emotion, is an important site of governance – and that attention to a theology of the state is warranted.

The very idea of a truth commission provoked a national soul searching that sometimes turned up in the oddest places. There was, for example, the elderly Afrikaner couple with concerned looks on their faces who approached me one day on the steps of St. George's Cathedral in Cape Town (the Anglican church of Archbishop Tutu). Where could they find "the bishop?" they asked me. When I said he was away, they looked crestfallen. I asked why they wanted to see him. "To confess to the Truth Commission," they said. "You see, we realize now that we did not treat black people very well and now we want to make a fresh start." I explained that the TRC was a very formal process "with lawyers and official documents" and that it was meant for murderers and torturers and not for ordinary people like themselves who could have behaved better.

The real effects of the TRC are and will continue to be felt in small ripples like these, in community and church meetings where people can now talk about what happened to them, how they behaved, and how they might begin to set the record straight. Long after the formal TRC has disbanded and all the grief counselors have returned to business as usual, a multitude of little Tics will still be needed to help ordinary people deal with the many perversions and horrors of apartheid.

So I will end, finally, with the story of Hennie's redemption. Hennie was, at the time I first knew him, an Afrikaner security guard for the University of Cape Town. He frequently dropped by our home in 1993–4 and I feared at the time that either he was a spy or he had a special fondness for one of our adult daughters. But he seemed genuinely curious and well intentioned. I ran into Hennie again in Cape Town in 1996 during the spontaneous celebration of South Africa's winning the All-Africa Soccer Cup that year. Hennie was simply beside himself with excitement. He tried to whirl me around in the street as he struggled in his rather broken English to find just the right words to express the magnitude of the moment. "Did you see the game?" he asked. I did, I said, and on a big screen at the new and decidedly integrated Manneberg Pub in downtown Cape Town. "*Both* goals?" he probed. "I did," I replied.

"And did you see our president [Mandela] right there out on the field? Do you know what this means for us?" And without waiting for an answer, Hennie continued:

> It means we white people are not all, 100 percent bad. And God is willing to forgive us. Imagine – that He would give *us*, of all people, such great heroes! It is a sign that we are going in a good way now. We are not hated any more. Before in the old South Africa it was like we were Fat Elvis – sick, disgusting, bloated, ugly. And now, in the new, we are like skinny Elvis – young, handsome, strong. In the new South Africa we have all been reborn.

In his awkward way, Hennie invoked the "miracle [of rebirth] that saves the world" to which Hannah Arendt (1958) referred in *The Human Condition* – the emergence of new men and women made possible through hope and optimism. Their little stories illustrate history working itself out as grace – no, not Divine grace – but the human grace of those millions of black South Africans who have not raised their hands in righteous anger and vengeance and who are still willing to take a risk on the birth of a new nation.

REFERENCES

Arendt, Hannah, 1958 *The Human Condition*. Chicago: University of Chicago Press.

Boraine, Alex, 2000. *A Country Unmasked: Inside South Africa's Truth and Reconciliation Commission*. Oxford: Oxford University Press.

Crapanzano, Vincent, 1985 *Waiting: The Whites of South Africa*. New York: Vintage.

Das, Veena, with Arthur Kleinman, Margaret Lock, Michelle Ramphele, and Pamela Reynolds, eds., 2001 *Remaking a World: Violence, Social Suffering, and Recovery*. Berkeley: University of California Press.

Das, Veena, with Arthur Kleinman, Michelle Ramphele, and Pamela Reynolds, eds., 2000 *Violence and Subjectivity*. Berkeley: University of California Press.

Gobodo-Madikizela, Pumla, 2003 *A Human Being Died That Night: A South African Story of Forgiveness*. Boston, MA: Houghton-Mifflin.

Goffman, Erving, 1963 *Stigma: Notes on the Management of Spoiled Identity*. Englewood Cliffs, NJ: Prentice-Hall.

Hamber, Brandon and Wilson, Richard, 2002 Symbolic Closure through Memory, Reparation, and Revenge in Post-Conflict Societies. *Journal of Human Rights* 1 (1): 35–53.

Ignatieff, Michael, 1997 "Digging up the Dead." *New Yorker*, November 10, 1997, pp. 85–93.

James, Wilmot and Linda Van de Vijver (eds.) 2000 *After the Truth and Reconciliation Commission: Reflections on Truth and Reconciliation in South Africa*. Athens, GA: Ohio University Press; Cape Town: David Philip.

Jeffery, Anthea, 1999 *The Truth about the TRC* (Spotlight Series). Johannesburg: South African Institute of Race Relations.

Kleinman, Arthur, with Veena Das and Margaret Lock, eds., 1997 *Social Suffering*. Berkeley: University of California Press.

Levinas, Immanuel, 1988 "Useless Suffering," trans. R. Cohen. In *The Provocation of Levinas*, ed. R. Bernasconi and D. Wood. New York: Routledge and Kegan Paul.

Nuttall, Sarah and Coetzee, Carli (eds.) 1998 *Negotiating the Past: The Making of Memory in South Africa*. Cape Town: Oxford University Press.

Malan, Rian, 1990 *My Traitor's Heart: A South African Exile Returns to Face His Country, His Tribe, and his Conscience*. New York: Atlantic Monthly Press.

Ross, Fiona, 2003 *Bearing Witness: Women and the Truth and Reconciliation Commission in South Africa*. London: Pluto Press.

Sachs, Albie, 2000 *Soft Vengeance of a Freedom Fighter*. Berkeley: University of California Press.

Scheper-Hughes, Nancy 1992 *Death without Weeping: The Violence of Everyday Life in Brazil*. Berkeley: University of California Press.

— 1994 "The Last White Christmas: The Heidelberg Pub Massacre (South Africa)." *American Anthropologist* 96 (4) (December): 1–28.

— 1995 "Who's the Killer? Popular Justice and Human Rights in a South African Squatter Camp." *Social Justice* 22 (3): 143–164.

— 1996 Positively FW: An Interview with Deputy President F. W. De Klerk. *Democracy in Action* (May).

— 2004 "Mixed Feelings: Spoiled Identities in the New South Africa." *Kroeber Anthropological Society Papers*. No. 89/90, pp. 219–248.

Tutu, Desmond, 2000 *No Future without Forgiveness*. London: Rider.

Young, Alan, 1995 *The Harmony of Illusions: Inventing Post-Traumatic Stress Disorder*. Princeton, NJ: Princeton University Press.

Afterword

Catherine Lutz

Self-consciously or not, intellectual work is always constituted in relationship to history and culture. Scholarship in psychocultural studies is no exception. North American ideologies of self, including especially the assumptions of individualism and fascination with self-awareness, have both nurtured the field of *psychological* anthropology and marginalized psychological *anthropology* in relation to psychology and psychiatry. Much work in psychological anthropology, as in other disciplines, was done to explicitly or tacitly address culturally defined problems in, and use cultural categories of, the United States, where most psychological anthropologists do their work. From the famous early example of Mead's work on the newly turbulent adolescence associated with young people's new dependency and place (or lack of such) in a changing educational and economic system (see di Leonardo 1998) and the World War II work of Benedict and others in managing understandings of the enemy at home and abroad, this tendency extends to Scheper-Hughes's (1992) work critiquing both the effects of universalized attachment theory and how extreme privation and exploitation affect relationships between mothers and their children.

From nearly constituting the field of US anthropology in the 1940s, 1950s, and 1960s, psychological anthropology became a sub-field with the turn to history and politics across the disciplines, a turn that occurred to people observing rebellions at home and the idea of "Vietnam" abroad. Then it appeared that Marx, Weber, De Beauvoir, and DuBois had more to say to anthropology than Freud or the academic psychologists still relatively insulated in their well-funded labs from those cultural forces of the late 1960s and 1970s. Some psychocultural work in the 1970s and 1980s, however, was involved in a broader cultural critique that began with Freud's *Civilization and its Discontents*, continued in Frankfurt School analyses (Marcuse 1964), and was brought into confrontation with the civil rights, feminist, and Vietnam War era questioning of received notions of civilizational discourse that defined the normal and charted individual and group goals (Riesman 1977). Many efforts have been made as well to draw links between, or to erode altogether, the conceptual divide between the notions of the individual and of society. The dualisms of self and society, of scientific and interpretive method, of nature and culture, and of emotion and thought, have been just a few of the central culturally constituted elements that have undergone debate and revision.

More than many fields of intellectual endeavor, psychological anthropology can provide tools for reflecting on the knowledge creation process itself within these historical contexts. Given the observation of historical sociologists that US social science has tended to be remarkably ahistorical in comparison with other social sciences, it might seem odd to turn to US psychocultural studies for insight into such matters. To those who associate this field exclusively with the synchronic study of individuals rather than persons-in-context-and-history, this might seem a symptom in the guise of a cure. The examples of work that contradict this image are far too many (for just a few recent, fine examples, see Cole 2001; Holland and Lave 2000; Luhrmann 2000; Mageo 2002; O'Nell 1996; Scheper-Hughes 1992). Psychocultural research can suggest how the "splitting and silences" that Ewing (this volume) identifies in migrants under stress could also be evident in academic work, where they might result from the contradictions of scholars' everyday life in particular national and historical contexts. In so doing, it can open up newer areas for investigation. This volume demonstrates how many ways psychological anthropologists have found and are finding to understand how what is taken for knowledge about selves and self-processes is emergent, politicized, and culturally grounded.

Many essays in this book speak to the interwoven concerns of psychological anthropologists and other sociocultural anthropologists, downplaying the distinctiveness of the field. So, for example, the studies of self with which psychological anthropologists are associated and the ubiquitous studies of identity in the field more generally mutually entail though only occasionally address each other (but see Ewing, and Linger, this volume). We can argue that they need to do so more often, particularly given the increased attention to plural and fragmented or contradictory identities (Sokefeld 1999).

What remain distinctive are psychological anthropologists' own identities, as Linger (this volume) notes, as "dissenters" who "place greater emphases on mental processes, individual particularities, experiential immediacies, and personal agency." When combined with dissent from the dominant rationality in US society and in the academy from which it springs and only sometimes distinguishes itself, this kind of psychological anthropological scholarship can provide what C. Wright Mills defined as the essence of the sociological or anthropological imagination itself. That imagination enables us "to grasp history and biography and the relations between the two within society." It is the route, he said, by which "the personal uneasiness of individuals is focused upon explicit troubles and the indifference of publics is transformed into involvement with public issues" (Mills 1959: 65). The movement from uneasiness to action, from anomic individuals to fully collaborative political actors or citizens, has never been more necessary given the success of capitalism in making a simplistic maximizing or entrepreneurial subject the alpha and omega of both acceptable scholarship and citizenship. Social change and alternative modernities will require the movement for which these chapters provide a partial charter.

Together, history and historical self-awareness have brought this field to the point where some scholars feel that much new ground of contemporary and urgent relevance can be explored by the new generation of psychological anthropologists.

Whether these research areas are termed modernities, crises, or alternative futures, they explicitly take on the dilemmas, capacities, and suffering associated with current sociohistorical formations. The social changes and problems that come into sharper view for this kind of anthropology are often defined by how they engage individualism and individuality and how two or more people co-construct each other's articulated ideas, desires, and practice. Examples include the intersubjective worlds engendered by computer life; the emotions medicalized and medicated by huge health institutions; the emotions of alienation and oppression which are the material organized by activists and evangelical missions, both groups connected in global networks to some degree; and the embodiment of ubiquitous commercial images of ideal female beauty and submissiveness in unprecedented rates of eating disorders and violence against women.

These concerns are most evident in parts three and four of this book – "Ambivalence, Alienation, and Belonging" and "Aggression, Dominance, and Violence" – where processes such as racism, corporate downsizing, genocide, gated communities, and immigration are both historicized and understood as conditions of persons. Ewing, for example, argued that immigrant identities are shaped not only by trauma and dislocation but also by cultural processes that give them meaning, as do the broadest international conditions such as the history and relative power of the countries between which a person migrates. Even in the more basic areas of psychocultural research that this volume covers, from consciousness to memory to dreaming, crisis and history are everywhere. Time can be seen, as Birth argues, as an integrated biosociocultural experience of the world; elaborated through cultural models, it can be reshaped on both social and individual biological levels by dint of globalization, which places people – from immigrants to stockbrokers – simultaneously in multiple time zones, creating new conflicts and possibilities. Greenfield, Garro, and Cole each thoroughly historicize the learning, cognitive, and memory processes that they have studied in Mexico, Canada, and Madagascar.

Future psychocultural research can expand into many other realms of contemporary life in a changing world of accumulation, forms of work and consumption; these range from understanding how people respond to environmental crisis to the nature of spiritual longing in commercial culture. The present moment of human history and human evolution in fact increasingly presses on scholars to address it. Poverty, child death, iatrogenic disease, war, and political oppression – all problems which were promised to wither away with modernity and with the triumph of free markets, positive science, and liberal democracy – are with us with more vengeance than ever. Some problems have morphed and/or worsened in ways that demand action-oriented research: global warming, global empire, global trafficking in women, arms, and genetically altered crops; massive migrations prompted by war, oppression, and the search for missing work, migrations that increasingly hybridize and pluralize identities and selves; increased inequality, and media and digital technologies permit unprecedented colonization of consciousness. So, too, are there unprecedented levels of motivation and movement among people opposed to the negative effects of globalization, corporatism, plunder of the environment, and war and empire. The largest single mobilization of human beings on a single day for a "single" purpose in 2003 requires research in the interest of understanding the personal, cultural, and social sources of this motivation and its potential for creating individuals capable of making change happen. Such research would reveal as well the great variety of reasons and great varieties of individual strategies and capacities for participating in political life. This kind of research will hopefully grow to become the future of the field of psychocultural studies.

REFERENCES

Cole, Jennifer, 2001 *Forget Colonialism? Sacrifice and the Art of Memory in Madagascar.* Berkeley: University of California Press.

di Leonardo, Micaela, 1998 *Exotics at Home: Anthropologies, Others, and American Modernity.* Chicago: University of Chicago Press.

Freud, Sigmund, 1961 *Civilization and its Discontents.* New York: W. W. Norton.

Holland, Dorothy and Jean Lave, eds., 2000 *History in Person: Enduring Struggles, Contentious Practice, Intimate Identities.* Santa Fe, NM: School of American Research Press.

Luhrmann, Tanya M., 2000 *Of Two Minds: The Growing Disorder in American Psychiatry.* New York: Knopf.

Mageo, Jeannette Marie, ed., 2002 *Power and the Self.* New York: Cambridge University Press.

Marcuse, Herbert, 1964 *One Dimensional Man: Studies in Ideology of Advanced Industrial Society.* Boston, MA: Beacon Press.

Mills, C. Wright, 1959 *The Sociological Imagination.* Oxford: Oxford University Press.

O'Nell, Theresa Deleane, 1996 *Disciplined Hearts: Hearts, Identity, and Depression in an American Indian Community.* Berkeley: University of California Press.

Riesman, Paul, 1977 *Freedom in Fulani Social Life: An Introspective Ethnography.* Chicago: University of Chicago Press.

Scheper-Hughes, Nancy, 1992 *Death Without Weeping: the Violence of Everyday Life in Brazil.* Berkeley: University of California Press.

Sokefeld, Martin, 1999 Debating Self, Identity, and Culture in Anthropology. *Current Anthropology* 40 (4): 417–447 (see especially commentary by Ewing and Mageo).

Index